5-2-00

THE AMERICAN LANDSCAPE

THE AMERICAN LANDSCAPE

A Critical Anthology of Prose and Poetry

John Conron

Middlebury College

New York
Oxford University Press
London 1973 Toronto

 Library of Congress Catalogue Card Number: 73-90323

Selections from works by the following authors were made possible by the kind permission of their respective publishers and representatives:

E. C. L. Adams: *Congaree Sketches.* Reprinted by permission of The University of North Carolina Press.

A. R. Ammons: *Uplands, New Poems.* Copyright © 1970 by A. R. Ammons; reprinted by permission of W. W. Norton & Company, Inc.

Brother Antoninus: *The Crooked Lines of God.* Reprinted by permission of University of Detroit Press.

B. A. Botkin: *Lay My Burden Down.* Copyright © 1945 by the University of Chicago; reprinted by permission of The University of Chicago Press.

Richard Brautigan: *Trout Fishing in America.* Copyright © 1967 by Richard Brautigan; reprinted by permission of Seymour Lawrence/Delacorte Press.

Rachel Carson: *Silent Spring.* Copyright © 1962 by Rachel L. Carson; reprinted by permission of Houghton Mifflin Company.

J. M. Cohen, trans.: *The Four Voyages of Christopher Columbus.* Copyright © 1969 by J. M. Cohen; reprinted by permission of Penguin Books Ltd.

Robert Coover: *Pricksongs & Descants.* Copyright © 1969 by Robert Coover; reprinted by permission of the publisher, E. P. Dutton & Co., Inc.

Printed in the United States of America

Henry Miller: *The Air-Conditioned Nightmare.* Copyright 1945 by New Directions Publishing Corporation; reprinted by permission of New Directions Publishing Corporation.

N. Scott Momaday: *House Made of Dawn.* Copyright © 1968 by N. Scott Momaday; reprinted by permission of Harper & Row, Publishers, Inc.

John Frederick Nims: *Knowledge of the Evening, Poems 1950–1960.* Reprinted by permission of Rutgers University Press, New Brunswick, New Jersey, 1960.

Robert Pack: *Nothing But Light.* Reprinted by permission of Rutgers University Press, New Brunswick, New Jersey, 1972.

Theodore Roethke: *Collected Poems of Theodore Roethke.* Copyright © 1960 by Beatrice Roethke, Administratrix of the Estate of Theodore Roethke; reprinted by permission of Doubleday & Company, Inc.

Constance Rourke: Abridged from *Davy Crockett.* Copyright 1934 by Harcourt Brace Jovanovich, Inc.; renewed, 1962, by Alice D. Fore; reprinted by permission of the publishers.

Mari Sandoz: *Old Jules.* Copyright © 1935 by Mari Sandoz; copyright renewed; reprinted by permission of McIntosh and Otis, Inc.

John Steinbeck: *The Grapes of Wrath.* Copyright 1939, © 1967 by John Steinbeck; reprinted by permission of The Viking Press, Inc.

Wallace Stevens: *The Collected Poems of Wallace Stevens.* "Looking Across the Fields and Watching the Birds Fly," copyright 1952 by Wallace Stevens; "Snow Man," copyright 1923 and renewed 1951 by Wallace Stevens; reprinted by permission of Alfred A. Knopf, Inc.

Edwin Way Teale: *Adventures in Nature.* Copyright © 1942, 1959 by Edwin Way Teale; reprinted by permission of Dodd, Mead & Company, Inc.

Frank Waters: *Masked Gods: Navaho and Pueblo Ceremonialism.* © 1950 by Frank Waters; reprinted by permission of The Swallow Press, Chicago.

E. B. White: *One Man's Meat.* Copyright 1939 by E. B. White; renewed 1967 by E. B. White; reprinted by permission of Harper & Row, Publishers, Inc.

William Carlos Williams: *Collected Earlier Poems.* Copyright 1938 by New Directions Publishing Corporation; reprinted by permission of New Directions Publishing Corporation.

For my father
John J. Conron
1900–1952

"When you read," he taught us, "form pictures in your mind."

Acknowledgments

In making this book, I have incurred many debts that cannot be repaid, but only acknowledged. The influence of the work of Howard Mumford Jones and Leo Marx particularly is acknowledged in the Introductions, but it is so general that it needs voicing here as well.

More general still but no less palpable to me is the influence of Professor Austin Warren, a man who taught not doctrine but groundedness and range.

David Littlefield and Larry Chase read portions of the introductory material, and their comments kept me going at it. Howard Munford's reading, affectionately rigorous, both kept me going and kept me thinking.

In my search for illustrations for the book I was given kind as well as professional help from Mr. Arno Jakobsen at the Brooklyn Museum, from Mrs. Eliane Zuesse at the Cooper-Hewitt Museum, and from Mr. Leroy Bellamy and Mr. Jerry Kerns at the Library of Congress.

The Middlebury College Research Committee was unfailingly generous with its faculty grants. Without that support and without the research assistance of Warren Koombs and especially of Ken Seward, this project would have floundered.

So it would have, too, without Cheryl.

Finally, there are those people, students and faculty alike, from both Middlebury College and the University of Michigan and too numerous to name here, who have made the academic community, for me, a place generous in spirit, bold in conversation. It is enough if they take this book as part of that conversation.

Contents

Deformations: Twentieth-Century Landscapes of Ruin 3

E. B. White, Walden (1939) 7
Henry Miller, *from* From the Grand Canyon to Burbank (1945) 11
Aldo Leopold, *from* A Sand County Almanac (1949)
Illinois Bus Ride 17
Thinking Like a Mountain 19
Rachel Carson, *from* Silent Spring (1962) 21
from Realms of the Soil
Norman Mailer, *from* Of a Fire on the Moon (1969) 25
[Cape Kennedy]
Robert Frost, A Brook in the City (1930) 36
Robert Lowell, The Mouth of the Hudson (1964) 37
John Frederick Nims, Decline and Fall (1960) 38
W. S. Merwin, Burning Mountain (1960) 40
William Gass, In the Heart of the Heart of the Country (1967) 41
Richard Brautigan, The Cleveland Wrecking Yard (1967) 62
Robert Coover, The Magic Poker (1969) 67

Early Explorations 85

Adam of Bremen, *from* Descriptio Insularum Aquilonis (1076)
[The Island of Wineland] 89

Christopher Columbus, *from* Letter . . . Describing . . . His First Voyage . . . (1493) 89
[Hispaniola]
Giovanni da Verrazzano, *from* Letter to the King (1524) 95
[The Coast of the New World]
Peter Martyr, *from* Decades of the New World (1533)
[Dariena] 100
[The Gold Regions] 102
Pedro de Castaneda, *from* Expedition to Cibola (1540) 103
[The Grand Canyon]
Arthur Barlowe, *from* First Voyage to Virginia (1584) 104
Michael Drayton, Ode to the Virginian Voyage (?1605) 108
John Brereton, *from* Briefe and True Relation (1602) 110
[The Cape Cod Area]

The Cultivation of the Promised Land, 1620–1800 113

William Bradford, *from* Of Plymouth Plantation (1620) 117
Edward Johnson, *from* Wonder-Working Providence of Sion's Saviour in New England (1653) 121
"Of the laborious worke Christ's people have in planting this Wildernesse, set forth in the building the Towne of Concord, being the first in-lande Towne"
Robert Beverley, *from* The History and Present State of Virginia (1705) 125
Of the Wild Fruits of the Country
Hector St. Jean de Crèvecœur, *from* Letters from an American Farmer (1782) 130
from What Is an American

Eighteenth-Century Perspectives: Natural History and the Sublime 141

William Bartram, *from* Travels (1791)
[A Trip up the Altamaha River] 147
[Ephemera: St. John's River] 150
[Salt Springs] 152
[A Sylvan Scene] 155
Thomas Jefferson, *from* Notes on Virginia (1784)
[The Confluence of the Shenandoah and Potomac Rivers] 158
[The Natural Bridge, Virginia] 160

The Poetry of Scene: An American Grand Tour 163

Nathaniel Willis, View from West Point (1840) 169
Nathaniel Hawthorne, *from* The Canal Boat (1846) 170
Horatio Parsons, *from* The Book of Niagara Falls (1836) 174
Nathaniel Willis, *from* Black Mountain—Lake George (1840) 181
Caldwell, Lake George (1840)
Timothy Dwight, *from* Travels in New England and New York (1821–1822) 184
[View from Mount Holyoke]
Nathaniel Hawthorne, *from* Notch of the White Mountains (1835) 186
Henry James, *from* The American Scene (1907) 188
from New England: An Autumn Impression

Landscape in the Great Theater of Human Events 193

Washington Irving, The Legend of Sleepy Hollow (1820) 197
James Fenimore Cooper, *from* The Last of the Mohicans (1826) 219
[Panorama: The Siege of Fort William Henry]

Landscape as Idea: The Transcendentalists 225

Henry David Thoreau, *from* Walden (1854) 233
[Spring]
from Cape Cod (1864) 236
[The Beach]
from The Maine Woods (1864) 245
from Ktaadn
John Muir, *from* The Mountains of California (1894)
from A Near View of the High Sierra 253
A Wind-storm in the Forests 264

Landscape as Idea: Romantic Prose and Poetry 271

Nathaniel Hawthorne, Sights from a Steeple (1831) 275
The Ambitious Guest (1835) 279
Edgar Allan Poe, The Island of the Fay (1841) 286
Frederick Douglass, *from* Narrative of the Life of Frederick Douglass, An American Slave (1845) 290
William Cullen Bryant, A Forest Hymn (1825) 292
Ralph Waldo Emerson, Each and All (1839) 295

Henry David Thoreau, Haze (1843) 297
Low-Anchored Cloud (1843) 298
Emily Dickinson, #824: The Wind begun to knead the Grass (?1864) 299
#550: I cross till I am weary (?1862) 299
#797: By my window I have for Scenery (?1863) 300
#1278: The Mountains stood in Haze— (?1873) 301
#1343: A single Clover Plank (?1875) 301
Walt Whitman, When Lilacs Last in the Dooryard Bloom'd (1865) 302
Song of the Redwood-Tree (1874) 310
A Voice from Death (1889) 314

The Ways West: Explorers, Travelers, and Emigrants 317

Meriwether Lewis, *from* The Journals of Lewis and Clark (1809) 323
[The Great Falls of the Missouri]
Prince Maxmilian, *from* Travels in the Interior of North America (1839) 326
[Rock Formations: The Missouri]
Washington Irving *from* Astoria (1836)
[Prairie Country] 330
[The Great American Desert] 331
John C. Frémont, *from* Report of the Exploring Expedition to the Rocky Mountains (1845) 334
[Frémont's Peak]
George W. Kendall, *from* Across the Great Southwestern Prairies (1845) 340
[Lost on the Prairie]
Nathaniel Pitt Langford, *from* The Discovery of Yellowstone Park (1905) 343
John Wesley Powell, *from* The Exploration of the Colorado River and Its Canyons (1895) 347
from The Grand Canyon (1895)
Mark Twain, *from* Roughing It (1872)
[Carson City, Nevada] 353
[Pocket Mining: Tuolumne, California] 357
Walt Whitman, *from* Specimen Days (1882) 360
[Western Tour]
Richard Harding Davis, *from* The West from a Car Window (1892) 365

William Gilpin, *from* The Central Gold Region (1860) 372
The Great Basin of the Mississippi
C. C. Coffin, Dakota Wheat Fields (1880) 377
Mari Sandoz, *from* Old Jules (1935) 379
from Hail on the Panhandle
Frank Norris, *from* The Octopus (1901) 383
[Planting: San Joaquin Valley]
John Steinbeck, *from* The Grapes of Wrath (1939) 386
[Exodus]

Landscape as Environment: Local Color Landscapes 395

Bret Harte, The Luck of Roaring Camp (1868) 397
Kate Chopin, Beyond The Bayou (1894) 405

Landscape as Antagonist: The Literary Naturalists 411

Stephen Crane, The Blue Hotel (1898) 415
William Faulkner, *from* The Wild Palms (1927) 437
from Old Man

Landscape into Myth and Ritual 449

Frank Waters, *from* Masked Gods (1950)
The Rock 453
The Canyon 455
Creation Myth (Zũni) 458
Night Chant (Navaho) 459
Rain Song (Pima) 462
Three Black American Folk Tales
Big Swamps of the Congaree 462
The Promised Land 463
Big Corn 463
Zora Neale Hurston, *from* Mules and Men (1935) 464
[Hoodoo Doctor]
The Reverend C. C. Lovelace, *from* The Wounds of Jesus 468
Constance Rourke, *from* Davy Crockett (1934) 474
from Sunrise in His Pocket

Affirming the Ancient Connections: Twentieth-Century Symbiotic Landscapes 477

Ernest Hemingway, Big Two-Hearted River, (1925)
Part 1 483
Part 2 489

Edwin Way Teale, Night in the Garden (1942) 497
Loren Eiseley, The Flow of the River (1957) 503
Jack Kerouac, Alone on a Mountaintop (1960) 509
N. Scott Momaday, The Priest of the Sun (1958) 519
William Carlos Williams, Flowers by the Sea (1935) 525
Dawn (1917) 525
The Trees (1934) 526
Wallace Stevens, Looking Across the Fields and Watching the Birds Fly (1954) 528
The Snow Man (1923) 529
Robert Frost, Desert Places (1939) 530
Directive (1949) 531
West-Running Brook (1930) 532
Robinson Jeffers, Apology for Bad Dreams (1930) 535
Theodore Roethke, Meditation at Oyster River (1960) 538
Robert Hayden, A Road in Kentucky (1966) 540
Ballad of Nat Turner (1966) 540
Michael S. Harper, Oak (1972) 543
Dead Oaks (1972) 544
A. R. Ammons, Conserving the Magnitude of Uselessness (1970) 545
Possibility Along a Line of Difference (1970) 546
Robert Pack, The Hummingbird (1972) 547
Make Way (1973) 548
Denise Levertov, A Tree Telling of Orpheus (1966) 549
Brother Antoninus, Advent (?1949) 554
The South Coast (1959) 554

Appendix

William Bartram, Introduction to Travels (1971) 559
Thomas Cole, Essay on American Scenery (1835) 568
Ralph Waldo Emerson, Nature (1836) 579
Aldo Leopold, *from* Round River (1953)
Conservation 608

Further Reading 616

Introduction

Our perspectives on the subject of landscape seem mostly confined by our urban technological culture to those of the laboratory microscope and the environmental planning report. Certainly the languages we most trust on the subject are the languages which give voice to those perspectives: that of biology ("bacteria," "protozoa," "arthropods," "biota," "symbiosis," and so on) and that of corporate management ("resources," "waste," "efficiency," "benefit," "control," "utilization"). Still, the experts who use these vocabularies, however limited those vocabularies are, have made us aware again of a grand truth: that we live in a world of which urban technology is only a part. This world we have come to conceive as a symbiotic web which stretches from city to farm to wilderness, from particular landscapes and the organisms that inhabit them to continental land-masses, all so profoundly interconnected that what shocks the web in one place shocks the whole web. Even at a time when only something like 2 per cent of our land is wilderness and only about 4 per cent of our people work at farming the land, the experts have come to convince us that this web is more healthily maintained in natural landscapes (or "biotic systems") than it is in our technological cityscapes. Thus, though most of us do not live in any proximity to natural landscapes, we do not need to be convinced of their material relevance.

We are less convinced, however, of the value or even the existence of any spiritual connection between man and landscape. We seem to have surrendered our trust in our imaginative and ideal perspectives on landscape, even though they are as rooted and recurrent as our dreams; even though, inseparable from any rounded notion of what landscape really is, they equally illuminate the spatial and cultural continuum in which we take our place. We have come to associate these perspectives with what one scientist calls "the nature loving, or 'oh my!' attitude"—with, that is, escapism, effete sentimentality, and simplistic and banal pieties. There is a kind of justice in that association. We really have indulged ourselves with our own sentimental posturings in the name of "nature."

But "landscape" is an old and still necessary way of arranging and expressing what we see and imagine about our earth-space, and it is no more limited to the "oh my!" response than it is to the notion of "utilization." If it is not entirely a matter of attitude, it is also not entirely a matter of matter. "Landscape" means, quite simply, the land's shape as it is seen from a particular and defined perspective. Land has no definable shape without that perspective. What is the shape of America? It has one shape when we see it from the moon, another, much more detailed but less extensive shape, when we see it flowing by a car window on Route 66 or enveloping us as we stand on an elevation in the Green Mountains or in a Michigan beanfield.

When, furthermore, we consider that "perspective" has a double meaning, that it applies not only to a physical outlook but also to a psychic outlook, we come to see that landscape includes both a physical and an ideal shape. It is both a cluster of physical facts seen from a physically locatable point of view and the projection, the visible image, of a personal or cultural point of view—an ideal design of hopes, needs, values, and ideas which both shapes and takes shape in landscape. The billions of sense impressions that impinge upon him at a given point in space the biologist might "shape" as a biotic system, the painter as an interplay of line, texture, and light, the poet as an interplay of painterly impressions and mental associations. How else can the impingements be given coherence? The biologist's or painter's or poet's visible image of a landscape gives human shape, human access, to the physical facts of a landscape, and the landscape in turn becomes the concrete embodiment of the biologist's or painter's or poet's hopes, needs, values, and ideas.

In no culture has this been more evident than in America, and in no culture has the spatial construct of landscape been more indispensable, for we seem to see ourselves as a people living in space more than in time, in an environment more than in a history. "SPACE," as the poet-critic Charles Olson observes, "is the central fact to man born in America." A growing body of critical scholarship in the area of American studies attests to the primacy of that fact. In politics, we imagine a government centralized or decentralized in space—a government whose domestic affairs center on the notions of land as "living room" and real estate and of the citizen as freeholder or homeowner; thus, our history of colonial settlement, territorial annexation, land grants, property rights, slavery, land improvement, conservation, preservation. In commerce, we have both imagined and realized a technology of speed and waste—a technology geared to the conquest of terrain and distance and based on the assumption of inexaustible natural resources: the "myth of abundance." In religion, we have been preoccupied less with theology than with the rich, timeless, and harmonious landscape of Eden and with the deformed and tormented or lifeless landscapes of hell; and we have worked to realize the one and anxiously seen the other realizing itself around us. In manners and morals, we have conceived the polarities of boundless space and of walled gardens (farms, suburban tracts, city and national parks); conceived the polarities of the Open Road and of cultivation, rootless pilgrimage and rooted growth; conceived grand dreams rising to fill a grand space and experienced the dream-driven deformations of that space; experienced the anxious fear arising from the loneliness of living in space and from impotence in the face of time, change, and death; experienced the claustrophobia generated by immigration, the close of the frontier, diminishing wilderness, overpopulation, and the shrinking of "private space." Such a catalogue touches only some of the more obvious connections between the transcontinental earth-space America and visible images its people have embodied in it.

The literature of American landscape has both reflected and influenced these connections. That literature, as this book defines it, is anything written in a descriptive mode about American landscape, and it thus includes as equally significant to an understanding of landscape the writings of explorers, settlers, travelers, natural scientists, visionaries, fiction writers, and poets. The literature included here is a representative record of American landscape, a record of the changes in our earth-space and in our imaginative and ideal perceptions of it. The book is arranged to present the various perspectives and historical phases which constitute our connection to American landscape, and it is illustrated, as far as possible, by the sketches, water colors, paintings, and photographs of artists who shared in these perspectives. The landscapes included are chiefly but not exclusively natural landscapes which incorporate both the visible facts and the visible images of wilderness, cultivation, and ruin. Strictly speaking, none are cityscapes, though some are set in cities. The Appendix includes a representative sampling of expository nature literature—theories of nature and of natural landscape—ranging from the eighteenth century to the present.

The literature of eco-crisis, a part of the aroused and abrasive expository literature of the last decade or so, is only minimally represented here, in part because it is so well represented in other available anthologies, in part because, having a logic of its own, it does not usually incorporate the art of landscape. The literature of eco-crisis is a literature of awakening. As such, it tends to present land as a matter of debate, or as an abstraction difficult to visualize, though we need to visualize. Even our dreams demonstrate the profoundly human need to ground ideas and emotions in images—to give them a place in the landscape of the mind. But to argue this is only to suggest what descriptive literature can contribute, in the way of complement rather than rivalry, to our reappraisal of the man-land relationship in America. The literature of eco-crisis awakens us to the effects and the future of that relationship, descriptive literature leads us into its motives and its history, and both converge on the present.

The writings represented reflect in their own ways the growing physical presence and psychic adjustments of America's immigrant inhabitants. The writings range the continental United States and the Caribbean area, and they span perspectives from that of the European Renaissance (Columbus celebrating an Edenic Haiti, for example, or Peter Martyr describing a living tree of gold) to those of the mid-twentieth century (Richard Brautigan inspecting pre-fab sections of a used trout stream in a wrecking yard, Loren Eiseley recounting an experience of symbiosis in the North Platte River). To at least two significant minority groups—Indians and Southern Blacks—the landscape traditionally seems less a "scene" to be described than a milieu in which they are totally immersed and which is therefore a vital part of them. Their distinctive perspective is felt most strongly in the sections Landscape into Myth and Affirming the Ancient Connections. For the rest, the perspective is largely the American counterpart of what we call Western civilization.

The thesis of the book is implied in its arrangement. The first of thirteen sections focuses on contemporary landscapes of ruin; the last, on contemporary landscapes of harmony. The sections in between sketch the complex perspectives that have led to both. More specifically, the first three sections suggest a connection between ruin and the impulse, aided increasingly by technology, not simply to cultivate but to subdue and dominate landscape. The last ten sections, with significant exceptions, focus less on domination and ruin than on coexistence and celebration. Coexistence had to be learned in two stages: the first stage, ca. 1780–1860, had to do with the imaginative and idealized connections between man and land—a psychic ecology, if you will. The second stage, ca. 1860 to the present, has had to do with both a psychic and a physical ecology.

Each of the thirteen sections has an introduction, and each introduction treats an aspect of the visible images or the literary art of landscape. The introductions avoid extensive paraphrase of the selections, attending instead to the historical and cultural perspectives which (often only implicitly) inform the sections. They are designed to provide, cumulatively, both a history and a method for sophisticated analysis of the landscapes they introduce. For example, the first three introductions focus on the sources of and the attitudes implied in dominant images and metaphors; the fourth introduction considers the subject of physical perspective as well as the concerns of natural history and the aesthetics of the sublime; the sixth, eighth, tenth, and eleventh form a brief history of setting in nineteenth-century American fiction.

The sections are meant to be self-explanatory in plan, range, and connection to each other, but a general statement here about two related methods of analyzing literary landscapes might be helpful. (Both methods are used in the introductions that follow.)

One method is based on the assumption that recurrent, related, or extended metaphors (metaphors, similes, symbols) in the work of a given writer or of a given period or culture are refractions of a world-view. These recurrences or relations signal a frame of reference, a construct or spectrum of constructs, through which a writer both perceives raw fact and appearances and gives them, or sees in them, design and significance. Metaphor expresses things by analogy—by comparing something that has to be expressed (what critics call the tenor) with something that expresses it (the vehicle). Metaphor can image ideas or idealize images; it can express unknown or inexpressible things in terms of known or expressible things, unfamiliar in terms of familiar things or familiar in terms of unfamiliar things. Metaphor can be simply ornamental, but it can also be, as Frost put it, "the profoundest thinking we have." What was it like? That is an invitation to metaphor. In a writer's response to that invitation—in his choice of a vehicle, a construct, a frame of reference, and in the implications of that choice—one can sense how he views and values the world. Even when he is not consciously responding to that invitation, his use of a characteristic vocabulary or of recurrent images, can implicitly signal how he views and values the world. I have already suggested, for example, our own attraction to the vocabularies of biology and corporate management in rendering landscapes.

Often in the writings included in this book, recurrent or related metaphors (and vocabularies and images) evoke an ideal design of landscape. The introductions to Early Explorations and The Cultivation of the Promised Land, for example, trace some of the features and some of the implications of landscape as a paradisaical garden, and the introduction to Limning the New World deals with both that design, as it is applied to wilderness landscapes, and with the Newtonian design of landscape as a system of mechanisms in a mechanistic clockwork universe. The reader can add to these his own natural history of such metaphoric designs, in which landscape is variously perceived in terms of a palace, a household, or some other kind of building; a work of art, a book, a bible; a field of energies in which forms evolve (Darwinism) or are transformed from one state to another (ecology); an incarnation of spirit or mind; an organism (Romanticism, biology); a personified being; a community.

Often in these landscapes, there are other constructs, or other impulses, at work in addition to the ideal design, and they form what Poe would have called an "undercurrent," which might either contradict or expand the design. In the reports of the maritime explorers, for example, the obvious visions of riches, violence, and conquest appear in sharp and artless contrast to the evocation of a paradise—an intricate interplay between things of the spirit and things of the flesh, between ideal and appetite. In the works of the American Renaissance, on the other hand, the surface design is that of the painterly or geographical scene, and the ideal design is left implicit in an undercurrent of subtly related metaphors. To examine the interplay of such metaphoric constructs and impulses is to begin to sense the interplay of perception, motive, and ideal which constitute a writer's or a culture's world view.

The other method of analyzing verbal landscapes is grounded on the concept and the techniques of literary setting. How can a place in which events "take place" be represented in the time-flow of language? That, in its broadest sense, is the problem of setting, and it is a problem shared by anyone who would render a landscape in language—explorer, naturalist, tourist, and literary artist alike.

The problem of setting is a complex one. Like characterization, which is also basically descriptive, setting demands that a mass of visible facts and mental impressions be given order and coherence. But where, in physical space and in the spatial arts, this mass appears to exist simultaneously, it must be rendered sequentially in language: first one fact or impression, then another. In language a given landscape can exist only as a sequence of specific details which accumulate as the sequence progresses. But how can the details be arranged so that they will not only accumulate, but also connect to each other as parts of a living picture?

Up until the eighteenth century, this question apparently had little significance and no real answer. For lack of an answer, the only resort is a list—the kind of list the maritime explorers made. The list is a sort of stockman's inventory, and in it the landscape exists as nothing more than the sum of its disparate objects: these kinds of trees and plants, those kinds of animals, and so on. Even the images in such a list are more diffuse than concrete: steep mountains, broad rivers, and so on.

During the late eighteenth and early nineteenth centuries in America there evolved in the art of description four combinable but distinct answers to the problem of reproducing a coherent and detailed landscape. They are still with us.

The simplest answer to the problem is an orientation from a *fixed point of view:* I stand at the eastern edge of a field, facing a tree in the middle of the field; behind the tree is a glow in the rain clouds where the sun is; the field is laid out in front of me, stretching left as far as I can see and right to the top of a gradual rise. Here the landscape is organized, from where I locate myself at the edge of it, in terms of a coherent visual logic: foreground to background, left to right. Most of the pre-nineteenth-century literary landscapes are organized this way; even the travelogues are descriptions from a series of temporarily fixed points of view.

A more complex answer to the problem is to organize the landscape around physical movement: I walk toward the tree; wet, empty furrows ripple under my feet; the tree balloons and spreads as I approach it. Movement thus energizes the heart of the sentence, the verb, and consciously or no it activates description, it suggests that landscape is animate rather than just inertly there. Think, for example, of Ichabod Crane's terrifying ride through space—a ride composed only of sudden encounters with objects and beings, or of Thoreau's pilgrim's progress along the beach at Cape Cod, the landscape and his meditations mutually unfolding as he goes. Nineteenth-century writers learned early how to collect a landscape around movement, if not their own, then that of water or wind or of lines that invited the eye to move along them; and they were, at the same time, increasingly preoccupied with landscape as a field of vitalistic, animistic, and (later in the century) mechanistic energies.

These two techniques develop a visual logic. Two other techniques play off visual with cognitive logic. In the first of these, the significant detail of a landscape is arranged in terms of a *metaphoric frame image:* the furrows in the field are like corduroy; the field is a flat, slightly mussed piece of grayish-brown corduroy on which the tree sticks like a burr. The vehicle of the metaphor (here, corduroy) provides a frame of reference for the appearance of the landscape. It also acts in the way that a painterly foreground acts: it picks up and projects the dominant motif or impression; it acts to organize and to give access to the significant details of the whole. In the metaphoric frame image, it is as if some part of the viewer's consciousness (his mental landscape) acts as the foreground to the outer landscape. This technique is part of the conscious art of the picturesque sketch (see The Poetry of Scene), and writers as early as Irving and Thoreau are masters of it. Witness, for example, a hungry Ichabod Crane's perception of a landscape as a huge banquet or Thoreau's perception of the Cape Cod headlands as an oriental carpet. And it is with this technique that the approach to landscape as literary setting intersects with the approach to landscape as metaphor, which examines the constructs through which a writer both perceives raw fact and appearances and gives them, or sees in them, design and significance.

In the fourth technique, a *dominant impression* arranges the significant details of a landscape in terms of its effect on the perceiver ("impression" means literally a mark on the mind). If I am a painter or a hunter or a tourist, I will naturally ascribe different values to the field. If I am cold, I will describe the field in images which emphasize the chill I feel: gray light, rigidity, starkness, even loneliness. And perhaps the field has a presence imparted to it by some memorable event: it is part of a glacial deposit or the place where a battle was fought or a crime committed, or it is part of a farm, worked for three generations, which I have just sold or bought. Perhaps in its exhausted or richly fertile soil, in the tired sag and decay or the strong, clean assertiveness of its buildings, it even embodies the way I view the world. All of these things will affect my perception of a landscape, and all of them can be conveyed, explicitly or implicitly, by the art of impressionistic description. That is the art we have demanded of the short story since Poe, for example.

There are other ways of organizing verbal landscapes, but they depend much less on visual than on cognitive logic. They are techniques of exposition, of the sort to be found, say, in the Renaissance "relation" and in its descendant the nature essay. Any coherent description of place, however, will depend, artfully or not, on one of the four techniques of literary setting or on some combination of them. And in analyzing a description in terms of its techniques, one can analyze as well the implications of the writer's perspective. What constructs does he bring as a frame of reference, a design, to his description? And what are the implications of the physical perspective he chooses? Looking down from a prominence or up from a depression each have their psychic implications for landscape just as they do for dreams. A landscape described from a fixed point of view, furthermore, is described literally as a matter of scenery: like the scenery on a proscenium stage it is set off from the perceiver as a backdrop to human action; it is part of a show that goes on outside of him, apart from him, "out there." The impressionistic landscape, on the other hand, is the expression of both a physical and a psychic immersion in landscape. It presents a landscape as an environment continuous with, analogous to, the perceiver's inner environment.

The approaches to landscape as metaphor and as setting can illuminate not only individual texts, but also their historical contexts. The histories of metaphor and of setting are integral parts of the history of literature itself, in its various relations to landscape—in its imagined and its observed relations to landscape, in its fictions as well as in its "objective" reports. The notion of landscape as environment, for example, developed in fiction as it did in other areas of American culture. In Romantic fiction, as in the landscapes of the Transcendentalists, the environment was conceived of as chiefly psychic, a projection of individual will; and fiction writers enveloped their dreamers in soft, dusky, undulating landscapes, their wrathful or tormented characters in landscapes of sublime frenzy (storms, thunder, jagged cliffs), and their passionate or obsessive characters in landscapes kindled by fire or fiery light. The realists and other survivors of the Civil War, less dream-driven and less preoccupied with projections of individualistic spirit, were drawn to the physical and regional character of landscape and to its relationship with the physical and cultural aspects of environment. If they were, in a way, environmentalists, their successors the literary naturalists were determinists who saw the environment, physical and cultural, as an omnipotent antagonist, a remorseless agent of people's fate. Since the naturalists, however, and coinciding with the emergence of ecology in the 1920's, fictional landscapes have come again to serve more passive and more healing environmental functions, though they remain (in Hemingway and Faulkner, for example) insistently true to matters of physical fact and appearance.

The histories of metaphor and of setting are integral parts of the history (yet to be written) of literature in its various relations to landscape. And the history of this literature is, in turn, an integral part of the history, and the quality of the relationship between Americans and that vague, blurred galaxy of land masses, myths, ideals, fears, and hungers which they inhabit.

Note on the texts. A three-dot ellipsis indicates the cutting of less than a sentence; a four-dot ellipsis indicates the cutting of more. The dates given for the texts are the dates of first publication in book form. The exceptions to this are the short description by Adam of Bremen and the poetry of Emily Dickinson, for which the approximate dates of composition are given (both were published long after their deaths). No dates are given for the folk material in Landscape into Myth and Ritual. For ease of reading the spelling has been somewhat modernized in most pre-eighteenth-century English-language texts, and modern translations have normally been used for non-English texts.

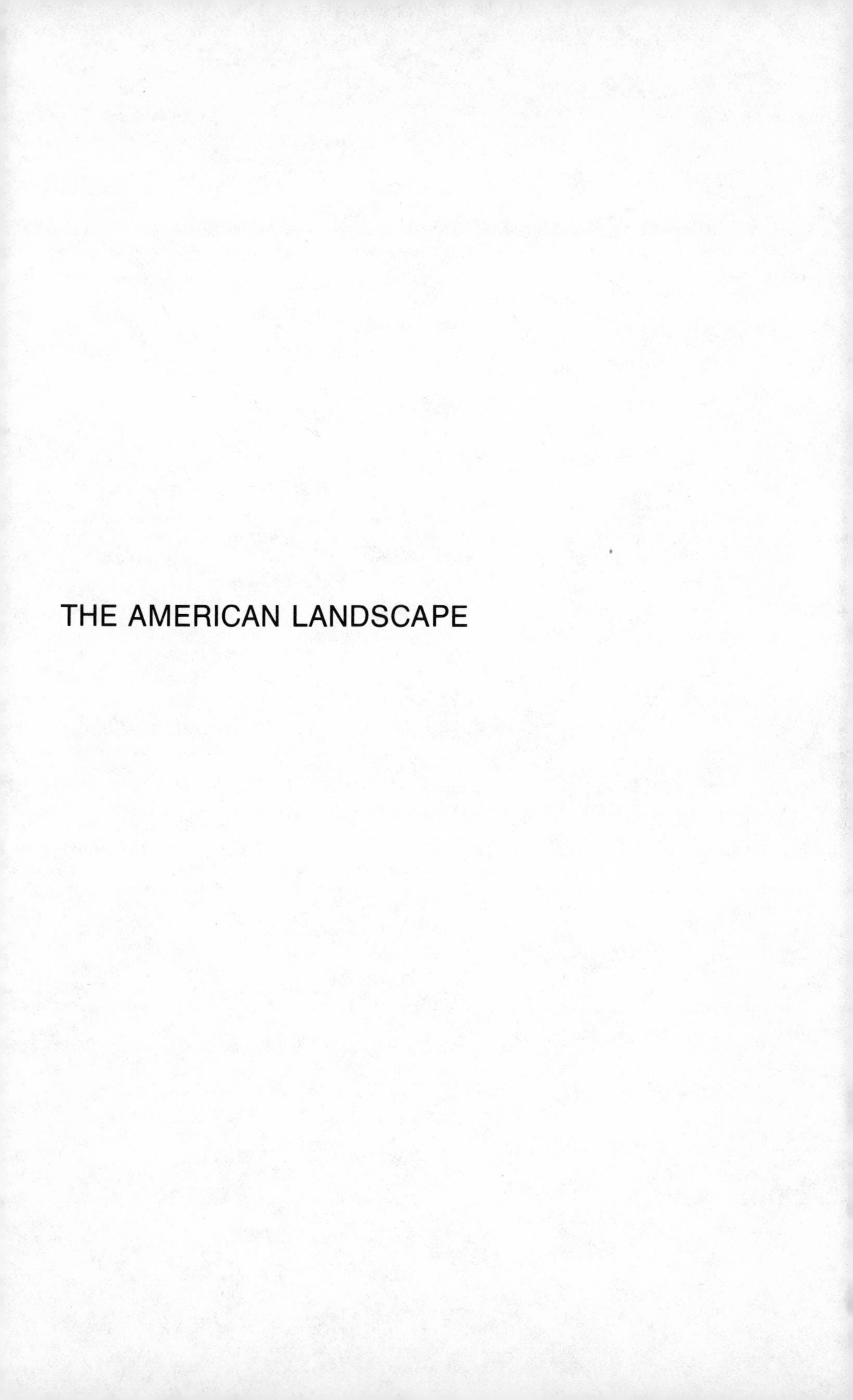

THE AMERICAN LANDSCAPE

Deformations

Twentieth-Century Landscapes of Ruin

These fragments I have shored against my ruins . . .
T. S. Eliot, *The Waste Land*

Twentieth-century Americans have come to see that there are many kinds and degrees of ruin. There is, first of all, that state of natural ruin which all landmarks—from mountains and trees to old civilizations—come to and which both saddens and fascinates, attracts and repels. Picturesque ruin is the softening, crumbling effect of a building or a tree abandoned to the elements and in the process of returning to them. It is, traditionally, a reminder of the state to which all humans, their monuments, their artifacts, and intimate spaces must go: *sic transit gloria mundi.* Grotesque ruin is more organic. It involves the processes of dissolution and corruption (both physical and moral) or the reassertion of wild things—plants and animals—into an urban or garden landscape.

Like their spiritual kin the Romantics, many of the writers represented here are preoccupied with the picturesque tension between brilliance and decay, fecundity and barrenness, continuity and discontinuity. They have, too, a certain "delight in destruction"—in what ages and venerably or grotesquely dies and in what, surprisingly, survives. Re-creating pastoral landscapes deserted or otherwise transformed by the American commitment to urban technology, they hover between the worlds of the picturesque and the grotesque in a lunar but fecund terrain in which both the surfaces of objects and their significances have become disturbingly unfamiliar, distorted, incongruous, disproportionate; in which (nature gone wild) night and nightmare dominate, the real seems dreamt and nocturnal beings (bats, snakes, and predators chiefly) creep and flutter through viny thickets; or in which a mineral silence reigns. In such landscapes everything seems to change shapes and beings, the inanimate taking on a life of its own, the human becoming, through metaphor, monstrous, ghostly, or inanimate.

However nightmarish the landscape of natural ruin might be, it is not as overwhelming as the landscape of what might be called technological ruin, in which nature is wounded, sickened, or deformed. The first of many degrees of technological ruin is the deformation of surfaces and appearances caused by the accumulation of refuse or by acts of vandalism, as in E. B. White's "Walden" and Robert Coover's "The Magic Poker," with its gutted, smeared, graffito-covered summer house.

Then there is the more elemental ruin caused directly by technology—by war or by extraction, refining, and even construction operations. The spirit of technology is progressivist, and to the progressivist natural ruin is a denial of progress, an unhygienic, nonfunctional obstacle, a reminder of death in a commitment to a productive present and a liberated future. But after the Civil War, technology itself began to create a surprising and even terrifying landscape of ruin. Sublime in its size and power, the machine created in the surrounding landscape an apocalyptic speed-up of the processes of dissolution, and what it did not dissolve it deformed by mutation or it obliterated. This was as true on the farm as it was in the city, though in the city the process was more spectacular.

Technological ruin begins with mutilation differing only in intensity from the process Edward Johnson described when the Puritans began to attack the virgin soil of the New World (see the section, The Cultivation of the Promised Land). In technological ruin, however, not only are plant and animal life killed off and the earth gouged, slashed, and stripped, but, often, nothing is put back in their place. What is left is characterized by burns, gouges, mazes, muddles, and heaps. The record of a human or natural past, the record of creation, is obliterated. All landmarks are obliterated, and the landscape thus becomes as unchartable in space as it is in time. The pattern and the effect, though less extreme than I describe, are recognizable even in Aldo Leopold's "Thinking Like a Mountain": first the wolf (the genius, the animistic spirit) of the mountain is mutilated, then comes the maze of deer trails.

At its worst extreme, technological ruin "creates" a landscape of desolation: shapeless, lifeless, primordial. T. S. Eliot's *The Waste Land* represents a large literature of such landscapes which appeared after World War I. Eliot's generation witnessed in the war in France and in the urbanization of the Eastern seaboard at home a technological cataclysm beyond its comprehension, and it was shocked into a perception of it which had the surreal clarity of a nightmare. Other writers (William Gass, for example) have come to see such ruin not so much in terms of cataclysm as in terms of entropy: a draining away of energy, of value, of meaning; a reduction of life to absurdity and paralysis. Recent literature, on the other hand, if the fiction of Robert Coover is representative, shows less of an imaginative engagement with entropy than with the grotesque mutation and persistence, however diminished, of life. It shares with ecology the growing conviction that life—even (as Rachel Carson's "Realms of the Insects" demonstrates) the life of insects which Americans have committed themselves to kill—cannot be killed but only terribly changed. Cataclysm, entropy, grotesqueness—these are the perspectives modern and contemporary literature brings to the landscape of technological ruin.

When the technological process involves construction, the landscape of ruin becomes disguised by architectural cosmetics which, for most contemporary observers, are only a more subtle manifestation of ruin—a projection of the sick anxiety or despair in the American mind which causes or is caused by deformation. From such a perspective Richard Brautigan renders his "Cleveland Wrecking Yard" and Norman Mailer his Cape Kennedy—a swamp landscape converted into a technological "cathedral." And though Mailer is unable to decide whether it is a cathedral to life or to death, he suggests that the landscape has been created by a culture which (he writes elsewhere in *Of a Fire on the Moon*) has witnessed deformation even at the level of the elements:

> the oncoming world of parallel colostomies draining into the same main line, and the air of earth cities become carbon monoxide and lead, sulphur dioxide and ash, nitrogen oxide and other particulates of the noxious, earth staggering with sewages which did not rot, synthetics, aluminums, oils and pesticides, fertilizers, detergents and nuclear spews, acids and plastics and salts in the soil, cakes of suffocation in the rivers, hazes of nitrogen effluent to cut off the light from the sky, a burgeoning of artifivicials to addict the soils, another year of pollutions to choke the planet.

Especially in fiction and poetry, the tones communicated in these landscapes of technological and spiritual ruin are extraordinarily complex. Agent and object, cause and effect, can no longer clearly be determined even though more recent writers are aware of the ecological processes involved; and the imagination seems no longer able to contain or define the forces at work, though it can render their effect. Clearly the forces are technological, unselectively violent and uncontrollable; the agents, in some incomprehensible way, ourselves; and the effects, visible. But a just sense of causality and thus of moral scrutiny is frustrated by the very scope and pervasiveness of the forces at work, and thus the human responses to the violence of technological ruin have no comprehensible object and no apparent effect. The attitudes which result from this are the attitudes of a person who is both victimizer and victim; they range in tone from a profound funereal sadness (Nims) to a numb, apathetic inertia (Lowell, Gass) to a rage equal to the violence it rages over (Leopold, Mailer). Always there is a sense of disorientation and often a deeply felt sense of humiliation, horror, or terror: humiliation at the loss of control over one's life, at having passively to endure the same violations as the landscape; horror at the prospect of prolonged sickness and suffering, at the spectacle of organic decay and mutilation; terror at the magnitude and the aimlessness of the forces at work and at the sublime obscurity (Lowell's hellish yellow haze, Merwin's subterranean fire) with which they invest the landscape and the mind perceiving it. Often, too, there is an undefined sense of guilt, a sense of having become as sick or mad as the landscape, of having somehow participated in its ruin.

The spatial relationships in these landscapes are as disconnected as the values and emotions invested in them. Things in them exist apart from each other in a fragmented or grotesquely incongruous whole—the integral with the deformed and the mutilated. And just as these landscapes disrupt the connections between past and present, this and that, so the literary techniques which render them disrupt the flow or the logic of language itself. The technique most used is that of *juxtaposition.* In *The Waste Land,* which revolutionized the technique, Eliot juxtaposed fragments of dialogue, description, and literary allusions as if they were all that was left of order in an exploded civilization: "These fragments I have shored against my ruins." Eliot further juxtaposed with these fragments, which composed a post-war London cityscape, images of old pastoral landscapes (Spenser's "sweet Thames"), of deserts, and of the landscapes of purgatory and hell. Such model landscapes, juxtaposed with present ruin, recur in the works of writers as different as William Gass and Robert Lowell. There are other sorts of juxtaposition: Henry Miller surrealistically juxtaposes images of a pop civilization (a lake of condensed milk, streets like fried bananas) with a desert landscape of the Southwest; Robert Coover stages and restages the movements of his characters and the landscape they move in, as if in dream-sequences, and so on. The device of juxtaposition has many such uses and variations in the landscape of ruin.

In these and in other modern landscapes represented in this anthology, two thinly affirmative responses can be seen at work: nostalgia and irony. Nostalgia turns, for refuge from despair, to a golden but unrecoverable past: the pastoral landscape of one's youth (Brautigan, Hemingway) or of a golden age at once more simple and more civilized (White's Walden) or even of the creation itself as it is manifested in virginal water or wilderness. Nostalgia, it is said, is the great American theme, and indeed every contemporary movement to natural landscapes (few writers live there long) partakes in some degree of nostalgia. Nostalgia is escapist, and so it, too, dead-ends in despair. Irony, on the other hand, is, at its healthiest, a way of fighting back—a way of making moral judgments. An indictment or a purge, it savagely or comically juxtaposes the natural and the unnatural, dream and reality, past and present, awareness and fact, so that these might be sorted out, and it presides over the defeat and the tenuous re-creation of hope, if not in mercy then in justice, or else in some "separate peace."

Such a range of responses to the landscapes of technological ruin suggests that these landscapes are the most intense and faithful projections we have of our own anguished minds.

E. B. White

Walden

White's "Walden" is a narrative essay addressed as a kind of open letter to Henry David Thoreau. White's essay marks the centennial of Thoreau's experiment at Walden Pond (he moved into his cabin on Independence Day, 1845) by juxtaposing the deformed and "browbeaten" look of the contemporary landscape against the same landscape as Thoreau delineated and memorialized it in *Walden.* Even the expense account is an ironic echo of Thoreau's list of expenditures for living at minimal subsistence.

IT WAS JUNE and everywhere June was publishing her immemorial stanza; in the lilacs, in the syringa, in the freshly edged paths and the sweetness of moist beloved gardens, and the little wire wickets that preserved the tulips' front. Farmers were already moving the fruits of their toil into their yards, arranging the rhubarb, the asparagus, the strictly fresh eggs on the painted stands under the little shed roofs with the patent shingles. And though it was almost a hundred years since you had taken your ax and started cutting out your home on Walden Pond, I was interested to observe that the philosophical spirit was still alive in Massachusetts: in the center of a vacant lot some boys were assembling the framework of the rude shelter, their whole mind and skill concentrated in the rather inauspicious helter-skeleton of studs and rafters. They too were escaping from town, to live naturally, in a rich blend of savagery and philosophy.

That evening, after supper at the inn, I strolled out into the twilight to dream my shapeless transcendental dreams and see that the car was locked up for the night (first open the right front door, then reach over, straining, and pull up the handles of the left rear and the left front till you hear the click, then the handle of the right rear, then shut the right front but open it again, remembering that the key is still in the ignition switch, remove the key, shut the right front again with a bang, push the tiny keyhole cover to one side, insert key, turn, and withdraw). It is what we all do, Henry. It is called locking the car. It is said to confuse thieves and keep them from making off with the laprobe. Four doors to lock behind one robe. The driver himself never uses a laprobe, the free movement of his legs being vital to the operation of the vehicle; so that when he locks the car it is a pure and unselfish act. I have in my life gained very little essential heat from laprobes, yet I have ever been at pains to lock them up.

The evening was full of sounds, some of which would have stirred your memory. The robins still love the elms of New England villages at sundown. There is enough of the thrush in them to make song inevitable at the end of day, and enough of the tramp to make them hang round the dwellings of men. A robin, like many another American, dearly loves a white house with green blinds. Concord is still full of them.

Your fellow-townsmen were stirring abroad—not many afoot, most of them in their cars; and the sound which they made in Concord at evening was a rustling and a whispering. The sound lacks steadfastness and is wholly unlike that of a train. A train, as you know who lived so near the Fitchburg line, whistles once or twice sadly and is gone, trailing a memory in smoke, soothing to ear and mind. Automobiles, skirting a village green, are like flies that have gained the inner ear—they buzz, cease, pause, start, shift, stop, halt, brake, and the whole effect is a nervous polytone curiously disturbing.

As I wandered along, the toc toc of ping pong balls drifted from an attic window. In front of the Reuben Brown house a Buick was drawn up. At the wheel, motionless, his hat upon his head, a man sat, listening to Amos and Andy on the radio (it is a drama of many scenes and without an end). The deep voice of Andrew Brown, emerging from the car, although it originated more than two hundred miles away, was unstrained by distance. When you used to sit on the shore of your pond on Sunday morning, listening to the church bells of Acton and Concord, you were aware of the excellent filter of the intervening atmosphere. Science has attended to that, and sound now maintains its intensity without regard for distance. Properly sponsored, it goes on forever.

A fire engine, out for a trial spin, roared past Emerson's house, hot with readiness for public duty. Over the barn roofs the martins dipped and chittered. A swarthy daughter of an asparagus grower, in culottes, shirt, and bandanna, pedalled past on her bicycle. It was indeed a delicious evening, and I returned to the inn (I believe it was your house once) to rock with the old ladies on the concrete veranda.

Next morning early I started afoot for Walden, out Main Street and down Thoreau, past the depot and the Minuteman Chevrolet Company. The morning was fresh, and in a bean field along the way I flushed an agriculturalist, quietly studying his beans. Thoreau Street soon joined Number 126, an artery of the State. We number our highways nowadays, our speed being so great we can remember little of their quality or character and are lucky to remember their number. (Men have an indistinct notion that if they keep up this activity long enough all will at length ride somewhere, in next to no time.) Your pond is on 126.

I knew I must be nearing your woodland retreat when the Golden Pheasant lunchroom came into view—Sealtest ice cream, toasted sandwiches, hot frankfurters, waffles, tonics, and lunches. Were I the proprietor, I should add rice, Indian meal, and molasses—just for old time's sake. The Pheasant, incidentally, is for sale: a chance for some nature lover who wishes to set himself up beside a pond in the Concord atmosphere and live deliberately, fronting only the essential facts of life on Number 126. Beyond the Pheasant was a place called Walden Breezes, an oasis whose porch pillars were made of old green shutters sawed into lengths. On the porch was a distorting mirror, to give the traveler a comical image of himself, who had miraculously learned to gaze in an ordinary glass without smiling. Behind the Breezes, in a sun-parched clearing, dwelt your philosophical descendants in their trailers, each trailer the size of your hut, but all grouped together for the sake of congeniality. Trailer people leave the city, as you did, to discover solitude and in any weather, at any hour of the day or night, to improve the nick of time; but they soon collect in villages and get bogged deeper in the mud than ever. The camp behind Walden Breezes was just rousing itself to the morning. The ground was packed hard under the heel, and the sun came through the clearing to bake the soil and enlarge the wry smell of cramped housekeeping. Cushman's bakery truck had stopped to deliver an early basket of rolls. A camp dog, seeing me in the road, barked petulantly. A man emerged from one of the trailers and set forth with a bucket to draw water from some forest tap.

Leaving the highway I turned off into the woods toward the pond, which was apparent through the foliage. The floor of the forest was strewn with dried oak leaves and *Transcripts*. From beneath the flattened popcorn wrapper (*granum explosum*) peeped the frail violet. I followed a footpath and descended to the water's edge. The pond lay clear and blue in the morning light, as you have seen it so many times. In the shallows a man's waterlogged shirt undulated gently. A few flies came out to greet me and convoy me to your cove, past the No Bathing signs on which the fellows and the girls had scrawled their names. I felt strangely excited suddenly to be snooping around your premises, tiptoeing along watchfully, as though not to tread by mistake upon the intervening century. Before I got to the cove I heard something which seemed to me quite wonderful: I heard your frog, a full, clear *troonk,* guiding me, still hoarse and solemn, bridging the years as the robins had bridged them in the sweetness of the village evening. But he soon quit, and I came on a couple of young boys throwing stones at him.

Your front yard is marked by a bronze tablet set in a stone. Four small granite posts, a few feet away, show where the house was. On top of the tablet was a pair of faded blue bathing trunks with a white stripe. Back of it is a pile of stones, a sort of cairn, left by your visitors as a tribute I suppose. It is a rather ugly little heap of stones, Henry. In fact the hillside itself seems faded, browbeaten; a few tall skinny pines, bare of lower limbs, a smattering of young maples in suitable green, some birches and oaks, and a number of trees felled by the last big wind. It was from the bole of one of these fallen pines, torn up by the roots, that I extracted the stone which I added to the cairn—a sentimental act in which I was interrupted by a small terrier from a nearby picnic group, who confronted me and wanted to know about the stone.

I sat down for a while on one of the posts of your house to listen to the bluebottles and the dragonflies. The invaded glade sprawled shabby and mean at my feet, but the flies were tuned to the old vibration. There were the remains of a fire in your ruins, but I doubt that it was yours; also two beer bottles trodden into the soil and become part of earth. A young oak had taken root in your house, and two or three ferns, unrolling like the ticklers at a banquet. The only other furnishings were a DuBarry pattern sheet, a page torn from a picture magazine, and some crusts in wax paper.

Before I quit I walked clear round the pond and found the place where you used to sit on the northeast side to get the sun in the fall, and the beach where you got sand for scrubbing your floor. On the eastern side of the pond, where the highway borders it, the State has built dressing rooms for swimmers, a float with diving towers, drinking fountains of porcelain, and rowboats for hire. The pond is in fact a State Preserve, and carries a twenty-dollar fine for picking wild flowers, a decree signed in all solemnity by your fellow-citizens Walter C. Wardwell, Erson B. Barlow, and Nathaniel I. Bowditch. There was a smell of creosote where they had been building a wide wooden stairway to the road and the parking area. Swimmers and boaters were arriving: bodies plunged vigorously into the water and emerged wet and beautiful in the bright air. As I left, a boatload of town boys were splashing about in mid-pond, kidding and fooling, the young fellows singing at the tops of their lungs in a wild chorus:

Amer-ica, Amer-ica, God shed his grace on thee,
And crown thy good with brotherhood
From sea to shi-ning sea!

I walked back to town along the railroad, following your custom. The rails were expanding noisily in the hot sun, and on the slope of the roadbed the wild grape and the blackberry sent up their creepers to the track.

The expense of my brief sojourn in Concord was:

Canvas shoes	$1.95	
Baseball bat	.25	gifts to take back
Left-handed fielder's glove	1.25	to a boy
Hotels and meals	4.25	
In all	$7.70	

As you see, this amount was almost what you spent for food for eight months. I cannot defend the shoes or the expenditure for shelter and food; they reveal a meanness and grossness in my nature which you would find contemptible. The baseball equipment, however, is the kind of impediment with which you were never on even terms. You must remember that the house where you practiced the sort of economy which I respect was haunted only by mice and squirrels. You never had to cope with a short-stop.

1939

Henry Miller

From From the Grand Canyon to Burbank

Miller, surrealist, anarchist, urbanite, and self-avowed hater both of technology and of nature, returned from Paris in the early forties and took a long journey by second-hand Buick across the United States to reacclimate himself. *The Air-Conditioned Nightmare* (1945), from which "Grand Canyon to Burbank" comes, is the record of what he saw and found: a perversion, as the title suggests, of the American Dream. "From the Grand Canyon to Burbank" is his vision of the deserts of the Southwest: a surrealistic nightmare and no more a sanctuary than the cities are.

I LEFT GRAND CANYON about nine o'clock in the morning of a warm day, looking forward to a serene and beautiful toboggan slide from the clouds to sea level. Now, when I look back on it, I have difficulty in remembering whether Barstow came before or after Needles. I remember vaguely getting to Kingman towards sundown. That soothing noise, as of tiny bracelets passing through a wringer, which is the thing I like best about the engine, had changed to a frightening clatter, as if the clutch, the rear end, the differential, the carburetor, the thermostat and all the nuts, bolts and ball bearings would drop out any minute. . . .

At Needles I went to bed immediately after supper, planning to get up about five the next morning. But at three-thirty I heard the cocks crowing and feeling quite refreshed I took a shower and decided to start with the crack of dawn. I had breakfast, tanked up, and was on the road at four-thirty. It was coolish at that hour—about seventy-five or eighty degrees, I guess. The gauge read about 170. I figured that before the real heat commenced I ought to be in Barstow—say by nine o'clock in the morning surely. Now and then a crazy bird seemed to fly through the car, making a strange chirping which I had been hearing ever since leaving the Ozarks. It was the kind of music the lugs make when they're too tight or too loose. I never knew for sure whether it was the car or the creatures of the air, and sometimes I wondered if a bird had become a prisoner in the back of the car and was perhaps dying of thirst or melancholy.

As I was pulling out of town a New York car slowed up alongside of me and a woman cried out ecstatically—"Hello there, New York!" She was one of those panicky ones who get an attack of hysteria in the middle of nowhere. They were going at a leisurely pace, about forty-five miles an hour, and I thought I'd just hang on to their tail. I clung to them for about three miles and then I saw that the gauge was climbing up over 190. I slowed to a walk and began doing some mental calculations. Back in Albuquerque, when I visited that wizard of automotive repairing, Hugh Dutter, I had learned that there was a difference between the reading of the gauge and the thermometer reading. A difference of fifteen degrees, supposedly in my favor, though it never really worked out that way in practice. Hugh Dutter had done everything possible to overcome the heating problem—except to boil out the radiator. But that was my own fault. I told him I had had that done about four thousand miles back. It was only when I got to Joseph City, Arizona, where I met an old Indian trader, that I realized there was nothing to do but have her cleaned out again. Bushman, that was the man's name, was kind enough to ride into Winslow with me in order to put me in the right hands. There I met his son-in-law, another automotive wizard, and I waited four hours or so while the radiator was boiled out, the timing re-timed, the fan belt changed, the points tickled up, the valves unloosened, the carburetor calibrated, and so on. All to the tune of a modest four dollars. It was wonderful, after that operation, to ride into Flagstaff in the heat of the afternoon with the gauge reading 130! I could scarcely believe my eyes. Of course, about an hour later, pulling up a long slope on my way to Cameron, just when it was getting real chilly, the damned thing boiled over. But once I got out of the forest and into the no-man's land where the mountains are wine-colored, the earth pea green, the mesas pink, blue, black and white, everything was lovely. For about forty miles I don't think I passed a human habitation. But that can happen of course most anywhere west of the big cities. Only here it's terrifying. Three cars passed me and then there was a stretch of silence and emptiness, a steady, sinister ebbing of all human life, of plant and vegetable life, of light itself. Suddenly, out of nowhere, it seemed, three horsemen galloped into the center of the road about fifty yards ahead of me. They just materialized, as it were. For a moment I thought it might be a hold-up. But no, they pranced a moment or two in the middle of the road, waved me a greeting, and then spurred their horses on into the phantasmal emptiness of dusk, disappearing in the space of a few seconds. What was amazing to me was that they seemed to have a sense of direction; they galloped off as if they were going somewhere when obviously there was nowhere to go to. When I got to Cameron I nearly passed it. Luckily there was a gas station, a few shacks, a hotel and some hogans by the side of the road. "Where's Cameron?" I asked, thinking it lay hidden on the other side of the bridge. "You're in it," said the man at the gas station. I was so fascinated by the eeriness of the décor that before inquiring for a room I walked down to the Little Colorado River and took a good look at the canyon there. I didn't know until the next morning that I was camping beside the Painted Desert which I had left the previous morning. I thought only that I had come to some very definite end, some hidden navel of the world where the rivers disappear and the hot magma pushes the granite up into pinkish veins, like geodesic haemorrhoids.

Well, anyway, to get back. Where was I? Somehow, ever since I hit Tucumcari I have become completely disoriented. On the license plates in New Mexico it reads: "The Land of Enchantment." And that it is, by God! There's a huge rectangle which embraces parts of four States—Utah, Colorado, New Mexico and Arizona—and which is nothing but enchantment, sorcery, illusionismus, phantasmagoria. Perhaps the secret of the American continent is contained in this wild, forbidding and partially unexplored territory. It is the land of the Indian par excellence. Everything is hypnagogic, chthonian and super-celestial. Here Nature has gone gaga and dada. Man is just an irruption, like a wart or a pimple. Man is not wanted here. Red men, yes, but then they are so far removed from what we think of as man that they seem like another species. Embedded in the rocks are their glyphs and hieroglyphs. Not to speak of the footprints of dinosaurs and other lumbering antediluvian beasts. When you come to the Grand Canyon it's as though Nature were breaking out into supplication. On an average it's only ten to eighteen miles from rim to rim of the Canyon, but it takes two days to traverse it on foot or horseback. It takes four days for the mail to travel from one side to the other, a fantastic journey in which your letters pass through four States. Animals and birds rarely cross the abyss. The trees and vegetation differ from one plateau to the other. Passing from top to bottom you go through practically all the climatic changes known on this globe, except the Arctic and Antarctic extremes. Between two formations of rock there was, so the scientists say, an interval of 500,000,000 years. It's mad, completely mad, and at the same time so grandiose, so sublime, so illusory, that when you come upon it for the first time you break down and weep with joy. *I* did, at least. For over thirty years I had been aching to see this huge hole in the earth. Like Phaestos, Mycenae, Epidauros, it is one of the few spots on this earth which not only come up to all expectation but surpass it. My friend Bushman, who had been a guide here for a number of years, had told me some fantastic yarns about the Grand Canyon. I can believe anything that any one might tell me about it, whether it has to do with geological eras and formations, freaks of nature in animal or plant life, or Indian legends. If some one were to tell me that the peaks and mesas and amphitheatres which are so fittingly called Tower of Set, Cheop's Pyramid, Shiva Temple, Osiris Temple, Isis Temple, etc. were the creation of fugitive Egyptians, Hindus, Persians, Chaldeans, Babylonians, Ethiopians, Chinese or Tibetans, I would lend a credulous ear. The Grand Canyon is an enigma and no matter how much we learn we shall never know the ultimate truth about it. . . .

As I was saying, I was just entering the desert that lies between Needles and Barstow. It was six o'clock in the cool of a desert morning and I was sitting on the running board waiting for the engine to cool off. This repeated itself at regular intervals, every twenty or thirty miles, as I said before. When I had covered about fifty miles or so the car slowed down of itself, found its natural rhythm, as it were, and nothing I could do would make it change its pace. I was condemned to crawl along at twenty to twenty-five miles an hour. When I got to a place called Amboy, I believe it was, I had a cool, consoling chat with an old desert rat who was the incarnation of peace, serenity and charity. "Don't fret yourself," he said. "You'll get there in good time. If not to-day why to-morrow. It makes no difference." Some one had stolen his peanut slot machine during the night. It didn't disturb him in the least. He put it down to human nature. "Some folks make you feel like a king," he said, "and others are lower than worms. We learn a lot about human nature watching the cars pass by." He had warned me that there would come a forty mile stretch which would seem like the longest forty miles I had ever covered. "I've done it hundreds of times," he said, "and each time the miles seem to stretch out more and more."

And by God he was right! It must have happened soon after I took leave of him. I had only travelled about five miles when I had to pull up by the side of the road and practice the beatitudes. I got under a shed with a tin roof and patiently twiddled my thumbs. On the wall was a sort of hieroglyphic nomenclature of the engine—the parts that go wrong and make it heat up. There were so many things, according to this graph, which could bring on fever and dysentery that I wondered how any one could ever lay his finger on the trouble without first getting a diploma from Henry Ford's School of Mechanical Diabolism. Moreover, it seemed to me that all the tender, troublesome parts touched on had been treated, in the case of my *charabanc*. Age alone could account for a great deal, it seemed to me. My own organism wasn't functioning any too handsomely, and I'm not exactly an old model, as they say.

Well, inch by inch then. "Don't fret!" that's what I kept telling myself. The new models were whizzing by at seventy-five and eighty miles an hour. Air-conditioned, most likely. For them it was nothing to traverse the desert—a matter of a couple of hours—with the radio bringing them Bing Crosby or Count Basie.

I passed Ludlow upside down. Gold was lying about everywhere in big bright nuggets. There was a lake of pure condensed milk which had frozen in the night. There were yucca palms, or if not yucca date and if not date then cocoanut—and oleanders and striped sea bass from the Everglades. The heat was rippling up slant-wise, like Jacob's Ladder seen through a corrugated mirror. The sun had become a gory omelette frying itself to a crisp. The cicadas were cricketing and that mysterious bird in the back of the car had somehow found its way under my feet between the clutch and the brake. Everything was dragging, including the minature piano and the steam calliope which had become entangled in the universal during the previous night's underwater passage. It was a grand cacophony of heat and mystification, the engine boiling in oil like an antique instrument, the tires expanding like dead toads, the nuts falling out like old teeth. The first ten miles seemed like a hundred, the second ten miles like a thousand, and the rest of the way just humanly incalculable.

I got to Barstow about one in the afternoon, after passing another examination by the plant, lice and vegetable inspectors at Daggett or some such ungodly place. I hadn't eaten since four in the morning and yet I had no appetite whatever. I ordered a steak, swallowed a sliver of it, and dove into the iced tea. As I was sitting there lucubrating and testifying in all languages I espied two women whom I recognized as guests of the Bright Angel Lodge. They had left the Grand Canyon in the morning and would probably have dinner in Calgary or Ottawa. I felt like an overheated slug. My brain-pan was vaporized. I never thought of Olsen, of course. I was racking my brains to try to remember whether I had started from Flagstaff, Needles or Winslow. Suddenly I recalled an excursion I had made that day—or was it three days ago?—to Meteor Crater. Where the devil *was* Meteor Crater? I felt slightly hallucinated. The bartender was icing a glass. Meanwhile the owner of the restaurant had taken a squirt gun and was killing flies on the screen door outside. It was Mother's Day. That told me it was Sunday. I had hoped to sit quietly in the shade in Barstow and wait for the sun to set. But you can't sit for hours in a restaurant unless you eat and drink. I grew fidgety. I decided to go to the telegraph office and send a ready made Mother's Day greeting from Barstow. It was sizzling outdoors. The street was just a fried banana flaming with rum and creosote. The houses were wilting, sagging to their knees, threatening to melt into glue or glucose. Only the gas stations seemed capable of surviving. They looked cool, efficient, inviting. They were impeccable and full of mockery. They had nothing to do with human life. There was no distress in them.

The telegraph office was in the railway station. I sat on a bench in the shade, after dispatching my telegram, and floated back to the year 1913, the same month and perhaps the same day, when first I saw Barstow through the window of a railway coach. The train was still standing at the station, just as it had been twenty-eight years ago. Nothing had changed except that I had dragged my carcass halfway around the globe and back again in the meantime. The thing that was most vivid in my memory, curiously enough, was the smell and sight of oranges hanging on the trees. The smell mostly. It was like getting close to a woman for the first time—the woman you never dared hope to meet. I remembered other things too, which had more to do with lemons than with oranges. The job I took near Chula Vista, burning brush all day in a broiling sun. The poster on the wall in San Diego, advertising a coming series of lectures by Emma Goldman—something that altered the whole course of my life. Looking for a job on a cattle ranch near San Pedro, thinking that I would become a cowboy because I was fed up with books. Nights, standing on the porch of the bunk house and looking towards Point Loma, wondering if I had understood that queer book in the library at Brooklyn—*Esoteric Buddhism.* Coming back to it in Paris about twenty years later and going quite daffy over it. No, nothing had radically altered. Confirmations, corroborations rather than disillusionment. At eighteen I was as much of a philosopher as I will ever be. An anarchist at heart, a non-partisan spirit, a free lancer and a free-booter. Strong friendships, strong hatreds, detesting everything lukewarm or compromising. Well, I hadn't liked California then and I had a premonition I wouldn't like it now. One enthusiasm completely vanished—the desire to see the Pacific Ocean. The Pacific leaves me indifferent. That part of it, at any rate, which washes the California shore. Venice, Redondo, Long Beach—I haven't visited them yet, though I'm only a few minutes away from them, being at this precise chronological moment of aberration in the celluloid city of Hollywood.

Well, the car had cooled off and so had I a bit. I had grown a little wistful, in fact. On to San Bernardino!

For twenty miles out of Barstow you ride over a washboard amidst sand dunes reminiscent of Bergen Beach or Canarsie. After a while you notice farms and trees, heavy green trees waving in the breeze. Suddenly the world has grown human again—because of the trees. Slowly, gradually, you begin climbing. And the trees and the farms and the houses climb with you. Every thousand feet there is a big sign indicating the altitude. The landscape becomes thermometric. Around you rugged, towering mountain ranges fading almost to extinction in the dancing heat waves of mid-afternoon. Some of them, indeed, have completely vanished, leaving only the pink snow shimmering in the heavens—like an ice cream cone without the cone. Others leave just a cardboard façade exposed—to indicate their substantiality.

Somewhere about a mile up towards God and his winged satellites the whole works comes toppling down on you. All the ranges converge suddenly—like a publicity stunt. Then comes a burst of green, the wildest, greenest green imaginable, as if to prove beyond the shadow of a doubt that California is indeed the Paradise it boasts of being. Everything but the ocean seems jammed into this mile-high circus at sixty miles an hour. It wasn't I who got the thrill—it was a man inside me trying to recapture the imagined thrill of the pioneers who came through this pass on foot and on horseback. Seated in an automobile, hemmed in by a horde of Sunday afternoon maniacs, one can't possibly experience the emotion which such a scene should produce in the human breast. I want to go back through that pass—Cajon Pass—on foot, holding my hat reverently in my hand and saluting the Creator. I would like it to be winter with a light covering of snow on the ground and a little sleigh under me such as Jean Cocteau used when he was a boy. I'd like to coast down into San Bernardino doing a belly-wopper. And if there are oranges ripening maybe God would be kind enough to put a few within reach so that I could pluck them at eighty miles an hour and give them to the poor. Of course the oranges are at Riverside, but with a light sleigh and a thin dry blanket of snow what are a few geographical dislocations!

The important thing to remember is that California begins at Cajon Pass a mile up in the air. Anything prior to that is vestigial and vestibulary. Barstow is in Nevada and Ludlow is a fiction or a mirage. As for Needles, it's on the ocean bed in another time, probably Tertiary or Mesozoic.

By the time I got to Burbank it was dark and full of embryonic aeroplanes. A flock of mechanical students were sitting on the curb along the Main Street eating dry sandwiches and washing them down with Coca-Colas. I tried to summon a feeling of devotion in memory of Luther Burbank but the traffic was too thick and there was no parking space. I couldn't see any connection between Luther and the town that was named after him. Or perhaps they had named it after another Burbank, the king of soda water or popcorn or laminated valves. I stopped at a drug store and took a Bromo Seltzer—for "simple headaches." The real California began to make itself felt. I wanted to puke. But you have to get a permit to vomit in public. So I drove into a hotel and took a beautiful room with a radio apparatus that looked like a repository for dirty linen. Bing Crosby was crooning away—the same old song which I had heard in Chattanooga, Boswell's Tavern, Chickamauga and other places. I wanted Connie Boswell but they were all out of her for the moment. I took my socks off and hung them around the knob of the dial to choke it off. It was eight o'clock and I had awakened at dawn about five days ago, it seemed. There were no beetles or bed-bugs—just the steady roar of traffic on the concrete strip. And Bing Crosby, of course, somewhere out in the blue on the invisible ether waves owned by the five-and-ten cent store.

1945

Aldo Leopold

From A Sand County Almanac

Leopold, Iowa-born, served with the U.S. Forest Service in the territories of Arizona and New Mexico (1909–1924) and in Wisconsin (1924–1933) during a time when "progress began to do away with" wild things. Later he was a professor at the University of Wisconsin. He died in 1948, fighting a brush fire. The three sketches which follow are from "Sketches Here and There," Part II of *Sand County Almanac.* They recount, in Leopold's words, "some of the episodes in my life that taught me, gradually and sometimes painfully, that the company is out of step. These episodes, scattered over the continent and through forty years of time, present a fair sample of the issues that bear the collective label: conservation." Leopold's essay "Conservation" (see Appendix) describes the conservationist's perspective on landscape. The sketches delineate, in particular landscapes, some of the destructive processes conservation has committed itself to stop, or at least to retard.

Illinois Bus Ride

A FARMER AND HIS SON are out in the yard, pulling a crosscut saw through the innards of an ancient cottonwood. The tree is so large and so old that only a foot of blade is left to pull on.

Time was when that tree was a buoy in the prairie sea. George Rogers Clark may have camped under it; buffalo may have nooned in its shade, switching flies. Every spring it roosted fluttering pigeons. It is the best historical library short of the State College, but once a year it sheds cotton on the farmer's window screens. Of these two facts, only the second is important.

The State College tells farmers that Chinese elms do not clog screens, and hence are preferable to cottonwoods. It likewise pontificates on cherry preserves, Bang's disease, hybrid corn, and beautifying the farm home. The only thing it does not know about farms is where they came from. Its job is to make Illinois safe for soybeans.

I am sitting in a 60-mile-an-hour bus sailing over a highway originally laid out for horse and buggy. The ribbon of concrete has been widened and widened until the field fences threaten to topple into the road cuts. In the narrow thread of sod between the shaved banks and the toppling fences grow the relics of what once was Illinois: the prairie.

No one in the bus sees these relics. A worried farmer, his fertilizer bill projecting from his shirt pocket, looks blankly at the lupines, lespedezas, or Baptisias that originally pumped nitrogen out of the prairie air and into his black loamy acres. He does not distinguish them from the parvenu quack-grass in which they grow. Were I to ask him why his corn makes a hundred bushels, while that of non-prairie states does well to make thirty, he would probably answer that Illinois soil is better. Were I to ask him the name of that white spike of pea-like flowers hugging the fence, he would shake his head. A weed, likely.

A cemetery flashes by, its borders alight with prairie puccoons. There are no puccoons elsewhere; dog-fennels and sowthistles supply the yellow motif for the modern landscape. Puccoons converse only with the dead.

Through the open window I hear the heart-stirring whistle of an upland plover; time was when his forebears followed the buffalo as they trudged shoulder-deep through an illimitable garden of forgotten blooms. A boy spies the bird and remarks to his father: there goes a snipe.

The sign says, "You are entering the Green River Soil Conservation District." In smaller type is a list of who is cooperating; the letters are too small to be read from a moving bus. It must be a roster of who's who in conservation.

The sign is neatly painted. It stands in a creek-bottom pasture so short you could play golf on it. Near by is the graceful loop of an old dry creek bed. The new creek bed is ditched straight as a ruler; it has been "uncurled" by the county engineer to hurry the run-off. On the hill in the background are contoured strip-crops; they have been "curled" by the erosion engineer to retard the run-off. The water must be confused by so much advice.

Everything on this farm spells money in the bank. The farmstead abounds in fresh paint, steel, and concrete. A date on the barn commemorates the founding fathers. The roof bristles with lightning rods, the weathercock is proud with new gilt. Even the pigs look solvent.

The old oaks in the woodlot are without issue. There are no hedges, brush patches, fencerows, or other signs of shiftless husbandry. The cornfield has fat steers, but probably no quail. The fences stand on narrow ribbons of sod; whoever plowed that close to barbed wires must have been saying, "Waste not, want not."

In the creek-bottom pasture, flood trash is lodged high in the bushes. The creek banks are raw; chunks of Illinois have sloughed off and moved seaward. Patches of giant ragweed mark where freshets have thrown down the silt they could not carry. Just who is solvent? For how long?

The highway stretches like a taut tape across the corn, oats, and clover fields; the bus ticks off the opulent miles; the passengers talk and talk and talk. About what? About baseball, taxes, sons-in-law, movies, motors, and funerals, but never about the heaving groundswell of Illinois that washes the windows of the speeding bus. Illinois has no genesis, no history, no shoals or deeps, no tides of life and death. To them Illinois is only the sea on which they sail to ports unknown.

Thinking Like a Mountain

A DEEP CHESTY BAWL echoes from rimrock to rimrock, rolls down the mountain, and fades into the far blackness of the night. It is an outburst of wild defiant sorrow, and of contempt for all the adversities of the world.

Every living thing (and perhaps many a dead one as well) pays heed to that call. To the deer it is a reminder of the way of all flesh, to the pine a forecast of midnight scuffles and of blood upon the snow, to the coyote a promise of gleanings to come, to the cowman a threat of red ink at the bank, to the hunter a challenge of fang against bullet. Yet behind these obvious and immediate hopes and fears there lies a deeper meaning, known only to the mountain itself. Only the mountain has lived long enough to listen objectively to the howl of a wolf.

Those unable to decipher the hidden meaning know nevertheless that it is there, for it is felt in all wolf country, and distinguishes that country from all other land. It tingles in the spine of all who hear wolves by night, or who scan their tracks by day. Even without sight or sound of wolf, it is implicit in a hundred small events: the midnight whinny of a pack horse, the rattle of rolling rocks, the bound of a fleeing deer, the way shadows lie under the spruces. Only the ineducable tyro can fail to sense the presence or absence of wolves, or the fact that mountains have a secret opinion about them.

My own conviction on this score dates from the day I saw a wolf die. We were eating lunch on a high rimrock, at the foot of which a turbulent river elbowed its way. We saw what we thought was a doe fording the torrent, her breast awash in white water. When she climbed the bank toward us and shook out her tail, we realized our error: it was a wolf. A half-dozen others, evidently grown pups, sprang from the willows and all joined in a welcoming mêlée of wagging tails and playful maulings. What was literally a pile of wolves writhed and tumbled in the center of an open flat at the foot of our rimrock.

In those days we had never heard of passing up a chance to kill a wolf. In a second we were pumping lead into the pack, but with more excitement than accuracy: how to aim a steep downhill shot is always confusing. When our rifles were empty, the old wolf was down, and a pup was dragging a leg into impassable slide-rocks.

We reached the old wolf in time to watch a fierce green fire dying in her eyes. I realized then, and have known ever since, that there was something new to me in those eyes—something known only to her and to the mountain. I was young then, and full of trigger-itch; I thought that because fewer wolves meant more deer, that no wolves would mean hunters' paradise. But after seeing the green fire die, I sensed that neither the wolf nor the mountain agreed with such a view.

Since then I have lived to see state after state extirpate its wolves. I have watched the face of many a newly wolfless mountain, and seen the south-facing slopes wrinkle with a maze of new deer trails. I have seen every edible bush and seedling browsed, first to anaemic desuetude, and then to death. I have seen every edible tree defoilated to the height of a saddlehorn. Such a mountain looks as if someone had given God a new pruning shears, and forbidden Him all other exercise. In the end the starved bones of the hoped-for deer herd, dead of its own too-much, bleach with the bones of the dead sage, or molder under the high-lined junipers.

I now suspect that just as a deer herd lives in mortal fear of its wolves, so does a mountain live in mortal fear of its deer. And perhaps with better cause, for while a buck pulled down by wolves can be replaced in two or three years, a range pulled down by too many deer may fail of replacement in as many decades.

So also with cows. The cowman who cleans his range of wolves does not realize that he is taking over the wolf's job of trimming the herd to fit the range. He has not learned to think like a mountain. Hence we have dustbowls, and rivers washing the future into the sea.

We all strive for safety, prosperity, comfort, long life, and dullness. The deer strives with his supple legs, the cowman with trap and poison, the statesman with pen, the most of us with machines, votes, and dollars, but it all comes to the same thing: peace in our time. A measure of success in this is all well enough, and perhaps is a requisite to objective thinking, but too much safety seems to yield only danger in the long run. Perhaps this is behind Thoreau's dictum: In wildness is the salvation of the world. Perhaps this is the hidden meaning in the howl of the wolf, long known among mountains, but seldom perceived among men.

1949

Rachel Carson

From Silent Spring

A biologist, Rachel Carson taught at the University of Maryland and at the Johns Hopkins University before she joined the U.S. Fish and Wildlife Service. *Silent Spring,* a best seller, could be said to be the first book to awaken an ecological conscience in contemporary America. It delineates the side-effects suffered in the ecological community by the uncontrolled use of pesticides.

From Realms of the Soil

THE THIN LAYER of soil that forms a patchy covering over the continents controls our own existence and that of every other animal of the land. Without soil, land plants as we know them could not grow, and without plants no animals could survive.

Yet if our agriculture-based life depends on the soil, it is equally true that soil depends on life, its very origins and the maintenance of its true nature being intimately related to living plants and animals. For soil is in part a creation of life, born of a marvelous interaction of life and nonlife long eons ago. The parent materials were gathered together as volcanoes poured them out in fiery streams, as waters running over the bare rocks of the continents wore away even the hardest granite, and as the chisels of frost and ice split and shattered the rocks. Then living things began to work their creative magic and little by little these inert materials became soil. Lichens, the rocks' first covering, aided the process of disintegration by their acid secretions and made a lodging place for other life. Mosses took hold in the little pockets of simple soil—soil formed by crumbling bits of lichen, by the husks of minute insect life, by the debris of a fauna beginning its emergence from the sea.

Life not only formed the soil, but other living things of incredible abundance and diversity now exist within it; if this were not so the soil would be a dead and sterile thing. By their presence and by their activities the myriad organisms of the soil make it capable of supporting the earth's green mantle.

The soil exists in a state of constant change, taking part in cycles that have no beginning and no end. New materials are constantly being contributed as rocks disintegrate, as organic matter decays, and as nitrogen and other gases are brought down in rain from the skies. At the same time other materials are being taken away, borrowed for temporary use by living creatures. Subtle and vastly important chemical changes are constantly in progress, converting elements derived from air and water into forms suitable for use by plants. In all these changes living organisms are active agents.

There are few studies more fascinating, and at the same time more neglected, than those of the teeming populations that exist in the dark realms of the soil. We know too little of the threads that bind the soil organisms to each other and to their world, and to the world above.

Perhaps the most essential organisms in the soil are the smallest—the invisible hosts of bacteria and of thread-like fungi. Statistics of their abundance take us at once into astronomical figures. A teaspoonful of topsoil may contain billions of bacteria. In spite of their minute size, the total weight of this host of bacteria in the top foot of a single acre of soil may be as much as a thousand pounds. Ray fungi, growing in long threadlike filaments, are somewhat less numerous than the bacteria, yet because they are larger their total weight in a given amount of soil may be about the same. With small green cells called algae, these make up the microscopic plant life of the soil.

Bacteria, fungi, and algae are the principal agents of decay, reducing plant and animal residues to their component minerals. The vast cyclic movements of chemical elements such as carbon and nitrogen through soil and air and living tissue could not proceed without these microplants. Without the mitrogen-fixing bacteria, for example, plants would starve for want of nitrogen, though surrounded by a sea of nitrogen-containing air. Other organisms form carbon dioxide, which, as carbonic acid, aids in dissolving rock. Still other soil microbes perform various oxidations and reductions by which minerals such as iron, manganese, and sulfur are transformed and made available to plants.

Also present in prodigious numbers are microscopic mites and primitive wingless insects called springtails. Despite their small size they play an important part in breaking down the residues of plants, aiding in the slow conversion of the litter of the forest floor to soil. The specialization of some of these minute creatures for their task is almost incredible. Several species of mites, for example, can begin life only within the fallen needles of a spruce tree. Sheltered here, they digest out the inner tissues of the needle. When the mites have completed their development only the outer layer of cells remains. The truly staggering task of dealing with the tremendous amount of plant material in the annual leaf fall belongs to some of the small insects of the soil and the forest floor. They macerate and digest the leaves, and aid in mixing the decomposed matter with the surface soil.

Besides all this horde of minute but ceaselessly toiling creatures there are of course many larger forms, for soil life runs the gamut from bacteria to mammals. Some are permanent residents of the dark subsurface layers; some hibernate or spend definite parts of their life cycles in underground chambers; some freely come and go between their burrows and the upper world. In general the effect of all this habitation of the soil is to aerate it and improve both its drainage and the penetration of water throughout the layers of plant growth.

Of all the larger inhabitants of the soil, probably none is more important than the earthworm. Over three quarters of a century ago, Charles Darwin published a book titled *The Formation of Vegetable Mould, through the Actions of Worms, with Observations on Their Habits.* In it he gave the world its first understanding of the fundamental role of earthworms as geologic agents for the transport of soil—a picture of surface rocks being gradually covered by fine soil brought up from below by the worms, in annual amounts running to many tons to the acre in most favorable areas. At the same time, quantities of organic matter contained in leaves and grass (as much as 20 pounds to the square yard in six months) are drawn down into the burrows and incorporated in soil. Darwin's calculations showed that the toil of earthworms might add a layer of soil an inch to an inch and a half thick in a ten-year period. And this is by no means all they do: their burrows aerate the soil, keep it well drained, and aid the penetration of plant roots. The presence of earthworms increases the nitrifying powers of the soil bacteria and decreases putrification of the soil. Organic matter is broken down as it passes through the digestive tracts of the worms and the soil is enriched by their excretory products.

This soil community, then, consists of a web of interwoven lives, each in some way related to the others—the living creatures depending on the soil, but the soil in turn a vital element of the earth only so long as this community within it flourishes.

The problem that concerns us here is one that has received little consideration: What happens to these incredibly numerous and vitally necessary inhabitants of the soil when poisonous chemicals are carried down into their world, either introduced directly as soil ''sterilants'' or borne on the rain that has picked up a lethal contamination as it filters through the leaf canopy of forest and orchard and cropland? Is it reasonable to suppose that we can apply a broad-spectrum insecticide to kill the burrowing larval stages of a crop-destroying insect, for example, without also killing the ''good'' insects whose function may be the essential one of breaking down organic matter? Or can we use a nonspecific fungicide without also killing the fungi that inhabit the roots of many trees in a beneficial association that aids the tree in extracting nutrients from the soil?

The plain truth is that this critically important subject of the ecology of the soil has been largely neglected even by scientists and almost completely ignored by control men. Chemical control of insects seems to have proceeded on the assumption that the soil could and would sustain any amount of insult via the introduction of poisons without striking back. The very nature of the world of the soil has been largely ignored.

From the few studies that have been made, a picture of the impact of pesticides on the soil is slowly emerging. It is not surprising that the studies are not always in agreement, for soil types vary so enormously that what causes damage in one may be innocuous in another. Light sandy soils suffer far more heavily than humus types. Combinations of chemicals seem to do more harm then separate applications. Despite the varying results, enough solid evidence of harm is accumulating to cause apprehension on the part of many scientists.

Under some conditions the chemical conversions and transformations that lie at the very heart of the living world are affected. Nitrification, which makes atmospheric nitrogen available to plants, is an example. The herbicide 2,4-D causes a temporary interruption of nitrification. In recent experiments in Florida, lindane, heptachlor, and BHC (benzene hexachloride) reduced nitrification after only two weeks in soil; BHC and DDT had significantly detrimental effects a year after treatment. In other experiments BHC, aldrin, lindane, heptachlor, and DDD all prevented nitrogen-fixing bacteria from forming the necessary root nodules on leguminous plants. A curious but beneficial relation between fungi and the roots of higher plants is seriously disrupted.

Sometimes the problem is one of upsetting that delicate balance of populations by which nature accomplishes far-reaching aims. Explosive increases in some kinds of soil organisms have occurred when others have been reduced by insecticides, disturbing the relation of predator to prey. Such changes could easily alter the metabolic activity of the soil and affect its productivity. They could also mean that potentially harmful organisms, formerly held in check, could escape from their natural controls and rise to pest status.

One of the most important things to remember about insecticides in soil is their long persistence, measured not in months but in years. Aldrin has been recovered after four years, both as traces and more abundantly as converted to dieldrin. Enough toxaphene remains in sandy soil ten years after its application to kill termites. Benzene hexachloride persists at least eleven years, heptachlor or a more toxic derived chemical, at least nine. Chlordane has been recovered twelve years after its application, in the amount of 15 per cent of the original quantity.

Seemingly moderate applications of insecticides over a period of years may build up fantastic quantities in soil. Since the chlorinated hydrocarbons are persistent and long-lasting, each application is merely added to the quantity remaining from the previous one. The old legend that "a pound of DDT to the acre is harmless'' means nothing if spraying is repeated. Potato soils have been found to contain up to 15 pounds of DDT per acre, corn soils up to 19. A cranberry bog under study contained 34.5 pounds to the acre. Soils from apple orchards seem to reach the peak of contamination, with DDT accumulating at a rate that almost keeps pace with its rate of annual application. Even in a single season, with orchards sprayed four or more times, DDT residues may build up to peaks of 30 to 50 pounds. With repeated spraying over the years the range between trees is from 26 to 60 pounds to the acre; under trees, up to 113 pounds. . . .

We are therefore confronted with a second problem. We must not only be concerned with what is happening to the soil; we must wonder to what extent insecticides are absorbed from contaminated soils and introduced into plant tissues. Much depends on the type of soil, the crop, and the nature and concentration of the insecticide. Soil high in organic matter releases smaller quantities of poisons than others. Carrots absorb more insecticide than any other crop studied; if the chemical used happens to be lindane, carrots actually accumulate higher concentrations than are present in the soil. In the future it may become necessary to analyze soils for insecticides before planting certain food crops. Otherwise even unsprayed crops may take up enough insecticide merely from the soil to render them unfit for market. . . .

As applications of pesticides continue and the virtually indestructible residues continue to build up in the soil, it is almost certain that we are heading for trouble. This was the consensus of a group of specialists who met at Syracuse University in 1960 to discuss the ecology of the soil. These men summed up the hazards of using ''such potent and little-understood tools'' as chemicals and radiation: ''A few false moves on the part of man may result in destruction of soil productivity and the arthropods may well take over.''

1962

Norman Mailer

From Of a Fire on the Moon

For Mailer, the moon-flight of Apollo II, which landed men on the moon for the first time, raises a moral question about America which he is unable to answer but only to amplify and elaborate. Is the Space Program "the noblest expression of the Twentieth Century or the quintessential statement of our lunacy"?—the lunacy of that technological deformation of the earth which he describes elsewhere in the book and which is quoted in the introduction to this section. In the excerpt which follows he examines the landscape of Cape Kennedy for any hints of an answer, any amplification of the question.

[Cape Kennedy]

WE MOVE on to Florida and the launch. If Aquarius had spent a week in Houston, he was to put in ten days on Cape Canaveral. He was loose in some real tropics at last with swamp and coconut palms. It was encouraging. Technology and the tropics were not built to hide everything from each other.

Let us take the tour. On Merritt Island and old Cape Canaveral now Cape Kennedy, the Space Center has been installed, a twenty-mile stretch between the Intracoastal Waterway and the Atlantic, a terrain of marshland and scrub where raccoon, bobcat and alligator are still reported, and moors and truncated dunes lie low before the sea. It is country beaten by the wind and water, not dissimilar to Hatteras, Chincoteague and the National Seashore on Cape Cod, unspectacular country, uninhabited by men in normal times and normal occupations, for there are few trees and only occasional palms as ravaged and scabby as the matted backside of a monkey, a flat land of heat and water and birds, indeed birds no less impressive to Aquarius than ibis, curlew, plover and tern, hawks and vultures gliding fine as squadrons in formation, even bald eagles, ospreys and owls. In the brackish water are saltwater trout, redfish, largemouth bass, and bream. It is country for hunting, for fishing, and for men who seek mosquitoes; it was next to uninhabited before the war. Now, first spaceport—think on it! first *space*port—of an industry which pay salaries to perhaps so much as half a million men and some women before it is through, and has spent more than four billion dollars a year for average the last few years, a spaceport which is focus to the aerospace industries, a congeries of the richest corporations supplying NASA. Yet this port to the moon, Mars, Venus, solar system and the beyond is a first clue to space, for it is surprisingly empty, mournful beyond belief for the tropics, and its road through the Air Force Base and the Space Center pass by empty marshes, deserted dune grass, and lonely signs. Every quarter-mile or so along that low grassy ridge toward the side of the sea is a road sign pointing to an old launch complex which on exploration turns out to consist of an unoccupied road and a launching tower for rockets no longer fired, and so left to commune by itself on a modest field of concrete, a tall, rust-red vertical structure of iron girders surrounded by abandoned blockhouses and utility sheds. To Aquarius the early history of the Space Program is contained in these empty launch towers, now as isolated and private as grain elevators by the side of railroad tracks in the flat prairies of Nebraska, Kansas, and the Dakotas, the town low before them, the quiet whine of the wind like the sound of surf off a sea of wheat. It was the grain elevator which communed on prairie nights with the stars. Here in the cricket-dinning tympani of Florida's dunes and marshes, the launching towers of rockets now obsolete give that same sense of the sentinel in a field of space, stand already as monoliths and artifacts of a prehistoric period when rockets usually exploded in the first few hundred feet of their flight.

Yes, the Cape has given a turn to Aquarius. If at Houston he still remained attached to a somewhat disembodied ego (which felt like a balloon on a tether)—if for all his extorted admiration at the self-sufficiency of NASA and its world, he could still not quite like it, quite rid himself of the idea that finally space travel proposed a future world of brains attached to wires, his ego was therefore of use. He would pull in the string from time to time to criticize what he saw. If he were heard to utter "This is not unimpressive," when encountering some perfection of cooperation or technique, he was also ready to whisper—in his heart at least—that the Manned Spacecraft Center was not the coziest home for the human heart. Indeed, it was so cold that one could finally walk away from it like from a chill corridor in a dream. The beauties of MSC went on in the minds of technicians, but the soul of a visitor felt locked in the vault with an air conditioner. So it was attractive to think that one could end the dream, unlock the door, and walk away.

That was hardly possible on the Cape. If the abandoned launch towers and the hot lonely ocean breeze opened vistas of the West and thoughts of how many of the most important events in America seemed to take place in all the lonely spaces—as if the Twentieth Century had become the domain of all the great and empty territories (the Saharas, the Siberias, and the Minutemen in the buried silos of the West)—that was forced to give way to a sense of huge activity and gargantuan dimensions. If MSC near Houston was a brain, then Cape Kennedy was the body, and at Launch Complex 39, up twenty miles to the north of Cocoa Beach and Canaveral, were found the bones and muscles of a Colossus. Here the big components of Saturn V came in by cargo plane, came by ship through the Panama Canal and by barge through the Gulf, came from Los Angeles and Sacramento, from Huntsville in Alabama to Michoud in Louisiana, and from Michoud to the Cape; here at Complex 39 the parts were assembled in a mammoth cube of an edifice with a smaller box attached, the Vehicle Assembly Building, 526 feet high, a building just about as large as the combined volume of the Merchandise Mart in Chicago and the Pentagon. Covering eight acres, enclosing 129 million cubic feet, the Vehicle Assembly Building was nonetheless windowless, and decorated from the outside in huge concentric rectangles of green-gray, and charcoal-gray, ivory-gray and light blue-gray; it looked like a block of wood colored by an Op Art painter, but since it was over fifty stories high, it also looked like the walls of a gargantuan suburban department store. If by volume it was when built the largest building in the world, the Vehicle Assembly Building, as one saw it standing on the flat filled-in marshes of the Cape, had to be also a fair candidate for the ugliest building in the world. Viewed from any external approach it was the architectural fungoid of them all.

Once inside, however, it was conceivably one of the more beautiful buildings in the world. Large enough to assemble as many as four moongoing Apollo-Saturn vehicles at once, it was therefore open enough to offer interior space for four tall bays, each of these niches tall enough to house the full rocket, which was thirty-six stories high. Since the rocket in turn sat on a transporter, called a crawler, of some dimension itself, the doors to the four bays were each over forty stories and therefore high enough and wide enough to take in through their portals the UN Building or the Statue of Liberty. Yet for all its size, the VAB was without decoration inside, rather a veritable shipyard and rigging of steel girders which supported whole floors capable of being elevated and lowered, then rolled in and out like steel file drawers in order to encircle each rocket with adjustable working platforms from either side. Since some of these platforms had three complete stories contained within them, the interior of the VAB was a complexity of buildings within buildings which had been first maneuvered then suspended ten and twenty and thirty stories above the ground. Because the sides were usually open, one could look out from the platforms to other constellations of girders and buildings and could look down from whichever great height to the floor of the VAB, sometimes as much as forty stories below. Note however: one was still inside a closed space, and the light which filtered through translucent panels rising from floor to ceiling was dim, hardly brighter than the light in a church or an old railroad terminal. One lost in consequence any familiar sense of recognition—you could have been up in the rigging of a bridge built beneath the dome of some partially constructed and enormous subterranean city, or you could have been standing on the scaffolding of an unfinished but monumental cathedral, beautiful in this dim light, this smoky concatenation of structure upon structure, of breadths and vertigos and volumes of open space beneath the ceiling, tantalizing views of immense rockets hidden by their clusters of work platforms. One did not always know whether one was on a floor, a platform, a bridge, a fixed or impermanent part of this huge shifting ironwork of girders and suspended walkways. It was like being in the back of the stage at an opera house, the view as complex, yet the ceiling was visible from the floor and the ceiling was more than fifty stories up, since above the rockets were yet some massive traveling overhead cranes. To look down from the upper stages of the rocket, or from the highest level where the crew would sit, was to open oneself to a study of the dimensions of one's fear of heights. Down, down, a long throw of the soul down, down again, still falling was the floor of the building, forty floors below. The breath came back into the chest from an abyss. And in one corner of the floor like a stamp on the edge of a large envelope was a roped-in square of several hundred tourists gawking up at the yellow cranes and the battleship-gray girders.

Taken originally on a tour by a guide, Aquarius had spent the good part of a day in this building, and was back again twice to be given a more intimate trip and a peek into the three stages and the Command and Service Module of Apollo 12, which was then being prepared for its flight in November. Looking into any portion of the interior of a rocket was like looking into the abdominal cavity of a submarine or a whale. Green metal walls, green and blue tanks, pipes and proliferations of pipes, black blocks of electrical boxes and gray blocks of such boxes gave an offering of those zones of silence which reside at the center of machines, a hint of that ancient dark beneath the hatch in the hold of the bow—such zones of silence came over him. He could not even be amused at the curtained walls of white and the in-sucking wind of the dust collectors and the electrical shoe polishers, the white smocks and the interns' caps they were obliged to put on before they could peer through the hatch of the Command Module, and see the habitation of the astronauts. A gray conical innerland of hundreds of buttons and switches looked back at him, and three reclining seats vaguely reminiscent of instruments of torture. Three dentists' chairs side by side! Yes, he could have found the white outfits they were wearing a touch comic—if dust they were to protect the machine against, then garments they could wear, but why white, why the white hospital walls? And thought that of course they would keep it like the sterile room in a delivery ward, for indeed there was something about space which spoke of men preparing to deliver the babies they would themselves bear. The aim of technique was to parallel nature, and the interior of the VAB was the antechamber of a new Creation.

So, it was probably the Vehicle Assembly Building which encouraged Aquarius to release the string of the balloon and let his ego float off to whatever would receive it. It was not that he suddenly decided to adopt the Space Program, or even approve it in part, it was just that he came to recognize that whatever was in store, a Leviathan was most certainly ready to ascend the heavens—whether for good or ill he might never know—but he was standing at least in the first cathedral of the age of technology, and he might as well recognize that the world would change, that the world *had* changed, even as he had thought to be pushing and shoving on it with *his* mighty ego. And it had changed in ways he did not recognize, had never anticipated, and could possibly not comprehend now. The change was mightier than he had counted on. The full brawn of the rocket came over him in this cavernous womb of an immensity, this giant cathedral of a machine designed to put together another machine which would voyage through space. Yes, this emergence of a ship to travel the ether was no event he could measure by any philosophy he had been able to put together in his brain. . . .

II

Saturn V would take off from a plain of gray-green moor and marsh, no factory or habitation within three and a half miles. Saturn V had almost six million pounds of fuel. So it would take the equivalent of thirty thousand strong men to raise it an inch. It would take liquid oxygen, liquid hydrogen and a very high grade of kerosene called RP-1. It had hydrazine, unsymmetrical dimethylhydrazine, and nitrogen tetroxide in the Service Module. It was in effect a bomb, thirty-three feet wide—the length of a long living room. Corporation executives earning $50,000 a year just begin to think of a thirty-three-foot living room for themselves. And it was the height of a football field set on end. Sometimes they described it as a thirty-six-story building (ten feet to a floor) but a football field was clear measure of size, and this bomb, 363 feet high, 33 feet wide at the base, would blow if it blew with a force kin to one million pounds of TNT. That was like an old-fashioned bombing raid in World War II—one thousand planes each carrying one thousand pounds of bombs. So Saturn V would devastate an area if ever it went. Flight Control, the Press Site and the VIP stands were located therefore three and a half empty miles away across barren moors which, having been built by dredging fill into marshland, looked as if a bomb had gone off on them already.

On the night before the launch of Apollo 11, in the heart of Brevard County, in that stretch which runs from Melbourne through Eau Gallie, and Cocoa, to Titusville, on the coastal strip from Patrick Air Force Base through Cocoa Beach and Cape Canaveral to the Cape Kennedy Air Force Station and above to the Space Center and Launch Pad 39, through all that several hundred square miles of town and water and flat swampy waste of wilderness, through cultivated tropical gardens, and back roads by rivers lined with palms, through all the evening din of crickets, cicadas, beetles, bees, mosquitoes, grasshoppers and wasps some portion of a million people began to foregather on all the beaches and available islands and causeways and bridges and promontories which would give clear view of the flight from six miles and ten miles and fifteen miles away. Tomorrow most of them would need field glasses to follow the flight up from the pad and out of sight over the sea down a chain of Caribbean isles, but they would have a view—they knew tonight that if the skies were clear they would have their view because they were encamped only where the line of sight was unimpeded to Launch Pad 39 on the horizon. There one could certainly see Apollo 11 on her Saturn V, see her for seven, nine, eleven miles away; she was lit up. A play of giant arc lights, as voluminous in candlepower as the lights for an old-fashioned Hollywood premiere, was directed on the spaceship from every side. On U.S. 1 in Titusville, eleven miles from Cape Kennedy across Merritt Island and the Banana and Indian rivers, all that clear shot across the evening waters, at an artillery range of twenty thousand yards, two hundred football fields away, by an encampment of tourists up from southern Florida, Everglades, Miami, and the Keys; in from Tampa, and Orlando; down from Daytona, St. Augustine, Gainesville, and Jacksonville; come from Fort Myers and Fort Lauderdale, from Sarasota, St. Petersburg, Lakeland,

Ocala and Tallahassee, come from all the towns of Georgia and points farther north and west as well as every itinerant camper in the area from all of the ambulatory camping-out families of the fifty states, and tourists down on economy flights for a week in cheap hot summer Florida and now slung out in the back seats of rented cars, on U.S. 1 in Titusville, in an encampment of every variety of camper, was a view of the spaceship across flat land and waters, and she looked like a shrine with the lights upon her. In the distance she glowed for all the world like some white stone Madonna in the mountains, welcoming footsore travelers at dusk. Perhaps it was an unforeseen game of the lighting, but America had not had its movie premieres for nothing, nor its Rockettes in Radio City and fifty million squares tooling the tourist miles over the years to Big Town to buy a ticket to spectacle and back home again. If you were going to have a Hollywood premiere and arc lights, a million out to watch and a spaceship which looked across the evening flutter like the light on the Shrine of Our Lady outside any church in South Brooklyn or Bay Ridge, then by God you might just as well have this spectacle on the premiere trip to the moon. That deserved a searchlight or two! And the campers stared across the waters in their bivouac off Route 1 in Titusville, campers sat on the banks of the Indian River at twilight and waited for the tropical night to pass its hold on the hours.

There were new industries in America these years. After five decades of suspense movies, and movies of the Wild West, after the adventures of several generations of men in two world wars and Korea and Vietnam, after sixteen years of *Playboy* and American iconization of the gravity-defying breast and the sun-ripened buttock, after ten years of the greatest professional football, after a hundred years and more of a tradition that the frontier was open and would never close, and after twenty more perplexing technological years when prosperity came to nearly every White pocket, and technology put out its plastic, its superhighways, its supermarkets, its appliances, its suburbs, its smog, and its intimation that the frontier was damn shut, shut like a boulder on a rabbit burrow, America had erupted from this pressure between its love of adventure and its fear that adventure was not completely shut down; America had spewed out on the road. The country had become a nation of campers, of cars toting trailers, of cars pulling tent-trailers, of truck-campers, top-of-car tent packs, Volkswagen buses converted to ambulatory bedrooms, jeeps with Chic Sale houses built on the back, Land-Rovers with bunks, Broncos with more bunks—any way a man could get out of the house with his buddies or his family or his grandmother, and take to the road and find some ten by twenty feet of parking grass not posted, not tenanted, and not too muddy, he would camp. All over America in the summer the night fields were now filled with Americans sleeping on air mattresses which reposed on plastic cloth floors of plastic cloth tents—what a sweet smell of Corporate Chemical, what a vat and void to mix with all the balmy fermy chlorophylls and pollens of nature! America the Sanitary, and America the Wild, went out to sleep in the woods, Sanitary-Lobe and Wild-Lobe nesting together neatly, schizophrenic twins in the skull case of the good family American.

So they were out tonight, some portion of a million, all drawn on the lines of sight in Brevard County, and on every highway and causeway in the area the ground was covered with cars and campers, the shelter-roof extension of one family's tent near to topping the picnic blanket spread out behind the tailgate of the next station wagon, and the open trunk lid of a twelve- or fifteen-year-old Dodge convertible (rusty, top all rent, peeling friction tape and dirty white adhesive tape chasing a flap of a patch) stood next to both, part of the family sleeping in the trunk, the others with their good dirty feet out the windows. It was hardly just middle-class America here tonight, rather every echo of hard trade-union beer-binge paunch-gut-and-muscle, and lean whippy redneck honky-tonk clans out to bird-watch in the morning with redeye in the shot glass. There were tourists and not inelegant campers which spoke of peanut butter and jelly, watercress, and cucumber—suburban campers—but there was also the raw gasoline of expectation in the air, and families of poor Okies. One felt the whole South stirring on this night. Quiet pious Baptists, out somewhere on their porches (kin to some of the redneck and Okie—Okie for Okeechobee!—and working class here) seemed to be waiting over an arc of a thousand miles, certainly all the way from Cape Kennedy across Florida along the Gulf of Mexico to Houston and the Manned Spacecraft Center and back again, all across that belt of Fundamentalist piety, hot dry tempers burning like closed-up balefire against the humidity of the swamps, religion and lust to work their combat in the tropical nights, yes all over the South they had to be praying, yes even more than everywhere for the safety of this shot, the astronauts part of that family of concern which White Southerners could share with each other out of the sweet deep wells of their Christian hearts, what was left of them. It was not hard to have a vision of mothers and grandmothers looking like spinsters, silver-rimmed glasses to shield your skin from their eyes of burning faith, predictable turkey wattles on the neck: they would be praying for America tonight—thoughts of America served to replace the tender sense of the Virgin in Protestant hearts. And out here on the campgrounds of Brevard County, out on all the scorched shoulders and oil-coated grass of the available highway, were men getting ready to drink with their wives, middle-aged, green-eyed Southern mill workers with sunburned freckled skin, reddish hair, hard mechanic's muscles in their forearms, wife a trinity of worrying mother, fattening slattern, and give-me-a-drink-and-I'll-holler-happy sort of bitch. Dutiful work, devotion to family and property, their sloven property! mingy propriety, real raucous bustouts—that sort of South, married out of high school, oats half-sown like three quarters of all America over thirty, and their boys on the hunt through the encampment looking for opposite numbers, other boys or—Gods of fornication with them!—girls without bank locks on their bloomersl You can expect nothing less on a night so filled with heat, human meat, bubbles of fear, prayer soft as love, and tropical sex in every sauce. . . .

And men and women, tired from work and travel, sat in their cars and sat outside their cars on aluminum pipe and plastic-webbing folding chairs, and fanned themselves, and looked across the miles at the shrine. Out a car window projected the sole of a dirty foot. The big toe pointed straight up to Heaven in parallel to Saturn V. . . .

IV

The two hours of sleep were more worthy of Atlas than Aquarius, for in his dreams he held up a portion of the State of Florida. Aquarius had been covering the moon shot from July first to this morning of the sixteenth. The mildest form of purgatory was to spend two weeks in a motel.

Everybody complained that the tension accompanying the preparations for Apollo 11 had been less than launchings in the past. Cocoa Beach itself had altered. The old days of honky-tonks on the strip of highway and rockets threatening to carve a furrow down the beach were now gone. Money had come in and industry, space technicians and their families, Supermarkets, motels churches, and real estate developments had been put up. In the restaurants, public address systems broke into the mood of a meal to call patrons to the phone. The paper doilies under the plate carried legends: AMERICA'S SPACE PROGRAM BENEFITS ALL MANKIND—*Your Souvenir of Apollo 11 Lunar Landing*. Better Color Telvision. Water Purification at Less Cost. New Paints and Plastics. Lunar Walker for the Handicapped. Laser Surgery. Solar Power. So forth. Cocoa Beach had been one of the five places on the Atlantic Seaboard which deserved the title "Wild West of the East," but Cocoa Beach deserved it no longer. As the doily revealed, it was part of the Brevard Economic Development Council. Until the last few days when the Press arrived in hundreds then thousands, there had been monotonous hours when it was necessary to remind oneself that three men were leaving for the moon in less than a week.

But in the dark morning before dawn on the sixteenth, in the black hour of 4 A.M., the night air a wet and lightless forest in the nose, one was finally scared. It was not unlike awakening in a convoy with invasion of a foreign beach scheduled for the hours ahead, an awakening in the dark of the sort one will always remember, for such nights live only on a few mornings of one's life. Somewhere not so far from here, the astronauts were getting up as well. And the ghosts of old Indians.

In that long-ago of prairie spaces when the wind was the message of America, Indians had lived beneath the moon, stared at the moon, lived in greater intimacy with the moon than any European. Who could say the ride of the Indian with whisky in his veins was not some conflagration of messages derived from the silences of the moon? Now tonight were the ghosts of old Indians awakening in the prairies and the swamps? Did the echo of the wind through the abandoned launch towers of the Cape strike a resonance across two thousand miles to the grain elevators by the side of railroad tracks in the mournful empty windings of the West? The country had been virgin once, an all but empty continent with lavender and orange in the rocks, pink in the sky, an aura of blue in the deep green of the forest—now, not four centuries even spent, the buffalo were gone, and the Indians; the swamps were filled; the air stank with every exhaust from man and machine. All the while we had been composing our songs to the moon and driving the Indian onto the reservation, had we also been getting ready to go to the moon out of some deep recognition that we had already killed the nerve which gave life to the earth? Yet the moon by every appearance knew more about disease and the emanations of disease than the oldest leper on earth. ''Of what can you dream?'' said the moon. ''I am battered beyond belief and you think to violate me now?''

Driving through the night, passing again the families and tourists who were waiting for morning on the banks of the causeway, showing a Press Pass to the guard at the gate, and being waved on in silence, yes near to conspiratorial silence, there was the tangible sense of time running in parallel, the million-headed witness now traveling to a point where the place would cross the time and the conscious eye of the nation would be there to witness this event. By television would they witness it. That would be an experience like getting conceived in a test tube.

Out at the Press Site, Saturn V was visible across the near distance of three and a half miles. It was the nearest Aquarius had approached on this long night, and it was indeed the nearest anyone would come but the launching crew and the three astronauts. As Apollo-Saturn stood on its concrete pad six thousand yards away across a lagoon from the small grandstand built for the Press, its details now visible, it looked less like a shrine, but all the more a presence. A squad of floodlights played upon it, and their beams reflecting from the thin night haze displayed a fan of separate lights across the sky on down into the surface of the lagoon, a bending and glancing of rays worthy of a diamond upon a mirror. In the black wet night, back of the floor lamps, lightning flickered, so regularly that one might have been looking at a lighthouse rotating its flare—somewhere down the horizon, a potency of storm was speaking up in the response of the Caribbean. Long far-off rolls of thunder.

Staring across the water, Aquarius took a long study. His binoculars appeared to lock him into collaboration with Saturn V, as if the rocket had the power to keep those binoculars pressed to his nose, as if finally Aquarius and Saturn V were now linked into some concupiscence of mission like a one-night stand which might leave its unexpected consequence upon him. What a vehicle was the spaceship! A planet-traveler massive as a destroyer, delicate as a silver arrow. At the moment if lifted off from the earth it would be burning as much oxygen as is consumed by half a billion people taking their breath—that was twice, no, more than twice the population of America. What a deep breath must then have been concentrated into the liquid oxygen cooled to 297 degrees below zero and thereby turning air to cloud at every hint of contact with the pipes which were in turn contained within other pipes two feet thick to insulate the fuel. Model of an ogress, umbilical cords of every thickness and sinuosity, snakes and cables and ropes and constrictors thick as tree trunks passed in cluster from swing-arms and the walkways of the launching tower into the thin-skinned walls of the rocket; a Medusa's head of umbilicals loading fuel, charging batteries, testing circuits; a complexity of interrelation between the launching tower and the rocket so simplified by the swing-arms that Apollo-Saturn resting on her pad did not look distraught but calm, like a silver-white ship standing erect by an iron tree with nine horizontal branches. There were clouds about both, strings of small firm well-puffed little clouds drifting off at right angles from the rocket at each place where an umbilical from an oxygen pipe had been disconnected; the clouds gave Saturn V the brow of a philosopher in contemplation above his thought, yes, the cloud belonged to Saturn V, it nuzzled at it, a new cloud not many hours old. And the light from the floodlamps reflected from the white icy skin of the wall. Sainted Leviathan, ship of space, she was a planetary traveler. . . .

They got back to the Press Site at seven-thirty. The sun was clearly up and burning through a haze. In the distance, through binoculars, Saturn V now looked gray, a near-white gray, a gray palpability among other grays. Everything was gray, the Launch Pad, the tower, the vehicle, the sky. The rocket looked as if it were already on the moon. Only the sun gave a platinum edge to the outline of Saturn and the cryogenic cloud.

Aquarius, still brooding over the astronauts, came to the gloomy conclusion that even if you comprehended them (came to some whole notion that they were finally good and noble men, or men who were brave but not without malignity), you would still be inhibited from saying in confidence that the Space Program was for good or ill since History often used the best of men for the worst of purposes and discarded them when the machines of new intent were ready. As often History had used the worst of men to convert an unhealthy era to a new clime. But like a dive into a dream, explorations of these questions would only open into deeper questions. Standing in the early morning heat he had an instinct that before all was done the questions would travel through the unmapped continent of America's undetermined heart.

1969

Robert Frost

A Brook in the City

The symbolic dimensions of this poem are evoked and suggested by those qualities of the brook which Frost chooses to emphasize: "strength/ and impulse"; and by the way in which he characterizes the process of urbanization: "square," "wear," "cemented," "sent," "dispose," "thrown." The landscape becomes psychological as well as physical.

The farmhouse lingers, though averse to square
With the new city street it has to wear
A number in. But what about the brook
That held the house as in an elbow-crook?
I ask as one who knew the brook, its strength
And impulse, having dipped a finger length
And made it leap my knuckle, having tossed
A flower to try its currents where they crossed.
The meadow grass could be cemented down
From growing under pavements of a town;
The apple trees be sent to hearthstone flame.
Is water wood to serve a brook the same?
How else dispose of an immortal force
No longer needed? Staunch it at its source
With cinder loads dumped down? The brook was thrown
Deep in a sewer dungeon under stone
In fetid darkness still to live and run—
And all for nothing it had ever done,
Except forget to go in fear perhaps.
No one would know except for ancient maps
That such a brook ran water. But I wonder
If from its being kept forever under,
The thoughts may not have risen that so keep
This new-built city from both work and sleep.

1921

Robert Lowell

The Mouth of the Hudson

"The Mouth of the Hudson" evokes a static, hopelessly jumbled, and soulless landscape. The fact that the poet-observer cannot image the "thirty states" in the freight trains suggests that even the consolation open to such romantic figures in the ruins of a technological landscape as the hobo of the thirties (Dos Passos' "Vag," Hart Crane's hoboes in "The River" section of *The Bridge*) and Jack Kerouac's beat "educated penniless rake" of the fifties is closed to him. The image of a sulphurous yellow sun (or fog) is a signature of the French symbolists and of Eliot, who used it to symbolize a purgatorial no man's land.

(*For Esther Brooks*)

A single man stands like a bird-watcher,
and scuffles the pepper and salt snow
from a discarded, gray
Westinghouse Electric cable drum.
He cannot discover America by counting
the chains of condemned freight-trains
from thirty states. They jolt and jar
and junk in the siding below him.
He has trouble with his balance.
His eyes drop,
and he drifts with the wild ice
ticking seaward down the Hudson,
like the blank sides of a jig-saw puzzle.

The ice ticks seaward like a clock.
A Negro toasts
Wheat-seeds over the coke-fumes
of a punctured barrel.
Chemical air
sweeps in from New Jersey,
and smells of coffee.

Across the river,
ledges of suburban factories tan
in the sulphur-yellow sun
of the unforgivable landscape.

1964

John Frederick Nims

Decline and Fall

"Decline and Fall" evokes not only the inevitable ruin of civilizations, and cities, but also the ruins that succeeding civilizations make of ruin.

We had a city also. Hand in hand
Wandered happy as travellers our own land.
Murmured in turn the hearsay of each stone
Or, where a legend faltered, lived our own.
The far-seen obelisk my father set
(Pinning two roads forever where they met)
Waved us in wandering circles, turned our tread
Where once morass engulfed that passionate head.

Cornice rose in ranges, rose so high
It saw no sky, that forum, but noon sky.
Marble shone like shallows; columns too
Streamed with cool light as rocks in breakers do.

O marble many-colored as reach of thought,
Tones so recollected and so distraught.
Golden: like swimmers when the August shore
Brightens their folklore poses more and more.
Or grey with silver: moon's whirling spell
Over the breathless olives we knew well;
Ivory as shoulders there that summer-dressed
Curve to come shyly naked, then find rest
(The tresses love dishevelled leaning dazed
And grateful). Or the wayward stone that blazed
As cheeks do. Or as eyes half-lowered flare.
Violet as veins are, love knows where.
Fine coral as the shy and wild tonguetip,
Undersea coral, rich as inner lip.

There was a stone to build on!
Friezes ran
In strong chorales that where they closed began;
And statues: each a wrung or ringing phrase
In the soul's passionate cadence of her days.

O stone so matched and massive, worked so well,
Who could believe it when the first brick fell?

Who could imagine the unlucky word
Would darken to the worldwide sigh we heard?
How our eyes wrenched together and held fast
Each face tightening to a chalky cast
(So poor a copy of one hour before).
Who could believe the gloom, the funnelled roar
Of cornice falling, forum falling, all
Falling? Or dream it fallen? Not a wall
With eaves to route the rain. The rivers swelled
Till roads groped in lakebottom. Nothing held
Clean edge or corner. Caking, the black flood
Left every luminous room tunnels of mud.
Earth shook: the columns walked, in midair clashed,
And the steep stone exploded as it crashed.

Soon the barbarian swarmed like locusts blown
Between the flood and spasm of our stone.
Grunted to tug their huts and marble sties
Where friezes broke like foam in the blue skies.
Blue noses poked, recoiling as they found
Our young and glad-eyed statues underground;
Singing salvation, the lewd chisel pecks
At boy and girl: one mutilated sex.
All our high moments cheapened—greed and grime
Charred them in rickety stithies to quicklime.
Murderous world. That town that seemed a star
Rose in our soul. And there the ruins are.
We'll not walk there again. Who'd wish to walk
Where the rats gather and grey tourists talk?
Who'd walk there even alive? Or bid his ghost
Trail phosphor on the melancholy coast?

1960

W. S. Merwin

Burning Mountain

"Burning Mountain" evokes a landscape "fissured" by a smouldering coal mine. Merwin, who was born in New York and raised in Scranton, Pennsylvania, makes this a symbol of natural rather than technological deformation: it is the microcosm of a universe governed by the law of entropy—the slow, inevitable loss of energy (fire) which in time will turn the earth into a burned-out meteor.

No blacker than others in winter, but
The hushed snow never arrives on that slope.
An emanation of steam on damp days,
With a faint hiss, if you listen some places,
Yes, and if you pause to notice, an odor,
Even so near the chimneyed city, these
Betray what the mountain has at heart. And all night,
Here and there, popping in and out of their holes
Like ground-hogs gone nocturnal, the shy flames.

Unnatural, but no mystery.
Many are still alive to testify
Of the miner who left his lamp hanging
Lit in the shaft and took the lift, and never
Missed a thing till, half-way home to supper
The bells' clangor caught him. He was the last
You'd have expected such a thing from;
The worrying kind, whose old-womanish
Precautions had been a joke for years.

Smothered and silent, for some miles the fire
Still riddles the fissured hill, deviously
Wasting and inextinguishable. They
Have sealed off all the veins they could find,
Thus at least setting limits to it, we trust.
It consumes itself, but so slowly it will outlast
Our time and our grandchildren's, curious
But not unique: there was always one of these
Nearby, wherever we moved, when I was a child.

Under it, not far, the molten core
Of the earth recedes from its thin crust
Which all the fires we light cannot prevent
From cooling. Not a good day's walk above it
The meteors burn out in the air to fall

Harmless in empty fields, if at all.
Before long it practically seemed normal,
With its farms on it, and wells of good water,
Still cold, that should last us, and our grandchildren.

1960

William Gass

In the Heart of the Heart of the Country

"My fictions," Gass has written, "are, by and large, experimental constructions; that is, I try to make things out of words the way a sculptor might make a statue out of stone. Readers will therefore find very little in the way of character or story in my stories. Working in the tradition of the Symbolist poets, I regard the techniques of fiction (for the contemporary artist) as in no way distinct from the strategies of the long poem." "In the Heart of the Heart of the Country" is a "voice" story—a story less concerned with plot than with the spoken and unspoken revelations of the speaker's state of mind. Covertly the speaker reveals his own history as overtly he reveals, in a sequence of journal-like observations, his relationship to the landscape and the environment in which he finds himself. Something of what he is doing in B . . . , Indiana, is suggested by his ironic allusion to Yeats's Symbolist poem "Sailing to Byzantium" in the opening sentence. In Yeats's poem Byzantium is "the artifice of eternity"; in Gass's world "the cities are swollen and poisonous with people," and the speaker has retreated to a pastoral sanctuary only to find that there "the modern husbandman uses chemicals from cylinders and sacks, spike-ball-and-claw machines, metal sheds, and cost accounting."

Gass is currently Professor of Philosophy at Washington University in St. Louis. Richard Brautigan, Robert Coover (whose stories follow), and he represent the experimentalist impulse in contemporary fiction.

A PLACE

So I have sailed the seas and come . . .

to B . . .

a small town fastened to a field in Indiana. Twice there have been twelve hundred people here to answer to the census. The town is outstandingly neat and shady, and always puts its best side to the highway. On one lawn there's even a wood or plastic iron deer.

You can reach us by crossing a creek. In the spring the lawns are green, the forsythia is singing, and even the railroad that guts the town has straight bright rails which hum when the train is coming, and the train itself has a welcome horning sound.

Down the back streets the asphalt crumbles into gravel. There's Westbrook's, with the geraniums, Horsefall's, Mott's. The sidewalk shatters. Gravel dust rises like breath behind the wagons. And I am in retirement from love.

WEATHER

In the midwest, around the lower Lakes, the sky in the winter is heavy and close, and it is a rare day, a day to remark on, when the sky lifts and allows the heart up. I am keeping count, and as I write this page, it is eleven days since I have seen the sun.

MY HOUSE

There's a row of headless maples behind my house, cut to free the passage of electric wires. High stumps, ten feet tall, remain, and I climb these like a boy to watch the country sail away from me. They are ordinary fields, a little more uneven than they should be, since in the spring they puddle. The topsoil's thin, but only moderately stony. Corn is grown one year, soybeans another. At dusk starlings darken the single tree—a larch—which stands in the middle. When the sky moves, fields move under it. I feel, on my perch, that I've lost my years. It's as though I were living at last in my eyes, as I have always dreamed of doing, and I think then I know why I've come here: to see, and so to go out against new things—oh god how easily—like air in a breeze. It's true there are moments—foolish moments, ecstasy on a tree stump—when I'm all but gone, scattered I like to think like seed, for I'm the sort now in the fool's position of having love left over which I'd like to lose; what good is it now to me, candy ungiven after Halloween?

A PERSON

There are vacant lots on either side of Billy Holsclaw's house. As the weather improves, they fill with hollyhocks. From spring through fall, Billy collects coal and wood and puts the lumps and pieces in piles near his door, for keeping warm is his one work. I see him most often on mild days sitting on his doorsill in the sun. I notice he's squinting a little, which is perhaps the reason he doesn't cackle as I pass. His house is the size of a single garage, and very old. It shed its paint with its youth, and its boards are a warped and weathered gray. So is Billy. He wears a short lumpy faded black coat when it's cold, otherwise he always goes about in the same loose, grease-spotted shirt and trousers. I suspect his galluses were yellow once, when they were new.

WIRES

These wires offend me. Three trees were maimed on their account, and now these wires deface the sky. They cross like a fence in front of me, enclosing the crows with the clouds. I can't reach in, but like a stick, I throw my feelings over. What is it that offends me? I am on my stump, I've built a platform there and the wires prevent my going out. The cut trees, black wires, all the beyond birds therefore anger me. When I've wormed through a fence to reach a meadow, do I ever feel the same about the field?

THE CHURCH

The church has a steeple like a hat of a witch, and five birds, all doves, perch in its gutters.

MY HOUSE

Leaves move in the windows. I cannot tell you yet how beautiful it is, what it means. But they do move. They move in the glass.

POLITICS

. . . for all those not in love.

I've heard Batista described as a Mason. A farmer who'd seen him in Miami made this claim. He's as nice a fellow as you'd ever want to meet. Of Castro, of course, no one speaks.

For all those not in love there's law: to rule . . . to regulate . . . to rectify. I cannot write the poetry of such proposals, the poetry of politics, though sometimes—often—always now—I am in that uneasy peace of equal powers which makes a State; then I communicate by passing papers, proclamations, orders, through my bowels. Yet I was not a State with you, nor were we both together any Indiana. A squad of Pershing Rifles at the moment, I make myself Right Face! Legislation packs the screw of my intestines. Well, king of the classroom's king of the hill. You used to waddle when you walked because my sperm between your legs was draining to a towel. Teacher, poet, folded lover—like the politician, like those drunkards, ill, or those who faucet-off while pissing heartily to preach upon the force and fullness of that stream, or pause from vomiting to praise the purity and passion of their puke—I chant, I beg, I orate, I command, I sing—

Come back to Indiana—not too late!
(Or will you be a ranger to the end?)

Good-bye . . . Good-bye . . . oh, I shall always wait
You, Larry, traveler—
stranger,
son,
—my friend—

my little girl, my poem by heart, my self, my childhood.

But I've heard Batista described as a Mason. That dries up my pity, melts my hate. Back from the garage where I have overheard it, I slap the mended fender of my car to laugh, and listen to the metal stinging tartly in my hand.

PEOPLE

Their hair in curlers and their heads wrapped in loud scarves, young mothers, fattish in trousers, lounge about in the speedwash, smoking cigarettes, eating candy, drinking pop, thumbing magazines, and screaming at their children above the whir and rumble of the machines.

At the bank a young man freshly pressed is letting himself in with a key. Along the street, delicately teetering, many grandfathers move in a dream. During the murderous heat of summer, they perch on window ledges, their feet dangling just inside the narrow shelf of shade the store has made, staring steadily into the street. Where their consciousness has gone I can't say. It's not in the eyes. Perhaps it's diffuse, all temperature and skin, like an infant's, though more mild. Near the corner there are several large overalled men employed in standing. A truck turns to be weighed on the scales at the Feed and Grain. Images drift on the drugstore window. The wind has blown the smell of cattle into town. Our eyes have been driven in like the eyes of the old men. And there's no one to have mercy on us.

VITAL DATA

There are two restaurants here and a tearoom. two bars. one bank, three barbers, one with a green shade with which he blinds his window. two groceries. a dealer in Fords. one drug, one hardware, and one appliance store. several that sell feed, grain, and farm equipment. an antique shop. a poolroom. a laundromat. three doctors. a dentist. a plumber. a vet. a funeral home in elegant repair the color of a buttercup. numerous beauty parlors which open and shut like night-blooming plants. a tiny dime and department store of no width but several floors. a hutch, homemade, where you can order, after lying down or squirming in, furniture that's been fashioned from bent lengths of stainless tubing, glowing plastic, metallic thread, and clear shellac. an American Legion Post and a root beer stand. little agencies for this and that: cosmetics, brushes, insurance, greeting cards and garden produce—anything—sample shoes—which do their business out of hats and satchels, over coffee cups and dissolving sugar. a factory for making paper sacks and pasteboard boxes that's lodged in an old brick building bearing the legend OPERA HOUSE, still faintly golden, on its roof. a library given by Carnegie. a post office. a school. a railroad station. fire station. lumberyard. telephone company. welding shop. garage . . . and spotted through the town from one end to the other in a line along the highway, gas stations to the number five.

EDUCATION

In 1833, Colin Goodykoontz, an itinerant preacher with a name from a fairy-tale, summed up the situation in one Indiana town this way:

> Ignorance and her squalid brood. A universal dearth of intellect. Total abstinence from literature is very generally practiced. . . . There is not a scholar in grammar or geography, or a *teacher capable* of *instructing* in them, to my knowledge. . . . Others are supplied a few months of the year with the most antiquated & unreasonable forms of teaching reading, writing & cyphering. . . . Need I stop to remind you of the host of loathsome reptiles such a stagnant pool is fitted to breed! Croaking jealousy; bloated bigotry; coiling suspicion; wormish blindness; crocodile malice!

Things have changed since then, but in none of the respects mentioned.

BUSINESS

One side section of street is blocked off with sawhorses. Hard, thin, bitter men in blue jeans, cowboy boots and hats, untruck a dinky carnival. The merchants are promoting themselves. There will be free rides, raucous music, parades and coneys, pop, popcorn, candy, cones, awards and drawings, with all you can endure of pinch, push, bawl, shove, shout, scream, shriek, and bellow. Children pedal past on decorated bicycles, their wheels a blur of color, streaming crinkled paper and excited dogs. A little later there's a pet show for a prize—dogs, cats, birds, sheep, ponies, goats—none of which wins. The whirlabouts whirl about. The Ferris wheel climbs dizzily into the sky as far as a tall man on tiptoe might be persuaded to reach, and the irritated operators measure the height and weight of every child with sour eyes to see if they are safe for the machines. An electrical megaphone repeatedly trumpets the names of the generous sponsors. The following day they do not allow the refuse to remain long in the street.

MY HOUSE, THIS PLACE AND BODY

I have met with some mischance, wings withering, as Plato says obscurely, and across the breadth of Ohio, like heaven on a table, I've fallen as far as the poet, to the sixth sort of body, this house in B, in Indiana, with its blue and gray bewitching windows, holy magical insides. Great thick evergreens protect its entry. And I live *in*.

Lost in the corn rows, I remember feeling just another stalk, and thus this country takes me over in the way I occupy myself when I am well . . . completely—to the edge of both my house and body. No one notices, when they walk by, that I am brimming in the doorways. My house, this place and body, I've come in mourning to be born in. To anybody else it's pretty silly: love.

Why should I feel a loss? How am I bereft? She was never mine; she was a fiction, always a golden tomgirl, barefoot, with an adolescent's slouch and a boy's taste for sports and fishing, a figure out of Twain, or worse, in Riley. Age cannot be kind.

There's little hand-in-hand here . . . not in B. No one touches except in rage. Occasionally girls will twine their arms about each other and lurch along, school out, toward home and play. I dreamed my lips would drift down your back like a skiff on a river. I'd follow a vein with the point of my finger, hold your bare feet in my naked hands.

THE SAME PERSON

Billy Holsclaw lives alone—how alone it is impossible to fathom. In the post office he talks greedily to me about the weather. His head bobs on a wild flood of words, and I take this violence to be a measure of his eagerness for speech. He badly needs a shave, coal dust has layered his face, he spits when he speaks, and his fingers pick at his tatters. He wobbles out in the wind when I leave him, a paper sack mashed in the fold of his arm, the leaves blowing past him, and our encounter drives me sadly home to poetry—where there's no answer. Billy closes his door and carries coal or wood to his fire and closes his eyes, and there's simply no way of knowing how lonely and empty he is or whether he's as vacant and barren and loveless as the rest of us are—here in the heart of the country.

WEATHER

For we're always out of luck here. That's just how it is—for instance in the winter. The sides of the buildings, the roofs, the limbs of the trees are gray. Streets, sidewalks, faces, feelings—they are gray. Speech is gray, and the grass where it shows. Every flank and front, each top is gray. Everything is gray: hair, eyes, window glass, the hawkers' bills and touters' posters, lips, teeth, poles and metal signs—they're gray, quite gray. Cars are gray. Boots, shoes, suits, hats, gloves are gray. Horses, sheep, and cows, cats killed in the road, squirrels in the same way, sparrows, doves, and pigeons, all are gray, everything is gray, and everyone is out of luck who lives here.

A similar haze turns the summer sky milky, and the air muffles your head and shoulders like a sweater you've got caught in. In the summer light, too, the sky darkens a moment when you open your eyes. The heat is pure distraction. Steeped in our fluids, miserable in the folds of our bodies, we can scarcely think of anything but our sticky parts. Hot cyclonic winds and storms of dust crisscross the country. In many places, given an indifferent push, the wind will still coast for miles, gathering resource and edge as it goes, cunning and force. According to the season, paper, leaves, field litter, seeds, snow, fill up the fences. Sometimes I think the land is flat because the winds have leveled it, they blow so constantly. In any case, a gale can grow in a field of corn that's as hot as a draft from hell, and to receive it is one of the most dismaying experiences of this life, though the smart of the same wind in winter is more humiliating, and in that sense even worse. But in the spring it rains as well, and the trees fill with ice.

PLACE

Many small Midwestern towns are nothing more than rural slums, and this community could easily become one. Principally during the first decade of the century, though there were many earlier instances, well-to-do farmers moved to town and built fine homes to contain them in their retirement. Others desired a more social life, and so lived in, driving to their fields like storekeepers to their businesses. These houses are now dying like the bereaved who inhabit them; they are slowly losing their senses—deafness, blindness, forgetfulness, mumbling, an insecure gait, an uncontrollable trembling has overcome them. Some kind of Northern Snopes will occupy them next: large-familied, Catholic, Democratic, scrambling, vigorous, poor; and since the parents will work in larger, nearby towns, the children will be loosed upon themselves and upon the hapless neighbors much as the fabulous Khan loosed his legendary horde. These Snopes will undertake makeshift repairs with materials that other people have thrown away; paint halfway round their house, then quit; almost certainly maintain an ugly loud cantankerous dog and underfeed a pair of cats to keep the rodents down. They will collect piles of possibly useful junk in the back yard, park their cars in the front, live largely leaning over engines, give not a hoot for the land, the old community, the hallowed ways, the established clans. Weakening widow ladies have already begun to hire large rude youths from families such as these to rake and mow and tidy the grounds they will inherit.

PEOPLE

In the cinders at the station boys sit smoking steadily in darkened cars, their arms bent out the windows, white shirts glowing behind the glass. Nine o'clock is the best time. They sit in a line facing the highway—two or three or four of them—idling their engines. As you walk by a machine may growl at you or a pair of headlights flare up briefly. In a moment one will pull out, spinning cinders behind it, to stalk impatiently up and down the dark streets or roar half a mile into the country before returning to its place in line and pulling up.

MY HOUSE, MY CAT, MY COMPANY

I must organize myself. I must, as they say, pull myself together, dump this cat from my lap, stir—yes, resolve, move, do. But do what? My will is like the rosy dustlike light in this room: soft, diffuse, and gently comforting. It lets me do . . . anything . . . nothing. My ears hear what they happen to; I eat what's put before me; my eyes see what blunders into them; my thoughts are not thoughts, they are dreams. I'm empty or I'm full . . . depending; and I cannot choose. I sink my claws in Tick's fur and scratch the bones of his back until his rear rises amorously. Mr. Tick, I murmur, I must organize myself. I must pull myself together. And Mr. Tick rolls over on his belly, all ooze.

I spill Mr. Tick when I've rubbed his stomach. Shoo. He steps away slowly, his long tail rhyming with his paws. How beautifully he moves, I think; how beautifully, like you, he commands his loving, how beautifully he accepts. So I rise and wander from room to room, up and down, gazing through most of my forty-one windows. How well this house receives its loving too. Let out like Mr. Tick, my eyes sink in the shrubbery. I am not here; I've passed the glass, passed second-story spaces, flown by branches, brilliant berries, to the ground, grass high in seed and leafage every season; and it is the same as when I passed above you in my aged, ardent body; it's, in short, a kind of love; and I am learning to restore myself, my house, my body, by paying court to gardens, cats, and running water, and with neighbors keeping company.

Mrs. Desmond is my right-hand friend; she's eighty-five. A thin white mist of hair, fine and tangled, manifests the climate of her mind. She is habitually suspicious, fretful, nervous. Burglars break in at noon. Children trespass. Even now they are shaking the pear tree, stealing rhubarb, denting lawn. Flies caught in the screens and numbed by frost awake in the heat to buzz and scrape the metal cloth and frighten her, though she is deaf to me, and consequently cannot hear them. Boards creak, the wind whistles across the chimney mouth, drafts cruise like fish through the hollow rooms. It is herself she hears, her own flesh failing, for only death will preserve her from those daily chores she climbs like stairs, and all that anxious waiting. Is it now, she wonders. No? Then: is it now?

We do not converse. She visits me to talk. My task to murmur. She talks about her grandsons, her daughter who lives in Delphi, her sister or her husband—both gone—obscure friends—dead—obscurer aunts and uncles—lost—ancient neighbors, members of her church or of her clubs—passed or passing on; and in this way she brings the ends of her life together with a terrifying rush: she is a girl, a wife, a mother, widow, all at once. All at once—appalling—but I believe it; I wince in expectation of the clap. Her talk's a fence—a shade drawn, window fastened, door that's locked—for no one dies taking tea in a kitchen; and as her years compress and begin to jumble, I really believe in the brevity of life; I sweat in my wonder; death is the dog down the street, the angry gander, bedroom spider, goblin who's come to get her; and it occurs to me that in my listening posture I'm the boy who suffered the winds of my grandfather with an exactly similar politeness, that I am, right now, all my ages, out in elbows, as angular as badly stacked cards. Thus was I, when I loved you, every man I could be, youth and child—far from enough—and you, so strangely ambiguous a being, met me, heart for spade, play after play, the whole run of our suits.

Mr. Tick, you do me honor. You not only lie in my lap, but you remain alive there, coiled like a fetus. Through your deep nap, I feel you hum. You are, and are not, a machine. You are alive, alive exactly, and it means nothing to you—much to me. You are a cat—you cannot understand—you are a cat so easily. Your nature is not something you must rise to. You, not I, live in: in house, in skin, in shrubbery. Yes. I think I shall hat my head with a steeple; turn church; devour people. Mr. Tick, though, has a tail he can twitch, he need not fly his Fancy. Claws, not metrical schema, poetry his paws; while smoothing . . . smoothing . . . smoothing roughly, his tongue laps its neatness. O Mr. Tick, I know you; you are an electrical penis. Go on now, shoo. Mrs. Desmond doesn't like you. She thinks you will tangle yourself in her legs and she will fall. You murder her birds, she knows, and walk upon her roof with death in your jaws. I must gather myself together for a bound. What age is it I'm at right now, I wonder. The heart, don't they always say, keeps the true time. Mrs. Desmond is knocking. Faintly, you'd think, but she pounds. She's brought me a cucumber. I believe she believes I'm a woman. Come in, Mrs. Desmond, thank you, be my company, it looks lovely, and have tea. I'll slice it, crisp, with cream, for luncheon, each slice as thin as me.

POLITICS

O all ye isolate and separate powers, Sing! Sing, and sing in such a way that from a distance it will seem a harmony, a Strindberg play, a friendship ring . . . so happy—happy, happy, happy—as here we go hand in handling, up and down. Our union was a singing, though we were silent in the songs we sang like single notes are silent in a symphony. In no sense sober, we barbershopped together and never heard the discords in our music or saw ourselves as dirty, cheap, or silly. Yet cats have worn out better shoes than those thrown through our love songs at us. Hush. Be patient—prudent—politic. Still, Cleveland killed you, Mr. Crane. Were you not politic enough and fond of being beaten? Like a piece of sewage, the city shat you from its stern three hundred miles from history—beyond the loving reach of sailors. Well, I'm not a poet who puts Paris to his temple in his youth to blow himself from Idaho, or—fancy that—Missouri. My god, I said, this is my country, but must my country go so far as Terre Haute or Whiting, go so far as Gary?

When the Russians first announced the launching of their satellite, many people naturally refused to believe them. Later others were outraged that they had sent a dog around the earth. I wouldn't want to take that mutt from out that metal flying thing if he's still living when he lands, our own dog catcher said; anybody knows you shut a dog up by himself to toss around the first thing he'll be setting on to do you let him out is bite somebody.

This Midwest. A dissonance of parts and people, we are a consonance of Towns. Like a man grown fat in everything but heart, we overlabor; our outlook never really urban, never rural either, we enlarge and linger at the same time, as Alice both changed and remained in her story. You are blond. I put my hand upon your belly; feel it tremble from my trembling. We always drive large cars in my section of the country. How could you be a comfort to me now?

MORE VITAL DATA

The town is exactly fifty houses, trailers, stores, and miscellaneous buildings long, but in places no streets deep. It takes on width as you drive south, always adding to the east. Most of the dwellings are fairly spacious farm houses in the customary white, with wide wraparound porches and tall narrow windows, though there are many of the grander kind—fretted, scalloped, turreted, and decorated with clapboards set at angles or on end, with stained-glass windows at the stair landings and lots of wrought iron full of fancy curls—and a few of these look like castles in their rarer brick. Old stables serve as garages now, and the lots are large to contain them and the vegetable and flower gardens which, ultimately, widows plant and weed and then entirely disappear in. The shade is ample, the grass is good, the sky a glorious fall violet; the apple trees are heavy and red, the roads are calm and empty; corn has sifted from the chains of tractored wagons to speckle the streets with gold and with the russet fragments of the cob, and a man would be a fool who wanted, blessed with this, to live anywhere else in the world.

EDUCATION

Buses like great orange animals move through the early light to school. There the children will be taught to read and warned against Communism. By Miss Janet Jakes. That's not her name. Her name is Helen something—Scott or James. A teacher twenty years. She's now worn fine and smooth, and has a face, Wilfred says, like a mail-order ax. Her voice is hoarse, and she has a cough. For she screams abuse. The children stare, their faces blank. This is the thirteenth week. They are used to it. You will all, she shouts, you will all draw pictures of me. No. She is a Mrs.—someone's missus. And in silence they set to work while Miss Jakes jabs hairpins in her hair. Wilfred says an ax, but she has those rimless tinted glasses, graying hair, an almost dimpled chin. I must concentrate. I must stop making up things. I must give myself to life; let it mold me: that's what they say in *Wisdom's Monthly Digest* every day. Enough, enough—you've been at it long enough; and the children rise formally a row at a time to present their work to her desk. No, she wears rims; it's her chin that's dimpleless. Well, it will take more than a tablespoon of features to sweeten that face. So she grimly shuffles their sheets, examines her reflection crayoned on them. I would not dare . . . allow a child . . . to put a line around me. Though now and then she smiles like a nick in the blade, in the end these drawings depress her. I could not bear it—how can she ask?—that anyone

. . . draw me. Her anger's lit. That's why she does it: flame. There go her eyes; the pink in her glasses brightens, dims. She is a pumpkin, and her rage is breathing like the candle in. No, she shouts, no—the cartoon trembling—no, John Mauck, John Stewart Mauck, this will not do. The picture flutters from her fingers. You've made me too muscular.

I work on my poetry. I remember my friends, associates, my students, by their names. Their names are Maypop, Dormouse, Upsydaisy. Their names are Gladiolus, Callow Bladder, Prince and Princess Oleo, Hieronymus, Cardinal Mummum, Mr. Fitchew, The Silken Howdah, Spot. Sometimes you're Tom Sawyer, Huckleberry Finn; it is perpetually summer; your buttocks are my pillow; we are adrift on a raft; your back is our river. Sometimes you are Major Barbara, sometimes a goddess who kills men in battle, sometimes you are soft like a shower of water; you are bread in my mouth.

I do not work on my poetry. I forget my friends, associates, my students, and their names: Gramophone, Blowgun, Pickle, Serenade . . . Marge the Barge, Arena, Uberhaupt . . . Doctor Dildoe, The Fog Machine. For I am now in B, in Indiana: out of job and out of patience, out of love and time and money, out of bread and out of body, in a temper, Mrs. Desmond, out of tea. So shut your fist up, bitch, you bag of death; go bang another door; go die, my dearie. Die, life-deaf old lady. Spill your breath. Fall over like a frozen board. Gray hair grows from the nose of your mind. You are a skull already—*memento mori*—the foreskin retracts from your teeth. Will your plastic gums last longer than your bones, and color their grinning? And is your twot still hazel-hairy, or are you bald as a ditch? . . . bitch . . . . bitch . . . . bitch. I wanted to be famous, but you bring me age—my emptiness. Was it *that* which I thought would balloon me above the rest? Love? where are you? . . . love me. I want to rise so high, I said, that when I shit I won't miss anybody.

BUSINESS

For most people, business is poor. Nearby cities have siphoned off all but a neighborhood trade. Except for feed and grain and farm supplies, you stand a chance to sell only what one runs out to buy. Chevrolet has quit, and Frigidaire. A locker plant has left its afterimage. The lumberyard has been, so far, six months about its going. Gas stations change hands clumsily, a restaurant becomes available, a grocery closes. One day they came and knocked the cornices from the watch repair and pasted campaign posters on the windows. Torn across, by now, by boys, they urge you still to vote for half an orange beblazoned man who as a whole one failed two years ago to win at his election. Everywhere, in this manner, the past speaks, and it mostly speaks of failure. The empty stores, the old signs and dusty fixtures, the debris in alleys, the flaking paint and rusty gutters, the heavy locks and sagging boards: they say the same disagreeable things. What do the sightless windows see, I wonder, when the sun throws a passerby against them? Here a stair unfolds toward the street—dark, rickety, and treacherous—and I always feel, as I pass it, that if I just went carefully up and turned the corner at the landing, I would find myself out of the world. But I've never had the courage.

THAT SAME PERSON

The weeds catch up with Billy. In pursuit of the hollyhocks, they rise in coarse clumps all around the front of his house. Billy has to stamp down a circle by his door like a dog or cat does turning round to nest up, they're so thick. What particularly troubles me is that winter will find the weeds still standing stiff and tindery to take the sparks which Billy's little mortarless chimney spouts. It's true that fires are fun here. The town whistle, which otherwise only blows for noon (and there's no noon on Sunday), signals the direction of the fire by the length and number of its blasts, the volunteer firemen rush past in their cars and trucks, houses empty their owners along the street every time like an illustration in a children's book. There are many bikes, too, and barking dogs, and sometimes—halleluiah—the fire's right here in town—a vacant lot of weeds and stubble flaming up. But I'd rather it weren't Billy or Billy's lot or house. Quite selfishly I want him to remain the way he is—counting his sticks and logs, sitting on his sill in the soft early sun—though I'm not sure what his presence means to me . . . or to anyone. Nevertheless, I keep wondering whether, given time, I might not someday find a figure in our language which would serve him faithfully, and furnish his poverty and loneliness richly out.

WIRES

Where sparrows sit like fists. Doves fly the steeple. In mist the wires change perspective, rise and twist. If they led to you, I would know what they were. Thoughts passing often, like the starlings who flock these fields at evening to sleep in the trees beyond, would form a family of paths like this; they'd foot down the natural height of air to just about a birds perch. But they do not lead to you.

> Of whose beauty it was sung
> She shall make the old man young.

They fasten me.

If I walked straight on, in my present mood, I would reach the Wabash. It's not a mood in which I'd choose to conjure you. Similes dangle like baubles from me. This time of year the river is slow and shallow, the clay banks crack in the sun, weeds surprise the sandbars. The air is moist and I am sweating. It's impossible to rhyme in this dust. Everything—sky, the cornfield, stump, wild daisies, my old clothes and pressless feelings—seem fabricated for installment purchase. Yes. Christ. I am suffering a summer Christmas; and I cannot walk under the wires. The sparrows scatter like handfuls of gravel. Really, wires are voices in thin strips. They are words wound in cables. Bars of connection.

WEATHER

I would rather it were the weather that was to blame for what I am and what my friends and neighbors are—we who live here in the heart of the country. Better the weather, the wind, the pale dying snow . . . the snow—why not the snow? There's never much really, not around the lower Lakes anyway, not enough to boast about, not enough to be useful. My father tells how the snow in the Dakotas would sweep to the roofs of the barns in the old days, and he and his friends could sled on the crust that would form because the snow was so fiercely driven. In Bemidji trees have been known to explode. That would be something—if the trees in Davenport or Francisville or Carbondale or Niles were to go blam some winter—blam! blam! blam! all the way down the gray, cindery, snow-sick streets.

A cold fall rain is blackening the trees or the air is like lilac and full of parachuting seeds. Who cares to live in any season but his own? Still I suspect the secret's in this snow, the secret of our sickness, if we could only diagnose it, for we are all dying like the elms in Urbana. This snow—like our skin it covers the country. Later dust will do it. Right now—snow. Mud presently. But it is snow without any laughter in it, a pale gray pudding thinly spread on stiff toast, and if that seems a strange description, it's accurate all the same. Of course soot blackens everything, but apart from that, we are never sufficiently cold here. The flakes as they come, alive and burning, we cannot retain, for if our temperatures fall, they rise promptly again, just as, in the summer, they bob about in the same feckless way. Suppose though . . . suppose they were to rise some August, climb and rise, and then hang in the hundreds like a hawk through December, what a desert we could make of ourselves—from Chicago to Cairo, from Hammond to Columbus—what beautiful Death Valleys.

PLACE

I would rather it were the weather. It drives us in upon ourselves—an unlucky fate. Of course there is enough to stir our wonder anywhere; there's enough to love, anywhere, if one is strong enough, if one is diligent enough, if one is perceptive, patient, kind enough—whatever it takes; and surely it's better to live in the country, to live on a prairie by a drawing of rivers, in Iowa or Illinois or Indiana, say, than in any city, in any stinking fog of human beings, in any blooming orchard of machines. It ought to be. The cities are swollen and poisonous with people. It ought to be better. Man has never been a fit environment for man—for rats, maybe, rats do nicely, or for dogs or cats and the household beetle.

And how long the street is, nowadays. These endless walls are fallen to keep back the tides of earth. Brick could be beautiful but we have covered it gradually with gray industrial vomits. Age does not make concrete genial, and asphalt is always—like America—twenty-one, until it breaks up in crumbs like stale cake. The brick, the asphalt, the concrete, the dancing signs and garish posters, the feed and excrement of the automobile, the litter of its inhabitants: they compose, they decorate, they line our streets, and there is nowhere, nowadays, our streets can't reach.

A man in the city has no natural thing by which to measure himself. His parks are potted plants. Nothing can live and remain free where he resides but the pigeon, starling, sparrow, spider, cockroach, mouse, moth, fly and weed, and he laments the existence of even these and makes his plans to poison them. The zoo? There *is* the zoo. Through its bars the city man stares at the great cats and dully sucks his ice. Living, alas, among men and their marvels, the city man supposes that his happiness depends on establishing, somehow, a special kind of harmonious accord with others. The novelists of the city, of slums and crowds, they call it love—and break their pens.

Wordsworth feared the accumulation of men in cities. He foresaw their "degrading thirst after outrageous stimulation," and some of their hunger for love. Living in a city, among so many, dwelling in the heat and tumult of incessant movement, a man's affairs are touch and go—that's all. It's not surprising that the novelists of the slums, the cities, and the crowds, should find that sex is but a scratch to ease a tickle, that we're most human when we're sitting on the john, and that the justest image of our life is in full passage through the plumbing.

> That man, immur'd in cities, still retains
> His inborn inextinguishable thirst
> Of rural scenes, compensating his loss
> By supplemental shifts, the best he may.

Come into the country, then. The air nimbly and sweetly recommends itself unto our gentle senses. Here, growling tractors tear the earth. Dust roils up behind them. Drivers sit jouncing bright umbrellas. They wear refrigerated hats and steer by looking at the tracks they've cut behind them, their transistors blaring. Close to the land, are they? good companions to the soil? Tell me: do they live in harmony with the alternating seasons?

It's a lie of old poetry. The modern husbandman uses chemicals from cylinders and sacks, spike-ball-and-claw machines, metal sheds, and cost accounting. Nature in the old sense does not matter. It does not exist. Our farmer's only mystical attachment is to parity. And if he does not realize that cows and corn are simply different kinds of chemical engine, he cannot expect to make a go of it.

It isn't necessary to suppose our cows have feelings; our neighbor hasn't as many as he used to have either; but think of it this way a moment, you can correct for the human imputations later: how would it feel to nurse those strange tentacled calves with their rubber, glass, and metal lips, their stainless eyes?

PEOPLE

Aunt Pet's still able to drive her car—a high square Ford—even though she walks with difficulty and a stout stick. She has a watery gaze, a smooth plump face despite her age, and jet black hair in a bun. She has the slowest smile of anyone I ever saw, but she hates dogs, and not very long ago cracked the back of one she cornered in her garden. To prove her vigor she will tell you this, her smile breaking gently while she raises the knob of her stick to the level of your eyes.

HOUSE, MY BREATH AND WINDOW

My window is a grave, and all that lies within it's dead. No snow is falling. There's no haze. It is not still, not silent. Its images are not an animal that waits, for movement is no demonstration. I have seen the sea slack, life bubble through a body without a trace, its spheres impervious as soda's. Downwound, the whore at wagtag clicks and clacks. Leaves wiggle. Grass sways. A bird chirps, pecks the ground. An auto wheel in penning circles keeps its rigid spokes. These images are stones; they are memorials. Beneath this sea lies sea: god rest it . . . rest the world beyond my window, me in front of my reflection, above this page, my shade. Death is not so still, so silent, since silence implies a falling quiet, stillness a stopping, containing, holding in; for death is time in a clock, like Mr. Tick, electric . . . like wind through a windup poet. And my blear floats out to visible against the glass, befog its country and bespill myself. The mist lifts slowly from the fields in the morning. No one now would say: the Earth throws back its covers; it is rising from sleep. Why is the feeling foolish? The image is too Greek. I used to gaze at you so wantonly your body blushed. Imagine: wonder: that my eyes could cause such flowering. Ah, my friend, your face is pale, the weather cloudy; a street has been felled through your chin, bare trees do nothing, houses take root in their rectangles, a steeple stands up in your head. You speak of loving; then give me a kiss. The pane is cold. On icy mornings the fog rises to greet me (as you always did); the barns and other buildings, rather than ghostly, seem all the more substantial for looming, as if they grew in themselves while I watched (as you always did). Oh my approach, I suppose, was like breath in a rubber monkey. Nevertheless, on the road along the Wabash in the morning, though the trees are sometimes obscured by fog, their reflection floats serenely on the river, reasoning the banks, the sycamores in French rows. Magically, the world tips. I'm led to think that only those who grow down live (which will scarcely win me twenty-five from *Wisdom's Monthly Digest*), but I find I write that only those who live down grow; and what I write, I hold, whatever I really know. My every word's inverted, or reversed—or I am. I held you, too, that way. You were so utterly provisional, subject to my change. I could inflate your bosom with a kiss, disperse your skin with gentleness, enter your vagina from within, and make my love emerge like a fresh sex. The pane is cold. Honesty is cold, my inside lover. The sun looks, through the mist, like a plum on the tree of heaven, or a bruise on the slope of your belly. Which? The grass crawls with frost. We meet on this window, the world and I, inelegantly, swimmers of the glass; and swung wrong way round to one another, the world seems in. The world—how grand, how monumental, grave and deadly, that word is: the world, my house and poetry. All poets have their inside lovers. Wee penis does not belong to me, or any of this foggery. It is *his* property which he's thrust through what's womanly of me to set down this. These wooden houses in their squares, gray streets and fallen sidewalks, standing trees, your name I've written sentimentally across my breath into the whitening air, pale birds: they exist in me now because of him. I gazed with what intensity . . . A bush in the excitement of its roses could not have bloomed so beautifully as you did then. It was a look I'd like to give this page. For that is poetry: to bring within about, to change.

POLITICS

Sports, politics, and religion are the three passions of the badly educated. They are the Midwest's open sores. Ugly to see, a source of constant discontent, they sap the body's strength. Appalling quantities of money, time, and energy are wasted on them. The rural mind is narrow, passionate, and reckless on these matters. Greed, however shortsighted and direct, will not alone account for it. I have known men, for instance, who for years have voted squarely against their interests. Nor have I ever noticed that their surly Christian views prevented them from urging forward the smithereening, say, of Russia, China, Cuba, or Korea. And they tend to back their country like they back their local team: they have a fanatical desire to win; yelling is their forte; and if things go badly, they are inclined to sack the coach. All in all, then, Birch is a good name. It stands for the bigot's stick, the wild-child-tamer's cane.

Forgetfulness—is that their object?

Oh, I was new, I thought. A fresh start: new cunt, new climate, and new country—there you were, and I was pioneer, and had no history. That language hurts me, too, my dear. You'll never hear it.

FINAL VITAL DATA

The Modern Homemakers' Demonstration Club. The Prairie Home Demonstration Club. The Night-outers' Home Demonstration Club. The IOOF, FFF,

VFW, WCTU, WSCS, 4-H, 40 and 8, Psi Iota Chi, and PTA. The Boy and Girl Scouts, Rainbows, Masons, Indians and Rebekah Lodge. Also the Past Noble Grand Club of the Rebekah Lodge. As well as the Moose and the Ladies of the Moose. The Elks, the Eagles, the Jaynettes and the Eastern Star. The Women's Literary Club, the Hobby Club, the Art Club, the Sunshine Society, the Dorcas Society, the Pythian Sisters, the Pilgrim Youth Fellowship, the American Legion, the American Legion Auxiliary, the American Legion Junior Auxiliary, the Gardez Club, the Bridge for Fun Club, the What-can-you-do? Club, the Get Together Club, the Coterie Club, the Worthwhile Club, the Let's Help Our Town Club, the No Name Club, the Forget-me-not Club, the Merry-go-round Club. . . .

EDUCATION

Has a quarter disappeared from Paula Frosty's pocket book? Imagine the landscape of that face: no crayon could engender it; soft wax is wrong; thin wire in trifling snips might do the trick. Paula Frosty and Christopher Roger accuse the pale and splotchy Cheryl Pipes. But Miss Jakes, I *saw* her. Miss Jakes is so extremely vexed she snaps her pencil. What else is missing? I appoint you a detective, John: search her desk. Gum, candy, paper, pencils, marble, round eraser—whose? A thief. I can't watch her all the time, I'm here to teach. Poor pale fossetted Cheryl, it's determined, can't return the money because she took it home and spent it. Cindy, Janice, John, and Pete—you four who sit around her—you will be detectives this whole term to watch her. A thief. In all my time. Miss Jakes turns, unfists, and turns again. I'll handle you, she cries. To think. A thief. In all my years. Then she writes on the blackboard the name of Cheryl Pipes and beneath that the figure twenty-five with a large sign for cents. Now Cheryl, she says, this won't be taken off until you bring that money out of home, out of home straight up to here, Miss Jakes says, tapping her desk.

Which is three days.

ANOTHER PERSON

I was raking leaves when Uncle Halley introduced himself to me. He said his name came from the comet, and that his mother had borne him prematurely in her fright of it. I thought of Hobbes, whom fear of the Spanish Armada had hurried into birth, and so I believed Uncle Halley to honor the philosopher, though Uncle Halley is a liar, and neither the one hundred twenty-nine nor the fifty-three he ought to be. That fall the leaves had burned themselves out on the trees, the leaf lobes had curled, and now they flocked noisily down the street and were broken in the wires of my rake. Uncle Halley was himself (like Mrs. Desmond and history generally) both deaf and implacable, and he shooed me down his basement stairs to a room set aside there for stacks of newspapers reaching to the ceiling, boxes of leaflets and letters and programs, racks of photo albums, scrapbooks, bundles of rolled-up posters and maps, flags and pennants and slanting piles of dusty magazines devoted mostly to motoring and the Christian ethic. I saw a bird cage, a tray of butterflies, a bugle, a stiff straw boater, and all kinds of tassels tied to a coat tree. He still possessed and had on display the steering lever from his first car, a linen duster, driving gloves and goggles, photographs along the wall of himself, his friends, and his various machines, a shell from the first war, a record of ''Ramona'' nailed through its hole to a post, walking sticks and fanciful umbrellas, shoes of all sorts (his baby shoes, their counters broken, were held in sorrow beneath my nose—they had not been bronzed, but he might have them done someday before he died, he said), countless boxes of medals, pins, beads, trinkets, toys, and keys (I scarcely saw—they flowed like jewels from his palms), pictures of downtown when it was only a path by the railroad station, a brightly colored globe of the world with a dent in Poland, antique guns, belt buckles, buttons, souvenir plates and cups and saucers (I can't remember all of it—I won't), but I recall how shamefully, how rudely, how abruptly, I fled, a good story in my mouth but death in my nostrils; and how afterward I busily, righteously, burned my leaves as if I were purging the world of its years. I still wonder if this town—its life, and mine now—isn't really a record like the one of ''Ramona'' that I used to crank around on my grandmother's mahogany Victrola through lonely rainy days as a kid.

THE FIRST PERSON

Billy's like the coal he's found: spilled, mislaid, discarded. The sky's no comfort. His house and his body are dying together. His windows are boarded. And now he's reduced to his hands. I suspect he has glaucoma. At any rate he can scarcely see, and weeds his yard of rubble on his hands and knees. Perhaps he's a surgeon cleansing a wound or an ardent and tactile lover. I watch, I must say, apprehensively. Like mine-war detectors, his hands graze in circles ahead of him. Your nipples were the color of your eyes. Pebble. Snarl of paper. Length of twine. He leans down closely, picks up something silvery, holds it near his nose. Foil? cap? coin? He has within him—what, I wonder? Does he know more now because he fingers everything and has to sniff to see? It would be romantic cruelty to think so. He bends the down on your arms like a breeze. You wrote me: something is strange when we don't understand. I write in return: I think when I loved you I fell to my death.

Billy, I could read to you from Beddoes; he's your man perhaps; he held with dying, freed his blood of its arteries; and he said that there were many wretched love-ill fools like me lying alongside the last bone of their former selves, as full of spirit and speech, nonetheless, as Mrs. Desmond, Uncle Halley and the Ferris wheel, Aunt Pet, Miss Jakes, Ramona or the megaphone; yet I reverse him finally, Billy, on no evidence but braggadocio, and I declare that though my inner organs were devoured long ago, the worm which swallowed down my parts still throbs and glows like a crystal palace.

Yes, you were younger. I was Uncle Halley, the museum man and infrequent meteor. Here is my first piece of ass. They weren't so flat in those days, had more round, more juice. And over here's the sperm I've spilled, nicely jarred and clearly labeled. Look at this tape like lengths of intestine where I've stored my spew, the endless worm of words I've written, a hundred million emissions or more: oh I was quite a man right from the start; even when unconscious in my cradle, from crotch to cranium, I was erectile tissue; though mostly, after the manner approved by Plato, I had intercourse by eye. Never mind, old Holsclaw, you are blind. We pull down darkness when we go to bed; put out like Oedipus the actually offending organ, and train our touch to lies. All cats are gray, says Mr. Tick; so under cover of glaucoma you are sack gray too, and cannot be distinguished from a stallion.

I must pull myself together, get a grip, just as they say, but I feel spilled, bewildered, quite mislaid. I did not restore my house to its youth, but to its age. Hunting, you hitch through the hollyhocks. I'm inclined to say you aren't half the cripple I am, for there is nothing left of me but mouth. However, I resist the impulse. It is another lie of poetry. My organs are all there, though it's there where I fail—at the roots of my experience. Poet of the spiritual, Rilke, weren't you? yet that's what you said. Poetry, like love, is—in and out—a physical caress. I can't tolerate any more of my sophistries about spirit, mind, and breath. Body equals being, and if your weight goes down, you are the less.

HOUSEHOLD APPLES

I knew nothing about apples. Why should I? My country came in my childhood, and I dreamed of sitting among the blooms like the bees. I failed to spray the pear tree too. I doubled up under them at first, admiring the sturdy low branches I should have pruned, and later I acclaimed the blossoms. Shortly after the fruit formed there were falls—not many—apples the size of goodish stones which made me wobble on my ankles when I walked about the yard. Sometimes a piece crushed by a heel would cling on the shoe to track the house. I gathered a few and heaved them over the wires. A slingshot would have been splendid. Hard, an unattractive green, the worms had them. Before long I realized the worms had them all. Even as the apples reddened, lit their tree, they were being swallowed. The birds preferred the pears, which were small—sugar pears I think they're called—with thick skins of graying green that ripen on toward violet. So the fruit fell, and once I made some applesauce by quartering and paring hundreds; but mostly I did nothing, left them, until suddenly, overnight it seemed, in that ugly late September heat we often have in Indiana, my problem was upon me.

My childhood came in the country. I remember, now, the flies on our snowy luncheon table. As we cleared away they would settle, fastidiously scrub themselves and stroll to the crumbs to feed where I would kill them in crowds with a swatter. It was quite a game to catch them taking off. I struck heavily since I didn't mind a few stains; they'd wash. The swatter was a square of screen bound down in red cloth. It drove no air ahead of it to give them warning. They might have thought they'd flown headlong into a summered window. The faint pink dot where they had died did not rub out as I'd supposed, and after years of use our luncheon linen would faintly, pinkly, speckle.

The country became my childhood. Flies braided themselves on the flypaper in my grandmother's house. I can smell the bakery and the grocery and the stables and the dairy in that small Dakota town I knew as a kid; knew as I dreamed I'd know your body, as I've known nothing, before or since; knew as the flies knew, in the honest, unchaste sense: the burned house, hose-wet, which drew a mist of insects like the blue smoke of its smolder, and gangs of boys, moist-lipped, destructive as its burning. Flies have always impressed me; they are so persistently alive. Now they were coating the ground beneath my trees. Some were ordinary flies; there were the large blue-green ones; there were swarms of fruit flies too, and the red-spotted scavenger beetle; there were a few wasps, several sorts of bees and butterflies—checkers, sulphurs, monarchs, commas, question marks—and delicate dragonflies . . . but principally houseflies and horseflies and bottleflies, flies and more flies in clusters around the rotting fruit. They loved the pears. Inside, they fed. If you picked up a pear, they flew, and the pear became skin and stem. They were everywhere the fruit was: in the tree still—apples like a hive for them—or where the fruit littered the ground, squashing itself as you stepped . . . there was no help for it. The flies droned, feasting on the sweet juice. No one could go near the trees; I could not climb; so I determined at last to labor like Hercules. There were fruit baskets in the barn. Collecting them and kneeling under the branches, I began to gather remains. Deep in the strong rich smell of the fruit, I began to hum myself. The fruit caved in at the touch. Glistening red apples, my lifting disclosed, had families of beetles, flies, and bugs, devouring their rotten undersides. There were streams of flies; there were lakes and cataracts and rivers of flies, seas and oceans. The hum was heavier, higher, than the hum of the bees when they came to the blooms in the spring, though the bees were there, among the flies, ignoring me—ignoring everyone. As my work went on and juice covered my hands and arms, they would form a sleeve, black and moving, like knotty wool. No caress could have been more indifferently complete. Still I rose fearfully, ramming my head in the branches, apples bumping against me before falling, bursting with bugs. I'd snap my hand sharply but the flies would cling to the sweet. I could toss a whole cluster into a basket from several feet. As the pear or apple lit, they would explosively rise, like monads for a moment, windowless, certainly, with respect to one another, sugar their harmony. I had to admit, though, despite my distaste, that my arm had never been more alive, oftener or more gently kissed. Those hundreds of feet were light. In washing them off, I pretended the hose was a pump. What have I missed? Childhood is a lie of poetry.

THE CHURCH

Friday night. Girls in dark skirts and white blouses sit in ranks and scream in concert. They carry funnels loosely stuffed with orange and black paper which they shake wildly, and small megaphones through which, as drilled, they direct and magnify their shouting. Their leaders, barely pubescent girls, prance and shake and whirl their skirts above their bloomers. The young men, leaping, extend their arms and race through puddles of amber light, their bodies glistening. In a lull, though it rarely occurs, you can hear the squeak of tennis shoes against the floor. Then the yelling begins again, and then continues; fathers, mothers, neighbors joining in to form a single pulsing ululation—a cry of the whole community—for in this gymnasium each body becomes the bodies beside it, pressed as they are together, thigh to thigh, and the same shudder runs through all of them, and runs toward the same release. Only the ball moves serenely through this dazzling din. Obedient to law it scarcely speaks but caroms quietly and lives at peace.

BUSINESS

It is the week of Christmas and the stores, to accommodate the rush they hope for, are remaining open in the evening. You can see snow falling in the cones of the street lamps. The roads are filling—undisturbed. Strings of red and green lights droop over the principal highway, and the water tower wears a star. The windows of the stores have been bedizened. Shamelessly they beckon. But I am alone, leaning against a pole—no . . . there is no one in sight. They're all at home, perhaps by their instruments, tuning in on their evenings, and like Ramona, tirelessly playing and replaying themselves. There's a speaker perched in the tower, and through the boughs of falling snow and over the vacant streets, it drapes the twisted and metallic strains of a tune that can barely be distinguished—yes, I believe it's one of the jolly ones, it's "Joy to the World." There's no one to hear the music but myself, and though I'm listening, I'm no longer certain. Perhaps the record's playing something else.

1967

Richard Brautigan

The Cleveland Wrecking Yard

For most of the book, *Trout Fishing in America* is not literally about trout fishing in America; the fishing is a symbolic metaphor which evokes a pastoral landscape and the qualities of health, innocence, and optimism, which are part of the American vision of the pastoral. In the twentieth-century landscape of ruin, both the pastoral landscape and the pastoral values are momentary, discontinuous, and metamorphic; so, too, is Brautigan's symbolic metaphor, which can appear as a trout stream, a person, a book, or even, in "The Cleveland Wrecking Yard," a prefabricated construction. Like William Gass's speaker, Richard Brautigan's speaker is not so much a character as a perspective, an attitude; unlike Gass's speaker, Brautigan's speaker—perpetually optimistic, innocent, good-humored, but also cunning—will allow nothing to disconfirm his pastoralism, even technological artifice.

UNTIL RECENTLY my knowledge about the Cleveland Wrecking Yard had come from a couple of friends who'd bought things there. One of them bought a huge window: the frame, glass and everything for just a few dollars. It was a fine-looking window.

Then he chopped a hole in the side of his house up on Potrero Hill and put the window in. Now he has a panoramic view of the San Francisco County Hospital.

He can practically look right down into the wards and see old magazines eroded like the Grand Canyon from endless readings. He can practically hear the patients thinking about breakfast: *I hate milk,* and thinking about dinner: *I hate peas,* and then he can watch the hospital slowly drown at night, hopelessly entangled in huge bunches of brick seaweed.

He bought that window at the Cleveland Wrecking Yard.

My other friend bought an iron roof at the Cleveland Wrecking Yard and took the roof down to Big Sur in an old station wagon and then he carried the iron roof on his back up the side of a mountain. He carried up half the roof on his back. It was no picnic. Then he bought a mule, George, from Pleasanton. George carried up the other half of the roof.

The mule didn't like what was happening at all. He lost a lot of weight because of the ticks, and the smell of the wildcats up on the plateau made him too nervous to graze there. My friend said jokingly that George had lost around two hundred pounds. The good wine country around Pleasanton in the Livermore Valley probably had looked a lot better to George than the wild side of the Santa Lucia Mountains.

My friend's place was a shack right beside a huge fireplace where there had once been a great mansion during the 1920s, built by a famous movie actor. The mansion was built before there was even a road down at Big Sur. The mansion had been brought over the mountains on the backs of mules, strung out like ants, bringing visions of the good life to the poison oak, the ticks, and the salmon.

The mansion was on a promontory, high over the Pacific. Money could see farther in the 1920s, and one could look out and see whales and the Hawaiian Islands and the Kuomintang in China.

The mansion burned down years ago.

The actor died.

His mules were made into soap.

His mistresses became bird nests of wrinkles.

Now only the fireplace remains as a sort of Carthaginian homage to Hollywood.

I was down there a few weeks ago to see my friend's roof. I wouldn't have passed up the chance for a million dollars, as they say. The roof looked like a colander to me. If that roof and the rain were running against each other at Bay Meadows, I'd bet on the rain and plan to spend my winnings at the World's Fair in Seattle.

My own experience with the Cleveland Wrecking Yard began two days ago when I heard about a used trout stream they had on sale out at the Yard. So I caught the Number 15 bus on Columbus Avenue and went out there for the first time.

There were two Negro boys sitting behind me on the bus. They were talking about Chubby Checker and the Twist. They thought that Chubby Checker was only fifteen years old because he didn't have a mustache. Then they talked about some other guy who did the twist forty-four hours in a row until he saw George Washington crossing the Delaware.

"Man, that's what I call twisting," one of the kids said.

"I don't think I could twist no forty-four hours in a row," the other kid said. "That's a lot of twisting."

I got off the bus right next to an abandoned Time Gasoline filling station and an abandoned fifty-cent self-service car wash. There was a long field on one side of the filling station. The field had once been covered with a housing project during the war, put there for the shipyard workers.

On the other side of the Time filling station was the Cleveland Wrecking Yard. I walked down there to have a look at the used trout stream. The Cleveland Wrecking Yard has a very long front window filled with signs and merchandise.

There was a sign in the window advertising a laundry marking machine for $65.00. The original cost of the machine was $175.00. Quite a saving.

There was another sign advertising new and used two and three ton hoists. I wondered how many hoists it would take to move a trout stream.

There was another sign that said:

THE FAMILY GIFT CENTER, GIFT SUGGESTIONS FOR THE ENTIRE FAMILY

The window was filled with hundreds of items for the entire family. *Daddy, do you know what I want for Christmas? What, son? A bathroom. Mommy, do you know what I want for Christmas? What, Patricia? Some roofing material.*

There were jungle hammocks in the window for distant relatives and dollar-ten-cent gallons of earth-brown enamel paint for other loved ones.

There was also a big sign that said:

USED TROUT STREAM FOR SALE.
MUST BE SEEN TO BE APPRECIATED.

I went inside and looked at some ship's lanterns that were for sale next to the door. Then a salesman came up to me and said in a pleasant voice, "Can I help you?"

"Yes," I said. "I'm curious about the trout stream you have for sale. Can you tell me something about it? How are you selling it?"

"We're selling it by the foot length. You can buy as little as you want or you can buy all we've got left. A man came in here this morning and bought 563 feet. He's going to give it to his niece for a birthday present," the salesman said.

"We're selling the waterfalls separately of course, and the trees and birds, flowers, grass and ferns we're also selling extra. The insects we're giving away free with a minimum purchase of ten feet of stream."

"How much are you selling the stream for?" I asked.

"Six dollars and fifty-cents a foot," he said. "That's for the first hundred feet. After that it's five dollars a foot."

"How much are the birds?" I asked.

"Thirty-five cents apiece," he said. "But of course they're used. We can't guarantee anything."

"How wide is the stream?" I asked. "You said you were selling it by the length, didn't you?"

"Yes," he said. "We're selling it by the length. Its width runs between five and eleven feet. You don't have to pay anything extra for width. It's not a big stream, but it's very pleasant."

"What kinds of animals do you have?" I asked.

"We only have three deer left," he said.

"Oh . . . What about flowers?"

"By the dozen," he said.

"Is the stream clear?" I asked.

"Sir," the salesman said. "I wouldn't want you to think that we would ever sell a murky trout stream here. We always make sure they're running crystal clear before we even think about moving them."

"Where did the stream come from?" I asked.

"Colorado," he said. "We moved it with loving care. We've never damaged a trout stream yet. We treat them all as if they were china."

"You're probably asked this all the time, but how's fishing in the stream?" I asked.

"Very good," he said. "Mostly German browns, but there are a few rainbows."

"What do the trout cost?" I asked.

"They come with the stream," he said. "Of course it's all luck. You never know how many you're going to get or how big they are. But the fishing's very good, you might say it's excellent. Both bait and dry fly," he said smiling.

"Where's the stream at?" I asked. "I'd like to take a look at it."

"It's around in back," he said. "You go straight through that door and then turn right until you're outside. It's stacked in lengths. You can't miss it. The waterfalls are upstairs in the used pumbing department."

"What about the animals?"

"Well, what's left of the animals are straight back from the stream. You'll see a bunch of our trucks parked on a road by the railroad tracks. Turn right on the road and follow it down past the piles of lumber. The animal shed's right at the end of the lot."

"Thanks," I said. "I think I'll look at the waterfalls first. You don't have to come with me. Just tell me how to get there and I'll find my own way."

"All right," he said. "Go up those stairs. You'll see a bunch of doors and windows, turn left and you'll find the used plumbing department. Here's my card if you need any help."

"Okay," I said. "You've been a great help already. Thanks a lot. I'll take a look around."

"Good luck," he said.

I went upstairs and there were thousands of doors there, I'd never seen so many doors before in my life. You could have built an entire city out of those doors. Doorstown. And there were enough windows up there to build a little suburb entirely out of windows. Windowville.

I turned left and went back and saw the faint glow of pearl-colored light. The light got stronger and stronger as I went farther back, and then I was in the used plumbing department, surrounded by hundreds of toilets.

The toilets were stacked on shelves. They were stacked five toilets high. There was a skylight above the toilets that made them glow like the Great Taboo Pearl of the South Sea movies.

Stacked over against the wall were the waterfalls. There were about a dozen of them, ranging from a drop of a few feet to a drop of ten or fifteen feet.

There was one waterfall that was over sixty feet long. There were tags on the pieces of the big falls describing the correct order for putting the falls back together again.

The waterfalls all had price tags on them. They were more expensive than the stream. The waterfalls were selling for $19.00 a foot.

I went into another room where there were piles of sweet-smelling lumber, glowing a soft yellow from a different color skylight above the lumber. In the shadows at the edge of the room under the sloping roof of the building were many sinks and urinals covered with dust, and there was also another waterfall about seventeen feet long, lying there in two lengths and already beginning to gather dust.

I had seen all I wanted of the waterfalls, and now I was very curious about the trout stream, so I followed the salesman's directions and ended up outside the building.

O I had never in my life seen anything like that trout stream. It was stacked in piles of various lengths: ten, fifteen, twenty feet, etc. There was one pile of hundred-foot lengths. There was also a box of scraps. The scraps were in odd sizes ranging from six inches to a couple of feet.

There was a loudspeaker on the side of the building and soft music was coming out. It was a cloudy day and seagulls were circling high overhead.

Behind the stream were big bundles of trees and bushes. They were covered with sheets of patched canvas. You could see the tops and roots sticking out the ends of the bundles.

I went up close and looked at the lengths of stream. I could see some trout in them. I saw one good fish. I saw some crawdads crawling around the rocks at the bottom.

It looked like a fine stream. I put my hand in the water. It was cold and felt good.

I decided to go around to the side and look at the animals. I saw where the trucks were parked beside the railroad tracks. I followed the road down past the piles of lumber, back to the shed where the animals were.

The salesman had been right. They were practically out of animals. About the only thing they had left in any abundance were mice. There were hundreds of mice.

Beside the shed was a huge wire birdcage, maybe fifty feet high, filled with many kinds of birds. The top of the cage had a piece of canvas over it, so the birds wouldn't get wet when it rained. There were woodpeckers and wild canaries and sparrows.

On my way back to where the trout stream was piled, I found the insects. They were inside a prefabricated steel building that was selling for eighty-cents a square foot. There was a sign over the door. It said

INSECTS

1967

Robert Coover

The Magic Poker

The grotesque and ruined island in "The Magic Poker" is, as the story-teller confesses, his invention, but gradually he comes to think of it as "somehow real, . . . its condition of ruin not so much an aesthetic design as an historical denouement." Its recent history is told and re-told as a sequence of alternating possibilities, part fairy tale and part local "legend," something "archetypal and even maybe beautiful, a blend of eros and wisdom, sex and sensibility, music and myth." Perhaps it is the two men who blend eros and wisdom; the two women, sex and sensibility; and the story itself, music and myth. (The music involves the technique of *incremental repetition:* an image or theme which, as in music, repeats itself and each time adds new meaning or variations of meaning. The central image is, of course, the poker, but each of the characters has his own distinctive images and themes, and each is connected in his own way to the landscape.)

I WANDER THE ISLAND, inventing it. I make a sun for it, and trees—pines and birch and dogwood and firs—and cause the water to lap the pebbles of its abandoned shores. This, and more: I deposit shadows and dampness, spin webs, and scatter ruins. Yes: ruins. A mansion and guest cabins and boat houses and docks. Terraces, too, and bath houses and even an observation tower. All gutted and window-busted and autographed and shat upon. I impose a hot midday silence, a profound and heavy stillness. But anything can happen.

This small and secretive bay, here just below what was once the caretaker's cabin and not far from the main boat house, probably once possessed its own system of docks, built out to protect boats from the big rocks along the shore. At least the refuse—the long bony planks of gray lumber heaped up at one end of the bay—would suggest that. But aside from the planks, the bay is now only a bay, shallow, floored with rocks and cans and bottles. Schools of silver fish, thin as fingernails, fog the bottom, and dragonflies dart and hover over its placid surface. The harsh snarl of the boat motor—for indeed a boat has been approaching, coming in off the lake into this small bay—breaks off abruptly, as the boat carves a long gentle arc through the bay, and slides, scraping bottom, toward a shallow pebbly corner. There are two girls in the boat.

Bedded deep in the grass, near the path up to the first guest cabin, lies a wrought-iron poker. It is long and slender with an intricately worked handle, and it is orange with rust. It lies shadowed, not by trees, but by the grass that has grown up wildly around it. I put it there.

The caretaker's son, left behind when the island was deserted, crouches naked in the brambly fringe of the forest overlooking the bay. He watches, scratching himself, as the boat scrapes to a stop and the girls stand—then he scampers through the trees and bushes to the guest cabin.

The girl standing forward—fashionbook-trim in tight gold pants, ruffled blouse, silk neckscarf—hesitates, makes one false start, then jumps from the boat, her sandaled heel catching the water's edge. She utters a short irritable cry, hops up on a rock, stumbles, lands finally in dry weeds on the other side. She turns her heel up and frowns down over her shoulder at it. Tiny muscles in front of her ears tense and ripple. She brushes anxiously at a thick black fly in front of her face, and asks peevishly: ''What do I do *now,* Karen?''

I arrange the guest cabin. I rot the porch and tatter the screen door and infest the walls. I tear out the light switches, gut the mattresses, smash the windows, and shit on the bathroom floor. I rust the pipes, kick in the papered walls, unhinge doors. Really, there's nothing to it. In fact, it's a pleasure.

Once, earlier in this age, a family with great wealth purchased this entire island, here up on the border, and built on it all these houses, these cabins and the mansion up there on the promontory, and the boat house, docks, bath houses, observation tower. They tamed the island some, seeded lawn grass, contrived their own sewage system with indoor appurtenances, generated electricity for the rooms inside and for the japanese lanterns and postlamps without, and they came up here from time to time in the summers. They used to maintain a caretaker on the island year round, housed him in the cabin by the boat house, but then the patriarch of the family died, and the rest had other things to do. They stopped coming to the island and forgot about caretaking.

The one in gold pants watches as the girl still in the boat switches the motor into neutral and upends it, picks up a yellowish-gray rope from the bottom, and tosses it ashore to her. She reaches for it straight-armed, then shies from it, letting it fall to the ground. She takes it up with two fingers and a thumb and holds it out in front of her. The other girl, Karen (she wears a light yellow dress with a beige cardigan over it), pushes a toolkit under a seat, gazes thoughtfully about the boat, then jumps out. Her canvas shoes splash in the water's edge, but she pays no notice. She takes the rope from the girl in gold pants, loops it around a birch near the shore, smiles warmly, and then, with a nod, leads the way up the path.

At the main house, the mansion, there is a kind of veranda or terrace, a balcony of sorts, high out on the promontory, offering a spectacular view of the lake with its wide interconnected expanses of blue and its many islands. Poised there now, gazing thoughtfully out on that view, is a tall slender man, dressed in slacks, white turtleneck shirt, and navy-blue jacket, smoking a pipe, leaning against the stone parapet. Has he heard a boat come to the island? He is unsure. The sound of the motor seemed to diminish, to grow more distant, before it stopped. Yet, on water, especially around islands, one can never trust what he hears.

Also this, then: the mansion with its many rooms, its debris, its fireplaces and wasps' nests, its musty basement, its grand hexagonal loggia and bright red doors. Though the two girls will not come here for a while—first, they have the guest cabin to explore, the poker to find—I have been busy. In the loggia, I have placed a green piano. I have pulled out its wires, chipped and yellowed its ivory keys, and cracked its green paint. I am nothing if not thorough, a real stickler for detail. I have dismembered the piano's pedals and dropped an old boot in its body (this, too, I've designed: it is horizontal and harp-shaped). The broken wires hang like rusted hairs.

The caretaker's son watches for their approach through a shattered window of the guest cabin. He is stout and hairy, muscular, dark, with short bowed legs and a rounded spiny back. The hair on his head is long, and a thin young beard sprouts on his chin and upper lip. His genitals hang thick and heavy and his buttocks are shaggy. His small eyes dart to and fro: where are they?

In the bay, the sun's light has been constant and oppressive; along the path, it is mottled and varied. Even in this variety, though, there is a kind of monotony, a determined patterning that wants a good wind. Through these patterns move the two girls, Karen long-striding with soft steps and expectant smile, the other girl hurrying behind, halting, hurrying again, slapping her arms, her legs, the back of her neck, cursing plaintively. Each time she passes between the two trees, the girl in pants stops, claws the space with her hands, runs through, but spiderwebs keep diving and tangling into her hair just the same.

Between two trees on the path, a large spider—black with a red heart on its abdomen—weaves an intricate web. The girl stops short, terrified. Nimbly, the shiny black creature works, as though spelling out some terrible message for her alone. How did Karen pass through here without brushing into it? The girl takes a step backward, holding her hands to her face. Which way around? To the left it is dark, to the right sunny: she chooses the sunny side and there, not far from the path, comes upon a wrought-iron poker, long and slender with an intricately worked handle. She bends low, her golden haunches gleaming over the grass: how beautiful it is! On a strange impulse, she kisses it—POOF! before her stands a tall slender man, handsome, dressed in dark slacks, white turtleneck shirt, and jacket, smoking a pipe. He smiles down at her. "Thank you," he says, and takes her hand.

Karen is some distance in front, almost out of sight, when the other girl discovers, bedded in the grass, a wrought-iron poker. Orange with rust, it is long and slender with an elaborate handle. She crouches to examine it, her haunches curving golden above the bluegreen grass, her long black hair drifting lightly down over her small shoulders and wafting in front of her fineboned face. "Oh!" she says softly. "How strange! How beautiful!" Squeamishly, she touches it, grips it, picks it up, turns it over. Not so rusty on the underside—but bugs! *millions* of them! She drops the thing, shudders, stands, wipes her hand several times on her pants, again. A few steps away, she pauses, glances back, then around at everything about her, concentrating, memorizing the place probably. She hurries on up the path and sees her sister already at the first guest cabin.

The girl in gold pants? yes. The other one, Karen? also. In fact, they are sisters. I have brought two sisters to this invented island, and shall, in time, send them home again. I have dressed them and may well choose to undress them. I have given one three marriages, the other none at all, nor is that the end of my beneficence and cruelty. It might even be argued that I have invented their common parents. No, I have not. We have options that may, I admit, seem strangely limited to some . . .

She crouches, haunches flexing golden above the bluegreen grass, and kisses the strange poker, kisses its handle and its long rusted shaft. Nothing. Only a harsh unpleasant taste. I am a fool, she thinks, a silly romantic fool. Yet why else has she been diverted to this small meadow? She kisses the tip—POOF! "Thank you," he says, smiling down at her. He bows to kiss her cheek and take her hand.

The guest cabin is built of rough-hewn logs, hardly the fruit of necessity, given the funds at hand, but probably it was thought fashionable; proof of traffic with other cultures is adequately provided by its gabled roof and log columns. It is here, on the shaded porch, where Karen is standing, waiting for her sister. Karen waves when she sees her, ducking down there along the path; then she turns and enters the cabin through the broken front door.

He knows that one. He's been there before. He crouches inside the door, his hairy body tense. She enters, staring straight at him. He grunts. She smiles, backing away. "Karen!" His small eyes dart to the doorway, and he shrinks back into the shadows.

She kisses the rusted iron poker, kisses its ornate handle, its long rusted shaft, kisses the tip. Nothing happens. Only a rotten taste in her mouth. Something is wrong. "Karen!"

"Karen!" the girl in pants calls from outside the guest cabin. "Karen, I just found the most beautiful thing!" The second step of the porch is rotted away. She hops over it onto the porch, drags open the tattered screen door. "Karen, I—*oh, good God!* look what they've *done* to this house! Just *look!*" Karen, about to enter the kitchen, turns back, smiling, as her sister surveys the room: "The walls all smashed in, even the plugs in the wall and the light switches pulled out! Think of it, Karen! They even had electricity! Out here on this island, so far from everything civilized! And, see, what beautiful paper they had on the walls! And now just look at it! It's so—oh! what a dreadful beautiful beastly thing all at once!"

But where is the caretaker's son? I don't know. He was here, shrinking into the shadows, when Karen's sister entered. Yet, though she catalogues the room's disrepair, there is no mention of the caretaker's son. This is awkward. Didn't I invent him myself, along with the girls and the man in the turtleneck shirt? Didn't I round his back and stunt his legs and cause the hair to hang between his buttocks? I don't know. The girls, yes, and the tall man in the shirt—to be sure, he's one of the first of my inventions. But the caretaker's son? To tell the truth, I sometimes wonder if it was not he who invented me . . .

The caretaker's son, genitals hanging hard and heavy, eyes aglitter, shrinks back into the shadows as the girl approaches, and then goes bounding silently into the empty rooms. Behind an unhinged door, he peek stealthily at the declaiming girl in gold pants, then slips, almost instinctively, into the bathroom to hide. It was here, after all, where first they met.

Karen passes quietly through the house, as though familiar with it. In the kitchen, she picks up a chipped blue teakettle, peers inside. All rust. She thumps it, the sound is dull. She sets it on a bench in the sunlight. On all sides, there are broken things: rubble really. Windows gape, shards of glass in the edges pointing out the middle spaces. The mattresses on the floors have been slashed with knives. What little there is of wood is warped. The girl in tight gold pants and silk neckscarf moves, chattering, in and out of rooms. She opens a white door, steps into a bathroom, steps quickly out again. "Judas God!" she gasps, clearly horrified. Karen turns, eyebrows raised in concern. "Don't go in there, Karen! *Don't go in there!*" She clutches one hand to her ruffled blouse. "About a hundred million people have gone to the *bath*room in there!" Exiting the bathroom behind her, a lone fly swims lazily past her elbow into the close warm air of the kitchen. It circles over a cracked table—the table bearing newspapers, shreds of wallpaper, tin cans, a stiff black washcloth—then settles on a counter near a rusted pipeless sink. It chafes its rear legs, walks past the blue teakettle's shadow into a band of pure sunlight stretched out along the counter, and sits there.

The tall man stands, one foot up on the stone parapet, gazing out on the blue sunlit lake, drawing meditatively on his pipe. He has been deeply moved by the desolation of this island. And yet, it is only the desolation of artifact, is it not, the ruin of man's civilized arrogance, nature reclaiming her own. Even the willful mutilations: a kind of instinctive response to the futile artifices of imposed order, after all. But such reasoning does not appease him. Leaning against his raised knee, staring out upon the vast wilderness, hoping indeed he has heard a boat come here, he puffs vigorously on his pipe and affirms reason, man, order. Are we merely blind brutes loosed in a system of mindless energy, impotent, misdirected, and insolent? "No," he says aloud, "we are not."

She peeks into the bathroom; yes, he is in there, crouching obscurely, shaggily, but eyes aglitter, behind the stool. She hears his urgent grunt and smiles. "Oh, Karen!" cries the other girl from the rear of the house. "It's so very sad!" Hastily, Karen steps out into the hallway, eases the bathroom door shut, her heart pounding.

"Oh, Karen, it's so very sad!" That's the girl in the gold pants again, of course. Now she is gazing out a window. At: high weeds and grass, crowding young birches, red rattan chair with the seat smashed out, backdrop of gray-trunked pines. She is thinking of her three wrecked marriages, her affairs, and her desolation of spirit. The broken rattan chair somehow communicates to her a sensation of real physical pain. Where have all the Princes gone? she wonders. "I mean, it's not the ones who stole the things, you know, the scavengers. I've seen people in Paris and Mexico and Algiers, lots of places, scooping rotten oranges and fishheads out of the heaped-up gutters and eating them, and

I didn't blame them, I didn't dis*like* them, I felt *sorry* for them. I even felt sorry for them if they were just doing it to be stealing something, to get something for nothing, even if they weren't hungry or anything. But it isn't the people who look for things they want or need or even don't need and take them, it's the people who just *destroy,* destroy because—God! because they just *want* to destroy! Lust! That's all, Karen! See? Somebody just went around these rooms driving his fist in the walls because he had to hurt, it didn't matter who or what, or maybe he kicked them with his feet, and bashed the windows and ripped the curtains and then went to the *bath*room on it all! Oh my God! *Why?* Why would anybody want to *do* that?'' The window in front of Karen (she has long since turned her back) is, but for one panel, still whole. In the excepted panel, the rupture in the glass is now spanned by a spiderweb more intricate than a butterfly's wing, than a system of stars, its silver paths seeming to imitate or perhaps merely to extend the delicate tracery of the fractured glass still surrounding the hole. It is a new web, for nothing has entered it yet to alter its original construction. Karen's hand reaches toward it, but then withdraws. ''Karen, let's get out of here!''

The girls have gone. The caretaker's son bounds about the guest cabin, holding himself with one hand, smashing walls and busting windows with the other, grunting happily as he goes. He leaps up onto the kitchen counter, watches the two girls from the window, as they wind their way up to the main mansion, then squats joyfully over the blue teakettle, depositing . . . a love letter, so to speak.

A love letter! Wait a minute, this is getting out of hand! What happened to that poker, I was doing much better with the poker, I had something going there, archetypal and even maybe beautiful, a blend of eros and wisdom, sex and sensibility, music and myth. But what am I going to do with shit in a rusty teakettle? No, no, there's nothing to be gained by burdening our fabrications with impieties. Enough that the skin of the world is littered with our contentious artifice, lepered with the stigmata of human aggression and despair, without suffering our songs to be flatted by savagery. Back to the poker.

''Thank you,'' he says, smiling down at her, her haunches gleaming golden over the shadowed grass. ''But, tell me, how did you know to kiss it?'' ''Call it woman's intuition,'' she replies, laughing lightly, and rises with an appreciative glance. ''But the neglected state that it was in, it must have tasted simply dreadful,'' he apologizes, and kisses her gently on the cheek. ''What momentary bitterness I might have suffered,'' she responds, ''has been more than indemnified by the sweetness of your disenchantment.'' ''My disenchantment?

Oh no, my dear, there *are* no disenchantments, merely progressions and styles of possession. To exist is to be spell-bound.'' She collapses, marveling, at his feet.

Karen, alone on the path to the mansion, pauses. Where is her sister? Has something distracted her? Has she strayed? Perhaps she has gone on ahead. Well, it hardly matters, what can happen on a desolate island? they'll meet soon enough at the mansion. In fact, Karen isn't even thinking about her sister, she's staring silently, entranced at a small green snake, stretched across the path. Is it dozing? Or simply unafraid? Maybe it's never seen a real person before, doesn't know what people can do. It's possible: few people come here now, and it looks like a very young snake. Slender, wriggly, green, and shiny. No, probably it's asleep. Smiling, Karen leaves the path, circling away from the snake so as not to disturb it. To the right of the path is a small clearing and the sun is hot there; to the left it is cool and shadowed in the gathering forest. Karen moves that way, in under the trees, picking the flowers that grow wildly here. Her cardigan catches on brambles and birch seedlings, so she pulls it off, tosses it loosely over her shoulder, hooked on one finger. She hears, not far away, a sound not unlike soft footfalls. Curious, she wanders that way to see who or what it is.

The path up to the main house, the mansion, is not even mottled, the sun does not reach back here at all, it is dark and damp-smelling, an ambience of mushrooms and crickets and fingery rustles and dead brown leaves never quite dry, or so it might seem to the girl in gold pants, were she to come this way. Where is she? His small eyes dart to and fro. Here, beside the path, trees have collapsed and rotted, seedlings and underbrush have sprung up, and lichens have crept softly over all surfaces, alive and dead. Strange creatures abide here.

''Call it woman's intuition,'' she says with a light laugh. He appraises her fineboned features, her delicate hands, her soft maidenly breasts under the ruffled blouse, her firm haunches gleaming golden over the shadowed grass. He pulls her gently to her feet, kisses her cheek. ''You are enchantingly beautiful, my dear!'' he whispers. ''Wouldn't you like to lie with me here awhile?'' ''Of course,'' she replies, and kisses his cheek in return, ''but these pants are an awful bother to remove, and my sister awaits us. Come! Let us go up to the mansion!''

A small green snake lies motionless across the path. The girl approaching does not see it, sees only the insects flicking damply, the girl in tight pants which are still golden here in the deep shadows. Her hand flutters ceaselessly before her face, it was surely the bugs that drove these people away from here finally,

"Karen, is this the right way?", and she very nearly walks right on the snake, which has perhaps been dozing, but which now switches with a frantic whip of its shiny green tail off into the damp leaves. The girl starts at the sudden whirring shush at her feet, spins around clutching her hands to her upper arms, expecting the worst, but though staring wide-eyed right at the sound, she can see nothing. Why did she ever let her sister talk her into coming here? *"Karen!"* She runs, ignoring the webs now, right through all the gnats and flies, on up the path, crying out her sister's name.

The caretaker's son, poised gingerly on a moss-covered rock, peeking through thick branches, watches the girl come up the path. Karen watches the caretaker's son. From the rear, his prominent feature is his back, broad and rounded, humped almost, where tufts of dark hair sprout randomly. His head is just a small hairy lump beyond the mound of heavy back. His arms are as long as his legs are short, and the elbows like the knees, turn outward. Thick hair grows between his buttocks and down his thighs. Smiling, she picks up a pebble to toss at him, but then she hears her sister call her name.

Leaning against his raised knee, smoking his pipe, the tall man on the parapet stares out on the wilderness, contemplating the island's ruin. Trees have collapsed upon one another, and vast areas of the island, once cleared and no doubt the stage for garden parties famous for miles around, are now virtually impassable. Brambles and bunchberries grow wildly amid saxifrage and shinleaf, and everything in sight is mottled with moss. Lichens: the symbiotic union, he recalls, of fungi and algae. He smiles and at the same moment, as though it has been brought into being by his smile, hears a voice on the garden path. A girl. How charming, he's to have company, after all! At least two, for he heard the voice on the path behind the mansion, and below him, slipping surefootedly through the trees and bushes, moves another creature in a yellow dress, carrying a beige sweater over her shoulder. She looks a little simple, not his type really, but then dissimilar organisms can, at times, enjoy mutually advantageous partnerships, can they not? He knocks the ashes from his pipe and refills the bowl.

At times, I forget that this arrangement is my own invention. I begin to think of the island as somehow real, its objects solid and intractable, its condition of ruin not so much an aesthetic design as an historical denouement. I find myself peering into blue teakettles, batting at spiderwebs, and contemplating a greenish-gray growth on the side of a stone parapet. I wonder if others might wander here without my knowing it; I wonder if I might die and the teakettle remain. "I have brought two sisters to this invented island," I say. This is no extravagance. It is indeed I who burdens them with curiosity and history, appetite and rhetoric. If they have names and griefs, I have provided them. "In fact," I add, "without me they'd have no cunts." This is not (I interrupt here to tell you that I have done all that I shall do. I return here to bring you this news, since this seemed as good a place as any. Though you have more to face, and even more to suffer from me, this is in fact the last thing I shall say to you. But can the end be in the middle? Yes, yes, it always is . . .) meant to alarm, merely to make a truth manifest—yet *I* am myself somewhat alarmed. It is one thing to discover the shag of hair between my buttocks, quite another to find myself tugging the tight gold pants off Karen's sister. Or perhaps it is the same thing, yet troubling in either case. Where does this illusion come from, this sensation of "hardness" in a blue teakettle or an iron poker, golden haunches or a green piano?

In the hexagonal loggia of the mansion stands a grand piano, painted bright green, though chipped and cracked now with age and abuse. One can easily imagine a child at such a piano, a piano so glad and ready, perhaps two children, and the sun is shining—no, rather, there is a storm on the lake, the sky is in a fury, all black and pitching, the children are inside here, out of the wind and storm, the little girl on the right, the boy on the left, pushing at each other a bit, staking out property lines on the keys, a grandmother, or perhaps just a lady, yet why not a grandmother? sitting on a window-bench gazing out on the frothy blue-black lake, and the children are playing "Chopsticks," laughing, a little noisy surely, and the grandmother, or lady, looks over from time to time, forms a patient smile if they chance to glance up at her, then—well, but it's only a supposition, who knows whether there were children or if they cared a damn about a green piano even on a bad day, "Chopsticks" least of all? No, it's only a piece of fancy, the kind of fancy that is passing through the mind of the girl in gold pants who now reaches down, strikes a key. There is no sound, of course. The ivory is chipped and yellowed, the pedals dismembered, the wires torn out and hanging like rusted hairs. The girl wonders at her own unkemptness, feels a lock loose on her forehead, but there are no mirrors. Stolen or broken. She stares about her, nostalgically absorbed for some reason, at the elegantly timbered roof of the loggia, at the enormous stone fireplace, at the old shoe in the doorway, the wasps' nests over one broken-out window. She sighs, steps out on the terrace, steep and proud over the lake. "It's a sad place," she says aloud.

The tall man in the navy-blue jacket stands, one foot up on the stone parapet, gazing out on the blue sunlit lake, drawing meditatively on his pipe, while being sketched by the girl in the tight gold pants. "I somehow expected to find you here," she says. "I've been waiting for you," replies the man. Her three-quarters view of him from the rear allows her to include only the tip of his nose in her sketch, the edge of his pipebowl, the collar of his white turtleneck shirt. "I was afraid there might be others," she says. "Others?" "Yes. Children perhaps. Or somebody's grandmother. I saw so many names everywhere I went, on walls and doors and trees and even scratched into that green piano." She is carefully filling in on her sketch the dark contours of his navy-blue jacket. "No," he says, "whoever they were, they left here long ago." "It's a sad place," she says, "and all too much like my own life." He nods. "You mean, the losing struggle against inscrutable blind forces, young dreams brought to ruin?" "Yes, something like that," she says. "And getting kicked in and gutted and shat upon." "Mmm." He straightens. "Just a moment," she says, and he resumes his pose. The girl has accomplished a reasonable likeness of the tall man, except that his legs are stubby (perhaps she failed to center her drawing properly, and ran out of space at the bottom of the paper) and his buttocks are bare and shaggy.

"It's a sad place," he says, contemplating the vast wilderness. He turns to find her grinning and wiggling her ears at him. "Karen, you're mocking me!" he complains, laughing. She props one foot up on the stone parapet, leans against her leg, sticks an iron poker between her teeth, and scowls out upon the lake. "Come on! Stop it!" he laughs. She puffs on the iron poker, blowing imaginary smokerings, then turns it into a walking stick and hobbles about imitating an old granny chasing young children. Next, she puts the poker to her shoulder like a rifle and conducts an inspection of all the broken windows facing on the terrace, scowling or weeping broadly before each one. The man has slumped to the terrace floor, doubled up with laughter. Suddenly, Karen discovers an unbroken window. She leaps up and down, does a somersault, pirouettes, jumps up and clicks her heels together. She points at it, kisses it, points again. "Yes, yes!" the man laughs, "I see it, Karen!" She points to herself, then at the window, to herself again. "You? You're like the window, Karen?" he asks, puzzled, but still laughing. She nods her head vigorously, thrusts the iron poker into his hands. It is dirty and rusty and he feels clumsy with the thing. "I don't understand . . ." She grabs it out of his hands and—*crash!*—drives it through the window. "Oh no, Karen! No, no . . . .!"

"It's a sad place." Karen has joined her sister on the terrace, the balcony, and they gaze out at the lake, two girls alone on a desolate island. "Sad and yet all too right for me, I suppose. Oh, I don't regret any of it, Karen. No, I was wrong, wrong as always, but I don't regret it. It'd be silly to be all pinched and morbid about it, wouldn't it, Karen?" The girl, of course, is talking about the failure of her third marriage. "Things are done and they are undone and then we get ready to do them again." Karen looks at her shyly, then turns her gentle gaze back out across the lake, blue with a river's muted blue under this afternoon sun. "The sun!" the girl in gold pants exclaims, though it is not clear why she thought of it. She tries to explain that she is like the sun somehow, or the sun is like her, but she becomes confused. Finally, she interrupts herself to blurt out: "Oh, Karen! *I'm so miserable!*" Karen looks up anxiously: there are no tears in her sister's eyes, but she is biting down painfully on her lower lip. Karen offers a smile, a little awkward, not quite understanding perhaps, and finally her sister, eyes closing a moment, then fluttering open, smiles wanly in return. A moment of grace settles between them, but Karen turns her back on it clumsily.

"No, Karen! Please! Stop! " The man, collapsed to the terrace floor, has tears of laughter running down his cheeks. Karen has found an old shoe and is now holding it up at arm's length, making broad silent motions with her upper torso and free arm as though declaiming upon the sadness of the shoe. She sets the shoe on the terrace floor and squats down over it, covering it with the skirt of her yellow dress. "No, Karen! No!" She leaps up, whacks her heels together in midair, picks up the shoe and peers inside. A broad smile spreads across her face, and she does a little dance, holding the shoe aloft. With a little curtsy, she presents the shoe to the man. "No! Please!" Warily, but still laughing, he looks inside. "What's this? Oh no! A flower! Karen, this is too much!" She runs into the mansion, returns carrying the green piano on her back. She drops it so hard, one leg breaks off. She finds an iron poker, props the piano up with it, sits down on an imaginary stool to play. She lifts her hands high over her head, then comes driving down with extravagant magisterial gestures. The piano, of course, has been completely disemboweled, so no sounds emerge, but up and down the broken keyboard Karen's stubby fingers fly, arriving at last, with a crescendo of violent flourishes, at a grand climactic coda, which she delivers with such force as to buckle the two remaining legs of the piano and send it all crashing to the terrace floor. "No, Karen! Oh my God!" Out of the wreckage, a wild goose springs, honking in holy terror, goes flapping out over the lake. Karen carries the piano back inside, there's a splintering crash, and she returns wielding the poker. "Careful!" She holds the poker up with two hands and does a little dance, toes turned outward, hippety-hopping about the terrace. She stops abruptly over the man, thrusts the poker in front of his nose, then slowly brings it to her own lips and kisses it. She makes a wry face. "Oh, Karen! Whoo! Please! You're killing me!" She kisses the handle, the shaft, the tip. She wrinkles her nose and shudders, lifts her skirt and wipes her tongue with it. She scowls at the poker. She takes a firm grip on the poking end and bats the handle a couple times against the stone parapet as though testing it. "Oh, Karen! Oh!" Then she lifts it high over her head and brings it down with all her might—WHAM!—POOF! it is the caretaker's son, yowling with pain. She lets go and spins away from him, as he strikes out at her in distress and fury. She tumbles into a corner of the terrace and cowers there, whimpering, pale and terrified, as the caretaker's son, breathing heavily, back stooped and buttocks tensed, circles her, prepared to spring. Suddenly, she dashes for the parapet and leaps over, the caretaker's son bounding after, and off they go, scrambling frantically through the trees and brambles, leaving the tall man in the white turtleneck shirt alone and limp from laughter on the terrace.

There is a storm on the lake. Two children play ''Chopsticks'' on the green piano. Their grandmother stirs the embers in the fireplace with an iron poker, then returns to her seat on the windowbench. The children glance over at her and she smiles at them. Suddenly a strange naked creature comes bounding into the loggia, grinning idiotically. The children and their grandmother scream with terror and race from the room and on out of the mansion, running for their lives. The visitor leaps up on the piano bench and squats there, staring quizzically at the ivory keys. He reaches for one and it sounds a note—he jerks his hand back in fright. He reaches for another—a different note. He brings his fist down—BLAM! Aha! Again: BLAM! Excitedly, he leaps up and down on the piano bench, banging his fists on the piano keyboard. He hops up on the piano, finds wires inside, and pulls them out. TWANG! TWANG! He holds his genitals with one hand and rips out the wires with the other, grunting with delight. Then he spies the iron poker. He grabs it up, admires it, then bounds joyfully around the room, smashing windows and wrecking furniture. The girl in gold pants enters and takes the poker away from him. ''Lust! That's all it is!'' she scolds. She whacks him on the nates with the poker, and, yelping with pain and astonishment, he bounds away, leaping over the stone parapet, and slinks off through the brambly forest.

''Lust!'' she says, ''that's all it is!'' Her sketch is nearly complete. ''And they're not the worst ones. The worst ones are the ones who just let it happen. If they'd kept their caretaker here . . .'' The man smiles. ''There never was a caretaker,'' he explains. ''Really! But I thought—!'' ''No,'' he says, ''that's just a legend of the island.'' She seems taken aback by this new knowledge. ''Then . . . then I don't understand . . .'' He relights his pipe, wanders over to appraise her sketch. He laughs when he sees the shaggy buttocks. ''Marvelous!'' he exclaims, ''but a poor likeness, I'm afraid! Look!'' He lowers his dark slacks and shows her his hindend, smooth as marble and hairless as a movie starlet's. Her curiosity is caught, however, not by his barbered buttocks, but by the hair around his genitals: the tight neat curls fan out in both directions like the wings of an eagle, or a wild goose . . .

The two sisters return to the loggia, their visit nearly concluded, the one in gold pants still trying to explain about herself and the sun, about consuming herself with an outer fire, while harboring an icecold center within. Her gaze falls once more on the green piano. It is obvious she still has something more to say. But now as she declaims, she has less of an audience. Karen stands distractedly before the green piano. Haltingly she lifts a finger, strikes a key. No note, only a dull thuck. Her sister reveals a new insight she has just obtained about it not being the people who steal or even those who wantonly destroy, but those who let it happen, who just don't give a proper damn. She provides instances. Once, Karen nods, but maybe only at something she has thought to herself. Her finger lifts, strikes. Thuck! Again. Thuck! Her whole arm drives the strong blunt finger. Thuck! Thuck! There is something genuinely beautiful about the girl in gold pants and silk neckscarf as she gestures and speaks. Her eyes are sorrowful and wise. Thuck! Karen strikes the key. Suddenly, her sister breaks off her message. "Oh, I'm sorry, Karen!" she says. She stares at the piano, then runs out of room.

I am disappearing. You have no doubt noticed. Yes, and by some no doubt calculable formula of event and pagination. But before we drift apart to a distance beyond the reach of confessions (though I warn you: like Zeno's turtle, I am with you always), listen: it's just as I feared, my invented island is really taking its place in world geography. Why, this island sounds very much like the old Dahlberg place on Jackfish Island up on Rainy Lake, people say, and I wonder: can it be happening? Someone tells me: I understand somebody bought the place recently and plans to fix it up, maybe put a resort there or something. On *my* island? Extraordinary!—and yet it seems possible. I look on a map: yes, there's Rainy Lake, there's Jackfish Island. Who invented this map? Well, I must have, surely. And the Dahlbergs, too, of course, and the people who told me about them. Yes, and perhaps tomorrow I will invent Chicago and Jesus Christ and the history of the moon. Just as I have invented you, dear reader, while lying here in the afternoon sun, bedded deeply in the bluegreen grass like an old iron poker. . . .

There is a storm on the lake and the water is frothy and black. The wind howls around the corner of the stone parapet and the pine trees shake and creak. The two children playing "Chopsticks" on the green piano are arguing about the jurisdiction of the bench and keyboard. "Come over here," their grandmother says from her seat by the window, "and I'll tell you the story of 'The Magic Poker'. . ."

Once upon a time, a family of wealthy Minnesotans bought an island on Rainy Lake up on the Canadian border. They built a home on it and guest cabins and boat houses and an observation tower. They installed an electric generator and a sewage system with indoor toilets, maintained a caretaker, and constructed docks and bath houses. Did they name it Jackfish Island, or did it bear that name when they bought it? The legend does not say, nor should it. What it does say, however, is that when the family abandoned the island, they left behind an iron poker, which, years later, on a visit to the island, a beautiful young girl, not quite a princess perhaps, yet altogether equal to the occasion, kissed. And when she did so, something quite extraordinary happened. . . .

Once upon a time there was an island visited by ruin and inhabited by strange woodland creatures. Some thought it had once had a caretaker who had either died or found another job elsewhere. Others said, no, there was never a caretaker, that was only a childish legend. Others believed there was indeed a caretaker and he lived there yet and was in fact responsible for the island's tragic condition. All this is neither here nor there. What is certainly beyond dispute it that no one who visited the island, whether searching for its legendary Magic Poker or avenging the loss of a loved one, ever came back. Only their names were left, inscribed hastily on walls and ceilings and carved on trees.

Once upon a time, two sisters visited a desolate island. They walked its paths with their proclivities and scruples, dreaming their dreams and sorrowing their sorrows. They scared a snake and probably a bird or two, broke a few windows (there were few left to break), and gazed meditatively out upon the lake from the terrace of the main house. They wrote their names above the stone fireplace in the hexagonal loggia and shat in the soundbox of an old green piano. One of them did anyway; the other one couldn't get her pants down. On the island, they found a beautiful iron poker, and when they went home, they took it with them.

The girl in gold pants hastens out of the big house and down the dark path where earlier the snake slept and past the gutted guest cabin and on down the mottled path toward the boat. To either side of her, flies and bees mumble indolently under the summer sun. A small speckled frog who will not live out the day squats staring on a stone, burps, hops into a darkness. A white moth drifts silently into the web of a spider, flutters there awhile before his execution. Suddenly, there on the path mottled with sunlight, the girl stops short, her breath coming in short gasps, looking around her. Wasn't this—? Yes, yes, it is the place! A smile begins to form. And in fact, there it is! She waits for Karen.

Once upon a time there was a beautiful young Princess in tight gold pants, so very tight in fact that no one could remove them from her. Knights came from far and wide, and they huffed and they puffed, and they grunted and they groaned, but the pants would not come down. One rash Knight even went so far as to jam the blade of his sword down the front of the gold pants, striving to pry them from her, but he succeeded only in shattering his sword, much to his lifelong dismay and ignominy. The King at last delivered a Proclamation. "Whosoever shall succed in pulling my daughter's pants down," he declared, "shall have her for his bride!" Since this was perhaps not the most tempting of trophies, the Princess having been married off three times already in previous competitions, the King added: "And moreover he shall have bestowed upon him the Magic Poker, whose powers and prodigies are well-known in the Kingdom!" "The Old Man's got his bloody cart before his horse," one Knight complained sourly to a companion upon hearing the Proclamation. "If I had the bloody Poker, you could damn well bet I'd have no trouble gettin' the bloody pants off her!" Now, it chanced that this heedless remark was overheard by a peculiar little gnome-like creature, huddling naked and unshaven in the brush alongside the road, and no sooner had the words been uttered than this strange fellow determined to steal the Magic Poker and win the beauty for himself. Such an enterprise might well have seemed impossible for even the most dauntless of Knights, much less for so hapless a creature as this poor naked brute with the shaggy loins, but the truth, always stranger than fiction, was that his father had once been the King's Official Caretaker, and the son had grown up among the mysteries and secret chambers of the Court. Imagine the entire Kingdom's astonishment, therefore, when, the very next day, the Caretaker's son appeared, squat, naked, and hirsute, before the King and with grunts and broad gestures made manifest his intention to quit the Princess of her pants and win the prizes for himself! "Indeed!" cried her father. The King's laughter boomed throughout the Palace, and all the Knights and Ladies joined in, creating the jolliest of uproars. "Bring my daughter here at once!" the King thundered, delighted by the droll spectacle. The Princess, amused, but at the same time somewhat afrighted of the strange little man, stepped timidly forward, her golden haunches gleaming in the bright lights of the Palace. The Caretaker's son promptly drew forth the Magic Poker, pointed it at the Princess, and—POOF!—the gold pants dropped—plop!—to the Palace floor. "Oh's!" and "Ah's!" of amazement and admiration rose up in excited chorus from the crowd of nobles attending this most extraordinary moment. Flushed, trembling, impatient, the Princess grasped the Magic Poker and kissed it—POOF!—a handsome Knight in shining armor of white and navy blue stood before her, smoking a pipe. He drew his sword and slew the Caretaker's son. Then, smiling at the maiden standing in her puddle of gold pants, he sheathed his sword, knocked the ashes from his pipe bowl, and knelt before the King. "Your Majesty," he said, "I have slain the monster and rescued your daughter!" "Not at all," replied the King gloomily. "You have made her a widow. Kiss the fool, my dear!" "No, please!" the Knight begged. "Stop!"

"Look, Karen, look! See what I found! Do you think we can take it? It doesn't hurt, does it, I mean, what with everything else—? It's just beautiful and I can scour off the rust and—?'' Karen glances at the poker in the grass, shrugs, smiles in assent, turns to stride on down the rise toward the boat, a small white edge of which can be glimpsed through the trees, below, at the end of the path. ''Karen—? Could you please—?'' Karen turns around, gazes quizzically at her sister, head tilted to one side—then laughs, a low grunting sound, something like a half-gargle, walks back and picks up the poker, brushes off the insects with her hand. Her sister, delighted, reaches for it, but Karen grunts again, keeps it, carries it down to their boat. There, she washes it clean in the lake water, scrubbing it with sand. She dries it on her dress. ''Don't get your dress dirty, Karen! It's rusty anyway. We'll clean it when we get home.'' Karen holds it between them a moment before tossing it into the boat, and they both smile to see it. Wet still, it glistens, sparkling with flecks of rainbow-colored light in the sunshine.

The tall man stands poised before her, smoking his pipe, one hand in the pocket of his navy-blue jacket. Besides the jacket, he wears only a white turtleneck shirt. The girl in gold pants is kissing him. From the tip of his crown to the least of his toes. Nothing happens. Only a bitter wild goose taste in the mouth. Something is wrong. ''Karen!'' Karen laughs, a low grunting sound, then takes hold of the man and lifts her skirts. ''No, Karen! Please!'' he cries, laughing. ''Stop!'' POOF! From her skirts, Karen withdraws a wrought-iron poker, long and slender with an intricately worked handle. ''It's beautiful, Karen!'' her sister exclaims and reaches for it. Karen grunts again, holds it up between them a moment, and they both smile to see it. It glistens in the sunshine, a handsome souvenir of a beautiful day.

Soon the bay is still again, the silver fish and the dragonflies are returned, and only the slightest murmur near the shore by the old waterlogged lumber betrays the recent disquiet. The boat is already far out on the lake, its stern confronting us in retreat. The family who prepared this land does not know the girls have been here, nor would it astonish them to hear of it. As a matter of fact, with that touch of the divinity common to the rich, they have probably forgotten why they built all the things on this island in the first place, or whatever possessed them seriously to concern themselves, to squander good hours, over the selection of this or that object to decorate the newly made spaces or to do the things that had usually to be done, over the selection of this or that iron poker, for example. The boat is almost out of sight, so distant in fact, it's no longer possible to see its occupants or even to know how many there are—all just a blurred speck on the bright sheen laid on the lake by the lowering sun. The lake is calm. Here, a few shadows lengthen, a frog dies, a strange creature lies slain, a tanager sings.

1969

Early Explorations

When the bark of Columbus nears the shore of America;—
before it, the beach lined with savages, fleeing out of all their huts of cane;
the sea behind; and the purple mountains of the Indian Archipelago around,
can we separate the man from the living picture?

Emerson, *Nature*

Off the Azores in February 1493, Christopher Columbus wrote, in a letter about his discovery of Hispaniola (now Haiti), the first authenticated description of the New World. Before that letter there had been, since ancient times, mythic traditions and vague claims of the discovery of bountiful and blessed islands in the western Atlantic. Elysium and Atlantis lay there, the Isles of the Blest described by Hesiod and Pindar and the Fortunate Isles described by Horace. Among the medieval Celts it was told how Bran and Maeldune discovered there an archipelago of Happy Isles, which included the Isle of Laughter and the Isle of Women, and how the bard Oisin was brought to Tir na nOg, the Land of Youth. And among the Norse the saga *The Vinland History of the Flat Island Book* told, with a claim to historical fact, how Leif Erikson found a land west of Greenland, where he felled trees and gathered large numbers of grapes "and from its products Leif gave the land a name, and called it Vinland"—Wineland. These are only a few of the old traditions, and the brief passage from Adam of Bremen is meant to suggest how shadowy and sometimes terrifying the terrain of the New World was in those traditions.

Columbus, though he had set out for an equally exotic Orient and thought he had found it, gave the first precise geographical location to a part of the New World, and he thus inaugurated the first extensive explorations of it. The actual discovery of the New World, however, did not displace the old traditions but seemed indeed to affirm them. Columbus himself, for example, made two more voyages, and on the third, off the Orinoco River, he thought Paradise, a nipple-shaped mountain on the breast of the earth, to be the river's source.

In the century following Columbus's first voyage, the Spanish and the Portuguese combed the Caribbean and the Gulf Coast; and the Spanish penetrated Mexico, fanning out north to the American Southwest (where Coronado discovered the Grand Canyon), the California Coast and the Great Plains, and south to Brazil and Peru. Meanwhile the French had discovered the St. Lawrence River, which they followed to the Great Lakes and then, finding the Mississippi River, rode it down to its mouth at New Orleans. British and Dutch explorations probed the East Coast of the New World: the British from Florida to Virginia, where they established short-lived colonies at Roanoke Island (1584 and 1587) and at Jamestown (1607); the Dutch around the mouth of the Hudson River, where they established a colony in 1623; and the British again from Cape Cod to Newfoundland, planting another short-lived colony at Popham, Maine (1607), and the first two colonies to take enduring root in the New World, Plymouth Plantation (1620) and Massachusetts Bay Colony (1630). In the process of these explorations, the New World was transformed from an archipelago of mythic islands to a land mass of two continents—a wilderness whose coastline stretched and twisted from the Arctic through the Torrid to the Antarctic Zones. In the process, too, the motive to discover led to the desire to settle.

Read in full, the reports of the maritime explorers are disappointingly thin and formulaic: no explorer sent up articulate and melodious wonder-songs (as Fitzgerald's Nick Carroway would have had it in the ending of *The Great Gatsby*). The forms these reports take leave little room for lyricism. There are *ship's logs* or *journals,* giving a serial account of days, locations, ship's affairs, and brief notes about landfalls, terrain, and encounters with "natives." More usual is the *letter,* written retrospectively to the financiers of the voyage or to influential friends, briefly narrating the highlights of the voyage and describing the lands and the people discovered. The reports of Columbus, Verrazzano, Castaneda, Drake, and Barlowe included here are letters. Finally, there is the more elaborate *relation* or *particular description,* a geographical area-study drawn from available journals and letters, often by a scholar who has never seen the New World. The selections from Adam of Bremen and Peter Martyr can be called relations.

No poets traveled to the New World in the age of exploration, as no poets have yet traveled to the moon—except vicariously, imaginatively. And so, when the explorers' descriptions are factual, they are implacably matter-of-fact. They provide a rough verbal map on which are located landmarks helpful to navigation, hazards to be avoided, safe harbors, potential settlement sites, and exploitable natural resources, which were what the explorers were committed to find. The landscapes thus emerge clustered around a line—a line traced by the magic, orienting numbers of latitude and longitude—at one end of which lies home and at the other, the splendid treasures of the New World. Around that line the landscapes take shape chiefly as a list, an inventory of the bounty awaiting the entrepreneur or the colonist bold enough to come and take it.

But the explorers' descriptions are not always so matter-of-fact. Often the reader feels the imaginative energy of a Renaissance mind trying to come to terms with the unfamiliar and the inexpressible, trying to assert dominion over the "living picture." The Adamic act of naming islands and other landmarks is one kind of assertion; the name talismanically characterizes a place or extends the domain of a monarch. Another is the use of direct comparison or simile in which the unfamiliar and the natural are compared to the familiar and the civilized: Castaneda sights rocks in the Grand Canyon "bigger than the great tower of Seville," for example, and Brereton speaks of trees (possibly sumac) "of an Orange colour, in feeling soft and smoothe like Velvet."

Often, too, the reader sees how the old wonder-giving traditions kept their hold on the imaginations of the explorers. These traditions provided at least three ideal designs by which the explorers and other Renaissance writers could arrange and shape the landscapes of the New World.

The first ideal was what might be called *the landscape as mine.* With an eye for the bountiful commodities, the explorers descriptively inventoried all natural food-stores, from fishing grounds to groves of fruit and spice trees: fish, fruit and so on were what travelers might subsist upon when they came here; spices and other delicacies were valuable exports. They got equally excited at the particularly fine stretches of timber, which could be used for building houses and ships (up until the Revolution, for example, the British crown took for shipmasts from its colonial preserves all white pines of twenty-four-inch diameter). And the least hint of precious mineral deposits which might be mined pushed them to near rapture. Every Indian settlement was scrutinized for jewels or gold artifacts; every Indian who could talk was asked, or so it seems, about gold. The impulse to find and extract such treasures, particularly gold and pearls, might not alone account for the heroic exploits of the explorers, but it is true, writes Howard Mumford Jones,

> . . . that superhuman exploits would not have been undertaken without the dream of reward. . . . Gold, pearls, and precious stones were tangible, were concrete evidence of success, were proof that the New World was, if not the kingdom of Prester John, the empire of the great Khan, or Asia heavy with the wealth of Ormuz and of Ind, then next door to it, or a passage to it, or better still, a richer and more wonderful land. . . . The fixed idea of Renaissance man [was] that gold, silver, precious stones, and pearls were easily to be found anywhere from the Arctic Circle to the Straits of Magellan.

The New World came to seem indeed a "more wonderful land" than the rich, exotic lands of the Orient to which the explorers had been trying to find passage; and the second ideal design they brought with them (the Spanish most notably) gave substance to that wonder. The ideal was that of *the romance landscape*—the landscape they could behold in the works of the Italian romancers (Ariosto, for example), in Spenser's *Faerie Queene,* in Malory's *Morte d'Arthur,* in Shakespeare's *The Tempest* (written shortly after the founding of Jamestown). The romance landscape is a landscape of magic, miracles, and prodigies; it is both lovely and terrifying in earthly and in unearthly ways; it is both providential and demonic. Such an ideal seems at least partly to inform Peter Martyr's accounts of magical water and a living tree of gold, and it could very well be behind Verrazzano's wanting to take home an Indian child as a kind of talismanic souvenir.

The third ideal design, a design Americans came to impose physically on their transcontinental nation during the eighteenth and nineteenth centuries, was that of *the garden in the wilderness.* From the Renaissance on, the ideal designs of the garden and the wilderness have been amazingly adaptable, if not to say plastic. Literally, the term "wilderness" was applied to any place uninhabitable because it was impenetrable or barren, unfarmable: an ocean, a forest, a mountain, a desert. The term "garden," on the other hand, was applied to any place habitable, fruitful, civilized: an island such as Columbus's Hispaniola or even Peter Martyr's Dariena (where elements of wilderness and garden are intermixed); a stretch of "beautiful fields and broad plains" such as Verrazzano saw in the vicinity of Virginia; a clearing such as Bradford was to see on Cape Cod; a farm carved from Northern deciduous forest; a pastoral meadow where sheep and cattle grazed.

By the end of the eighteenth century, on the other hand, natural historians could image a forest or swamp as a kind of wild garden, divinely maintained. And by the end of the nineteenth century, the literary naturalists could image the city, that fruit of the garden of civilization, as a wilderness—a desert or a jungle ruled by savage laws of survival.

The ideal design of the garden depended, among other things, on whether it was already there to be found or had instead to be carved out of the wilderness by settlers. If found, it usually gave rise to the ideal of paradise ("paradise" means literally "walled garden"—a garden walled off from the wilderness): an Eden or a millennial Golden Age. If it had to be carved out by settlers, it usually gave rise to the ideal of the Promised Land or the pastoral (see next section). In both cases, the ideal designs were amalgams of Christian and classical traditions.

For the explorers and their contemporaries, the ideal that gave shape to the landscapes of the New World, especially those in its temperate and tropical zones, was an Edenic garden or a Golden Age, such as Hesiod had conjured. In virgin soil, corn grew to the size of trees, its kernels grew to the size of grapes; oxen, writes Peter Martyr, grew elephant-sized. Here man seemed not yet to have suffered his diminishment, his curse. Here there were no winter, no weeds or wild animals, no need to work, no deceit or treachery, no terror, chaos, or death. All was order, beauty, light, fragrance, peace, and plenty.

Outside these marvelous gardens, however, particularly in Northern latitudes, lay the terrors, physical and psychic, of a wilderness whose extent and power western Europeans had not experienced since the ancient times, when they had wandered in the gothic forests of northern Europe. The shape of the New World wilderness was the shape of the profoundest terror this race could imagine. The wilderness was by definition God-forsaken and thus barren both of fruit and of grace. It was the demented household, as Cotton Mather was to write, whose landlord was the Devil and whose tenants were his grotesquely gothic monsters (bats, crocodiles, and so on) and his wild minions the Indians, who ate human flesh. Its mountains were excrescences—warts, blisters—or deserts, like the deserts Adam and Eve had been driven into or which the Israelites wandered in for forty years. In its forests and jungles, writes Kenneth Clark in *Landscape into Art,* were not the "orderly decorative trees" to be found in the garden, but "menacing, organic growth, ready to smother and strangle any intruder." The wilderness was a place whose physical and psychic forces stripped men of their reason and therefore their souls. To enter it was to court not simply death but dissolution into a primeval and demonic miasma.

These are the ideal designs which gave shape to the landscapes of the New World. In one form or another they are still with us, and they help us to understand why, from Columbus on, we cannot "separate the man from the living picture."

Adam of Bremen

From Descriptio Insularum Aquilonis

Adam of Bremen, an ecclesiastical historian, drew much information for his *Descriptio Insularum Aquilonis* ("Discription of the Northern Islands") from the Danish king, Svend Estridson. Adam's Vinland or Wineland is most likely the present Newfoundland. His manuscript was written in 1076, but not published until 1595.

[The Island of Wineland]

SVEND ESTRIDSON, king of Denmark, spoke of an island in that ocean discovered by many, which is called Vinland, for the reason that vines grow wild there, which yield the best of wine. Moreover that grain unsown grows there abundantly, is not a fabulous fancy, but, from the accounts of the Danes, we know to be a fact. Beyond this island, it is said, that there is no habitable land in that ocean, but all those regions which are beyond are filled with insupportable ice and boundless gloom, to which Martian thus refers: "One day's sail beyond Thile the sea is frozen." This was assayed not long since by that very enterprising Northmen's prince, Harold, who explored the extent of the northern ocean with his ship, but was scarcely able by retreating to escape in safety from the gulf's enormous abyss, where before his eyes the vanishing bounds of earth were hidden in gloom.

1595

Christopher Columbus

From Letter . . . Describing . . . His First Voyage . . .

Like most reports from the New World which followed, the *Letter of Columbus to Various Persons Describing the Results of His First Voyage and Written on the Return Journey* (1493) mixes geography, surveys of natural resources, sketches of manners and morals, military intelligence, and Christian zeal. The geography is shadowy at best: Columbus's estimations of the size of Haiti (Hispaniola) and of Cuba are much inflated, and at one point he suggests that Haiti is part of the territories of the Grand Khan—the Asian mainland. The reports of gold are also inaccurate, and the "nightingale" he reports is a matter of literary convention rather than of fact (it was most likely a mockingbird). Among the exportable treasures he lists toward the end, mastic is an evergreen resin used as an astringent and an ingredient in varnish, chewing gum, and incense; aloes are a plant in the lily family whose juices are used as a laxative.

[Hispaniola]

SINCE I KNOW that you will be pleased at the great success with which the Lord has crowned my voyage, I write to inform you how in thirty-three days I crossed from the Canary Islands to the Indies, with the fleet which our most illustrious sovereigns gave me. I found very many islands with large populations and took possession of them all for their Highnesses: this I did by proclamation and unfurled the royal standard. No opposition was offered.

I named the first island that I found 'San Salvador', in honour of our Lord and Savior who has granted me this miracle. The Indians call it 'Guanahani'. The second island I named 'Santa Maria de Concepcion', the third 'Fernandina', the fourth 'Isabela' and the fifth 'Juana'; thus I renamed them all.

When I reached Cuba, I followed its north coast westwards, and found it so extensive that I thought this must be the mainland, the province of Cathay. Since there were no towns or villages on the coast, but only small groups of houses whose inhabitants fled as soon as we approached, I continued on my course, thinking that I should undoubtedly come to some great towns or cities. We continued for many leagues but found no change, except that the coast was bearing me northwards. This I wished to avoid, since winter was approaching and my plan was to journey south. As the wind was carrying me on I decided not to wait for a change of weather, but to turn back to a remarkable harbour which I had observed. From here I sent two men inland to discover whether there was a king or any great cities. They travelled for three days, finding only a large number of small villages and great numbers of people, but nothing more substantial. Therefore they returned.

I understood from some Indians whom I had captured elsewhere that this was an island, and so I followed the coast for 107 leagues to its eastward point. From there I saw another island eighteen leagues eastwards which I named 'Hispaniola'. I crossed to this island and followed its northern coast eastwards for 188 leagues continuously, as I had followed the coast of Cuba. All these islands are extremely fertile and this one is particularly so. It has many large harbours finer than any I know in Christian lands, and many large rivers. All this is marvellous. The land is high and has many ranges of hills, and mountains incomparably finer than Tenerife. All are most beautiful and various in shape, and all are accessible. They are covered with tall trees of different kinds which seem to reach the sky. I have heard that they never lose their leaves, which I can well believe, for I saw them as green and lovely as they are in Spain in May; some were flowering, some bore fruit and others were at different stages according to their nature. It was November but everywhere I went the nightingale and many other birds were singing. There are palms of six or eight different kinds—a marvellous sight because of their great variety—and the other trees, fruit, and plants are equally marvellous. There are splendid pine woods and broad fertile plains, and there is honey. There are many kinds of birds and varieties of fruit. In the interior are mines and a very large population.

Hispaniola is a wonder. The mountains and hills, the plains and meadow lands are both fertile and beautiful. They are most suitable for planting crops and for raising cattle of all kinds, and there are good sites for building towns and villages. The harbours are incredibly fine and there are many great rivers with broad channels and the majority contain gold. The trees, fruits and plants are very different from those of Cuba. In Hispaniola there are many spices and large mines of gold and other metals. . . .

The inhabitants of this island and all the rest that I discovered or heard of, go naked, as their mothers bore them, men and women alike. A few of the women, however, cover a single place with a leaf of a plant or a piece of cotton which they weave for the purpose. They have no iron or steel or arms and are not capable of using them, not because they are not strong and well built but because they are amazingly timid. All the weapons they have are canes cut at seeding time, at the end of which they fix a sharpened stick, but they have not the courage to make use of these, for very often when I have sent two or three men to a village to have conversation with them a great number of them have come out. But as soon as they saw my men all fled immediately, a father not even waiting for his son. And this is not because we have harmed any of them; on the contrary, wherever I have gone and been able to have conversation with them, I have given them some of the various things I had, a cloth and other articles, and received nothing in exchange. But they have still remained incurably timid. True, when they have been reassured and lost their fear, they are so ingenuous and so liberal with all of their possessions that no one who has not seen them would believe it. If one asks for anything they have they never say no. On the contrary, they offer a share to anyone with demonstrations of heartfelt affection, and they are immediately content with any small thing, valuable or valueless, that is given them. I forbade the men to give them bits of broken crockery, fragments of glass or tags of lace, though if they could get them they fancied them the finest jewels in the world. One sailor was known to have received gold to the weight of two and a half *castellanos* for the tag of a breeches lace, and others received much more for things of even less value. For newly minted *blancas* they would give everything they possessed, even two or three *castellanos* of gold or an arroba or two of spun cotton. They even took bits of broken hoops from the wine barrels and, as simple as animals, gave what they had. This seemed to me to be wrong and I forbade it.

I gave them a thousand pretty things that I had brought, in order to gain their love and incline them to become Christians. I hoped to win them to the love and service of their Highnesses and of the whole Spanish nation and to persuade them to collect and give us of the things which they possessed in abundance and which we needed. They have no religion and are not idolators; but all believe that power and goodness dwell in the sky and they are firmly convinced that I have come from the sky with these ships and people. In this belief they gave me a good reception everywhere, once they had overcome their fear; and this is not because they are stupid—far from it, they are men of great intelligence, for they navigate all of those seas, and give marvellously good account of everything—but because they have never before seen men clothed or ships like these.

As soon as I came to the Indies, at the first island I discovered I seized some natives, intending them to inquire and inform me about things in these parts. These men soon understood us, and we them, either by speech or signs and they were very useful to us. I still have them with me and despite all the conversation they have had with me they are still of the opinion that I come from the sky and have been the first to proclaim this wherever I have gone. Then others have gone running from house to house and to the neighboring villages shouting: 'Come, come and see the people from the sky, 'so, once they were reassured about us, all have come, men and women alike, and not one, old or young, has remained behind. All have brought us something to eat and drink which they have given with a great show of love. In all the islands they have very many canoes like oared *fustas*.

They are of various sizes, some as large as a *fusta* of eighteen benches. But they are not as broad, since they are hollowed out of a single tree. A *fusta* would not be able to keep up with them, however, for they are rowed at an incredible speed. In these they travel and transport their goods between the islands, which are innumerable. I have seen some of these canoes with eighty men in them, all rowing.

In all these islands I saw no great difference in the looks of the people, their customs or their language. On the other hand, all understand one another, which will be of singular assistance to the work of their conversion to our holy faith, on which I hope your Highnesses will decide, since they are very well disposed towards it.

I have already told you of my voyage of 107 leagues in a straight line from west to east along the coast of Cuba, according to which I reckon that the island is larger than England and Scotland put together.

One of these provinces is called Avan and there the people are born with tails, and these provinces cannot have a length of less than fifty or sixty leagues, according to the information I received from those Indians who I have with me and who know all the island.

The other island, Hispaniola, is greater in circumference than the whole of Spain from Collioure to Fuenterabia in the Basque province, since I travelled along one side for 188 great leagues in a straight line from west to east.

These islands are richer than I yet know or can say and I have taken possession of them in their Majesties' name and hold them all on their behalf and as completely at their disposition as the Kingdom of Castile. In this island of Hispaniola I have taken possession of a large town which is most conveniently located for the goldfields and for communications with the mainland both here, and there in the territories of the Grand Khan, with which there will be very profitable trade. I have named this town Villa de Navidad and have built a fort there. Its fortifications will by now be finished and I have left sufficient men to complete them. They have arms, artillery and provisions for more than a year, and a *fusta;* also a skilled shipwright who can build more.

I have established warm friendship with the king of that land, so much so, indeed, that he was proud to call me and treat me as a brother. But even should he change his attitude and attack the men of La Navidad, he and his people know nothing about arms and go naked, as I have already said; they are the most timorous people in the world. In fact, the men that I have left there would be enough to destroy the whole land, and the island holds no dangers for them so long as they maintain discipline.

In all these islands the men are seemingly content with one woman, but their chief or king is allowed more than twenty. The women appear to work more than the men and I have not been able to find out if they have private property. As far as I could see whatever a man had was shared among all the rest and this particularly applies to food.

I have not found the human monsters which many people expected. On the contrary, the whole population is very well made. They are not Negroes as in Guinea, and their hair is straight, for where they live the sun's rays do not strike too harshly, but they are strong nevertheless, despite the fact that Hispaniola is 20 to 21 degrees from the Equator.

There are high mountains in these islands and it was very cold this winter but the natives are used to this and withstand the weather, thanks to their food, which they eat heavily seasoned with very hot spices. Not only have I found no monsters but I have had no reports of any except at the island called 'Quaris' [Dominica?], which is second as you approach the Indies from the east, and which is inhabited by a people who are regarded in these islands as extremely fierce and who eat human flesh. They have many canoes in which they travel throughout the islands of the Indies, robbing and taking all they can. They are no more ill-shaped than any other natives of the Indies, though they are in the habit of wearing their hair long like women. They have bows and arrows with the same canes, tipped with splinters of wood, for lack of iron which they do not possess. They behave most savagely to the other peoples but I take no more account of them than the rest. It is these men who have relations with the women of Matinino [Martinique], where there are no men and which is the first island you come to on the way from Spain to the Indies. These women do not follow feminine occupations but use cane bows and arrows like those of the men and arm and protect themselves with plates of copper, of which they have much.

In another island, which I am told is larger than Hispaniola, the people have no hair. Here there is a vast quantity of gold, and from here and other islands I bring Indians as evidence.

In conclusion, to speak only of the results of this very hasty voyage, their Highnesses can see that I will give them as much gold as they require, if they will render me some very slight assistance; also I will give them all the spices and cotton they want, and as for mastic, which has so far been found only in Greece and the island of Chios and which the Genoese authorities have sold at their own price, I will bring back as large a cargo as their Highnesses may command. I will also bring them as much aloes as they ask and as many slaves, who will be taken from idolators. I believe also that I have found rhubarb and cinnamon and there will be countless other things in addition, which the people I have left there will discover. For I did not stay anywhere unless delayed by lack of wind except at the town of La Navidad, which I had to leave secure and well established. In fact I should have done much more if the ships had been reasonably serviceable, but of this enough.

Thus the eternal God, Our Lord, grants to all those who walk in his way victory over apparent impossibilities, and this voyage was pre-eminently a victory of this kind. For although there was much talk and writing of these lands, all was conjectural, without ocular evidence. In fact, those who accepted the stories judged rather by hearsay than on any tangible information. So all Christendom will be delighted that our Redeemer has given victory to our most illustrious King and Queen and their renowned kingdoms, in this great matter. They should hold great celebrations and render solemn thanks to the Holy Trinity with many solemn prayers, for the great triumph which they will have, by the conversion of so many people to our holy faith and for the temporal benefits which will follow, for not only Spain, but all Christendom will receive encouragement and profit.

This is a brief account of the facts

Written in the caravel off the Canary Islands

15 February 1493

At your orders
THE ADMIRAL

Giovanni da Verrazzano

From Letter to the King

Verrazzano, a Florentine, was sent in 1524 by a syndicate of French silk merchants in search of a passage to Cathay and the Asian silk markets. He sailed from Florida to Nova Scotia looking for such a passage (he thought he found an isthmus through the sand banks off the Carolinas), and in the process he became the first European to confirm that the New World had a continental coastline. His report is addressed to François I, king of France. Of the two landings described here, the first is in the area of Cape Fear, the second in the area of Kitty Hawk, North Carolina, which Verrazzano named Arcadia. The "pleasant situation among some steep hills" near the end of the excerpt is New York Bay (its Narrows and the bridge over them now have been named after him). The triangular island "about the bigness of Rhodes" is Block Island (so named by the Dutch), off Narragansett Bay, Rhode Island.

[The Coast of the New World]

ON THE 17TH of last January, we set sail from a desolate rock near the island of Madeira, belonging to his most Serene Majesty, the King of Portugal, with fifty men, having provisions sufficient for eight months, arms and other warlike munition and naval stores. Sailing westward with a light and pleasant easterly breeze, in twenty-five days we ran eight hundred leagues. On the 24th of February we encountered as violent a hurricane as any ship ever weathered, from which we escaped unhurt by the divine assistance and goodness, to the praise of the glorious and fortunate name of our good ship, that had been able to support the violent tossing of the waves. Pursuing our voyage towards the West, a little northwardly, in twenty-four days more, having run four hundred leagues, we reached a new country, which had never before been seen by any one, either in ancient or modern times. At first it appeared to be very low, but on approaching it to within a quarter of a league from the shore we perceived, by the light of the great fires near the coast, that it was inhabited. We perceived that it stretched to the south, and coasted along in that direction in search of some port, in which we might come to anchor, and examine into the nature of the country, but for fifty leagues we could find none in which we could lie securely. Seeing the coast still stretch to the south, we resolved to change our course and stand to the northward, and as we still had the same difficulty, we drew in with the land and sent a boat ashore. Many people who were seen coming to the sea-side fled at our approach, but occasionally stopping to look back upon us with astonishment, and some were at length induced, by various friendly signs, to come to us. These showed the greatest delight on beholding us, wondering at our dress, countenance and complexion. They then showed us by signs where we could more conveniently secure our boat, and offered us some of their provisions. That your Majesty may know all that we learned, while on shore, of their manners and customs of life, I will relate what we saw as briefly as possible. They go entirely naked, except that about the loins they wear skins of small animals like martens fastened by a girdle of plaited grass, to which they tie, all round the body, the tails of other animals hanging down to the knees; all other parts of the body and head are naked. Some wear garlands similar to birds' feathers.

The complexion of these people is black, not much different from that of the Ethiopians; their hair is black, and thick, and not very long; it is worn tied back upon their head in the form of a little tail. In person they are of good proportions, of middle stature, a little above our own, broad across the breast, strong in the arms, and well formed in the legs and other parts of the body; the only exception to their good looks is that they have broad faces, but not all, however, as we saw many that had sharp ones, with large black eyes and a fixed expression. They are not very strong in body, but acute in mind, active, and swift of foot, as far as we could judge by observation. In these last two particulars they resemble the people of the east, especially those the most remote. We could not learn a great many particulars of their usages on account of our short stay among them, and the distance of our ship from the shore.

We found not far from this another people whose mode of life we judged to be similar. The whole shore is covered with fine sand about fifteen feet thick, rising in the form of little hills about fifty paces broad. Ascending farther, we found several arms of the sea which make in through inlets, washing the shore on both sides as the coast runs. An outstretched country appears at a little distance rising somewhat above the sandy shore in beautiful fields and broad plains, covered with immense forests of trees, more or less dense, too various in colours, and too delightful and charming in appearance to be described. I do not believe that they are like the Hercynian forest or the rough wilds of Scythia, and the northern regions full of vines and common trees, but adorned with palms, laurels, cypresses, and other varieties unknown in Europe, that send forth the sweetest fragrance to a great distance, but which we could not examine more closely for the reasons before given, and not on account of any difficulty in traversing the woods, which, on the contrary, are easily penetated.

As the "East" stretches around this country, I think it cannot be devoid of the same medicinal and aromatic drugs, and various riches of gold and the like, as is denoted by the colour of the ground. It abounds also in animals, as deer, stags, hares, and many other similar, and with a great variety of birds for every kind of pleasant and delightful sport. It is plentifully supplied with lakes and ponds of running water, and being in the latitude of 34, the air is salubrious, pure and temperate, and free from the extremes of both heat and cold. There are no violent winds in these regions, the most prevalent are the northwest and west. In summer the season in which we were there, the sky is clear, with but little rain: if fogs and mists are at any time driven in by the south wind, they are instantly dissipated, and at once it becomes serene and bright again. The sea is calm not boisterous, and its waves are gentle. Although the whole coast is low and without harbours, it is not dangerous for navigation, being free from rocks and bold, so that within four or five fathoms from the shore there is twenty-four feet of water at all times of the tide, and this depth constantly increases in a uniform proportion. The holding ground is so good that no ship can part her cable, however violent the wind, as we proved by experience; for while riding at anchor on the coast, we were overtaken by a gale in the beginning of March, when the winds are high, as is usual in all countries, we found our anchor broken before it started from its hold or moved at all.

We set sail from this place, continuing to coast along the shore, which we found stretching out to the west; the inhabitants being numerous, we saw everywhere a multitude of fires. While at anchor on this coast, there being no harbour to enter, we sent the boat on shore with twenty-five men to obtain water, but it was not possible to land without endangering the boat, on account of the immense high surf thrown up by the sea, as it was an open roadstead. Many of the natives came to the beach, indicating by various friendly signs that we might trust ourselves on shore. One of their noble deeds of friendship deserves to be made known to your Majesty. A young sailor was attempting to swim ashore through the surf to carry them some knick-knacks, as little bells, looking-glasses, and other like trifles; when he came near to three or four of them he tossed the things to them, and turned to go back to the boat, but he was thrown over by the waves and so dashed by them that he lay as it were dead upon the beach. When these people saw him in that situation, they ran and took him up by the head, legs and arms, and carried him to a distance from the surf; the young man, finding himself borne off in this way, uttered very loud shrieks in fear and dismay, while they answered as they could in their language, showing him that he had no cause to fear. Afterwards they laid him down at the foot of a little hill, when they took off his shirt and trowsers, and examined him, expressing the greatest astonishment at the whiteness of his skin. Our sailors in the boat seeing a great fire made up, and their companion placed very near it, full of fear, as is usual in all cases of novelty, imagined that the natives were about to roast him for food. But as soon as he had recovered his strength after a short stay with them, showing by signs that he wished to return aboard, they hugged him with great affection, and accompanied him to the shore, then leaving him that he might feel more secure, they withdrew to a little hill, from which they watched him until he was safe in the boat. This young man remarked that these people were black like the others, that they had shining skins, middle stature, and sharper faces, and very delicate bodies and limbs, and that they were inferior in strength, but quick in their minds; this is all that he observed of them.

Departing hence, and always following the shore, which stretched to the north, we came in the space of fifty leagues to another land, which appeared very beautiful and full of the largest forests. We approached it, and going ashore with twenty men, we went back from the coast about two leagues, and found that the people had fled and hid themselves in the woods for fear. By searching around we discovered in the grass a very old woman and a young girl of about eighteen or twenty, who had concealed themselves for the same reason; the old woman carried two infants on her shoulders, and behind her neck a little boy of eight years; when we came up to them they began to shriek and make signs to the men who had fled to the woods. We gave them a part of our provisions which they accepted with delight, but the girl would not touch any; everything we offered her being thrown down in great anger. We took the little boy from the old woman to carry with us to France, and would have taken the girl also, but it was impossible because of the loud shrieks she uttered as we attempted to lead her away; having to pass some woods, and being far from the ship, we determined to leave her and take the boy only. We found them fairer than the others, and wearing a covering made of certain plants, which hung down from the branches of the trees, tying them together with threads of wild hemp; their heads are without covering and of the same shape as the others. Their food is a kind of pulse which there abounds, different in colour and size from ours, and of a very delicious flavor. Besides they take birds and fish for food, using snares and bows made of hard woods with reeds for arrows, in the ends of which they put the bones of fish and other animals. The animals in these regions are wilder than in Europe from being continually molested by the hunters. We saw many of their boats made of one tree twenty feet long and four feet broad, without the aid of stone, of iron or other kind of metal. In the whole country for the space of two hundred leagues, which we visited, we saw no stone of any sort. To hollow out their boats they burn out as much of a log as is requisite, and also from the prow and stern to make them float well on the sea. The land, in situation, fertility and beauty, is like the other, abounding also in forests filled with various kinds of trees, but not of such fragrance, as it is more northern and colder.

We saw in this country many vines growing naturally, which entwine about the trees, and run up upon them as they do in the plains of Lombardy. These vines would doubtless produce excellent wine if they were properly cultivated and attended to, as we have often seen the grapes which they produce very sweet and pleasant, and not unlike our own. They must be held in estimation by them, as they carefully remove the shrubbery from around them, wherever they grow, to allow the fruit to ripen better. We also found wild roses, violets, lilies, and many sorts of fragrant flowers different from our own. We cannot describe their habitations, as they are in the interior of the country, but from various indications we conclude they must be formed of trees and shrubs. We saw also many grounds for conjecturing that they often sleep in the open air, without any covering but the sky. Of their other usages we know nothing; we believe, however, that all people we were among live in the same way.

After having remained here three days, riding at anchor on the coast, as we could find no harbour we determined to depart, and coast along the shore to the north-east, keeping sail on the vessel only by day, and coming to anchor by night. After proceeding one hundred leagues, we found a very pleasant situation among some steep hills, through which a very large river, deep at its mouth, forced its way to the sea; from the sea to the estuary of the river, any ship heavily laden might pass, with the help of the tide, which rises eight feet. But as we were riding at anchor in a good berth, we would not venture up in our vessel, without a knowledge of the mouth; therefore we took the boat, and entering the river we found the country on its banks well peopled, the inhabitants not differing much from the others, being dressed out with the feathers of birds of various colors. They came toward us with evident delight, raising shouts of admiration, and showing us where we could most securely land with our boat. We passed up this river, about half a league, when we found it formed a most beautiful lake three leagues in circuit, upon which they were rowing thirty or more of their small boats, from one shore to another, filled with multitudes who came to see us. All of a sudden, as is wont to happen to navigators, a violent contrary wind blew in from the sea, and forced us to return to our ship, greatly regretting to leave this region which seemed so commodious and delightful, and which we supposed must also contain great riches, as the hills showed many indications of minerals. Weighing anchor, we sailed fifty leagues toward the east, as the coast stretched in that direction, and always in sight of it; at length we discovered an island of a triangular form, about ten leagues from the mainland, in size about equal to the island of Rhodes, having many hills covered with trees, and well peopled, judging from the great number of fires which we saw all around its shores; we gave it the name of your Majesty's illustrious mother.

1524

Peter Martyr

From Decades of the New World

An Italian-born member of the Spanish Council of the Indies, Peter Martyr (Pietro Martire d'Anghiera) composed his *Decades* as a series of relations concerning the explorations and discoveries of voyages in the service of Spain. The book was first published in 1533 and translated into English in 1555 by Richard Eden. Eden's translation, with the spelling and punctuation somewhat modernized, is used here.

Dariena is from the Third Decade, Sixth Book; *Hispaniola,* from the Third Decade, Seventh Book; and *The Gold Regions* from the Third Decade, Eighth Book.

[Dariena]

LET US NOW . . . rehearse what they write of Dariena, and of their habitation there, which they calle Sancta Maria Antiqua, planted on the sea bankes of Dariena. The situation of the place hath no natural munition or defense: And the aire is more pestiferous than in Sardus. The Spanish inhabitours are all pale and yellowe, like unto them that have the yellowe jaundice. Whiche neverthe-less commeth not of the nature of the region as it is situate under the heaven. For in many regions being under the self same degree of latitude, having the pole of the same elevation, they find wholesome and temperate aire in such places where as the earth bringeth forth faire springs of water, or where whole-some rivers runne by bankes of pure earth without mudde: but moste especially where they inhabite the sides of the hilles and not the valleyes. But that habi-tation whiche in one of the bankes of the river of Dariena, is situate in a deepe valley, and environed on every side with highe hilles: By reason whereof, it re-ceiveth the sunne beames at noonetide directly perpendicular over their heades, and are therefore sore vexed by reflection of the beames bothe before, be-hinde, and from the sides. For it is the reflection of the sunne beames whiche causeth fervente heate, and not their accesse or nearenesse to the earth. Foras-muche as they are not passible in themselves as dothe manifestly appeare by the snowe lyinge continually unmolten upon certaine high mountaines, as youre holynesse knoweth righte well. The sunne beames therefore, falling on the mountaines, are reflected downeward into the valley by reason of the objecte of the droppes of the hilles, as it were the falle of a greate rounde sunne rolled frome the toppe of a mountaine. The valley therefore receiveth both those beames whiche falle directly theron, and also those whiche are reflected downwarde from every side of the mountaines. Their habitation therefore in Dariena is pernicious and unwholesome only of the particular nature of the place, and not by the situation of the region as it is placed under the heaven or neare to the sunne. The place is also contagious by the nature of the soile, by reason it is compassed aboute with muddy and stinkinge marshes, the infection whereof is not a little increased by the heate. The village itselfe, is in a marshe, and in manner a standinge puddle, where, of the droppes falling from the handes of the bond men while they water the pavementes of their houses, toades are engendered immediately, as I myselfe sawe in another place the droppes of that water turne into fleas in the summer season. Furthermore, wheresoever they digge the grounde the depthe of a handfull and a halfe, there springeth oute unwholesome and corrupte water of the nature of the river which runneth through the deepe and muddy channel of the valley, and so falleth into the sea. Now therefore they consule of removing their habitation. Necessitie caused them first to fasten their foote here, because that whiche first arrived in those landes were oppressed with suche urgente hunger, that they had no respecte to change the place althoughe they were thus vexed by the contagion of the soile and heate of the sunne, beside the corrupte water and infectious aire by reason of venemous vapours and exhalations risinge from the same. Another great incommoditie was, that the place was destitute of a commodious haven, being three leagues distante from the sea. But let us nowe speake somewhat of other particular thinges whiche chanced. Therefore shortly after that they were arrived, there happened many thinges whereof they had no knowledge before. A certaine well learned physician of Sivile, whome partely the authoritie of the bishop of Dariena, and partely the desire of golde had allured to those landes, was so scarred with lightninge in the nighte season lyinge in bedde with his wife, that the house and all the stuffe therein beinge sette on fire and burnte, he and his wife both sore scorched, ranne forthe cryinge and almoste naked, hardly escapinge the danger of deathe. At another time, as certaine of them stoode on the shore, a great Crocodile suddenly carried awaye a mastiff of a yeare and a halfe olde, as a kite shoulde have snatched up a chicken: And this even in the presence of them all, where the miserable dogge cried in vaine for the helpe of his master. In the nighte season they were tormented with the bitinge of battes whiche are there so noisome that if they bite any man in his sleepe, they putte him in danger of life, onely with drawinge of bloode: Insomuche that some have died thereof, fallinge as it were into a consumption through the maliciousnesse of the venemous wounde. If these battes chance to finde a cocke or a henne abroade in the night season, they bite them by the combes and so kill them. They also whiche wente laste into these regions do write that the lande is troubled with Crocodiles, Lions, and Tigers: But that they have nowe devised artes and engines howe to take them. Likewise that in the houses of their fellowes, that by reason of the rankenesse and fruitefulnesse of the grounde, kine, swine, and horses, do marvelously increase in these regions, and growe to a muche bigger quantitie than they whiche were of the first broode. Of the exceedinge highnesse of the trees with their fruites, of the garden herbes, fruites, plantes, and seedes whiche oure men broughte from Spaine and sowed and set the same in these regions, likewise of the hartes and other foure footed beastes both tame and wilde, also of divers kindes of foules, birdes, and fishes, they write even as we have declared in the decades before.

The Gold Regions

THERE IS ALSO another region in Hispaniola named Cotohy after the same name. . . . It hath mountaines, vales, and plaines. But because it is barren, it is not muche inhabited. Yet is it richest in golde: For the originall of the abundance of gold, beginneth here: Insomuche that it is not gathered in smalle graines and sparkes as in other places: but is founde whole, massie, and pure, amonge certaine softe stones and in the veines of rockes, by breakinge the stones whereof they followe the veines of golde. They have founde by experience, that the veine of golde is a livinge tree: And that the same by all wayes that it spreadeth and springeth from the roote by the softe pores and passages of the earth, putteth forth branches even unto the uppermost part of the earth, & ceaseth not until it discover itself unto the open aire: At whiche time, it shineth forth certaine beautifull colours instead of flowers, rounde stones of golden earth instead of fruites, and thinne plates instead of leaves. These are they which are dispersed throughout the whole Islande by the course of the rivers, eruptions of the springes oute of the mountaines, and violent falles of the floodes. For they thinke that such graines are not engendered where they are gathered: especially on the dry land: but otherwise in the rivers. They say that the roote of the golde tree extendeth to the center of the earth & taketh nourishment of increase. For the deeper that they digge, they find the trunkes thereof to be so much the greater as farre as they maye followe it for abundance of water springing in the mountaines. Of the branches of this tree, they finde some as smalle as a threade, and others as bigge as a manne's finger accordinge to the largenesse or straightnesse of the riftes and cleftes. They have sometimes chanced upon whole caves sustained and borne up as it were with golden pillars: And this in the wayes by whiche the branches ascende: The whiche beinge filled with the substance of the trunke creepinge from beneath, the branche maketh it self waye by whiche it may passe oute. It is oftentimes divided by encounteringe with some kinde of harde stone. Yet is it in other cleftes nourished by the exhalations and virtue of the roote. But now perhappes you will aske me what plentie of golde is brought from thence. You shall therefore understande that only oute of Hispaniola, the sum of foure hundredth and sometimes five hundreth thousande ducates of gold is brought yearely into Spaine: as may be gathered by the fifthe portion due to the kinge's Exchecker, which amounteth to the sum of a hundredth and fourscore, or fourescore and ten thousand Castellanes of golde, and sometimes more. What is to be thought of the Islande of Cuba and Sancti Iohannis (otherwise cauled Burichena) being both very riche in golde, we will declare further hereafter. To have saide thus muche of golde, it shall suffice.

1533

Pedro de Castaneda

From Expedition to Cibola

Castaneda was a private soldier in the army of Coronado, who set out from Mexico City on an expedition to the fabled Seven Cities of Cibola (actually villages of the ancestors of the Zuñi Indians in western New Mexico) and ranged as far as the plains of Texas, Kansas, and Nebraska. They found no gold, but they were the first to see the Grand Canyon, which Castaneda rather matter of factly describes. Coronado's expedition (1540–1542) and that of DeSoto's, which ranged through the Gulf States as far as Texas (1539–1543), gave the first extensive reports of the New World's continental interior.

[The Grand Canyon]

THEY STARTED from here loaded with provisions, for they had to go through a desert country before reaching the inhabited region, which the Indians said was more than twenty days' journey. After they had gone twenty days they came to the banks of the river, which seemed to be more than three or four leagues in an air line across to the other bank of the stream which flowed between them [Grand Canyon of Colorado]. This country was elevated and full of low twisted pines, very cold, and lying open toward the north, so that, this being the warm season, no one could live there on account of the cold. They spent three days on this bank looking for a passage down to the river, which looked from above as if the water was six feet across, although the Indians said it was half a league wide. It was impossible to descend, for after these three days Captain Melgosa and one Juan Galeras and another companion, who were the three lightest and most agile men, made an attempt to go down at the least difficult place, and went down until those who were above were unable to keep sight of them. They returned about four o'clock in the afternoon, not having succeeded in reaching the bottom on account of the great difficulties which they found, because what seemed to be easy from above was not so, but instead very hard and difficult. They said that they had been down about a third of the way and that the river seemed very large from the place which they reached, and that from what they saw they thought the Indians had given the width correctly. Those who stayed above had estimated that some huge rocks on the sides of the cliffs seemed to be about as tall as a man, but those who went down swore that when they reached these rocks they were bigger than the great tower of Seville. They did not go farther up the river, because they could not get water. Before this they had to go a league or two inland every day late in the evening in order to find water, and the guides said that if they should go four days farther it would not be possible to go on, because there was no water within three or four days, for when they travel across this region themselves they take with them women loaded with water in gourds, and bury the gourds of water along the way, to use when they return, and besides this, they travel in one day over what it takes us two days to accomplish.

1540

Arthur Barlowe

From First Voyage to Virginia

Barlowe's was the first English voyage to Virginia. Sir Walter Raleigh commissioned the voyage, and Barlowe sent his report to him in 1584. Like other English reports represented here, it was included in Richard Hakluyt's *The Principal Navigations, Voyages, Traffiques and Discoveries of the English Nation* (1599–1600), which did for English explorations of the New World what Peter Martyr's *Decades* did for the Spanish and Johann De Laet's *Novus Orbis* did for the Dutch explorations. The spelling has been somewhat modernized.

THE 27 DAY OF APRILL, in the yeere of our redemption, 1584 we departed the West of England, with two barkes well furnished with men and victuals, having received our last and perfect directions by your letters, confirming the former instructions, and commandements delivered by yourselfe at our leaving the river of Thames. And I thinke it a matter both unnecessary, for the manifest discoverie of the Countrey, as also for tediousnesse sake, to remember unto you the diurnall of our course, sailing thither and returning: only I have presumed to present unto you this briefe discourse, by which you may judge how profitable this land is like to succeede, as well to yourselfe, (by whose direction and charge, and by whose servants this our discoverie hath beene performed) as also to her Highnesse, and the Common wealth, in which we hope your wisdome will be satisfied, considering that as much by us hath beene brought to light, as by those small meanes, and number of men we had, could any way have bene expected, or hoped for.

The tenth of May we arrived at the Canaries, and the tenth of June in this present yeere, we were fallen with the Islands of the West Indies. . . .

The second of July, we found shoale water, where we smelt so sweet and so strong a smell, as if we had beene in the midst of some delicate garden abounding with all kinde of odoriferous flowers, by which we were assured, that the land could not be farre distant: and keeping good watch, and bearing but slacke saile, the fourth of the same month we arrived upon the coast, which we supposed to be a continent and firme lande, and we sailed along the same a hundred and twentie English miles before we could finde any entrance, or river issuing into the Sea. The first that appeared unto us, we entered, though not without some difficultie, & cast anker about three harquebuz-shot within the havens mouth, on the left hand of the same: and after thankes given to God for our safe arrival thither, we manned our boats, and went to view the land next adjoining, and "to take possession of the same, in the right of the Queenes most excellent Majestie, as rightfull Queene, and Princesse of the same, and after delivered the same over to your use, according to her Majesties grant, and letters patent, under her Highnesse great Seale. Which being performed, according to the ceremonies used in such enterprises, we viewed the land about us, being, whereas we first landed, very sandie and low towards the waters side, but so full of grapes, as the very beating and surge of the Sea overflowed them. . . .

We passed from the Sea side towardes the toppes of those hilles next adjoining, being but of meane heigth, and from thence we behelde the Sea on both sides to the North, and to the South, finding no ende any of both wayes. This lande lay stretching itselfe to the West, which after we found to be but an Island of twentie miles long, and not above sixe miles broade. Under the banke or hill whereon we stoode, we behelde the valleyes replenished with goodly Cedar trees, and having discharged our harquebuz-shot, such a flocke of Cranes (the most part white) arose under us, with such a cry redoubled by many ecchoes, as if an armie of men had shouted all together.

This Island had many goodly woodes full of Deere, Conies, Hares, and Fowle, even in the middest of Summer in incredible abundance. The woodes are not such as you finde in Bohemia, Moscovia, or Hercynia, barren and fruitless, but the highest and reddest Cedars in the world, farre bettering the Cedars of the Azores, of the Indies, or Lybanus, Pines, Cypress, Sassaphras, the Lentisk, or the tree that beareth the Masticke, the tree that beareth the rine of blacke Cinnamon, of which Master Winter brought from the streights of Magellan, and many other of excellent smell and qualitie. We remained by the side of this Island two whole dayes before we saw any people of the Countrey: the third day we espied one small boate rowing towardes us, having in it three persons: this boat came to the Island side, foure harquebuz-shot from our shippes, and there two of the people remaining, the third came along the shoreside towards us, and we being then all within board, he walked up and downe upon the point of the land next unto us: then the Master and the Pilot of the Admirall, Simon Ferdinando, and the Captaine Philip Amadas, myselfe, and others rowed to the land, whose coming this fellow attended, never making any show of feare or doubt. And after he had spoken of many things not understood by us, we brought him with his owne good liking, aboard the ships, and gave him a shirt, a hat, & some other things, and made him taste of our wine, and our meat, which he liked very well: and after having viewed both barks, he departed, and went to his own boate againe, which he had left in a little Cove or Creeke adjoining: as soon as he was two bow shot into the water, he fell to fishing, and in lesse then halfe an houre, he had laden his boate as deepe as it could swimme, with which he came againe to the point of lande, and there he divided his fish into two parts, pointing one part to the ship, and the other to the pinnesse: which after he had (as much as he might) requited the former benefites received, departed out of our sight.

The next day there came unto us diverse boates, and in one of them the Kings brother, accompanied with fortie or fiftie men, very handsome and goodly people, and in their behaviour as mannerly and civill as any in Europe. His name was Granganimeo, and the king is called Wingina, the country Wingandacoa, and now by her Majestie Virginia. . . .

The Kings brother had great liking of our armour, a sword, and divers other things which we had: and offered to lay a great boxe of pearle in gage for them: but we refused it for this time, because we would not make them knowe, that we esteemed thereof, untill we had understoode in what places of the countrey the pearle grew: which now your Worshippe doeth very well understand. . . .

The soile is the most plentifull, sweete, fruitfull and wholesome of all the worlde: there are above fourteene severall sweete smelling timber trees, and the most part of their underwoods are Bayes, and such like: they have those Oakes that we have, but farre greater and better. After they had beene divers times aboard our shippes, myselfe with seven more went twentie mile into the River that runneth towarde the Citie of Skicoak, which River they call Occam: and the evening following, we came to an Island, which they call Roanoak, distant from the harbour by which we entered, seven leagues: and at the North end thereof was a village of nine houses, built of Cedar, and fortified round about with sharpe trees, to keepe out their enemies, and the entrance into it made like a turne pike very artificially: when we came towardes it, standing neare unto the waters side, the wife of Granganimo, the kings brother came running out to meete us very cheerefully and friendly. . . .

After we had thus dried ourselves, she brought us into the inner roome, where she set on the board standing along the house, some wheate like furmentie, sodden Venison and roasted, fish sodden, boyled and roasted, Melons rawe, and sodden, rootes of divers kindes, and divers fruites: their drinke is commonly water, but while the grape lasteth, they drinke wine, and for want of caskes to keepe it, all the yeare after they drink water, but it is sodden with Ginger in it, and blacke Cinnamon, and sometimes Sassaphras, and divers other wholesome, and medicinable herbes and trees. We were entertained with all love and kindnesse, and with as much bountie (after their manner) as they could possibly devise. We found the people most gentle, loving, and faithfull, voide of all guile and treason, and such as live after the manner of the golden age. The people only care howe to defend themselves from the cold in their short winter, and to feed themselves with such meat as the soile affordeth:

their meate is very well sodden and they make broth very sweet and savorie: their vessels are earthen pots, very large, white and sweete, their dishes are wooden platters of sweet timber: within the place where they feede was their lodging, and within that their Idoll, which they worship, of whome they speake incredible things. . . .

Beyond this Island called Roanoak, are maine Islands very plentifull of fruits and other naturall increases, together with many townes, and villages, along the side of the continent, some bounding upon the Islands, and some stretching up further into the land.

When we first had sight of this countrey, some thought the first land we saw to be the continent: but after we entered into the Haven, we saw before us another mighty long Sea: for there lyeth along the coast a tracte of Islands, two hundreth miles in length, adjoining to the Ocean sea, and betweene the Islands, two or three entrances: when you are entered betweene them (these Islands being very narrow for the most part, as in most places sixe miles broad, in some places lesse, in fewe more) then there appeareth another great Sea, containing in breadth in some places, forty, and in some fifty, in some twenty miles over, before you come unto the continent: and in this enclosed Sea there are above an hundreth Islands of divers bignesses, whereof one is sixteene miles long, at which we were, finding it a most pleasant and fertile ground, replenished with goodly Cedars, and divers other sweete woods, full of Currants, of flaxe, and many other notable commodities, which we at that time had no leisure to view. . . .

Thus Sir, we have acquainted you with the particulars of our discovery made this present voyage, as farre forth as the shortnesse of the time we there continued would afford us to take view of: and so contenting our selves with this service at this time, which we hope hereafter to enlarge, as occasion and assistance shall be given, we resolved to leave the country, and to apply our selves to returne for England, which we did accordingly, and arrived safely in the West of England about the middest of September.

And whereas wee have above certified you of the countrey taken in possession by us, to her Majesties use, and so to yours by her Majesties grant, we thought good for the better assurance thereof, to record some of the particular Gentlemen, & men of accompt, who then were present, as witnesses of the same. . . .

We brought home also two of the Savages being lustie men, whose names were Wanchese and Manteo.

1584

Michael Drayton

Ode to the Virginian Voyage

Based on Barlowe's report, with its images of fruitfulness and fragrance and its allusions to a golden age, Drayton's poem represents (with Andrew Marvell's "Bermudas," based on John Smith's *Historie of Virginia,* and with other pastoral poems and plays of the English Renaissance) the close ties between the explorers' perceptions and literary traditions. Drayton's poem appeared in his *Poems Lyrick and Pastoral,* ca. 1605.

You brave heroic minds
Worthy your country's name,
  That honor still pursue,
  Go, and subdue,
Whilst loit'ring hinds
Lurk here at home, with shame.

Britons, you stay too long;
Quickly aboard bestow you,
  And with a merry gale
  Swell your stretched sail,
With vows as strong
As the winds that blow you.

Your course securely steer,
West and by south forth keep,
  Rocks, lee-shores, nor shoals,
  When Æolus scowls,
You need not fear,
So absolute the deep.

And cheerfully at sea,
Success you still entice,
  To get the pearl and gold,
  And ours to hold,
Virginia,
Earth's only paradise,

Where nature hath in store
Fowl, venison, and fish,
  And the fruitful'st soil
  Without your toil
Three harvests more,
All greater than your wish.

And the ambitious vine
Crowns with his purple mass,
  The cedar reaching high
  To kiss the sky,
The cypress, pine,
And useful sassafras.

To whose the golden age
Still nature's laws doth give,
  No other cares that tend,
  But them to defend
From winter's age,
That long there doth not live.

Whenas the luscious smell
Of that delicious land,
  Above the seas that flows,
  The clear wind throws,
Your hearts to swell
Approaching the dear strand,

In kenning of the shore,
Thanks to God first given,
  O you, the happi'st men,
  Be frolic then,
Let cannons roar,
Frighting the wide heaven.

And in regions far
Such heroes bring ye forth
  As those from whom we came,
  And plant our name
Under that star
Not known unto our north.

And as there plenty grows
Of laurel everywhere,
  Apollo's sacred tree,
  You it may see
A poet's brows
To crown, that may sing there.

Thy voyages attend,
Industrious Hakluÿt,
  Whose reading shall enflame
  Men to seek fame,
And much commend
To after times thy wit.

?1605

John Brereton

From Briefe and True Relation

Brereton accompanied Captain Bartholomew Gosnold to Cape Cod (so named by Gosnold) in 1602. His description of the area, addressed to Sir Walter Raleigh, was the earliest English description of what was to become part of the Massachusetts Bay Colony. His discovery of sassafras precipitated a number of subsequent voyages in search of that herbal panacea for "the French pox, . . . the plague and many other maladies."

[The Cape Cod Area]

FROM THIS PLACE we sailed round about this headland, almost all the points of the compasse, the shore very bolde; but as no coast is free from dangers, so I am persuaded, this is as free as any; the land somewhat lowe, full of goodly woods, but in some places plaine: at length we were come amongst many faire Islands, which we had partly discerned at first landing; all lying within a league or two of another, and the outermost not above sixe or seven leagues from the maine: but comming to an anker under one of them [Martha's Vineyard?], which was about three or foure leagues from the maine, captaine Gosnold, myselfe, and some others, went ashore and going round about it, we found it to be foure English miles in compasse, without house or inhabitant, saving a little old house made of boughs, covered with barke, an olde piece of a weire of the Indians, to catch fish, and one or two places where they had made fires. The chieftest trees of this Island are Beeches, and Cedars; the outward parts all overgrowne with lowe bushie trees, three or foure foot in height, which beare some kinde of fruits, as appeared by their blossomes; Strawberries, red and white, as sweet and much bigger than ours in England, Raspberries, Goose-berries, Hurtleberries, and such; an incredible store of Vines, as well in the woodie part of the Island, where they run upon every tree, as on the outward parts, that we could not go for treading upon them: also, many springs of excellent sweet water, and a great standing lake of fresh water, neare the sea side, an English mile in compasse, which is maintained with the springs running exceeding pleasantly through the woodie grounds which are very rockie. Here also in this Island, great store of Deere which we saw, and other beasts, as appeared by their tracks, as also divers fowles, as Cranes, Hernshaws, Bitterns, Geese, Mallards, Teales, and other fowles, in great plenty; also great store of Pease, which grow in certaine plots the Island over. On the North side of this Island we found many huge bones and ribbes of Whales. This Island, as also all the rest of these Islands are full of all sorts of stones fit for building; the sea sides all covered with stones, many of them glistering and shining like minerall stones, and very rockie: also, the rest of these Islands are replenished with these commodities, and upon some of them, inhabitants; as upon an Island to the Northward, and within two leagues of this; yet we found no townes, nor many of their houses, although we saw manie Indians, which are tall big boned men, all naked, saving they cover their privy parts with a blacke tewed skin, much like a Black-smithes apron, tied about their middle and betweene their legs behinde: they gave us of their fish readie boiled (which they carried in a basket made of twiggs, not unlike our osier) whereof we did eat, and judged them to be fresh water fish: they gave us also of their Tabacco, which they drinke greene, but dried into powder, very strong and pleasant, and much better than any I have tasted in England: the necks of their pipes are made of clay hard dried (whereof in that Island is a great store both red and white) the other part, is a piece of hollow copper, very finely closed and cemented together: we gave unto them certaine trifles, as knives, points, and such like, which they much esteemed. From thence we went to another Island [Cuttyhunk], to the Northwest of this, and within a league or two of the maine, which we found to be greater than before we imagined, being 16 English miles at the least in compasse; for it containeth many pieces or necks of land, which differ nothing from severall Islands, saving that certaine banks of small breadth do like bridges joine them to this Island: on the outside of this Island are many plaine places of grasse, abundance of Strawberries and other berries before mentioned: in mid-May we did sowe in this Island (as for triall) in sundry places, Wheat, Barley, Oats, and Pease, which in fourteene dayes were sprung up nine inches and more: The soile is fat and lustie; the upper crust of gray colour; but a foot or lesse in depth, of the colour of our hempelands in England; and being thus apt for these and the like graines; the sowing or setting (after the ground is cleansed) is no greater labour than if you should set or sowe in one of our best prepared gardens in England. This Island is full of high timbered Oaks, their leaves thrive so broad as ours Cedars, strait and tall; Beech, Elme, Hollie, Walnut trees in abundance, the fruit as bigge as ours, as appeared by those we found under the trees, which had lain all the yeare ungathered; Hazelnut trees,

Cherry trees, the leafe, barke and bignesse not differing from ours in England, but the stalke beareth the blossomes or fruit at the end thereof, like a cluster of Grapes, forty or fifty in a bunch; Sassafras trees plentie all the Island over, a tree of high price and profit; also other divers fruit trees, some of them with strange barks, of an Orange colour, in feeling soft and smoothe like Velvet: in the thickest part of the woods, you may see a furlong or more round about. On the Northwest side of this Island, neare to the sea side, is a standing Lake of fresh water, almost three English miles in compasse, in the middest whereof stands a plot of woodie ground, an acre in quantitie or not above: This Lake is full of small Tortoises, and exceedingly frequented with all sorts of fowles before rehearsed which breed, some lowe on the banks, and others on lowe trees about this Lake in great abundance, whose young ones of all sorts we tooke and eat at our pleasure: but all these fowles are much bigger than ours in England. Also, in every Island, and almost in every part of every Island, are great store of Ground nuts, fortie together on a string, some of them as bigge as hennes egges; they grow not two inches under ground: the which nuts we found to be as good as potatoes. Also divers sorts of shell-fish, as Scallops, Muscles, Cockles, Lobsters, Crabs, Oysters, and Whelks, exceeding good and very great. But not to cloy you with particular rehearsal of such things as God and Nature hath bestowed on these places, in comparison whereof the most fertile part of all England is (of itselfe) but barren; we went in our light-horseman from this Island to the maine, right against this Island some two leagues off, where coming ashore, we stood a while like men ravished at the beautye and delicacie of this sweet soile; for besides divers cleere Lakes of fresh water (whereof we saw no end) were Meadowes very large and full of greene grasse; even the most woody places (I speak only of such as I saw) doe growe so distinct and apart, one tree from another, upon greene grassie ground, somewhat higher than the Plaines, as if Nature would show herselfe above her power, artificiall. Hard by, we espied seven Indians, and coming up to them at first they expressed some feare, but being emboldened by our courteous usage, and some trifles which we gave them, they followed us to a necke of land, which we imagined had beene severed from the maine; but finding it otherwise, we perceived a broad harbour or rivers mouth which ranne up into the maine: but because the day was so farre spent, we were forced to returne to the Island from whence we came, leaving the discoverie of this harbour, for a time of better leisure: of the goodness of which harbour, as also of many others thereabouts, there is small doubt, considering that all the Islands, as also the maine (where we were) [Buzzard's Bay] is all rockie ground and broken lands.

1602

The Cultivation of the Promised Land, 1620–1800

Thus hath the Lord been pleased to turn one of the most hideous,
boundless, and unknown Wildernesses in the world . . .
to a well-ordered Commonwealth.

Edward Johnson, *Wonder-Working Providence* (1653)

From the beginning, the relationship between the immigrant farmer and the virgin soil of the New World testifies to the durable adaptability of the ideal design of the garden in the wilderness. On the southern coast, as the accounts of Verrazano and Barlowe in the preceding section suggest, the garden seemed already there—seemed Edenic. On the northern coast and later in the continental interior, however, the garden had to be carved out of the wilderness: first by cutting back deciduous forest, then by penetrating the iron-like topsoil of the prairies, then by irrigating the "deserts" of the far West. For this reason and because, in Massachusetts, the Calvinist Puritans could not countenance the possibility of an earthly Eden for fallen man, the ideal design of the garden became that of the Promised Land.

In Eden, Adam had dominion over all living things, but his dominion was a passive one. He was to share with every other creature the food of "the green plants"—food which he did not have to cultivate himself (Genesis 2:28–30). Adam's was not a mandate for struggle or change but a mandate for the preservation of a self-sustaining ecological order. But the dominion that God promised Abraham and granted to his descendants through Moses was a dominion over a post-Edenic landscape. The Promised Land to which God led Moses and the Chosen People was a desert country transformed into a garden by virtue of the "seasonal rain" which God allowed to fall on it. The terms of God's covenant with His Chosen People were these: they would redeem the spiritual wilderness in themselves by worshipping Him and adhering to His commandments, and they would undertake the task of cultivating Canaan by farming and by raising livestock. If they did these things faithfully, God would bless them and protect their garden on the one hand from wilderness by sending the seasonal rain, and on the other hand from their enemies by giving them the militant strength to defend themselves (Deuteronomy 11).

The Puritans believed themselves to be New Israelites. England had been their

Egypt, and there they had made a new Abrahamic covenant with God; Holland and the Atlantic had in some ways been the desert wilderness through which they had wandered in prayerful waiting; and Massachusetts was their New Canaan, where they must continue the work of the Reformation in redeeming the physical and spiritual wilderness of a fallen world.

The selection from William Bradford, a taciturn man given to understatement and plain style, only hints at the ideal of the garden which he brings with him. Off Cape Cod in its November bleakness (which is also the bleakness of his own momentary doubt) he takes note that there is "no Pisgah" to be seen—no mountain like that from which God gave Moses a lovely panoramic view of the Promised Land he and his people were to take dominion over. Later, ashore, Bradford writes of the thickets and the thorns which "were ready to tear their clothes and armor in pieces,"—ready, that is, to overcome them and turn them wild. Only after finding faint signs of a cultivated landscape—a field, a cache of corn, a spring—is Bradford's Abrahamic vision tenuously confirmed: he and his men return to the ship like "the men from Eshcol," Moses' scouts returning from their first reconnaissance of Canaan.

Thus began the Puritans' convenant to occupy the wilderness of North America; to fight a holy war against all it stood for; to bring pastoral order and, as Cotton Mather wrote, "the cleare sunshine of the Gospell" to its "thick antichristian darkness"; and to receive as their victory-share the fruits of the garden and the grace of the Lord. The passage from Edward Johnson describes one battle—ironically, at Concord, Massachusetts, where Emerson was later to live "emparadised" on his farm—in the American war for dominion over the landscape. One needs only a look at Johnson's verbs to see how fiercely that battle was fought and how close his energies are to those that would create the landscapes of technological ruin.

By the end of the seventeenth century, the battle for Massachusetts Bay Colony had largely been won, and a Puritan named Samuel Sewall could look out over the landscape of Plum Island, off Newbury, to see the Abrahamic covenant confirmed in the contrast between an arrogant ocean-wilderness and a humble, submissive island-garden:

> And as long as Plum Island shall faithfully keep the commanded post, notwithstanding all the hectoring words and hard blows of the proud and boisterous ocean; . . . as long as any cattle shall be fed with the grass growing in the meadows which do humbly bow down themselves before Turkey Hill; as long as any sheep shall walk upon Old Town Hill, and shall from thence pleasantly look down upon the river Parker and the fruitful marshes lying beneath; as long as any free and harmless doves shall find a white oak or other tree within the township to perch or feed or build a careless nest upon, and shall voluntarily present themselves to perform the office of gleaners after barley harvest; as long as nature shall not grow old and dote, but shall constantly remember to give the rows of Indian corn their education by pairs: so long shall Christians be born there, and being first made meet, shall from thence be translated, to be made partakers of the Inheritance of the saints in light.

From the seventeenth into the twentieth century the war against the wilderness, though it became for many people less of a holy war than the Puritans had made it, rolled across America's continental interior. By the late eighteenth century, the garden-landscape which sprang up behind the frontier battle zone, in occupied territory, began to be seen in more secular terms. The ideals of Eden and of the Promised Land persisted (in the selection from John Steinbeck in The Ways West, for example, California is a Promised Land), but they were largely incorporated into a third ideal—the pastoral.

The source of the pastoral ideal was not Biblical but classical. It had originated in the pastoral idylls and eclogues of Theocritus, Bion, Moschus, and especially Vergil, and it had been reinvigorated during the English Renaissance. Shakespeare's *The Tempest,* as Leo Marx observes in *The Machine in the Garden,* was one of the greatest expressions of the pastoral ideal during that time, and it was one of many works in which Renaissance writers played with the possibility of "the unspoiled terrain of the New World as a possible setting for a pastoral utopia." But "a fully articulated pastoral idea of America did not emerge until the end of the eighteenth century." Jefferson's vision of America was basically pastoral; so, too, were the visions of Hector St. Jean de Crèvecoeur, who is represented here.

The pastoral setting is traditionally an oasis-like meadow or pasture. In its American variations it can be an island, a forest clearing, a hut beside Walden, a raft floating down the Mississippi. And its inhabitants, traditionally shepherds, can range from freemen and husbandmen seen at their virtuous labors or in repose to Romantic travelers and poet-dreamers seen at their rapt meditations. As with the garden as Promised Land, the American pastoral garden is usually cultivated by human hands. But as with the Edenic garden, the dominant themes of the pastoral garden are harmony, serenity, and fruitfulness. "In the pastoral economy," writes Marx,

> nature supplies most of the herdman's needs and, even better, nature does virtually all of the work. A similar accommodation with the idealized landscape is the basis for the herdman's less tangible satisfactions: the woods 'echo back' the notes of his pipe. It is as if the consciousness of the musician shared a principle of order with the landscape and, indeed, the external universe. The echo, a recurrent device in pastoral, is another metaphor of reciprocity. It evokes that sense of relatedness between man and not-man which lends a metaphysical aspect to the mode; it is a hint of the quasi-religious experience to be developed in the romantic pastoralism of Wordsworth, Emerson, and Thoreau.

Perhaps the chief difference between the pastoral garden and those of Eden or the Promised Land is that, while the latter two are surrounded by wilderness, the pastoral is a kind of middle country between wilderness on the one hand, and on the other, civilization with all of its mechanistic complexity, corruption, and other distontents. That is the configuration which Crèvecœur's pastoral landscape takes: on the one side a Europe "too thickly planted," a culture in which men "withered, and were mowed down by want, hunger, and war"; on the other side a frontier in which men's "actions are regulated by the wildness of the neighborhood"; and in between them, "a people of cultivation" and a garden landscape with "the embryos of all the arts, sciences, and ingenuity which flourish in Europe."

It is clear from Crèvecœur's essay that the pastoral is not simply a concrete landscape but the embodiment as well of a whole nexus of social, economic, and political dreams. For the ideal of the cultivated garden seemed to define the work of a nation. Not only in the culture of the soil, but also in the culture of the individual and the community, the work was that of clearing away chaos and old entanglements; of converting the waste places, in Crèvecœur's words, "into a pleasing meadow, the rough ridge into a fine field"; of planting and reaping a fruit wholesome to body, mind, and spirit. Even in the cities, traditionally anathema to the pastoral ideal, men like Thomas Paine were preoccupied with nursing the infant Republic through its tender "seed-time," or, like Benjamin Franklin, with "weeding" vices from the "gardens" of their souls. Emerson, who found in the wilderness "something more dear and connate than in streets or villages," nevertheless lived "emparadised" on his Concord farm; and his friend Thoreau, sojourner in the wilderness, nevertheless spent most of his time studying "the smooth but still varied landscape" of Concord and its rural environs.

The special pathos of the ideal of the pastoral garden was that, while it seemed to give shape to a nation, it was nevertheless a nostalgic and unattainable dream. It was, furthermore, a dream which invited its own disintegration. It had little or no influence on human ethics; it created an enormous tolerance for waste of natural resources (wasn't the supply endless?); and while it envisioned an uncrowded place, it drew multitudes of emigrants. In the American archetype of the pastoral, as Leo Marx observes, it is not usually wilderness but civilization which overwhelms the pastoral sanctuary. When the walls of the American dream-garden were breached, what woke us from the lovely sleep was not, as Crèvecœur might have had it, "the yell of the savage, the screech of the owl, or the hissing of the snake," but the yell, the screech, and the hiss of mechanization: the machine in the garden (see The Ways West).

William Bradford

From Of Plymouth Plantation

William Bradford converted to Congregationalism, a radical Puritan sect, at age twelve; with a small group of Puritans from Yorkshire, he endured persecution and self-imposed exile in Holland while still in his teens; and he crossed with them to the New World when he was thirty. He was governor of Plymouth for a total of thirty-three years between 1621 and 1656. The period covered in this excerpt is November 1620–December 1621. He wrote the first ten chapters of his history (including the material reprinted here) in 1630. He did not write the book for publication but for his descendants, as "a perpetual monument to a high enterprise"—the highest point of which was, for him, the first few years at Plymouth. After that period, the history breaks down into a fragmented chronicle dominated by divisiveness and commercialism. The spelling has been somewhat modernized.

AFTER THEY HAD ENJOYED faire winds and weather for a season, they were encountered many times with crosse winds, and mette with many fierce stormes, with which the shipe was shroudly shaken, and her upper works made very leakie; and one of the maine beames in the midd ships was bowed & cracked, which put them in some fear that the shipe could not be able to performe the voyage. . . . In sundrie of these stormes the winds were so fierce, & the seas so high, as they could not beare a knote of saile, but were forced to hull, for diverse days together. . . . But to omite other things, (that I may be briefe,) after longe beating at sea they fell with that land which is called Cape Cod; the which being made & certainly knowne to be it, they were not a litle joyfull. After some deliberation had amongst them selves & with the master of the ship, they tacked aboute and resolved to stande for the southward (the wind & weather being faire) to finde some place aboute Hudsons river for their habitation. But after they had sailed that course about halfe the day, they fell amongst dangerous shoals and roaring breakers, and they were so farr entangled therewith as they conceived themselves in great danger; & the wind shrinking upon them withall, they resolved to bear up againe for the Cape, and thought themselves happy to gett out of those dangers before night overtooke them, as by Gods providence they did. And the next day they gott into the Cape-harbor wher they ridd in safetie. A word or two by the way of this cape; it was thus first named by Capten Gosnold & his company, Anno: 1602, and after by Capten Smith was called Cape James; but it retains the former name amongst seamen. Also that pointe which first showed those dangerous shoals unto them, they called Pointe Care, & Tuckers Terrour; but the French & Dutch to this day call it Malabarr, by reason of those perilous shoals, and the losses they have suffered there.

Being thus arrived in a good harbor and brought safe to land, they fell upon their knees & blessed the God of heaven, who had brought them over the vast & furious ocean, and delivered them from all the periles & miseries thereof, againe to set their feete on the firme and stable earth, their proper elemente. And no marvell if they were thus joyefull, seeing wise Seneca was so affected with sailing a few miles on the coast of his owne Italy; as he affirmed, that he had rather remaine twentie years on his way by land, than pass by sea to any place in a short time; so tedious & dreadfull was the same unto him.

But here I cannot but stay and make a pause, and stand half amazed at this poore peoples presente condition; and so I thinke will the reader too, when he well considers the same. Being thus passed the vast ocean, and a sea of troubles before in their preparation (as may be remembered by that which wente before), they had now no friends to wellcome them, nor inns to entertaine or refresh their weatherbeaten bodys, no houses or much less townes to repaire to, to seeke for succoure. It is recorded in scripture as a mercie to the apostle & his shipwrecked company, that the barbarians showed them no smalle kindness in refreshing them, but these savage barbarians, when they mette with them (as after will appeare) were readier to fill their sides full of arrows than otherwise. And for the season it was winter, and they that know the winters of that countrie know them to be sharp & violent, & subjecte to cruell & fierce stormes, dangerous to travell to known places, much more to search an unknown coast. Besides, what could they see but a hideous & desolate wilderness, full of wild beasts & wild men? and what multitudes there might be of them they knew not. Neither could they, as it were, goe up to the top of Pisgah, to view from this wilderness a more goodly countrie to feed their hopes; for which way soever they turned their eyes (save upward to the heavens) they could have little solace or content in respecte of any outward objects. For summer being done, all things stand upon them with a weatherbeaten face; and the whole countrie, full of woods & thickets, represented a wild & savage hew. If they looked behind them, there was the mighty ocean which they had passed, and was now as a maine barr & gulfe to seperate them from all the civill parts of the world. If it be said they had a ship to succour them, it is true; but what heard they daily from the master & company? but that with speede they should looke out a place with their shallop, where they would be at some near distance; for the season was such as he would not stirr from thence till a safe harbor was discovered by them where they would be, and he might goe without danger; and that victalls consumed apace, but he must & would keepe sufficient for them selves & their returne. Yea, it was muttered by some, that if they gott not a place in time, they would turne them & their goods ashore & leave them. Let it also be considered what weake hopes of supply & succoure they left behind them, that might bear up their minds in this sad condition and trialls they were under; and they could not but be very smalle. It is true, indeed, the affections & love of their brethren at Leyden was cordiall & entire towards them, but they had litle power to help them, or them selves; and how the case stoode betweene them & the merchants at their coming away, hath allready been declared. What could now sustaine them but the spirit of God & his grace? May not & ought not the children of these fathers, rightly say: *Our fathers were Englishmen which came over this great ocean, and were ready to perish in this wilderness*. . . .

Being thus arrived at Cap Cod the 11. of November, and necessitie calling them to looke out a place for habitation, (as well as the masters & mariners importunitie,) they having brought a large shallop with them out of England, stowed in quarters in the ship, they now gott her out & sett their carpenters to worke to trim her up; but being much bruised & shattered in the shipe with foule weather, they saw she would be longe in mending. Wherupon a few of them tendered themselves to goe by land and discovere those nearest places, whilst the shallop was in mending; and the rather because as they wente into that harbor there seemed to be an opening some 2. or 3 leagues off, which the master judged to be a river. It was conceived there might be some danger in the attempte, yet seeing them resolute, they were permited to goe, being 16. of them well armed, under the conduct of Captain Standish, having such instructions given them as was thought meete. They sett forth the 15. of November and when they had marched aboute the space of a mile by the sea side, they espied 5. or 6. persons with a dogg coming towards them, who were savages; but they fled from them, & ran up into the woods, and the English followed them, partly to see if they could speake with them, and partly to discover if there might not be more of them lying in ambush. But the Indians seeing themselves thus followed, they againe forsooke the woods, & rane away on the sands as hard as they could, so as they could not come near them, but followed them by the tracte of their feet sundrie miles, and saw that they had come the same way. So, night coming on, they made their rendevous & set out their sentinels, and rested in quiete *that night,* and the next morning followed their tracte till they had headed a great creeke, & so left the sands, & turned another way into the woods. But they still followed them by guess, hopeing to find their dwellings; but they soone lost them & themselves, falling into such thickets as were ready to tear their cloaths & armore in pieces, but were most distresed for want of drinke. But at length they found water & refreshed themselves, being the first New-England water they drunke of, and was now in their great thirste as pleasante unto them as wine or beer had been in foretimes. Afterwards they directed their course to come to the other shore, for they knew it was a necke of land they were to crosse over, and so at length gott to the sea-side, and marched to this supposed river, & by the way found a pond of clear fresh water, and shortly after a good quantitie of clear ground where the Indians had formerly set corne, and some of their graves. And proceeding further they saw new-stubble where corne had been set the same year, also they found where lately a house had been, where some planks and a great kettle was remaining, and heaps of sand newly paddled with their hands, which they, digging up, found in them diverse faire Indian baskets filled with corne, and some in eares, faire and good, of diverse colours, which seemed to them a very goodly sight, (having never seen any such before). This was near the place of that supposed river they came to seek; unto which they wente and found it to open itselfe into 2. armes with a high cliffe of sand in the enterance, but more like to be creekes of salte water than any fresh, for ought they saw; and that there was good harborage for their shallope; leaving it further to be discovered by their shallop when she was ready. So their time limited them being expired, they returned to the ship, lest they should be in fear of their safetie; and tooke with them parte of the corne, and buried up the rest, and so like the men from Eshcoll carried with them of the fruits of the land, & showed their brethren; of which, & their returne, they were marvelously glad, and their hearts encouraged. . . .

In November, about that time twelfe month that themselves came, there came in a small ship to them unexpected or looked for, in which came Mr. Cushman . . . and with him 35. persons to remaine & live in the plantation; which did not a litle rejoice them. And they when they came ashore and found all well, and saw plenty of victals in every house, were no less glade. For most of them were lusty younge men, and many of them wild enough, who little considered whither or aboute what they wente, till they came into the harbore at Cap Cod, and there saw nothing but a naked and barren place. They then begane to thinke what should become of them, if the people here were dead or cut off by the Indians. They begane to consulte (upon some speeches that some of the seamen had cast out) to take the sails from the yard lest the ship should gett away and leave them there. But the master hearing of it, gave them good words, and told them if anything but well should have befallen the people here, he hoped he had victalls enough to carry them to Virginia, and whilst he had a bitt they should have their parte; which gave them good satisfaction. So they were all landed; but there was not so much as bisket-cake or any other victalls for them, neither had they any bedding, but some sorry things they had in their cabins, not pot, nor pan, to dresse any meate in; nor over-many cloaths, for many of them had brusht away their coats & cloaks at Plimoth as they came. But there was sent over some burching-lane suits in the ship, out of which they were supplied. The plantation was glad of this addition of strength, but could have wished that many of them had been of better condition, and all of them better furnished with provisions; but that could not now be helpte. . . .

Soone after this ships departure, the great people of the Narragansetts, in a braving manner, sente a messenger unto them with a bundle of arrows tied aboute with a great snake-skine; which their interpretours told them was a threatening & a challenge. Upon which the Governor, with the advice of others, sente them a round answere, that if they had rather have warre than peace, they might begine when they would; they had done them no wrong, neither did they fear them, or should they find them unprovided. And by another messenger sente the snake-skine back with bullets in it; but they would not receive it, but sent it back againe. But these things I doe but mention, because they are more at large allready put forth in printe, by Mr. Winslow, at the requeste of some friends. And it is likely the reason was their owne ambition, who, (since the death of so many of the Indians,) thought to domineer & lord it over the rest, & conceived the English would be a barr in their way, and saw that Massasoit took shelter allready under their wings.

But this made them the more carefully to looke to themselves, so as they agreed to enclose their dwellings with a good strong pale, and make flankers in convenient places, with gates to shut, which were every night locked, and a watch kept, and when neede required there was also warding in the day time. And the company was by the Captaine and the Governor advice, divided into 4. squadrons, and every one had ther quarter apointed them, unto which they were to repaire upon any suddene alarme. And if there should be any crie of fire, a company were appointed for a guard, with muskets, whilst others quenchet the same, to prevent Indian treachery. This was accomplished very cheerfully, and the towne impailed round by the beginning of March, in which every family had a pretty garden plote secured. And herewith I shall end this year.

1620

Edward Johnson

From Wonder-Working Providence of Sion's Saviour in New England (1653)

Johnson sailed with John Winthrop in 1630 to help plant the Massachusetts Bay Colony. He returned to England in 1631 but came back to the New World again in 1636 to participate in the "wilderness work" of settling the town of Woburn. He served as captain of Woburn's militia company. His book, a history of New England settlement to 1651, was written at various periods of time from 1650 to 1651. The settlement described in the excerpt is that of Concord, Massachusetts. The spelling has been somewhat modernized.

Of the laborious worke Christ's people have in planting this wildernesse, set forth in the building the Towne of Concord, being the first in-lande Towne.

NOW because it is one of the admirable acts of Christ['s] Providence in leading his people forth into these Westerne Fields, in his providing of Huts for them, to defend them from the bitter stormes this place is subject unto, therefore here is a short Epitome of the manner how they placed downe their dwellings in this

Desart Wildernesse, the Lord being pleased to hide from the Eyes of his people the difficulties they are to encounter withall in a new Plantation, that they might not thereby be hindered from taking the worke in hand; upon some inquiry of the Indians, who lived to the North-west of the Bay, one Captaine Simon Willard being acquainted with them, by reason of his Trade, became a chiefe instrument in erecting this Town, the land they purchase of the Indians, and with much difficulties traveling through watery swamps, they discover the fitnesse of the place, sometimes passing through the Thickets, where their hands are forced to make way for their bodies passage, and their feete clambering over the crossed Trees, which when they missed they sunke unto an uncertaine bottome in water, and wade up to the knees, tumbling sometimes higher and sometimes lower, wearied with this toile, they at end of this meete with a scorching plaine, yet not so plaine, but that the ragged Bushes scratch their legs foully, even to wearing their stockings to their bare skin in two or three houres; if they be not otherwise well-defended with Bootes or Buskings, their flesh will be torne: (that some being forced to passe on without further provision) have had the blood trickle downe at every step, and in the time of Summer, the Sun casts such a reflecting heate from the sweet Ferne, whose scent is very strong so that some herewith have been very neare fainting, although they have very able bodies to undergoe much travell, and this not to be endured for one day, but for many, and verily did not the Lord encourage their naturall parts (with hopes of a new and strange discovery, expecting every houre to see some rare sight never seene before) they were never able to hold out, and breake through: but above all, the thirsting desires these servants of Christ have had to Plant his Churches, among whom the forenamed Mr. Jones shall not be forgotten.

In Desart's depth where Wolves and Beares abide,
There Jones sits down a wary watch to keepe,
O're Christs deare flock, who now are wandered wide;
But not from him, whose eyes ne're close with sleepe.
Surely it suites thy melancholy minde,
Thus solitary for to spend thy dayes,
Much more thy soule in Christ content doth finde,
To worke for him, who thee to joy will raise.
Leading thy son to Land yet more remote,
To feede his flock upon this Westerne waste:
Exhort him then Christs Kingdome to promote;
That he with thee of lasting joyes may taste.

Yet farther to tell of the hard labours this people found in Planting this Wildernesse, after some dayes spent in search, toiling in the daytime as formerly is said; like true Jacobites they rest them on the Rocks where the night takes them, their short repast is some small pittance of Bread, if it hold out, but as for Drinke, they have plenty, the Countrey being well watered in all places that yet are found out. Their farther hardship is to travell, sometimes they know not whither, bewildered indeed without sight of Sun, their compasse miscarrying in crouding through the Bushes, they sadly search up and down for a known way, the Indian paths being not above one foot broad, so that a man may travell many dayes and never find one. But to be sure the directing Providence of Christ hath beene better unto them than many paths, as might here be inserted, did not haste call my Pen away to more weighty matters; yet by the way a touch thus, it befell with a servant maide, who was travelling about three or foure miles from one Towne to another, losing her selfe in the Woods, had a very diligent search made after her for the space of three dayes, and could not possibly be found, then being given over as quite lost, after three dayes and nights, the Lord was pleased to bring her feeble body to her own home in safety, to the great admiration of all that heard of it. This intricate worke no whit daunted these resolved servants of Christ to goe on with the worke in hand, but lying in the open aire, while the watery clouds poure down all the night season, and sometimes the driving Snow dissolving on their backs, they keep their wet cloathes warme with a continued fire, till the renewed morning give fresh opportunity of further travell; after they have thus found out a place of abode, they burrow themselves in the Earth for their first shelter under some Hill-side, casting the Earth aloft upon Timber; they make a smoaky fire against the Earth at the highest side, and thus these poore servants of Christ provide shelter for themselves, their Wives and little ones, keeping off the short showers from their Lodgings, but the long raines penetrate through to their great disturbance in the night season: yet in these poore Wigwames they sing Psalms, pray and praise their God, till they can provide them houses, which ordinarily was not wont to be with many till the Earth, by the Lords blessing, brought forth Bread to feed them, their Wives and little ones, which with sore labours they attaine every one that can lift a hoe to strike it into the Earth, standing stoutly to their labours, and teare up the Rootes and Bushes, which the first yeare beares them a very thin crop, till the sward of the Earth be rotten, and therefore they have been forced to cut their bread very thin for a long season. But the Lord is pleased to provide for them great store of Fish in the spring time, and especially Alewives about the bignesse of a Herring; many thousands of these, they used to put under their Indian Corne, which they plant in Hills five foot asunder, and assuredly when the Lord created this Corne, he had a speciall eye to supply these peoples wants with it, for ordinarily five or six graines doth produce six hundred.

As for flesh they looked not for any in those times (although now they have plenty) unlesse they could barter with the Indians for Venison or Raccoons, whose flesh is not much inferior unto Lambe, the toile of a new Plantation being like the labours of Hercules never at an end, yet are none so barbarously bent (under the Mattacusets especially) but with a new Plantation they ordinarily gather into Church fellowship, so that Pastors and people suffer the inconveniences together, which is a great meanes to season the sore labours they undergoe, and verily the edge of their appetite was greater to spiritual duties at their first coming in time of wants, than afterward: many in new Plantations have been forced to go barefoot, and bareleg, till these latter dayes, and some in time of Frost and Snow: Yet were they then very healthy more than now they are: in this Wildernesse-worke men of Estates speed no better than others, and some much worse for want of being inured to such hard labour, having laid out their estate upon cattell at five and twenty pound a Cow, when they came to winter them with inland Hay, and feed upon such wild Fother as was never cut before, they could not hold out the Winter, but ordinarily the first or second yeare after their coming up to a new Plantation, many of their cattell died, especially if they wanted Saltmarshes: and also those, who supposed they should feed upon Swines flesh were cut short, the Wolves commonly feeding themselves before them, who never leave neither flesh nor bones, if they be not scared away before they have made an end of their meale. As for those who laid out their Estate upon Sheepe, they speed worst of any at the beginning (although some have sped the best of any now) for untill the Land be often fed with other Cattell Sheepe cannot live; And therefore they never thrived until these latter dayes: Horse had then no better successe, which made many an honest Gentleman travell a foot for a long time, and some have even perished with extreame heate in their travells: as also the want of English graine, Wheate, Barley and Rye proved a sore affliction to some stomacks, who could not live upon Indian Bread and water, yet were they compelled to it till Cattell increased, and the Plowes could but goe: instead of Apples and Peares, they had Pomkins and Squashes of divers kinds. Their lonesome condition was very grievous to some, which was much aggravated by continuall feare of the Indians approach, whose cruelties were much spoken of, and more especially during the time of the Pequot wars.

Thus this poore people populate this howling Desart, marching manfully on (the Lord assisting) through the greatest difficulties, and forest labours that ever any with such weak means have done.

1653

Robert Beverley

From The History and Present State of Virginia

Beverley owned a plantation of 6,000 acres, Beverley Park, in King and Queen County, Virginia. Like Jefferson and other eighteenth-century men of leisure, he devoted his time to the study of books and of nature and to schemes for agricultural improvement (one he proposed was a wine industry). In his description of the present state of Virginia, written nearly a century after the earliest Virginia settlers landed at Jamestown, he criticizes his countrymen for misusing their wild garden either by not making a more cultivated garden out of it or by draining the soil with a one-crop economy in the land they do cultivate. "Thus," he writes, "they depend altogether upon the liberality of nature without endeavoring to improve its gifts by art and industry." He seems to waver between the ideal designs of Eden and of the Promised Land.

Of the Wild Fruits of the Country

OF FRUITS natural to the Country there is great Abundance, but the several Species of them, are produced according to the Difference of the Soil, and the various Situation of the Country: It being impossible that one Piece of Ground, should produce so many different Kinds intermix'd. Of the better Sorts of the wild Fruits, that I have met with, I will barely give you the Names, not designing a Natural History. And when I have done that, possibly I may not mention one half of what the Country affords, because I never went out of my Way, to enquire after any Thing of this Nature.

Of stoned Fruits, I have met with Three good Sorts, *viz.* Cherries, Plums, and Persimmons.

1. Of Cherries natural to the Country, and growing wild in the Woods, I have seen Three Sorts. Two of these grow upon Trees, as big as the common *English* white Oak, whereof one grows in Bunches like Grapes. Both these Sorts are black without, and but one of them red within; that which is red within, is more palatable than the *English* black Cherry, as being without its bitterness. The Other, which hangs on the Branch like Grapes, is Water-colour'd within, of a faintish Sweet, and greedily devour'd by the small Birds. The Third sort is call'd the *Indian* Cherry, and grows higher up in the Country, than the Others do. It is commonly found by the Sides of Rivers, and Branches, on small slender Trees, scarce able to support themselves, about the Bigness of the Peach-Trees in *England*. This is certainly the most delicious Cherry in the World; it is of a dark Purple when ripe, and grows upon a single Stalk, like the *English* Cherry, but is very small; though, I suppose, it may be made larger by Cultivation, if any Body wou'd mind it. These too are so greedily devour'd by the small Birds, that they won't let them remain on the Tree, long enough to

ripen; by which Means, they are rarely known to any, and much more rarely tasted; though perhaps at the same time, they grow just by the Houses.

2. The Plums which I have observ'd to grow wild there, are of Two sorts, the Black, and the Murrey Plum, both which are small, and have much the same Relish with the Damasine.

3. The Persimmon is by *Hariot* call'd the *Indian* Plum; and so *Smith, Purchase,* and *Du Lake* [De Laet], call it after him; but I can't perceive that any of those Authors, had ever heard of the Sorts I have just now mention'd, they growing high up in the Country. These Persimmons amongst them retain their *Indian* Name. They are of several Sizes, between the Bigness of a Damasine and a Burgamot Pear. The Taste of them is so very rough, it is not to be endured, till they are fully ripe, and then they are a pleasant Fruit. Of these some *Vertuosi* make an agreeable kind of Beer; to which Purpose they dry them in Cakes, and lay them up for Use. These, like most other Fruits there, grow as thick upon the Trees, as Ropes of Onions; the Branches very often break down by the mighty Weight of the Fruit. . . .

The Honey and Sugar-Trees are likewise spontaneous, near the Heads of the Rivers. The Honey-Tree bears a thick swelling Pod, full of Honey, appearing at a Distance like the bending Pod of a Bean or Pea. The Sugar-Tree yields a kind of Sap or Juice, which by boiling is made into Sugar. This Juice is drawn out, by wounding the Trunk of the Tree, and placing a Receiver under the Wound. The *Indians* make One Pound of Sugar, out of Eight Pounds of the Liquor. Some of this Sugar I examined very carefully. It was bright and moist, with a large full Grain; the Sweetness of it being like that of good Muscovada.

Though this Discovery has not been made by the *English* above Twelve or Fourteen Years; yet it has been known among the *Indians,* longer than any now living can remember. It was found out by the *English* after this manner. The Soldiers which were kept on the Land Frontiers, to clear them of the *Indians,* taking their Range through a Piece of low Ground, about Forty Miles above the inhabited Parts of *Patowmeck* River, and resting themselves in the Woods of those low Grounds, observ'd an inspissate Juice, like Molasses, distilling from the Tree. The Heat of the Sun had candied some of this Juice, which gave the Men a Curiosity to taste it. They found it sweet, and by this Process of Nature, learn'd to improve it into Sugar. But these Trees growing so far above the Christian Inhabitants, it hath not yet been tried, whether for Quantity, or Quality it may be worth while to cultivate this Discovery. . . .

All over the Country, is interspers'd here and there, a surprizing Variety of curious Plants and Flowers. . . .

There's the Rattle-Snake-Root, to which no Remedy was ever yet found comparable; for it effectually cures the Bite of a Rattle-Snake, which sometimes has been mortal in Two Minutes. If this Medicine be early applied, it presently removes the Infection, and in Two or Three Hours, restores the Patient to as perfect Health, as if he had never been hurt. This operates by violent Vomit; and Sweat.

The *James-Town* Weed (which resembles the Thorny Apple of *Peru,* and I take to be the Plant so call'd) is supposed to be one of the greatest Coolers in the World. This being an early Plant, was gather'd very young for a boil'd Salad, by some of the Soldiers sent thither, to pacifie the Troubles of *Bacon;* and some of them eat plentifully of it, the Effect of which was a very pleasant Comedy; for they turn'd natural Fools upon it for several Days: One would blow up a Feather in the Air; another wou'd dart Straws at it with much Fury; and another stark naked was sitting up in a Corner, like a Monkey, grinning and making Mows at them; a Fourth would fondly kiss, and paw his Companions, and snear in their Faces, with a Countenance more antick, than any in a *Dutch* Droll. In this frantick Condition they were confined, lest they should in their Folly destroy themselves; though it was observed, that all their Actions were full of Innocence and good Nature. Indeed, they were not very cleanly; for they would have wallow'd in their own Excrements, if they had not been prevented. A Thousand such simple Tricks they play'd, and after Eleven Days, return'd to themselves again, not remembring any thing that had pass'd.

Of spontaneous Flowers they have an unknown Variety: The finest Crown Imperial in the World; the Cardinal-Flower, so much extoll'd for its Scarlet Colour, is almost in every Branch; the Moccasin Flower, and a Thousand others, not yet known, to *English* Herbalists. Almost all the Year round, the Levels and Vales are beautified with Flowers of one Kind or other, which make their Woods as fragrant as a Garden. From these Materials their wild Bees make vast Quantities of Honey, but their Magazines are very often rifled, by Bears, Raccoons, and such like liquorish Vermine.

About Two Years ago, walking out to take the Air, I found, a little without my Pasture Fence, a Flower as big as a Tulip, and upon a Stalk resembling the Stalk of a Tulip. The Flower was of a Flesh Colour, having a Down upon one End, while the other was plain. The Form of it resembled the *Pudenda* of a Man and Woman lovingly join'd in one. Not long after I had discover'd this Rarity, and while it was still in Bloom, I drew a grave Gentleman, about an Hundred Yards, out of his Way, to see this Curiosity, not telling him any thing more, than that it was a Rarity, and such, perhaps, as he had never seen, nor heard of. When we arrived at the Place, I gather'd one of them, and put it into his Hand, which he had no sooner cast his Eye upon, but he threw it away with Indignation, as being asham'd of this Waggery of Nature. It was impossible to perswade him to touch it again, or so much as to squint towards so immodest a Representation. Neither would I presume to mention such an Indecency, but that I thought it unpardonable, to omit a Production so extraordinary. . . .

Of the Temperature of the Climate, and the Inconveniencies attending it.

THE NATURAL TEMPERATURE of the Inha[bit]ed part of the Country, is hot and moist: tho' this Moisture I take to be occasion'd by the abundance of low Grounds, Marshes, Creeks, and Rivers, which are every where among their lower Settlements; but more backward in the Woods, where they are now Seating, and making new Plantations, they have abundance of high and dry Land, where there are only Crystal Streams of Water, which flow gently from their Springs, and divide themselves into innumerable Branches, to moisten and enrich the adjacent Lands.

The Country is in a very happy Situation, between the extreams of Heat and Cold, but inclining rather to the first. Certainly it must be a happy Climate, since it is very near of the same Latitude with the Land of Promise. Besides, As *Judœa* was full of Rivers, and Branches of Rivers; So is *Virginia:* As that was seated upon a great Bay and Sea, wherein were all the conveniences for Shipping and Trade; So is *Virginia.* Had that fertility of Soil? So has *Virginia,* equal to any Land in the known World. In fine, if any one impartially considers all the Advantages of this Country, as Nature made it; he must allow it to be as fine a Place, as any in the Universe; but I confess I am asham'd to say any thing of its Improvements, because I must at the same time reproach my Country-Men wth a Laziness that is unpardonable. If there be any excuse for them in this Matter, 'tis the exceeding plenty of good things, with which Nature has blest them; for where God Almighty is so Merciful as to work for People, they never work for themselves.

All the Countries in the World, seated in or near the Latitude of *Virginia,* are esteem'd the Fruitfullest, and Pleasantest of all Clymates. As for Example, *Canaan, Syria, Persia,* great part of *India, China* and *Japan,* the *Morea, Spain, Portugal,* and the Coast of *Barbary,* none of which differ many Degrees of Latitude from *Virginia.* These are reckon'd the Gardens of the World, while *Virginia* is unjustly neglected by its own Inhabitants, and abus'd by other People.

That which makes this Country most unfortunate, is, that it must submit to receive its Character from the Mouths not only of unfit, but very unequal Judges; For, all its Reproaches happen after this manner.

Many of the Merchants and others that go thither from *England,* make no distinction between a cold, and a hot Country: but wisely go sweltering about in their thick Cloaths all the Summer, because they used to do so in their *Northern* Climate; and then unfairly complain of the heat of the Country. They greedily Surfeit with their delicious Fruits, and are guilty of great Intemperance, through the exceeding Generosity of the Inhabitants; by which means they fall Sick, and then unjustly complain of the unhealthiness of the Country. In the next place, the Sailers for want of Towns there, are put to the hardship of rowling most of the Tobacco, a Mile or more, to the Water-side; this Splinters their Hands sometimes, and provokes 'em to curse the Country. Such Exercise, and a bright Sun, makes them hot, and then they imprudently fall to drinking cold Water, or perhaps New Cyder, which in its Season, they find at every Planter's House; Or else they greedily devour all the green Fruit, and unripe Trash they can meet with, and so fall into Fluxes, Fevers, and the Belly-Ach; and then, to spare their own Indiscretion, they in their Tarpawlin Language, cry, God D—— the Country. This is the true State of the case, as to the Complaints of its being Sickly; For, by the most impartial Observation I can make, if People will be perswaded to be Temperate, and take due care of themselves, I believe it is as healthy a Country, as any under Heaven: but the extraordinary pleasantness of the Weather, and the goodness of the Fruit, lead People into many Temptations. The clearness and brightness of the Sky, add new vigour to their Spirits, and perfectly remove all Splenetick and sullen Thoughts. Here they enjoy all the benefits of a warm Sun, and by their shady Groves, are protected from its Inconvenience. Here all their Senses are entertain'd with an endless Succession of Native Pleasures. Their Eyes are ravished with the Beauties of naked Nature. Their Ears are Serenaded with the perpetual murmur of Brooks, and the thorow-base which the Wind plays, when it wantons through the Trees; the merry Birds too, join their pleasing Notes to this rural Consort, especially the Mock-birds, who love Society so well, that whenever they see Mankind, they will perch upon a Twigg very near them, and sing the sweetest wild Airs in the World: But what is most remarkable in these Melodious Animals, they will frequently fly at small distances before a Traveller, warbling out their Notes several Miles on end, and by their Musick, make a Man forget the Fatigues of his Journey. Their Taste is regaled with the most delicious Fruits, which without Art, they have in great Variety and Perfection. And then their smell is refreshed with an eternal fragrancy of Flowers and Sweets, with which Nature perfumes and adorns the Woods almost the whole year round.

Have you pleasure in a Garden? All things thrive in it, most surpriseingly; you can't walk by a Bed of Flowers, but besides the entertainment of their Beauty, your Eyes will be saluted with the charming colours of the Humming Bird, which revels among the Flowers, and licks off the Dew and Honey from their tender Leaves, on which it only feeds. It's size is not half so large as an *English* Wren, and its colour is a glorious shining mixture of Scarlet, Green, and Gold. Colonel *Byrd,* in his Garden, which is the finest in that Country, has a Summer-House set round with the *Indian* Honey-Suckle, which all the Summer is continually full of sweet Flowers, in which these Birds delight exceedingly. Upon these Flowers, I have seen ten or a dozen of these Beautiful

Creatures together, which sported about me so familiarly, that with their little Wings they often fann'd my Face.

1705

Hector St. Jean de Crèvecœur

From Letters from An American Farmer

As an officer with the French army of Montcalm in Canada during the French and Indian War (1754–1763), Crèvecœur mapped and surveyed areas around the Great Lakes and in Ohio and later participated in the siege of Fort William Henry (see Cooper's panorama in Landscape into Art). After the French defeat, he traveled New York, Pennsylvania, and the southern colonies and by 1765 settled down as a farmer at Pine Hill in Orange County, New York. A loyalist to the British crown, he had to leave the new United States during the Revolution but later returned as French consul (1783–1790). He shared with his friend John Bartram (William's father) a deep curiosity about natural history, and with Thomas Jefferson a physiocratic belief in the cultivated landscape as the basis both of wealth and of manners and morals.

Letters from An American Farmer was first published in London. The correspondent of Crèvecœur's letters was represented as a "Mr. F. B." of London; his own name, as author, is Anglicized to J. (for James) Hector St. John.

From What is an American

I WISH I could be acquainted with the feelings and thoughts which must agitate the heart and present themselves to the mind of an enlightened Englishman, when he first lands on this continent. He must greatly rejoice that he lived at a time to see this fair country discovered and settled; he must necessarily feel a share of national pride, when he views the chain of settlements which embellishes these extended shores. When he says to himself, this is the work of my countrymen, who, when convulsed by factions, afflicted by a variety of miseries and wants, restless and impatient, took refuge here. They brought along with them their national genius, to which they principally owe what liberty they enjoy, and what substance they possess. Here he sees the industry of his native country displayed in a new manner, and traces in their works the embryos of all the arts, sciences, and ingenuity which flourish in Europe. Here he beholds fair cities, substantial villages, extensive fields, an immense country filled with decent houses, good roads, orchards, meadows, and bridges, where an hundred years ago all was wild, woody, and uncultivated! What a train of pleasing ideas this fair spectacle must suggest; it is a prospect which must inspire a good citizen with the most heartfelt pleasure. The difficulty consists in the manner of viewing so extensive a scene. He is arrived on a new continent; a modern society offers itself to his contemplation, different from what he had hitherto seen. It is not composed, as in Europe, of great lords who possess everything, and of a herd of people who have nothing. Here are no aristocratical families, no courts, no kings, no bishops, no ecclesiastical dominion, no invisible power giving to a few a very visible one; no great manufacturers employing thousands, no great refinements of luxury. The rich and the poor are not so far removed from each other as they are in Europe. Some few towns excepted, we are all tillers of the earth, from Nova Scotia to West Florida. We are a people of cultivators, scattered over an immense territory, communicating with each other by means of good roads and navigable rivers, united by the silken bands of mild government, all respecting the laws, without dreading their power, because they are equitable. We are all animated with the spirit of an industry which is unfettered and unrestrained, because each person works for himself. If he travels through our rural districts he views not the hostile castle, and the haughty mansion, contrasted with the clay-built hut and miserable cabin, where cattle and men help to keep each other warm, and dwell in meanness, smoke, and indigence. A pleasing uniformity of decent competence appears throughout our habitations. The meanest of our log-houses is a dry and comfortable habitation. Lawyer or merchant are the fairest titles our towns afford; that of a farmer is the only appellation of the rural inhabitants of our country. It must take some time ere he can reconcile himself to our dictionary, which is but short in words of dignity, and names of honour. There, on a Sunday, he sees a congregation of respectable farmers and their wives, all clad in neat homespun, well mounted, or riding in their own humble waggons. There is not among them an esquire, saving the unlettered magistrate. There he sees a parson as simple as his flock, a farmer who does not riot on the labour of others. We have no princes, for whom we toil, starve, and bleed: we are the most perfect society now existing in the world. Here man is free as he ought to be; nor is this pleasing equality so transitory as many others are. Many ages will not see the shores of our great lakes replenished with inland nations, nor the unknown bounds of North America entirely peopled. Who can tell how far it extends? Who can tell the millions of men whom it will feed and contain? for no European foot has as yet travelled half the extent of this mighty continent!

The next wish of this traveller will be to know whence came all these people? they are a mixture of English, Scotch, Irish, French, Dutch, Germans, and Swedes. From this promiscuous breed, that race now called Americans have arisen. The eastern provinces must indeed be excepted, as being the unmixed descendants of Englishmen. I have heard many wish that they had been more intermixed also: for my part I am no wisher, and think it much better as it has happened. They exhibit a most conspicuous figure in this great and variegated picture; they too enter for a great share in the pleasing perspective displayed in these thirteen provinces. I know it is fashionable to reflect on them, but I respect them for what they have done; for the accuracy and wisdom with which they have settled their territory; for the decency of their manners; for their early love of letters; their ancient college, the first in this hemisphere; for their industry; which to me who am but a farmer, is the criterion of everything. There never was a people, situated as they are, who with so ungrateful a soil have done more in so short a time. Do you think that the monarchical ingredients which are more prevalent in other governments, have purged them from all foul stains? Their histories assert the contrary.

In this great American asylum, the poor of Europe have by some means met together, and in consequence of various causes; to what purpose should they ask one another what countrymen they are? Alas, two thirds of them had no country. Can a wretch who wanders about, who works and starves, whose life is a continual scene of sore affliction or pinching penury; can that man call England or any other kingdom his country? A country that had no bread for him, whose fields procured him no harvest, who met with nothing but the frowns of the rich, the severity of the laws, with jails and punishments; who owned not a single foot of the extensive surface of this planet? No! urged by a variety of motives, here they came. Every thing has tended to regenerate them; new laws, a new mode of living, a new social system; here they are become men: in Europe they were as so many useless plants, wanting vegetative mould, and refreshing showers; they withered, and were mowed down by want, hunger, and war; but now by the power of transplantation, like all other plants they have taken root and flourished! Formerly they were not numbered in any civil lists of their country, except in those of the poor; here they rank as citizens. By what invisible power has this surprising metamorphosis been performed? By that of the laws and that of their industry. The laws, the indulgent laws, protect them as they arrive, stamping on them the symbol of adoption; they receive ample rewards for their labours; these accumulated rewards procure them lands; those lands confer on them the title of freemen, and to that title every benefit is affixed with men can possibly require. This is the great operation daily performed by our laws. . . .

What attachment can a poor European emigrant have for a country where he had nothing? The knowledge of the language, the love of a few kindred as poor as himself, were the only cords that tied him: his country is now that which gives him land, bread, protection, and consequence: *Ubi panis ibi patria,* is the motto of all emigrants. What then is the American, this new man? He is either an European, or the descendant of an European, hence that strange mixture of blood, which you will find in no other country. I could point out to you a family whose grandfather was an Englishman, whose wife was Dutch, whose son married a French woman, and whose present four sons have now four wives of different nations. *He* is an American, who, leaving behind him all his ancient prejudices and manners, receives new ones from the new mode of life he has embraced, the new government he obeys, and the new rank he holds. He becomes an American by being received in the broad lap of our great *Alma Mater*. Here individuals of all nations are melted into a new race of men, whose labours and posterity will one day cause great changes in the world. Americans are the western pilgrims, who are carrying along with them that great mass of arts, sciences, vigour, and industry which began long since in the east; they will finish the great circle. The Americans were once scattered all over Europe; here they are incorporated into one of the finest systems of population which has ever appeared, and which will hereafter become distinct by the power of the different climates they inhabit. The American ought therefore to love this country much better than that wherein either he or his forefathers were born. Here the rewards of his industry follow with equal steps the progress of his labour; his labour is founded on the basis of nature, *self-interest;* can it want a stronger allurement? Wives and children, who before in vain demanded of him a morsel of bread, now, fat and frolicsome, gladly help their father to clear those fields whence exuberant crops are to arise to feed and to clothe them all; without any part being claimed, either by a despotic prince, a rich abbot, or a mighty lord. Here religion demands but little of him; a small voluntary salary to the minister, and gratitude to God; can he refuse these? The American is a new man, who acts upon new principles; he must therefore entertain new ideas, and form new opinions. From involuntary idleness, servile dependence, penury, and useless labour, he has passed to toils of a very different nature, rewarded by ample subsistence.—This is an American.

British America is divided into many provinces, forming a large association, scattered along a coast 1500 miles extent and about 200 wide. This society I would fain examine, at least such as it appears in the middle provinces; if it does not afford that variety of tinges and gradations which may be observed in Europe, we have colours peculiar to ourselves. For instance, it is natural to conceive that those who live near the sea, must be very different from those who live in the woods; the intermediate space will afford a separate and distinct class.

Men are like plants; the goodness and flavour of the fruit proceeds from the peculiar soil and exposition in which they grow. We are nothing but what we derive from the air we breathe, the climate we inhabit, the government we obey, the system of religion we profess, and the nature of our employment. Here you will find but few crimes; these have acquired as yet no root among us. I wish I was able to trace all my ideas; if my ignorance prevents me from describing them properly, I hope I shall be able to delineate a few of the outlines, which are all I propose.

Those who live near the sea, feed more on fish than on flesh, and often encounter that boisterous element. This renders them more bold and enterprising; this leads them to neglect the confined occupations of the land. They see and converse with a variety of people, their intercourse with mankind becomes extensive. The sea inspires them with a love of traffic, a desire of transporting produce from one place to another; and leads them to a variety of resources which supply the place of labour. Those who inhabit the middle settlements, by far the most numerous, must be very different; the simple cultivation of the earth purifies them, but the indulgences of the government, the soft remonstrances of religion, the rank of independent freeholders, must necessarily inspire them with sentiments, very little known in Europe among people of the same class. What do I say? Europe has no such class of men; the early knowledge they acquire, the early bargains they make, give them a great degree of sagacity. As freemen they will be litigious; pride and obstinacy are often the cause of law suits; the nature of our laws and governments may be another. As citizens it is easy to imagine, that they will carefully read the newspapers, enter into every political disquisition, freely blame or censure governors and others. As farmers they will be careful and anxious to get as much as they can, because what they get is their own. As northern men they will love the cheerful cup. As Christians, religion curbs them not in their opinions; the general indulgence leaves every one to think for themselves in spiritual matters; the laws inspect our actions, our thoughts are left to God. Industry, good living, selfishness, litigiousness, country politics, the pride of freemen, religious indifference, and their characteristics. If you recede still farther from the sea, you will come into more modern settlements; they exhibit the same strong lineaments, in a ruder appearance. Religion seems to have still less influence, and their manners are less improved.

Now we arrive near the great woods, near the last inhabited districts; there men seem to be placed still farther beyond the reach of government, which in some measure leaves them to themselves. How can it pervade every corner; as they were driven there by misfortunes, necessity of beginnings, desire of acquiring large tracts of land, idleness, frequent want of economy, ancient debts; the re-union of such people does not afford a very pleasing spectacle. When discord, want of unity and friendship; when either drunkenness or idleness prevail in such remote districts; contention, inactivity, and wretchedness must ensue. There are not the same remedies to these evils as in a long established community. The few magistrates they have, are in general little better than the rest; they are often in a perfect state of war; that of man against man, sometimes decided by blows, sometimes by means of the law; that of man against every wild inhabitant of these venerable woods, of which they are come to dispossess them. There men appear to be no better than carnivorous animals of a superior rank, living on the flesh of wild animals when they can catch them, and when they are not able, they subsist on grain. He who would wish to see

America in its proper light, and have a true idea of its feeble beginnings and barbarous rudiments, must visit our extended line of frontiers where the last settlers dwell, and where he may see the first labours of settlement, the mode of clearing the earth, in all their different appearances; where men are wholly left dependent on their native tempers, and on the spur of uncertain industry, which often fails when not sanctified by the efficacy of a few moral rules. There, remote from the power of example and check of shame, many families exhibit the most hideous parts of our society. They are a kind of forlorn hope, preceding by ten or twelve years the most respectable army of veterans which come after them. In that space, prosperity will polish some, vice and the law will drive off the rest, who uniting again with others like themselves will recede still farther; making room for more industrious people, who will finish their improvements, convert the loghouse into a convenient habitation, and rejoicing that the first heavy labours are finished, will change in a few years that hitherto barbarous country into a fine fertile, well regulated district. Such is our progress, such is the march of the Europeans toward the interior parts of this continent. In all societies there are off-casts; this impure part serves as our precursors or pioneers; my father himself was one of that class, but he came upon honest principles, and was therefore one of the few who held fast; by good conduct and temperance, he transmitted to me his fair inheritance, when not above one in fourteen of his contemporaries had the same good fortune.

Forty years ago this smiling country was thus inhabited; it is now purged, a general decency of manners prevails throughout, and such has been the fate of our best countries.

Exclusive of those general characteristics, each province has its own, founded on the government, climate, mode of husbandry, customs, and peculiarity of circumstances. Europeans submit insensibly to these great powers, and become, in the course of a few generations, not only Americans in general, but either Pennsylvanians, Virginians, or provincials under some other name. Whoever traverses the continent must easily observe those strong differences, which will grow more evident in time. The inhabitants of Canada, Massachusetts, the middle provinces, the southern ones will be as different as their climates; their only points of unity will be those of religion and language. . . .

But to return to our back settlers. I must tell you, that there is something in the proximity of the woods, which is very singular. It is with men as it is with the plants and animals that grow and live in the forests; they are entirely different from those that live in the plains. I will candidly tell you all my thoughts but you are not to expect that I shall advance any reasons. By living in or near the woods, their actions are regulated by the wildness of the neighbourhood. The deer often come to eat their grain, the wolves to destroy their sheep, the bears to kill their hogs, the foxes to catch their poultry. This surrounding hostility immediately puts the gun into their hands; they watch these animals, they kill some; and thus by defending their property, they soon become professed hunters: this is the progress; once hunters, farewell to the plough. The chase renders them ferocious, gloomy, and unsociable; a hunter wants no neighbour, he rather hates them, because he dreads the competition. In a little time their success in the woods makes them neglect their tillage. They trust to the natural fecundity of the earth, and therefore do little; carelessness in fencing often exposes what little they sow to destruction; they are not at home to watch; in order therefore to make up the deficiency, they go oftener to the woods. That new mode of life brings along with it a new set of manners, which I cannot easily describe. These new manners being grafted on the old stock, produce a strange sort of lawless profligacy, the impressions of which are indelible. The manners of the Indian natives are respectable, compared with this European medley. Their wives and children live in sloth and inactivity; and having no proper pursuits, you may judge what education the latter receive. Their tender minds have nothing else to contemplate but the example of their parents; like them they grow up a mongrel breed, half civilised, half savage, except nature stamps on them some constitutional propensities. That rich, that voluptuous sentiment is gone that struck them so forcibly; the possession of their freeholds no longer conveys to their minds the same pleasure and pride. To all these reasons you must add, their lonely situation, and you cannot imagine what an effect on manners the great distances they live from each other has! Consider one of the last settlements in its first view: of what is it composed? Europeans who have not that sufficient share of knowledge they ought to have, in order to prosper; people who have suddenly passed from oppression, dread of government, and fear of laws, into the unlimited freedom of the woods. This sudden change must have a very great effect on most men, and on that class particularly. Eating of wild meat, whatever you may think, tends to alter their temper: though all the proof I can adduce, is, that I have seen it: and having no place of worship to resort to, what little society this might afford is denied them. The Sunday meetings, exclusive of religious benefits, were the only social bonds that might have inspired them with some degree of emulation in neatness. Is it then surprising to see men thus situated, immersed in great and heavy labours, degenerate a little? It is rather a wonder the effect is not more diffusive. The Moravians and the Quakers are the only instances in exception to what I have advanced. The first never settle singly, it is a colony of the society which emigrates; they carry with them their forms, worship, rules, and decency: the others never begin so hard, they are always able to buy improvements, in which there is a great advantage, for by that time the country is recovered from its first barbarity. Thus our bad people are those who are half cultivators and half hunters; and the worst of them are those who have degenerated altogether into the hunting state. As old ploughmen and new men of the woods, as Europeans and new made Indians, they contract the vices of both; they adopt the moroseness and ferocity of a native, without his mildness, or even his industry at home. If manners are not refined, at least they are rendered simple and inoffensive by tilling the earth; all our wants are supplied by it, our time is divided between labour and rest, and leaves none for the commission of great misdeeds. As hunters it is divided between the toil of the chase, the idleness of repose, or the indulgence of inebriation. Hunting is but a licentious idle life, and if it does not always pervert good dispositions; yet, when it is united with bad luck, it leads to want: want stimulates that propensity to rapacity and injustice, too natural to needy men, which is the fatal gradation. After this explanation of the effects which follow by living in the woods, shall we yet vainly flatter ourselves with the hope of converting the Indians? We should rather begin with converting our back-settlers; and now if I dare mention the name of religion, its sweet accents would be lost in the immensity of these woods. Men thus placed are not fit either to receive or remember its mild instructions; they want temples and ministers, but as soon as men cease to remain at home, and begin to lead an erratic life, let them be either tawny or white, they cease to be its disciples.

Thus have I faintly and imperfectly endeavoured to trace our society from the sea to our woods! yet you must not imagine that every person who moves back, acts upon the same principles, or falls into the same degeneracy. Many families carry with them all their decency of conduct, purity of morals, and respect of religion; but these are scarce, the power of example is sometimes irresistible. Even among these back-settlers, their depravity is greater or less, according to what nation or province they belong. Were I to adduce proofs of this, I might be accused of partiality. If there happens to be some rich intervals, some fertile bottoms, in those remote districts, the people will there prefer tilling the land to hunting, and will attach themselves to it; but even on these fertile spots you may plainly perceive the inhabitants to acquire a great degree of rusticity and selfishness.

It is in consequence of this straggling situation, and the astonishing power it has on manners, that the backsettlers of both the Carolinas, Virginia, and many other parts, have been long a set of lawless people; it has been even dangerous to travel among them. Government can do nothing in so extensive a country, better it should wink at these irregularities, than that it should use means inconsistent with its usual mildness. Time will efface those stains: in proportion as the great body of population approaches them they will reform, and become polished and subordinate. Whatever has been said of the four New England provinces, no such degeneracy of manners has ever tarnished their annals; their backsettlers have been kept within the bounds of decency, and government, by means of wise laws, and by the influence of religion. What a detestable idea such people must have given to the natives of the Europeans! They trade with them, the worst of people are permitted to do that which none but persons of the best characters should be employed in. They get drunk with them, and often defraud the Indians. Their avarice, removed from the eyes of their superiors, knows no bounds; and aided by the little superiority of knowledge, these traders deceive them, and even sometimes shed blood. Hence those shocking violations, those sudden devastations which have so often stained our frontiers, when hundreds of innocent people have been sacrificed for the crimes of a few. It was in consequence of such behaviour, that the Indians took the hatchet against the Virginians in 1774. Thus are our first steps trod, thus are our first trees felled, in general, by the most vicious of our people; and thus the path is opened for the arrival of a second and better class, the true American freeholders; the most respectable set of people in this part of the world: respectable for their industry, their happy independence, the great share of freedom they possess, the good regulation of their families, and for extending the trade and the dominion of our mother country.

Europe contains hardly any other distinctions but lords and tenants; this fair country alone is settled by freeholders, the possessors of the soil they cultivate, members of the government they obey, and the framers of their own laws, by means of their representatives. This is a thought which you have taught me to cherish; our difference from Europe, far from diminishing, rather adds to our usefulness and consequence as men and subjects. Had our forefathers remained there, they would only have crowded it, and perhaps prolonged those convulsions which had shook it so long. Every industrious European who transports himself here, may be compared to a sprout growing at the foot of a great tree; it enjoys and draws but a little portion of sap; wrench it from the parent roots, transplant it, and it will become a tree bearing fruit also. . . .

An European, when he first arrives, seems limited in his intentions, as well as in his views; but he very suddenly alters his scale; two hundred miles formerly appeared a very great distance, it is now but a trifle; he no sooner breathes our air than he forms schemes, and embarks in designs he never would have thought of in his own country. There the plenitude of society confines many useful ideas, and often extinguishes the most laudable schemes which here ripen into maturity. Thus Europeans become Americans. . . .

Whenever I hear of any new settlement, I pay it a visit once or twice a year, on purpose to observe the different steps each settler takes, the gradual improvements, the different tempers of each family, on which their prosperity in a great nature depends; their different modifications of industry, their ingenuity, and contrivance; for being all poor, their life requires sagacity and prudence. . . . What a happy change it must be, to descend from the high, sterile, bleak lands of Scotland, where everything is barren and cold, to rest on some fertile farms in these middle provinces! Such a transition must have afforded the most pleasing satisfaction.

The following dialogue passed at an out-settlement, where I lately paid a visit:

Well, friend, how do you do now; I am come fifty odd miles on purpose to see you; how do you go on with your new cutting and slashing? Very well, good Sir, we learn the use of the axe bravely, we shall make it out; we have a belly full of victuals every day, our cows run about, and come home full of milk, our hogs get fat of themselves in the woods: Oh, this is a good country! God bless the king, and William Penn; we shall do very well by and by, if we keep our healths. Your loghouse looks neat and light, where did you get these shingles? One of our neighbours is a New-England man, and he showed us how to split them out of chestnut-trees. Now for a barn, but all in good time, here are fine trees to build with. Who is to frame it, sure you don't understand that work yet? A countryman of ours who has been in America these ten years, offers to wait for his money until the second crop is lodged in it. What did you give for your land? Thirty-five shillings per acre, payable in seven years. How many acres have you got? An hundred and fifty. That is enough to begin with; is not your land pretty hard to clear? Yes, Sir, hard enough, but it would be harder still if it were ready cleared, for then we should have no timber, and I love the woods much; and the land is nothing without them. Have not you found out any bees yet? No, Sir; and if we had we should not know what to do with them. I will tell you by and by. You are very kind. Farewell, honest man, God prosper you; whenever you travel toward ——, inquire for J.S. He will entertain you kindly, provided you bring him good tidings from your family and farm. In this manner I often visit them,and carefully examine their houses, their modes of ingenuity, their different ways; and make them all relate all they know, and describe all they feel. These are scenes which I believe you would willingly share with me. I well remember your philanthropic turn of mind. Is it not better to contemplate under these humble roofs, the rudiments of future wealth and population, than to behold the accumulated bundles of litigious papers in the office of a lawyer? To examine how the world is gradually settled, how the howling swamp is converted into a pleasing meadow, the rough ridge into a fine field; and to hear the cheerful whistling, the rural song, where there was no sound heard before, save the yell of the savage, the screech of the owl or the hissing of the snake? Here an European, fatigued with luxury, riches, and pleasures, may find a sweet relaxation in a series of interesting scenes, as affecting as they are new. England, which now contains so many domes, so many castles, was once like this; a place woody and marshy; its inhabitants, now the favourite nation for arts and commerce, were once painted like our neighbours. The country will flourish in its turn, and the same observations will be made which I have just delineated. Posterity will look back with avidity and pleasure, to trace, if possible, the era of this or that particular settlement.

1782

Eighteenth-Century Perspectives

Natural History and the Sublime

The eighteenth century was a period of major change both in attitudes toward landscape and in ways of rendering it. Science had come to posit the model of a universe which was sun-centered (and not, as Christian tradition held, man-centered), vast beyond imagination and yet subject to the intricate harmony of natural laws which governed all being, from flowers to farmers to governments to galaxies. Scientists ("natural historians") began studying in this light the objects and processes of the natural world. Meanwhile painters and aesthetic philosophers, trying to assess the relative values of landscapes (the word itself was a borrowing from seventeenth-century Dutch artists), were producing a complex aesthetics which distinguished the sublime, the beautiful, and, later, the picturesque. At the same time, Deists were looking to the natural world as the true source of divine revelation.

All of these ideas, so the new liberal orthodoxy held, were accessible if not self-evident to anybody who would look for them in galaxies or in earthly landscapes —especially in wilderness landscapes, untouched by man.

In America, the full implications of these ideas were not felt until about the second decade of the nineteenth century. But in the last two decades of the eighteenth century, their initial impact can be observed in the works of travelers and natural historians. There, three new concepts of landscape can be distinguished: *landscape as natural history*, *landscape as sublime scenery*, and *landscape as scripture*.

LANDSCAPE AS NATURAL HISTORY

In the deciduous forest and the sub-tropical savannah and jungle of the eastern seaboard, natural history was chiefly a matter of botany and zoology. But as it was practiced in eighteenth-century America, natural history did not confine itself to these specialized interests. Indeed, having no rigorously limited interest or methodology, it attended to any conceivable fact or process related to the landscape: its geography and geology; its climate and soils; its "animal and vegetable productions." Where a landscape was inhabited (a cultivated garden) the work of natural history generally included a relation of the garden's human history and sociological sketches of the inhabitants, whether Indians, frontiersmen, or farmers: their appearances, their institutions, their manners and morals, and particularly their relation to the land. Where a landscape was uninhabited (a wilderness) the work gave voice to a redemptive or at least undemonizing vision of the wilderness as a garden divinely created and naturally maintained: a huge, exotic herbarium, tree farm, and zoo with its own community, its own ways of enacting and illuminating the laws that governed the universe.

In such a work, professional training was often less necessary than the equipment of any literate traveler: energy and curiosity, a liberal education, an observant eye, and an ability to picture landscapes and the life they supported in accurate, detailed sketches—verbal or linear or both. It did not hurt to have in addition the literary skill to bind these descriptions into a coherent episodic narrative not so different, say, from *Robinson Crusoe.* Bartram's *Travels,* for example, takes the form of a Deistic "pilgrimage" through some of the American "rooms" and "scenes" of that "boundless palace of the sovereign Creator," the earth.

The professional qualifications of the two writers represented here are characteristically mixed. Bartram, less formally trained than European scientists but certainly as skilled in field work, wrote his *Travels Through North & South Carolina, Georgia, East & West Florida* as a record of his search for specimens for his English patron, Dr. John Fothergill. Bartram was a scientist, though he clearly refused to limit himself to scientific observations in his work of natural history. Jefferson, on the other hand, was more like a literate traveler with a little knowledge of painting and of natural history, and he is simply responding to the demands of correspondents when he makes his observations on the natural history of the New World. His *Notes on Virignia,* for example, is a response to a set of queries from the Secretary of the French Legation in Philadelphia on matters ranging from Virginia's laws, religions, customs, and Indians to its "mines and other subterranean riches," its "trees, plants, fruits, etc.," its mountains (*Query IV,* which is excerpted here) and its "cascades and caverns" (*Query V,* which is also excerpted here).

Almost all eighteenth-century natural histories are responses to the demands of Old World scientists for more objective knowledge of the New World. More artfully and more factually than the letters and relations of the maritime explorers and the early settlers, these reports provide for laboratory analysis (like the moon landings) close-up pictures from the field. They leave the experts to decide which sketches and which scenes are scientifically significant, and they seem fully aware that to the readership beyond the laboratories—to a public hungry for knowledge of nature and of the New World—nothing seen here was insignificant.

What animates and humanizes these landscapes are the verbs and the metaphors. The verbs, transitive and dynamic, register not only motion and feelings (the feelings are often vitalistically ascribed to animals and even to plants) but also natural processes: the processes of organic growth and of geological "disrupture and avulsion" by fire and water, what Jefferson calls "the most powerful agents of nature."

The metaphors form two rich clusters. One cluster, distinctively neo-classical, images both garden and wilderness in terms of urban environment and ritual. Trees and plants are thus grandly or gravely robed or cosmetically painted with foliage. Wind, birds, and water appear as musicians. Animals and even landscapes move with processional dignity, and by their bearing and their actions they personify the benevolent ideals of a civilized society. The land itself, in Bartram's world, is endowed with enough benevolence to "receive" or "liberate" rivers or, as a gracious host, to "present" to the traveler a "bountiful repast." At the heart of these metaphors is the suggestion that each species of life—each "tribe" or "race," whether humans or trout or oaks—is united in a "great chain of being," each link of which demonstrates the grandeur and beauty of immutable natural law and virtue.

The other cluster of metaphor, basically Newtonian, images the natural world as a functioning structure. In this metaphor, God is conceived of as the master constructionist, and the earth and its "productions" become examples of what Bartram calls "the divine and inimitable workmanship." Every natural object can thus be described as a work of art or craft: a painting, a work of furniture or architecture or an efficiently designed machine. To Bartram, for example, the yellow trumpet flower resembled "a silken canopy": "the yellow pendant petals are the curtains," and the hollow leaves, he discovered, were also a marvelously efficient "reservoir." And in trees and rock formations both he and Jefferson could see canopies, arches, and columns—details of the splendid natural architecture of the New World.

SUBLIME SCENERY

As natural historians and other eighteenth-century travelers sought access to wilderness landscapes, they were confronted with a problem of value. Of what value was the wilderness-as-it-is? It was not apparently useful until it began to be mined for its resources. It was not, of course, pastoral. It was not beautiful in the harmonious, symmetrical, and humanly proportionate way that a work of art or a formal garden could be beautiful, for it was too rugged, irregular, and vast. To give value to wilderness-as-it-is, English painters and aesthetic philosophers resurrected from antiquity the concept of the *sublime.* By the time of Bartram and Jefferson, this concept had taken permanent root in American thought.

In his "Philosophical Enquiry into . . . the Sublime and Beautiful" (1756), Edmund Burke listed seven qualities which could make a landscape sublime: *obscurity* (darkness or mist); *power* (as of a storm or waterfall); *privation* (darkness, emptiness, silence, solitude—as of an ocean, a virgin forest, a prairie, or a desert); *vastness* (length, height, and most especially depth, which immerses the perceiver and leads his eye into remote distances); *the sense of infinity or eternity or duration; difficulty of access or traversal* (as of a mountain or desert); and *magnificence* (as of a sunset). One or more of these qualities, as the examples suggest, was present in a wide spectrum of natural landscapes. But as it turned out, the most recurrent sources of sublimity in eighteenth- and early nineteenth-century America were night, mountains, storms, cataracts, caverns, wilderness forest, prairies, and deserts. These were consecrated as Romantic icons.

From the start, the sublime was a phenomenon described not so much in physical as in psychic terms. "It gives me pleasure," wrote Burke, "to see nature in these great though terrible scenes. It fills the mind with grand ideas, and turns the soul in upon itself." The sublime was valued because it struck into motion, like sympathetic tuning forks, a loosely connected sequence of mental states. First, it produced pleasurably intense sensations or emotions: awe, terror, solemnity, elevation, rapture, floodings of "selfish pleasure," or "wild delight." Then, through such impressions (literally, "marks on the mind"), the sublime gave rise, by association, to "grand ideas," and description shaded into reverie, meditation, exposition.

The sublime landscape, in short, as the eighteenth-century English critic William Gilpin wrote, had "the power of furnishing images *analogous to the various feelings, and sensations of the mind.*" Through these images, wrote the precursor of Wordsworth and Coleridge, Emerson and Poe, the imagination "collects its scattered ideas, transposes, combines, and shifts them into a thousand forms." The kind of grand ideas to which the sublime gave rise in America can be seen, in this section, in Bartram's description of a storm on the Alatamaha River. By the 1820's, as later sections show, meditations on the sublime could take any number of directions: personal, nationalistic, historical, primitivistic, as well as religious.

The value of the sublime depends to great extent upon perspective. Few farmers learned to value storms or deserts for the "grand ideas" they might give rise to; few explorers could learn to distinguish the great from the terrible in the cliffs, mountains, torrents, and deserts they had to cross. Usually the perceiver was a man of taste and leisure, a tourist; and usually he had to find a vantage point from which the sublime occupied the middle or background, its danger thus defused. For example, before Jefferson visited the Natural Bridge of Virginia (which was on his property), tourists had found the experience—standing atop the bridge—"painful" and "intolerable." Jefferson, an architect and a reader of Burke, stood below the bridge, saw in it the form of an arch "springing up to heaven," and considered the scene "delightful."

The perspective best suited to a sublime landscape, as Jefferson discovered, is the panorama; and his sketch of the confluence of the Shenandoah and the Potomac rivers is one of the first panoramic sketches of the American landscape. The *fixed panorama,* of the sort Jefferson uses, is a very natural perspective. Standing on a hillside or mountaintop or on some other eminence (Hawthorne's steeple, Ishmael's masthead, and so on), or by the side of a lake, which both opens out a sublime panorama of forest and reflects it, the perceiver takes in an unobstructed view in all directions; and quite naturally grand ideas rise to fill the grand sweep of space. In the *moving panorama,* viewed from a boat or carriage or viewed over the course of a journey (Bartram's riverscape, for example), a sequence of scenes, characters, and events unfolds in the manner of a procession. To such a procession the Romantic dreamer could later add "fanciful" re-enactments of past events, prophetic visions of the future, and revelations of the immanent laws which permeate the "scenes and shows" of life. For Transcendentalists, the panorama would become sublimely cosmic in perspective. Transcendentalism, Emerson wrote in *Nature,*

> . . . beholds the whole circle of persons and things, of actions and events, of country and religion, not as painfully accumulated, atom after atom, act after act, in an aged creeping Past, but as one vast picture which God paints on the instant eternity for the contemplation of the soul.

Because it gives, in the words of the eighteenth-century English critic George Turnbull, a "very large and as it were, unbounded Prospect to the Eye," the panorama is in itself a sublime perspective. And what other perspective could do such justice to a continent both resplendent and awful with such sublimity?

LANDSCAPE AS SCRIPTURE

The most profound and comprehensive concept of landscape in the late eighteenth and early nineteenth century—the age's ideal design—was that of the Deists' *landscape as scripture.* Both writers represented here were Deists, and as such they renounced sectarian Christianity in favor of an ecumenical benevolent ethics and they proselytized for the study of nature as the source of both useful knowledge and religious insight. For them, Christ was only a prophet, and God the Father, located somewhere out in the infinite darkness of the Newtonian universe, was too sublimely unimaginable and ineffable to hear and answer prayer or to reveal Himself directly to individuals. His grace and illumination could be experienced only through His works. "THE WORD OF GOD IS THE CREATION WE BEHOLD," proclaimed Thomas Paine in *The Age of Reason* (1794), and the truths of the Word were accessible to any student of the creation:

> Do we want to contemplate his power? We see it in the immensity of the creation. . . . His wisdom? We see it in the unchangeable order by which the incomprehensible whole is governed. . . . His munificence? We see it in the abundance with which he fills the earth. . . . His mercy? We see it in his not witholding that abundance even from the unthankful.

"Search not the book called the Scripture, which any hand might make," went Paine's Deist manifesto, "but the scripture called the Creation."

As scripture, landscape could be read on four levels of meaning: the literal, the typological or symbolic, the allegorical, and the apocalyptic. The levels and the ways of locating them had been part of the tradition of scriptural exigesis begun in the medieval Church and handed down, as modified by the Reformation, to the Puritans and their descendants. In America, they were applied more randomly than systematically, more intuitively than rationally, but they nevertheless began to synthesize the perceptions which natural history, aesthetics, and Deist ethics brought to landscape.

Natural history gave landscape its *literal* meaning by describing it as a collection of objects in space and processes in time. Artists of the picturesque could also render it literally as a composed mass of surfaces, textures, and other appearances.

The aesthetic perception of landscape as sublime or, somewhat later, as picturesque scenery (see *The Poetry of Scene*) gave landscape its *typological* or *symbolic* dimension of meaning. Every feature of the landscape could be seen, at this level of meaning, as an incarnate attribute of God or of the human mind. Thus mountains could be seen as expressions of spiritual elevation or of the vastness, grandeur, and infinite duration of God. Lakes could be seen as "types" of spiritual reflection and peacefulness or of God's benevolent blessing (Thoreau would make Walden Pond the serene "earth's eye" which reflected the depths of its soul). Winds and waterfalls could be types of God's power or of his "unceasing change and everlasting duration," or types of the poet's voice speaking as "the passive instrument played on by the elements." Forests could be types of human society—an assembly of the vibrantly young, the venerably old, and the dying—or gothic temples of a kingly God. The interested reader can extend or make for himself such a list of the symbolic properties of pre-Romantic and Romantic landscapes in America.

The third level of meaning, the *allegorical,* emerged from the landscape's "shadows," where concrete objects, half dissolved, revealed the universal laws and virtues which informed all being. In the Introduction to his *Travels,* for example, Bartram exacts a lesson in maternal love from a she-bear's wailing for her lost cub, and in an excerpt included here he ponders the implicit teaching in the short life of the May fly. And in *Nature* Emerson would declare that "every farm is a mute gospel," that the "sea-beaten rock" teaches the fisherman firmness and that "the pantomime of brutes" teaches industry and providence. At the allegorical level of meaning everything in the landscape was a teaching.

The fourth level of meaning, the *apocalyptic,* could be reached when the "grand ideas" called up by the sublime vastness and magnificence of the American landscape projected on the landscape the millenial promise of a pastoral Golden Age or an earthly city of God or (for the Transcendentalists) an experience of transcendent being.

The Deist era in America was not a long one (it was over by the end of the eighteenth century), but its ideal design of the landscape as scripture was to provide Emerson, in *Nature* (1836), a means of opening out his comprehensive "idea of creation." Through Emerson this design was to become one of the century's greatest gifts to American culture.

William Bartram

From Travels

William was a son of the Philadelphia botanist John Bartram, a friend of Jefferson, and a failure at every business venture he tried. He was inspired by the work of his father and of another naturalist, Mark Catesby, to become a sometime field botanist. His one extended field trip, to the Southern colonies from 1773 to 1777, was made possible by the encouragement and assistance of an English naturalist, Dr. John Fothergill; the trip ended when the Revolution cut off Bartram from his patron, and he never made another. He was certainly influenced by Edmund Burke, by Alexander Pope, and by other pre-Romantics (he makes the first extensive use of the notion of the sublime in American literature), and he was aware of painterly as well as scientific perspectives on natural landscape. Like other naturalists and travelers, he kept detailed field journals as well as sketching and collecting specimens on his field trip, and his *Travels* was composed from these journals. After long delays, the book was published in Philadelphia in 1791.

The four excerpts included here are located in different areas of the South. The Altamaha River is in east Georgia, and Bartram probably traveled up it in 1776. The St. John's River is in northeast Florida, and he traveled that in the spring of 1774. The Salt Springs are located in the northwest corner of Lake George in Florida (the St. John's flows into this lake), and the narrative is probably the composite of two visits—one in the early summer, one in the late summer of 1774. (From this description, Coleridge drew much of the imagery of "Kubla Khan"; his River Alph, for example, is drawn from the Salt Springs Run, which connects the springs to Lake George.) The "sylvan scene" in the last excerpt is located in the area of Cowee, North Carolina, which Bartram visited in the spring of 1775. The "brisk flowing creek" of paragraph 3 is Rose Creek; the "Jore village" is in the vicinity of Burningtown; and the "fine little river" in paragraph 4 is probably Burningtown Creek. The Cherokee "hamdrayades" (tree nymphs, the 'local geniuses' of the forest in classical Greek and Roman landscapes) are only the culmination of the intermittently classical perspective in which Bartram perceives the landscape. In paragraph 3, the "Fields of Pharsalia" and "the Vale of Tempe" (a valley between Mounts Ossa and Olympus) are both located in Thessaly, a region in Greece, characterized, like Cowee, by its high mountains, plunging rivers, and its nymphs and other magic beings. The benevolent vitalism of Bartram's landscape can be seen in the verbs he chooses. The rich sensuality is characteristic of tropical and Southern landscapes (and noticeable for its absence in the Puritan landscapes of New England).

[A Trip up the Altamaha River]

HAVING COMPLETED my Hortus Siccus, and made up my collections of seeds and growing roots, the fruits of my late western tour, and sent them to Charleston, to be forwarded to Europe, I spent the remaining part of this season in botanical excursions to the low countries, between Carolina and East Florida, and collected seeds, roots, and specimens, making drawings of such curious subjects as could not be preserved in their native state of excellence.

During this recess from the high road of my travels, having obtained the use of a neat light cypress canoe, at Broughton Island, a plantation, the property of the Hon. Henry Laurens, Esq. where I stored myself with necessaries, for the voyage, and resolved upon a trip up the Alatamaha.

I ascended this beautiful river, on whose fruitful banks the generous and true sons of liberty securely dwell, fifty miles above the white settlements.

How gently flow thy peaceful floods, O Alatamaha! How sublimely rise to view, on thy elevated shores, yon Magnolian groves, from whose tops the surrounding expanse is perfumed, by clouds of incense, blended with the exhaling balm of the Liquid-amber, and odours continually arising from circumambient aromatic groves of Illicium, Myrica, Laurus, and Bignonia.

When wearied, with working my canoe against the impetuous current (which becomes stronger by reason of the mighty floods of the river, with collected force, pressing through the first hilly ascents, where the shores on each side the river present to view rocky cliffs rising above the surface of the water, in nearly flat horizontal masses, washed smooth by the descending floods, and which appear to be a composition, or concrete, of sandy lime-stone) I resigned my bark to the friendly current, reserving to myself the control of the helm. My progress was rendered delightful by the sylvan elegance of the groves, chearful meadows, and high distant forests, which in grand order presented themselves to view. The winding banks of the river, and the high projecting promontories, unfolded fresh scenes of grandeur and sublimity. The deep forests and distant hills re-echoed the chearing social lowings of domestic herds. The air was filled with the loud and shrill whooping of the wary sharp-sighted crane. Behold, on yon decayed, defoliated Cypress tree, the solitary wood-pelican, dejectedly perched upon its utmost elevated spire; he there, like an ancient venerable sage, sets himself up as a mark of derision, for the safety of his kindred tribes. The crying-bird, another faithful guardian, screaming in the gloomy thickets, warns the feathered tribes of approaching peril; and the plumage of the swift sailing squadrons of Spanish curlews (white as the immaculate robe of innocence) gleam in the cerulean skies.

Thus secure and tranquil, and meditating on the marvellous scenes of primitive nature, as yet unmodified by the hand of man, I gently descended the peaceful stream, on whose polished surface were depicted the mutable shadows from its pensile banks; whilst myriads of finny inhabitants sported in its pellucid floods.

The glorious sovereign of day, cloathed in light refulgent, rolling on his gilded chariot, speeds to revisit the western realms. Grey pensive eve now admonishes us of gloomy night's hasty approach: I am roused by care to seek a place of secure repose, ere darkness comes on.

Drawing near the high shores, I ascended the steep banks, where stood a venerable oak. An ancient Indian field, verdured o'er with succulent grass, and checquered with coppices of fragrant shrubs, offers to my view the Myrica cerifera, Magnolia glauca, Laurus benzoin, Laur. Borbonia, Rhamnus frangula, Prunus Chicasaw, Prun. Lauro cerasa, and others. It was nearly encircled with an open forest of stately pines (Pinus palustris) through which appears the extensive savanna, the secure range of the swift roebuck. In front of my landing, and due east, I had a fine prospect of the river and low lands on each side, which gradually widened to the sea coast, and gave me an unconfined prospect, whilst the far distant sea coast islands, like a coronet, limited the hoary horizon.

My barque being securely moored, and having reconnoitered the surrounding groves, and collected fire-wood, I spread my skins and blanket by my chearful fire, under the protecting shade of the hospitable Live-oak, and reclined my head on my hard but healthy couch. I listened, undisturbed, to the divine hymns of the feathered songsters of the groves, whilst the softly whispering breezes faintly died away.

The sun now below the western horizon, the moon majestically rising in the east; again the tuneful birds become inspired; how melodious is the social mock-bird! the groves resound the unceasing cries of the whip-poor-will; the moon about an hour above the horizon; lo! a dark eclipse of her glorious brightness comes slowly on; at length, a silver thread alone encircles her temples: at this boding change, an universal silence prevails.

Nature now weary, I resigned myself to rest; the night passed over; the cool dews of the morning awake me; my fire burnt low; the blue smoke scarce rises above the moistened embers; all is gloomy: the late starry skies, now overcast by thick clouds, I am warned to rise and be going. The livid purple clouds thicken on the frowning brows of the morning; the tumultuous winds from the east now exert their power. O peaceful Alatamaha! gentle by nature! how thou art ruffled! thy wavy surface disfigures every object, presenting them obscurely to the sight, and they at length totally disappear, whilst the furious winds and sweeping rains bend the lofty groves, and prostrate the quaking grass, driving the affrighted creatures to their dens and caverns.

The tempest now relaxes, its impetus is spent, and a calm serenity gradually takes place; by noon they break away, the blue sky appears, the fulgid sun-beams spread abroad their animating light, and the steady western wind resumes his peaceful reign. The waters are purified, the waves subside, and the beautiful river regains its native calmness: so it is with the varied and mutable scenes of human events on the stream of life. The higher powers and affections of the soul are so blended and connected with the inferior passions, that the most painful feelings are excited in the mind when the latter are crossed: thus in the moral system, which we have planned for our conduct, as a ladder whereby to mount to the summit of terrestrial glory and happiness, and from whence we perhaps meditated our flight to heaven itself, at the very moment when we vainly imagine ourselves to have attained its point, some unforeseen accident intervenes, and surprises us; the chain is violently shaken, we quit our hold and fall: the well contrived system at once becomes a chaos; every idea of happiness recedes; the splendour of glory darkens, and at length totally disappears; every pleasing object is defaced, all is deranged, and the flattering scene passes quite away, a gloomy cloud pervades the understanding, and when we see our progress retarded, and our best intentions frustrated, we are apt to deviate from the admonitions and convictions of virtue, to shut our eyes upon our guide and protector, doubt of his power, and despair of his assistance. But let us wait and rely on our God, who in due time will shine forth in brightness, dissipate the envious cloud, and reveal to us how finite and circumscribed is human power, when assuming to itself independent wisdom.

[Ephemera: St. John's River]

LEAVING PICOLATA, I continued to ascend [St. John's] river. I observed this day, during my progress up the river, incredible numbers of small flying insects, of the genus, termed by naturalists, Ephemera, continually emerging from the shallow water, near shore, some of them immediately taking their flight to the land, whilst myriads, crept up the grass and herbage, where remaining, for a short time, as they acquired sufficient strength, they took their flight also, following their kindred, to the main land. This resurrection from the deep, if I may so express it, commences early in the morning, and ceases after the sun is up. At evening they are seen in clouds of innumerable millions, swarming and wantoning in the still air, gradually drawing near the river, descend upon its surface, and there quickly end their day, after committing their eggs to the deep; which being for a little while tossed about, enveloped in a viscid scum, are hatched, and the little Larvae descend into their secure and dark habitation, in the oozy bed beneath, where they remain, gradually increasing in size, until the returning spring; they then change to a Nymph, when the genial heat brings them, as it were, into existence, and they again arise into the world. This fly seems to be delicious food for birds, frogs and fish. In the morning, when they arise, and in the evening, when they return, the tumult is great indeed, and the surface of the water along shore broken into bubbles, or spirted into the air, by the contending aquatic tribes, and such is the avidity of the fish and frogs, that they spring into the air, after this delicious prey.

Early in the evening, after a pleasant days voyage, I made a convenient and safe harbour, in a little lagoon, under an elevated bank, on the West shore of the river, where I shall intreat the reader's patience, whilst we behold the closing scene of the short-lived Ephemera, and communicate to each other the reflections which so singular an exhibition might rationally suggest to an inquisitive mind. Our place of observation is happily situated, under the protecting shade of majestic Live Oaks, glorious Magnolias and the fragrant Orange, open to the view of the great river, and still waters of the lagoon just before us.

At the cool eves approach, the sweet enchanting melody of the feathered songsters gradually ceases, and they betake themselves to their leafy coverts for security and repose.

Solemnly and slowly move onward, to the river's shore, the rustling clouds of the Ephemera. How awful the procession! innumerable millions of winged beings, voluntarily verging on to destruction, to the brink of the grave, where they behold bands of their enemies with wide open jaws, ready to receive them. But as if insensible of their danger, gay and tranquil each meets his beloved mate, in the still air, inimitably bedecked in their new nuptial robes. What eye can trace them, in their varied wanton amorous chaces, bounding and fluttering on the odoriferous air? with what peace, love and joy, do they end the last moments of their existence?

I think we may assert, without any fear of exaggeration, that there are annually of these beautiful winged beings, which rise into existence, and for a few moments take a transient view of the glory of the Creator's works, a number greater than the whole race of mankind that have ever existed since the creation; and that only, from the shores of this river. How many then must have been produced since the creation, when we consider the number of large rivers in America, in comparison with which, this river is but a brook or rivulet.

The importance of the existence of these beautiful and delicately formed little creatures, in the creation, whose frame and organization is equally wonderful, more delicate, and perhaps as complicated as that of the most perfect human being, is well worth a few moments contemplation; I mean particularly when they appear in the fly state. And if we consider the very short period, of that stage of existence, which we may reasonably suppose, to be the only space of their life that admits of pleasure and enjoyment, what a lesson doth it not afford us of the vanity of our own pursuits.

Their whole existence in this world, is but one compleat year, and at least three hundred and sixty days of that time, they are in the form of an ugly grub, buried in mud, eighteen inches under water, and in this condition scarcely locomotive, as each Larva or grub, has but its own narrow solitary cell, from which it never travels, or moves, but in a perpendicular progression, of a few inches, up and down, from the bottom to the surface of the mud, in order to intercept the passing atoms for its food, and get a momentary respiration of fresh air; and even here it must be perpetually on its guard, in order to escape the troops of fish and shrimps, watching to catch it, and from whom it has no escape, but by instantly retreating back into its cell. One would be apt almost to imagine them created merely for the food of fish and other animals.

[Salt Springs]

HOW GLORIOUS the powerful sun, minister of the Most High, in the rule and government of this earth, leaves our hemisphere, retiring from our sight beyond the western forests! I behold with gratitude his departing smiles, tinging the fleecy roseate clouds, now riding far away on the Eastern horizon; behold they vanish from sight in the azure skies!

All now silent and peaceable, I suddenly fell asleep. At midnight I awake; when raising my head erect, I find myself alone in the wilderness of Florida, on the shores of Lake George. Alone indeed, but under the care of the Almighty, and protected by the invisible hand of my guardian angel.

When quite awake, I started at the heavy tread of some animal, the dry limbs of trees upon the ground crack under his feet, the close shrubby thickets part and bend under him as he rushes off.

I rekindled up my sleepy fire, lay in contact the exfoliated smoking brands damp with the dew of heaven.

The bright flame ascends and illuminates the ground and groves around me. . . .

The morning being clear, I set sail with a favourable breeze, coasting along the shores; when on a sudden the waters became transparent, and discovered the sandy bottom, and the several nations of fish, passing and repassing each other. Following this course I was led to the cape of the little river, descending from Six mile Springs, and meandering six miles from its source, through green meadows. I entered this pellucid stream, sailing over the heads of innumerable squadrons of fish, which, although many feet deep in the water, were distinctly to be seen; I passed by charming islets of flourishing trees, as Palm, Red Bay, Ash, Maple, Nussa and others. As I approached the distant high forest on the main, the river widens, floating fields of the green Pistia surrounded me, the rapid stream winding through them. What an alluring scene was now before me! A vast bason or little lake of crystal waters, half encircled by swelling hills, clad with Orange and odoriferous Illisium groves. The towering Magnolia itself a grove, and the exalted Palm, as if conscious of their transcendent glories, tossed about their lofty heads, painting, with mutable shades, the green floating fields beneath. The social prattling coot enrobed in blue, and the squeeling water-hen, with wings half expanded, tripped after each other, over the watery mirror.

I put in at an ancient landing place, which is a sloping ascent to a level grassy plain, an old Indian field. As I intended to make my most considerable collections at this place, I proceeded immediately to fix my encampment but a few yards from my safe harbour, where I securely fastened my boat to a Live Oak which overshadowed my port.

After collecting a good quantity of fire-wood, as it was about the middle of the afternoon, I resolved to reconnoiter the ground about my encampment: having penetrated the groves next to me, I came to the open forests, consisting of exceedingly tall strait Pines (Pinus Palustris) that stood at a considerable distance from each other, through which appeared at N. W. an almost unlimited plain of grassy savannas, embellished with a chain of shallow ponds, as far as the sight could reach. Here is a species of Magnolia that associates with the Gordonia lasianthus; it is a tall tree, sixty or eighty feet in height; the trunk strait; its head terminating in the form of a sharp cone; the leaves are oblong, lanceolate, of a fine deep green, and glaucous beneath; the flowers are large, perfectly white and extremely fragrant; with respect to its flowers and leaves, it differs very little from the Magnolia glauca. The silvery whiteness of the leaves of this tree, had a striking and pleasing effect on the sight, as it stood amidst the dark green of the Quercus dentata, Nyssa sylvatica, Nys. aquatica, Gordonia lasianthus and many others of the same hue. The tall aspiring Gordonia lasianthus, which now stood in my view in all its splendour, is every way deserving of our admiration. Its thick foliage, of a dark green colour, is flowered over with large milk-white fragrant blossoms, on long slender elastic peduncles, at the extremities of its numerous branches, from the bosom of the leaves, and renewed every morning; and that in such incredible profusion, that the tree appears silvered over with them, and the ground beneath covered with the fallen flowers. It at the same time continually pushes forth new twigs, with young buds on them; and in the winter and spring the third year's leaves, now partly concealed by the new and perfect ones, are gradually changing colour, from green to golden yellow, from that to a scarlet, from scarlet to crimson; and lastly to a brownish purple, and then fall to the ground. So that the Gordonia lasianthus may be said to change and renew its garments every morning throughout the year; and every day appears with unfading lustre. . . .

On the left hand of those open forests and savannas, as we turn our eyes Southward, South-west and West, we behold an endless wild desert, the upper stratum of the earth of which is a fine white sand, with small pebbles, and at some distance appears entirely covered with low trees and shrubs of various kinds, and of equal height. . . .

I now directed my steps towards my encampment, in a different direction. I seated myself upon a swelling green knoll, at the head of the crystal bason. Near me, on the left, was a point or projection of an entire grove of the aromatic Illisium Floridanum; on my right and all around behind me, was a fruitful Orange grove, with Palms and Magnolias interspersed; in front, just under my feet was the inchanting and amazing crystal fountain, which incessantly threw up, from dark, rocky caverns below, tons of water every minute, forming a bason, capacious enough for large shallops to ride in, and a creek of four or five feet depth of water, and near twenty yards over, which meanders six miles through green meadows, pouring its limpid waters into the great Lake George, where they seem to remain pure and unmixed. About twenty yards from the upper edge of the bason, and directly opposite to the mouth or outlet to the creek, is a continual and amazing ebullition, where the waters are thrown up in such abundance and amazing force, as to jet and swell up two or three feet above the common surface: white sand and small particles of shells are thrown up with the waters, near to the top, when they diverge from the center, subside with the expanding flood, and gently sink again, forming a large rim or funnel round about the aperture or mouth of the fountain, which is a vast perforation through a bed of rocks, the ragged points of which are projected out on every side. Thus far I know to be matter of real fact, and I have related it as near as I could conceive or express myself. But there are yet remaining scenes inexpressibly admirable and pleasing.

Behold, for instance, a vast circular expanse before you, the waters of which are so extremely clear as to be absolutely diaphanous or transparent as the ether; the margin of the bason ornamented with a great variety of fruitful and floriferous trees, shrubs and plants, the pendant golden Orange dancing on the surface of the pellucid waters, the balmy air vibrates the melody of the merry birds, tenants of the encircling aromatic grove.

At the same instant innumerable bands of fish are seen, some cloathed in the most brilliant colours; the voracious crocodile stretched along at full length, as the great trunk of a tree in size, the devouring garfish, inimical trout, and all the varieties of gilded painted bream, the barbed catfish, dreaded sting-ray, skate and flounder, spotted bass, sheeps head and ominous drum; all in their separate bands and communities, with free and unsuspicious intercourse performing their evolutions: there are no signs of enmity, no attempt to devour each other; the different bands seem peaceably and complaisantly to move a little aside, as it were to make room for others to pass by.

But behold yet something far more admirable, see whole armies descending into an abyss, into the mouth of the bubbling fountain, they disappear! are they gone forever? is it real? I raise my eyes with terror and astonishment,—I look down again to the fountain with anxiety, when behold them as it were emerging from the blue ether of another world, apparently at a vast distance, at their first appearance, no bigger than flies or minnows, now gradually enlarging, their brilliant colours begin to paint the fluid.

Now they come forward rapidly, and instantly emerge, with the elastic expanding column of crystalline waters, into the circular bason or funnel, see now how gently they rise, some upright, others obliquely, or seem to lay as it were on their sides, suffering themselves to be gently lifted or born up, by the expanding fluid towards the surface, sailing or floating like butterflies in the cerulean ether: then again they as gently descend, diverge and move off; when they rally, form again and rejoin their kindred tribes.

This amazing and delightful scene, though real, appears at first but as a piece of excellent painting; there seems no medium, you imagine the picture to be within a few inches of your eyes, and that you may without the least difficulty touch any one of the fish, or put your finger upon the crocodile's eye, when it really is twenty or thirty feet under water.

And although this paradise of fish, may seem to exhibit a just representation of the peaceable and happy state of nature which existed before the fall, yet in reality it is a mere representation; for the nature of the fish is the same as if they were in lake George or the river; but here the water or element in which they live and move, is so perfectly clear and transparent, it places them all on an equality with regard to their ability to injure or escape from one another; (as all river fish of prey, or such as feed upon each other, as well as the unwieldy crocodile, take their prey by surprise; secreting themselves under covert or in ambush, until an opportunity offers, when they rush suddenly upon them:) but here is no covert, no ambush, here the trout freely passes by the very nose of the alligator and laughs in his face, and the bream by the trout.

But what is really surprising, that the consciousness of each others safety or some other latent cause, should so absolutely alter their conduct, for here is not the least attempt made to injure or disturb one another.

[A Sylvan Scene]

NEXT DAY AFTER MY ARRIVAL [at Cowee, North Carolina] I crossed the river in a canoe, on a visit to a trader who resided amongst the habitations on the other shore.

After dinner, on his mentioning some curious scenes amongst the hills, some miles distance from the river, we agreed to spend the afternoon in observations on the mountains.

After riding near two miles through Indian plantations of Corn, which was well cultivated, kept clean of weeds and was well advanced, being near eighteen inches in height, and the Beans planted at the Corn-hills were above ground; we leave the fields on our right, turning towards the mountains and ascending through a delightful green vale or lawn, which conducted us in amongst the pyramidal hills and crossing a brisk flowing creek, meandering through the meads which continued near two miles, dividing and branching in amongst the hills; we then mounted their steep ascents, rising gradually by ridges or steps one above another, frequently crossing narrow, fertile dales as we ascended; the air feels cool and animating, being charged with the fragrant breath of the mountain beauties, the blooming mountain cluster Rose, blushing Rhododendron and fair Lilly of the valley: having now attained the summit of this very elevated ridge, we enjoyed a fine prospect indeed; the enchanting Vale of Keowe, perhaps as celebrated for fertility, fruitfulness and beautiful prospects as the Fields of Pharsalia or the Vale of Tempe: the town, the elevated peaks of the Jore mountains, a very distant prospect of the Jore village in a beautiful lawn, lifted up many thousand feet higher than our present situation, besides a view of many other villages and settlements on the sides of the mountains, at various distances and elevations; the silver rivulets gliding by them and snow white cataracts glimmering on the sides of the lofty hills; the bold promontories of the Jore mountain stepping into the Tanase river, whilst his foaming waters rushed between them.

After viewing this very entertaining scene we began to descend the mountain on the other side, which exhibited the same order of gradations of ridges and vales as on our ascent, and at length rested on a very expansive, fertile plain, amidst the towering hills, over which we rode a long time, through magnificent high forests, extensive green fields, meadows and lawns. Here had formerly been a very flourishing settlement, but the Indians deserted it in search of fresh planting land, which they soon found in a rich vale but a few miles distance over a ridge of hills. Soon after entering on these charming, sequestered, prolific fields, we came to a fine little river, which crossing, and riding over fruitful strawberry beds and green lawns, on the sides of a circular ridge of hills in front of us, and going round the bases of this promontory, came to a fine meadow on an arm of the vale, through which meandered a brook, its humid vapours bedewing the fragrant strawberries which hung in heavy red clusters over the grassy verge; we crossed the rivulet, then rising a sloping, green, turfy ascent, alighted on the borders of a grand forest of stately trees, which we penetrated on foot a little distance to a horse-stamp, where was a large squadron of those useful creatures, belonging to my friend and companion, the trader, on the sight of whom they assembled together from all quarters; some at a distance saluted him with shrill neighings of gratitude, or came prancing up to lick the salt out of his hand; whilst the younger and more timorous came galloping onward, but coyly wheeled off, and fetching a circuit stood aloof, but as soon as their lord and master strewed the crystalline salty bait on the hard beaten ground, they all, old and young, docile and timorous, soon formed themselves in ranks and fell to licking up the delicious morsel.

It was a fine sight; more beautiful creatures I never saw; there were of them of all colours, sizes and dispositions. Every year as they become of age he sends off a troop of them down to Charleston, where they are sold to the highest bidder.

Having paid our attention to this useful part of the creation, who, if they are under our dominion, have consequently a right to our protection and favour, we returned to our trusty servants that were regaling themselves in the exuberant sweet pastures and strawberry fields in sight, and mounted again; proceeding on our return to town, continued through part of this high forest skirting on the meadows; began to ascend the hills of a ridge which we were under the necessity of crossing, and having gained its summit, enjoyed a most enchanting view, a vast expanse of green meadows and strawberry fields; a meandering river gliding through, saluting in its various turnings the swelling, green, turfy knolls, embellished with parterres of flowers and fruitful strawberry beds; flocks of turkeys strolling about them; herds of deer prancing in the meads or bounding over the hills; companies of young, innocent Cherokee virgins, some busily gathering the rich fragrant fruit, others having already filled their baskets, lay reclined under the shade of floriferous and fragrant native bowers of Magnolia, Azalea, Philadelphus, perfumed Calycanthus, sweet Yellow Jessamine and cerulian Glycine frutescens, disclosing their beauties to the fluttering breeze, and bathing their limbs in the cool fleeting streams; whilst other parties, more gay and libertine, were yet collecting strawberries or wantonly chasing their companions, tantalising them, staining their lips and cheeks with the rich fruit.

This sylvan scene of primitive innocence was enchanting, and perhaps too enticing for hearty young men long to continue idle spectators.

In fine, nature prevailing over reason, we wished at least to have a more active part in their delicious sports. Thus precipitately resolving, we cautiously made our approaches, yet undiscovered, almost to the joyous scene of action. Now, although we meant no other than an innocent frolic with this gay assembly of hamadryades, we shall leave it to the person of feeling and sensibility to form an idea to what lengths our passions might have hurried us, thus warmed and excited, had it not been for the vigilance and care of some envious matrons who lay in ambush, and espying us gave the alarm, time enough for the nymphs to rally and assemble together; we however pursued and gained ground on a group of them, who had incautiously strolled to a greater distance from their guardians, and finding their retreat now like to be cut off, took shelter under cover of a little grove, but on perceiving themselves to be discovered by us, kept their station, peeping through the bushes; when observing our approaches, they confidently discovered themselves and decently advanced to meet us, half unveiling their blooming faces, incarnated with the modest maiden blush, and with native innocence and cheerfulness, presented their baskets, merrily telling us their fruit was ripe and sound.

We accepted a basket, sat down and regaled ourselves on the delicious fruit, encircled by the whole assembly of the innocently jocose sylvan nymphs; by this time the several parties under the conduct of the elder matrons, had disposed themselves in companies on the green, turfy banks.

My young companion, the trader, by concessions and suitable apologies for the bold intrusion, having compromised the matter with them, engaged them to bring their collections to his house at a stipulated price, we parted friendly.

And now taking leave of these Elysian fields, we again mounted the hills, which we crossed, and traversing obliquely their flowery beds, arrived in town in the cool of the evening.

1791

Thomas Jefferson

From Notes on Virginia

Like his contemporaries Franklin and Bartram, Jefferson had a versatile, wide-ranging mind, especially for "useful truths," and, like Robert Beverley, a member of the Virginia aristocracy, he had the means and the leisure for nature study. In addition to forty years of political life, he designed and built a house and a formal garden on his Virginia plantation, Monticello (10,000 acres, 200 slaves). Having studied natural science under Dr. William Small at William and Mary, he experimented in agriculture, and made field trips for purposes of geography, botany, and paleontology. He periodically kept detailed records of natural phenomena on his plantation and elsewhere in Virginia, and from the records he composed *Notes on Virginia,* first published in Paris in 1784. The excerpts are from Queries IV and V.

[The Confluence of the Shenandoah and Potomac Rivers]

FOR THE PARTICULAR GEOGRAPHY of our mountains I must refer to Fry and Jefferson's map of Virginia; and to Evans's analysis of his map of America, for a more philosophical view of them than is to be found in any other work. It is worthy of notice, that our mountains are not solitary and scattered confusedly over the face of the country; but that they commence at about one hundred and fifty miles from the sea-coast, are disposed in ridges, one behind another, running nearly parallel with the sea-coast, though rather approaching it as they advance northeastwardly. To the south-west, as the tract of country between the sea-coast and the Mississippi becomes narrower, the mountains converge into a single ridge, which, as it approaches the Gulf of Mexico, subsides into plain country, and gives rise to some of the waters of that gulf, and particularly to a river called the Apalachicola, probably from the Apalachies, an Indian nation formerly residing on it. Hence the mountains giving rise to that river, and seen from its various parts, were called the Apalachian mountains, being in fact the end or termination only of the great ridges passing through the continent. European geographers, however, extended the name northwardly as far as the mountains extended; some giving it, after their separation into different ridges, to the Blue Ridge, others to the North Mountain, others to the Alleghany, others to the Laurel Ridge, as may be seen by their different maps. But the fact

I believe is, that none of these ridges were ever known by that name to the inhabitants, either native or emigrant, but as they saw them so called in European maps. In the same direction, generally, are the veins of limestone, coal, and other minerals hitherto discovered; and so range the falls of our great rivers. But the courses of the great rivers are at right angles with these. James and Potomac penetrate through all the ridges of mountains eastward of the Alleghany; that is broken by no water course. It is in fact the spine of the country between the Atlantic on one side, and the Mississippi and St. Lawrence on the other. The passage of the Potomac through the Blue Ridge is, perhaps, one of the most stupendous scenes in nature. You stand on a very high point of land. On your right comes up the Shenandoah, having ranged along the foot of the mountain an hundred miles to seek a vent. On your left approaches the Potomac, in quest of a passage also. In the moment of their junction, they rush together against the mountain, rend it asunder, and pass off to the sea. The first glance of this scene hurries our senses into the opinion, that this earth has been created in time, that the mountains were formed first, that the rivers began to flow afterwards, that in this place, particularly, they have been dammed up by the Blue Ridge of mountains, and have formed an ocean which filled the whole valley; that continuing to rise they have at length broken over at this spot, and have torn the mountain down from its summit to its base. The piles of rock on each hand, but particularly on the Shenandoah, the evident marks of their disrupture and avulsion from their beds by the most powerful agents of nature, corroborate the impression. But the distant finishing which nature has given to the picture is of a very different character. It is a true contrast to the foreground. It is as placid and delightful as that is wild and tremendous. For the mountain being cloven asunder, she presents to your eye, through the cleft, a small catch of smooth blue horizon, at an infinite distance in the plain country, inviting you, as it were, from the riot and tumult roaring around, to pass through the breach and participate of the calm below. Here the eye ultimately composes itself; and that way, too, the road happens actually to lead. You cross the Potomac above the junction, pass along its side through the base of the mountain for three miles, its terrible precipices hanging in fragments over you, and within about twenty miles reach Frederic town, and the fine country round that. This scene is worth a voyage across the Atlantic. Yet here, as in the neighborhood of the Natural Bridge, are people who have passed their lives within half a dozen miles, and have never been to survey these monuments of a war between rivers and mountains, which must have shaken the earth itself to its centre.

The height of our mountains has not yet been estimated with any degree of exactness. The Alleghany being the great ridge which divides the waters of the Atlantic from those of the Mississippi, its summit is doubtless more elevated above the ocean than that of any other mountain. But its relative height, compared with the base on which it stands, is not so great as that of some others, the country rising behind the successive ridges like the steps of stairs. The mountains of the Blue Ridge, and of these the Peaks of Otter, are thought to be of a greater height, measured from their base, than any others in our country, and perhaps in North America. From data, which may found a tolerable conjecture, we suppose the highest peak to be about four thousand feet perpendicular, which is not a fifth part of the height of the mountains of South America, nor one-third of the height which would be necessary in our latitude to preserve ice in the open air unmelted through the year. The ridge of mountains next beyond the Blue Ridge, called by us the North mountain, is of the greatest extent; for which reason they were named by the Indians the Endless mountains.

A substance supposed to be pumice, found floating on the Mississippi, has induced a conjecture that there is a volcano on some of its waters; and as these are mostly known to their sources, except the Missouri, our expectations of verifying the conjecture would of course be led to the mountains which divide the waters of the Mexican Gulf from those of the South Sea; but no volcano having ever yet been known at such a distance from the sea, we must rather suppose that this floating substance has been erroneously deemed pumice.

[The Natural Bridge, Virginia]

. . . THE NATURAL BRIDGE, the most sublime of nature's works, though not comprehended under the present head, must not be pretermitted. It is on the ascent of a hill, which seems to have been cloven through its length by some great convulsion. The fissure, just at the bridge, is, by some admeasurements, two hundred and seventy feet deep, by others only two hundred and five. It is about forty-five feet wide at the bottom and ninety feet at the top; this of course determines the length of the bridge, and its height from the water. Its breadth in the middle is about sixty feet, but more at the ends, and the thickness of the mass, at the summit of the arch, about forty feet. A part of this thickness is constituted by a coat of earth, which gives growth to many large trees. The residue, with the hill on both sides, is one solid rock of limestone. The arch approaches the semi-elliptical form; but the larger axis of the ellipsis, which would be the cord of the arch, is many times longer than the transverse. Though the sides of this bridge are provided in some parts with a parapet of fixed rocks, yet few men have resolution to walk to them, and look over into the abyss. You involuntarily fall on your hands and feet, creep to the parapet, and peep over it. Looking down from this height about a minute gave me a violent head-ache. If the view from the top be painful and intolerable, that from below is delightful in an equal extreme. It is impossible for the emotions arising from the sublime to be felt beyond what they are here; so beautiful an arch, so elevated, so light, and springing as it were up to heaven! The rapture of the spectator is really indescribable! The fissure continuing narrow, deep, and straight, for a considerable distance above and below the bridge, opens a short but very pleasing view of the North mountain on one side, and the Blue Ridge on the other, at the distance each of them of about five miles. This bridge is in the county of Rockbridge, to which it has given name, and affords a public and commodious passage over a valley which cannot be crossed elsewhere for a considerable distance. The stream passing under it is called Cedar creek. It is a water of James river, and sufficient in the driest seasons to turn a grist-mill, though its fountain is not more than two miles above.

1784

The Poetry of Scene

An American Grand Tour

In the late eighteenth century and on into the nineteenth, the growing taste for natural scenery had two expressions. On the one hand (in England more than in America), people of cultivation began to create their own scenes in elaborately landscaped formal gardens and, on the other, they began to take tours (literally, circular journeys) without any specific object other than that of discovering sublime, beautiful, and picturesque "poetry" in natural landscapes, particularly wilderness landscapes. This poetry, this aesthetically pleasing fusion of mind and scenery, they sought, as William Gilpin wrote, "among all ingredients of the landscape—trees—rocks—broken-grounds, woods—rivers—lakes—plains—vallies—mountains—and distances." In Europe, the Grand Tour in quest of these and other "ingredients" became part of a young person's education. Toting Claude glasses, which framed and tinted the vistas they found, and journals or sketchbooks, in which they recorded their rapt impressions, they made their pilgrimages to the Alps, the Rhine, the Italian lakes.

By the third decade of the nineteenth century, it was possible to take an American version of the Grand Tour. The tour began with a sail up the Hudson (the "American Rhine") from New York City to Albany, a sail punctuated by stops at a series of vantage points, such as the one Nathaniel Willis describes at West Point, from which the river and the mountain scenery of the Catskills could be seen to best effect.

Albany was a junction. From there one could travel north to Lake George to behold the American version of Loch Katrine or Lake Como. To the west, the Erie Canal, which helped to usher in the age of tourism in America, had recently opened the region of northern New York all the way to Lake Erie and Niagara Falls, that sublimity of sublimities. From canal boats, as Hawthorne's sketch illustrates, the alternation of pastoral and wilderness landscapes became a sort of moving panorama, to be viewed at leisure from the comfort of a deck chair or dining table. The canal, wrote Melville in *Moby Dick,* flowed, like a "green-turfed flowery Nile,"

> for three hundred and sixty miles . . . through numerous populous cities and most thriving villages; through long, dismal, uninhabited swamps, and affluent, cultivated fields, unrivalled for fertility; . . . through the holy-of-holies of great forests; on Roman arches over Indian rivers; through sun and shade; by happy hearts or broken; through all the wide contrasting scenery of those noble Mohawk counties. . . .

East from Albany, one traveled by railroad and stagecoach through the Berkshires to Mount Holyoke and the stunning river scenery of the Connecticut Oxbow. That scene, represented here by Dwight's verbal sketch and Thomas Cole's painting, was visited by about three thousand tourists in 1837 alone. From Mount Holyoke, the American tourist could travel north by stagecoach to New Hampshire and the White Mountains—the last and in many ways the crowning natural scenery on the Grand Tour, for until the Rockies were discovered, New Hampshire was America's Switzerland and the White Mountains, as Hawthorne's sketch implies, its nearest approximation of the Alps.

During the 1820's and 1830's, America's Grand Tour was the fulfillment of the Romantic traveler's dream. It abounded in everything he could desire of the poetry of scene: river, waterfall, and lake scenes; mountain vistas; forest, pastoral, and urban landscapes; and glimpses of the picturesque life of a cross-section of American society, from backwoodsmen, rivermen, farmers, and villagers to city folk. Here the traveler could experience the entire panoply of American progress from wilderness to civilization.

By the end of the 1830's, however, there were newer and more picturesque places to travel. Spreading west, railroads and steamers opened out more and more "new and highly interesting natural scenery." The irony was that the speed and comfort a railroad could offer the tourist lessened the capacity for experiencing a sublime scene. Or perhaps—as the conqueror of distance—technology was itself sublime, though in a way no lover of scenery could appreciate. At any rate, by the time Frémont came to explore the Rockies, he was not very far in the vanguard of the tourists or the trains.

PICTURESQUE SCENERY AND THE ART OF THE SKETCH

In natural landscapes as in art, the ideal of beauty gave value to symmetry and luxuriance and the ideal of sublimity gave value to vastness and power. As men of sensibility thought about it, however, few landscapes seemed pure embodiments of these values. In the New World particularly, pastoral landscapes seemed still too rough to be beautiful but too tame to be sublime; wilderness landscape seemed to embody not one or the other ideal but complex combinations of both: luxuriance and power, symmetry and discontinuity. The ideal which embraced the rough, the complex, and the discontinuous in landscape, the ideal which came more and more to include both beauty and sublimity, was that of the *picturesque.*

The picturesque was a visual more than an emotional impressionism, and one of its most important literary functions was to temper the sensationalism which the sublime had given rise to. It focused more on the composition of the scene than on the viewer's sensibility. In its attention to surfaces, it demanded a painterly eye—an eye that could disassociate the traditional meaning of an object from its appearance; an eye that could focus on an object's appearance and its relation to other appearances in the landscape. The language of the picturesque is basically a language of color, texture, and light.

In literature, however, the picturesque was not a *purely* visual impressionism. A contemporary critic, Martin Price, characterizes one of its leading features as that of "play." Visually, play refers to the plasticity of an object (the degree of curve or give to it), or to the relative lightness of an object, or to the texture of light and shadow (the "play" of light). But the term "play" also refers to an activity of the mind. Mental play, such as the picturesque gave rise to, could perceive familiar things in strikingly unfamiliar ways and vice versa; it could find pleasure in such unpleasant and grotesque things as ruins and follies; and, most important, it could strike into motion the faculties of wit or of fancy—those faculties which make strikingly novel connections, whether by metaphor or by association, between landscape and ideas.

The organic form of the picturesque was, of course, the sketch, whether painterly or verbal. Tentative, unfinished, concerned only with catching the "general outline" and the "leading features" of a landscape, the sketch is a medium that is cool enough, plastic enough, to harbor the spirit of play in both of its meanings. Critics of the picturesque distinguished three kinds of sketches. The rough sketch (Willis's, for example), traced in a notebook or sketchbook by a traveler at the scene, ignored the effect of light and concentrated instead on the general lay of the landscape and on the significant details of its primary forms. The finished or "adorned" sketch (Hawthorne's and James's, for example), executed retrospectively, attended more closely to matters of composition, expression, and lighting effect. These matters it left as much to artistic license as to accurate and detailed observation, for even in the finished sketch there was room, as Poe would write, "for general ideas only"; there was no room at all for "mere Flemish devotion to matter of fact." The third kind of sketch, the "scene of fancy," begins not as an observed landscape but as a dream-like mood projected into an imagined landscape. The scene of fancy (Poe's "Island of the Fay," for example) gathered "the most admirable parts of nature" and recomposed them according to the rules of art and the demands of the mood; it was an invitation to symbolic or, more often, to allegorical reading.

The picturesque sketch concerns itself with three painterly principles: those of composition, expression, and effect. According to Gilpin, whose definitions held good for American painters and writers up until the Civil War, *composition* is a matter chiefly of cosmetically repairing those areas (ugly lines, bald spots) where the lines of nature "run false." Even more important, it is a way of giving shape and access to the landscape by way of a foreground, whose function "resembles those deep tones in music, which gives a value to all the lighter parts; and harmonize the whole." The foreground projects the dominant mood and motif and acts as a kind of frame or filter through which the eye passes to the middle and background, which extend and elaborate. In the verbal sketch, a frame image or a dominant impression can serve the function of a foreground.

Expression is the art of organically adapting form to subject: "the art of giving each object, that particular touch, whether smooth or rough, which best expresses its form." Expression is a matter of texture—of the quality and play of the lines which render the landscape. In Romantic literature, particularly in poetry, concern for expression gave rise to the notion of organic form.

The principle of *effect,* finally, includes not only the "simple illumination of objects" but, more important, the balancing of "large masses" of light and shadow. Effect is the art of determining where in the sketch "the full tone of shade must prevail—where the full effusion of light—or where the various degrees of each." It is the principle by which the artist of the picturesque achieves a tenuous unity of impression over his complex and shifting landscape. And that unity of impression was what writers as different as Emerson and Poe were searching for when they began attending with great care to the quality and play of light in landscape. They discovered in their own ways the profound analogy between play of light and play of vision, the quality of shadow and the quality of mood and meditation. The sky became "the soul of scenery" and its emanations could be seen as emanations of divine being as well as of light, the being existing like the light in a spectrum which ranged from the brightly benevolent to the darkly sublime. To these emanations, the visionary artist could join the sympathetic emanations of his own soul.

THE AMERICANIZATION OF THE SUBLIME AND THE PICTURESQUE

"If the admirer of nature can turn his amusements to a higher purpose," wrote Gilpin, "if its scenes can inspire him with religious awe . . . it is so much the better." But the picturesque was still at base an art of the eye, and "the eye . . . has nothing to do with moral sentiments, and is conversant with visible forms." As the travelers represented in this section practiced it (Hawthorne and James excepted), the poetry of scene remained largely an art of the eye. When they did aspire to a "higher purpose," that purpose usually had to do with the resolution of a national inferiority complex. As a matter of national pride, Americans had to find a way of matching, if not surpassing, the aesthetic resources of Europe, and the resource they settled on was landscape.

The concepts of the sublime and the picturesque in landscape, however, were themselves European concepts rooted in European landscapes, and American landscapes seemed not to measure up to their standards. American mountains (the Adirondacks, the White Mountains, and the Green Mountains) could not, as Thomas Cole observed, "vie in altitude with the snow-crowned Alps"; and furthermore they were "generally clothed to the summit by dense forests, while those of Europe are mostly bare, or merely tinted by grass or heath" and "are on this account more picturesque in form, and there is a grandeur in their nakedness." "The great defect in American lakes," wrote Nathaniel Willis, was that unlike the lakes of England or Italy they tend to fatigue the eye with a "vast, unrelieved expanse of water, without islands and promontories" (Lake George was a magnificent exception).

What finally relieved American travelers of their inferiority complex was the discovery of two unmatchable qualities which seemed to make up for all the defects in the landscapes of the American Grand Tour. One quality was energy: a sublime kinetic energy, as in Niagara Falls, or an equally sublime potential energy, as in the "utter and unbroken solitude" of the wilderness, over which (Cole wrote at Franconia Notch, New Hampshire) "brooded the spirit of repose, and the silent energy of nature stirred the soul to its inmost depths." The other quality was that of a pristine—an Edenic—freshness and brilliance in the water, the air, and especially the light. The "purity and transparency" of American lakes and rivers, for example, was for Cole, as it was for other less artful travelers, "a circumstance which greatly contributes to the beauty of landscape; for the reflections of surrounding objects, trees, mountains, sky, are most perfect in the clearest water; and the most perfect is the most beautiful."

Nathaniel Willis

View from West Point

"View from West Point" and the two sketches of Lake George and its environs, which appear later in this section, are from Willis's *American Scenery* (2 vols. London, 1840). The book is illustrated with plates made from drawings by William Bartlett, an English draughtsman, who made an American tour with Willis in 1837 and 1838—the one making verbal, the other linear, sketches of memorable landscapes. To his sketches Willis often added local legends and histories in an attempt to lend a degree of human association to the landscape, if not to make it a scene in "the great theater of human events." Cooper's panorama (see Landscape into Art) gives another view of Lake George at an epic moment in its history.

OF THE RIVER SCENERY of America, the Hudson, at West Point, is doubtless the boldest and most beautiful. This powerful river writhes through the highlands in abrupt curves, reminding one, when the tide runs strongly down, of Laocoon in the enlacing folds of the serpent. The different spurs of mountain ranges which meet here, abut upon the river in bold precipices from five to fifteen hundred feet from the water's edge; the foliage hangs to them, from base to summit, with the tenacity and bright verdure of moss; and the stream below, deprived of the slant lights which brighten its depths elsewhere, flows on with a sombre and dark green shadow in its bosom, as if frowning at the narrow gorge into which its broad-breasted waters are driven.

Back from the bluff of West Point extends a natural platform of near half a mile square, high, level, and beautifully amphitheatred with wood and rock. This is the site of the Military Academy, and a splendid natural parade. When the tents of the summer camp are shining on the field—the flag, with its blood-bright stripes, waving against the foliage of the hills—the trumpet echoing from bluff to bluff, and the compact batallion cutting its trice-line across the green-sward—there are few more fairy spots in this working-day world.

On the extreme edge of the summit, overlooking the river, stands a marble shaft, pointing like a bright finger to glory, the tomb of the soldier and patriot Kosciusko. The military colleges and other buildings skirt the parade on the side of the mountain; and forward, toward the river, on the western edge, stands a spacious hotel, from the verandahs of which the traveller gets a view through the highlands, that he remembers till he dies. Right up before him, with the smooth curve of an eagle's ascent, rises the "old cro' nest" of the culprit Fay, a bright green mountain, that thrusts its topmost pine into the sky; the Donderbarrak, or (if it is not sacrilege to translate so fine a name for a mountain,) the *Thunder-chamber,* heaves its round shoulder beyond; back from the opposite shore, as if it recoiled from these, leans the bold cliff of Breknock; and then looking out, as if from a cavern, into the sun-light, the eye drops beyond upon a sheet of wide-spreading water, with an emerald island in its bosom; the white buildings of Newburgh creeping back to the plains beyond, and in the far, far distance, the wavy and blue line of the Kattskills, as if it were the dim-seen edge of an outer horizon.

The passage through the highlands at West Point still bears the old name of Wey-gat, or Wind-gate; and one of the prettiest moving dioramas conceivable, is the working through the gorge of the myriad sailing-craft of the river. The sloops which ply upon the Hudson, by the way, are remarkable for their picturesque beauty, and for the enormous quantity of sail they carry on in all weathers; and nothing is more beautiful than the little fleets of from six to a dozen, all tacking or scudding together, like so many white sea-birds on the wing. Up they come, with a dashing breeze, under Anthony's Nose, and the Sugar-Loaf, and giving the rocky toe of West Point a wide berth, all down helm, and round into the bay; when—just as the peak of Crow Nest slides its shadow over the mainsail—slap comes the wind aback, and the whole fleet is in a flutter. The channel is narrow and serpentine, the wind baffling, and small room to beat; but the little craft are worked merrily and well; and dodging about, as if to escape some invisible imp in the air, they gain point after point, till at last they get the Donderbarrak behind them, and fall once more into the regular current of the wind.

1840

Nathaniel Hawthorne

From The Canal Boat

During the 1830's, Hawthorne made it a practice to take an annual summer "excursion of a few weeks." Three notable excursions were to the White Mountains (1832), the Berkshires in western Massachusetts (1838; there are many landscape sketches from this trip in his *American Notebooks*), and to Ticonderoga, Niagara Falls, and perhaps Detroit (1833 or 1834). From the latter came "My Visit to Niagara," "Sketches from Memory" (1835), and "Old Ticonderoga" (1836). This excerpt is from one of the "Sketches from Memory," which appeared in *Mosses from an Old Manse* (1846).

I WAS INCLINED to be poetical about the Grand Canal. In my imagination De Witt Clinton was an enchanter, who had waved his magic wand from the Hudson to Lake Erie and united them by a watery highway, crowded with the commerce of two worlds, till then inaccessible to each other. This simple and mighty conception had conferred inestimable value on spots which Nature seemed to have thrown carelessly into the great body of the earth, without foreseeing that they could ever attain importance. I pictured the surprise of the sleepy Dutchmen when the new river first glittered by their doors, bringing them hard cash or foreign commodities in exchange for their hitherto unmarketable produce. Surely the water of this canal must be the most fertilizing of all fluids; for it causes towns, with their masses of brick and stone, their churches and theatres, their business and hubbub, their luxury and refinement, their gay dames and polished citizens, to spring up, till in time the wondrous stream may flow between two continuous lines of buildings, through one thronged street, from Buffalo to Albany. I embarked about thirty miles below Utica, determining to voyage along the whole extent of the canal at least twice in the course of the summer.

Behold us, then, fairly afloat, with three horses harnessed to our vessel, like the steeds of Neptune to a huge scallop shell in mythological pictures. Bound to a distant port, we had neither chart nor compass, nor cared about the wind, nor felt the heaving of a billow, nor dreaded shipwreck, however fierce the tempest, in our adventurous navigation of an interminable mud puddle; for a mud puddle it seemed, and as dark and turbid as if every kennel in the land paid contribution to it. With an imperceptible current, it holds its drowsy way through all the dismal swamps and unimpressive scenery that could be found between the great lakes and the sea-coast. Yet there is variety enough, both on the surface of the canal and along its banks, to amuse the traveller, if an overpowering tedium did not deaden his perceptions.

Sometimes we met a black and rusty-looking vessel, laden with lumber, salt from Syracuse, or Genesee flour, and shaped at both ends like a square-toed boot, as if it had two sterns, and were fated always to advance backward. On its deck would be a square hut, and a woman seen through the window at her household work, with a little tribe of children, who perhaps had been born in this strange dwelling and knew no other home. Thus, while the husband smoked his pipe at the helm, and the eldest son rode one of the horses, on went the family, traveling hundreds of miles in their own house and carrying their fireside with them. The most frequent species of craft were the "line boars," which had a cabin at each end, and a great bulk of barrels, bales, and boxes in the midst, or light packets, like our own, decked all over with a row of curtained windows from stem to stern, and a drowsy face at every one. Once we encountered a boat of rude construction, painted all in gloomy black, and manned by three Indians, who gazed at us in silence and with a singular fixedness of eye. Perhaps these three alone, among the ancient possessors of the land, had attempted to derive benefit from the white man's mighty projects and float along the current of his enterprise. . . .

Had I been on my feet at the time instead of sailing slowly along in a dirty canal boat, I should often have paused to contemplate the diversified panorama along the banks of the canal. Sometimes the scene was a forest, dark, dense, and impervious, breaking away occasionally and receding from a lonely tract, covered with dismal black stumps where, on the verge of the canal, might be seen a log cottage and a sallow-faced woman at the window. Lean and aguish, she looked like poverty personified, half-clothed, half-fed, and dwelling in a desert, while a tide of wealth was sweeping by her door. Two or three miles farther would bring us to a lock, where the slight impediment to navigation had created a little mart of trade. Here would be found commodities of all sorts, enumerated in yellow letters on the window shutters of a small grocery store, the owner of which had set his soul to the gathering of coppers and small change, buying and selling through the week, and counting his gains on the blessed Sabbath. The next scene might be the dwelling-houses and stores of a thriving village, built of wood or small gray stones, a church spire rising in the midst, and generally two taverns, bearing over their piazzas the pompous titles of "hotel," "exchange," "tontine," or "coffee-house." Passing on, we glide now into the unquiet heart of an inland city,—of Utica, for instance,—and find ourselves amid piles of brick, crowded docks and quays, rich warehouses, and a busy population. We feel the eager and hurrying spirit of the place, like a stream and eddy whirling us along with it. Through the thickest of the tumult goes the canal, flowing between lofty rows of buildings and arched bridges of hewn stone. Onward, also, go we, till the hum and bustle of struggling enterprise die away behind us and we are threading an avenue of the ancient woods again.

This sounds not amiss in description, but was so tiresome in reality that we were driven to the most childish expedients for amusement. An English traveller paraded the deck, with a rifle in his walking stick, and waged war on squirrels and woodpeckers, sometimes sending an unsuccessful bullet among flocks of tame ducks and geese which abound in the dirty water of the canal. I, also, pelted these foolish birds with apples, and smiled at the ridiculous earnestness of their scrambles for the prize while the apple bobbed about like a thing of life. . . .

The crimson curtain being let down between the ladies and gentlemen, the cabin became a bedchamber for twenty persons, who were laid on shelves one above another. For a long time our various incommodities kept us all awake except five or six, who were accustomed to sleep nightly amid the uproar of their own snoring, and had little to dread from any other species of disturbance. . . .

Finally all was hushed in that quarter. Still I was more broad awake than through the whole preceding day, and felt a feverish impulse to toss my limbs miles apart and appease the unquietness of mind by that of matter. Forgetting that my berth was hardly so wide as a coffin, I turned suddenly over, and fell like an avalanche on the floor, to the disturbance of the whole community of sleepers. As there were no bones broken, I blessed the accident and went on deck. A lantern was burning at each end of the boat, and one of the crew was stationed at the bows, keeping watch as mariners do on the ocean. Though the rain had ceased, the sky was all one cloud, and the darkness so intense that there seemed to be no world except the little space on which our lantern glimmered. Yet it was an impressive scene.

We were traversing the "long level," a dead flat between Utica and Syracuse, where the canal has not rise or fall enough to require a lock for nearly seventy miles. There can hardly be a more dismal tract of country. The forest which covers it consisting chiefly of white cedar, black ash, and other trees that live in excessive moisture, is now decayed and death-struck by the partial draining of the swamp into the great ditch of the canal. Sometimes, indeed, our lights were reflected from pools of stagnant water which stretched far in among the trunks of the trees, beneath dense masses of dark foliage. But generally the tall stems and intermingled branches were naked, and brought into strong relief amid the surrounding gloom by the whiteness of their decay. Often we beheld the prostrate form of some old sylvan giant which had fallen and crushed down smaller trees under its immense ruin. In spots where destruction had been riotous, the lanterns showed perhaps a hundred trunks, erect, half overthrown, extended along the ground, resting on their shattered limbs or tossing them desperately into the darkness, but all of one ashy white, all naked together, in desolate confusion. Thus growing out of the night as we drew nigh, and vanishing as we glided on, based on obscurity, and overhung and bounded by it, the scene was ghostlike—the very land of unsubstantial things, whither dreams might betake themselves when they quit the slumberer's brain.

My fancy found another emblem. The wild nature of America had been driven to this desert-place by the encroachments of civilized man. And even here, where the savage queen was throned on the ruins of her empire, did we penetrate, a vulgar and worldly throng, intruding on her latest solitude. In other lands decay sits among fallen palaces; but here her home is in the forests.

Looking ahead, I discerned a distant light, announcing the approach of another boat, which soon passed us, and proved to be a rusty old scow—just such a craft as the "Flying Dutchman" would navigate on the canal. Perhaps it was that celebrated personage himself whom I imperfectly distinguished at the helm, in a glazed cap and rough greatcoat, with a pipe in his mouth, leaving the fumes of tobacco a hundred yards behind. Shortly after our boatman blew a horn, sending a long and melancholy note through the forest avenue, as a signal for some watcher in the wilderness to be ready with a change of horses. We had proceeded a mile or two with our fresh team when the tow rope got entangled in a fallen branch on the edge of the canal and caused a momentary delay, during which I went to examine the phosphoric light of an old tree a little within the forest. It was not the first delusive radiance that I had followed.

The tree lay along the ground, and was wholly converted into a mass of diseased splendor, which threw a ghastliness around. Being full of conceits that night, I called it a frigid fire, a funeral light, illumining decay and death, an emblem of fame that gleams around the dead man without warming him, or of genius when it owes its brilliancy to moral rottenness, and was thinking that such ghostlike torches were just fit to light up this dead forest or to blaze coldly in tombs, when, starting from my abstraction, I looked up the canal. I recollected myself, and discovered the lanterns glimmering far away.

"Boat ahoy!" shouted I, making a trumpet of my closed fists.

Though the cry must have rung for miles along that hollow passage of the woods, it produced no effect. These packet boats make up for their snail-like pace by never loitering day nor night, especially for those who have paid their fare. Indeed, the captain had an interest in getting rid of me, for I was his creditor for a breakfast.

"They are gone, Heaven be praised!" ejaculated I; "for I cannot possibly overtake them. Here am I, on the 'long level,' at midnight, with the comfortable prospect of a walk to Syracuse, where my baggage will be left. And now to find a house or shed wherein to pass the night." So thinking aloud, I took a flambeau from the old tree, burning, but consuming not, to light my steps withal, and, like a jack-o'-the-lantern, set out on my midnight tour.

1846

Horatio Parsons

From The Book of Niagara Falls

Parsons's guide book to Niagara Falls, part of the literature spawned by the Romantic vogue of tourism—a literature which included sketchbooks, gift books, summer books, travelogues, poems, and essays, came handily pocket-sized.

THE FALLS—TERRAPIN BRIDGE AND TOWER

THE BROAD RIVER, as it comes thundering and foaming down the declivity of the rapids, at length leaps the cataract, three-fourths of a mile in width, and falls, as it were, to the central caves of the earth. The mind, filled with amazement, recoils at the spectacle, and loses for a moment, its equilibrium. The trembling of the earth, the mighty rush and conflict and deafening roar of the water, the clouds of mist sparkling with rainbows, produce an effect upon the beholder, often quite overpowering; and it is only after the scene has become somewhat familiar to the eye, the ear, and the imagination, that its real grandeur and sublimity is properly realized and felt. . . .

The water on the American side, as ascertained by frequent measurement, falls 164 feet, and on the Canada side, 158 feet. The fall on the Canada side, embracing much the largest channel of the river, is called, from the shape of the precipice, the "Crescent or Horse-shoe Fall," and near to this a bridge, called the Terrapin Bridge, has been constructed, 300 feet in length, from Goat Island, and projecting ten feet over the Falls. Near the termination of this bridge, in the water, and on the very verge of the precipice, a stone tower, forty-five feet high, with winding steps to the top, was erected in the year 1833, from which, or from the end of the bridge, the effect of the Falls upon the beholder is most awfully sublime and utterly indescribable. The sublime, arising from obscurity, is here experienced in its greatest force. The eye, unable to discover the bottom of the Falls, or even to penetrate the mist that seems to hang as a veil over the amazing and terrific scene, gives place to the imagination, and the mind is instinctively elevated and filled with majestic dread. Here is

"All that expands the spirit, yet appals."

"It seems to be the good pleasure of God, that men shall learn his Omnipotence by evidence addressed to the senses as well as the understanding, and that there shall be on earth continual illustrations of his mighty power; of creation we are ascertained by faith, not by sight; the heavenly bodies, though vast, are distant, and roll silently in their courses. But the earth by its quakings, the volcano by its fires, the ocean by its mountain waves, and the floods of Niagara by the majesty of their power and ceaseless thunderings, proclaim to the eye, and to the ear, and to the heart, the omnipotence of God. From these far distant sources and multitudinous dispersions, He called them into the capacious reservoirs of the north, and bid them hasten their accumulating tide to this scene of wonders, and for ages the obedient waters have rolled and thundered his praise.

"In beholding this deluge of created Omnipotence, the thought, how irresistible is the displeasure of God, rushes upon the soul. It requires but a little aid of the imagination to behold in this ceaseless flow of waters, the stream of His indignation, which shall beat upon the wicked, in the gulf below the eternal pit; and in the cloud of exhalation, the smoke of their torment, which ascendeth up for ever and ever. With these associations, all is dark, terrific and dreadful, till from the midst of this darkness and these mighty thunderings, the bow, brilliant type of mercy, arises, and spreads its broad arch over the agitated waters, proclaiming that the Omnipotence which rolls the stream is associated with mercy as well as with justice." . . . .

The solar and lunar bows, the river above and below, and indeed the whole scenery of the Falls and rapids, appear to better advantage from this point than from any other; and no visiter on either side should presume to leave the Falls without visiting this tower and bridge. From the top of the tower especially, he will realize the force and beauty of the following description, which with the change of a single word, applies admirably to this matchless scene:

> "The roar of waters! From the headlong height
> *Niagara* cleaves the wave-worn precipice;
> The fall of waters! rapid as the light,
> The flashing mass foams shaking the abyss;
> The hell of waters! where they howl and hiss,
> And boil in endless torture; while the sweat
> Of their great agony, wrung out from this
> Their Phlegethon, curls round the rocks of jet
> That gird the gulf around, in pitiless horror set.
>
> And mounts in spray the skies, and thence again
> Returns in an unceasing shower, which round
> With its unemptied cloud of gentle rain
> Is an eternal April to the ground,
> Making it all one emerald;—how profound
> The gulf!—and how the giant element
> From rock to rock leaps with delirious bound,
> Crushing the cliffs, which downward worn and rent,
> With his fierce footsteps, yield in chasms a fearful vent.
>
> . . . .
> . . . . . . Look back!
> Lo! where it comes like an eternity,
> As if to sweep down all things in its track,
> Charming the eye with dread,—a matchless cataract,
> Horribly beautiful! but on the verge,
> From side to side, beneath the glittering morn,
> An Iris sits, amid the infernal surge,
> Like Hope upon a death-bed, and, unworn
> Its steady dies, while all around is torn
> By the distracted waters, bears serene
> Its brilliant hues with all their beams unshorn,
> Resembling, 'mid the torture of the scene,
> Love watching Madness with unalterable mien."

The lunar bow, seen at night, in the time of full moon, appears like a brightly illuminated arch, reaching from side to side, and is an object of great attraction,—especially as the world presents only a few other places where such a bow is ever seen,

> "Hung on the curling mist, the moonlight bow
> Arches the perilous river."

Goat Island, in a moonlight night, is the resort of great multitudes, where they find themselves introduced to a scene of unrivalled beauty and magnificence. The rapids at such a time sparkle with phosphoric splendor, and nature around wears an irresistible charm of loveliness. There is

"A silver light, which hallowing tree and tower,
Sheds beauty and deep softness o'er the whole."

The writer once had the pleasure of joining a lovely couple in marriage, about 11 o'clock on one of the brightest nights he has ever known, in full view of this enchanting scene, and then of taking a romantic excursion with the party around the island. This was poetry indeed; it was one of those bright and verdant oases sometimes met with in the journey of life. May all their days be equally bright and their rambles equally pleasant.

BIDDLE STAIRCASE—ÆOLUS' CAVE

At the lower end of Goat Island, about one-third across it, a stair-case, erected in the year 1829, at the expense of Nicholas Biddle, Esq., of Philadelphia, gives visiters an opportunity of descending below the bank and of passing a considerable distance behind the two main sheets of water. The descent from the top of the island to the margin of the river is 185 feet. A common flight of steps leads down 40 feet to the perpendicular spiral steps, 90 in number, which are enclosed in a building in the shape of a hexagon resting on a firm foundation at the bottom. From the foot of the building there are three paths leading to the most important points of observation, one of which leads to the river below, 80 feet, where visiters will find one of the finest fishing places in this part of the world. All the varieties of fish existing in Lake Ontario are found here, among which are sturgeon, pike, pickerel, black and white bass, herrings, catfish, eels, &c. Here was Sam Patch's jumping place. The path at the left of the staircase leads to the great Crescent Fall, where, when the wind blows up the river, a safe and delightful passage is opened behind the sheet of water.

The path at the right leads to a magnificent Cave, appropriately named when it was first discovered, twenty five years since, Æolus' Cave, or Cave of the Winds. This cave is about 120 feet across, 50 feet wide and 100 feet high; it is situated directly behind the Centre Fall, which at the bottom is more than 100 feet wide, and were the rocks excavated a little and a few steps made, visiters could safely pass into and entirely through the cave behind the sheet of water. Beyond this cave at the foot of Luna Island, there is an open space where persons may amuse themselves at leisure upon the rocks, over which the floods are pouring, and then venture in as far as they please behind the whole American Fall. . . .

The cave itself is the *ne plus ultra* of wonders, a visit to which no person ought to omit. Ladies and gentlemen can very often, when the wind blows down the river, pass a considerable distance behind the sheet of water within the cave without getting wet at all. The view presented to a person while in the cave, in connexion with the tremendous and astounding roar of waters, which, owing to the echoes or reverberations, is apparently a hundred times greater here than any where else, will enable him to appreciate the following beautiful and graphic lines of Brainard,—especially as there is always in the afternoon when the sun shines, a bright rain-bow visible directly within the cave and behind the sheet of water.

> "The thoughts are strange that crowd into my brain,
> While I look upwards to thee. It would seem,
> As if God poured thee from his hollow hand,
> And hung his bow upon thy awful front,
> And spoke in that loud voice, which seemed to him
> Who dwelt in Patmos for his Saviour's sake,
> 'The sound of many waters;' and had bade
> Thy flood to chronicle the ages back,
> And notch His centuries in the eternal rocks.
>
> Deep calleth unto deep. And what are we,
> That hear the question of that voice sublime?
> Oh! what are all the notes that ever rung
> From war's vain trumpet by thy thundering side?
> Yea, what is all the riot man can make
> In his short life, to thy unceasing roar!
> And yet, bold babbler, what art thou to Him
> Who drowned a world, and heaped the waters far
> Above its loftiest mountains?—a light wave,
> That breaks and whispers of its Maker's might."

How little and insignificant do the efforts of man appear, when measured by this exhibition of Omnipotence! The earthquake, the volcano, the wide-spread conflagration, the shock of contending armies are sublime and terrific spectacles, though short in their continuance and limited in their effects; but here, ever since the flood probably, the deafening and incessant roar of the mightiest cataract on the globe has called upon the children of men to fall down and adore their Maker. . . .

SUMMER AND WINTER SCENERY

The surrounding scenery on both sides of the river is in good keeping with the magnificence of the Falls. It is just what it should be,—grand, striking, and unique. By most visiters it is seen only in summer. But in the winter it is also inimitably and indescribably beautiful. The trees and shrubbery on Goat and other islands and on the banks of the river near the Falls, are covered with transparent sleet, presenting an appearance of "icy brilliants," or rather of millions of glittering chandeliers of all sizes and descriptions, and giving one a most a vivid idea of fairy land,

> "For every shrub and every blade of grass
> And every pointed thorn seems wrought in glass.
> The frighted birds the rattling branches shun,
> Which wave and glitter in the distant sun."

The scene presents a splendid counterpart to Goldsmith's description of the subterranean grottos of Paros and Antiparos. The mist from the Falls freezes upon the trees so gradually and to such thickness, that it often bears a most exact resemblance to Alabaster; and this, set off by the dazzling colors of the rainbows that arch the river from twenty different points, seems, by natural association, to raise the imagination to that world, where the streets are of pure gold, the gates of pearl, and night is unknown.

> "Look, the massy trunks
> Are cased in the pure crystal; branch and twig
> Shine in the lucid covering; each light rod,
> Nodding and twinkling in the stirring breeze,
> Is studded with its trembling water-drops,
> Still streaming, as they move, with colored light.
> But round the parent stem, the long, low boughs
> Bend in a glittering ring, and arbors hide
> The glassy floor. O! you might deem the spot
> The spacious cavern of some virgin mine,
> Deep in the womb of earth, where the gems grow;
> And diamonds put forth radiant rods, and bud
> With amethyst and topaz, and the place
> Lit up most royally with the pure beam
> That dwells in them; or, haply the vast hall
> Of fairy palace, that outlasts the night,
> And fades not in the glory of the sun;
> Where crystal columns send forth slender shafts,
> And crossing arches, and fantastic aisles
> Wind from the sight in brightness, and are lost
> Among the crowded pillars."

The winter scenery about the Falls is peculiar, a sight of which is worth a journey of one thousand miles. Myriads of wild ducks and geese spend the day in and above the rapids, and regularly take their departure for Lake Ontario every night before dark; though some are often found in the morning with a broken leg or wing, and sometimes dead, in the river below the Falls. This generally happens after a very dark or foggy night; and it is supposed that, as they always have their heads up stream, while in the water, they are carried down insensibly by the rapids, till they find themselves going over the precipice, and then, in attempting to fly, they dive into the sheet of water, and are buried for a time under the Falls or upon the rocks.

Dead fish, too, of almost all sizes and descriptions, weighing from one to seventy pounds, are found floating in the eddies below the Falls, forming a dainty repast for gulls, loons, hawks, and eagles. The splendid gyrations of the gulls, and their fearless approaches, enveloped in clouds of mist, up to the boiling caldron directly under the Falls, attract much attention. But the eagle, fierce, daring, contemplative, and tyrannical, takes his stand upon the point of some projecting rock, or the dry limb of a gigantic tree, and watches with excited interest the movements of the whole feathered tribes below. Standing there in lordly pride and dignity, in an instant his eye kindles and his ardor rises as he sees the fish-hawk emerge from the deep, screaming with exultation at his success. He darts forth like lightning, and gives furious chase. The hawk, perceiving his danger, utters a scream of despair and drops his fish; and the eagle instantly seizes the fish in the air, and bears his ill-gotten booty to his lofty eyrie.

Sometimes during a part of the winter, the ice is driven by the wind from Lake Erie, and poured over the Falls in such immense quantities as to fill and block up the river between the banks, for a mile or more, to the depth of from thirty to fifty feet, so that people cross the ice to Canada, on foot, for weeks together. . . .

WHIRLPOOL

One mile farther down leads to a tremendous whirlpool, resembling very much, in its appearance and gyrations, the celebrated Mælstrom on the coast of Norway. Logs and trees are sometimes whirled around for days together in its outer circles, while in the centre they are drawn down perpendicularly with great force, are soon shot out again at the distance of many rods, and occasionally thrust into the channel to pass down the river. The river here makes nearly a right angle, which occasions the whirlpool,—is narrower than at any other place,—not more than thirty rods in width,—and the current runs with such amazing velocity as to rise up in the middle ten feet above the sides. This has been ascertained by actual measurement.

"Resistless, roaring, dreadful, down it comes,—
There, gathering triple force, rapid and deep,—
It boils, and wheels, and foams, and thunders through."

There is a path leading down the bank to the whirlpool on both sides, and, though somewhat difficult to descend and ascend, it is accomplished almost every day on the American side, by gentlemen, and often by ladies.

A brisk and very refreshing breeze is felt there during the hottest and stillest days of summer; and no place is better fitted to elevate and expand the mind. The whirlpool is a phenomenon of great interest as seen even from the top of the bank, especially if a small telescope be used; but to have any adequate idea of its power and motion, visiters ought to descend to the water's edge, and walk some distance up the river. The rapids here are much more powerful and terrific than they are above the Falls, and appear like a flood of watery brilliants rushing along.

Having written thus far, the writer laid down his pen, and started off on a fresh visit to the whirlpool; and now, having spent half a day there in mute astonishment and admiration, and walked more than a mile by the river's edge, he is utterly at a loss what language to use in describing it. Of the above tame and meagre description he is ashamed; and yet he can think of no language, no imagery, no comparison, that will not fall immeasurably short of conveying a just idea of the scene. He can only say, soberly and earnestly, that no gentleman ought hereafter to acknowledge that he had seen the Falls of Niagara, unless he could also say, he had seen the Whirlpool from the water's edge. . . .

This place has been consecrated by some fabulous tales of wonder and of peril which it is not necessary here to repeat.

1836

Nathaniel Willis

From Black Mountain—Lake George

THE MOUNTAINS on the shore of this exquisite lake consist of two great ranges, bordering it from north to south. The western range passes westward of the north-west bay, at the head of which a vast spar, shooting towards the south-east, forms the whole of the peninsula between that bay and the lake. Both these ranges alternately approach the lake, so as to constitute a considerable part of its shores, and recede from it again to the distance sometimes of two or three miles.

The summits of these mountains are of almost every figure, from the arch, to the bold, bluff, and sharp cone. In some instances, the loftier ones are bald, solemn, and forbidding; in others, they are clothed and crowned with verdure. It is the peculiarity of Lake George, that, while all the world agrees to speak only of its loveliness, it is surrounded by features of the highest grandeur and sublimity. The Black Mountain is one of these; and there is every variety of chasm, crag, promontory, and peak, which a painter would require for the noblest composition of mountain scenery. The atmospheric changes here, too, are almost always violent; and storms are so frequent, that there is scarce a traveller to Lake George in the summer who has not seen it in a thunderstorm. . . .

Caldwell, Lake George

IN THE FUTURE POETRY of America, Lake George will hold the place of Loch Katrine in Scotland. The best idea that can be given of it, indeed, to a person who has seen Loch Katrine, is to say, that it is the Trosachs on a little larger scale. There is the same remarkably clear water in both,—the same jutting and bold shores, small green islands, and bright vegetation; and the same profusion of nooks and bays. It struck me at Loch Katrine, that the waters seemed to have overflowed the dells of an undulating country, and left nothing visible but the small green hilltops loaded with vegetation. The impression was owing, no doubt, to the reach of the shrubs and grass to the very edge of the water; and the same thing produces the same effect at Lake George. When the bosom of the lake is tranquil, the small islands, with their reflections below, look like globes of heaped-up leaves suspended in the air.

The extraordinary purity of the waters of Lake George procured for it the name of Lake Sacrament; and every stranger is struck with their singular transparency. It is singular, that the waters on every side of it,—those of Lake Champlain, for example, of the Hudson, and of the whole region between the Green Mountains and the Mississippi,—are more or less impregnated with lime, while Lake George alone is pellucid and pure. It receives its waters, probably, from subjacent springs.

The surface of this lake is said to be one hundred feet higher than Lake Champlain. Another, and probably a more correct estimate, makes the difference three hundred. There are three steps to the falls, which form the outlet into the latter lake; and the lower one, when the snow is melting in spring, is a cataract of uncommon beauty. Lake George is frozen over from three to four months; and it is remarked of it, that the ice does not sink, as in Lake Champlain, but gradually dissolves.

Before it became a part of the fashionable tour, this lake was a solitude, appropriated more particularly by the deer and the eagle. Both have nearly disappeared. The echo of the steam-boat, that has now taken the place of the noiseless canoe,—and the peppering of fancy sportsmen, that have followed the far-between but more effectual shots of the borderer's rifle,—have drawn from its shores these and other circumstances of romance. The only poetry of scene which can take the place of that of nature, is historical and legendary; and ages must lapse, and generations pass away, and many changes come over the land, before that time. We are in the interregnum, now, least favourable for poetry.

Caldwell is a flourishing town, built at the end of the lake, and remarkable for nothing, in itself, but a famous hotel, where scenery-hunters dine. We turn from this too succulent theme, to give an extract from the works of a grave and eminent divine; proving, by its glowing enthusiasm, the effect of this lovely scenery even on minds of the most serious bent.

"The whole scenery of this lake is greatly enhanced in beauty and splendour, by the progressive change which the traveller sailing on its bosom perpetually finds in his position, and by the unceasing variegations of light and shade which attend his progress. The gradual and the sudden openings of scoops and basins, of islands and points, of promontories and summits—the continual change of their forms, and their equally gradual and sudden disappearance,—impart to every object a brilliancy, life, and motion, scarcely inferior to that which is seen in the images formed by the camera-obscura, and in strength and distinctness greatly superior. Light and shade are here not only far more diversified, but are much more obvious, intense, and flowing, than in smooth, open countries. Every thing, whether on the land or water, was here affected by the changes of the day; and the eye, without forecast, found itself, however disposed on ordinary occasions to inattention, instinctively engaged, and fastened with emotions approximating to rapture. The shadows of the mountains, particularly on the west, floating slowly over the bosom of the lake, and then softly ascending that of the mountains on the east, presented to us, in a wide expanse, the uncommon and most pleasing image of one vast range of mountains slowly moving up the ascent of another.

"On the evening of Friday, the 1st of October, while we were returning from Ticonderoga, we were presented with a prospect superior to any which I ever beheld. An opening lay before us, between the mountains on the west and those on the east, gilded by the departing sunbeams. The lake, alternately glassy and gently rippled, of a light and exquisite sapphire, gay and brilliant with the tremulous lustre already mentioned floating upon its surface, stretched in prospect to a vast distance, through a great variety of larger and smaller apertures. In the chasm, formed by the mountains, lay a multitude of islands, differing in size, shape, and umbrage, and clothed in deeply-shaded green. Beyond them, and often partly hidden behind the tall and variously-figured trees with which they were tufted, rose, in the west and south-west, a long range of distant mountains, tinged with a deep misty azure, and crowned with an immense succession of lofty pines. Above the mountains, and above each other, were extended in great numbers long streaming clouds, of the happiest forms, and painted with red and orange light, in all their diversities of tincture.

"To complete the scenery of this lake, the efforts of cultivation are obviously wanting. The hand of the husbandman has already begun to clear these grounds; and will, at no great distance of time, adorn them with all the smiling scenes of agriculture. It does not demand the gift of prophecy to foresee, that the villas of opulence and refinement will, within half a century, add here all the elegances of art to the beauty and majesty of nature.''

1840

Timothy Dwight

From Travels in New England and New York

Dwight was president of Yale from 1795 to his death in 1817. He was one of the earliest American Grand Tourists; his first of many excursions in New England and New York was in 1797. The landscapes he described in his book of letters (though landscape, he wrote, was not his primary interest) excited great public interest.

By the 1830's Mount Holyoke, like other scenic points on the Grand Tour, had accommodated itself to tourists: ladders assisted them up the steepest parts of the ascent, and at the top they could have ginger beer at a shelter as they viewed the Connecticut Oxbow. In 1837, over two thousand tourists made the ascent.

Travels in New England and New York was published in 4 vols., 1821–1822; this selection is from Vol. I, Letter XXXV.

[View from Mount Holyoke]

FROM MOUNT HOLYOKE, on the Southern side of this township, at the distance of three miles from the church, is seen the richest prospect in New-England, and not improbably in the United States. The mountain is about one thousand one hundred feet above the surface of the River; but in the place of ascent is of so gradual an acclivity, that two-thirds of the elevation may be easily gained on horseback. On the highest part of the summit, the inhabitants have cleared away the trees and shrubs, so as to open the prospect in the most advantageous manner. From this spot the eye is presented with a vast expansion to the South, comprehending the Southern part of the County of Hampshire, and a portion of the State of Connecticut. The Middletown Mountains, the Blue Mountains at Southington, both at the distance of sixty miles, and the whole extent of the Connecticut valley to Middletown, together with the long ranges by which it is bordered, appear in full view. The variety of farms, fields, and forests, of churches and villages, of hills and vallies, of mountains and plains, comprised in this scene, can neither be described nor imagined.

South-Westward, Mount Tom with its various summits, a narrow range running in a direct line with Mount Holyoke, intercepts the prospect; and furnishes a fine substitute for more distant objects.

In the Connecticut valley, North of these Mountains, expands a bason about twenty miles long from the North-East to the South-West, and about fifteen miles wide in the opposite direction, limited on the Western side of the River by Mount Tom on the South, and the Green Mountains running in a circuitous direction on the Western and Northern border, and, on the Eastern, by a semi-ellipsis, formed of Mount Holyoke, a part of the Lyme range, and Mount Toby, a commanding eminence, which shoots out as a spur near Connecticut River. Between the last mentioned height, and the Green Mountains, rises on the Western margin of the River the Sugar-loaf; a fine abrupt cone; the termination of Deerfield Mountain; with a noble vista on each side, opening into distant regions, gradually withdrawing from the sight. In this bason lie the townships of Northampton, South-Hampton, East-Hampton, West-Hampton, Hatfield, Williamsburg, and Whately, on the West; and Hadley, Amherst, Leverett, and Sunderland, on the East, of the River. A great number of others are presented on the summits of the mountains, and subjacent hills.

But the most exquisite scenery of the whole landscape is formed by the River, and its extended margin of beautiful intervals. The River turns four times to the East, and three times to the West, within twelve miles; and within that distance makes a progress of twenty-four. It is generally one-fourth of a mile wide: and its banks are beautifully alternated with a fringing of shrubs, green lawns, and lofty trees. The intervals, which in this view border it in continual succession, are fields containing from five hundred to five thousand acres, formed like terraced gardens; lowest near the River, and rising, as they recede from it, by regular gradations. These fields are distributed into an immense multitude of lots, separated only by imaginary lines, and devoted to all the various cultivation of the climate. Meadows are here seen, containing from five to five hundred acres, interspersed with beautiful and lofty forest trees rising every where at little distances, and at times with orchards, of considerable extent, and covered with exquisite verdure. Here spread, also, vast expansions of arable ground, in which the different lots exactly resemble garden-beds, distinguishable from each other only by the different kinds of vegetation, and exhibiting all its varied hues from the dark green of the maize to the brilliant gold of the barley. One range of these lots is separated from another by a straight road, running, like an alley, from one to two or three miles in length, with here and there a brook, or mill-stream, winding through the whole. A perfect neatness and brilliancy is every where diffused; without a neglected spot to tarnish the lustre, or excite a wish in the mind for a higher finish. All these objects united present here a collection of beauties, to which I know no parallel. When the eye traces this majestic stream, meandering with a singular course through these delightful fields, wandering in one place five miles to gain one, and in another four to gain seventy yards; enclosing, almost immediately beneath, an island of twenty acres, exquisite in its form and verdure, and adorned on the Northern end with a beautiful grove; forcing its way between these mountains, exhibiting itself like a vast canal six or eight miles below them, and occasionally reappearing at greater and greater distances in its passage to the ocean: when it marks the sprightly towns, which rise upon its banks, and the numerous churches, which gem the whole landscape in its neighbourhood: when it explores the lofty forests, wildly contrasted with the rich scene of cultivation, which it has just examined, and presenting all the varieties of woodland vegetation: when it ascends higher, and marks the perpetually varying and undulating arches of the hills, the points and crowns of the nearer and detached mountains, and the long continued ranges of the more distant ones; particularly of the Green Mountains, receding Northward beyond the reach of the eye: when last of all it fastens upon the Monadnoc in the North-East, and in the North-West upon Saddle Mountain, ascending, each, at the distance of fifty miles in dim and misty grandeur, far above all the other objects in view: it will be difficult not to say, that with these exquisite varieties of beauty and grandeur the relish for landscape is filled; neither a wish for higher perfection, nor an idea of what it is, remaining in the mind.

1821–1822

Nathaniel Hawthorne

From Notch of the White Mountains

Hawthorne's first sketch of the Notch appeared in "Sketches from Memory," which he included in *Mosses from an Old Manse* (1846). Later the Notch became the setting for his "The Ambitious Guest" (see Landscape as Idea), a story based on an event which occurred there in 1826, when a landslide buried the fleeing inhabitants of the Willey cottage and left the cottage itself untouched.

The Notch's popularity as a tourist attraction is suggested by the accommodations made for them by Ethan Allan Crawford, the mountain man and guide who lived at the top of it: by 1815 he had made his house an inn; by 1819 he had cut a path up Mount Washington; by 1824 he had placed on the summit a sheet of lead and an iron pencil with which tourists could leave their names. Thomas Cole stayed at Crawford House in the spring of 1827, Hawthorne in the fall of 1832. Timothy Dwight had visited it long before.

IT WAS NOW the middle of September. We had come since sunrise from Bartlett, passing up through the valley of the Saco, which extends between mountainous walls, sometimes with a steep ascent, but often as level as a church aisle. All that day and two preceding ones we had been loitering towards the heart of the White Mountains,—those old crystal hills, whose mysterious brilliancy had gleamed upon our distant wanderings before we thought of visiting them. Height after height had risen and towered one above another till the clouds began to hang below the peaks. Down their slopes were the red pathways of the slides, those avalanches of earth, stones and trees, which descend into the hollows, leaving vestiges of their track hardly to be effaced by the vegetation of ages. We had mountains behind us and mountains on each side, and a group of mightier ones ahead. Still our road went up along the Saco, right towards the centre of that group, as if to climb above the clouds in its passage to the farther region.

In old times the settlers used to be astounded by the inroads of the northern Indians coming down upon them from this mountain rampart through some defile known only to themselves. It is, indeed, a wondrous path. A demon, it might be fancied, or one of the Titans, was travelling up the valley, elbowing the heights carelessly aside as he passed, till at length a great mountain took its stand directly across his intended road. He tarries not for such an obstacle, but, rending it asunder a thousand feet from peak to base, discloses its treasures of hidden minerals, its sunless waters, all the secrets of the mountain's inmost heart, with a mighty fracture of rugged precipices on each side. This is the Notch of the White Hills. Shame on me that I have attempted to describe it by so mean an image—feeling, as I do, that it is one of those symbolic scenes which lead the mind to the sentiment, though not to the conception, of Omnipotence.

We had now reached a narrow passage, which showed almost the appearance of having been cut by human strength and artifice in the solid rock. There was a wall of granite on each side, high and precipitous, especially on our right, and so smooth that a few evergreens could hardly find foothold enough to grow there. This is the entrance, or, in the direction we were going, the extremity, of the romantic defile of the Notch. Before emerging from it, the rattling of wheels approached behind us, and a stage-coach rumbled out of the mountain, with seats on top and trunks behind, and a smart driver, in a drab greatcoat, touching the wheel horses with the whipstock and reining in the leaders. To my mind there was a sort of poetry in such an incident, hardly inferior to what would have accompanied the painted array of an Indian war party gliding forth from the same wild chasm. All the passengers, except a very fat lady on the back seat, had alighted. One was a mineralogist, a scientific, green-spectacled figure in black, bearing a heavy hammer, with which he did great damage to the precipices, and put the fragments in his pocket. Another was a well-dressed young man, who carried an opera glass set in gold, and seemed to be making a quotation from some of Byron's rhapsodies on mountain scenery. There was also a trader, returning from Portland to the upper part of Vermont; and a fair young girl, with a very faint bloom like one of those pale and delicate flowers which sometimes occur among alpine cliffs.

They disappeared, and we followed them, passing through a deep pine forest, which for some miles allowed us to see nothing but its own dismal shade. Towards nightfall we reached a level amphitheatre, surrounded by a great rampart of hills, which shut out the sunshine long before it left the external world. It was here that we obtained our first view, except at a distance, of the principal group of mountains. They are majestic, and even awful, when contemplated in a proper mood, yet, by their breadth of base and the long ridges which support them, give the idea of immense bulk rather than of towering height. Mount Washington, indeed, looked near to heaven: he was white with snow a mile downward, and had caught the only cloud that was sailing through the atmosphere to veil his head. Let us forget the other names of American statesmen that have been stamped upon these hills, but still call the loftiest WASHINGTON. Mountains are Earth's undecaying monuments. They must stand while she endures, and never should be consecrated to the mere great men of their own age and country, but to the mighty ones alone, whose glory is universal, and whom all time will render illustrious.

The air, not often sultry in this elevated region, nearly two thousand feet above the sea, was now sharp and cold, like that of a clear November evening in the lowlands. By morning, probably, there would be a frost, if not a snowfall, on the grass and rye, and an icy surface over the standing water. I was glad to perceive a prospect of comfortable quarters in a house which we were approaching, and of pleasant company in the guests who were assembled at the door.

1835

Henry James

From The American Scene

One of the long line of American expatriate artists, James returned to America for two years (1903–1905) in search of new perspectives on his native culture. What he found, in the end, was that America's "material and political power" was "almost cruelly charmless"—an opinion confirmed by most of his contemporaries. But what he found is perhaps less significant than how and where he looked: his first attraction was the "Arcadian" New Hampshire; his second was that center of American power, New York City. He ends the book with an essay written earlier, in the 1870's, on another center of American power, Niagara Falls.

From New England: An Autumn Impression

I WOKE UP, by a quick transition, in the New Hampshire mountains, in the deep valleys and the wide woodlands, on the forest-fringed slopes, the far-seeing crests of the high places, and by the side of the liberal streams and the lonely lakes; things full, at first, of the sweetness of belated recognition, that of the sense of some bedimmed summer of the distant prime flushing back into life and asking to give again as much as possible of what it had given before—all in spite, too, of much unacquaintedness, of the newness, to my eyes, through the mild September glow, of the particular rich region. I call it rich without compunction, despite its several poverties, caring little that half the charm, or half the response to it, may have been shamelessly "subjective"; since that but slightly shifts the ground of the beauty of the impression. When you wander about in Arcadia you ask as few questions as possible. That *is* Arcadia in fact, and questions drop, or at least get themselves deferred and shiftlessly shirked; in conformity with which truth the New England hills and woods—since they were not all, for the weeks to come, of mere New Hampshire—the mild September glow and even the clear October blaze were things to play on the chords of memory and association, to say nothing of those of surprise, with an admirable art of their own. The tune may have dropped at last, but it succeeded for a month in being strangely sweet, and in producing, quite with intensity, the fine illusion. Here, moreover, was "interest" of the sort—quite the contrary—that involved a consideration of the millions spent; a fact none the fainter, into the bargain, for having its curious, unexpected, inscrutable side.

Why was the whole connotation so *delicately* Arcadian, like that of the Arcadia of an old tapestry, an old legend, an old love-story in fifteen volumes, one of those of Mademoiselle de Scuderi? Why, in default of other elements of the higher finish, did all the woodwalks and nestled nooks and shallow, carpeted dells, why did most of the larger views themselves, the outlooks to purple crag and blue horizon, insist on referring themselves to the idyllic *type* in its purity?—as if the higher finish, even at the hand of nature, were in some sort a perversion, and hillsides and rocky eminences and wild orchards, in short any common sequestered spot, could strike one as the more exquisitely and ideally Sicilian, Theocritan, poetic, romantic, academic, from their not bearing the burden of too much history. The history was there in its degree, and one came upon it, on sunny afternoons, in the form of the classic abandoned farm of the rude forefather who had lost patience with his fate. These scenes of old, hard New England effort, defeated by the soil and the climate and reclaimed by nature and time—the crumbled, lonely chimney-stack, the overgrown threshold, the dried-up well, the cart-track vague and lost—these seemed the only notes to interfere, in their meagreness, with the queer *other,* the larger, eloquence that one kept reading into the picture. Even the wild legend, immediately local, of the Indian who, having, a hundred years ago, murdered a husbandman, was pursued, by roused avengers, to the topmost peak of Chocorua Mountain, and thence, to escape, took his leap into the abyss—even so sharp an echo of a definite far-off past, enriching the effect of an admirable silvered summit (for Chocorua Mountain carries its grey head quite with the grandest air), spent itself in the mere idleness of the undiscriminated, tangled actual. There was one thinkable reason, of course, for everything, which hung there as a possible answer to any question, should any question insist. Did one by chance exaggerate, did one rhapsodize amiss, and was the apparent superior charm of the whole thing mainly but an accident of one's own situation, the state of having happened to be deprived to excess—that is for too long—of naturalism in *quantity?* Here it was in such quantity as one hadn't for years had to deal with; and that might by itself be a luxury corrupting the judgment.

It was absurd, perhaps, to have one's head so easily turned; but there was perfect convenience, at least, in the way the parts of the impression fell together and took a particular light. This light, from whatever source proceeding, cast an irresistible spell, bathed the picture in the confessed resignation of early autumn, the charming sadness that resigned itself with a silent smile. I say "silent" because the voice of the air had dropped as forever, dropped to a stillness exquisite, day by day, for a pilgrim from a land of stentorous breathing, one of the windiest corners of the world; the leaves of the forest turned, one by one, to crimson and to gold, but never broke off: all the the enhancement of this strange conscious hush of the landscape, which kept one in presence as of a world created, a stage set, a sort of ample capacity constituted, for—well, for things that wouldn't, after all, happen: more the pity for them, and for me and for you. This view of so many of the high places of the hills and deep places of the woods, the lost trails and wasted bowers, the vague, empty, rock-roughened pastures, the lonely intervals where the afternoon lingered and the hidden ponds over which the season itself seemed to bend as a young bedizened, a slightly melodramatic mother, before taking some guilty flight, hangs over the crib of her sleeping child—these things put you, so far as you were preoccupied with the human history of places, into a mood in which appreciation became a positive wantonness and the sense of quality, plucking up unexpectedly a spirit, fairly threatened to take the game into its hands. You discovered, when once it was stirred, an elegance in the commonest objects, and a mystery even in accidents that really represented, perhaps, mere plainness unashamed. Why otherwise, for instance, the inveterate charm of the silver-grey rock cropping through thinly-grassed acres with a placed and "composed" felicity that suggested the furniture of a drawing-room? The great boulders in the woods, the pulpit-stones, the couchant and rampant beast, the isolated cliffs and lichened cathedrals, had all, seen, as one passed, through their drizzle of forest light, a special New Hampshire beauty; but I never tired of finding myself of a sudden in some lonely confined place, that was yet at the same time both wide and bright, where I could recognize, after the fashion of the old New Hampshire sociability, every facility for spending the day. There was the oddity—the place was furnished by its own good taste; its bosky ring shut it in, the two or three gaps of the old forgotten enclosure made symmetrical doors, the sweet old stones had the surface of grey velvet, and the scattered wild apples were like figures in the carpet.

It might be an ado about trifles—and half the poetry, roundabout, the poetry in solution in the air, was doubtless but the alertness of the touch of autumn, the imprisoned painter, the Bohemian with a rusty jacket, who had already broken out with palette and brush; yet the way the colour begins in those days to be dabbed, the way, here and there, for a start, a solitary maple on a woodside flames in single scarlet, recalls nothing so much as the daughter of a noble house dressed for a fancy-ball, with the whole family gathered round to admire her before she goes. One speaks, at the same time, of the orchards; but there are properly no orchards where half the countryside shows, all September, the easiest, most familiar sacrifice to Pomona. The apple-tree, in New England, plays the part of the olive in Italy, charges itself with the effect of detail, for the most part otherwise too scantly produced, and, engaged in this charming care, becomes infinitely decorative and delicate. What it must do for the too under-dressed land in May and June is easily supposable; but its office in the early autumn is to scatter coral and gold. The apples are everywhere and every interval, every old clearing, an orchard; they have "run down" from neglect and shrunken from cheapness—you pick them up from under your feet but to bite into them, for fellowship, and throw them away; but as you catch their young brightness in the blue air, where they suggest strings of strange-coloured pearls tangled in the knotted boughs, as you note their manner of swarming for a brief and wasted gaiety, they seem to ask to be praised only by the cheerful shepherd and the oaten pipe. The question of the encircled waters too, larger and smaller—that again was perhaps an ado about trifles; but you can't, in such conditions, and especially at first, resist the appeal of their extraordinarily mild faces and wooded brims, with the various choice spots where the great straight pines, interspaced beside them, and yielding to small strands as finely curved as the eyebrows of beauty, make the sacred grove and the American classic temple, the temple for the worship of the evening sky, the cult of the Indian canoe, of Fenimore Cooper, of W. C. Bryant, of the immortalizable water-fowl. They look too much alike, the lakes and the ponds, and this is, indeed, all over the world, too much a reproach to lakes and ponds—to all save the pick of the family, say, like George and Champlain; the American idea, moreover, is too inveterately that woods shall grow thick to the water. Yet there is no feature of grace the landscape could so ill spare—let alone one's not knowing what other, what baser, promiscuity mightn't oppress the banks if that of the free overgrowth didn't. Each surface of this sort is a breathing-space in the large monotony; the rich recurrence of water gives a polish to the manner itself, so to speak, of nature; thanks to which, in any case, the memory of a characteristic perfection attaches, I find, to certain hours of declining day spent, in a shallow cove, on a fallen log, by the scarce-heard plash of the largest liquid expanse under Chocorua; a situation interfused with every properest item of sunset and evening star, of darkening circle of forest, of boat that, across the water, put noiselessly out—of analogy, in short, with every typical triumph of the American landscape "school," now as rococo as so many squares of ingenious woolwork, but the remembered delight of our childhood. On *terra firma,* in New England, too often dusty or scrubby, the guarantee is small that some object at variance, cruelly at variance, with the glamour of the landscape school may not "put out." But that boat across the water is safe, is sustaining as far as it goes; it puts out from the cove of romance, from the inlet of poetry, and glides straight over, with muffled oar, to the—well, to the right place.

1907

Landscape in the Great Theater of Human Events

One major discordance between American landscape and the European standards of sublimity and picturesqueness, a discordance which American tourists tried to resolve (see The Poetry of Scene), had to do with the quality of its "visible forms." A second major discordance, more abstract, had to do with what Thomas Cole termed "the want of associations" in American landscape, "such as arise amid the scenes of the old world." "The glorious scenes of the old world," he wrote in his "Essay on American Scenery," formed a "ground which has been the great theater of human events—those mountains, woods, and streams, made sacred in our minds by heroic deeds and immortal song. . . ." Few American landscapes had been hallowed as scenes in "the great theater of human events"—as scenes made memorable by heroic deeds or immortal poetry, scenes "peopled with the gigantic associations of the storied past."

Both James Fenimore Cooper and Washington Irving were acutely aware of this deficiency. "My native country was full of youthful promise," wrote Irving in "The Author's Account of Himself," "Europe was rich in the accumulated treasures of age. Her very ruins told the history of times gone by, and every mouldering stone was a chronicle." Nevertheless, Cooper set out to capture in the landscapes of northern New York a poetry of scene which would locate and evoke historical associations, and Irving set out to capture in the Catskills and the Hudson River valley a poetry of scene which would locate and evoke legendary associations. Cooper and Irving (and, later, Hawthorne) were the writers who best succeeded in delineating American landscapes as scenes in "the great theater of human events."

The fiction of both writers elaborately combines several strands of interest. In Cooper's novels, the dominant strand is usually a romantic fiction of adventure or love, and other strands delineate what he calls in *The Prairie* "incidents and scenes . . . connected with" the American past. *The Last of the Mohicans* thus includes a narration of the siege of Fort William Henry during the French and Indian War and an elaborate descriptive panorama (excerpted here) of the actual place in which the siege took place.

Irving's "Sleepy Hollow" is also a romantic fiction, or a comic caricature of one, which describes the triangle involving Ichabod Crane, Brom Bones, and Katrina Van Tassel. At the same time it satirically delineates the manners and morals of a predominantly Dutch-American community in Tarrytown, New York, amid incidents and scenes which are not so much factual as legendary history. In the work of both Cooper and Irving the leading characters are fictional, but they are representative of an actual time and place in the American past, and of a people whose manners and morals are as accurately represented as its landscape.

The scenes—the landscapes—in the work of both writers are conceived and executed in painterly terms which bear a marked resemblance to the work of the painters of the Hudson River School. The scale is characteristically panoramic, the perspective such that an "opening" leads the eye into the depths of the landscape. The composition involves a picturesque roughness and play of line and texture, and it emphasizes the effects of light: in Cooper, the peaceful, pristine, and dreamy glow of sunrise or dusk; in Irving, both dusk and the sublimely terrifying obscurity of night. These scenes were sketched elaborately enough to be called, in the language of the times, "accessories"—ornamental illustrations—to the interwoven plots.

But their function is not simply ornamental. They have a reciprocal relationship with their human inhabitants: on the one hand, they act as a moral measure by which humans can be judged; on the other, they are consecrated by heroic acts or by legendary imaginings.

The moral measure which Cooper's landscapes provide combines the best virtues of both civilization and wilderness, and its place is in the border landscapes between these two grounds, the median between extremes. The more "in keeping" the characters' sentiments and acts are with this landscape, the higher they are in Cooper's moral hierarchy. At the top of the hierarchy move Natty Bumppo and Chingachgook, and at the bottom move renegade Indians, professional soldiers, and trappers who destroy in the name of profit or even of civilization. A close reading of the Cooper passage will reveal such a hierarchy even here. The setting of the siege connects the landscape to what Cole called "the gigantic associations of a storied past"; the actions of the fictional characters on the mountaintop connect the landscape to a moral design.

In "Sleepy Hollow," on the other hand, the moral measure which the landscape provides is pastoral in character—an invitation to industry and rootedness, to a healthful peace, to a conservative resistance to change. And yet picturesquely balanced against this moral atmosphere in Sleepy Hollow, partly a check against its tendency to smug complacency, are the unmistakable elements of a sublime wildness: night, a grotesque tree, a deformed ghost. The tree provides a historical association, the spirit both a historical and legendary one. The spirit (such was the poverty of legendary associations in the landscape of Sleepy Hollow) Irving drew not from Ichabod's Connecticut Yankee "anecdotes of witchcraft, and of the direful omens and portentous sights and sounds in the air"; not even, in actual fact, from the Dutch wives' "marvelous tales of ghosts and goblins, and haunted fields, and haunted brooks, and haunted bridges, and haunted houses." Instead, as critics have discovered, he borrowed a legend from the storied past of Old World Germany: one source for his headless horseman was probably Musaeus's *Volksmärchen der Deutschen;* another, Bürger's "Der Wilde Jäger." To this legend he gave an American history and an American place and so made it the "dominant spirit," the *genius loci,* of Sleepy Hollow, New York. It was his way of giving the American landscape the gigantic associations of a storied past, even if the past had to be borrowed, so that every mouldering stone in it might become a chronicle.

Washington Irving

The Legend of Sleepy Hollow

Found Among the Papers of the Late Diedrich Knickerbocker

In a memoir he wrote in 1851, Irving recalled his boyhood on the Hudson River:

> The scenery of the Hudson, the Kaatskill Mountains had the most witching effect on my boyish imagination. Never shall I forget the effect upon me of the first view of them predominating over a wide extent of country, part wild, woody, and rugged; part softened away into all the graces of cultivation.

Though he spent most of his life in New York City and in Europe (it was during his stay there that he wrote *The Sketch Book,* which appeared serially in 1819–1820), he finally settled at Sunnyside, near Tarrytown ("Sleepy Hollow"). In "The Legend of Sleepy Hollow" Irving realized the sublime "witching effect" of the Hudson and the Catskills by blending German legend with legends of the American Revolution. Irving's Postscript to the story is omitted here. For more details on the story, see the introduction to this section.

A pleasing land of drowsy head it was,
  Of dreams that wave before the half-shut eye,
And of gay castles in the clouds that pass,
  For ever flushing round a summer sky.

Castle of Indolence

IN THE BOSOM of one of those spacious coves which indent the eastern shore of the Hudson, at that broad expansion of the river denominated by the ancient Dutch navigators the Tappan Zee, and where they always prudently shortened sail, and implored the protection of St. Nicholas when they crossed, there lies a small market-town or rural port, which by some is called Greensburgh, but which is more generally and properly known by the name of Tarry Town. This name was given, we are told, in former days, by the good housewives of the adjacent country, from the inveterate propensity of their husbands to linger about the village tavern on market days. Be that as it may, I do not vouch for the fact, but merely advert to it, for the sake of being precise and authentic. Not far from this village, perhaps about two miles, there is a little valley, or rather lap of land, among high hills, which is one of the quietest places in the whole world. A small brook glides through it, with just murmur enough to lull one to repose; and the occasional whistle of a quail, or tapping of a woodpecker, is almost the only sound that ever breaks in upon the uniform tranquillity.

I recollect that, when a stripling, my first exploit in squirrel-shooting was in a grove of tall walnut-trees that shades one side of the valley. I had wandered into it at noon time, when all nature is peculiarly quiet, and was startled by the roar of my own gun, as it broke the Sabbath stillness around, and was prolonged and reverberated by the angry echoes. If ever I should wish for a retreat, whither I might steal from the world and its distractions, and dream quietly away the remnant of a troubled life, I know of none more promising than this little valley.

From the listless repose of the place, and the peculiar character of its inhabitants, who are descendants from the original Dutch settlers, this sequestered glen has long been known by the name of SLEEPY HOLLOW, and its rustic lads are called Sleepy Hollow Boys throughout all the neighboring country. A drowsy, dreamy influence seems to hang over the land, and to pervade the very atmosphere. Some say that the place was bewitched by a high German doctor, during the early days of the settlement; others, that an old Indian chief, the prophet or wizard of his tribe, held his powwows there before the country was discovered by Master Hendrick Hudson. Certain it is, the place still continues under the sway of some witching power, that holds a spell over the minds of the good people, causing them to walk in a continual reverie. They are given to all kinds of marvellous beliefs; are subject to trances and visions; and frequently see strange sights, and hear music and voices in the air. The whole neighborhood abounds with local tales, haunted spots, and twilight superstitions; stars shoot and meteors glare oftener across the valley than in any other part of the country, and the nightmare, with her whole nine fold, seems to make it the favorite scene of her gambols.

The dominant spirit, however, that haunts this enchanted region, and seems to be commander-in-chief of all the powers of the air, is the apparition of a figure on horseback without a head. It is said by some to be the ghost of a Hessian trooper, whose head had been carried away by a cannon-ball, in some nameless battle during the revolutionary war; and who is ever and anon seen by the country folk, hurrying along in the gloom of night, as if on the wings of the wind. His haunts are not confined to the valley, but extend at times to the adjacent roads, and especially to the vicinity of a church at no great distance. Indeed, certain of the most authentic historians of those parts, who have been careful in collecting and collating the floating facts concerning this spectre, allege that the body of the trooper, having been buried in the church-yard, the ghost rides forth to the scene of battle in nightly quest of his head; and that the rushing speed with which he sometimes passes along the Hollow, like a midnight blast, is owing to his being belated, and in a hurry to get back to the church-yard before daybreak.

Such is the general purport of this legendary superstition, which has furnished materials for many a wild story in that region of shadows; and the spectre is known, at all the country firesides, by the name of the Headless Horseman of Sleepy Hollow.

It is remarkable that the visionary propensity I have mentioned is not confined to the native inhabitants of the valley, but is unconsciously imbibed by every one who resides there for a time. However wide awake they may have been before they entered that sleepy region, they are sure, in a little time, to inhale the witching influence of the air, and begin to grow imaginative—to dream dreams, and see apparitions.

I mention this peaceful spot with all possible laud; for it is in such little retired Dutch valleys, found here and there embosomed in the great State of New-York, that population, manners, and customs, remain fixed; while the great torrent of migration and improvement, which is making such incessant changes in other parts of this restless country, sweeps by them unobserved. They are like those little nooks of still water which border a rapid stream; where we may see the straw and bubble riding quietly at anchor, or slowly revolving in their mimic harbor, undisturbed by the rush of the passing current. Though many years have elapsed since I trod the drowsy shades of Sleepy Hollow, yet I question whether I should not still find the same trees and the same families vegetating in its sheltered bosom.

In this by-place of nature, there abode, in a remote period of American history, that is to say, some thirty years since, a worthy wight of the name of Ichabod Crane; who sojourned, or, as he expressed it, "tarried," in Sleepy Hollow, for the purpose of instructing the children of the vicinity. He was a native of Connecticut; a State which supplies the Union with pioneers for the mind as well as for the forest, and sends forth yearly its legions of frontier woodsmen and country schoolmasters. The cognomen of Crane was not inapplicable to his person. He was tall, but exceedingly lank, with narrow shoulders, long arms and legs, hands that dangled a mile out of his sleeves, feet that might have served for shovels, and his whole frame most loosely hung together. His head was small, and flat at top, with huge ears, large green glassy eyes, and a long snipe nose, so that it looked like a weather-cock, perched upon his spindle neck, to tell which way the wind blew. To see him striding along the profile of a hill on a windy day, with his clothes bagging and fluttering about him, one might have mistaken him for the genius of famine descending upon the earth, or some scarecrow eloped from a cornfield.

His school-house was a low building of one large room, rudely constructed of logs; the windows partly glazed, and partly patched with leaves of old copy-books. It was most ingeniously secured at vacant hours, by a withe twisted in the handle of the door, and stakes set against the window shutters; so that, though a thief might get in with perfect ease, he would find some embarrassment in getting out; an idea most probably borrowed by the architect, Yost Van Houten, from the mystery of an eel-pot. The school-house stood in a rather lonely but pleasant situation, just at the foot of a woody hill, with a brook running close by, and a formidable birch tree growing at one end of it.

From hence the low murmur of his pupils' voices, conning over their lessons, might be heard in a drowsy summer's day, like the hum of a bee-hive; interrupted now and then by the authoritative voice of the master, in the tone of menace or command; or, peradventure, by the appalling sound of the birch, as he urged some tardy loiterer along the flowery path of knowledge. Truth to say, he was a conscientious man, and ever bore in mind the golden maxim, "Spare the rod and spoil the child."—Ichabod Crane's scholars certainly were not spoiled.

I would not have it imagined, however, that he was one of those cruel potentates of the school, who joy in the smart of their subjects; on the contrary, he administered justice with discrimination rather than severity; taking the burthen off the backs of the weak, and laying it on those of the strong. Your mere puny stripling, that winced at the least flourish of the rod, was passed by with indulgence; but the claims of justice were satisfied by inflicting a double portion on some little, tough, wrong-headed, broad-skirted Dutch urchin, who sulked and swelled and grew dogged and sullen beneath the birch. All this he called "doing his duty by their parents"; and he never inflicted a chastisement without following it by the assurance, so consolatory to the smarting urchin, that "he would remember it, and thank him for it the longest day he had to live."

When school hours were over, he was even the companion and playmate of the larger boys; and on holiday afternoons would convoy some of the smaller ones home, who happened to have pretty sisters, or good housewives for mothers, noted for the comforts of the cupboard. Indeed it behooved him to keep on good terms with his pupils. The revenue arising from his school was small, and would have been scarcely sufficient to furnish him with daily bread, for he was a huge feeder, and though lank, had the dilating powers of an anaconda; but to help out his maintenance, he was, according to country custom in those parts, boarded and lodged at the houses of the farmers, whose children he instructed. With these he lived successively a week at a time; thus going the rounds of the neighborhood, with all his worldly effects tied up in a cotton handkerchief.

That all this might not be too onerous on the purses of his rustic patrons, who are apt to consider the costs of schooling a grievous burden, and schoolmasters as mere drones, he had various ways of rendering himself both useful and agreeable. He assisted the farmers occasionally in the lighter labors of their farms; helped to make hay; mended the fences; took the horses to water; drove the cows from pasture; and cut wood for the winter fire. He laid aside, too, all the dominant dignity and absolute sway with which he lorded it in his little empire, the school, and became wonderfully gentle and ingratiating. He found favor in the eyes of the mothers, by petting the children, particularly the youngest; and like the lion bold, which whilom so magnanimously the lamb did hold, he would sit with a child on one knee, and rock a cradle with his foot for whole hours together.

In addition to his other vocations, he was the singing-master of the neighborhood, and picked up many bright shillings by instructing the young folks in psalmody. It was a matter of no little vanity to him, on Sundays, to take his station in front of the church gallery, with a band of chosen singers; where, in his own mind, he completely carried away the palm from the parson. Certain it is, his voice resounded far above all the rest of the congregation; and there are peculiar quavers still to be heard in that church, and which may even be heard half a mile off, quite to the opposite side of the mill-pond, on a still Sunday morning, which are said to be legitimately descended from the nose of Ichabod Crane. Thus, by divers little make-shifts in that ingenious way which is commonly denominated "by hook and by crook," the worthy pedagogue got on tolerably enough, and was thought, by all who understood nothing of the labor of headwork, to have a wonderfully easy life of it.

The schoolmaster is generally a man of some importance in the female circle of a rural neighborhood; being considered a kind of idle gentlemanlike personage, of vastly superior taste and accomplishments to the rough country swains, and, indeed, inferior in learning only to the parson. His appearance, therefore, is apt to occasion some little stir at the tea-table of a farmhouse, and the addition of a supernumerary dish of cakes or sweetmeats, or peradventure, the parade of a silver tea-pot. Our man of letters, therefore, was peculiarly happy in the smiles of all the country damsels. How he would figure among them in the churchyard, between services on Sundays! gathering grapes for them from the wild vines that overrun the surrounding trees; reciting for their amusement all the epitaphs on the tombstones; or sauntering, with a whole bevy of them, along the banks of the adjacent mill-pond; while the more bashful country bumpkins hung sheepishly back, envying his superior elegance and address.

From his half itinerant life, also, he was a kind of travelling gazette, carrying the whole budget of local gossip from house to house; so that his appearance was always greeted with satisfaction. He was, moreover, esteemed by the women as a man of great erudition, for he had read several books quite through, and was a perfect master of Cotton Mather's history of New England Witchcraft, in which, by the way, he most firmly and potently believed.

He was, in fact, an odd mixture of small shrewdness and simple credulity. His appetite for the marvellous, and his powers of digesting it, were equally extraordinary; and both had been increased by his residence in this spellbound region. No tale was too gross or monstrous for his capacious swallow. It was often his delight, after his school was dismissed in the afternoon, to stretch himself on the rich bed of clover, bordering the little brook that whimpered by his school-house, and there con over old Mather's direful tales, until the gathering dusk of the evening made the printed page a mere mist before his eyes. Then, as he wended his way, by swamp and stream and awful woodland, to the farmhouse where he happened to be quartered, every sound of nature, at that witching hour, fluttered his excited imagination: the moan of the whip-poor-will from the hill-side; the boding cry of the tree-toad, that harbinger of storm; the dreary hooting of the screech-owl, or the sudden rustling in the thicket of birds frightened from their roost. The fire-flies, too, which sparkled most vividly in the darkest places, now and then startled him, as one of uncommon brightness would stream across his path; and if, by chance, a huge blockhead of a beetle came winging his blundering flight against him, the poor varlet was ready to give up the ghost, with the idea that he was struck with a witch's token. His only resource on such occasions, either to drown thought, or drive away evil spirits, was to sing psalm tunes;—and the good people of Sleepy Hollow, as they sat by their doors of an evening, were often filled with awe, at hearing his nasal melody, "in linked sweetness long drawn out," floating from the distant hill, or along the dusky road.

Another of his sources of fearful pleasure was, to pass long winter evenings with the old Dutch wives, as they sat spinning by the fire, with a row of apples roasting and spluttering along the hearth, and listen to their marvellous tales of ghosts and goblins, and haunted fields, and haunted brooks, and haunted bridges, and haunted houses, and particularly of the headless horseman, or galloping Hessian of the Hollow, as they sometimes called him. He would delight them equally by his anecdotes of witchcraft, and of the direful omens and portentous sights and sounds in the air, which prevailed in the earlier times of Connecticut; and would frighten them wofully with speculations upon comets and shooting stars; and with the alarming fact that the world did absolutely turn round, and that they were half the time topsy-turvy!

But if there was a pleasure in all this, while snugly cuddling in the chimney corner of a chamber that was all of a ruddy glow from the crackling wood fire, and where, of course, no spectre dared to show his face, it was dearly purchased by the terrors of his subsequent walk homewards. What fearful shapes and shadows beset his path amidst the dim and ghastly glare of a snowy night!—With what wistful look did he eye every trembling ray of light streaming across the waste fields from some distant window!—How often was he appalled by some shrub covered with snow, which, like a sheeted spectre, beset his very path!—How often did he shrink with curdling awe at the sound of his own steps on the frosty crust beneath his feet; and dread to look over his shoulder, lest he should behold some uncouth being tramping close behind him!—and how often was he thrown into complete dismay by some rushing blast, howling among the trees, in the idea that it was the Galloping Hessian on one of his nightly scourings!

All these, however, were mere terrors of the night, phantoms of the mind that walk in darkness; and though he had seen many spectres in his time, and been more than once beset by Satan in divers shapes, in his lonely perambulations, yet daylight put an end to all these evils; and he would have passed a pleasant life of it, in despite of the devil and all his works, if his path had not been crossed by a being that causes more perplexity to mortal man than ghosts, goblins, and the whole race of witches put together, and that was—a woman.

Among the musical disciples who assembled, one evening in each week, to receive his instructions in psalmody, was Katrina Van Tassel, the daughter and only child of a substantial Dutch farmer. She was a blooming lass of fresh eighteen; plump as a partridge; ripe and melting and rosy cheeked as one of her father's peaches, and universally famed, not merely for her beauty, but her vast expectations. She was withal a little of a coquette, as might be perceived even in her dress, which was a mixture of ancient and modern fashions, as most suited to set off her charms. She wore the ornaments of pure yellow gold, which her great-great-grandmother had brought over from Saardam; the tempting stomacher of the older time; and withal a provokingly short petticoat, to display the prettiest foot and ankle in the country round.

Ichabod Crane had a soft and foolish heart towards the sex; and it is not to be wondered at, that so tempting a morsel soon found favor in his eyes; more especially after he had visited her in her paternal mansion. Old Baltus Van Tassel was a perfect picture of a thriving, contented, liberal-hearted farmer. He seldom, it is true, sent either his eyes or his thoughts beyond the boundaries of his own farm; but within those every thing was snug, happy, and well-conditioned. He was satisfied with his wealth, but not proud of it; and piqued himself upon the hearty abundance, rather than the style in which he lived. His stronghold was situated on the banks of the Hudson, in one of those green, sheltered, fertile nooks, in which the Dutch farmers are so fond of nestling. A great elm-tree spread its broad branches over it; at the foot of which bubbled up a spring of the softest and sweetest water, in a little well, formed of a barrel; and then stole sparkling away through the grass, to a neighboring brook, that bubbled along among alders and dwarf willows. Hard by the farmhouse was a vast barn, that might have served for a church; every window and crevice of which seemed bursting forth with the treasures of the farm; the flail was busily resounding within it from morning to night; swallows and martins skimmed twittering about the eaves; and rows of pigeons, some with one eye turned up, as if watching the weather, some with their heads under their wings, or buried in their bosoms, and others swelling, and cooing, and bowing about their dames, were enjoying the sunshine on the roof. Sleek unwieldy porkers were grunting in the repose and abundance of their pens; whence sallied forth, now and then, troops of sucking pigs, as if to snuff the air. A stately squadron of snowy geese were riding in an adjoining pond, convoying whole fleets of ducks; regiments of turkeys were gobbling through the farmyard, and guinea fowls fretting about it, like ill-tempered housewives, with their peevish discontented cry. Before the barn door strutted the gallant cock, that pattern of a husband, a warrior, and a fine gentleman, clapping his burnished wings, and crowing in the pride and gladness of his heart—sometimes tearing up the earth with his feet, and then generously calling his ever-hungry family of wives and children to enjoy the rich morsel which he had discovered.

The pedagogue's mouth watered, as he looked upon this sumptuous promise of luxurious winter fare. In his devouring mind's eye he pictured to himself every roasting-pig running about with a pudding in his belly, and an apple in his mouth; the pigeons were snugly put to bed in a comfortable pie, and tucked in with a coverlet of crust; the geese were swimming in their own gravy; and the ducks pairing cosily in dishes, like snug married couples, with a decent competency of onion sauce. In the porkers he saw carved out the future sleek side of bacon, and juicy relishing ham; not a turkey but he beheld daintily trussed up, with its gizzard under its wing, and, peradventure, a necklace of savory sausages; and even bright chanticleer himself lay sprawling on his back, in a side-dish, with uplifted claws, as if craving that quarter which his chivalrous spirit disdained to ask while living.

As the enraptured Ichabod fancied all this, and as he rolled his great green eyes over the fat meadowlands, the rich fields of wheat, of rye, of buckwheat, and Indian corn, and the orchards burthened with ruddy fruit, which surrounded the warm tenement of Van Tassel, his heart yearned after the damsel who was to inherit these domains, and his imagination expanded with the idea, how they might be readily turned into cash, and the money invested in immense tracts of wild land, and shingle palaces in the wilderness. Nay, his busy fancy already realized his hopes, and presented to him the blooming Katrina, with a whole family of children, mounted on the top of a wagon loaded with household trumpery, with pots and kettles dangling beneath; and he beheld himself bestriding a pacing mare, with a colt at her heels, setting out for Kentucky, Tennessee, or the Lord knows where.

When he entered the house the conquest of his heart was complete. It was one of those spacious farmhouses, with high-ridged, but lowly-sloping roofs, built in the style handed down from the first Dutch settlers; the low projecting eaves forming a piazza along the front, capable of being closed up in bad weather. Under this were hung flails, harness, various utensils of husbandry, and nets for fishing in the neighboring river. Benches were built along the sides for summer use; and a great spinning-wheel at one end, and a churn at the other, showed the various uses to which this important porch might be devoted. From this piazza the wondering Ichabod entered the hall, which formed the centre of the mansion and the place of usual residence. Here, rows of resplendent pewter, ranged on a long dresser, dazzled his eyes. In one corner stood a huge bag of wool ready to be spun; in another a quantity of linsey-woolsey just from the loom; ears of Indian corn, and strings of dried apples and peaches, hung in gay festoons along the walls, mingled with the gaud of red peppers; and a door left ajar gave him a peep into the best parlor, where the claw-footed chairs, and dark mahogany tables, shone like mirrors; andirons, with their accompanying shovel and tongs, glistened from their covert of asparagus tops; mock-oranges and conchshells decorated the mantel-piece; strings of various colored birds' eggs were suspended above it: a great ostrich egg was hung from the centre of the room, and a corner cupboard, knowingly left open, displayed immense treasures of old silver and well-mended china.

From the moment Ichabod laid his eyes upon these regions of delight, the peace of his mind was at an end, and his only study was how to gain the affections of the peerless daughter of Van Tassel. In this enterprise, however, he had more real difficulties than generally fell to the lot of a knight-errant of yore, who seldom had any thing but giants, enchanters, fiery dragons, and such like easily-conquered adversaries, to contend with; and had to make his way merely through gates of iron and brass, and walls of adamant, to the castle keep, where the lady of his heart was confined; all which he achieved as easily as a man would carve his way to the centre of a Christmas pie; and then the lady gave him her hand as a matter of course. Ichabod, on the contrary, had to win his way to the heart of a country coquette, beset with a labyrinth of whims and caprices, which were for ever presenting new difficulties and impediments; and he had to encounter a host of fearful adversaries of real flesh and blood, and numerous rustic admirers, who beset every portal to her heart; keeping a watchful and angry eye upon each other, but ready to fly out in the common cause against any new competitor.

Among these the most formidable was a burly, roaring, roystering blade, of the name of Abraham, or, according to the Dutch abbreviation, Brom Van Brunt, the hero of the country round, which rang with his feats of strength and hardihood. He was broad-shouldered and double-jointed, with short curly black hair, and a bluff, but not unpleasant countenance, having a mingled air of fun and arrogance. From his Herculean frame and great powers of limb, he had received the nickname of BROM BONES, by which he was universally known. He was famed for great knowledge and skill in horsemanship, being as dexterous on horseback as a Tartar. He was foremost at all races and cock-fights; and, with the ascendency which bodily strength acquires in rustic life, was the umpire in all disputes, setting his hat on one side, and giving his decisions with an air and tone admitting of no gainsay or appeal. He was always ready for either a fight or a frolic; but had more mischief than ill-will in his composition; and, with all his over-bearing roughness, there was a strong dash of waggish good humor at bottom. He had three or four boon companions, who regarded him as their model, and at the head of whom he scoured the country, attending every scene of feud or merriment for miles round. In cold weather he was distinguished by a fur cap, surmounted with a flaunting fox's tail; and when the folks at a country gathering descried this well-known crest at a distance, whisking about among a squad of hard riders, they always stood by for a squall. Sometimes his crew could be heard dashing along past the farmhouses at midnight, with whoop and halloo, like a troop of Don Cossacks; and the old dames, startled out of their sleep, would listen for a moment till the hurry-scurry had clattered by, and then exclaim, "Ay, there goes Brom Bones and his gang!" The neighbors looked upon him with a mixture of awe, admiration, and good will; and when any madcap prank, or rustic brawl, occurred in the vicinity, always shook their heads, and warranted Brom Bones was at the bottom of it.

This rantipole hero had for some time singled out the blooming Katrina for the object of his uncouth gallantries, and though his amorous toyings were something like the gentle caresses and endearment of a bear, yet it was whispered that she did not altogether discourage his hopes. Certain it is, his advances were signals for rival candidates to retire, who felt no inclination to cross a lion in his amours; insomuch, that when his horse was seen tied to Van Tassel's paling, on a Sunday night, a sure sign that his master was courting, or, as it is termed, "sparking," within, all other suitors passed by in despair, and carried the war into other quarters.

Such was the formidable rival with whom Ichabod Crane had to contend, and, considering all things, a stouter man than he would have shrunk from the competition, and a wiser man would have despaired. He had, however, a happy mixture of pliability and perseverance in his nature; he was in form and spirit like a supple-jack—yielding, but tough; though he bent, he never broke; and though he bowed beneath the slightest pressure, yet, the moment it was away—jerk! he was as erect, and carried his head as high as ever.

To have taken the field openly against his rival would have been madness; for he was not a man to be thwarted in his amours, any more than the stormy lover, Achilles. Ichabod, therefore, made his advances in a quiet and gently-insinuating manner. Under cover of his character of singing-master, he made frequent visits at the farmhouse; not that he had any thing to apprehend from the meddlesome interference of parents, which is so often a stumbling-block in the path of lovers. Balt Van Tassel was an easy indulgent soul; he loved his daughter better even than his pipe, and like a reasonable man and an excellent father, let her have her way in every thing. His notable little wife, too, had enough to do to attend to her housekeeping and manage her poultry; for, as she sagely observed, ducks and geese are foolish things, and must be looked after, but girls can take care of themselves. Thus while the busy dame bustled about the house, or plied her spinning-wheel at one end of the piazza, honest Balt would sit smoking his evening pipe at the other, watching the achievements of a little wooden warrior, who, armed with a sword in each hand, was most valiantly fighting the wind on the pinnacle of the barn. In the mean time, Ichabod would carry on his suit with the daughter by the side of the spring under the great elm, or sauntering along in the twilight, that hour so favorable to the lover's eloquence.

I profess not to know how women's hearts are wooed and won. To me they have always been matters of riddle and admiration. Some seem to have but one vulnerable point, or door of access; while others have a thousand avenues, and may be captured in a thousand different ways. It is a great triumph of skill to gain the former, but a still greater proof of generalship to maintain possession of the latter, for the man must battle for his fortress at every door and window. He who wins a thousand common hearts is therefore entitled to some renown; but he who keeps undisputed sway over the heart of a coquette, is indeed a hero. Certain it is, this was not the case with the redoubtable Brom Bones; and from the moment Ichabod Crane made his advances, the interests of the former evidently declined; his horse was no longer seen tied at the palings on Sunday nights, and a deadly feud gradually arose between him and the preceptor of Sleepy Hollow.

Brom, who had a degree of rough chivalry in his nature, would fain have carried matters to open warfare, and have settled their pretensions to the lady, according to the mode of those most concise and simple reasoners, the knights-errant of yore—by single combat; but Ichabod was too conscious of the superior might of his adversary to enter the lists against him: he had overheard a boast of Bones, that he would "double the schoolmaster up, and lay him on a shelf of his own school-house"; and he was too wary to give him an opportunity. There was something extremely provoking in this obstinately pacific system; it left Brom no alternative but to draw upon the funds of rustic waggery in his disposition, and to play off boorish practical jokes upon his rival: Ichabod became the object of whimsical persecution to Bones, and his gang of rough riders. They harried his hitherto peaceful domains; smoked out his singing school, by stopping up the chimney; broke into the school-house at night, in spite of its formidable fastenings of withe and window stakes, and turned every thing topsy-turvy: so that the poor schoolmaster began to think all the witches in the country held their meetings there. But what was still more annoying, Brom took all opportunities of turning him into ridicule in presence of his mistress, and had a scoundrel dog whom he taught to whine in the most ludicrous manner, and introduced as a rival of Ichabod's to instruct her in psalmody.

In this way matters went on for some time, without producing any material effect on the relative situation of the contending powers. On a fine autumnal afternoon, Ichabod, in pensive mood, sat enthroned on the lofty stool whence he usually watched all the concerns of his little literary realm. In his hand he swayed a ferule, that sceptre of despotic power; the birch of justice reposed on three nails, behind the throne, a constant terror to evil doers; while on the desk before him might be seen sundry contraband articles and prohibited weapons, detected upon the persons of idle urchins; such as half-munched apples, popguns, whirligigs, fly-cages, and whole legions of rampant little paper game-cocks. Apparently there had been some appalling act of justice recently inflicted, for his scholars were all busily intent upon their books, or slyly whispering behind them with one eye kept upon the master; and a kind of buzzing stillness reigned throughout the schoolroom. It was suddenly interrupted by the appearance of a negro, in tow-cloth jacket and trowsers, a round-crowned fragment of a hat, like the cap of Mercury, and mounted on the back of a ragged, wild, half-broken colt, which he managed with a rope by way of halter. He came clattering up to the school door with an invitation to Ichabod to attend a merry-making or "quilting frolic," to be held that evening at Mynheer Van Tassel's; and having delivered his message with that air of importance, and effort at fine language, which a negro is apt to display on petty embassies of the kind, he dashed over the brook, and was seen scampering away up the hollow, full of the importance and hurry of his mission.

All was now bustle and hubbub in the late quiet schoolroom. The scholars were hurried through their lessons, without stopping at trifles; those who were nimble skipped over half with impunity, and those who were tardy, had a smart application now and then in the rear, to quicken their speed, or help them over a tall word. Books were flung aside without being put away on the shelves, ink-stands were overturned, benches thrown down, and the whole school was turned loose an hour before the usual time, bursting forth like a legion of young imps, yelping and racketing about the green, in joy at their early emancipation.

The gallant Ichabod now spent at least an extra hour at his toilet, brushing and furbishing up his best, and indeed only suit of rusty black, and arranging his looks [locks] by a bit of broken looking-glass, that hung up in the school-house. That he might make his appearance before his mistress in the true style of a cavalier, he borrowed a horse from the farmer with whom he was domiciliated, a choleric old Dutchman, of the name of Hans Van Ripper, and, thus gallantly mounted, issued forth, like a knight-errant in quest of adventures. But it is meet I should, in the true spirit of romantic story, give some account of the looks and equipments of my hero and his steed. The animal he bestrode was a broken-down plough-horse, that had outlived almost every thing but his viciousness. He was gaunt and shagged, with a ewe neck and a head like a hammer; his rusty mane and tail were tangled and knotted with burrs; one eye had lost its pupil, and was glaring and spectral; but the other had the gleam of a genuine devil in it. Still he must have had fire and mettle in his day, if we may judge from the name he bore of Gunpowder. He had, in fact, been a favorite steed of his master's, the choleric Van Ripper, who was a furious rider, and had infused, very probably, some of his own spirit into the animal; for, old and broken-down as he looked, there was more of the lurking devil in him than in any young filly in the country.

Ichabod was a suitable figure for such a steed. He rode with short stirrups, which brought his knees nearly up to the pommel of the saddle; his sharp elbows stuck out like grasshoppers'; he carried his whip perpendicularly in his hand, like a sceptre, and, as his horse jogged on, the motion of his arms was not unlike the flapping of a pair of wings. A small wool hat rested on the top of his nose, for so his scanty strip of forehead might be called; and the skirts of his black coat fluttered out almost to the horse's tail. Such was the appearance of Ichabod and his steed, as they shambled out of the gate of Hans Van Ripper, and it was altogether such an apparition as is seldom to be met with in broad daylight.

It was, as I have said, a fine autumnal day, the sky was clear and serene, and nature wore that rich and golden livery which we always associate with the idea of abundance. The forests had put on their sober brown and yellow, while some trees of the tenderer kind had been nipped by the frosts into brilliant dyes of orange, purple, and scarlet. Streaming files of wild ducks began to make their appearance high in the air; the bark of the squirrel might be heard from the groves of beech and hickory nuts, and the pensive whistle of the quail at intervals from the neighboring stubble-field.

The small birds were taking their farewell banquets. In the fulness of their revelry, they fluttered, chirping and frolicking, from bush to bush, and tree to tree, capricious from the very profusion and variety around them. There was the honest cock-robin, the favorite game of stripling sportsmen, with its loud querulous note; and the twittering blackbirds flying in sable clouds; and the golden-winged woodpecker, with his crimson crest, his broad black gorget, and splendid plumage; and the cedar bird, with its red-tipt wings and yellow-tipt tail, and its little monteiro cap of feathers; and the blue jay, that noisy coxcomb, in his gay light-blue coat and white underclothes; screaming and chattering, nodding and bobbing and bowing, and pretending to be on good terms with every songster of the grove.

As Ichabod jogged slowly on his way, his eye, ever open to every symptom of culinary abundance, ranged with delight over the treasures of jolly autumn. On all sides he beheld vast store of apples; some hanging in oppressive opulence on the trees; some gathered into baskets and barrels for the market; others heaped up in rich piles for the cider-press. Farther on he beheld great fields of Indian corn, with its golden ears peeping from their leafy coverts, and holding out the promise of cakes and hasty pudding; and the yellow pumpkins lying beneath them, turning up their fair round bellies to the sun, and giving ample prospects of the most luxurious of pies; and anon he passed the fragrant buckwheat fields, breathing the odor of the bee-hive, and as he beheld them, soft anticipations stole over his mind of dainty slapjacks, well buttered, and garnished with honey or treacle, by the delicate little dimpled hand of Katrina Van Tassel.

Thus feeding his mind with many sweet thoughts and "sugared suppositions," he journeyed along the sides of a range of hills which look out upon some of the goodliest scenes of the mighty Hudson. The sun gradually wheeled his broad disk down into the west. The wide bosom of the Tappan Zee lay motionless and glassy, excepting that here and there a gentle undulation waved and prolonged the blue shadow of the distant mountain. A few amber clouds floated in the sky, without a breath of air to move them. The horizon was of a fine golden tint, changing gradually into a pure apple green, and from that into the deep blue of the mid-heaven. A slanting ray lingered on the woody crests of the precipices that overhung some parts of the river, giving greater depth to the dark-gray and purple of their rocky sides. A sloop was loitering in the distance, dropping slowly down with the tide, her sail hanging uselessly against the mast; and as the reflection of the sky gleamed along the still water, it seemed as if the vessel was suspended in the air.

It was toward evening that Ichabod arrived at the castle of the Heer Van Tassel, which he found thronged with the pride and flower of the adjacent country. Old farmers, a spare leathern-faced race, in homespun coats and breeches, blue stockings, huge shoes, and magnificent pewter buckles. Their brisk withered little dames, in close crimped caps, longwaisted shortgown, homespun petticoats, with scissors and pin-cushions, and gay calico pockets hanging on the outside. Buxom lasses, almost as antiquated as their mothers, excepting where a straw hat, a fine ribbon, or perhaps a white frock, gave symptoms of city innovation. The sons, in short square-skirted coats with rows of stupendous brass buttons, and their hair generally queued in the fashion of the times, especially if they could procure an eel-skin for the purpose, it being esteemed, throughout the country, as a potent nourisher and strengthener of the hair.

Brom Bones, however, was the hero of the scene, having come to the gathering on his favorite steed Daredevil, a creature, like himself, full of mettle and mischief, and which no one but himself could manage. He was, in fact, noted for preferring vicious animals, given to all kinds of tricks, which kept the rider in constant risk of his neck, for he held a tractable well-broken horse as unworthy of a lad of spirit.

Fain would I pause to swell upon the world of charms that burst upon the enraptured gaze of my hero, as he entered the state parlor of Van Tassel's mansion. Not those of the bevy of buxom lasses, with their luxurious display of red and white; but the ample charms of a genuine Dutch country tea-table, in the sumptuous time of autumn. Such heaped-up platters of cakes of various and almost indescribable kinds, known only to experienced Dutch housewives! There was the doughty dough-nut, the tenderer oly koek, and the crisp and crumbling cruller; sweet cakes and short cakes, ginger cakes and honey cakes, and the whole family of cakes. And then there were apple pies and peach pies and pumpkin pies; besides slices of ham and smoked beef; and moreover delectable dishes of preserved plums, and peaches, and pears, and quinces; not to mention broiled shad and roasted chickens; together with bowls of milk and cream, all mingled higgledy-piggledy, pretty much as I have enumerated them, with the motherly tea-pot sending up its clouds of vapor from the midst—Heaven bless the mark! I want breath and time to discuss this banquet as it deserves, and am too eager to get on with my story. Happily, Ichabod Crane was not in so great a hurry as his historian, but did ample justice to every dainty.

He was a kind and thankful creature, whose heart dilated in proportion as his skin was filled with good cheer; and whose spirits rose with eating as some men's do with drink. He could not help, too, rolling his large eyes round him as he ate, and chuckling with the possibility that he might one day be lord of all this scene of almost unimaginable luxury and splendor. Then, he thought, how soon he'd turn his back upon the old school-house; snap his fingers in the face of Hans Van Ripper, and every other niggardly patron, and kick any itinerant pedagogue out of doors that should dare to call him comrade!

Old Baltus Van Tassel moved about among his guests with a face dilated with content and good humor, round and jolly as the harvest moon. His hospitable attentions were brief, but expressive, being confined to a shake of the hand, a slap on the shoulder a loud laugh, and a pressing invitation to "fall to, and help themselves."

And now the sound of the music from the common room, or hall, summoned to the dance. The musician was an old grayheaded negro, who had been the itinerant orchestra of the neighborhood for more than half a century. His instrument was as old and battered as himself. The greater part of the time he scraped on two or three strings, accompanying every movement of the bow with a motion of the head; bowing almost to the ground, and stamping with his foot whenever a fresh couple were to start.

Ichabod prided himself upon his dancing as much as upon his vocal powers. Not a limb, not a fibre about him was idle; and to have seen his loosely hung frame in full motion, and clattering about the room, you would have thought Saint Vitus himself, that blessed patron of the dance, was figuring before you in person. He was the admiration of all the negroes; who, having gathered, of all ages and sizes, from the farm and the neighborhood, stood forming a pyramid of shining black faces at every door and window, gazing with delight at the scene, rolling their white eye-balls, and showing grinning rows of ivory from ear to ear. How could the flogger of urchins be otherwise than animated and joyous? the lady of his heart was his partner in the dance, and smiling graciously in reply to all his amorous oglings; while Brom Bones, sorely smitten with love and jealousy, sat brooding by himself in one corner.

When the dance was at an end, Ichabod was attracted to a knot of the sager folks, who, with old Van Tassel, sat smoking at one end of the piazza, gossiping over former times, and drawing out long stories about the war.

This neighborhood, at the time of which I am speaking, was one of those highly-favored places which abound with chronicle and great men. The British and American line had run near it during the war; it had, therefore, been the scene of marauding, and infested with refugees, cow-boys, and all kinds of border chivalry. Just sufficient time had elapsed to enable each story-teller to dress up his tale with a little becoming fiction, and, in the indistinctness of his recollection, to make himself the hero of every exploit.

There was the story of Doffue Martling, a large blue-beared Dutchman, who had nearly taken a British frigate with an old iron nine-pounder from a mud breastwork, only that his gun burst at the sixth discharge. And there was an old gentleman who shall be nameless, being too rich a mynheer to be lightly mentioned, who, in the battle of Whiteplains, being an excellent master of defence, parried a musket ball with a small sword, insomuch that he absolutely felt it whiz round the blade, and glance off at the hilt: in proof of which, he was ready at any time to show the sword, with the hilt a little bent. There were several more that had been equally great in the field, not one of whom but was persuaded that he had a considerable hand in bringing the war to a happy termination.

But all these were nothing to the tales of ghosts and apparitions that succeeded. The neighborhood is rich in legendary treasures of the kind. Local tales and superstitions thrive best in these sheltered long-settled retreats; but are trampled under foot by the shifting throng that forms the population of most of our country places. Besides, there is no encouragement for ghosts in most of our villages, for they have scarcely had time to finish their first nap, and turn themselves in their graves, before their surviving friends have travelled away from the neighborhood; so that when they turn out at night to walk their rounds, they have no acquaintance left to call upon. This is perhaps the reason why we so seldom hear of ghosts except in our long-established Dutch communities.

The immediate cause, however, of the prevalence of supernatural stories in these parts, was doubtless owing to the vicinity of Sleepy Hollow. There was a contagion in the very air that blew from that haunted region; it breathed forth an atmosphere of dreams and fancies infecting all the land. Several of the Sleepy Hollow people were present at Van Tassel's, and, as usual, were doling out their wild and wonderful legends. Many dismal tales were told about funeral trains, and mourning cries and wailings heard and seen about the great tree where the unfortunate Major André was taken, and which stood in the neighborhood. Some mention was made also of the woman in white, that haunted the dark glen at Raven Rock, and was often heard to shriek on winter nights before a storm, having perished there in the snow. The chief part of the stories, however, turned upon the favorite spectre of Sleepy Hollow, the headless horseman, who had been heard several times of late, patrolling the country; and, it was said, tethered his horse nightly among the graves in the churchyard.

The sequestered situation of this church seems always to have made it a favorite haunt of troubled spirits. It stands on a knoll, surrounded by locust-trees and lofty elms, from among which its decent whitewashed walls shine modestly forth, like Christian purity beaming through the shades of retirement. A gentle slope descends from it to a silver sheet of water, bordered by high trees, between which, peeps may be caught at the blue hills of the Hudson. To look upon its grass-grown yard, where the sunbeams seem to sleep so quietly, one would think that there at least the dead might rest in peace. On one side of the church extends a wide woody dell, along which raves a large brook among broken rocks and trunks of fallen trees. Over a deep black part of the stream, not far from the church, was formerly thrown a wooden bridge; the road that led to it, and the bridge itself, were thickly shaded by overhanging trees, which cast a gloom about it, even in the daytime; but occasioned a fearful darkness at night. This was one of the favorite haunts of the headless horseman; and the place where he was most frequently encountered. The tale was told of old Brouwer, a most heretical disbeliever in ghosts, how he met the horseman returning from his foray into Sleepy Hollow, and was obliged to get up behind him; how they galloped over bush and brake, over hill and swamp, until they reached the bridge; when the horseman suddenly turned into a skeleton, threw old Brouwer into the brook, and sprang away over the tree-tops with a clap of thunder.

This story was immediately matched by a thrice marvellous adventure of Brom Bones, who made light of the galloping Hessian as an arrant jockey. He affirmed that, on returning one night from the neighboring village of Sing Sing, he had been overtaken by this midnight trooper; that he had offered to race with him for a bowl of punch, and should have won it too, for Daredevil beat the goblin-horse all hollow, but, just as they came to the church-bridge, the Hessian bolted, and vanished in a flash of fire.

All these tales, told in the drowsy undertone with which men talk in the dark, the countenances of the listeners only now and then receiving a casual gleam from the glare of a pipe, sank deep in the mind of Ichabod. He repaid them in kind with large extracts from his invaluable author, Cotton Mather, and added many marvellous events that had taken place in his native State of Connecticut, and fearful sights which he had seen in his nightly walks about Sleepy Hollow.

The revel now gradually broke up. The old farmers gathered together their families in their wagons, and were heard for some time rattling along the hollow roads, and over the distant hills. Some of the damsels mounted on pillions behind their favorite swains, and their light-hearted laughter, mingling with the clatter of hoofs, echoed along the silent woodlands, sounding fainter and fainter until they gradually died away—and the late scene of noise and frolic was all silent and deserted. Ichabod only lingered behind, according to the custom of country lovers, to have a tête-à-tête with the heiress, fully convinced that he was now on the high road to success. What passed at his interview I will not pretend to say, for in fact I do not know. Something, however, I fear me, must have gone wrong, for he certainly sallied forth, after no very great interval, with an air quite desolate and chop-fallen—Oh these women! these women! Could that girl have been playing off any of her coquettish tricks?—Was her encouragement of the poor pedagogue all a mere sham to secure her conquest of his rival?—Heaven only knows, not I!—Let it suffice to say, Ichabod stole forth with the air of one who had been sacking a hen-roost, rather than a fair lady's heart. Without looking to the right or left to notice the scene of rural wealth, on which he had so often gloated, he went straight to the stable, and with several hearty cuffs and kicks, roused his steed most uncourteously from the comfortable quarters in which he was soundly sleeping, dreaming of mountains of corn and oats, and whole valleys of timothy and clover.

It was the very witching time of night that Ichabod, heavy-hearted and crest-fallen, pursued his travel homewards, along the sides of the lofty hills which rise above Tarry Town, and which he had traversed so cheerily in the afternoon. The hour was as dismal as himself. Far below him, the Tappan Zee spread its dusky and indistinct waste of waters, with here and there the tall mast of a sloop, riding quietly at anchor under the land. In the dead hush of midnight, he could even hear the barking of the watch dog from the opposite shore of the Hudson; but it was so vague and faint as only to give an idea of his distance from this faithful companion of man. Now and then, too, the long-drawn crowing of a cock, accidentally awakened, would sound far, far off, from some farmhouse away among the hills—but it was like a dreaming sound in his ear. No signs of life occurred near him, but occasionally the melancholy chirp of a cricket, or perhaps the guttural twang of a bull-frog, from a neighboring marsh, as if sleeping uncomfortably, and turning suddenly in his bed.

All the stories of ghosts and goblins that he had heard in the afternoon, now came crowding upon his recollection. The night grew darker and darker; the stars seemed to sink deeper in the sky, and driving clouds occasionally hid them from his sight. He had never felt so lonely and dismal. He was, moreover, approaching the very place where many of the scenes of the ghost stories had been laid. In the centre of the road stood an enormous tulip-tree, which towered like a giant above all the other trees of the neighborhood, and formed a kind of landmark. Its limbs were gnarled, and fantastic, large enough to form trunks for ordinary trees, twisting down almost to the earth, and rising again into the air. It was connected with the tragical story of the unfortunate André, who had been taken prisoner hard by; and was universally known by the name of Major André's tree. The common people regarded it with a mixture of respect and superstition, partly out of sympathy for the fate of its ill-starred namesake, and partly from the tales of strange sights and doleful lamentations told concerning it.

As Ichabod approached his fearful tree, he began to whistle: he thought his whistle was answered—it was but a blast sweeping sharply through the dry branches. As he approached a little nearer, he thought he saw something white, hanging in the midst of the tree—he paused and ceased whistling; but on looking more narrowly, perceived that it was a place where the tree had been scathed by lightning, and the white wood laid bare. Suddenly he heard a groan—his teeth chattered and his knees smote against the saddle; it was but the rubbing of one huge bough upon another, as they were swayed about by the breeze. He passed the tree in safety, but new perils lay before him.

About two hundred yards from the tree a small brook crossed the road, and ran into a marshy and thickly-wooded glen, known by the name of Wiley's swamp. A few rough logs, laid side by side, served for a bridge over this stream. On that side of the road where the brook entered the wood, a group of oaks and chestnuts, matted thick with wild grapevines, threw a cavernous gloom over it. To pass this bridge was the severest trial. It was at this identical spot that the unfortunate André was captured, and under the covert of those chestnuts and vines were the sturdy yeomen concealed who surprised him. This has ever since been considered a haunted stream, and fearful are the feelings of the schoolboy who has to pass it alone after dark.

As he approached the stream his heart began to thump; he summoned up, however, all his resolution, gave his horse half a score of kicks in the ribs, and attempted to dash briskly across the bridge; but instead of starting forward, the perverse old animal made a lateral movement, and ran broadside against the fence. Ichabod, whose fears increased with the delay, jerked the reins on the other side, and kicked lustily with the contrary foot: it was all in vain; his steed started, it is true, but it was only to plunge to the opposite side of the road into a thicket of brambles and alder bushes. The schoolmaster now bestowed both whip and heel upon the starveling ribs of old Gunpowder, who dashed forward, snuffling and snorting, but came to a stand just by the bridge, with a suddenness that had nearly sent his rider sprawling over his head. Just at this moment a plashy tramp by the side of the bridge caught the sensitive ear of Ichabod. In the dark shadow of the grove, on the margin of the brook, he beheld something huge, misshapen, black and towering. It stirred not, but seemed gathered up in the gloom, like some gigantic monster ready to spring upon the traveller.

The hair of the affrighted pedagogue rose upon his head with terror. What was to be done? To turn and fly was now too late; and besides, what chance was there of escaping ghost or goblin, if such it was, which could ride upon the wings of the wind? Summoning up, therefore, a show of courage, he demanded in stammering accents—"Who are you?" He received no reply. He repeated his demand in a still more agitated voice. Still there was no answer. Once more he cudgelled the sides of the inflexible Gunpowder, and, shutting his eyes, broke forth with involuntary fervor into a psalm tune. Just then the shadowy object of alarm put itself in motion, and, with a scramble and a bound, stood at once in the middle of the road. Though the night was dark and dismal, yet the form of the unknown might now in some degree be ascertained. He appeared to be a horseman of large dimensions, and mounted on a black horse of powerful frame. He made no offer of molestation or sociability, but kept aloof on one side of the road, jogging along on the blind side of old Gunpowder, who had now got over his fright and waywardness.

Ichabod, who had no relish for this strange midnight companion, and bethought himself of the adventure of Brom Bones with the Galloping Hessian, now quickened his steed, in hopes of leaving him behind. The stranger, however quickened his horse to an equal pace. Ichabod pulled up, and fell into a walk, thinking to lag behind—the other did the same. His heart began to sink within him; he endeavored to resume his psalm tune, but his parched tongue clove to the roof of his mouth, and he could not utter a stave. There was something in the moody and dogged silence of this pertinacious companion, that was mysterious and appalling. It was soon fearfully accounted for. On mounting a rising ground, which brought the figure of his fellow-traveller in relief against the sky, gigantic in height, and muffled in a cloak, Ichabod was horror-struck, on perceiving that he was headless!—but his horror was still more increased, on observing that the head, which should have arrested on his shoulders, was carried before him on the pommel of the saddle: his terror rose to desperation; he rained a shower of kicks and blows upon Gunpowder, hoping, by a sudden movement, to give his companion the slip—but the spectre started full jump with him. Away then they dashed, through thick and thin; stones flying, and sparks flashing at every bound. Ichabod's flimsy garments fluttered in the air, as he stretched his long lank body away over his horse's head, in the eagerness of his flight.

They had now reached the road which turns off to Sleepy Hollow; but Gunpowder, who seemed possessed with a demon, instead of keeping up it, made an opposite turn, and plunged headlong down hill to the left. This road leads through a sandy hollow, shaded by trees for about a quarter of a mile, where it crosses the bridge famous in the goblin story, and just beyond swells the green knoll on which stands the whitewashed church.

As yet the panic of the steed had given his unskilful rider an apparent advantage in the chase; but just as he had got half way through the hollow, the girths of the saddle gave way, and he felt it slipping from under him. He seized it by the pommel, and endeavored to hold it firm, but in vain; and had just time to save himself by clasping old Gunpowder round the neck, when the saddle fell to the earth, and he heard it trampled under foot by his pursuer. For a moment the terror of Hans Van Ripper's wrath passed across his mind—for it was his Sunday saddle; but this was no time for petty fears; the goblin was hard on his haunches; and (unskilful rider that he was!) he had much ado to maintain his seat; sometimes slipping on one side, sometimes on another, and sometimes jolted on the high ridge of his horse's back-bone, with a violence that he verily feared would cleave him asunder.

An opening in the trees now cheered him with the hopes that the church bridge was at hand. The wavering reflection of a silver star in the bosom of the brook told him that he was not mistaken. He saw the walls of the church dimly glaring under the trees beyond. He recollected the place where Brom Bones's ghostly competitor had disappeared. "If I can but reach that bridge," thought Ichabod, "I am safe." Just then he heard the black steed panting and blowing close behind him; he even fancied that he felt his hot breath. Another convulsive kick in the ribs and old Gunpowder sprang upon the bridge; he thundered over the resounding planks; he gained the opposite side; and now Ichabod cast a look behind to see if his pursuer should vanish, according to rule, in a flash of fire and brimstone. Just then he saw the goblin rising in his stirrups, and in the very act of hurling his head at him. Ichabod endeavored to dodge the horrible missile, but too late. It encountered his cranium with a tremendous crash—he was tumbled headlong into the dust, and Gunpowder, the black steed, and the goblin rider, passed by like a whirlwind.

The next morning the old horse was found without his saddle, and with the bridle under his feet, soberly cropping the grass at his master's gate. Ichabod did not make his appearance at breakfast—dinner-hour came, but no Ichabod. The boys assembled at the school-house, and strolled idly about the banks of the brook; but no schoolmaster. Hans Van Ripper now began to feel some uneasiness about the fate of poor Ichabod, and his saddle. An inquiry was set on foot, and after diligent investigation they came upon his traces. In one part of the road leading to the church was found the saddle trampled in the dirt; the tracks of horses's hoofs deeply dented in the road, and evidently at furious speed, were traced to the bridge, beyond which, on the bank of a broad part of the brook, where the water ran deep and black, was found the hat of the unfortunate Ichabod, and close beside it a shattered pumpkin.

The brook was searched, but the body of the schoolmaster was not to be discovered. Hans Van Ripper, as executor of his estate, examined the bundle which contained all his worldly effects. They consisted of two shirts and a half; two stocks for the neck; a pair or two of worsted stockings; an old pair of corduroy small-clothes; a rusty razor; a book of psalm tunes, full of dogs' ears; and a broken pitch-pipe. As to the books and furniture of the schoolhouse, they belonged to the community, excepting Cotton Mather's History of Witchcraft, a New England Almanac, and a book of dreams and fortune-telling; in which last was a sheet of foolscap much scribbled and blotted in several fruitless attempts to make a copy of verses in honor of the heiress of Van Tassel. These magic books and the poetic scrawl were forthwith consigned to the flames by

Hans Van Ripper; who from that time forward determined to send his children no more to school; observing, that he never knew any good come of this same reading and writing. Whatever money the schoolmaster possessed, and he had received his quarter's pay but a day or two before, he must have had about his person at the time of his disappearance.

The mysterious event caused much speculation at the church on the following Sunday. Knots of gazers and gossips were collected in the churchyard, at the bridge, and at the spot where the hat and pumpkin had been found. The stories of Brouwer, of Bones, and a whole budget of others, were called to mind; and when they had diligently considered them all, and compared them with the symptoms of the present case, they shook their heads, and came to the conclusion that Ichabod had been carried off by the galloping Hessian. As he was a bachelor, and in nobody's debt, nobody troubled his head any more about him. The school was removed to a different quarter of the hollow, and another pedagogue reigned in his stead.

It is true, an old farmer, who had been down to New York on a visit several years after, and from whom his account of the ghostly adventure was received, brought home the intelligence that Ichabod Crane was still alive; that he had left the neighborhood, partly through fear of the goblin and Hans Van Ripper, and partly in mortification at having been suddenly dismissed by the heiress; that he had changed his quarters to a distant part of the country; had kept school and studied law at the same time, had been admitted to the bar, turned politician, electioneered, written for the newspapers, and finally had been made a justice of the Ten Pound Court. Brom Bones too, who, shortly after his rival's disappearance, conducted the blooming Katrina in triumph to the altar, was observed to look exceedingly knowing whenever the story of Ichabod was related, and always burst into a hearty laugh at the mention of the pumpkin; which led some to suspect that he knew more about the matter than he chose to tell.

The old country wives, however, who are the best judges of these matters, maintain to this day that Ichabod was spirited away by supernatural means; and it is a favorite story often told about the neighborhood round the winter evening fire. The bridge became more than ever an object of superstitious awe, and that may be the reason why the road has been altered of late years, so as to approach the church by the border of the mill-pond. The school-house being deserted, soon fell to decay, and was reported to be haunted by the ghost of the unfortunate pedagogue; and the plough boy, loitering homeward of a still summer evening, has often fancied his voice at a distance, chanting a melancholy psalm tune among the tranquil solitudes of Sleepy Hollow.

1820

James Fenimore Cooper

From The Last of the Mohicans

Cooper spent most of his life at his family estate (now Cooperstown) at Otsego Lake, New York, writing something like thirty-five novels as well as books of travel, history, and social commentary. His fictional life of Natty Bumppo, a kind of frontier knight in a New World romance, composes the five *Leather-Stocking Tales.* Natty is the first of many American heroes who move in such border-landscapes as the ocean, the prairie, the mountains, the Mississippi River, and the Midwest and even in such psychic border-grounds as those of Hawthorne and Poe and, currently, Ken Kesey (with his "Edge City") and Kurt Vonnegut.

The Last of the Mohicans is set in the Lake George area in 1757, the year in which French and Indian forces under Montcalm sailed down Lake Champlain and into Lake George to capture the British Fort William Henry and establish a fort at Ticonderoga. The party in the excerpt is trying to reach the besieged Fort William Henry, and it consists of Natty (Hawk-eye), Major Duncan Heyward, Cora and Alice Munro (the "two sisters," daughters of the commander at the fort), David Gamut, an itinerant music master, and a small party of Mohicans led by Uncas (the last of the Mohicans). The land they traverse is between Ballston, New York, and Lake George ("the Horicon"); the "block-house" in the opening sentence is a deserted ruin in which the party has taken momentary cover from pursuing Hurons. In the Introduction, Cooper writes that the scene he panoramically describes has been little changed since 1757: the Indians have deserted it, the fort is now a ruin, there are a few villages and "well-attended watering-places" (for vacationers), but the wilderness there is otherwise "nearly a wilderness still."

The excerpt is from Chapters 14 and 15.

[Panorama: The Siege of Fort William Henry]

DURING THE RAPID MOVEMENT from the block-house, and until the party was deeply buried in the forest, each individual was too much interested in the escape to hazard a word, even in whispers. The scout resumed his post in the advance, though his steps, after he had thrown a safe distance between himself and his enemies, were more deliberate than in their previous march, in consequence of his utter ignorance of the localities of the surrounding woods. More than once he halted to consult with his confederates, the Mohicans, pointing upward at the moon, and examining the barks of the trees with care. In these brief pauses Heyward and the sister listened, with senses rendered doubly acute by danger, to detect any symptoms which might announce the proximity of their foes. At such moments it seemed as if a vast range of country lay buried in eternal sleep, not the least sound arising from the forest, unless it was the distant and scarcely audible rippling of a water-course. Birds, beasts, and men appeared to slumber alike, if, indeed, any of the latter were to be found in that wide tract of wilderness. But the sounds of the rivulet, feeble and murmuring as they were, relieved the guides at once from no trifling embarrassment, and toward it they immediately held their way.

When the banks of the little stream were gained, Hawk-eye made another halt; and, taking the moccasins from his feet, he invited Heyward and Gamut to follow his example. He then entered the water, and for near an hour they traveled in the bed of the brook, leaving no trail. The moon had already sunk into an immense pile of black clouds, which lay impending above the western horizon, when they issued from the low and devious water-course to rise again to the right and level of the sandy but wooded plain. Here the scout seemed to be once more at home, for he held on his way with the certainty and diligence of a man who moved in the security of his own knowledge. The path soon became more uneven, and the travelers could plainly perceive that the mountains drew nigher to them on each hand, and that they were, in truth, about entering one of their gorges. . . .

Hawk-eye soon deviated from the line of their retreat, and, striking off toward the mountains which form the western boundary of the narrow plain, he led his followers, with swift steps, deep within the shadows that were cast from their high and broken summits. The route was now painful, lying over ground ragged with rocks, and intersected with ravines, and their progress proportionately slow. Bleak and black hills lay on every side of them, compensating in some degree for the additional toil of the march, by the sense of security they imparted. At length the party began slowly to rise a steep and rugged ascent, by a path that curiously wound among rocks and trees, avoiding the one, and supported by the other, in a manner that showed it had been devised by men long practiced in the arts of the wilderness. As they gradually rose from the level of the valleys, the thick darkness which usually precedes the approach of day began to disperse, and objects were seen in the plain and palpable colors with which they had been gifted by Nature. When they issued from the stunted woods which clung to the barren sides of the mountain, upon a flat and mossy rock that formed its summit, they met the morning, as it came blushing above the green pines of a hill that lay on the opposite side of the valley of the Horicon.

The scout now told the sisters to dismount; and taking the bridles from the mouths, and the saddles off the backs of the jaded beasts, he turned them loose, to glean a scanty subsistence among the shrubs and meager herbage of that elevated region.

"Go," he said, "and seek your food where Natur' gives it you; and beware that you become not food for ravenous wolves yourselves, among these hills."

"Have we no further need of them?" demanded Heyward.

"See, and judge with your own eyes," said the scout, advancing toward the eastern brow of the mountain, whither he beckoned for the whole party to follow; "if it was as easy to look into the heart of man as it is to spy out the nakedness of Montcalm's camp from this spot, hypocrites would grow scarce, and the cunning of a Mingo might prove a losing game, compared to the honesty of a Delaware."

When the travelers reached the verge of the precipice, they saw at a glance the truth of the scout's declaration, and the admirable foresight with which he had led them to their commanding station. The mountain on which they stood, elevated, perhaps, a thousand feet in the air, was a high cone that rose a little in advance of that range which stretches for miles along the western shores of the lake, until meeting its sister-piles, beyond the water, it ran off toward the Canadas, in confused and broken masses of rock thinly sprinkled with evergreens. Immediately at the feet of the party, the southern shore of the Horicon swept in a broad semicircle, from mountain to mountain, marking a wide strand that soon rose into an uneven and somewhat elevated plain. To the north, stretched the limpid and, as it appeared from that dizzy height, the narrow sheet of the "holy lake," indented with numberless bays, embellished by fantastic headlands, and dotted with countless islands. At the distance of a few leagues, the bed of the waters became lost among mountains, or was wrapped in the masses of vapor that came slowly rolling along their bosom, before a light morning air. But a narrow opening in the crest of the hills pointed out the passage by which they found their way still further north, to spread their pure and ample sheet again, before pouring out their tribute into the distant Champlain. To the south stretched the defile or, rather, broken plain, so often mentioned. For several miles in this direction, the mountains appeared reluctant to yield their dominion, but within reach of the eye they diverged, and finally melted into the level and sandy lands across which we have accompanied our adventurers in their double journey. Along both ranges of hills, which bounded the opposite sides of the lake and valley, clouds of light vapor were rising in spiral wreaths from the uninhabited woods, looking like the smokes of hidden cottages; or rolled lazily down the declivities, to mingle with the fogs of the lower land. A single, solitary, snow-white cloud floated above the valley, and marked the spot beneath which lay the silent pool of the "bloody pond."

Directly on the shore of the lake, and nearer to its western than to its eastern margin, lay the extensive earthen ramparts and low buildings of William Henry. Two of the sweeping bastions appeared to rest on the water which washed their bases, while a deep ditch and extensive morasses guarded its other sides and angles. The land had been cleared of wood for a reasonable distance around the work, but every other part of the scene lay in the green livery of Nature, except where the limpid water mellowed the view, or the bold rocks thrust their black and naked heads above the undulating outline of the mountain-ranges. In its front might be seen the scattered sentinels, who held a weary watch against their numerous foes; and, within the walls themselves, the travelers looked down upon men still drowsy with a night of vigilance. Toward the southeast, but in immediate contact with the fort, was an intrenched camp, posted on a rocky eminence, that would have been far more eligible for the work itself, in which Hawk-eye pointed out the presence of those auxiliary regiments that had so recently left the Hudson in their company. From the woods, a little further to the south, rose numerous dark and lurid smokes, that were easily to be distinguished from the pure exhalations of the springs, and which the scout also showed to Heyward as evidence that the enemy lay in force in that direction.

But the spectacle which most concerned the young soldier was on the western bank of the lake, though quite near to its southern termination. On a strip of land, which appeared, from his stand, too narrow to contain such an army, but which, in truth, extended many hundreds of yards from the shores of the Horicon to the base of the mountain, were to be seen the white tents and military engines of an encampment of ten thousand men. Batteries were already thrown up in their front, and even while the spectators above them were looking down, with such different emotions, on a scene which lay like a map beneath their feet, the roar of artillery rose from the valley, and passed off in thundering echoes along the eastern hills.

''Morning is just touching them below,'' said the deliberate and musing scout, ''and the watchers have a mind to wake up the sleepers by the sound of cannon. We are a few hours too late! Montcalm has already filled the woods with his accursed Iroquois.''

''The place is, indeed, invested,'' returned Duncan, ''but is there no expedient by which we may enter? Capture in the works would be far preferable to falling again into the hands of roving Indians. . . .

''If I had but one of the thousand boats which lie empty along that shore, it might be done. Ha! here will soon be an end of the firing, for yonder comes a fog that will turn day to night, and make an Indian arrow more dangerous than a molded cannon. Now, if you are equal to the work, and will follow, I will make a push; for I long to get down into that camp, if it be only to scatter some Mingo dogs that I see lurking in the skirts of yonder thicket of birch.''

''We are equal,'' said Cora, firmly; ''on such an errand we will follow to any danger.''

The scout turned to her with a smile of honest and cordial approbation, as he answered:

''I would I had a thousand men, of brawny limbs and quick eyes, that feared death as little as you! I'd send them jabbering Frenchers back into their den again afore the week has ended, howling like so many fettered hounds or hungry wolves. But stir,'' he added, turning from her to the rest of the party, ''the fog comes rolling down so fast we shall have but just the time to meet it on the plain and use it as a cover. Remember, if any accident should befall me to keep the air blowing on your left cheek—or rather, follow the Mohicans; they'd scent their way be it in day or be it at night."

He then waved his hand for them to follow, and threw himself down the steep declivity with free but careful footsteps. Heyward assisted the sisters to descend, and in a few minutes they were all far down a mountain whose sides they had climbed with so much toil and pain.

A few succeeding days were passed amid the privations, the uproar, and the dangers of the siege, which was vigorously pressed by a power against whose approaches Munro possessed no competent means of resistance. It appeared as if Webb, with his army, which lay slumbering on the banks of the Hudson, had utterly forgotten the strait to which his countrymen were reduced. Montcalm had filled the woods of the portage with his savages, every yell and whoop from whom rang through the British encampment, chilling the hearts of the men who were already but too much disposed to magnify the danger.

Not so, however, with the besieged. Animated by the words, and stimulated by the examples of their leaders, they had found their courage, and maintained their ancient reputation, with a zeal that did justice to the stern character of their commander. As if satisfied with the toil of marching through the wilderness to encounter his enemy, the French general, though of approved skill, had neglected to seize the adjacent mountains; whence the besieged might have been exterminated with impunity, and which, in the more modern warfare of the country, would not have been neglected for a single hour. This sort of contempt for eminences, or rather dread of the labor of ascending them, might have been termed the besetting weakness of the warfare of the period. It originated in the simplicity of the Indian contests, in which, from the nature of the combats and the density of the forests, fortresses were rare and artillery next to useless. The carelessness engendered by these usages descended even to the war of the Revolution, and lost the States the important fortress of Ticonderoga, opening a way for the army of Burgoyne into what was then the bosom of the country. We look back at this ignorance, or infatuation, whichever it may be called, with wonder, knowing that the neglect of an eminence, whose difficulties, like those of Mount Defiance, have been so greatly exaggerated, would, at the present time, prove fatal to the reputation of the engineer who had planned the works at their base, or to that of the general whose lot it was to defend them.

The tourist, the valetudinarian, or the amateur of the beauties of Nature, who, in the train of his four-in-hand, now rolls through the scenes we have attempted to describe, in quest of information, health, or pleasure or floats steadily toward his object on those artificial waters * which have sprung up under the

* The Erie Canal—ed.

administration of a statesman who has dared to stake his political character on the hazardous issue, is not to suppose that his ancestors traversed those hills, or struggled with the same currents, with equal facility. The transportation of a single heavy gun was often considered equal to a victory gained; if, happily, the difficulties of the passage had not so far separated it from its necessary concomitant, the ammunition, as to render it no more than a useless tube of unwieldy iron.

1826

Landscape as Idea

The Transcendentalists

The world is a temple whose walls are
covered with emblems, pictures, and
commandments of the Deity . . .

Emerson, "The Poet"

If the connections between man and land are not to fall victim to shallowness, reductiveness, embarrassing sentimentality, or neglect, they must be examined, in Emerson's phrase, with "new eyes." Man must somehow come to see himself as part of the symbiotic web of created beings. Man, God, nature, and civilization must be seen, as Emerson urged in *Nature* (1836), in terms of a synthesizing "idea of Creation."

The early natural historians conceived of landscape as an array of structures and natural processes. Romantic painters and tourists conceived of it as an array of theatrical "scenes"—shot through with sublimity, beauty, or picturesqueness—in "the great theater of human events" or in the even greater theater of creation. Deists and their Romantic descendants conceived of landscape as a series of pages in "the scripture called the Creation." With Emerson as chief theorist and Thoreau and Muir as chief practitioners, the Transcendentalists inherited and refined these conceptions and gathered them into a coherent whole. Their synthesis still permeates the literature of the American landscape.

NATURAL HISTORY

The first care of a man settling in the country should be to open the face of the earth to himself by a little knowledge of Nature, or a great deal if he can; of birds, plants, rocks, astronomy.

So Emerson wrote in *Nature,* and though he himself had only "a little knowledge" of natural history, his two disciples Henry Thoreau and John Muir came to learn "a great deal" of it. Thoreau, a self-taught field naturalist, takes great delight in naming and describing everything from sand formations in a railroad cut in spring to such "anomalous" sea life as washed up on the shores of Cape Cod. (His

"Mount Katahdin," on the other hand, is grounded more in the literary associations of a Grand Tourist than in the factual observations of the amateur scientist.) Muir, too—that self-described "poetic-trampo-geologist-bot. and ornith-naturalist, etc.!!!"—lovingly renders not only the plants, trees, and animals of the California Sierras, but also their geological formations and processes—the actions of snow, wind, storms, and glaciers.

Natural history was not an end in itself for any of these men. For each of them, "to open the face of the earth to himself" is to come to experience it as the face of non-human creation and, ideally, as the face of God. "Is not the landscape," Emerson asks, "every glimpse of which hath a grandeur, the face of him?" For the Transcendentalists the values of natural history were to see clearly the natural facts and processes of creation and thus to ground (by metaphor, symbol, pun, and other synthesizing devices) their felt connections between the human spirit and the non-human earth. "The use of natural history," Emerson declares in *Nature,* is to give us aid in supernatural history," that is, the divine history of creation.

> Every natural fact is a symbol of some spiritual fact. Every appearance in nature corresponds to some state of the mind, and that state of mind can only be described by presenting that natural appearance as its picture . . . Light and darkness are our familiar expression for knowledge and ignorance; and heat for love. Visible distance behind and before us, is respectively our image of memory and hope.

In the landscapes of the Transcendentalists presented here, natural facts and processes become raised to the level of spiritual significance by symbolic analogies. If tourists and artists were seeking access to landscapes as historical or legendary settings in the great theater of human events, the Transcendentalists were seeking access to landscape as settings in a theater of Idea—that divine idea of creation which charged, shaped, and guided all being, or that human idea of creation which could give witness to the symbiotic unity of being. For each of the passages presented here the following declaration from *Nature* might serve as touchstone:

> . . . The most trivial of these facts, the habit of a plant, the organs, or work, or noise of an insect, applied to the illustration of a fact in intellectual philosophy, or in any way associated to human nature, affects us in the most lively and agreeable manner. The seed of a plant,—to what affecting analogies in the nature of man, is that little fruit made use of, in all discourse up to the voice of Paul, who calls the human corpse a seed . . . The motion of the earth round its axis, and round the sun, makes the day, and the year. These are certain amounts of brute light and heat. But is there no *intent of an analogy* between man's life and the season? And do the seasons gain no grandeur or pathos from that analogy? The instincts of the ant are very unimportant, considered as the ant's, but the moment a *ray of relation* is seen to extend from it to man, and the little drudge is seen to be a monitor, a little body with a mighty heart, then all its habits, even that said to be recently observed, that it never sleeps, become sublime. (Italics mine.)

PAINTERLY LANDSCAPES

New eyes. What is, appears. Go out to walk with a painter, and you shall see for the first time groups, colors, clouds, and keepings, and shall have the pleasure of discovering resources in a hitherto barren ground, of finding as good as a new sense in such skill to use an old one.

Emerson's *Journal* (1837)

Emerson was a reader of William Gilpin and a friend of Ellery Channing, that poet, he wrote, who "always speaks of the landscape as of a painting," and it was probably through the ministry of these two men that Emerson had his eyes opened to the painterly aspect of the "outward creation": to the world of visible appearances, of "scenes and shows." As with natural history he theorized about it, and Thoreau and Muir incorporated it into their art. The poetry of scene, transcendentalized, is best illustrated here by Thoreau's "Mount Katahdin" and by Muir's "Wind-Storm in the Forests."

In *Nature* Emerson considers, as Poe does in his literary criticism, the two basic considerations of the scenic sketch: its composition in terms of "outline, color, motion, and grouping" (Muir would later add to these the matters of foreground, middleground, and background); and, most important, the principle of "unity of impression," chiefly an effect of light. These principles had already been adumbrated and put into practice by earlier literary landscapists (see The Poetry of Scene for definitions and examples), and Emerson was simply affirming them when he wrote that, in the apprehension of landscape as scene, the ideal of the serious artist is to catch the "integrity of impression made by manifold natural objects." "Nothing is beautiful alone," he wrote in his journal (the theme recurs in his poem "Each and All"), "nothing but is beautiful in the whole."

What Emerson added to the painterly apprehension of landscape was a new dimension to the meaning of unity.

For unity of composition, he writes in *Nature,* the eye itself is "the best composer":

> By the mutual action of its structure and of the laws of light, perspective is produced, which integrates every mass of objects, of whatever character so ever, into a well colored and shaded globe, so that where the particular objects are mean and unaffecting, the landscape which they compose is round and symmetrical.

For unity of impression, however, light itself is "the best of painters." Emerson rediscovered and refined the properties of light not so much as physical illumination but as a metaphor for spiritual illumination. The sky for Thomas Cole is "the soul of scenery"; for Emerson the sky-soul's light is the "general grace" which emanates from it.

> There is no object so foul that intense light will not make beautiful. And the stimulus it affords to the sense, and a sort of infinitude which it hath, like space and time, make all matter gay.

Light for the Transcendentalists not only unifies and transfigures landscape, it impressionistically fuses the outer landscape to the inner landscape of the mind:

> Not the sun or the summer alone, but every hour and season yields its tribute of delight; for every hour and change corresponds to and authorizes a different state of mind, from breathless noon to grimmest midnight.

A little later in *Nature* Emerson formulates a kind of book of hours in which are catalogued the changing effects of light on the impressionistic landscape of the mind. Dawn, he writes, shall be his Assyria—his impression of exotic splendor and magnificence; the sunset shall be his Paphos—his impression of ecstatic, Grecian, sensuality; moonrise shall be his "unimaginable realms of faerie; broad noon shall be my England of the senses and the understanding; the night shall be my Germany of mystic philosophy and dreams."

The application of this brief book of hours seems endless. None of the Romantics, for example, are noon or afternoon writers—except, possibly, Emerson himself in his adumbration of a landscape both of "the senses and the understanding." The picturesque and beautiful landscapes of Romantic poets and fiction writers are characteristically set at dawn or dusk. Their sublime landscapes are recurrently set at midnight, or at least in dark forests or darkening stormlight, where red firelight often adds its tones of passion and moonlight its cool, weird fusion of objects, and animate presences.

It is possible to formulate from the writings presented in this anthology not only an amplified book of hours and moods but also a book of months and seasons in which, by their impressionistic effects on the mind, April could be taken as a kind of dawn, October a kind of dusk, December a kind of midnight, and so on. It is possible, too, to formulate a catalogue of motions, in which wind (gentle or stormy), the flow of water (a brook, a waterfall, a flood), or the flow of line or color complement or even substitute for the impressionistic effects of light.

Clearly it is as a source of metaphor more than as a phenomenon in itself that light matters to Emerson and other Romantics. And so it is with the whole painterly conception of the landscape as scene: its value is not so much the scene itself as the scene transcendentalized by analogies between it and the "idea of Creation." "The shows of day, the dewy morning, the rainbow, mountains, . . . and the like," Emerson declares, "if too eagerly hunted, become shows merely, and mock us with their unreality . . . The presence of a higher, namely, spiritual element" is necessary to see the true perfection of natural beauty. Emerson's apprehension of that higher element in the properties of landscape, and particularly in the properties of light and motion, had the effect of reaffirming in America the ancient spiritual connections a century before ecologists were to reaffirm the physical connections between Americans and their earth-space. He strengthened the possibility that Americans could accept at least some landscapes as they are, without the paradoxically necessary but destructive urge to occupy, re-shape and dominate them.

To see the spiritual dimension of a landscape for Emerson is to see it with "the eye of Reason"—to see, through a sympathetic act of imagination, its expression and its grace. Not to experience this dimension, not to listen to what natural objects teach, is to degenerate into a post-Edenic state in a ruined landscape where

> we are as much strangers in nature as we are aliens from God. We do not understand the notes of birds. The fox and deer run away from us; the bear and tiger rend us. We do not know the uses of more than a few plants, as corn and the apple, the potato and the vine.

LANDSCAPE AS SCRIPTURE

Through natural science and the painterly apprehension of landscape the Transcendentalists sought to establish the visible facts and appearances of landscape. Through a conviction that every landscape is the face of God, they sought to experience and interpret the spiritual signifiance of those facts and appearances. There are "manifold visions in the direction of every object," writes Thoreau in *A Week on the Concord and Merrimack Rivers,* "and even the most opaque reflect the heavens from their surface." Thoreau's puns are characteristic of the play of his mind between landscape and idea: what of "the heavens" do the surfaces of earthly objects reflect? There is both a physical and a spiritual answer to that question. They reflect beams of light, of course, but on reflection they also reflect beams of the heavenly. For the Transcendentalists, one has only to jostle surfaces playfully to see further into things, for every natural fact or appearance has its manifold levels of significance if it can be seen freshly, with new eyes.

The object of the Transcendentalists' impulse to make landscapes signify was not simply the knowledge but the experience of transcendent being—an experience in which, as Emerson describes it,

> a spiritual life has been imparted to nature; . . . the solid seeming block of matter has been pervaded and dissolved by a thought; . . . and this feeble human being has penetrated the vast masses of nature with an informing soul and has recognized itself in their harmony, that is, seized their law.

For Emerson, the earth was a "remoter and inferior incarnation of God"; for Muir, natural objects were the "terrestrial manifestations of God" and landscape, a "window opening into heaven, a mirror reflecting the Creator."

To experience the transcendent dimension of being in landscape, the observer must immerse himself in it: "you bathe in these spirit beams," Muir counsels in an Emersonian way, "turning round and round, as if warming at a camp-fire. Presently you lose consciousness of your separate existence; you blend with the landscape and become part and parcel of nature." Bathing, blending, washing, penetrating, pervading, interfusing, wedding—this is the vocabulary of the transcendental experience. Undergoing it the participant-observer senses a dimming, a diffusion, even a transparency in the landscape—the concrete and the immediate giving up their claims on his consciousness. (This is why all Romantics are preoccupied with the soft light of the dawn, the dusk, and the moon; with mist, fog, cloud, and the diffusing effect of distance; with the blending and shifting effects of water: "Meditation and water are wedded forever," muses Melville's skeptical visionary Ishmael. In such atmospheres as these it is easier to loose the bonds of the concrete.) In such atmospheres as these—informing them, given form by them; apprehended by the inner eye as evanescent flickers or motions or distant gleams—move the transcendent presences—the "grand ideas," the intimations of an immanent God. In the experience of transcendence, writes Emerson, "the universe becomes transparent, and the light of higher laws than its own shines through it."

The most intense of the experiences of transcendence presented here are Thoreau's "Spring" and Muir's "Windstorm in the Forests." In "Spring" the one "idea" of a leaf traced in clay comes to be seen as an idea of informing all of the living shapes of the earth, and the "one hillside" on which it is found comes to illustrate "the principle of all the operations of Nature," which makes everything "plastic like clay in the hands of the potter." Muir's experience rises from his immersion in a wind "measured and bestowed with love" on a Douglass pine forest.

Such experiences are testimonies to the apocalyptic meaning in the Transcendentalists' version of landscape as scripture, that ideal design of landscape which they inherited from the Deists and then modified and refined (see Eighteenth-Century Perspectives). But if they aspired to this dimension of significance, they did not neglect the other, less intense, dimensions: the typological or symbolic and the allegorical. These can emerge at any point in the landscapes of the Transcendentalists.

"Nature," writes Emerson in "The Poet," "offers all her creatures . . . as a picture-language. Being used as a type, a second wonderful value appears in the object, far better than its old value . . . The world is a temple whose walls are covered with emblems, pictures, and commandments of the Deity . . ." In *Nature* he had already offered abundant examples—examples which suggest that Transcendentalist symbolism is less fixed and more freely associational than the traditional Christian typology. Its point of orientation is not so much the Bible as the human mind and its culture (particularly its art and its ethics).

> Who looks upon a river in a meditative hour and is not *reminded of the flux of all things?* Throw a stone into the stream, and the circles that propagate themselves are the beautiful *type of all influence.* Man is conscious of a universal soul within or behind his individual life, wherein, *as in a firmament,* the natures of Justice, Truth, Love, Freedom, *arise and shine.* This universal soul, he calls Reason: it is not mine, or thine, or his, but we are its . . . *And the blue sky in which the private earth is buried, the sky with its eternal calm, and full of everlasting orbs, is the type of Reason.* (Italics mine.)

In the selections of Thoreau and Muir, the symbolic dimension of fact and appearance is sometimes made explicit. More often though, it is left implicit in the juxtaposition of a landscape and a reminiscence or meditation (the dominant impression of the one giving rise to the theme of the other) or in clusters or strings of recurrent metaphors, symbols, and puns. The movement in Thoreau's *Cape Cod,* for example, is a movement along "a desert, with the view of an autumnal landscape of extraordinary brilliancy . . . on the one hand, and the ocean on the other." The ocean comes to signify a kind of wilderness, the beach a kind of naked chaos and the autumnal landscape both a "Promised Land" and an "artful house." Thoreau walks the beach and the barrier dunes until he has "harvested" what significance he can from the "unwearied and illimitable ocean" and the beach, whose "chaos

. . . only anomalous creatures can inhabit"—a place naked of art and redolent with that primal foam and slime of which "we, too, are products." Having made this symbolic connection and sifted through some of its implications, he climbs toward the Promised Land of vegetation—"Earth's artful house" in which "naked Nature" has come to be adorned and ameliorated.

The allegorical or moral dimension of fact and appearance opens out to these Transcendentalists (and to their Romantic contemporaries, especially Hawthorne and Poe) a sense of the laws which govern the masses of nature, vast and small alike. By allegorical interpretation, the Transcendentalist discovers that, as Emerson writes,

> All things with which we deal, preach to us. What is a farm but a mute gospel? The chaff and the wheat, weeds and plants, blight, rain, insects, sun,—it is a sacred emblem from the first furrow of spring to the last stack which the snow of winter overtakes in the fields . . . The moral influence of nature upon every individual is that amount of truth which it illustrates to him. Who can estimate this? Who can guess how much firmness the sea-beaten rock has taught the fisherman?

(Consider the pun on firmness: in the rock it is physical hardness; in the man it can be both that and spiritual steadfastness. "Every word which is used to express a moral or intellectual fact," Emerson writes elsewhere in *Nature,* "if traced to its root, is found to be borrowed from some material appearance.")

Like the typological, the allegorical dimension of fact and appearance is not always experienced consciously or made explicit in language. Consider, for example, Thoreau's response to the moral implication of the soft, gelatinous sea animal called "sun-squall" on Cape Cod: "What right has the sea to bear in its bosom such tender things as sea-jellies and mosses, when it has such a boisterous shore, that the stoutest fabrics are wrecked against it? Strange that it should undertake to dandle such delicate children in its arm." If the reader is to find an answer to Thoreau's question about the "right" of the sea he must look to the implications of the passage—especially to what precedes it—rather than to any direct discourse. Muir is only a little more direct in his allegorical interpretations. In "A Near View of the High Sierras," for example, Muir reflects in a desolate Sierra landscape that "the darkest scriptures of the mountains are illumined with bright passages of love." Saying that, he begins to note, over the course of the night, the softness of pine boughs, the presence of birds, the night wind, the "chorus" of a waterfall; and in the morning, the sun and the cassiope, a flower than which "no evangel speaks Nature's love more plainly."

All such ideas which arise from the landscape—whether symbolic, allegorical, or anagogical; whether explicit or implicit—should be considered Emersonianly: not only in themselves, but also in their contexts in the prose work. For like the world they reflect, these works are designed as temples "whose walls are covered with emblems, pictures, and commandments of the Deity."

Henry David Thoreau

From Walden

Like Bartram, Thoreau was only fitfully practical in his worldly calling. A Harvard graduate from a poor family, he supported himself by sometime work as a pencil maker (his father's trade), a caretaker at Emerson's house and tutor to Emerson's brother's children, a surveyor, and an odd-job man. Though drawn deeply into the politics of Abolitionism and civil disobedience, he early defined his true calling in terms of Emerson's "The American Scholar," the commencement address at his Harvard graduation. That calling involved a life of study and meditation—a life committed to the close observation of natural fact in landscape and of the great and the wise in literature, and to illuminating what he observed by discovering its correspondences in his own inner being. He was an accomplished field botanist, a common sense philosopher, and a fair student of Gilpin's art of the picturesque, and these were his perspectives on landscape. True wilderness, as the excerpt from "Mt. Ktaadn" shows, defeated his attempts to perceive the correspondences between outward and inward creation. *Walden* (1854) was one of only two books he finished writing in his lifetime; the other was *A Week on the Concord and Merrimack Rivers* (1849). The excerpt from "Spring" is representative of what he went to Walden to find, and found.

Spring

ONE ATTRACTION in coming to the woods to live was that I should have leisure and opportunity to see the Spring come in. . . .

Few phenomena gave me more delight than to observe the forms which thawing sand and clay assume in flowing down the sides of a deep cut on the railroad through which I passed on my way to the village, a phenomenon not very common on so large a scale, though the number of freshly exposed banks of the right material must have been greatly multiplied since railroads were invented. The material was sand of every degree of fineness and of various rich colors, commonly mixed with a little clay. When the frost comes out in the spring, and even in a thawing day in the winter, the sand begins to flow down the slopes like lava, sometimes bursting out through the snow and overflowing it where no sand was to be seen before. Innumerable little streams overlap and interlace one with another, exhibiting a sort of hybrid product, which obeys half way the law of currents, and half way that of vegetation. As it flows it takes the forms of sappy leaves or vines, making heaps of pulpy sprays a foot or more in depth, and resembling, as you look down on them, the laciniated, lobed, and imbricated thalluses of some lichens; or you are reminded of coral, of leopards' paws or birds' feet, of brains or lungs or bowels, and excrements of all kinds. It is a truly *grotesque* vegetation, whose forms and color we see imitated in bronze, a sort of architectural foliage more ancient and typical than acanthus, chicory, ivy, vine, or any vegetable leaves; destined perhaps, under some circumstances, to become a puzzle to future geologists. The whole cut impressed me as if it were a cave with its stalactites laid open to the light. The various shades of the sand are singularly rich and agreeable, embracing the different iron colors, brown, gray, yellowish, and reddish. When the flowing mass reaches the drain at the foot of the bank it spreads out flatter into *strands,* the separate streams losing their semi-cylindrical form and gradually becoming more flat and broad, running together as they are more moist, till they form an almost flat *sand,* still variously and beautifully shaded, but in which you can trace the original forms of vegetation; till at length, in the water itself, they are converted into *banks,* like those formed off the mouths of rivers, and the forms of vegetation are lost in the ripple-marks on the bottom.

The whole bank, which is from twenty to forty feet high, is sometimes overlaid with a mass of this kind of foliage, or sandy rupture, for a quarter of a mile on one or both sides, the produce of one spring day. What makes this sand foliage remarkable is its springing into existence thus suddenly. When I see on the one side the inert bank,—for the sun acts on one side first,—and on the other this luxuriant foliage, the creation of an hour, I am affected as if in a peculiar sense I stood in the laboratory of the Artist who made the world and me,—had come to where he was still at work, sporting on this bank, and with excess of energy strewing his fresh designs about. I feel as if I were nearer to the vitals of the globe, for this sandy overflow is something such a foliaceous mass as the vitals of the animal body. You find thus in the very sands an anticipation of the vegetable leaf. No wonder that the earth expresses itself outwardly in leaves, it so labors with the idea inwardly. The atoms have already learned this law, and are pregnant by it. The overhanging leaf sees here its prototype. *Internally,* whether in the globe or animal body, it is a moist thick *lobe,* a word especially applicable to the liver and lungs and the *leaves* of fat (γείβω, *labor, lapsus,* to flow or slip downward, a lapsing; λοβός, *globus,* lobe, globe; also lap, flap, and many other words); *externally,* a dry thin *leaf,* even as the *f* and *v* are a pressed and dried *b*. The radicals of *lobe* are *lb,* the soft mass of the *b* (single-lobed, or B, double-lobed), with the liquid *l* behind it pressing it forward. In globe, *glb,* the guttural *g* adds to the meaning the capacity of the throat. The feathers and wings of birds are still drier and thinner leaves. Thus, also, you pass from the lumpish grub in the earth to the airy and fluttering butterfly. The very globe continually transcends and translates itself, and becomes winged in its orbit. Even ice begins with delicate crystal leaves, as if it had flowed into moulds which the fronds of water-plants have impressed on the watery mirror. The whole tree itself is but one leaf, and rivers are still vaster leaves whose pulp is intervening earth, and towns and cities are the ova of insects in their axils.

When the sun withdraws the sand ceases to flow, but in the morning the streams will start once more and branch and branch again into a myriad of others. You here see perchance how blood-vessels are formed. If you look closely you observe that first there pushes forward from the thawing mass a stream of softened sand with a drop-like point, like the ball of the finger, feeling its way slowly and blindly downward, until at last with more heat and moisture, as the sun gets higher, the most fluid portion, in its effort to obey the law to which the most inert also yields, separates from the latter and forms for itself a meandering channel or artery within that, in which is seen a little silvery stream glancing like lightning from one stage of pulpy leaves or branches to another, and ever and anon swallowed up in the sand. It is wonderful how rapidly yet perfectly the sand organizes itself as it flows, using the best material its mass affords to form the sharp edges of its channel. Such are the sources of rivers. In the silicious matter which the water deposits is perhaps the bony system, and in the still finer soil and organic matter the fleshy fibre or cellular tissue. What is man but a mass of thawing clay? The ball of the human finger is but a drop congealed. The fingers and toes flow to their extent from the thawing mass of the body. Who knows what the human body would expand and flow out to under a more genial heaven? Is not the hand a spreading *palm* leaf with its lobes and veins? The ear may be regarded, fancifully, as a lichen, *Umbilicaria,* on the side of the head, with its lobe or drop. The lip—*labium,* from *labor* (?)—laps or lapses from the sides of the cavernous mouth. The nose is a manifest congealed drop or stalactite. The chin is a still larger drop, the confluent dripping of the face. The cheeks are a slide from the brows into the valley of the face, opposed and diffused by the cheek bones. Each rounded lobe of the vegetable leaf, too, is a thick and now loitering drop, larger or smaller; the lobes are the fingers of the leaf; and as many lobes as it has, in so many directions it tends to flow, and more heat or other genial influences would have caused it to flow yet farther.

Thus it seemed that this one hillside illustrated the principle of all the operations of Nature. The Maker of this earth but patented a leaf. What Champollion will decipher this hieroglyphic for us, that we may turn over a new leaf at last? This phenomenon is more exhilarating to me than the luxuriance and fertility of vineyards. True, it is somewhat excrementitious in its character, and there is no end to the heaps of liver, lights, and bowels, as if the globe were turned wrong side outward; but this suggests at least that Nature has some bowels, and there again is mother of humanity. This is the frost coming out of the ground; this is Spring. It precedes the green and flowery spring, as mythology precedes regular poetry. I know of nothing more purgative of winter fumes and indigestions. It convinces me that Earth is still in her swaddling-clothes, and stretches forth baby fingers on every side. Fresh curls spring from the baldest brow. There is nothing inorganic. These foliaceous heaps lie along the bank like the slag of a furnace, showing that Nature is "in full blast" within. The earth is not a mere fragment of dead history, stratum upon stratum like the leaves of a book, to be studied by geologists and antiquaries chiefly, but living poetry like the leaves of a tree, which precede flowers and fruit,—not a fossil earth, but a living earth; compared with whose great central life all animal and vegetable life is merely parasitic. Its throes will heave our exuviæ from their graves. You may melt your metals and cast them into the most beautiful moulds you can; they will never excite me like the forms which this molten earth flows out into. And not only it, but the institutions upon it are plastic like clay in the hands of the potter.

1854

From Cape Cod

Cape Cod was edited by Sophia Thoreau and Ellery Channing after Thoreau's death and published in 1865. Thoreau had kept journals of three excursions to the Cape (1849, 1855, and 1857), which totaled about three weeks. He twice walked the Atlantic side of the Cape from Eastham to Provincetown. From the journals he had written what would become the first four chapters of the book and published them in *Putnam's* magazine in 1855.

[The Beach]

AT LENGTH we reached the seemingly retreating boundary of the [Nauset] plain, and entered what had appeared at a distance an upland marsh, but proved to be dry sand covered with beach-grass, the bearberry, bayberry, shrub-oaks, and beach-plum, slightly ascending as we approached the shore; then, crossing over a belt of sand on which nothing grew, though the roar of the sea sounded scarcely louder than before, and we were prepared to go half a mile farther, we suddenly stood on the edge of a bluff overlooking the Atlantic.

Far below us was the beach, from half a dozen to a dozen rods in width, with a long line of breakers rushing to the strand. The sea was exceedingly dark and stormy, the sky completely overcast, the clouds still dropping rain, and the wind seemed to blow not so much as the exciting cause, as from sympathy with the already agitated ocean. The waves broke on the bars at some distance from the shore, and curving green or yellow as if over so many unseen dams, ten or twelve feet high, like a thousand waterfalls, rolled in foam to the sand. There was nothing but that savage ocean between us and Europe.

Having got down the bank, and as close to the water as we could, where the sand was the hardest, leaving the Nauset Lights behind us, we began to walk leisurely up the beach, in a northwest direction, toward Provincetown, which was about twenty-five miles distant, still sailing under our umbrellas with a strong aft wind, admiring in silence, as we walked, the great force of the ocean stream,—

ποταμοῖο μέγα σθένος 'Ωκεανοῖο.*

The white breakers were rushing to the shore; the foam ran up the sand, and then ran back as far as we could see—and we imagined how much farther along the Atlantic coast, before and behind us—as regularly, to compare great things with small, as the master of a choir beats time with his white wand; and ever and anon a higher wave caused us hastily to deviate from our path, and we looked back on our tracks filled with water and foam. The breakers looked like droves of a thousand wild horses of Neptune, rushing to the shore, with their white manes streaming far behind; and when, at length, the sun shone for a moment, their manes were rainbowtinted. Also, the long kelpweed was tossed up from time to time, like the tails of sea-cows sporting in the brine.

There was not a sail in sight, and we saw none that day,—for they had all sought harbors in the late storm, and had not been able to get out again; and the only human beings whom we saw on the beach for several days were one or two wreckers looking for drift-wood, and fragments of wrecked vessels. After an easterly storm in the spring, this beach is sometimes strewn with eastern wood from one end to the other, which, as it belongs to him who saves it, and the Cape is nearly destitute of wood, is a godsend to the inhabitants.

We soon met one of these wreckers,—a regular Cape Cod man, with whom we parleyed, with a bleached and weather-beaten face, within whose wrinkles I distinguished no particular feature. It was like an old sail endowed with life,—a hanging-cliff of weather-beaten flesh,—like one of the clay boulders which occurred in that sand-bank. He had on a hat which had seen salt water, and a coat of many pieces and colors, though it was mainly the color of the beach, as if it had been sanded. His variegated back—for his coat had many patches, even between the shoulders—was a rich study to us when we had passed him and looked around. It might have been dishonorable for him to have so many scars behind, it is true, if he had not had many more and more serious ones in front. He looked as if he sometimes saw a doughnut, but never descended to comfort; too grave to laugh, too tough to cry; as indifferent as a clam,—like a sea-clam with hat on and legs, that was out walking the strand. He may have been one of the Pilgrims,—Peregrine White, at least,—who has kept on the back side of the Cape, and let the centuries go by. . . .

The wrecker directed us to a slight depression, called Snow's Hollow, by which we ascended the bank,—for elsewhere, if not difficult, it was inconvenient to climb it on account of the sliding sand which filled our shoes. This sand-bank—the backbone of the Cape—rose directly from the beach to the height of a hundred feet or more above the ocean. It was with singular emotions that we

* Homer's *Iliad.* Book 18, 1. 606: "the great river-strength of the ocean." Thoreau writes later that he uses Greek from time to time "partly because it sounds like the ocean." The phonetic rendering of the line is roughly: pót-ă-mŏyó măy-gă sthén-ŏs ŏkáy-ăn-ŏyó—ed.

first stood upon it and discovered what a place we had chosen to walk on. On our right, beneath us, was the beach of smooth and gently-sloping sand, a dozen rods in width; next, the endless series of white breakers; further still, the light green water over the bar, which runs the whole length of the fore-arm of the Cape, and beyond this stretched the unwearied and illimitable ocean. On our left, extending back from the very edge of the bank, was a perfect desert of shining sand, from thirty to eighty rods in width, skirted in the distance by small sand-hills fifteen or twenty feet high; between which, however, in some places, the sand penetrated as much farther.

Next commenced the region of vegetation,—a succession of small hills and valleys covered with shrubbery, now glowing with the brightest imaginable autumnal tints; and beyond this were seen, here and there, the waters of the bay. Here, in Wellfleet, this pure sand plateau, known to sailors as the Table Lands of Eastham, on account of its appearance, as seen from the ocean, and because it once made a part of that town,—full fifty rods in width, and in many places much more, and sometimes full one hundred and fifty feet above the ocean,—stretched away northward from the southern boundary of the town, without a particle of vegetation,—as level almost as a table,—for two and a half or three miles, or as far as the eye could reach; slightly rising towards the ocean, then stooping to the beach, by as steep a slope as sand could lie on, and as regular as a military engineer could desire. It was like the escarped rampart of a stupendous fortress, whose glacis was the beach, and whose champaign the ocean.

From its surface we overlooked the greater part of the Cape. In short, we were traversing a desert, with the view of an autumnal landscape of extraordinary brilliancy, a sort of Promised Land, on the one hand, and the ocean on the other. . . . All the aspects of this desert are beautiful, whether you behold it in fair weather or foul, or when the sun is just breaking out after a storm, and shining on its moist surface in the distance, it is so white, and pure, and level, and each slight inequality and track is so distinctly revealed; and when your eyes slide off this, they fall on the ocean. In summer the mackerel gulls—which here have their nests among the neighboring sand-hills—pursue the traveler anxiously, now and then diving close to his head with a squeak, and he may see them, like swallows, chase some crow which has been feeding on the beach, almost across the Cape.

Though for some time I have not spoken of the roaring of the breakers, and the ceaseless flux and reflux of the waves, yet they did not for a moment cease to dash and roar, with such a tumult that, if you had been there, you could scarcely have heard my voice the while; and they are dashing and roaring this very moment, though it may be with less din and violence, for there the sea never rests. We were wholly absorbed by this spectacle and tumult, and like Chryses, though in a different mood from him, we walked silent along the shore of the resounding sea.

Βῆ δ' ἀκέων παρὰ θῖνα πολυφλοίσβοιο θαλάσσης.*

I put in a little Greek now and then, partly because it sounds so much like the ocean,—though I doubt if Homer's *Mediterranean Sea* ever sounded so loud as this. . . .

There was but little weed cast up here, and that kelp chiefly, there being scarcely a rock for rock-weed to adhere to. Who has not had a vision from some vessel's deck, when he had still his land legs on, of this great brown apron, drifting half upright, and quite submerged through the green water, clasping a stone or a deep-sea mussel in its unearthly fingers? I have seen it carrying a stone half as large as my head. We sometimes watched a mass of this cable-like weed, as it was tossed up on the crest of a breaker, waiting with interest to see it come in, as if there was some treasure buoyed up by it; but we were always surprised and disappointed at the insignificance of the mass which had attracted us. As we looked out over the water, the smallest objects floating on it appeared indefinitely large, we were so impressed by the vastness of the ocean, and each one bore so large a proportion to the whole ocean, which we saw. We were so often disappointed in the size of such things as came ashore, the ridiculous bits of wood or weed, with which the ocean labored, that we began to doubt whether the Atlantic itself would bear a still closer inspection, and would not turn out to be but a small pond, if it should come ashore to us.

This kelp, oar-weed, tangle, devil's apron, sole-leather, or ribbon-weed,—as various species are called,—appeared to us a singularly marine and fabulous product, a fit invention for Neptune to adorn his car with, or a freak of Proteus. All that is told of the sea has a fabulous sound to an inhabitant of the land, and all its products have a certain fabulous quality, as if they belonged to another planet, from seaweed to a sailor's yarn, or a fish story. In this element the animal and vegetable kingdoms meet and are strangely mingled. One species of kelp, according to Bory St. Vincent, has a stem fifteen hundred feet long, and hence is the longest vegetable known, and a brig's crew spent two days to no purpose collecting the trunks of another kind cast ashore on the Falkland Islands, mistaking it for drift-wood.

This species looked almost edible; at least, I thought that if I were starving, I would try it. One sailor told me that the cows ate it. It cut like cheese; for I took the earliest opportunity to sit down and deliberately whittle up a fathom or two of it, that I might become more intimately acquainted with it, see how it cut, and if it were hollow all the way through. The blade looked like a broad belt, whose edges had been quilled, or as if stretched by hammering, and it was also twisted spirally. The extremity was generally worn and ragged from the lashing of the waves. A piece of the stem which I carried home shrunk to one quarter of its size a week afterward, and was completely covered with crystals

* *Iliad*. Book 1, 1. 34: "silently he walked away beside the loud-roaring ocean." The phonetic rendering is roughly: báy ď'akěy-ówn pără thénă pǒlý-pȟlois-bǒýo tȟa-lăss-áce .—ed.

of salt like frost. The reader will excuse my greenness,—though it is not sea-greenness, like his, perchance,—for I live by a river shore, where this weed does not wash up. When we consider in what meadows it grew, and how it was raked, and in what kind of hay weather got in or out, we may well be curious about it. . . .

These weeds were the symbols of those grotesque and fabulous thoughts which have not yet got into the sheltered coves of literature.

> ''Ever drifting, drifting, drifting
> On the shifting
> Currents of the restless heart;''
> *And not yet* ''in books recorded
> They, like hoarded
> Household words, no more depart.''

The beach was also strewn with beautiful sea-jellies, which the wreckers called sun-squall, one of the lowest forms of animal life, some white, some wine-colored, and a foot in diameter. I at first thought that they were a tender part of some marine monster, which the storm or some other foe had mangled. What right has the sea to bear in its bosom such tender things as sea-jellies and mosses, when it has such a boisterous shore, that the stoutest fabrics are wrecked against it? Strange that it should undertake to dandle such delicate children in its arm. I did not at first recognize these for the same which I had formerly seen in myriads in Boston Harbor, rising, with a waving motion, to the surface, as if to meet the sun, and discoloring the waters far and wide, so that I seemed to be sailing through a mere sun-fish soup. They say that when you endeavor to take one up, it will spill out the other side of your hand like quicksilver.

Before the land rose out of the ocean, and became *dry* land, chaos reigned; and between high and low water mark, where she is partially disrobed and rising, a sort of chaos reigns still, which only anomalous creatures can inhabit. Mackerel-gulls were all the while flying over our heads and amid the breakers, sometimes two white ones pursuing a black one; quite at home in the storm, though they are as delicate organizations as sea-jellies and mosses; and we saw that they were adapted to their circumstances rather by their spirits than their bodies. Theirs must be an essentially wilder, that is less human, nature, than that of larks and robins. Their note was like the sound of some vibrating metal, and harmonized well with the scenery and the roar of the surf, as if one had rudely touched the strings of the lyre, which ever lies on the shore; a ragged shred of ocean music tossed aloft on the spray.

But if I were required to name a sound, the remembrance of which most perfectly revives the impression which the beach has made, it would be the dreary peep of the piping plover (*Charadrius melodus*) which haunts there.

Their voices, too, are heard as a fugacious part in the dirge which is ever played along the shore for those mariners who have been lost in the deep since first it was created. But through all this dreariness we seemed to have a pure and unqualified strain of eternal melody, for always the same strain which is a dirge to one household is a morning song of rejoicing to another. . . .

Still held on without a break the inland barrens and shrubbery, the desert and the high sand-bank with its even slope, the broad white beach, the breakers, the green water on the bar, and the Atlantic Ocean; and we traversed with delight new reaches of the shore; we took another lesson in sea-horses' manes and sea-cows' tails, in sea-jellies and sea-clams, with our new-gained experience. The sea ran hardly less than the day before. It seemed with every wave to be subsiding, because such was our expectation, and yet when hours had elapsed we could see no difference. But there it was, balancing itself, the restless ocean by our side, lurching in its gait. Each wave left the sand all braided or woven, as it were with a coarse woof and warp, and a distinct raised edge to its rapid work. We made no haste, since we wished to see the ocean at our leisure, and indeed that soft sand was no place in which to be in a hurry, for one mile there was as good as two elsewhere. Besides, we were obliged frequently to empty our shoes of the sand which one took in in climbing or descending the bank.

As we were walking close to the water's edge this morning, we turned round, by chance, and saw a large black object which the waves had just cast up on the beach behind us, yet too far off for us to distinguish what it was; and when we were about to return to it, two men came running from the bank, where no human beings had appeared before, as if they had come out of the sand, in order to save it before another wave took it. As we approached, it took successively the form of a huge fish, a drowned man, a sail or a net, and finally of a mass of tow-cloth, part of the cargo of the Franklin, which the men loaded into a cart.

Objects on the beach, whether men or inanimate things, look not only exceedingly grotesque, but much larger and more wonderful than they actually are. Lately, when approaching the seashore several degrees south of this, I saw before me, seemingly half a mile distant, what appeared like bold and rugged cliffs on the beach, fifteen feet high, and whitened by the sun and waves; but after a few steps it proved to be low heaps of rags,—part of the cargo of a wrecked vessel,—scarcely more than a foot in height.

Once also it was my business to go in search of the relics of a human body, mangled by sharks, which had just been cast up, a week after a wreck, having got the direction from a light-house: I should find it a mile or two distant over the sand, a dozen rods from the water, covered with a cloth, by a stick stuck up. I expected that I must look very narrowly to find so small an object, but the sandy beach, half a mile wide, and stretching farther than the eye could reach, was so perfectly smooth and bare, and the mirage toward the sea so magnifying, that when I was half a mile distant the insignificant sliver which marked the spot looked like a bleached spar, and the relics were as conspicuous as if they lay in state on that sandy plain, or a generation had labored to pile up their cairn there.

Close at hand they were simply some bones with a little flesh adhering to them, in fact, only a slight inequality in the sweep of the shore. There was nothing at all remarkable about them, and they were singularly inoffensive both to the senses and the imagination. But as I stood there they grew more and more imposing. They were alone with the beach and the sea, whose hollow roar seemed addressed to them, and I was impressed as if there was an understanding between them and the ocean which necessarily left me out, with my snivelling sympathies. That dead body had taken possession of the shore, and reigned over it as no living one could, in the name of a certain majesty which belonged to it.

We afterward saw many small pieces of tow-cloth washed up, and I learn that it continued to be found in good condition, even as late as November in that year, half a dozen bolts at a time.

We eagerly filled our pockets with the smooth round pebbles which in some places, even here, were thinly sprinkled over the sand, together with flat circular shells (*Scutellæ?*); but, as we had read, when they were dry they had lost their beauty, and at each sitting we emptied our pockets again of the least remarkable, until our collection was well culled. Every material was rolled into the pebble form by the waves; not only stones of various kinds, but the hard coal which some vessel had dropped, bits of glass, and in one instance a mass of peat three feet long, where there was nothing like it to be seen for many miles. All the great rivers of the globe are annually, if not constantly, discharging great quantities of lumber, which drifts to distant shores.

I have also seen very perfect pebbles of brick, and bars of Castile soap from a wreck rolled into perfect cylinders, and still spirally streaked with red, like a barber's pole. When a cargo of rags is washed ashore, every old pocket and bag-like recess will be filled to bursting with sand by being rolled on the beach; and on one occasion, the pockets in the clothing of the wrecked being thus puffed up, even after they had been ripped open by wreckers, deluded me into the hope of identifying them by the contents. A pair of gloves looked exactly as if filled by a hand. The water in such clothing is soon wrung out and evaporated, but the sand, which works itself into every seam, is not so easily got rid of. Sponges, which are picked up on the shore, as is well known, retain some of the sand of the beach to the latest day, in spite of every effort to extract it. . . .

The sea, vast and wild as it is, bears thus the waste and wrecks of human art to its remotest shore. There is no telling what it may not vomit up. It lets nothing lie; not even the giant clams which cling to its bottom. It is still heaving up the tow-cloth of the Franklin, and perhaps a piece of some old pirate's ship, wrecked more than a hundred years ago, comes ashore to-day. Some years since, when a vessel was wrecked here which had nutmegs in her cargo, they were strewn all along the beach, and for a considerable time were not spoiled by the salt water. Soon afterward, a fisherman caught a cod which was full of them. Why, then, might not the Spice-Islanders shake their nutmeg-trees into the ocean, and let all nations who stand in need of them pick them up? However, after a year, I found that the nutmegs from the Franklin had become soft.

I picked up a bottle half buried in the wet sand, covered with barnacles, but stoppled tight, and half full of red ale, which still smacked of juniper,—all that remained I fancied from the wreck of a rowdy world,—that great salt sea on the one hand, and this little sea of ale on the other, preserving their separate characters. What if it could tell us its adventures over countless ocean waves! Man would not be man through such ordeals as it had passed. But as I poured it slowly out on to the sand, it seemed to me that man himself was like a half-emptied bottle of pale ale, which Time had drunk so far, yet stoppled tight for a while, and drifting about in the ocean of circumstances, but destined erelong to mingle with the surrounding waves, or be spilled amid the sands of a distant shore. . . .

The Cape became narrower and narrower as we approached its wrist between Truro and Provincetown and the shore inclined more decidedly to the west. At the head of East Harbor Creek, the Atlantic is separated but by half a dozen rods of sand from the tide-waters of the Bay. From the Clay Pounds the bank flatted off for the last ten miles to the extremity at Race Point, though the highest parts, which are called "islands" from their appearance at a distance on the sea, were still seventy or eighty feet above the Atlantic, and afforded a good view of the latter, as well as a constant view of the Bay, there being no trees nor a hill sufficient to interrupt it. Also the sands began to invade the land more and more, until finally they had entire possession from sea to sea, at the narrowest part. For three or four miles between Truro and Provincetown there were no inhabitants from shore to shore, and there were but three or four houses for twice that distance. . . .

It was even more cold and windy to-day than before, and we were frequently glad to take shelter behind a sand-hill. None of the elements were resting. On the beach there is a ceaseless activity, always something going on, in storm and in calm, winter and summer, night and day. Even the sedentary man here enjoys a breadth of view which is almost equivalent to motion. In clear weather the laziest may look across the Bay as far as Plymouth at a glance, or over the Atlantic as far as human vision reaches, merely raising his eyelids; or if he is too lazy to look after all, he can hardly help *hearing* the ceaseless dash and roar of the breakers. The restless ocean may at any moment cast up a whale or a wrecked vessel at your feet. All the reporters in the world, the most rapid stenographers, could not report the news it brings. No creature could move slowly where there was so much life around. . . .

I used to see packs of half-wild dogs haunting the lonely beach on the south shore of Staten Island, in New York Bay, for the sake of the carrion there cast up; and I remember that once, when for a long time I had heard a furious barking in the tall grass of the marsh, a pack of half a dozen large dogs burst forth on to the beach, pursuing a little one which ran straight to me for protection, and I afforded it with some stones, though at some risk to myself; but the next day the little one was the first to bark at me. . . .

Sometimes, when I was approaching the carcass of a horse or ox which lay on the beach there, where there was no living creature in sight, a dog would unexpectedly emerge from it and slink away with a mouthful of offal.

The seashore is a sort of neutral ground, a most advantageous point from which to contemplate this world. It is even a trivial place. The waves forever rolling to the land are too far-traveled and untamable to be familiar. Creeping along the endless beach amid the sun-squawl and the foam, it occurs to us that we, too, are the product of sea-slime.

It is a wild, rank place, and there is no flattery in it. Strewn with crabs, horse-shoes, and razor-clams, and whatever the sea casts up,—a vast *morgue,* where famished dogs may range in packs, and crows come daily to glean the pittance which the tide leaves them. The carcasses of men and beasts together lie stately up upon its shelf, rotting and bleaching in the sun and waves, and each tide turns them in their beds, and tucks fresh sand under them. There is naked Nature,—inhumanly sincere, wasting no thought on man, nibbling at the cliffy shore where gulls wheel amid the spray. . . .

Before sunset, having already seen the mackerel fleet returning into the Bay, we left the seashore on the north of Provincetown, and made our way across the desert to the eastern extremity of the town. From the first high sand-hill, covered with beach-grass and bushes to its top, on the edge of the desert, we overlooked the shrubby hill and swamp country which surrounds Provincetown on the north, and protects it, in some measure, from the invading sand. Notwithstanding the universal barrenness, and the contiguity of the desert, I never saw an autumnal landscape so beautifully painted as this was.

It was like the richest rug imaginable spread over an uneven surface; no damask nor velvet, nor Tyrian dye or stuffs, nor the work of any loom, could ever match it. There was the incredibly bright red of the Huckleberry, and the reddish brown of the Bayberry, mingled with the bright and living green of small Pitch-Pines, and also the duller green of the Bayberry, Boxberry, and Plum, the yellowish green of the Shrub-Oaks, and the various golden and yellow and fawn-colored tints of the Birch and Maple and Aspen,—each making its own figure, and, in the midst, the few yellow sandslides on the sides of the hills looked like the white floor seen through rents in the rug.

Coming from the country as I did, and many autumnal woods as I had seen, this was perhaps the most novel and remarkable sight that I saw on the Cape. Probably the brightness of the tints was enhanced by contrast with the sand which surrounded this tract. This was a part of the furniture of Cape Cod. We had for days walked up the long and bleak piazza which runs along her Atlantic side, then over the sanded floor of her halls, and now we were being introduced into her boudoir. The hundred white sails crowding round Long Point into Provincetown Harbor, seen over the painted hills in front, looked like toy ships upon a mantel-piece.

The peculiarity of this autumnal landscape consisted in the lowness and thickness of the shrubbery, no less than in the brightness of the tints. It was like a thick stuff of worsted or a fleece, and looked as if a giant could take it up by the hem, or rather the tasseled fringe which trailed out on the sand, and shake it, though it needed not to be shaken. But no doubt the dust would fly in that case, for not a little has accumulated underneath it. Was it not such an autumnal landscape as this which suggested our high-colored rugs and carpets? Hereafter when I look on a richer rug than usual, and study its figures, I shall think, there are the huckleberry hills, and there the denser swamps of boxberry and blueberry; there the shrub-oak patches and the bayberries, there the maples and the birches and the pines. What other dyes are to be compared to these? They were warmer colors than I had associated with the New England coast.

After threading a swamp full of boxberry, and climbing several hills covered with shrub-oaks, without a path, where shipwrecked men would be in danger of perishing in the night, we came down upon the eastern extremity of the four planks which run the whole length of Provincetown street. This, which is the last town on the Cape, lies mainly in one street along the curving beach fronting the southeast. The sand-hills, covered with shrubbery and interposed with swamps and ponds, rose immediately behind it in the form of a crescent, which is from half a mile to a mile or more wide in the middle, and beyond these is the desert, which is the greater part of its territory, stretching to the sea on the east and west and north.

1864

From The Maine Woods

Thoreau traveled to the Maine backwoods in the summer of 1846 to visit "some of the lakes of Penobscot" (he considered them "the Lake-country of New England"—the New England counterpart to the Lake district of Wordsworth and Coleridge) and to climb Mount Katahdin. The mountain had not yet been much visited by whites, but he had evidently read the accounts of travelers who had climbed it in 1836,

1837, and 1845. His own account he wrote and published in *Atlantic* magazine. It was incorporated into *The Maine Woods* (1864) by Sophia Thoreau and Ellery Channing. The excerpt included here covers a two-day period (7–8 September 1846) beginning with his approach to the summit. He is accompanied by guides and by a friend.

From Ktaadn

AT LENGTH we reached an elevation sufficiently bare to afford a view of the summit, still distant and blue, almost as if retreating from us. A torrent, which proved to be the same we had crossed, was seen tumbling down in front, literally from out of the clouds. But this glimpse at our whereabouts was soon lost, and we were buried in the woods again. The wood was chiefly yellow birch, spruce, fir, mountain-ash, or round-wood, as the Maine people call it, and moose-wood. It was the worst kind of travelling; sometimes like the densest scrub-oak patches with us. The cornel, or bunch-berries, were very abundant, as well as Solomon's seal and moose-berries. Blueberries were distributed along our whole route; and in one place the bushes were drooping with the weight of the fruit, still as fresh as ever. It was the 7th of September. Such patches afforded a grateful repast, and served to bait the tired party forward. When any lagged behind, the cry of "blueberries" was most effectual to bring them up. Even at this elevation we passed through a moose-yard, formed by a large flat rock, four or five rods square, where they tread down the snow in winter. At length, fearing that if we held the direct course to the summit we should not find any water near our camping-ground, we gradually swerved to the west, till, at four o'clock, we struck again the torrent which I have mentioned, and here, in view of the summit, the weary party decided to camp that night.

While my companions were seeking a suitable spot for this purpose, I improved the little daylight that was left, in climbing the mountain alone. We were in a deep and narrow ravine, sloping up to the clouds, at an angle of nearly forty-five degrees, and hemmed in by walls of rock, which were at first covered with low trees, then with impenetrable thickets of scraggy birches and spruce-trees, and with moss, but at last bare of all vegetation but lichens, and almost continually draped in clouds. Following up the course of the torrent which occupied this,—and I mean to lay some emphasis on this word *up,*—pulling myself up by the side of perpendicular falls of twenty or thirty feet, by the roots of firs and birches, and then, perhaps, walking a level rod or two in the thin stream, for it took up the whole road, ascending by huge steps, as it were, a giant's stairway, down which a river flowed, I had soon cleared the trees, and paused on the successive shelves, to look back over the country. The torrent was from fifteen to thirty feet wide, without a tributary, and seemingly not diminishing in breadth as I advanced; but still it came rushing and roaring down, with a copious tide over and amidst masses of bare rock, from the very clouds, as though a waterspout had just burst over the mountain. Leaving this at last, I began to work my way, scarcely less arduous than Satan's anciently through Chaos, up the nearest, though not the highest peak. At first scrambling on all fours over the tops of ancient black spruce-trees (*Abies nigra*), old as the flood, from two to ten or twelve feet in height, their tops flat and spreading, and their foliage blue, and nipt with cold, as if for centuries they had ceased growing upward against the bleak sky, the solid cold. I walked some good rods erect upon the tops of these trees, which were overgrown with moss and mountain-cranberries. It seemed that in the course of time they had filled up the intervals between the huge rocks, and the cold wind had uniformly levelled all over. Here the principle of vegetation was hard put to it. There was apparently a belt of this kind running quite round the mountain, though, perhaps nowhere so remarkable as here. Once, slumping through, I looked down ten feet, into a dark and cavernous region, and saw the stem of a spruce, on whose top I stood, as on a mass of coarse basket-work, fully nine inches in diameter at the ground. These holes were bears' dens, and the bears were even then at home. This was the sort of garden I made my way *over,* for an eighth of a mile, at the risk, it is true, of treading on some of the plants, not seeing any path *through* it,—certainly the most treacherous and porous country I ever travelled.

> ''Nigh foundered on he fares,
> Treading the crude consistence, half on foot,
> Half flying.'' *

But nothing could exceed the toughness of the twigs,—not one snapped under my weight, for they had slowly grown. Having slumped, scrambled, rolled, bounced, and walked, by turns, over this scraggy country, I arrived upon a side-hill, or rather side-mountain, where rocks, gray, silent rocks, were the flocks and herds that pastured, chewing a rocky cud at sunset. They looked at me with hard gray eyes, without a bleat or a low. This brought me to the skirt of a cloud, and bounded my walk that night. But I had already seen that Maine country when I turned about, waving, flowing, rippling, down below.

When I returned to my companions, they had selected a camping-ground on the torrent's edge, and were resting on the ground; one was on the sick list, rolled in a blanket, on a damp shelf of rock. It was a savage and dreary scenery enough; so wildly rough, that they looked long to find a level and open space for the tent. We could not well camp higher, for want of fuel; and the trees here seemed so evergreen and sappy, that we almost doubted if they would acknowledge the influence of fire; but fire prevailed at last, and blazed here, too, like a

* Milton's *Paradise Lost.* Book 2, l. 941. The lines quoted here and in the following note refer to Satan's journey to the throne of Chaos after being banished from heaven—ed.

good citizen of the world. Even at this height we met with frequent traces of moose, as well as of bears. As here was no cedar, we made our bed of coarser feathered spruce; but at any rate the feathers were plucked from the live tree. It was, perhaps, even a more grand and desolate place for a night's lodging than the summit would have been, being in the neighborhood of those wild trees, and of the torrent. Some more aerial and finer-spirited winds rushed and roared through the ravine all night, from time to time arousing our fire, and dispersing the embers about. It was as if we lay in the very nest of a young whirlwind. At midnight, one of my bed-fellows, being startled in his dreams by the sudden blazing up to its top of a fir-tree, whose green boughs were dried by the heat, sprang up, with a cry, from his bed, thinking the world on fire, and drew the whole camp after him.

In the morning, after whetting our appetite on some raw pork, a wafer of hard bread, and a dipper of condensed cloud or waterspout, we all together began to make our way up the falls, which I have described; this time choosing the right hand, or highest peak, which was not the one I had approached before. But soon my companions were lost to my sight behind the mountain ridge in my rear, which still seemed ever retreating before me, and I climbed alone over huge rocks, loosely poised, a mile or more, still edging toward the clouds; for though the day was clear elsewhere, the summit was concealed by mist. The mountain seemed a vast aggregation of loose rocks, as if some time it had rained rocks, and they lay as they fell on the mountain sides, nowhere fairly at rest, but leaning on each other, all rocking-stones, with cavities between, but scarcely any soil or smoother shelf. They were the raw materials of a planet dropped from an unseen quarry, which the vast chemistry of nature would anon work up, or work down, into the smiling and verdant plains and valleys of earth. This was an undone extremity of the globe; as in lignite we see coal in the process of formation.

At length I entered within the skirts of the cloud which seemed forever drifting over the summit, and yet would never be gone, but was generated out of that pure air as fast as it flowed away; and when, a quarter of a mile farther. I reached the summit of the ridge, which those who have seen in clearer weather say is about five miles long, and contains a thousand acres of table-land, I was deep within the hostile ranks of clouds, and all objects were obscured by them. Now the wind would blow me out a yard of clear sunlight, wherein I stood; then a gray, dawning light was all it could accomplish, the cloud-line ever rising and falling with the wind's intensity. Sometimes it seemed as if the summit would be cleared in a few moments, and smile in sunshine: but what was gained on one side was lost on another. It was like sitting in a chimney and waiting for the smoke to blow away. It was, in fact, a cloud-factory,—these were the cloud-works, and the wind turned them off done from the cool, bare rocks. Occasionally, when the windy columns broke in to me, I caught sight of a dark, damp crag to the right or left; the mist driving ceaselessly between it and me. It reminded me of the creations of the old epic and dramatic poets, of Atlas, Vulcan, the Cyclops, and Prometheus. Such was Caucasus and the rock where Prometheus was bound. Æschylus had no doubt visited such scenery as this. It was vast, Titanic, and such as man never inhabits. Some part of the beholder, even some vital part, seems to escape through the loose grating of his ribs as he ascends. He is more lone than you can imagine. There is less of substantial thought and fair understanding in him, than in the plains where men inhabit. His reason is dispersed and shadowy, more thin and subtile, like the air. Vast, Titanic, inhuman Nature has got him at disadvantage, caught him alone, and pilfers him some of his divine faculty. She does not smile on him as in the plains. She seems to say sternly, why came ye here before your time? This ground is not prepared for you. Is it not enough that I smile in the valleys? I have never made this soil for thy feet, this air for thy breathing, these rocks for thy neighbors. I cannot pity nor fondle thee here, but forever relentlessly drive thee hence to where I *am* kind. Why seek me where I have not called thee, and then complain because you find me but a stepmother? Shouldst thous freeze or starve, or shudder thy life away, here is no shrine, nor alter, nor any access to my ear.

> "Chaos and ancient Night, I come no spy
> With purpose to explore or to disturb
> The secrets of your realm, but . . .
> . . . . as my way
> Lies through your spacious empire up to light." *

The tops of mountains are among the unfinished parts of the globe, whither it is a slight insult to the gods to climb and pry into their secrets, and try their effect on our humanity. Only daring and insolent men, perchance, go there. Simple races, as savages, do not climb mountains,—their tops are sacred and mysterious tracts never visited by them. Pomola is always angry with those who climb to the summit of Ktaadn.

According to Jackson, who, in his capacity of geological surveyor of the State, has accurately measured it,—the altitude of Ktaadn is 5,300 feet, or a little more than one mile above the level of the sea,—and he adds, "It is then evidently the highest point in the State of Maine, and is the most abrupt granite mountain in New England." The peculiarities of that spacious table-land on which I was standing, as well as the remarkable semi-circular precipice or basin on the eastern side, were all concealed by the mist. I had brought my whole pack to the top, not knowing but I should have to make my descent to the river, and possibly to the settled portion of the State alone, and by some other route,

* *Paradise Lost*. Book 2, 1. 974. Satan is now addressing Chaos and Night, who are "Powers / And Spirits of the nethermost abyss" of hell—ed.

and wishing to have a complete outfit with me. But at length, fearing that my companions would be anxious to reach the river before night, and knowing that the clouds might rest on the mountain for days, I was compelled to descend. Occasionally, as I came down, the wind would blow me a vista open, through which I could see the country eastward, boundless forests, and lakes, and streams, gleaming in the sun, some of them emptying into the East Branch. There were also new mountains in sight in that direction. Now and then some small bird of the sparrow family would flit away before me, unable to command its course, like a fragment of the gray rock blown off by the wind.

I found my companions where I had left them, on the side of the peak, gathering the mountain cranberries, which filled every crevice between the rocks, together with blueberries, which had a spicier flavor the higher up they grew, but were not the less agreeable to our palates. When the country is settled, and roads are made, these cranberries will perhaps become an article of commerce. From this elevation, just on the skirts of the clouds, we could overlook the country, west and south, for a hundred miles. There it was, the State of Maine, which we had seen on the map, but not much like that,—immeasurable forest for the sun to shine on, that eastern *stuff* we hear of in Massachusetts. No clearing, no house. It did not look as if a solitary traveller had cut so much as a walking-stick there. Countless lakes,—Moosehead in the southwest, forty miles long by ten wide, like a gleaming silver platter at the end of the table; Chesuncook, eighteen long by three wide, without an island; Millinocket, on the south, with its hundred islands; and a hundred others without a name; and mountains also, whose names, for the most part, are known only to the Indians. The forest looked like a firm grass sward, and the effect of these lakes in its midst has been well compared, by one who has since visited this same spot, to that of a "mirror broken into a thousand fragments, and wildly scattered over the grass, reflecting the full blaze of the sun." It was a large farm for somebody, when cleared. According to the Gazetteer, which was printed before the boundary question was settled, this single Penobscot county, in which we were, was larger than the whole State of Vermont, with its fourteen counties; and this was only a part of the wild lands of Maine. We are concerned now, however, about natural, not political limits. We were about eighty miles, as the bird flies, from Bangor, or one hundred and fifteen, as we had rode, and walked, and paddled. We had to console ourselves with the reflection that this view was probably as good as that from the peak, as far as it went; and what were a mountain without its attendant clouds and mists? Like ourselves, neither Bailey nor Jackson had obtained a clear view from the summit.

Setting out on our return to the river, still at an early hour in the day, we decided to follow the course of the torrent, which we supposed to be Murch Brook, as long as it would not lead us too far out of our way. We thus travelled about four miles in the very torrent itself, continually crossing and recrossing it, leaping from rock to rock, and jumping with the stream down falls of seven or eight feet, or sometimes sliding down on our backs in a thin sheet of water. This ravine had been the scene of an extraordinary freshet in the spring, apparently accompanied by a slide from the mountain. It must have been filled with a stream of stones and water, at least twenty feet above the present level of the torrent. For a rod or two, on either side of its channel, the trees were barked and splintered up to their tops, the birches bent over, twisted, and sometimes finely split, like a stablebroom; some, a foot in diameter, snapped off, and whole clumps of trees bent over with the weight of rocks piled on them. In one place we noticed a rock, two or three feet in diameter, lodged nearly twenty feet high in the crotch of a tree. For the whole four miles, we saw but one rill emptying in, and the volume of water did not seem to be increased from the first. We travelled thus very rapidly with a downward impetus, and grew remarkably expert at leaping from rock to rock, for leap we must, and leap we did, whether there was any rock at the right distance or not. It was a pleasant picture when the foremost turned about and looked up the winding ravine, walled in with rocks and the green forest, to see, at intervals of a rod or two, a red-shirted or green-jacketed mountaineer against the white torrent, leaping down the channel with his pack on his back, or pausing upon a convenient rock in the midst of the torrent to mend a rent in his clothes, or unstrap the dipper at his belt to take a draught of the water. At one place we were startled by seeing, on a little sandy shelf by the side of the stream, the fresh print of a man's foot, and for a moment realized how Robinson Crusoe felt in a similar case; but at last we remembered that we had struck this stream on our way up, though we could not have told where, and one had descended into the ravine for a drink. The cool air above, and the continual bathing of our bodies in mountain water, alternate foot, sitz, douche, and plunge baths, made this walk exceedingly refreshing, and we had travelled only a mile or two, after leaving the torrent, before every thread of our clothes was as dry as usual, owing perhaps to a peculiar quality in the atmosphere.

After leaving the torrent, being in doubt about our course, Tom threw down his pack at the foot of the loftiest spruce tree at hand, and shinned up the bare trunk, some twenty feet, and then climbed through the green tower, lost to our sight, until he held the topmost spray in his hand. . . . To Tom we cried, Where away does the summit bear? where the burnt lands? The last he could only conjecture; he descried, however, a little meadow and pond, lying probably in our course, which we concluded to steer for. On reaching this secluded meadow, we found fresh tracks of moose on the shore of the pond, and the water was still unsettled as if they had fled before us. A little farther, in a dense thicket, we seemed to be still on their trail. It was a small meadow, of a few acres, on the mountain side, concealed by the forest, and perhaps never seen by a white man before, where one would think that the moose might browse and bathe, and rest in peace. Pursuing this course, we soon reached the open land, which went sloping down some miles toward the Penobscot.

Perhaps I most fully realized that this was primeval, untamed, and forever untameable *Nature,* or whatever else men call it, while coming down this part of the mountain. We were passing over "Burnt Lands," burnt by lightning, perchance, though they showed no recent marks of fire, hardly so much as a charred stump, but looked rather like a natural pasture for the moose and deer, exceedingly wild and desolate, with occasional strips of timber crossing them, and low poplars springing up, and patches of blueberries here and there. I found myself traversing them familiarly, like some pasture run to waste, or partially reclaimed by man; but when I reflected what man, what brother or sister or kinsman of our race made it and claimed it, I expected the proprietor to rise up and dispute my passage. It is difficult to conceive of a region uninhabited by man. We habitually presume his presence and influence everywhere. And yet we have not seen pure Nature, unless we have seen her thus vast and drear and inhuman, though in the midst of cities. Nature was here something savage and awful, though beautiful. I looked with awe at the ground I trod on, to see what the Powers had made there, the form and fashion and material of their work. This was that Earth of which we have heard, made out of Chaos and Old Night. Here was no man's garden, but the unhandselled globe. It was not lawn, nor pasture, nor mead, nor woodland, nor lea, nor arable, nor waste-land. It was the fresh and natural surface of the planet Earth, as it was made for ever and ever,—to be the dwelling of man, we say—so Nature made it, and man may use it if he can. Man was not to be associated with it. It was Matter, vast, terrific,—not his Mother Earth that we have heard of, not for him to tread on, or be buried in,—no, it were being too familiar even to let his bones lie there,—the home, this, of Necessity and Fate. There was there felt the presence of a force not bound to be kind to man. It was a place for heathenism and superstitious rites,—to be inhabited by men nearer of kin to the rocks and to wild animals than we. We walked over it with a certain awe, stopping, from time to time, to pick the blueberries which grew there, and had a smart and spicy taste. Perchance where *our* wild pines stand, and leaves lie on their forest floor, in Concord, there were once reapers, and husbandmen planted grain; but here not even the surface had been scarred by man, but it was a specimen of what God saw fit to make this world. What is it to be admitted to a museum, to see a myriad of particular things, compared with being shown some star's surface, some hard matter in its home! I stand in awe of my body, this matter to which I am bound has become so strange to me. I fear not spirits, ghosts, of which I am one,—*that* my body might,—but I fear bodies, I tremble to meet them. What is this Titan that has possession of me? Talk of mysteries!—Think of our life in nature,—daily to be shown matter, to come in contact with it,—rocks, trees, wind on our cheeks! the *solid* earth! the *actual* world! the *common sense! Contact! Contact! Who* are we? *where* are we?

1864

John Muir

From The Mountains of California

Muir was a drop-out from the University of Wisconsin, where he had studied botany and geology and had showed a flair for mechanical inventions. In 1867 he began a field trip-pilgrimage from Indiana to the Gulf of Mexico to "study the inventions of God." Another such journey led him to the California Sierras in 1868. By 1890 he had earned enough at fruit-growing in California to retire from any practical calling. The year before he had begun, with Robert Underwood Johnson, a campaign to establish a National Park which would include the Yosemite Valley. As a result of the two men's efforts the Yosemite, Sequoia, and General Grant National parks were established in 1890. Muir's contributions included a series of descriptive essays on the Sierra landscape, which he composed from voluminous field journals (serious students of landscape in America have always kept such journals, verbally sketching in them their impressions and observations). The descriptive essays in turn became the basis for his first and greatest book, *The Mountains of California,* published in 1894. In the book, he wrote to a friend, he tried to describe the mountains as a traveler might come to see them. In the "opening chapter" ("The Sierra Nevada"), he wrote elsewhere, revealing his technique throughout the book, "I have ventured to drop into the poetry that I like, but have taken good care to place it between the bluffs and buttresses of bald, glacial geological facts." "A Near View of the High Sierra" takes place on Mount Ritter; "Wind-Storm in the Forests," in the Yuba River Valley.

From A Near View of the High Sierra

EARLY ONE BRIGHT MORNING in the middle of Indian summer, while the glacier meadows were still crisp with frost crystals, I set out from the foot of Mount Lyell, on my way down to Yosemite Valley, to replenish my exhausted store of bread and tea. I had spent the past summer, as many preceding ones, exploring the glaciers that lie on the head waters of the San Joaquin, Tuolumne, Merced, and Owen's rivers; measuring and studying their movements, trends, crevasses, moraines, etc., and the part they had played during the period of their greater extension in the creation and development of the landscapes of this alpine wonderland. The time for this kind of work was nearly over for the year, and I began to look forward with delight to the approaching winter with its wondrous storms, when I would be warmly snow-bound in my Yosemite cabin with plenty of bread and books; but a tinge of regret came on when I considered that possibly I might not see this favorite region again until the next summer, excepting distant views from the heights about the Yosemite walls.

To artists, few portions of the High Sierra are, strictly speaking, picturesque. The whole massive uplift of the range is one great picture, not clearly divisible into smaller ones; differing much in this respect from the older, and what may be called, riper mountains of the Coast Range. All the landscapes of the Sierra, as we have seen, were born again, remodeled from base to summit by the developing ice-floods of the last glacial winter. But all these new landscapes were not brought forth simultaneously; some of the highest, where the ice lingered longest, are tens of centuries younger than those of the warmer regions below them. In general, the younger the mountain-landscapes,—younger, I mean, with reference to the time of their emergence from the ice of the glacial period,—the less separable are they into artistic bits capable of being made into warm, sympathetic, lovable pictures with appreciable humanity in them.

Here, however, on the head waters of the Tuolumne, is a group of wild peaks on which the geologist may say that the sun has but just begun to shine, which is yet in a high degree picturesque, and in its main features so regular and evenly balanced as almost to appear conventional—one somber cluster of snow-laden peaks with gray pine-fringed granite bosses braided around its base, the whole surging free into the sky from the head of a magnificent valley, whose lofty walls are beveled away on both sides so as to embrace it all without admitting anything not strictly belonging to it. The foreground was now aflame with autumn colors, brown and purple and gold, ripe in the mellow sunshine; contrasting brightly with the deep, cobalt blue of the sky, and the black and gray, and pure, spiritual white of the rocks and glaciers. Down through the midst, the young Tuolumne was seen pouring from its crystal fountains, now resting in glassy pools as if changing back again into ice, now leaping in white cascades as if turning to snow; gliding right and left between granite bosses, then sweeping on through the smooth, meadowy levels of the valley, swaying pensively from side to side with calm, stately gestures past dipping willows and sedges, and around groves of arrowy pine; and throughout its whole eventful course, whether flowing fast or slow, singing loud or low, ever filling the landscape with spiritual animation, and manifesting the grandeur of its sources in every movement and tone.

Pursuing my lonely way down the valley, I turned again and again to gaze on the glorious picture, throwing up my arms to inclose it as in a frame. After long ages of growth in the darkness beneath the glaciers, through sunshine and storms, it seemed now to be ready and waiting for the elected artist, like yellow wheat for the reaper; and I could not help wishing that I might carry colors and brushes with me on my travels, and learn to paint. In the mean time I had to be content with photographs on my mind and sketches in my notebooks. At length, after I had rounded a precipitous headland that puts out from the west wall of the valley, every peak vanished from sight, and I pushed rapidly along the frozen meadows, over the divide between the waters of the Merced and Tuolumne, and down through the forests that clothe the slopes of Cloud's Rest, arriving in Yosemite in due time—which, with me, is *any* time. And, strange to say, among the first people I met here were two artists who, with letters of introduction, were awaiting my return. They inquired whether in the course of my explorations in the adjacent mountains I had ever come upon a landscape suitable for a large painting; whereupon I began a description of the one that had so lately excited my admiration. Then, as I went on further and further into details, their faces began to glow, and I offered to guide them to it, while they declared that they would gladly follow, far or near, whithersoever I could spare the time to lead them.

Since storms might come breaking down through the fine weather at any time, burying the colors in snow, and cutting off the artists' retreat, I advised getting ready at once.

I led them out of the valley by the Vernal and Nevada Falls, thence over the main dividing ridge to the Big Tuolumne Meadows, by the old Mono trail, and thence along the upper Tuolumne River to its head. This was my companions' first excursion into the High Sierra, and as I was almost always alone in my mountaineering, the way that the fresh beauty was reflected in their faces made for me a novel and interesting study. They naturally were affected most of all by the colors—the intense azure of the sky, the purplish grays of the granite, the red and browns of dry meadows, and the translucent purple and crimson of huckleberry bogs; the flaming yellow of aspen groves, the silvery flashing of the streams, and the bright green and blue of the glacier lakes. But the general expression of the scenery—rocky and savage—seemed sadly disappointing; and as they threaded the forest from ridge to ridge, eagerly scanning the landscapes as they were unfolded, they said: "All this is huge and sublime, but we see nothing as yet at all available for effective pictures. Art is long, and art is limited, you know; and here are foregrounds, middle-grounds, backgrounds, all alike; bare rock-waves, woods, groves, diminutive flecks of meadow, and strips of glittering water." "Never mind," I replied, "only bide a wee, and I will show you something you will like."

At length, toward the end of the second day, the Sierra Crown began to come into view, and when we had fairly rounded the projecting headland before mentioned, the whole picture stood revealed in the flush of the alpenglow. Their enthusiasm was excited beyond bounds, and the more impulsive of the two, a young Scotchman, dashed ahead, shouting and gesticulating and tossing his arms in the air like a madman. Here, at last, was a typical alpine landscape.

After feasting a while on the view, I proceeded to make camp in a sheltered grove a little way back from the meadow, where pine-boughs could be obtained for beds, and where there was plenty of dry wood for fires, while the artists ran here and there, along the river-bends and up the sides of the cañon, choosing foregrounds for sketches. After dark, when our tea was made and a rousing fire had been built, we began to make our plans. They decided to remain several days, at the least, while I concluded to make an excursion in the mean time to the untouched summit of Ritter.

It was now about the middle of October, the springtime of snow-flowers.

The first winter-clouds had already bloomed, and the peaks were strewn with fresh crystals, without, however, affecting the climbing to any dangerous extent. And as the weather was still profoundly calm, and the distance to the foot of the mountain only a little more than a day, I felt that I was running no great risk of being storm-bound.

Mount Ritter is king of the mountains of the middle portion of the High Sierra, as Shasta of the north and Whitney of the south sections. Moreover, as far as I know, it had never been climbed. I had explored the adjacent wilderness summer after summer, but my studies thus far had never drawn me to the top of it. Its height above sea-level is about 13,300 feet, and it is fenced round by steeply inclined glaciers, and cañons of tremendous depth and ruggedness, which render it almost inaccessible. But difficulties of this kind only exhilarate the mountaineer.

Next morning, the artists went heartily to their work and I to mine. Former experiences had given good reason to know that passionate storms, invisible as yet, might be brooding in the calm sun-gold; therefore, before bidding farewell, I warned the artists not to be alarmed should I fail to appear before a week or ten days, and advised them, in case a snow-storm should set in, to keep up big fires and shelter themselves as best they could, and on no account to become frightened and attempt to seek their way back to Yosemite alone through the drifts.

My general plan was simply this: to scale the cañon wall, cross over to the eastern flank of the range, and then make my way southward to the northern spurs of Mount Ritter in compliance with the intervening topography; for to push on directly southward from camp through the innumerable peaks and pinnacles that adorn this portion of the axis of the range, however interesting, would take too much time, besides being extremely difficult and dangerous at this time of year.

All my first day was pure pleasure; simply mountaineering indulgence, crossing the dry pathways of the ancient glaciers, tracing happy streams, and learning the habits of the birds and marmots in the groves and rocks. Before I had gone a mile from camp, I came to the foot of a white cascade that beats its way down a rugged gorge in the cañon wall, from a height of about nine hundred feet, and pours its throbbing waters into the Tuolumne. I was acquainted with its fountains, which, fortunately, lay in my course. What a fine traveling companion it proved to be, what songs it sang, and how passionately it told the mountain's own joy! Gladly I climbed along its dashing border, absorbing its divine music, and bathing from time to time in waftings of irised spray. Climbing higher, higher, new beauty came streaming on the sight: painted meadows, late-blooming gardens, peaks of rare architecture, lakes here and there, shining like silver, and glimpses of the forested middle region and the yellow lowlands far in the west. Beyond the range I saw the so-called Mono

Desert, lying dreamily silent in thick purple light—a desert of heavy sun-glare beheld from a desert of ice-burnished granite. Here the waters divide, shouting in glorious enthusiasm, and falling eastward to vanish in the volcanic sands and dry sky of the Great Basin, or westward to the Great Valley of California, and thence through the Bay of San Francisco and the Golden Gate to the sea.

Passing a little way down over the summit until I had reached an elevation of about 10,000 feet, I pushed on southward toward a group of savage peaks that stand guard about Ritter on the north and west, groping my way, and dealing instinctively with every obstacle as it presented itself. Here a huge gorge would be found cutting across my path, along the dizzy edge of which I scrambled until some less precipitous point was discovered where I might safely venture to the bottom and then, selecting some feasible portion of the opposite wall, reascend with the same slow caution. Massive, flat-topped spurs alternate with the gorges, plunging abruptly from the shoulders of the snowy peaks, and planting their feet in the warm desert. These were everywhere marked and adorned with characteristic sculptures of the ancient glaciers that swept over this entire region like one vast ice-wind, and the polished surfaces produced by the ponderous flood are still so perfectly preserved that in many places the sunlight reflected from them is about as trying to the eyes as sheets of snow.

God's glacial-mills grind slowly, but they have been kept in motion long enough in California to grind sufficient soil for a glorious abundance of life, though most of the grist has been carried to the lowlands, leaving these high regions comparatively lean and bare; while the post-glacial agents of erosion have not yet furnished sufficient available food over the general surface for more than a few tufts of the hardiest plants, chiefly carices and eriogonæ. And it is interesting to learn in this connection that the sparseness and repressed character of the vegetation at this height is caused more by want of soil than by harshness of climate; for, here and there, in sheltered hollows (countersunk beneath the general surface) into which a few rods of well-ground moraine chips have been dumped, we find groves of spruce and pine thirty to forty feet high, trimmed around the edges with willow and huckleberry bushes, and oftentimes still further by an outer ring of tall grasses, bright with lupines, larkspurs, and showy columbines, suggesting a climate by no means repressingly severe. All the streams, too, and the pools at this elevation are furnished with little gardens wherever soil can be made to lie, which, though making scarce any show at a distance, constitute charming surprises to the appreciative observer. In these bits of leafiness a few birds find grateful homes. Having no acquaintance with man, they fear no ill, and flock curiously about the stranger, almost allowing themselves to be taken in the hand. In so wild and so beautiful a region was spent my first day, every sight and sound inspiring, leading one far out of himself, yet feeding and building up his individuality.

Now came the solemn, silent evening. Long, blue, spiky shadows crept out across the snow-fields, while a rosy glow, at first scarce discernible, gradually deepened and suffused every mountain-top, flushing the glaciers and the harsh crags above them. This was the alpenglow, to me one of the most impressive of all the terrestrial manifestations of God. At the touch of this divine light, the mountains seemed to kindle to a rapt, religious consciousness, and stood hushed and waiting like devout worshipers. Just before the alpenglow began to fade, two crimson clouds came streaming across the summit like wings of flame, rendering the sublime scene yet more impressive; then came darkness and the stars.

Icy Ritter was still miles away, but I could proceed no farther that night. I found a good camp-ground on the rim of a glacier basin about 11,000 feet above the sea. A small lake nestles in the bottom of it, from which I got water for my tea, and a stormbeaten thicket near by furnished abundance of resiny fire-wood. Somber peaks, hacked and shattered, circled half-way around the horizon, wearing a savage aspect in the gloaming, and a waterfall chanted solemnly across the lake on its way down from the foot of a glacier. The fall and the lake and the glacier were almost equally bare; while the scraggy pines anchored in the rock-fissures were so dwarfed and shorn by storm-winds that you might walk over their tops. In tone and aspect the scene was one of the most desolate I ever beheld. But the darkest scriptures of the mountains are illumined with bright passages of love that never fail to make themselves felt when one is alone.

I made my bed in a nook of the pine-thicket, where the branches were pressed and crinkled overhead like a roof, and bent down around the sides. These are the best bedchambers the high mountains afford—snug as squirrel-nests, well ventilated, full of spicy odors, and with plenty of wind-played needles to sing one asleep. I little expected company, but, creeping in through a low side-door, I found five or six birds nestling among the tassels. The night-wind began to blow soon after dark; at first only a gentle breathing, but increasing toward midnight to a rough gale that fell upon my leafy roof in ragged surges like a cascade, bearing wild sounds from the crags overhead. The waterfall sang in chorus, filling the old ice-fountain with its solemn roar, and seeming to increase in power as the night advanced—fit voice for such a landscape. I had to creep out many times to the fire during the night, for it was biting cold and I had no blankets. Gladly I welcomed the morning star.

The dawn in the dry, wavering air of the desert was glorious. Everything encouraged my undertaking and betokened success. There was no cloud in the sky, no storm-tone in the wind. Breakfast of bread and tea was soon made. I fastened a hard, durable crust to my belt by way of provision, in case I should be compelled to pass a night on the mountain-top; then, securing the remainder of my little stock against wolves and wood-rats, I set forth free and hopeful.

How glorious a greeting the sun gives the mountains! To behold this alone is worth the pains of any excursion a thousand times over. The highest peaks burned like islands in a sea of liquid shade. Then the lower peaks and spires caught the glow, and long lances of light, streaming through many a notch and pass, fell thick on the frozen meadows. The majestic form of Ritter was full in sight, and I pushed rapidly on over rounded rock-bosses and pavements, my iron-shod shoes making a clanking sound, suddenly hushed now and then in rugs of bryanthus, and sedgy lake-margins soft as moss. Here, too, in this so-called "land of desolation," I met cassiope, growing in fringes among the battered rocks. Her blossoms had faded long ago, but they were still clinging with happy memories to the evergreen sprays, and still so beautiful as to thrill every fiber of one's being. Winter and summer, you may hear her voice, the low, sweet melody of her purple bells. No evangel among all the mountain plants speaks Nature's love more plainly than cassiope. Where she dwells, the redemption of the coldest solitude is complete. The very rocks and glaciers seem to feel her presence, and become imbued with her own fountain sweetness. All things were warming and awakening. Frozen rills began to flow, the marmots came out of their nests in boulder-piles and climbed sunny rocks to bask, and the dun-headed sparrows were flitting about seeking their breakfasts. The lakes seen from every ridge-top were brilliantly rippled and spangled, shimmering like the thickets of the low Dwarf Pines. The rocks, too, seemed responsive to the vital heat—rock-crystals and snow-crystals thrilling alike. I strode on exhilarated, as if never more to feel fatigue, limbs moving of themselves, every sense unfolding like the thawing flowers, to take part in the new day harmony.

All along my course thus far, excepting when down in the cañons, the landscapes were mostly open to me, and expansive, at least on one side. On the left were the purple plains of Mono, reposing dreamily and warm; on the right, the near peaks springing keenly into the thin sky with more and more impressive sublimity. But these larger views were at length lost. Rugged spurs, and moraines, and huge, projecting buttresses began to shut me in. Every feature became more rigidly alpine, without, however, producing any chilling effect; for going to the mountains is like going home. We always find that the strangest objects in these fountain wilds are in some degree familiar, and we look upon them with a vague sense of having seen them before.

On the southern shore of a frozen lake, I encountered an extensive field of hard, granular snow, up which I scampered in fine tone, intending to follow it to its head, and cross the rocky spur against which it leans, hoping thus to come direct upon the base of the main Ritter peak. The surface was pitted with oval hollows, made by stones and drifted pine-needles that had melted themselves into the mass by the radiation of absorbed sun-heat. These afforded good footholds, but the surface curved more and more steeply at the head, and the pits became shallower and less abundant, until I found myself in danger of being shed off like avalanching snow. I persisted, however, creeping on all fours, and shuffling up the smoothest places on my back, as I had often done on burnished granite, until, after slipping several times, I was compelled to retrace my course to the bottom, and make my way around the west end of the lake, and thence up to the summit of the divide between the head waters of Rush Creek and the northernmost tributaries of the San Joaquin.

Arriving on the summit of this dividing crest, one of the most exciting pieces of pure wilderness was disclosed that I ever discovered in all my mountaineering. There, immediately in front, loomed the majestic mass of Mount Ritter, with a glacier swooping down its face nearly to my feet, then curving westward and pouring its frozen flood into a dark blue lake, whose shores were bound with precipices of crystalline snow; while a deep chasm drawn between the divide and the glacier separated the massive picture from everything else. I could see only the one sublime mountain, the one glacier, the one lake; the whole veiled with one blue shadow—rock, ice, and water close together without a single leaf or sign of life. After gazing spellbound, I began instinctively to scrutinize every notch and gorge and weathered buttress of the mountain, with reference to making the ascent. The entire front above the glacier appeared as one tremendous precipice, slightly receding at the top, and bristling with spires and pinnacles set above one another in formidable array. Massive lichen-stained battlements stood forward here and there, hacked at the top with angular notches, and separated by frosty gullies and recesses that have been veiled in shadow ever since their creation; while to right and left, as far as I could see, were huge, crumbling buttresses, offering no hope to the climber. The head of the glacier sends up a few finger-like branches through narrow *couloirs;* but these seemed too steep and short to be available, especially as I had no ax with which to cut steps, and the numerous narrow-throated gullies down which stones and snow are avalanched seemed hopelessly steep, besides being interrupted by vertical cliffs; while the whole front was rendered still more terribly forbidding by the chill shadow and the gloomy blackness of the rocks.

Descending the divide in a hesitating mood, I picked my way across the yawning chasm at the foot, and climbed out upon the glacier. There were no meadows now to cheer with their brave colors, nor could I hear the dun-headed sparrows, whose cheery notes so often relieve the silence of our highest mountains. The only sounds were the gurgling of small rills down in the veins and crevasses of the glacier, and now and then the rattling report of falling stones, with the echoes they shot out into the crisp air.

I could not distinctly hope to reach the summit from this side, yet I moved on across the glacier as if driven by fate. Contending with myself, the season is too far spent, I said, and even should I be successful, I might be storm-bound on the mountain; and in the cloud-darkness, with the cliffs and crevasses covered with snow, how could I escape? No; I must wait till next summer. I would only approach the mountain now, and inspect it, creep about its flanks, learn what I could of its history, holding myself ready to flee on the approach of the first storm-cloud. But we little know until tried how much of the uncontrollable there is in us, urging across glaciers and torrents, and up dangerous heights, let the judgment forbid as it may.

I succeeded in gaining the foot of the cliff on the eastern extremity of the glacier, and there discovered the mouth of a narrow avalanche gully, through which I began to climb, intending to follow it as far as possible, and at least obtain some fine wild views for my pains. Its general course is oblique to the plane of the mountain-face, and the metamorphic slates of which the mountain is built are cut by cleavage planes in such a way that they weather off in angular blocks, giving rise to irregular steps that greatly facilitate climbing on the sheer places. I thus made my way into a wilderness of crumbling spires and battlements, built together in bewildering combinations, and glazed in many places with a thin coating of ice, which I had to hammer off with stones. The situation was becoming gradually more perilous; but, having passed several dangerous spots, I dared not think of descending; for, so steep was the entire ascent, one would inevitably fall to the glacier in case a single misstep were made. Knowing, therefore, the tried danger beneath, I became all the more anxious concerning the developments to be made above, and began to be conscious of a vague foreboding of what actually befell; not that I was given to fear, but rather because my instincts, usually so positive and true, seemed vitiated in some way, and were leading me astray. At length, after attaining an elevation of about 12,800 feet, I found myself at the foot of a sheer drop in the bed of the avalanche channel I was tracing, which seemed absolutely to bar further progress. It was only about forty-five or fifty feet high, and somewhat roughened by fissures and projections; but these seemed so slight and insecure, as footholds, that I tried hard to avoid the precipice altogether, by scaling the wall of the channel on either side. But, though less steep, the walls were smoother than the obstructing rock, and repeated efforts only showed that I must either go right ahead or turn back. The tried dangers beneath seemed even greater than that of the cliff in front; therefore, after scanning its face again and again, I began to scale it, picking my holds with intense caution. After gaining a point about half-way to the top, I was suddenly brought to a dead stop, with arms outspread, clinging close to the face of the rock, unable to move hand or foot either up or down. My doom appeared fixed. I *must* fall. There would be a moment of bewilderment, and then a lifeless rumble down the one general precipice to the glacier below.

When this final danger flashed upon me, I became nerve-shaken for the first time since setting foot on the mountains, and my mind seemed to fill with a stifling smoke. But this terrible eclipse lasted only a moment, when life blazed forth again with preternatural clearness. I seemed suddenly to become possessed of a new sense. The other self, bygone experiences, Instinct, or

Guardian Angel,—call it what you will,—came forward and assumed control. Then my trembling muscles became firm again, every rift and flaw in the rock was seen as through a microscope, and my limbs moved with a positiveness and precision with which I seemed to have nothing at all to do. Had I been borne aloft upon wings, my deliverance could not have been more complete.

Above this memorable spot, the face of the mountain is still more savagely hacked and torn. It is a maze of yawning chasms and gullies, in the angles of which rise beetling crags and piles of detached boulders that seem to have been gotten ready to be launched below. But the strange influx of strength I had received seemed inexhaustible. I found a way without effort, and soon stood upon the topmost crag in the blessed light.

How truly glorious the landscape circled around this noble summit!—giant mountains, valleys innumerable, glaciers and meadows, rivers and lakes, with the wide blue sky bent tenderly over them all. But in my first hour of freedom from that terrible shadow, the sunlight in which I was laving seemed all in all.

Looking southward along the axis of the range, the eye is first caught by a row of exceedingly sharp and slender spires, which rise openly to a height of about a thousand feet, above a series of short, residual glaciers that lean back against their bases; their fantastic sculpture and the unrelieved sharpness with which they spring out of the ice rendering them peculiarly wild and striking. These are "The Minarets." Beyond them you behold a sublime wilderness of mountains, their snowy summits towering together in crowded abundance, peak beyond peak, swelling higher, higher as they sweep on southward, until the culminating point of the range is reached on Mount Whitney, near the head of the Kern River, at an elevation of nearly 14,700 feet above the level of the sea.

Westward, the general flank of the range is seen flowing sublimely away from the sharp summits, in smooth undulations; a sea of huge gray granite waves dotted with lakes and meadows, and fluted with stupendous cañons that grow steadily deeper as they recede in the distance. Below this gray region lies the dark forest zone, broken here and there by upswelling ridges and domes; and yet beyond lies a yellow, hazy belt, marking the broad plain of the San Joaquin, bounded on its farther side by the blue mountains of the coast.

Turning now to the northward, there in the immediate foreground is the glorious Sierra Crown, with Cathedral Peak, a temple of marvelous architecture, a few degrees to the left of it; the gray, massive form of Mammoth Mountain to the right; while Mounts Ord, Gibbs, Dana, Conness, Tower Peak, Castle Peak, Silver Mountain, and a host of noble companions, as yet nameless, make a sublime show along the axis of the range.

Eastward, the whole region seems a land of desolation covered with beautiful light. The torrid volcanic basin of Mono, with its one bare lake fourteen miles long; Owen's Valley and the broad lava table-land at its head, dotted with craters, and the massive Inyo Range, rivaling even the Sierra in height;

these are spread, map-like, beneath you, with countless ranges beyond, passing and overlapping one another and fading on the glowing horizon.

At a distance of less than 3,000 feet below the summit of Mount Ritter you may find tributaries of the San Joaquin and Owen's rivers, bursting forth from the ice and snow of the glaciers that load its flanks; while a little to the north of here are found the highest affluents of the Tuolumne and Merced. Thus, the fountains of four of the principal rivers of California are within a radius of four or five miles.

Lakes are seen gleaming in all sorts of places,—round, or oval, or square, like very mirrors; others narrow and sinuous, drawn close around the peaks like silver zones, the highest reflecting only rocks, snow, and the sky. But neither these nor the glaciers, nor the bits of brown meadow and moorland that occur here and there, are large enough to make any marked impression upon the mighty wilderness of mountains. The eye, rejoicing in its freedom, roves about the vast expanse, yet returns again and again to the fountain peaks. Perhaps some one of the multitude excites special attention, some gigantic castle with turret and battlement, or some Gothic cathedral more abundantly spired than Milan's. But, generally, when looking for the first time from an all-embracing standpoint like this, the inexperienced observer is oppressed by the incomprehensible grandeur, variety, and abundance of the mountains rising shoulder to shoulder beyond the reach of vision; and it is only after they have been studied one by one, long and lovingly, that their far-reaching harmonies become manifest. Then, penetrate the wilderness where you may, the main telling features, to which all the surrounding topography is subordinate, are quickly perceived, and the most complicated clusters of peaks stand revealed harmoniously correlated and fashioned like works of art—eloquent monuments of the ancient ice-rivers that brought them into relief from the general mass of the range. The cañons, too, some of them a mile deep, mazing wildly through the mighty host of mountains, however lawless and ungovernable at first sight they appear, are at length recognized as the necessary effects of causes which followed each other in harmonious sequence—Nature's poems carved on tables of stone—the simplest and most emphatic of her glacial compositions.

Could we have been here to observe during the glacial period, we should have overlooked a wrinkled ocean of ice as continuous as that now covering the landscapes of Greenland; filling every valley and cañon with only the tops of the fountain peaks rising darkly above the rock-encumbered ice-waves like islets in a stormy sea—those islets the only hints of the glorious landscapes now smiling in the sun. Standing here in the deep, brooding silence all the wilderness seems motionless, as if the work of creation were done. But in the midst of this outer steadfastness we know there is incessant motion and change. Ever and anon, avalanches are falling from yonder peaks. These cliff-bound glaciers, seemingly wedged and immovable, are flowing like water and grinding the rocks beneath them. The lakes are lapping their granite shores and wearing them away, and every one of these rills and young rivers is fretting the air into music, and carrying the mountains to the plains. Here are the roots of all the life of the valleys, and here more simply than elsewhere is the eternal flux of nature manifested. Ice changing to water, lakes to meadows, and mountains to plains. And while we thus contemplate Nature's methods of landscape creation, and, reading the records she has carved on the rocks, reconstruct, however imperfectly, the landscapes of the past, we also learn that as these we now behold have succeeded those of the pre-glacial age, so they in turn are withering and vanishing to be succeeded by others yet unborn.

A Wind-storm in the Forests

THE MOUNTAIN WINDS, like the dew and rain, sunshine and snow, are measured and bestowed with love on the forests to develop their strength and beauty. However restricted the scope of other forest influences, that of the winds is universal. The snow bends and trims the upper forests every winter, the lightning strikes a single tree here and there, while avalanches mow down thousands at a swoop as a gardener trims out a bed of flowers. But the winds go to every tree, fingering every leaf and branch and furrowed bole; not one is forgotten; the Mountain Pine towering with outstretched arms on the rugged buttresses of the icy peaks, the lowliest and most retiring tenant of the dells; they seek and find them all, caressing them tenderly, bending them in lusty exercise, stimulating their growth, plucking off a leaf or limb as required, or removing an entire tree or grove, now whispering and cooing through the branches like a sleepy child, now roaring like the ocean; the winds blessing the forests, the forests the winds, with ineffable beauty and harmony as the sure result.

After one has seen pines six feet in diameter bending like grasses before a mountain gale, and ever and anon some giant falling with a crash that shakes the hills, it seems astonishing that any, save the lowest thickset trees, could ever have found a period sufficiently stormless to establish themselves; or, once established, that they should not, sooner or later, have been blown down. But when the storm is over, and we behold the same forests tranquil again, towering fresh and unscathed in erect majesty, and consider what centuries of storms have fallen upon them since they were first planted,—hail, to break the tender seedlings; lightning, to scorch and shatter; snow, winds, and avalanches, to crush and overwhelm,—while the manifest result of all this wild storm-culture is the glorious perfection we behold; then faith in Nature's forestry is established, and we cease to deplore the violence of her most destructive gales, or of any other storm-implement whatsoever.

1 Arrival of the English in Virginia. From Theodor de Bry's *America* (1590). The New York Public Library.

One of the many Renaissance views of the New World "landfall," Figure 1 picks up the general configurations of the cultivated garden islanded by wilderness—configurations which compose the most durable ideal design of American landscape. In Renaissance eyes, both the wilderness and the garden harbored supernatural and magic beings as well as real beings never seen before by Europeans. In the wilderness might be found demons, savages, panthers; in the garden, passionflowers, tobacco, trees of sorrow (Figures 2, 3, 4).

2 Tobacco. From Mathias Lobel's *Stirpium* (Antwerp, 1576).

3 Arbor Malenconico (Tree of Sorrow). From Durante's *Herbario Nuova* (Rome, 1585).

4 Passionflower. From Parkinson's *Paradisus* (London, 1629).

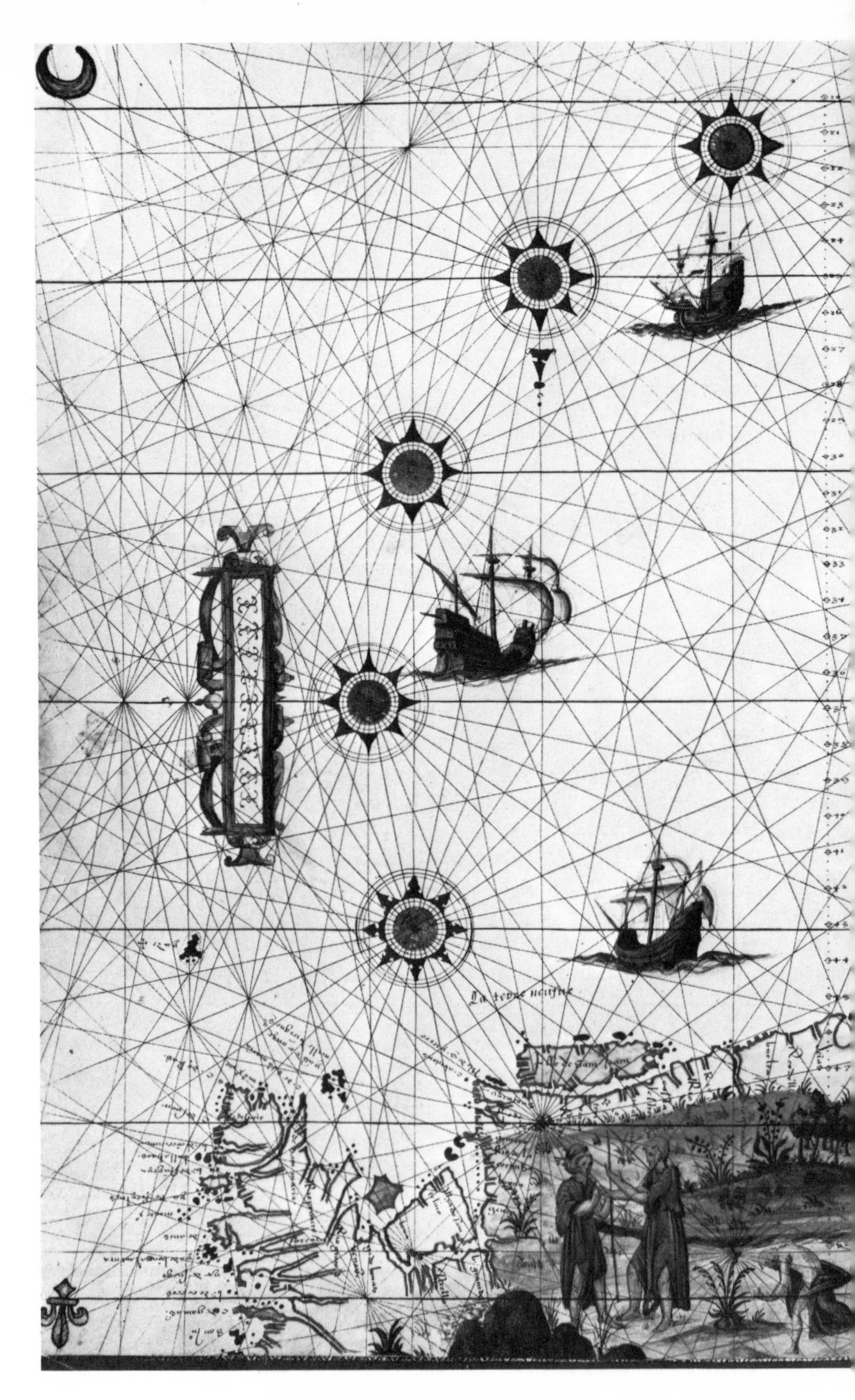

5 Map of the North Atlantic coast of the New World.

From what is now Canada, the viewer looks southward down the eastern coast of the New World to Florida (upper right). The mapmaker has visualized the continental interior as a natural garden composed of groves and mountains, cen-

From an anonymous atlas (*c.* 1540).

taurs, lions, and a sequence (right to left foreground) of beastly to upright men. Over all he has imposed the networks of grid lines which locate and fix the New World.

6 Edward Hicks, The Peaceable Kingdom (*c.* 1840-45). The Brooklyn Museum. Dick S. Ramsay Fund.

The middle ground idyllically commemorates William Penn's signing a peace treaty with Indians in the "peaceable kingdom" of Pennsylvania (Penn's woods). Out of the woods in the foreground come the symbols of millennial peace: an idyllic mix of carnivorous and herbivorous animals, children and cherubim. Here, as Isaiah promised, the lion might lie down with the lamb again and eat straw like the ox. On such millennial hopes many of the New World colonies were founded.

7 Peter Gordon, A View of Savannah (1734). The New York Public Library.

8 Anon., Adam and Eve (*c.* 1830). Gift of Edgar William and Bernice Chrysler Garbisch. Whitney Museum of Modern Art.

In sharp contrast to the ordered regularity of the cultivated garden and the city (the visible signs of virtuous industry), this natural garden is the visible sign of an Edenic world in which work is not necessary. Here are gathered many motifs that are recurrent in New World landscape paintings: the full clusters of grapes (fruits of the garden), water pure to the point of transparency, a soft bower of trees, and figures in serene repose.

◀ An emblem of civilization in the New World. The narrow strip of the foreground is a pastoral garden. The city, walled against both the river and the wilderness, takes shape as a rectangle of comfortingly regular houses and gardens—in contrast to the ruffled energy of the river and the amorphous dark of the forest.

9 Jasper Cropsey, Bareford Mountains, New Jersey (1850). Dick S. Ramsay Fund. The Brooklyn Museum.

Here the garden is a cultivated field of hay whose value Cropsey, a member of the Hudson River School, intensifies by kindling it with light.

10 Albert Bierstadt, Thunderstorm in the Rocky Mountains. Museum of Fine Arts, Boston.

Near the foreground is a sublimely aged and patriarchal tree (a signature motif of the Hudson River School); in the background, the darkening sublimity of the storm gathering over kingly mountains. Bierstadt's natural garden, where deer drink, appears in the middle ground as an agelessly serene and luminous island.

11 M. P. Wolcott, Mountain Home and Patches of Crops (September 1940). Near Hyden, Kentucky. Library of Congress, Washington, D.C.

A subsistence garden in the mountains of Kentucky, this has a design not too different, one imagines, from any mountain or backwoods garden from the eighteenth century on. Contoured rather than linear, it suggests a process of adaptation rather than of domination. Wolcott's photograph, like those of Vachon, Rothstein, Delano, and Feininger which follow, was taken under the auspices of the Farm Security Administration, which turned out a huge photographic catalogue of rural people, rituals, and landscapes during the Depression.

12 John Vachon, Harrowing the Ground Before Planting Corn (May 1940). Jasper County, Iowa. Library of Congress.

The photographs of Vachon and Garnett taken together suggest the effects of the machine in the garden from the nineteenth century on. The gardens grew so large that they made islands of the wilderness, whereas once they had been islanded by wilderness. Garnett's aerial photograph emphasizes the extent of cultivation made possible by the machine; Vachon's photograph reminds us of the relationship in scale between the marks of cultivation and the men who made them. Both remind us again that one of the major legacies of civilization in America was the imposition of linearity on landscape: from the grid lines of the map (Figure 5) to the furrow lines of the plough to the three-dimensional lines of building construction (Figures 7, 22, 23, and 24).

13 William A. Garnett, Erosion and Strip Farms West of Lancaster, California. Courtesy of the Photographer. ▶

14 George Inness, The Lackawanna Valley. National Gallery of Art, Washington, D.C.

With the progressivists, Inness and Gast see the machine as a natural part of the pastoral landscape and not an alien and deforming presence. Inness's railroad roundhouse thus has the look of a barn. Gast's Progress, carrying a "School Book," moves west, leaving in her wake the light and order of a mechanized civilization.

15 After John Gast, American Progress (1872/1873). Chromo-lithograph. Library of Congress.

16 Thomas Moran, Chama Below the Summit (1892). Cooper-Hewitt Museum of Design.

Here the machine is seen as deforming the landscape. In Moran's sketch the cuts of the railroad tracks break up the lines of the mountainside, and the train itself gives off a dark, deforming smudge. Rothstein's photograph images the desolation and the incongruous clutter of abandoned implements left behind when the harvest of a mine "field" has been extracted.

17 Arthur Rothstein, Abandoned Mine, Goldfield, Nevada (1940). Library of Congress.

18 John Vachon, Farmstead, Gaines County, Texas (1942). Library of Congress.

In contrast to Figure 15, these photographs suggest that the westward migration of the 1930's at least left landscapes of ruin in its wake; exhausted and drought-ridden fields and the ruins of settlement. The passage from John Steinbeck's *Grapes of Wrath* (see The Ways West) confirms this. Arthur K. Moore and Howard Mumford Jones are two of many historians who argue that from the beginning of settlement such ruins were a major cause of westward migration.

19 Jack Delano, Cut-over Land and Remains of Farm (1941). Santee-Cooper Basin, South Carolina. Library of Congress.

20 Dorothea Lange, Oklahoma Sharecroppers Entering California (1937). Library of Congress.

Off Cape Cod in November 1620, William Bradford gave voice to a moment of despair on having his dream of a New World Promised Land apparently disconfirmed: what he saw then (see The Cultivation of the Promised Land) was not the garden he expected but a "desert" wilderness. One senses the same disorienting mix of hope and despair in the postures of these migrant sharecroppers who, like Steinbeck's Joad family, have left their rented farms behind in a dustbowl only to find that the California Promised Land is also, apparently, a desert.

21 George Bellows, Pennsylvania Station Excavation (1909). A. Augustus Healy Fund. The Brooklyn Museum.

Bellows, a member of the Ash Can School of American painters, seems to equate this urban construction project with a geological upheaval. The visual deformations are balanced by a sense of the raw, transforming energies at work.

22, 23, 24 William A. Garnett, Subdivision under Construction, near Los Angeles. Courtesy of the Photographer.

The linear deformation of natural landscape to accommodate suburban tract housing. It is as if the orienting grid system of the map (see Figure 5) must be realized three-dimensionally on a landscape before people can locate themselves there.

For Europeans and their American descendants, the forest gave shape to the ▶
most profoundly imaginable terrors: being smothered or strangled by organic growth; being menaced or attacked by demonic beasts of prey; being dissolved and transformed in the primeval ooze of a swamp (see Introduction to Reports from the New World). The two landscapes pictured here, though softened by a Romantic perspective, suggest something of the terrors of forests and of jungle swamps. Bodmer's landscape is probably located in Indiana, Hamilton's in Louisiana.

25 Engraving after sketch by Karl Bodmer, Confluence of Fox River with the Wabash. From Maxmilian's *Travels* (1839).

26 James Hamilton, Bayou in Moonlight. Museum of Fine Arts, Boston.

27 Asher B. Durand, Woodland Interior. Museum of Fine Arts, Boston.

With the aesthetics of sublimity (see Introduction to Eighteenth-Century Perspectives), Romantics were able to ameliorate forest-terrors by perceiving forest clearings as protective bowers or even as natural Gothic cathedrals. Both Durand's painting and Bryant's "Forest Hymn" (see Landscape as Idea: Romantic Fiction and Poetry) locate in such a clearing the architectural and sacramentalizing attributes of a cathedral: columns, a vault, an aisle (here the streambed), an altar illuminated by a "window" (center background), and a crypt for the holy, patriarchal dead (foreground).

28 John Quidor, Ichabod Crane Pursued by the Headless Horseman. The Mabel Brady Garvan Collection. Yale University Art Gallery.

A terrified Ichabod Crane is here in flight from nothing more, or less, than a grotesque tree root—in flight, that is, from his forest-terrors—rather than from a supernatural headless horseman. The luminous tree might be the tulip tree of Irving's story, the tree under which Major André was captured. But Quidor, who illustrated several scenes from Irving's tales, apparently considers the headless horseman a projection of Ichabod's "fearful pleasure" at hearing "marvelous tales of ghosts and goblins," the local spirits of the forest.

Thon's disturbing superimposition of quarry face and forest at once suggests fossilized forest and organic rock. A mineral stillness informs the mysterious convolutions of forest shapes, which still conjure something of the old terrors. The quarried rock, one imagines, has been carried off to build cities.

29 William Thon, Quarry (*c.* 1952). Dick S. Ramsay Fund. The Brooklyn Museum.

30 Thomas Cole, A View of Two Lakes and Mountain House, Catskill Mountains, Morning (1844). The Brooklyn Museum. Dick S. Ramsay Fund.

The Mountain House in the Catskills was the seat and the schoolground of the Hudson River School of painters, and Cole sets it here in a perspective from North Mountain that includes his characteristic vista into infinity on the left and a view of two lakes on the right. "Like the eye in the human countenance," Cole wrote in his "Essay on American Scenery" (see Appendix), water "is the most expressive feature: in the unrippled lake, which mirrors all surrounding objects, we have the expression of tranquillity and peace—in the rapid stream, the headlong cataract, that of turbulence and impetuosity."

31 E. L. Cummings, The Magic Lake (1864). Frick Art Reference Library. Courtesy James Thomas Flexner.

Mrs. Cummings, a New Hampshire "folk painter," drew this scene from a theatrical melodrama as reproduced in a Currier and Ives print. Cherubs and a wingless Hecate float in the mist of the middleground on the left. The witch points at the moon from the foreground, and the frightened posture of the kneeling girl picks up the atmosphere of preternatural menace that pervades the landscape, from the bridge of weird structure that frames it to the unnatural stillness of the lake water.

32 Engraving from sketch by William H. Bartlett, View from Mount Holyoke (1840). From Nathaniel Willis's *American Scenery*.

Bartlett collaborated with Nathaniel Willis on the production of the travel book *American Scenery* (1840), Willis doing prose sketches and Bartlett linear sketches of the scenes they visited. Willis's sketch of Mount Holyoke is included in The Poetry of Scene. The structure at the left here was apparently a tourist shelter where ginger beer could be bought—one of the many accommodations made for tourists at this popular shrine on the American Grand Tour.

33 Thomas Cole, The Oxbow (The Connecticut River near Northampton, Massachusetts) (1846). The Metropolitan Museum of Art, New York. Gift of Mrs. Russell Sage.

34 Jasper Cropsey, Early Autumn on the Hudson. Museum of Fine Arts, Boston. Bequest of Maxim Karolik.

Figures 33-36 might be taken as a sequence that suggests the changing perceptions of wilderness during the nineteenth century: Cole's and Cropsey's riverscapes are romantic; Winslow Homer's and Kwiz and Allison's (Figures 35 and 36) are closer to the cataclysmic perspectives of the literary naturalists (see Landscape as Antagonist). In Cropsey's painting the viewer is brought down to the river's edge for a soft, spectacular composition of light, texture, and color, which emphasizes the serenely reflective qualities of water.

◀ Cole saw the same landscape as Willis and Bartlett (Figure 32) but painted Mount Holyoke as a sublime wilderness sublimely darkened by an oncoming storm and the landscape east of the river as a golden, glowing garden of cultivated farms. The river itself, with its beautiful sinuousness, is the element that balances wilderness and garden in picturesque tension. The painter, too, may be seen (in the middle foreground) as another link between the two worlds, though he finds himself on the wilderness side of the river.

35 Winslow Homer, Fishing the Rapids, Saguenay River, Quebec (1902). The Brooklyn Museum.

Here the viewer is brought out from a riverbank to the rim of a cauldron, a cataclysm of rapids, in the middle of which two figures stand on a rock in incongruous repose, their backs to us and the fury, one of them wielding a long, delicate fishing rod. The background, which almost completely walls out the sky, closes the river's fury in on itself.

36 Kwiz and Allison, Flood and Fire, Conemaugh Valley, Johnstown, Pennsylvania (1890). Library of Congress.

This is the Johnstown Flood, which destroyed four valley towns, overwhelmed Johnstown with thirty feet of silt and debris, and took some 2200 lives in May 1889 in the "peaceable kingdom" of Pennsylvania. Here, in contrast to Homer, the cataclysm is panoramic and thickly peopled with victims. In his poem "A Voice from Death" (see Landscape as Idea: Romantic Fiction and Poetry), a shaken Walt Whitman tried to make sense of the destruction this flood caused.

37 Engraving after sketch by Karl Bodmer, The Stone Walls on the Upper Missouri. From Prince Maxmilian's *Travels in the Interior of North America* (*c*. 1834).

Figures 37-41 are all Western landscapes, and most of them suggest the absolute appropriateness of the architectural metaphors travelers used to describe the rock configurations along Western rivers and in Western mountains. Bodmer accompanied Prince Maxmilian on a field trip up the Missouri River (*c*. 1834), Maxmilian doing prose sketches and Bodmer linear sketches of what they saw. These sandstone formations they saw in the area of what is now Fort Peck Reservoir, Montana. Maxmilian's descriptions can be found in The Ways West.

38 William H. Jackson, Pueblo of Walpi, Arizona, Showing Sheep Corrals in Center (*c*. 1875). Smithsonian Institution National Archives, Bureau of American Ethnology Collection.

39 Thomas Moran, Cliffs of the Rio Virgin, Southern Utah. Cooper-Hewitt Museum of Design (Smithsonian Institution), New York.

Moran accompanied John Wesley Powell on his second survey of the Great Plateau in 1873 (see The Ways West) and made detailed sketches of the Plateau, the Grand Canyon, and the tributary waters of the Colorado, including the Rio Virgin. The weirdness of the natural battlements Moran sketched here, in watercolor, is accentuated by a color spectrum dominated by purples.

◀ Taken on his second exploration (1875) of the little-known Mesa Verde, the country of the Cliff Dwellers, Jackson's photograph suggests that the architectural possibilities of rock were not simply metaphorical and not simply generated by geological forces. The pueblo pictured here, occupied by Moqui Indians, was situated on a mesa near the Canyon de Chelly.

40 William H. Jackson, Jupiter Terrace (1871). National Archives, U.S. Geological Survey. ▶

Jackson took this photograph as a member of F. V. Hayden's government survey of the headwaters of the Yellowstone River in 1871. Jackson was the official photographer and Thomas Moran the official artist on this expedition. Viewing the geysers and hot springs in this area a year earlier, Nathaniel Langford was reminded of the witches' scene in *Macbeth* (see The Ways West).

41 Andreas Feininger, Loveland Pass, Colorado (1942). Library of Congress.

Feininger's Farm Security Administration photograph catches the magnificent desolation of Western landscapes, composed only of primordial minerals, void of visible organisms, void of life. Only religion or a theory of evolution could place such landscapes into a humanly accessible design.

There are two trees in the Sierra forests that are never blown down, so long as they continue in sound health. These are the Juniper and the Dwarf Pine of the summit peaks. Their stiff, crooked roots grip the storm-beaten ledges like eagles' claws, while their lithe, cord-like branches bend round compliantly, offering but slight holds for winds, however violent. The other alpine conifers—the Needle Pine, Mountain Pine, Two-leaved Pine, and Hemlock Spruce—are never thinned out by this agent to any destructive extent, on account of their admirable toughness and the closeness of their growth. In general the same is true of the giants of the lower zones. The kingly Sugar Pine, towering aloft to a height of more than 200 feet, offers a fine mark to storm-winds; but it is not densely foliaged, and its long, horizontal arms swing round compliantly in the blast, like tresses of green, fluent algæ in a brook; while the Silver Firs in most places keep their ranks well together in united strength. The Yellow or Silver Pine is more frequently overturned than any other tree on the Sierra, because its leaves and branches form a larger mass in proportion to its height, while in many places it is planted sparsely, leaving open lanes through which storms may enter with full force. Furthermore, because it is distributed along the lower portion of the range, which was the first to be left bare on the breaking up of the ice-sheet at the close of the glacial winter, the soil it is growing upon has been longer exposed to post-glacial weathering, and consequently is in a more crumbling, decayed condition than the fresher soils farther up the range, and therefore offers a less secure anchorage for the roots.

While exploring the forest zones of Mount Shasta, I discovered the path of a hurricane strewn with thousands of pines of this species. Great and small had been uprooted or wrenched off by sheer force, making a clean gap, like that made by a snow avalanche. But hurricanes capable of doing this class of work are rare in the Sierra, and when we have explored the forests from one extremity of the range to the other, we are compelled to believe that they are the most beautiful on the face of the earth, however we may regard the agents that have made them so.

There is always something deeply exciting, not only in the sounds of winds in the woods, which exert more or less influence over every mind, but in their varied waterlike flow as manifested by the movements of the trees, especially those of the conifers. By no other trees are they rendered so extensively and impressively visible, not even by the lordly tropic palms or tree-ferns responsive to the gentlest breeze. The waving of a forest of the giant Sequoias is indescribably impressive and sublime, but the pines seem to me the best interpreters of winds. They are mighty waving goldenrods, ever in tune, singing and writing wind-music all their long century lives. Little, however, of this noble tree-waving and tree-music will you see or hear in the strictly alpine portion of the forests. The burly Juniper, whose girth sometimes more than equals its height, is about as rigid as the rocks on which it grows. The slender lash-like sprays of the Dwarf Pine stream out in wavering ripples, but the tallest and slenderest are far too unyielding to wave even in the heaviest gales. They only shake in quick, short vibrations. The Hemlock Spruce, however, and the Mountain Pine, and some of the tallest thickets of the Two-leaved species bow in storms with considerable scope and gracefulness. But it is only in the lower and middle zones that the meeting of winds and woods is to be seen in all its grandeur.

One of the most beautiful and exhilarating storms I ever enjoyed in the Sierra occurred in December, 1874, when I happened to be exploring one of the tributary valleys of the Yuba River. The sky and the ground and the trees had been thoroughly rain-washed and were dry again. The day was intensely pure, one of those incomparable bits of California winter, warm and balmy and full of white sparkling sunshine, redolent of all the purest influences of the spring, and at the same time enlivened with one of the most bracing wind-storms conceivable. Instead of camping out, as I usually do, I then chanced to be stopping at the house of a friend. But when the storm began to sound, I lost no time in pushing out into the woods to enjoy it. For on such occasions Nature has always something rare to show us, and the danger to life and limb is hardly greater than one would experience crouching deprecatingly beneath a roof.

It was still early morning when I found myself fairly adrift. Delicious sunshine came pouring over the hills, lighting the tops of the pines, and setting free a steam of summery fragrance that contrasted strangely with the wild tones of the storm. The air was mottled with pine-tassels and bright green plumes, that went flashing past in the sunlight like birds pursued. But there was not the slightest dustiness, nothing less pure than leaves, and ripe pollen, and flecks of withered bracken and moss. I heard trees falling for hours at the rate of one every two or three minutes; some uprooted, partly on account of the loose, water-soaked condition of the ground; others broken straight across, where some weakness caused by fire had determined the spot. The gestures of the various trees made a delightful study. Young Sugar Pines, light and feathery as squirrel-tails, were bowing almost to the ground; while the grand old patriarchs, whose massive boles had been tried in a hundred storms, waved solemnly above them, their long, arching branches streaming fluently on the gale, and every needle thrilling and ringing and shedding off keen lances of light like a diamond. The Douglas Spruces, with long sprays drawn out in level tresses, and needles massed in a gray, shimmering glow, presented a most striking appearance as they stood in bold relief along the hilltops. The madroños in the dells, with their red bark and large glossy leaves tilted every way, reflected the sunshine in throbbing spangles like those one so often sees on the rippled surface of a glacier lake. But the Silver Pines were now the most impressively beautiful of all. Colossal spires 200 feet in height waved like supple goldenrods chanting and bowing low as if in worship, while the whole mass of their long, tremulous foliage was kindled into one continuous blaze of white sun-fire. The force of the gale was such that the most steadfast monarch of them all rocked down to its roots with a motion plainly perceptible when one leaned against it. Nature was holding high festival, and every fiber of the most rigid giants thrilled with glad excitement.

I drifted on through the midst of this passionate music and motion, across many a glen, from ridge to ridge; often halting in the lee of a rock for shelter, or to gaze and listen. Even when the grand anthem had swelled to its highest pitch, I could distinctly hear the varying tones of individual trees,—Spruce, and Fir, and Pine, and leafless Oak,—and even the infinitely gentle rustle of the withered grasses at my feet. Each was expressing itself in its own way,—singing its own song, and making its own peculiar gestures,—manifesting a richness of variety to be found in no other forest I have yet seen. The coniferous woods of Canada, and the Carolinas, and Florida, are made up of trees that resemble one another about as nearly as blades of grass, and grow close together in much the same way. Coniferous trees, in general, seldom possess individual character, such as is manifest among Oaks and Elms. But the California forests are made up of a greater number of distinct species than any other in the world. And in them we find, not only a marked differentiation into special groups, but also a marked individuality in almost every tree, giving rise to storm effects indescribably glorious.

Toward midday, after a long, tingling scramble through copses of hazel and ceanothus, I gained the summit of the highest ridge in the neighborhood; and then it occurred to me that it would be a fine thing to climb one of the trees to obtain a wider outlook and get my ear close to the Æolian music of its topmost needles. But under the circumstances the choice of a tree was a serious matter. One whose instep was not very strong seemed in danger of being blown down, or of being struck by others in case they should fall; another was branchless to a considerable height above the ground, and at the same time too large to be grasped with arms and legs in climbing; while others were not favorably situated for clear views. After cautiously casting about, I made choice of the tallest of a group of Douglas Spruces that were growing close together like a tuft of grass, no one of which seemed likely to fall unless all the rest fell with it. Though comparatively young, they were about 100 feet high, and their lithe, brushy tops were rocking and swirling in wild ecstasy. Being accustomed to climb trees in making botanical studies, I experienced no difficulty in reaching the top of this one, and never before did I enjoy so noble an exhilaration of motion. The slender tops fairly flapped and swished in the passionate torrent, bending and swirling backward and forward, round and round, tracing indescribable combinations of vertical and horizontal curves, while I clung with muscles firm braced, like a bobolink on a reed.

In its widest sweeps my tree-top described an arc of from twenty to thirty degrees, but I felt sure of its elastic temper, having seen others of the same species still more severely tried—bent almost to the ground indeed, in heavy snows—without breaking a fiber. I was therefore safe, and free to take the wind into my pulses and enjoy the excited forest from my superb outlook. The view from here must be extremely beautiful in any weather. Now my eye roved over the piny hills and dales as over fields of waving grain, and felt the light running in ripples and broad swelling undulations across the valleys from ridge to ridge, as the shining foliage was stirred by corresponding waves of air. Oftentimes these waves of reflected light would break up suddenly into a kind of beaten foam, and again, after chasing one another in regular order, they would seem to bend forward in concentric curves, and disappear on some hillside, like sea-waves on a shelving shore. The quantity of light reflected from the bent needles was so great as to make whole groves appear as if covered with snow, while the black shadows beneath the trees greatly enhanced the effect of the silvery splendor.

Excepting only the shadows there was nothing somber in all this wild sea of pines. On the contrary, notwithstanding this was the winter season, the colors were remarkably beautiful. The shafts of the pine and libocedrus were brown and purple, and most of the foliage was well tinged with yellow; the laurel groves, with the pale undersides of their leaves turned upward, made masses of gray; and then there was many a dash of chocolate color from clumps of manzanita, and jet of vivid crimson from the bark of the madroños, while the ground on the hillsides, appearing here and there through openings between the groves, displayed masses of pale purple and brown.

The sounds of the storm corresponded gloriously with this wild exuberance of light and motion. The profound bass of the naked branches and boles booming like waterfalls; the quick, tense vibrations of the pine-needles, now rising to a shrill, whistling hiss, now falling to a silky murmur; the rustling of laurel groves in the dells, and the keen metallic click of leaf on leaf—all this was heard in easy analysis when the attention was calmly bent.

The varied gestures of the multitude were seen to fine advantage, so that one could recognize the different species at a distance of several miles by this means alone, as well as by their forms and colors, and the way they reflected the light. All seemed strong and comfortable, as if really enjoying the storm, while responding to its most enthusiastic greetings. We hear much nowadays concerning the universal struggle for existence, but no struggle in the common meaning of the word was manifest here; no recognition of danger by any tree; no deprecation; but rather an invincible gladness as remote from exultation as from fear.

I kept my lofty perch for hours, frequently closing my eyes to enjoy the music by itself, or to feast quietly on the delicious fragrance that was streaming past. The fragrance of the woods was less marked than that produced during warm rain, when so many balsamic buds and leaves are steeped like tea; but, from the chafing of resiny branches against each other, and the incessant attrition of myriads of needles, the gale was spiced to a very tonic degree. And besides the fragrance from these local sources there were traces of scents brought from afar. For this wind came first from the sea, rubbing against its fresh, briny waves, then distilled through the redwoods, threading rich ferny gulches, and spreading itself in broad undulating currents over many a flower-enameled ridge of the coast mountains, then across the golden plains, up the purple foot-hills, and into these piny woods with the varied incense gathered by the way.

Winds are advertisements of all they touch, however much or little we may be able to read them; telling their wanderings even by their scents alone. Mariners detect the flowery perfume of land-winds far at sea, and sea-winds carry the fragrance of dulse and tangle far inland, where it is quickly recognized, though mingled with the scents of a thousand land-flowers. As an illustration of this, I may tell here that I breathed sea-air on the Firth of Forth, in Scotland, while a boy; then was taken to Wisconsin, where I remained nineteen years; then, without in all this time having breathed one breath of the sea, I walked quietly, alone, from the middle of the Mississippi Valley to the Gulf of Mexico, on a botanical excursion, and while in Florida, far from the coast, my attention wholly bent on the splendid tropical vegetation about me, I suddenly recognized a sea-breeze, as it came sifting through the palmettos and blooming vine-tangles, which at once awakened and set free a thousand dormant associations, and made me a boy again in Scotland, as if all the intervening years had been annihilated.

Most people like to look at mountain rivers, and bear them in mind; but few care to look at the winds, though far more beautiful and sublime, and though they become at times about as visible as flowing water. When the north winds in winter are making upward sweeps over the curving summits of the High Sierra, the fact is sometimes published with flying snow-banners a mile long. Those portions of the winds thus embodied can scarce be wholly invisible, even to the darkest imagination. And when we look around over an agitated forest, we may see something of the wind that stirs it, by its effects upon the trees. Yonder it descends in a rush of waterlike ripples, and sweeps over the bending pines from hill to hill. Nearer, we see detached plumes and leaves, now speeding by on level currents, now whirling in eddies, or, escaping over the edges of the whirls, soaring aloft on grand, upswelling domes of air, or tossing on flame-like crests. Smooth, deep currents, cascades, falls, and swirling eddies, sing around every tree and leaf, and over all the varied topography of the region with telling changes of form, like mountain rivers conforming to the features of their channels.

After tracing the Sierra streams from their fountains to the plains, marking where they bloom white in falls, glide in crystal plumes, surge gray and foam-filled in boulder-choked gorges, and slip through the woods in long, tranquil reaches—after thus learning their language and forms in detail, we may at length hear them chanting all together in one grand anthem, and comprehend them all in clear inner vision, covering the range like lace. But even this spectacle is far less sublime and not a whit more substantial than what we may behold of these storm-streams of air in the mountain woods.

We all travel the milky way together, trees and men; but it never occurred to me until this storm-day, while swinging in the wind, that trees are travelers, in the ordinary sense. They make many journeys, not extensive ones, it is true; but our own little journeys, away and back again, are only little more than tree-wavings—many of them not so much.

When the storm began to abate, I dismounted and sauntered down through the calming woods. The storm-tones died away, and, turning toward the east, I beheld the countless hosts of the forests hushed and tranquil, towering above one another on the slopes of the hills like a devout audience. The setting sun filled them with amber light, and seemed to say, while they listened, "My peace I give unto you."

As I gazed on the impressive scene, all the so-called ruin of the storm was forgotten, and never before did these noble woods appear so fresh, so joyous, so immortal.

1894

Landscape as Idea

Romantic Prose and Poetry

The selections in this section are representative of the Romantic art of landscape in literature during the period 1830 to roughly 1860. They range from adorned sketches to sketches of fancy (see The Poetry of Scene), from landscapes observed to landscapes imagined or dreamed and described *as if* seen, with the surreal clarity of a dream. The landscapes observed are not precisely located in geographical space, for most of them are not concerned with hallowing particular places, in the manner of Irving and Cooper. The concern they all share is the relationship of landscape and idea, and in this they show their affinity to Emerson and the Transcendentalists.

Their similarity granted, their real differences need elaboration.

ROMANTIC PROSE

Members of the generation following Irving and Cooper, Poe and Hawthorne together employ all the modes of prose landscape description in currency during the period 1830–1860. Hawthorne, following Thoreau's direction, kept a journal of his travels and observations, and from that journal he composed travel sketches such as "The Erie Canal" (see The Poetry of Scene); a nature essay, "Buds and Bird-Voices;" and some of the settings for his stories. Both men wrote meditative sketches, which Poe called "essays," of which Poe's "The Island of the Fay" and Hawthorne's "Sights from a Steeple" are included here. In "The Domain of Arnheim" Poe embodied his theory of beauty in the description of a formal landscape garden. Hawthorne wrote many stories to evoke "storied and poetical associations" in New England landscapes—some of them, like "The Maypole of Merry Mount," with reference to the Puritan period and some of them, like "The Ambitious Guest," with reference to a more recent past. In their major short fiction, finally, landscape settings become either the occasion of insight into a transcendent, though not a Transcendentalist, reality or symbolic projections of a human psyche.

Hawthorne, more rooted and more sensitive to the spirit of place than Poe, locates most of his stories in New England, though he distances them in time. The locations of Poe's stories are much more indeterminate: his settings are distanced both in time and space. "No such combination of scenery exists in nature as the painter of genius may produce," he wrote in "The Domain of Arnheim." "No such paradises are to be found in reality as have glowed on the canvas of Claude."

Both writers are masters of the impressionistic sketch, though Poe is the more articulate theorist of literary impressionism. Like Emerson, Poe demands that landscape be pruned and diffused by literary art—pruned down to its outline and its significant details ("An outline frequently stirs the spirit more pleasantly than the most elaborate picture") and diffused by the effect of light or motion. For lighting both Poe and Hawthorne prefer what Poe calls "chiaro' scuro": "that blending of light and shade and shadow, where nothing is too distinct, yet where the idea is fully conveyed." Forest or dusklight have the effect of chiaroscuro; see, for example, "The Island of the Fay." So, too, does that mixture of moon and firelight which Hawthorne speaks of in the Custom House introduction to *The Scarlet Letter:* the moonlight makes "every object so minutely visible, yet so unlike a morning or noontide visibility"; it "spiritualizes" objects so that they "seem to lose their actual substance and become things of the intellect." And the warmer light of "a somewhat dim coal-fire" (bonfires and other conflagrations have a more luridly and sublimely passionate effect) "mingles itself with the cold spirituality of the moon beams, and communicates, as it were, a heart and sensibilities of human tenderness to the forms which fancy summons up." In the work of Hawthorne and Poe, as in that of the Transcendentalists, the effect of light thus fuses the physical and the psychic dimensions of landscape.

The object of these writers is to create in the reader a mental state receptive to the presence in the landscape of a supernatural or preternatural dimension of reality. Different impressions make the reader receptive to different aspects of this reality. "The Island of the Fay," for example, evokes an impression of beauty. The physical details of such a landscape blossom, interwreathe, undulate; the light sparkles and glows; the landscape as a whole projects a feeling of sensuality, of harmony, and of exhuberant repose such as fairies or angels might feel. "Sights from a Steeple," on the other hand, evokes an impression of picturesque complexity: pleasing shifts from beauty to sublimity, pathos to comedy, in a panoramic whole. From such a perspective, life becomes a kind of progression through various seasons and stations, through storm and sunshine. Such stories as "The Ambitious Guest" or "Descent into the Maelstrom" or "The Fall of the House of Usher," finally, evoke grand and terrible impressions of sublimity: everything is wildly lit; a whirl of detail excites, unsettles, and finally disorients the senses until the whole landscape pours, crashes, whirls; and the landscape projects a feeling of terrible unfamiliarity and of such overwhelming force as only the God-visited and the apocalypse-haunted feel.

What these two writers hope to perceive through their landscapes are "gleams" of the timeless essences which inform them. Their landscapes are both the occasion of reverie or revelation and the source of metaphor by which these mental motions are defined.

ROMANTIC POETRY

In both the poetry and the fiction the reader can discover two kinds of relationships between landscape and idea. In one relationship, idea precedes landscape (as in the sketch of fancy), and landscape becomes only the way of expressing the idea; it has no meaning in itself. This is allegory in its fullest sense, and it demonstrates the power of the mind to give its own abstract shape to the world. In the other relationship, in the adorned sketch, the landscape precedes and generates idea in the ways enumerated in The Transcendentalists: a concrete landscape is conceived of as scripture and is interpreted symbolically, allegorically, or anagogically. This suggests a more passive process of perceiving and valuing. The difference between the two relationships is the difference between, say, Emerson's "Each and All," with its allegorical dimensions of meaning, and Frederick Douglass's Way to the Promised Land or Emily Dickinson's "I cross till I am weary," which are both allegorized landscapes.

Poetry brings to the literary art of landscape a heightening of the principle of expression—a heightening of tone. The visual expressions of tone are color, texture, light, and shadow. The aural expressions of tone, which poetry amplifies, are *voice* and *rhythm.* Voice is a combination of the poem-speaker's attitude toward his subject (detached, celebrational, exultant, frightened, awed, joyful, and so on) and his attitude toward his audience (formal, teaching, confessional, and so on). The questions to ask of a landscape poem, or indeed of any verbal sketch, are these: what in the landscape is generating the writer's attitude toward the whole? And how important is that attitude in relation to the visible facts of the landscape? In the sublime landscape, for example, the attitude—the tone of the voice—comes to dominate the foreground as the emphasis shifts from the landscape *per se* to its effects on the perceiver's mind. To analyze the voice in a poem is to trace the shifting or implicit contours of emotion and thought which the landscape generates.

Rhythm is perhaps the most important vehicle of expression in a landscape poem. Rhythm, as it came to be regarded in the period 1830–1860, is not an ornament but an organic reflection of the dynamics of a landscape and the perceiver's responses to it. Rhythm can express both physical and psychic movement in landscape. The two chief rhythmic forms in poetry are *metrical form* and *free verse.* In metrical form, rhythm is measured by the regular recurrence of accented syllables, and the measurement—fast or slow, regular or irregular—can be adapted to physical or psychic motion. In free verse, the rhythms are the rhythms of the chant or litany—the incantational repetition of sounds (assonance, alliteration), words, and syntactic structures (balance, parallel construction)—or the rhythms of natural speech when it is charged with emotion or thought. Either of these rhythmic forms of poetry can bring into play all of the expressive resources of language right down to the repetition of consonants and vowels. Short vowels have the effect of speed and tightness; long vowels, of leisure and openness. In a beautiful landscape, liquid l's and humming nasals (m's and n's), and in a sublime landscape, plosive d's and b's, might suggest a sympathetic movement of the mouth as it shapes the sounds that will give shape to the landscape.

In the poems included here, such nuances of organic form can be discovered even as the poets themselves discovered and put into practice the idea of organic form first adumbrated by Emerson when he wrote in *The Poet* (1841):

> . . . It is not meters, but a meter-making argument that makes a poem,—a thought so passionate and alive that like the spirit of a plant or an animal it has an architecture of its own, and adorns nature with a new thing. The thought and the form are equal in the order of time, but in the order of genesis the thought is prior to the form.

Nathaniel Hawthorne

Sights from a Steeple

In this meditative sketch—probably, as it suggests, "drawn from the life"—correspondences are made between light and motion in the landscape and mood and motion in the figures which appear on it. The figures themselves form a kind of symbolic procession.

so! I have climbed high, and my reward is small. Here I stand, with wearied knees, earth, indeed, at a dizzy depth below, but heaven far, far beyond me still. Oh that I could soar up into the very zenith, where man never breathed, nor eagle ever flew, and where the ethereal azure melts away from the eye, and appears only a deepened shade of nothingness! And yet I shiver at that cold and solitary thought. What clouds are gathering in the golden west, with direful intent against the brightness and the warmth of this summer afternoon! They are ponderous air ships, black as death, and freighted with the tempest; and at intervals their thunder, the signal guns of that unearthly squadron, rolls distant along the deep of heaven. These nearer heaps of fleecy vapor—methinks I could roll and toss upon them the whole day long!—seem scattered here and there for the repose of tired pilgrims through the sky. Perhaps—for who can tell?—beautiful spirits are disporting themselves there, and will bless my mortal eye with the brief appearance of their curly locks of golden light, and laughing faces, fair and faint as the people of a rosy dream. Or, where the floating mass so imperfectly obstructs the color of the firmament, a slender foot and fairy limb, resting too heavily upon the frail support, may be thrust through, and suddenly withdrawn, while longing fancy follows them in vain. Yonder again is an airy archipelago, where the sun beams love to linger in their journeyings through space. Every one of those little clouds has been dipped and steeped in radiance, which the slightest pressure might disengage in silvery profusion, like water wrung from a sea-maid's hair. Bright they are as a young man's visions, and, like them, would be realized in chillness, obscurity, and tears. I will look on them no more.

In three parts of the visible circle, whose centre is this spire, I discern cultivated fields, villages, white country seats, the waving lines of rivulets, little placid lakes, and here and there a rising ground, that would fain be termed a hill. On the fourth side is the sea, stretching away towards a viewless boundary, blue and calm, except where the passing anger of a shadow flits across its surface, and is gone. Hitherward, a broad inlet penetrates far into the land; on the verge of the harbor, formed by its extremity, is a town; and over it am I, a watchman, all-heeding and unheeded. Oh that the multitude of chimneys could speak, like those of Madrid, and betray, in smoky whispers, the secrets of all who, since their first foundation, have assembled at the hearths within! Oh that the Limping Devil of Le Sage would perch beside me here, extend his wand over this contiguity of roofs, uncover every chamber, and make me familiar with their inhabitants! The most desirable mode of existence might be that of a spiritualized Paul Pry, hovering invisible round man and woman, witnessing their deeds, searching into their hearts, borrowing brightness from their felicity and shade from their sorrow, and retaining no emotion peculiar to himself. But none of these things are possible; and if I would know the interior of brick walls, or the mystery of human bosoms, I can but guess.

Yonder is a fair street, extending north and south. The stately mansions are placed each on its carpet of verdant grass, and a long flight of steps descends from every door to the pavement. Ornamental trees—the broad-leafed horse-chestnut, the elm so lofty and bending, the graceful but infrequent willow, and others whereof I know not the names—grow thrivingly among brick and stone. The oblique rays of the sun are intercepted by these green citizens, and by the houses, so that one side of the street is a shaded and pleasant walk. On its whole extent there is now but a single passenger, advancing from the upper end; and he, unless distance and the medium of a pocket spy-glass do him more than justice, is a fine young man of twenty. He saunters slowly forward, slapping his left hand with his folded gloves, bending his eyes upon the pavement, and sometimes raising them to throw a glance before him. Certainly, he has a pensive air. Is he in doubt, or in debt? Is he, if the question be allowable, in love? Does he strive to be melancholy and gentleman-like? Or, is he merely overcome by the heat? But I bid him farewell for the present. The door of one of the houses—an aristocratic edifice, with curtains of purple and gold waving from the windows, is now opened, and down the steps come two ladies, swinging their parasols, and lightly arrayed for a summer ramble. Both are young, both are pretty, but methinks the left-hand lass is the fairer of the twain; and, though she be so serious at this moment, I could swear that there is a treasure of gentle fun within her. They stand talking a little while upon the steps, and finally proceed up the street. Meantime, as their faces are now turned from me, I may look elsewhere.

Upon that wharf, and down the corresponding street, is a busy contrast to the quiet scene which I have just noticed. Business evidently has its centre there, and many a man is wasting the summer afternoon in labor and anxiety, in losing riches or in gaining them, where he would be wiser to flee away to some pleasant country village, or shaded lake in the forest, or wild and cool sea-beach. I see vessels unlading at the wharf, and precious merchandise strewn upon the ground, abundantly as at the bottom of the sea, that market whence no goods return, and where there is no captain nor supercargo to render an account of sales. Here, the clerks are diligent with their paper and pencils, and sailors ply the block and tackle that hang over the hold, accompanying their toil with cries, long drawn and roughly melodious, till the bales and puncheons ascend to upper air. At a little distance a group of gentlemen are assembled round the door of a warehouse. Grave seniors be they, and I would wager—if it were safe in these times to be responsible for any one—that the least eminent among them might vie with old Vicentio, that incomparable trafficker of Pisa. I can even select the wealthiest of the company. It is the elderly personage, in somewhat rusty black, with powdered hair, the superfluous whiteness of which is visible upon the cape of his coat. His twenty ships are wafted on some of their many courses by every breeze that blows, and his name—I will venture to say, though I know it not—is a familar sound among the far separated merchants of Europe and the Indies.

But I bestow too much of my attention in this quarter. On looking again to the long and shady walk, I perceive that the two fair girls have encountered the young man. After a sort of shyness in the recognition, he turns back with them. Moreover, he has sanctioned my taste in regard to his companions by placing himself on the inner side of the pavement, nearest the Venus to whom I—enacting, on a steeple top, the part of Paris on the top of Ida—adjudged the golden apple.

In two streets, converging at right angles towards my watchtower, I distinguish three different processions. One is a proud array of voluntary soldiers, in bright uniform, resembling, from the height whence I look down, the painted veterans that garrison the windows of a toyshop. And yet, it stirs my heart; their regular advance, their nodding plumes, the sunflash on their bayonets and musket barrels, the roll of their drums ascending past me, and the fife ever and anon piercing through—these things have wakened a war-like fire, peaceful though I be. Close to their rear marches a battalion of school-boys, ranged in crooked and irregular platoons, shouldering sticks, thumping a harsh and unripe clatter from an instrument of tin, and ridiculously aping the intricate manœuvres of the foremost band. Nevertheless, as slight differences are scarcely perceptible from a church spire, one might be tempted to ask, "Which are the boys?"—or rather, "Which the men?" But, leaving these, let us turn to the third procession, which, though sadder in outward show, may excite identical reflections in the thoughtful mind. It is a funeral. A hearse, drawn by a black and bony steed, and covered by a dusty pall; two or three coaches rumbling over the stones, their drivers half asleep; a dozen couple of careless mourners in their every-day attire; such was not the fashion of our fathers, when they carried a friend to his grave. There is now no doleful clang of the bell to proclaim sorrow to the town. Was the King of Terrors more awful in those days than in our own, that wisdom and philosophy have been able to produce this change? Not so. Here is a proof that he retains his proper majesty. The military men and the military boys are wheeling round the corner, and meet the funeral full in the face. Immediately the drum is silent, all but the tap that regulates each simultaneous footfall. The soldiers yield the path to the dusty hearse and unpretending train, and the children quit their ranks, and cluster on the sidewalks, with timorous and instinctive curiosity. The mourners enter the churchyard at the base of the steeple, and pause by an open grave among the burial stones; the lightning glimmers on them as they lower down the coffin, and the thunder rattles heavily while they throw the earth upon its lid. Verily, the shower is near, and I tremble for the young man and the girls, who have now disappeared from the long and shady street.

How various are the situations of the people covered by the roofs beneath me, and how diversified are the events at this moment befalling them! The new born, the aged, the dying, the strong in life, and the recent dead, are in the chambers of these many mansions. The full of hope, the happy, the miserable, and the desperate, dwell together within the circle of my glance. In some of the houses over which my eyes roam so coldly, guilt is entering into hearts that are still tenanted by a debased and trodden virtue,—guilt is on the very edge of commission, and the impending deed might be averted; guilt is done, and the criminal wonders if it be irrevocable. There are broad thoughts struggling in my mind, and, were I able to give them distinctness, they would make their way in eloquence. Lo! the raindrops are descending.

The clouds, within a little time, have gathered over all the sky, hanging heavily, as if about to drop in one unbroken mass upon the earth. At intervals, the lightning flashes from their brooding hearts, quivers, disappears, and then comes the thunder, travelling slowly after its twin-born flame. A strong wind has sprung up, howls through the darkened streets, and raises the dust in dense bodies, to rebel against the approaching storm. The disbanded soldiers fly, the funeral has already vanished like its dead, and all people hurry homeward—all that have a home; while a few lounge by the corners, or trudge on desperately, at their leisure. In a narrow lane, which communicates with the shady street, I discern the rich old merchant, putting himself to the top of his speed, lest the rain should convert his hair powder to a paste. Unhappy gentleman! By the slow vehemence and painful moderation wherewith he journeys, it is but too evident that Podagra has left its thrilling tenderness in his great toe. But yonder, at a far more rapid pace, come three other of my acquaintance, the two pretty girls and the young man, unseasonably interrupted in their walk. Their footsteps are supported by the risen dust,—the wind lends them its velocity,—they fly like three sea-birds driven landward by the tempestuous breeze. The ladies would not thus rival Atalanta if they but knew that any one were at leisure to observe them. Ah! as they hasten onward, laughing in the angry face of nature, a sudden catastrophe has chanced. At the corner where the narrow lane enters into the street, they come plump against the old merchant, whose tortoise motion has just brought him to that point. He likes not the sweet encounter; the darkness of the whole air gathers speedily upon his visage, and there is a pause on both sides. Finally, he thrusts aside the youth with little courtesy, seizes an arm of each of the two girls, and plods onward, like a magician with a prize of captive fairies. All this is easy to be understood. How disconsolate the poor lover stands! regardless of the rain that threatens an exceeding damage to his well-fashioned habiliments, till he catches a backward glance of mirth from a bright eye, and turns away with what ever comfort it conveys.

The old man and his daughters are safely housed, and now the storm lets loose its fury. In every dwelling I perceive the faces of the chambermaids as they shut down the windows, excluding the impetuous shower, and shrinking away from the quick fiery glare. The large drops descend with force upon the slated roofs, and rise again in smoke. There is a rush and roar, as of a river through the air, and muddy streams bubble majestically along the pavement, whirl their dusky foam into the kennel, and disappear beneath iron grates. Thus did Arethusa sink. I love not my station here aloft, in the midst of the tumult which I am powerless to direct or quell, with the blue lightning wrinkling on my brow, and the thunder muttering its first awful syllables in my ear. I will descend. Yet let me give another glance to the sea, where the foam breaks out in long white lines upon a broad expanse of blackness, or boils up in the far distant points, like snowy mountain tops in the eddies of a flood; and let me look once more at the green plain, and the little hills of the country, over which the giant of the storm is striding in robes of mist, and at the town, whose obscured and desolate streets might beseem a city of the dead; and turning a single moment to the sky, now gloomy as an author's prospects, I prepare to resume my station on lower earth. But stay! A little speck of azure has widened in the western heavens; the sunbeams find a passage, and go rejoicing through the tempest; and on yonder darkest cloud, born, like hallowed hopes, of the glory of another world and the trouble and tears of this, brightens forth the Rainbow!

1831

The Ambitious Guest

It is probable that Hawthorne heard the legend on which "The Ambitious Guest" is based in September 1832, when he stopped at Ethan Crawford's inn in the White Mountains (see The Poetry of Scene). He seems not to have known as much about painting as Poe, but he was able, as F. O. Matthiessen observes in *American Renaissance,* to create "sustained landscapes of low-pitched tones to heighten the effects of his foreground. He generally visualized his outdoor scenes in neutral 'gray and russet,' against which he projected" his brilliantly colored symbols. Here the "foregound" is an interior, the background an outdoor scene not so much visualized as heard. In writing of "The Hollow of the Three Hills," Poe said: "Mr. Hawthorne has wonderfully heightened his effect by making the ear, in place of the eye, the medium by which the fantasy is conveyed"; and the sounds Poe heard there had "an all-sufficient intelligence." Poe's observation applies to "The Ambitious Guest," if for "fantasy" one reads "allegory" or "moral sublime."

ONE SEPTEMBER NIGHT, a family had gathered round their hearth, and piled it high with the driftwood of mountain streams, the dry cones of the pine, and the splintered ruins of great trees that had come crashing down the precipice. Up the chimney roared the fire, and brightened the room with its broad blaze. The faces of the father and mother had a sober gladness; the children laughed; the eldest daughter was the image of Happiness at seventeen; and the aged grandmother, who sat knitting in the warmest place, was the image of Happiness grown old. They had found the "herb, heart's ease," in the bleakest spot of all New England. This family were situated in the Notch of the White Hills, where the wind was sharp throughout the year, and pitilessly cold in the winter, giving their cottage all its fresh inclemency before it descended on the valley of the Saco. They dwelt in a cold spot and a dangerous one; for a mountain towered above their heads, so steep that the stones would often rumble down its sides and startle them at midnight.

The daughter had just uttered some simple jest that filled them all with mirth, when the wind came through the Notch and seemed to pause before their cottage—rattling the door, with a sound of wailing and lamentation, before it passed into the valley. For a moment it saddened them, though there was nothing unusual in the tones. But the family were glad again when they perceived that the latch was lifted by some traveler, whose footsteps had been unheard amid the dreary blast which heralded his approach, and wailed as he was entering, and went moaning away from the door.

Though they dwelt in such a solitude, these people held daily converse with the world. The romantic pass of the Notch is a great artery, through which the lifeblood of internal commerce is continually throbbing between Maine, on one side, and the Green Mountains and the shores of the St. Lawrence, on the other. The stagecoach always drew up before the door of the cottage. The wayfarer, with no companion but his staff, paused here to exchange a word, that the sense of loneliness might not utterly overcome him ere he could pass through the cleft of the mountain, or reach the first house in the valley. And here the teamster, on his way to Portland market, would put up for the night; and, if a bachelor, might sit an hour beyond the usual bedtime, and steal a kiss from the mountain maid at parting. It was one of those primitive taverns where the traveler pays only for food and lodging, but meets with a homely kindness beyond all price. When the footsteps were heard, therefore, between the outer door and the inner one, the whole family rose up, grandmother, children, and all, as if about to welcome someone who belonged to them, and whose fate was linked with theirs.

The door was opened by a young man. His face at first wore the melancholy expression, almost despondency, of one who travels a wild and bleak road, at nightfall and alone, but soon brightened up when he saw the kindly warmth of his reception. He felt his heart spring forward to meet them all, from the old woman, who wiped a chair with her apron, to the little child that held out its arms to him. One glance and smile placed the stranger on a footing of innocent familiarity with the eldest daughter.

"Ah, this fire is the right thing!" cried he, "especially when there is such a pleasant circle round it. I am quite benumbed; for the Notch is just like the pipe of a great pair of bellows; it has blown a terrible blast in my face all the way from Bartlett."

"Then you are going towards Vermont?" said the master of the house, as he helped to take a light knapsack off the young man's shoulders.

"Yes; to Burlington, and far enough beyond," replied he. "I meant to have been at Ethan Crawford's tonight; but a pedestrian lingers along such a road as this. It is no matter; for, when I saw this good fire, and all your cheerful faces, I felt as if you had kindled it on purpose for me, and were waiting my arrival. So I shall sit down among you, and make myself at home."

The frank-hearted stranger had just drawn his chair to the fire when something like a heavy footstep was heard without, rushing down the steep side of the mountain, as with long and rapid strides, and taking such a leap in passing the cottage as to strike the opposite precipice. The family held their breath, because they knew the sound, and their guest held his by instinct.

"The old mountain has thrown a stone at us, for fear we should forget him," said the landlord, recovering himself. "He sometimes nods his head and threatens to come down; but we are old neighbors, and agree together pretty well upon the whole. Besides, we have a sure place of refuge hard by if he should be coming in good earnest."

Let us now suppose the stranger to have finished his supper of bear's meat; and, by his natural felicity of manner, to have placed himself on a footing of kindness with the whole family, so that they talked as freely together as if he belonged to their mountain brood. He was of a proud, yet gentle spirit—haughty and reserved among the rich and great; but ever ready to stoop his head to the lowly cottage door, and be like a brother or a son at the poor man's fireside. In the household of the Notch he found warmth and simplicity of feeling, the pervading intelligence of New England, and a poetry of native growth, which they had gathered when they little thought of it from the mountain peaks and chasms, and at the very threshold of their romantic and dangerous abode. He had traveled far and alone; his whole life, indeed, had been a solitary path; for, with the lofty caution of his nature, he had kept himself apart from those who might otherwise have been his companions. The family, too, though so kind and hospitable, had that consciousness of unity among themselves, and separation from the world at large, which, in every domestic circle, should still keep a holy place where no stranger may intrude. But this evening a prophetic sympathy impelled the refined and educated youth to pour out his heart before the simple mountaineers, and constrained them to answer him with the same free confidence. And thus it should have been. Is not the kindred of a common fate a closer tie than that of birth?

The secret of the young man's character was a high and abstracted ambition. He could have borne to live an undistinguished life, but not to be forgotten in the grave. Yearning desire had been transformed to hope; and hope, long cherished, had become like certainty that, obscurely as he journeyed now, a glory was to beam on all his pathway—though not, perhaps, while he was treading it. But when posterity should gaze back into the gloom of what was now the present, they would trace the brightness of his footsteps, brightening as meaner glories faded, and confess that a gifted one had passed from his cradle to his tomb with none to recognize him.

"As yet," cried the stranger, his cheek glowing and his eye flashing with enthusiasm, "as yet, I have done nothing. Were I to vanish from the earth tomorrow, none would know so much of me as you: that a nameless youth came up at nightfall from the valley of the Saco, and opened his heart to you in the evening, and passed through the Notch by sunrise, and was seen no more. Not a soul would ask, 'Who was he? Whither did the wanderer go?' But I cannot die till I have achieved my destiny. Then, let Death come! I shall have built my monument!"

There was a continual flow of natural emotion, gushing forth amid abstracted reverie, which enabled the family to understand this young man's sentiments, though so foreign from their own. With quick sensibility of the ludicrous, he blushed at the ardor into which he had been betrayed.

"You laugh at me," said he, taking the eldest daughter's hand, and laughing himself. "You think my ambition as nonsensical as if I were to freeze myself to death on the top of Mount Washington, only that people might spy at me from the country round about. And, truly, that would be a noble pedestal for a man's statue!"

"It is better to sit here by this fire," answered the girl, blushing, "and be comfortable and contented, though nobody thinks about us."

"I suppose," said her father, after a fit of musing, "there is something natural in what the young man says; and if my mind had been turned that way, I might have felt just the same. It is strange, wife, how his talk has set my head running on things that are pretty certain never to come to pass."

"Perhaps they may," observed the wife. "Is the man thinking what he will do when he is a widower?"

"No, no!" cried he, repelling the idea with reproachful kindness. "When I think of your death, Esther, I think of mine, too. But I was wishing we had a good farm in Bartlett, or Bethlehem, or Littleton, or some other township round the White Mountains; but not where they could tumble on our heads. I should want to stand well with my neighbors and be called Squire, and sent to General Court for a term or two; for a plain, honest man may do as much good there as a lawyer. And when I should be grown quite an old man, and you an old woman, so as not to be long apart, I might die happy enough in my bed, and leave you all crying around me. A slate gravestone would suit me as well as a marble one—with just my name and age, and a verse of a hymn, and something to let people know that I lived an honest man and died a Christian."

"There now!" exclaimed the stranger. "It is our nature to desire a monument, be it slate or marble, or a pillar of granite, or a glorious memory in the universal heart of man."

"We're in a strange way tonight," said the wife, with tears in her eyes. "They say it's a sign of something, when folks' minds go a wandering so. Hark to the children!"

They listened accordingly. The younger children had been put to bed in another room, but with an open door between, so that they could be heard talking busily among themselves. One and all seemed to have caught the infection from the fireside circle, and were outvying each other in wild wishes, and childish projects of what they would do when they came to be men and women. At length, a little boy, instead of addressing his brothers and sisters, called out to his mother.

"I'll tell you what I wish, Mother," cried he. "I want you and Father and Grandma'm, and all of us, and the stranger, too, to start right away, and go and take a drink out of the basin of the Flume!"

Nobody could help laughing at the child's notion of leaving a warm bed, and dragging them from a cheerful fire, to visit the basin of the Flume—a brook, which tumbles over the precipice, deep within the Notch. The boy had hardly spoken when a wagon rattled along the road, and stopped a moment before the door. It appeared to contain two or three men, who were cheering their hearts with the rough chorus of a song, which resounded, in broken notes, between the cliffs, while the singers hesitated whether to continue their journey or put up here for the night.

"Father," said the girl, "they are calling you by name."

But the good man doubted whether they had really called him, and was unwilling to show himself too solicitous of gain by inviting people to patronize his house. He therefore did not hurry to the door; and the lash being soon applied, the travelers plunged into the Notch, still singing and laughing, though their music and mirth came back drearily from the heart of the mountain.

"There, Mother!" cried the boy again. "They'd have given us a ride to the Flume."

Again they laughed at the child's pertinacious fancy for a night ramble. But it happened that a light cloud passed over the daughter's spirit; she looked gravely into the fire, and drew a breath that was almost a sigh. It forced its way, in spite of a little struggle to repress it. Then, starting and blushing, she looked quickly round the circle, as if they had caught a glimpse into her bosom. The stranger asked what she had been thinking of.

''Nothing,'' answered she, with a downcast smile. ''Only I felt lonesome just then.''

''Oh, I have always had a gift of feeling what is in other people's hearts,'' said he, half seriously. ''Shall I tell the secrets of yours? For I know what to think when a young girl shivers by a warm hearth, and complains of lonesomeness at her mother's side. Shall I put these feelings into words?''

''They would not be a girl's feelings any longer if they could be put into words,'' replied the mountain nymph, laughing, but avoiding his eye.

All this was said apart. Perhaps a germ of love was springing in their hearts, so pure that it might blossom in Paradise, since it could not be matured on earth; for women worship such gentle dignity as his; and the proud, contemplative, yet kindly soul is oftenest captivated by simplicity like hers. But while they spoke softly, and he was watching the happy sadness, the lightsome shadows, the shy yearnings of a maiden's nature, the wind through the Notch took a deeper and drearier sound. It seemed, as the fanciful stranger said, like the choral strain of the spirits of the blast, who in old Indian times had their dwelling among these mountains, and made their heights and recesses a sacred region. There was a wail along the road, as if a funeral were passing. To chase away the gloom, the family threw pine branches on their fire, till the dry leaves crackled and the flame arose, discovering once again a scene of peace and humble happiness. The light hovered about them fondly, and caressed them all. There were the little faces of the children, peeping from their bed apart, and here the father's frame of strength, the mother's subdued and careful mien, the high-browed youth, the budding girl, and the good old grandam, still knitting in the warmest place. The aged woman looked up from her task, and, with fingers ever busy, was the next to speak.

''Old folks have their notions,'' said she, ''as well as young ones. You've been wishing and planning; and letting your heads run on one thing and another, till you've set my mind a wandering, too. Now, what should an old woman wish for, when she can go but a step or two before she comes to her grave? Children, it will haunt me night and day till I tell you.''

''What is it, Mother?'' cried the husband and wife at once.

Then the old woman, with an air of mystery which drew the circle closer round the fire, informed them that she had provided her grave clothes some years before—a nice linen shroud, a cap with a muslin ruff, and everything of a finer sort than she had worn since her wedding day. But this evening an old superstition had strangely recurred to her. It used to be said, in her younger days, that if anything were amiss with a corpse, if only the ruff were not smooth, or the cap did not set right, the corpse in the coffin and beneath the clods would strive to put up its cold hands and arrange it. The bare thought made her nervous.

"Don't talk so, Grandmother!" said the girl shuddering.

"Now," continued the old woman, with singular earnestness, yet smiling strangely at her own folly, "I want one of you, my children—when your mother is dressed and in the coffin—I want one of you to hold a looking glass over my face. Who knows but I may take a glimpse at myself, and see whether all's right?"

"Old and young, we dream of graves and monuments," murmured the stranger youth. "I wonder how mariners feel when the ship is sinking, and they, unknown and undistinguished, are to be buried together in the ocean—that wide and nameless sepulcher?"

For a moment, the old woman's ghastly conception so engrossed the minds of her hearers that a sound abroad in the night, rising like the roar of a blast, had grown broad, deep, and terrible, before the fated group were conscious of it. The house and all within it trembled; the foundations of the earth seemed to be shaken, as if this awful sound were the peal of the last trump. Young and old exchanged one wild glance, and remained an instant, pale, affrighted, without utterance, or power to move. Then the same shriek burst simultaneously from all their lips.

"The Slide! The Slide!"

The simplest words must intimate, but not portray, the unutterable horror of the catastrophe. The victims rushed from their cottage, and sought refuge in what they deemed a safer spot—where, in contemplation of such an emergency, a sort of barrier had been reared. Alas! they had quitted their security, and fled right into the pathway of destruction. Down came the whole side of the mountain, in a cataract of ruin. Just before it reached the house, the stream broke into two branches—shivered not a window there, but overwhelmed the whole vicinity, blocked up the road, and annihilated everything in its dreadful course. Long ere the thunder of the great Slide had ceased to roar among the mountains, the mortal agony had been endured, and the victims were at peace. Their bodies were never found.

The next morning, the light smoke was seen stealing from the cottage chimney up the mountain side. Within, the fire was yet smoldering on the hearth, and the chairs in a circle round it, as if the inhabitants had but gone forth to view the devastation of the Slide, and would shortly return, to thank Heaven for their miraculous escape. All had left separate tokens, by which those who had known the family were made to shed a tear for each. Who has not heard their name? The story has been told far and wide, and will forever be a legend of these mountains. Poets have sung their fate.

There were circumstances which led some to suppose that a stranger had been received into the cottage on this awful night, and had shared the catastrophe of all its inmates. Others denied that there were sufficient grounds for such a conjecture. Woe for the high-souled youth, with his dream of earthly immortality! His name and person utterly unknown; his history, his way of life, his plans, a mystery never to be solved, his death and his existence equally a doubt! Whose was the agony of that death moment?

1835

Edgar Allan Poe

The Island of the Fay

A "scene of fancy" (see introduction to The Poetry of Scene), "The island of the Fay" is an invitation to allegory. There are no pat equations of object and idea, but the contrast of an Edenic West and a darkened, cultivated East, both with their influences on the fay (or fairy), suggests the influence of time and of settlement on the American continent.

Nullus enim locus sine genio est.[1]

—Servius

LA MUSIQUE," says Marmontel, in those "Contes Moraux" [2] which in all our translations, we have insisted upon calling "Moral Tales," as if in mockery of their spirit—"*la musique est le seul des talents qui jouissent de lui-même; tous les autres veulent des temoins.*" He here confounds the pleasure derivable from sweet sounds with the capacity for creating them. No more than any other *talent,* is that for music susceptible of complete enjoyment, where there is no second party to appreciate its exercise. And it is only in common with other talents that it produces *effects* which may be fully enjoyed in solitude. The idea which the *raconteur* has either failed to entertain clearly, or has sacrificed in its expression to his national love of *point,* is, doubtless, the very tenable one that the higher order of music is the most thoroughly estimated when we are exclusively alone. The proposition, in this form, will be admitted at once by those who love the lyre for its own sake, and for its spiritual uses. But there is one pleasure still within the reach of fallen mortality—and perhaps only one—which owes even more than does music to the accessory sentiment

[1] "No place is without its local spirit"—ed.

[2] Moraux is here derived from *mœurs,* and its meaning is "*fashionable*" or more strictly "of manners."

of seclusion. I mean the happiness experienced in the contemplation of natural scenery. In truth, the man who would behold aright the glory of God upon earth must in solitude behold that glory. To me, at least, the presence—not of human life only, but of life in any other form than that of the green things which grow upon the soil and are voiceless—is a stain upon the landscape—is at war with the genius of the scene. I love, indeed, to regard the dark valleys, and the gray rocks, and the waters that silently smile, and the forests that sigh in uneasy slumbers, and the proud watchful mountains that look down upon all,—I love to regard these as themselves but the colossal members of one vast animate and sentient whole—a whole whose form (that of the sphere) is the most perfect and most inclusive of all; whose path is among associate planets; whose meek handmaiden is the moon, whose mediate sovereign is the sun; whose life is eternity; whose thought is that of a God; whose enjoyment is knowledge; whose destinies are lost in immensity; whose cognizance of ourselves is akin with our own cognizance of the *animalculæ* [3] which infest the brain—a being which we, in consequence, regard as purely inanimate and material, much in the same manner as these *animalculæ* must thus regard us.

Our telescopes and our mathematical investigations assure us on every hand—notwithstanding the cant of the more ignorant of the priesthood—that space, and therefore that bulk, is an important consideration in the eyes of the Almighty. The cycles in which the stars move are those best adapted for the evolution, without collision, of the greatest possible number of bodies. The forms of those bodies are accurately such as, within a given surface, to include the greatest possible amount of matter;—while the surfaces themselves are so disposed as to accommodate a denser population than could be accommodated on the same surfaces otherwise arranged. Nor is it any argument against bulk being an object with God, that space itself is infinite; for there may be an infinity of matter to fill it. And since we see clearly that the endowment of matter with vitality is a principle—indeed, as far as our judgments extend, the *leading* principle in the operations of Deity,—it is scarcely logical to imagine it confined to the regions of the minute, where we daily trace it, and not extending to those of the august. As we find cycle within cycle without end,—yet all revolving around one far-distant centre which is the God-head, may we not analogically suppose in the same manner, life within life, the less with the greater, and all within the Spirit Divine? In short, we are madly erring, through self-esteem, in believing man, in either his temporal or future destinies, to be of more moment in the universe than that vast "clod of the valley" which he tills and contemns, and to which he denies a soul for no more profound reason than that he does not behold it in operation.[4]

[3] Microscopic animals—ed.

[4] Speaking of the tides, Pomponius Mela, in his treatise "*De Situ Orbis,*" says "either the world is a great animal, or" etc.

These fancies, and such as these, have always given to my meditations among the mountains and the forests, by the rivers and the ocean, a tinge of what the everyday world would not fail to term fantastic. My wanderings amid such scenes have been many, and far-searching, and often solitary; and the interest with which I have strayed through many a dim, deep valley, or gazed into the reflected Heaven of many a bright lake, has been an interest greatly deepened by the thought that I have strayed and gazed *alone*. What flippant Frenchman was it who said in allusion to the well-known work of Zimmerman, that, "*la solitude est une belle chose; mais il faut quelqu'un pour vous dire que la solitude est une belle chose?*" The epigram cannot be gainsayed; but the necessity is a thing that does not exist.

It was during one of my lonely journeyings, amid a far distant region of mountain locked within mountain, and sad rivers and melancholy tarns writhing or sleeping within all—that I chanced upon a certain rivulet and island. I came upon them suddenly in the leafy June, and threw myself upon the turf, beneath the branches of an unknown odorous shrub, that I might doze as I contemplated the scene. I felt that thus only should I look upon it—such was the character of phantasm which it wore.

On all sides—save to the west, where the sun was about sinking—arose the verdant walls of the forest. The little river which turned sharply in its course, and was thus immediately lost to sight, seemed to have no exit from its prison, but to be absorbed by the deep green foliage of the trees to the east—while in the opposite quarter (so it appeared to me as I lay at length and glanced upward) there poured down noiselessly and continuously into the valley, a rich golden and crimson waterfall from the sunset fountains of the sky.

About midway in the short vista which my dreamy vision took in, one small circular island, profusely verdured, reposed upon the bosom of the stream.

So blended blank and shadow there
That each seemed pendulous in air—

so mirror-like was the glassy water, that it was scarcely possible to say at what point upon the slope of the emerald turf its crystal dominion began.

My position enabled me to include in a single view both the eastern and western extremities of the islet; and I observed a singularly-marked difference in their aspects. The latter was all one radiant harem of garden beauties. It glowed and blushed beneath the eyes of the slant sunlight, and fairly laughed with flowers. The grass was short, springy, sweet-scented, and Asphodel-interspersed. The trees were lithe, mirthful, erect—bright, slender, and graceful,—of eastern figure and foliage, with bark smooth, glossy, and parti-colored. There seemed a deep sense of life and joy about all; and although no airs blew from out the heavens, yet every thing had motion through the gentle sweepings to and fro of innumerable butterflies, that might have been mistaken for tulips with wings.[5]

The other or eastern end of the isle was whelmed in the blackest shade. A sombre, yet beautiful and peaceful gloom here pervaded all things. The trees were dark in color, and mournful in form and attitude, wreathing themselves into sad, solemn, and spectral shapes that conveyed ideas of mortal sorrow and untimely death. The grass wore the deep tint of the cypress, and the heads of its blades hung droopingly, and hither and thither among it were many small unsightly hillocks, low and narrow, and not very long, that had the aspect of graves, but were not; although over and all about them the rue and the rosemary clambered. The shade of the trees fell heavily upon the water, and seemed to bury itself therein, impregnating the depths of the element with darkness. I fancied that each shadow, as the sun descended lower and lower, separated itself sullenly from the trunk that gave it birth, and thus became absorbed by the stream; while other shadows issued momently from the trees, taking the place of their predecessors thus entombed.

This idea, having once seized upon my fancy, greatly excited it, and I lost myself forthwith in revery. "If ever island were enchanted," said I to myself, "this is it. This is the haunt of the few gentle Fays who remain from the wreck of the race. Are these green tombs theirs?—or do they yield up their sweet lives as mankind yield up their own? In dying, do they not rather waste away mournfully, rendering unto God, little by little, their existence, as these trees render up shadow after shadow, exhausting their substance unto dissolution? What the wasting tree is to the water that imbibes its shade, growing thus blacker by what it preys upon, may not the life of the Fay be to the death which engulfs it?"

As I thus mused, with half-shut eyes, while the sun sank rapidly to rest, and eddying currents careered round and round the island, bearing upon their bosom large, dazzling, white flakes of the bark of the sycamore—flakes which, in their multiform positions upon the water, a quick imagination might have converted into any thing it pleased,—while I thus mused, it appeared to me that the form of one of those very Fays about whom I had been pondering made its way slowly into the darkness from out the light at the western end of the island. She stood erect in a singularly fragile canoe, and urged it with the mere phantom of an oar. While within the influence of the lingering sunbeams, her attitude seemed indicative of joy—but sorrow deformed it as she passed within the shade. Slowly she glided along, and at length rounded the islet and re-entered the region of light. "The revolution which has just been made by the Fay," continued, I, musingly, "is the cycle of the brief year of her life. She has floated through her winter and through her summer. She is a year nearer unto

[5] Florem putares nare per liquidum æthera.—*P. Commire.*

Death; for I did not fail to see that, as she came into the shade, her shadow fell from her, and was swallowed up in the dark water, making its blackness more black.''

And again the boat appeared and the Fay, but about the attitude of the latter there was more of care and uncertainty and less of elastic joy. She floated again from out the light and into the gloom (which deepened momently) and again her shadow fell from her into the ebony water, and became absorbed into its blackness. And again and again she made the circuit of the island, (while the sun rushed down to his slumbers), and at each issuing into the light there was more sorrow about her person, while it grew feebler and far fainter and more indistinct, and at each passage into the gloom there fell from her a darker shade, which became whelmed in a shadow more black. But at length when the sun had utterly departed, the Fay, now the mere ghost of her former self, went disconsolately with her boat into the region of the ebony floor, and that she issued thence at all I cannot say, for darkness fell over all things and I beheld her magical figure no more.

1841

Frederick Douglass

From Narrative of the Life of Frederick Douglass, An American Slave

In Douglass's sketch, the allegorical meaning is more overt than in Poe's, and the meaning, the imagined reality, has a more visible base in historical circumstance. Douglass is not dreaming but artfully reporting a state of mind by projecting it onto a landscape. In 1835, the year in which the excerpt from Douglass's autobiography takes place, Douglass had been hired out by his master, Thomas Auld, to work as a field hand on William Freeland's farm, located near Maryland's Chesapeake Bay. He was about sixteen. The escape attempt he refers to was foiled, and he would try twice more before escaping to freedom at twenty-one. The excerpt suggests one of the rhetorical uses to which landscape was put in the political and factual literature of the American Renaissance.

AT THE CLOSE of the year 1834, Mr. Freeland again hired me of my master, for the year 1835. But, by this time, I began to want to live *upon free land* as well as *with Freeland;* and I was no longer content, therefore, to live with him or any other slaveholder. I began, with the commencement of the year, to prepare myself for a final struggle, which should decide my fate one way or the other.

My tendency was upward. I was fast approaching manhood, and year after year had passed, and I was still a slave. These thoughts roused me—I must do something. I therefore resolved that 1835 should not pass without witnessing an attempt, on my part, to secure my liberty. But I was not willing to cherish this determination alone. My fellow-slaves were dear to me. I was anxious to have them participate with me in this, my life-giving determination. I therefore, though with great prudence, commenced early to ascertain their views and feelings in regard to their condition, and to imbue their minds with thoughts of freedom. I bent myself to devising ways and means for our escape, and meanwhile strove, on all fitting occasions, to impress them with the gross fraud and inhumanity of slavery. I went first to Henry, next to John, then to the others. I found, in them all, warm hearts and noble spirits. They were ready to hear, and ready to act when a feasible plan should be proposed. This was what I wanted. I talked to them of our want of manhood, if we submitted to our enslavement without at least one noble effort to be free. We met often, and consulted frequently, and told our hopes and fears, recounted the difficulties, real and imagined, which we should be called on to meet. At times we were almost disposed to give up, and try to content ourselves with our wretched lot; at others, we were firm and unbending in our determination to go. Whenever we suggested any plan, there was shrinking—the odds were fearful. Our path was beset with the greatest obstacles; and if we succeeded in gaining the end of it, our right to be free was yet questionable—we were yet liable to be returned to bondage. We could see no spot, this side of the ocean, where we could be free. We knew nothing about Canada. Our knowledge of the north did not extend farther than New York; and to go there, and be forever harassed with the frightful liability of being returned to slavery—with the certainty of being treated tenfold worse than before—the thought was truly a horrible one, and one which it was not easy to overcome. The case sometimes stood thus: At every gate through which we were to pass, we saw a watchman—at every ferry a guard—on every bridge a sentinel—and in every wood a patrol. We were hemmed in upon every side. Here were the difficulties, real or imagined—the good to be sought, and the evil to be shunned. On the one hand, there stood slavery, a stern reality, glaring frightfully upon us,—its robes already crimsoned with the blood of millions, and even now feasting itself greedily upon our own flesh. On the other hand, away back in the dim distance, under the flickering light of the north star, behind some craggy hill or snow-covered mountain, stood a doubtful freedom—half frozen—beckoning us to come and share its hospitality. This in itself was sometimes enough to stagger us; but when we permitted ourselves to survey the road, we were frequently appalled. Upon either side we saw grim death, assuming the most horrid shapes. Now it was starvation, causing us to eat our own flesh;—now we were contending with the waves, and were drowned;—now we were overtaken, and torn to pieces by the fangs of the terrible bloodhound. We were stung by scorpions, chased by wild beasts, bitten by snakes, and finally, after having nearly reached the desired spot,—after swimming rivers, encountering wild beasts, sleeping in the woods, suffering hunger and nakedness,—we were overtaken by our pursuers, and, in our resistance, we were shot dead upon the spot! I say, this picture sometimes appalled us, and made us

> rather bear those ills we had,
> Than fly to others, that we knew not of.

In coming to a fixed determination to run away, we did more than Patrick Henry, when he resolved upon liberty or death. With us it was a doubtful liberty at most, and almost certain death if we failed. For my part, I should prefer death to hopeless bondage.

1845

William Cullen Bryant

A Forest Hymn

Like Thoreau, Bryant was an amateur botanist and ambler, and he came to know well the Berkshire Mountains of western Massachusetts. He wrote "A Forest Hymn" in 1825 in Great Barrington, Massachusetts. Almost all of the details of the forest grove contribute to the metaphoric frame-image of a cathedral.

The groves were God's first temples. Ere man learned
To hew the shaft, and lay the architrave,
And spread the roof above them—ere he framed
The lofty vault, to gather and roll back
The sound of anthems; in the darkling wood,
Amid the cool and silence, he knelt down,
And offered to the Mightiest solemn thanks
And supplication. For his simple heart
Might not resist the sacred influences
Which, from the stilly twilight of the place,
And from the gray old trunks that high in heaven
Mingled their mossy boughs, and from the sound
Of the invisible breath that swayed at once
All their green tops, stole over him, and bowed
His spirit with the thought of boundless power

And inaccessible majesty. Ah, why
Should we, in the world's riper years, neglect
God's ancient sanctuaries, and adore
Only among the crowd, and under roofs
That our frail hands have raised? Let me, at least,
Here, in the shadow of this aged wood,
Offer one hymn—thrice happy, if it find
Acceptance in His ear.

Father, thy hand
Hath reared these venerable columns, thou
Didst weave this verdant roof. Thou didst look down
Upon the naked earth, and, forthwith, rose
All these fair ranks of trees. They, in thy sun,
Budded, and shook their green leaves in thy breeze,
And shot toward heaven. The century-living crow
Whose birth was in their tops, grew old and died
Among their branches, till, at last, they stood,
As now they stand, massy, and tall, and dark,
Fit shrine for humble worshipper to hold
Communion with his Maker. These dim vaults,
These winding aisles, of human pomp or pride
Report not. No fantastic carvings show
The boast of our vain race to change the form
Of thy fair works. But thou art here—thou fill'st
The solitude. Thou art in the soft winds
That run along the summit of these trees
In music; thou art in the cooler breath
That from the inmost darkness of the place
Comes, scarcely felt; the barky trunks, the ground,
The fresh moist ground, are all instinct with thee.
Here is continual worship;—Nature, here,
In the tranquillity that thou dost love,
Enjoys thy presence. Noiselessly, around,
From perch to perch, the solitary bird
Passes; and yon clear spring, that, midst its herbs,
Wells softly forth and wandering steeps the roots
Of half the mighty forest, tells no tale
Of all the good it does. Thou has not left
Thyself without a witness, in the shades,
Of thy perfections. Grandeur, strength, and grace
Are here to speak of thee. This mighty oak—

By whose immovable stem I stand and seem
Almost annihilated—not a prince,
In all that proud old world beyond the deep,
E'er wore his crown as loftily as he
Wears the green coronal of leaves with which
Thy hand had graced him. Nestled at his root
Is beauty, such as blooms not in the glare
Of the broad sun. That delicate forest flower,
With scented breath and look so like a smile,
Seems, as it issues from the shapeless mould,
An emanation of the indwelling Life.
A visible token of the upholding Love,
That are the soul of this great universe.

My heart is awed within me when I think
Of the great miracle that still goes on,
In silence, round me—the perpetual work
Of thy creation, finished, yet renewed
Forever. Written on thy works I read
The lesson of thy own eternity.
Lo! all grow old and die—but see again,
How on the faltering footsteps of decay
Youth presses—ever gay and beautiful youth
In all its beautiful forms. These lofty trees
Wave not less proudly that their ancestors
Moulder beneath them. Oh, there is not lost
One of earth's charms: upon her bosom yet,
After the flight of untold centuries,
The freshness of her far beginning lies
And yet shall lie. Life mocks the idle hate
Of his arch-enemy Death—yea, seats himself
Upon the tyrant's throne—the sepulchre,
And of the triumphs of his ghastly foe
Makes his own nourishment. For he came forth
From thine own bosom, and shall have no end.

There have been holy men who hid themselves
Deep in the woody wilderness, and gave
Their lives to thought and prayer, till they outlived
The generation born with them, nor seemed
Less aged than the hoary trees and rocks
Around them;—and there have been holy men
Who deemed it were not well to pass life thus.

But let me often to these solitudes
Retire, and in thy presence reassure
My feeble virtue. Here its enemies,
The passions, at thy plainer footsteps shrink
And tremble and are still. O God! when thou
Dost scare the world with tempests, set on fire
The heavens with falling thunderbolts, or fill,
With all the waters of the firmament,
The swift dark whirlwind that uproots the woods
And drowns the villages; when, at thy call,
Uprises the great deep and throws himself
Upon the continent, and overwhelms
Its cities—who forgets not, at the sight
Of these tremendous tokens of thy power,
His pride, and lays his strifes and follies by?
Oh, from these sterner aspects of thy face
Spare me and mine, nor let us need the wrath
Of the mad unchained elements to teach
Who rules them. Be it ours to meditate,
In these calm shades, thy milder majesty,
And to the beautiful order of thy works
Learn to conform the order of our lives.

1825

Ralph Waldo Emerson

Each and All

Emerson probably wrote this poem in 1834, about a year after he returned from a long trip to Europe. The opening lines suggest a European landscape: the enigmatic "red-cloaked clown," for example, he saw in northern Italy (what struck him was that even the poor wore such ornaments as "a scarlet cloak"). In May 1834, he recalled in his journal how, as a boy, he had been "charmed with the colors and forms" of shells on a beach and had taken some home, only to find "nothing that I gathered—nothing but some dry, ugly mussel and snail shells. Thence I learned that composition was more important than individual forms to effect." The theme of the poem, orchestrated and amplified by a series of such musings and observations, recalls other lines he wrote in his journal: "Nothing is beautiful alone. Nothing but is beautiful in the whole."

Little thinks, in the field, yon red-cloaked clown
Of thee from the hill-top looking down;
The heifer that lows in the upland farm,
Far-heard, lows not thine ear to charm;
The sexton, tolling his bell at noon,
Deems not that great Napoleon
Stops his horse, and lists with delight,
Whilst his files sweep round yon Alpine height;
Nor knowest thou what argument
Thy life to thy neighbor's creed has lent.
All are needed by each one;
Nothing is fair or good alone.
I thought the sparrow's note from heaven,
Singing at dawn on the alder bough;
I brought him home, in his nest, at even;
He sings the song, but it pleases not now,
For I did not bring home the river and sky;—
He sang to my ear,—they sang to my eye.
The delicate shells lay on the shore;
The bubbles of the latest wave
Fresh pearls to their enamel gave;
And the bellowing of the savage sea
Greeted their safe escape to me.
I wiped away the weeds and foam,
I fetch my sea-born treasures home;
But the poor, unsightly, noisome things
Had left their beauty on the shore
With the sun and the sand and the wild uproar.
The lover watched his graceful maid,
As 'mid the virgin train she strayed,
Nor knew her beauty's best attire
Was woven by the snow-white choir.
At last she came to his hermitage,
Like the bird from the woodlands to the cage;—
The gay enchantment was undone,
A gentle wife, but fairy none.
Then I said, "I covet truth;
Beauty is unripe childhood's cheat;
I leave it behind with the games of youth:"—
As I spoke, beneath my feet
The ground-pine curled its pretty wreath,
Running over the club-moss burrs;

I inhaled the violet's breath;
Around me stood the oaks and firs;
Pine-cones and acorns lay on the ground;
Over me soared the eternal sky,
Full of light and of deity;
Again I saw, again I heard,
The rolling river, the morning bird;—
Beauty through my senses stole;
I yielded myself to the perfect whole.

1839

Henry David Thoreau

Both "Haze" and "Low-Anchored Cloud" appeared, though not for the first time, in "Tuesday" in *A Week on the Concord and Merrimack Rivers* (1849). "Haze" follows this sentence: "The haze, the sun's dust of travel, had a Lethean influence on the land and its inhabitants, and all creatures resigned themselves to float upon the inappreciable tides of nature." And "Cloud" follows this sentence earlier in the chapter: "The fog, as it required more skill in the steering, enhanced the interest of our early voyage, and made the river seem indefinitely broad. A slight mist, through which objects are faintly visible, has the effect of expanding even ordinary streams, by a singular mirage, into the arms of the sea or inland lakes. In the present instance, it was even fragrant and invigorating, and we enjoyed it as a sort of earlier sunshine, or dewy and embryo light." "Is it not as language," Thoreau wrote in his journal (August 1853), "that all natural objects affect the poet? He sees a flower or other object, and it is beautiful or affecting to him because it is a symbol of his thought. . . ."

Haze

Woof of the sun, ethereal gauze,
Woven of Nature's richest stuffs,
Visible heat, air-water, and dry sea,
Last conquest of the eye;
Toil of the day displayed, sun-dust,
Aerial surf upon the shores of earth,
Ethereal estuary, frith of light,
Breakers of air, billows of heat,

Fine summer spray on inland seas;
Bird of the sun, transparent-winged
Owlet of noon, soft-pinioned,
From heath or stubble rising without song;
Establish thy serenity o'er the fields.

1843

Low-Anchored Cloud

Low-anchored cloud,
Newfoundland air,
Fountain-head and source of rivers,
Dew-cloth, dream drapery,
And napkin spred by fays;
Drifting meadow of the air,
Where bloom the daisied banks and violets,
And in whose fenny labyrinth
The bittern booms and heron wades;
Spirit of lakes and seas and rivers,
Bear only perfumes and the scent
Of healing herbs to just men's fields!

1843

Emily Dickinson

Emily Dickinson's fondness for idealized allegory and for symbolic undercurrents of meaning which evoke transcendent realities ("Grace," "Immortality," "the Invisible," and so on) makes her a poet of the American Renaissance. She herself recognized her debts to Emerson, as Whitman did his. But she was also, like Whitman, a witness to the discovery of a violent and heartless non-humanity in nature—a discovery made by the generation following the Civil War. She and Whitman thus bridge two ideal designs of landscape—landscape as idea and landscape as antagonist—and the tension in their later poetry is the tension between these two designs.

The dates given after the poems are the dates of composition rather than publication because none of them were published during her lifetime. After her death they were published in various volumes, though severely revised and edited by her executors. They were not published in their original form until 1960.

824

The Wind begun to knead the Grass—
As Women do a Dough—
He flung a Hand full at the Plain—
A Hand full at the Sky—
The Leaves unhooked themselves from Trees—
And started all abroad—
The Dust did scoop itself like Hands—
And throw away the Road—
The Wagons quickened on the Street—
The Thunders gossiped low—
The Lightning showed a Yellow Head—
And then a livid Toe—
The Birds put up the Bars to Nests—
The Cattle flung to Barns—
Then came one drop of Giant Rain—
And then, as if the Hands
That held the Dams—had parted hold—
The Waters Wrecked the Sky—
But overlooked my Father's House—
Just Quartering a Tree—

?1864

550

I cross till I am weary
A Mountain—in my mind—
More Mountains—then a Sea—
More Seas—And then
A Desert—find—

And My Horizon blocks
With steady—drifting—Grains
Of unconjectured quantity—
As Asiatic Rains—

Nor this—defeat my Pace—
It hinder from the West
But as an Enemy's Salute
One hurrying to Rest—

What merit had the Goal—
Except there intervene
Faint Doubt—and far Competitor—
To jeopardize the Gain?

At last—the Grace in sight—
I shout unto my feet—
I offer them the Whole of Heaven
The instant that we meet—

They strive—and yet delay—
They perish—Do we die—
Or is this Death's Experiment—
Reversed—in Victory?

?1862

797

By my Window have I for Scenery
Just a Sea—with a Stem—
If the Bird and the Farmer—deem it a "Pine"—
The Opinion will serve—for them—

It has no Port, nor a "Line"—but the Jays—
That split their route to the Sky—
Or a Squirrel, whose giddy Peninsula
May be easier reached—this way—

For Inlands—the Earth is the under side—
And the upper side—is the Sun—
And its Commerce—if Commerce it have—
Of Spice—I infer from the Odors borne—

Of its Voice—to affirm—when the Wind is within—
Can the Dumb—define the Divine?
The Definition of Melody—is—
That Definition is none—

It—suggests to our Faith—
They—suggest to our Sight—
When the latter—is put away

I shall meet with Conviction I somewhere met
That Immortality—

Was the Pine at my Window a ''Fellow
Of the Royal'' Infinity?
Apprehensions—are God's introductions—
To be hallowed—accordingly—

?1863

1278

The Mountains stood in Haze—
The Valleys stopped below
And went or waited as they liked
The River and the Sky.

At leisure was the Sun—
His interests of Fire
A little from remark withdrawn—
The Twilight spoke the Spire,

So soft upon the Scene
The Act of evening fell
We felt how neighborly a Thing
Was the Invisible.

?1873

1343

A single Clover Plank
Was all that saved a Bee
A Bee I personally knew
From sinking in the sky—

'Twixt Firmament above
And Firmament below
The Billows of Circumference
Were sweeping him away—

The idly swaying Plank
Responsible to nought

A sudden Freight of Wind assumed
And Bumble Bee was not—

This harrowing event
Transpiring in the Grass
Did not so much as wring from him
A wandering ''Alas''—

?1875

Walt Whitman

When Lilacs Last in the Dooryard Bloom'd

Composed in the weeks following Lincoln's assassination (14 April 1865), this poem was first published in the fall of 1865. It is an elegy for a man who has become a kind of genius of the American landscape, particularly its western frontier. Landscape enters directly into the poem in verse paragraph 11: as "pictures" conjured in response to the question "And what shall the pictures be that I hang on the walls / To adorn the burial house of him I love?" Three natural objects become, through incremental repetition, the symbols and the symbolic resolution of the elegy. Each of the symbols is grounded in experience and observation. On the evening of the assassination, Whitman recalled later, the stars appeared earlier than usual (a storm had just cleared) and Venus, "the western star," had "never been so large, so clear; it seems as if it told something, as if it held rapport indulgent with humanity, with us Americans." Whitman heard the news of the assassination the next morning in a house redolent with the smell of lilacs that grew in the dooryard. The hermit thrush was Whitman's own addition to the trinity, but he took several pages of notes on its song and its habits from his friend, the naturalist John Burroughs.

1

When lilacs last in the dooryard bloom'd,
And the great star early droop'd in the western sky in the night,
I mourn'd, and yet shall mourn with ever-returning spring.

Ever-returning spring, trinity sure to me you bring,
Lilac blooming perennial and drooping star in the west,
And thought of him I love.

2

O powerful western fallen star!
O shades of night—O moody, tearful night!
O great star disappear'd—O the black murk that hides the star!
O cruel hands that hold me powerless—O helpless soul of me!
O harsh surrounding cloud that will not free my soul.

3

In the dooryard fronting an old farm-house near the white-wash'd palings,
Stands the lilac-bush tall-growing with heart-shaped leaves of rich green,
With many a pointed blossom rising delicate, with the perfume strong I
love,
With every leaf a miracle—and from this bush in the dooryard,
With delicate-color'd blossoms and heart-shaped leaves of rich green,
A sprig with its flower I break.

4

In the swamp in secluded recesses,
A shy and hidden bird is warbling a song.

Solitary the thrush,
The hermit withdrawn to himself, avoiding the settlements,
Sings by himself a song.

Song of the bleeding throat,
Death's outlet song of life, (for well dear brother I know,
If thou wast not granted to sing thou would'st surely die.)

5

Over the breast of the spring, the land, amid cities,
Amid lanes and through old woods, where lately the violets peep'd from
the ground, spotting the gray debris,
Amid the grass in the fields each side of the lanes, passing the endless
grass,
Passing the yellow-spear'd wheat, every grain from its shroud in the dark-
brown fields uprisen,
Passing the apple-tree blows of white and pink in the orchards,
Carrying a corpse to where it shall rest in the grave,
Night and day journeys a coffin.

6

Coffin that passes through lanes and streets,
Through day and night with the great cloud darkening the land,

With the pomp of the inloop'd flags with the cities draped in black,
With the show of the States themselves as of crape-veil'd women standing,
With processions long and winding and the flambeaus of the night,
With the countless torches lit, with the silent sea of faces and the unbared heads,
With the waiting depot, the arriving coffin, and the sombre faces,
With dirges through the night, with the thousand voices rising strong and solemn,
With all the mournful voices of the dirges pour'd around the coffin,
The dim-lit churches and the shuddering organs—where amid these you journey,
With the tolling tolling bells' perpetual clang,
Here, coffin that slowly passes,
I give you my sprig of lilac.

7

(Nor for you, for one alone,
Blossoms and branches green to coffins all I bring,
For fresh as the morning, thus would I chant a song for you O sane and sacred death.

All over bouquets of roses,
O death, I cover you over with roses and early lilies,
But mostly and now the lilac that blooms the first,
Copious I break, I break the sprigs from the bushes,
With loaded arms I come, pouring for you,
For you and the coffins all of you O death.)

8

O western orb sailing the heaven,
Now I know what you must have meant as a month since I walk'd,
As I walk'd in silence the transparent shadowy night,
As I saw you had something to tell as you bent to me night after night,
As you droop'd from the sky low down as if to my side, (while the other stars all look'd on,)
As we wander'd together the solemn night, (for something I know not what kept me from sleep,)
As the night advanced, and I saw on the rim of the west how full you were of woe,
As I stood on the rising ground in the breeze in the cool transparent night,

As I watch'd where you pass'd and was lost in the netherward black of the
night,
As my soul in its trouble dissatisfied sank, as where you sad orb,
Concluded, dropt in the night, and was gone.

9

Sing on there in the swamp,
O singer bashful and tender, I hear your notes, I hear your call,
I hear, I come presently, I understand you,
But a moment I linger, for the lustrous star has detain'd me,
The star my departing comrade holds and detains me.

10

O how shall I warble myself for the dead one there I loved?
And how shall I deck my song for the large sweet soul that has gone?
And what shall my perfume be for the grave of him I love?

Sea-winds blown from east and west,
Blown from the Eastern sea and blown from the Western sea, till there on
the prairies meeting,
These and with these and the breath of my chant,
I'll perfume the grave of him I love.

11

O what shall I hang on the chamber walls?
And what shall the pictures be that I hang on the walls,
To adorn the burial-house of him I love?

Pictures of growing spring and farms and homes,
With the Fourth-month eve at sundown, and the gray smoke lucid and
bright,
With floods of the yellow gold of the gorgeous, indolent, sinking sun,
burning, expanding the air,
With the fresh sweet herbage under foot, and the pale green leaves of the
trees prolific,
In the distance the flowing glaze, the breast of the river, with a wind-
dapple here and there,
With ranging hills on the banks, with many a line against the sky, and
shadows,
And the city at hand with dwellings so dense, and stacks of chimneys,
And all the scenes of life and the workshops, and the workmen homeward
returning.

12

Lo, body and soul—this land,
My own Manhattan with spires, and the sparkling and hurrying tides, and the ships,
The varied and ample land, the South and the North in the light, Ohio's shores and flashing Missouri,
And ever the far-spreading prairies cover'd with grass and corn.

Lo, the most excellent sun so calm and haughty,
The violet and purple morn with just-felt breezes,
The gentle soft-born measureless light,
The miracle spreading bathing all, the fulfill'd noon,
The coming eve delicious, the welcome night and the stars,
Over my cities shining all, enveloping man and land.

13

Sing on, sing on you gray-brown bird,
Sing from the swamps, the recesses, pour your chant from the bushes,
Limitless out of the dusk, out of the cedars and pines.

Sing on dearest brother, warble your reedy song,
Loud human song, with voice of uttermost woe.

O liquid and free and tender!
O wild and loose to my soul—O wondrous singer,
You only I hear—yet the star holds me, (but will soon depart,)
Yet the lilac with mastering odor holds me.

14

Now while I sat in the day and look'd forth,
In the close of the day with its light and the fields of spring, and the farmers preparing their crops,
In the large unconscious scenery of my land with its lakes and forests,
In the heavenly aerial beauty, (after the perturb'd winds and the storms,)
Under the arching heavens of the afternoon swift passing, and the voices of children and women,
The many-moving sea-tides, and I saw the ships how they sail'd,
And the summer approaching with richness, and the fields all busy with labor,
And the infinite separate houses, how they all went on, each with its meals and minutia of daily usages,

And the streets how their throbbings throbb'd, and the cities pent—lo,
then and there,
Falling upon them all and among them all, enveloping me with the rest,
Appear'd the cloud, appear'd the long black trail,
And I knew death, its thought, and the sacred knowledge of death.
Then with the knowledge of death as walking one side of me,
And the thought of death close-walking the other side of me,
And I in the middle as with companions, and as holding the hands of companions,
I fled forth to the hiding receiving night that talks not,
Down to the shores of the water, the path by the swamp in the dimness,
To the solemn shadowy cedars and ghostly pines so still.

And the singer so shy to the rest receiv'd me,
The gray-brown bird I know receiv'd us comrades three,
And he sang the carol of death, and a verse for him I love.

From deep secluded recesses,
From the fragrant cedars and the ghostly pines so still,
Came the carol of the bird.

And the charm of the carol rapt me,
As I held as if by their hands my comrades in the night,
And the voice of my spirit tallied the song of the bird.

Come lovely and soothing death,
Undulate round the world, serenely arriving, arriving,
In the day, in the night, to all, to each,
Sooner or later delicate death.

Prais'd be the fathomless universe,
For life and joy, and for objects and knowledge curious,
And for love, sweet love—but praise! praise! praise!
For the sure-enwinding arms of cool-enfolding death.

Dark mother always gliding near with soft feet,
Have none chanted for thee a chant of fullest welcome?
Then I chant it for thee, I glorify thee above all,
I bring thee a song that when thou must indeed come, come unfalteringly.

Approach strong deliveress,
When it is so, when thou hast taken them I joyously sing the dead,

Lost in the loving floating ocean of thee,
Laved in the flood of thy bliss O death.

From me to thee glad serenades,
Dances for thee I propose saluting thee, adornments and feastings for thee,
And the sights of the open landscape and the high-spread sky are fitting,
And life and the fields, and the huge and thoughtful night.

The night in silence under many a star,
The ocean shore and the husky whispering wave whose voice I know,
And the soul turning to thee O vast and well-veil'd death,
And the body gratefully nestling close to thee.

Over the treetops I float thee a song,
Over the rising and sinking waves, over the myriad fields and the prairies wide,
Over the dense-pack'd cities all and the teeming wharves and ways,
I float this carol with joy to thee O death.

15

To the tally of my soul,
Loud and strong kept up the gray-brown bird,
With pure deliberate notes spreading filling the night.

Loud in the pines and cedars dim,
Clear in the freshness moist and the swamp-perfume,
And I with my comrades there in the night.

While my sight that was bound in my eyes unclosed,
As to long panoramas of visions.

And I saw askant the armies,
I saw as in noiseless dreams hundreds of battle-flags,
Borne through the smoke of the battles and pierc'd with missiles I saw them.
And carried hither and yon through the smoke, and torn and bloody,
And at last but a few shreds left on the staffs, (and all in silence,)
And the staffs all splinter'd and broken.

I saw battle-corpses, myriads of them,
And the white skeletons of young men, I saw them,

I saw the debris and debris of all the slain soldiers of the war,
But I saw they were not as was thought,
They themselves were fully at rest, they suffer'd not,
The living remain'd and suffer'd, the mother suffer'd,
And the wife and the child and the musing comrade suffer'd,
And the armies that remain'd suffer'd.

16

Passing the visions, passing the night,
Passing, unloosing the hold of my comrade's hands,
Passing the song of the hermit bird and the tallying song of my soul,
Victorious song, death's outlet song, yet varying ever-altering song,
As low and wailing, yet clear the notes, rising and falling, flooding the night,
Sadly sinking and fainting, as warning and warning, and yet again bursting with joy,
Covering the earth and filling the spread of the heaven,
As that powerful psalm in the night I heard from recesses,
Passing, I leave thee lilac with heart-shaped leaves,
I leave thee there in the door-yard, blooming, returning with spring.

I cease from my song for thee,
From my gaze on thee in the west, fronting the west, communing with thee,
O comrade lustrous with silver face in the night.

Yet each to keep and all, retrievements out of the night,
The song, the wondrous chant of the gray-brown bird,
And the tallying chant, the echo arous'd in my soul,
With the lustrous and drooping star with the countenance full of woe,
With the holders holding my hand nearing the call of the bird,
Comrades mine and I in the midst, and their memory ever to keep, for the dead I loved so well,
For the sweetest, wisest soul of all my days and lands—and this for his dear sake,
Lilac and star and bird twined with the chant of my soul,
There in the fragrant pines and the cedars dusk and dim.

1865

Song of the Redwood-Tree

Composed in the fall of 1873, the poem first appeared in *Harper's Magazine* in February 1874. Whitman noted to himself the theme of the poem in a manuscript draft: "The spinal idea of the poem[is that] I (the tree) have filled my time and fill'd it grandly All is prepared for you—my termination comes [to] prophecy a great race—great as the mountains and the trees Intersperse with *italic* (first person speaking). . . ." Later he wrote in a letter that he wanted the poem "to idealize our great Pacific half of America (the future *better half*)—". He had made two Western tours (see The Ways West), the first in 1848, to Ohio and Mississippi River country from New Orleans to the Great Lakes, the second in 1879, to St. Louis, Kansas City, and Colorado by railroad. In spite of his ecstatic discovery of the West, however, he locates the emotional center of this poem, as Edwin Fussell observes, in the heart of the doomed tree rather than in the "swarming and busy race settling and organizing everywhere."

1

A California song,
A prophecy and indirection, a thought impalpable to breathe as air,
A chorus of dryads, fading, departing, or hamadryads departing,
A murmuring, fateful, giant voice, out of the earth and sky,
Voice of a mighty dying tree in the redwood forest dense.

Farewell my brethren,
Farewell O earth and sky, farewell ye neighboring waters,
My time has ended, my term has come.

Along the northern coast,
Just back from the rock-bound shore and the caves,
In the saline air from the sea in the Mendocino country,
With the surge for base and accompaniment low and hoarse,
With crackling blows of axes sounding musically driven by strong arms,
Riven deep by the sharp tongues of the axes, there in the redwood forest dense,
I heard the mighty tree its death-chant chanting.

The choppers heard not, the camp shanties echoed not,
The quick-ear'd teamsters and chain and jack-screw men heard not,
As the wood-spirits came from their haunts of a thousand years to join the refrain,
But in my soul I plainly heard.

Murmuring out of its myriad leaves,
Down from its lofty top rising two hundred feet high,
Out of its stalwart trunk and limbs, out of its foot-thick bark,
That chant of the seasons and time, chant not of the past only but the future.

You untold life of me,
And all you venerable and innocent joys,
Perennial hardy life of me with joys 'mid rain and many a summer sun,
And the white snows and night and the wild winds;
O the great patient rugged joys, my soul's strong joys unreck'd by man,
(For know I bear the soul befitting me, I too have consciousness, identity,
And all the rocks and mountains have, and all the earth,)
Joys of the life befitting me and brothers mine,
Our time, our term has come.

Nor yield we mournfully majestic brothers,
We who have grandly fill'd our time;
With Nature's calm content, with tacit huge delight,
We welcome what we wrought for through the past,
And leave the field for them.
For them predicted long,
For a superber race, they too to grandly fill their time,
For them we abdicate, in them ourselves ye forest kings!
In them these skies and airs, these mountain peaks, Shasta, Nevadas,
These huge precipitous cliffs, this amplitude, these valleys, far Yosemite,
To be in them absorb'd, assimilated.

Then to a loftier strain,
Still prouder, more ecstatic rose the chant,
As if the heirs, the deities of the West,
Joining with master-tongue bore part.

Not wan from Asia's fetiches,[1]
Nor red from Europe's old dynastic slaughter-house,
(Area of murder-plots of thrones, with scent left yet of wars and scaffolds everywhere,)
But come from Nature's long and harmless throes, peacefully builded thence,
These virgin lands, lands of the Western shore,

[1] fetishes; objects worshipped because they have magical powers or are animated by spirits—ed.

To the new culminating man, to you, the empire new,
You promis'd long, we pledge, we dedicate.

You occult deep volitions,
You average spiritual manhood, purpose of all, pois'd on yourself, giving not taking law,
You womanhood divine, mistress and source of all, whence life and love and aught that comes from life and love,
You unseen moral essence of all the vast materials of America, (age upon age working in death the same as life,)
You that, sometimes known, oftener unknown, really shape and mould the New World, adjusting it to Time and Space,
You hidden national will lying in your abysms, conceal'd but ever alert,
You past and present purposes tenaciously pursued, may-be unconscious of yourselves,
Unswerv'd by all the passing errors, perturbations of the surface;
You vital, universal, deathless germs, beneath all creeds, arts, statutes, literatures,
Here build your homes for good, establish here, these areas entire, lands of the Western shore,
We pledge, we dedicate to you.

For man of you, your characteristic race,
Here may he hardy, sweet, gigantic grow, here tower proportionate to Nature,
Here climb the vast pure spaces unconfined, uncheck'd, by wall or roof,
Here laugh with storm or sun, here joy, here patiently inure,
Here heed himself, unfold himself, (not others' formulas heed,) here fill his time,
To duly fall, to aid, unreck'd at last,
To disappear, to serve.

Thus on the northern coast,
In the echo of teamsters' calls and the clinking chains, and the music of choppers' axes,
The falling trunk and limbs, the crash, the muffled shriek, the groan,
Such words combined from the redwood-tree, as of voices ecstatic, ancient and rustling,
The century-lasting, unseen dryads, singing, withdrawing,
All their recesses of forests and mountains leaving,
From the Cascade range to the Wasatch, or Idaho far, or Utah,
To the deities of the modern henceforth yielding,

The chorus and indications, the vistas of coming humanity, the settlements, features all,
In the Mendocino woods I caught.

2

The flashing and golden pageant of California,
The sudden and gorgeous drama, the sunny and ample lands,
The long and varied stretch from Puget sound to Colorado south,
Lands bathed in sweeter, rarer, healthier air, valley and mountain cliffs,
The fields of Nature long prepared and fallow, the silent, cyclic chemistry,
The slow and steady ages plodding, the unoccupied surface ripening, the rich ores forming beneath;
At last the New arriving, assuming, taking possession,
A swarming and busy race settling and organizing everywhere,
Ships coming in from the whole round world, and going out to the whole world,
To India and China and Australia and the thousand island paradises of the Pacific,
Populous cities, the latest inventions, the steamers on the rivers, the railroads, with many a thrifty farm, with machinery,
And wool and wheat and the grape, and diggings of yellow gold.

3

But more in you than these, lands of the Western shore,
(These but the means, the implements, the standing-ground,)
I see in you, certain to come, the promise of thousands of years, till now deferr'd,
Promis'd to be fulfill'd, our common kind, the race.

The new society at last, proportionate to Nature,
In man of you, more than your mountain peaks or stalwart trees imperial,
In woman more, far more, than all your gold or vines, or even vital air.

Fresh come, to a new world indeed, yet long prepared,
I see the genius of the modern, child of the real and ideal,
Clearing the ground for broad humanity, the true America, heir of the past so grand,
To build a grander future.

1874

A Voice from Death

"A Voice from Death" first appeared in the New York *World* on 7 June 1889, only a week after the Johnstown flood, a catastrophe which had an enormous emotional impact on the nation and which took 22,000 lives. Whitman images in the last stanza the "silent ever-swaying power" of the "elemental throes,/ In which and upon which we float, and every one of us is buoy'd." In *Nature,* Emerson had written: "As a plant upon the earth, so a man rests on the bosom of God; he is nourished by unfailing fountains, and draws at his need inexhaustible power." The differences between these two ideal images is an index of the differences between pre- and post-Civil War landscapes.

(*The Johnstown, Penn., cataclysm, May 31, 1889*)

A voice from Death, solemn and strange, in all his sweep and power,
With sudden, indescribable blow—towns drown'd—humanity by thousands slain,
The vaunted work of thrift, goods, dwellings, forge, street, iron bridge,
Dash'd pell-mell by the blow—yet usher'd life continuing on,
(Amid the rest, amid the rushing, whirling, wild debris,
A suffering woman saved—a baby safely born!)

Although I come and unannounc'd, in horror and in pang,
In pouring flood and fire, and wholesale elemental crash, (this voice so solemn, strange,)
I too a minister of Deity.

Yea, Death, we bow our faces, veil our eyes to thee,
We mourn the old, the young untimely drawn to thee,
The fair, the strong, the good, the capable,
The household wreck'd, the husband and the wife, the engulf'd forger in his forge,
The corpses in the whelming waters and the mud,
The gather'd thousands to their funeral mounds, and thousands never found or gather'd.

Then after burying, mourning the dead,
(Faithful to them found or unfound, forgetting not, bearing the past, here new musing,)
A day—a passing moment or an hour—America itself bends low,
Silent, resign'd, submissive.

War, death, cataclysm like this, America,
Take deep to thy proud prosperous heart.

E'en as I chant, lo! out of death, and out of ooze and slime,
The blossoms rapidly blooming, sympathy, help, love,
From West and East, from South and North and over sea,
Its hot-spurr'd hearts and hands humanity to human aid moves on;
And from within a thought and lesson yet.

Thou ever-darting Globe! through Space and Air!
Thou waters that encompass us!
Thou that in all the life and death of us, in action or in sleep!
Thou laws invisible that permeate them and all,
Thou that in all, and over all, and through and under all, incessant!
Thou! thou! the vital, universal, giant force resistless, sleepless, calm,
Holding Humanity as in thy open hand, as some ephemeral toy,
How ill to e'er forget thee!

For I too have forgotten,
(Wrapt in these little potencies of progress, politics, culture, wealth, inventions, civilization,)
Have lost my recognition of your silent ever-swaying power, ye mighty, elemental throes,
In which and upon which we float, and every one of us is buoy'd.

1889

The Ways West

Explorers, Travelers, and Emigrants

The scenery was extremely picturesque,
and notwithstanding our forlorn condition,
we were frequently obliged to stop and admire it.

John C. Frémont,
Report of the Exploring Expedition
to the Rocky Mountains in . . . 1842

The exploration and settlement of the West during the nineteenth century are in large part a sequel to the exploration and settlement of the eastern seaboard through the eighteenth century: they were a heroic effort in pursuit of the landscape as mine and the landscape as garden. Father Marquette discovered the mouth of the Missouri River, the main highway into the West, in 1673. The Lewis and Clark expedition (1804–1806) navigated the 2500 miles of the river from its mouth to its headwaters at Three Forks, Montana; crossed the continental divide through Lemhi Pass; took the Bitterroot River to Lolo Pass; portaged to the Snake River, and navigated the Snake to the Columbia River and the Pacific. Between the Great Bend of the Missouri in central North Dakota and the last hundred miles or so of the Columbia, they were in territory previously unknown to whites.

Into the territory they had opened up came the mountain men, the American vanguard of an international business in beaver furs. By 1807, the American fur trade had begun in earnest, and by the end of the 1830's it had peaked and was in decline. During that time, however, the fur traders discovered the second major highway in the West, an overland trail pioneered by Wilson P. Hunt. The selections from Irving's *Astoria* trace Hunt's route up the Missouri to the vicinity of the Platte River. From there Hunt's course followed the Platte (the river itself was unnavigable) through the "Great American Desert" to the Rockies. By the 1830's, wagon trains to resupply the trappers had beaten a road along this route to the Green River in Wyoming. John C. Frémont surveyed its route through the South Pass of the Rockies, under Frémont's Peak. By 1843, the year of the "Great Migration" west, this trail led from St. Louis to Oregon. By 1849, a major spur of the trail picked up the Humboldt River west of the Rockies, traversed an alkaline desert to the Sierras and deposited a torrent of fortune-seekers in the gold fields of California. For those who traveled its 2000 miles, the California-Oregon Trail was the "way" through desert and mountain wilderness to a garden or a mine.

This section is arranged into roughly two groupings. The first is a montage of the scenery to be viewed along the highways into the West when the viewers (explorers and other travelers), "notwithstanding [their] forlorn condition, . . . were frequently obliged to stop and admire it." (Powell's Grand Canyon and Langford's Yellowstone scenery are a sampling of the natural wonders of the wilderness which the highways missed.)

The second grouping, from post-Civil War literature of the West, delineates what Bret Harte came to call "the modifications of environment" in the cultivation of the West: the raw landscapes of mines and boom towns and the imposition of the new industrial order on Midwestern and Western farms. (The selections by Gilpin, Whitman, and Richard Harding Davis represent the boosters and debunkers of the "Myth of the West," which held that the West was the authentic America, wild, fresh, free of all the effete and corrupt influences of the East and the Old World.)

Like their maritime forebears (and for that matter, like their descendants, the astronauts), the Western explorers narrate their progress chiefly in terms of landmarks, often familiar enough not to need describing, or in terms of compass and sextant readings, which reduce the land to a series of orienting numbers. They continue to regard the land in terms of what can be hunted, picked, drunk, dug out, or cut down; they continue to collect their observations in bare factual lists in the form of reports to the government—reports not much more elaborate in general form than those of Columbus or Verrazzano. Maxmilian and Irving, on the other hand, represent the growing number of natural scientists and tourists who traveled west beginning in the 1830's, and they further represent the confluence in the literature of the West, including the literature of Western exploration, of the new ways of perceiving landscape. The perspectives which give shape and access to Western landscapes include not only those of garden and wilderness, but also those of natural history and the poetry of scene.

The garden is usually a prairie, a river bank, or a flower-strewn meadow in the Rockies. Often it is seen in terms of an oasis or an island in an oceanic desert, as rich and exotic as an oasis in North Africa or the Holy Land. Always it is fleshed out in images of calm, order, lushness, and plenty. The wilderness which surrounds these gardens emerges as a succession of landscapes too terrible and overwhelming to be easily valued as sublime: first, the fast and erratic, remorselessly destructive rivers, with their snags, quicksands, and rapids; then the prairies—flat, vast, monotonous, unearthly silent, and prone to such sudden catastrophes as fires, floods, and blizzards; then the weird and nearly unbreachable battlements of the Rockies; then the lifeless alkaline deserts east of the Sierras. The Western wilderness brought on, as Howard Mumford Jones observes in *The Age of Energy,* a sense not of demonic presences so much as a cosmic melancholy—a sense of the puniness and the futility of all human efforts.

> What could puny man achieve amid this combination of space and savagery? The environment dwarfed the individual, a moving speck on the Great Plains or an insect slowly crawling up the gigantic mountains or slowly moving through the difficult passes.

The increasingly complex and scientific values of natural history helped to give shape to Western landscapes from the very beginning. The Lewis and Clark expedition was commissioned by that amateur natural historian, President Thomas Jefferson, with special consideration for its "literary" (that is, non-commercial) purposes. Jefferson went so far as to send Lewis to Philadelphia for special training in botany, geology, and zoology. He made Clark the official geographer, who was to supervise the mapping of the Missouri and its branches and of another river (mythical as it turned out, the last vestige of the hypothetical "passage to India") which, "by it's course & communication with the waters of the Pacific Ocean, may offer the most direct & practicable water communication across this continent." As amateur field naturalists, they were to collect specimens of or describe, for interpretation by Jefferson's scientific correspondents, the "soil & face of the country, it's growth & vegetable productions"; native animals; minerals ("metals, limestone, pit coal & salt petre; salines & mineral waters"); the geology, especially any "Volcanic appearances"; and the climate

> . . . as characterized by the thermometer, by the proportion of rainy, cloudy & clear days, by lightening, hail, snow, ice, by the access & recess of frost, by the winds prevailing at different seasons, the dates at which particular plants put forth and lose their flowers, or leaf, times of appearance of particular birds, reptiles or insects.

As amateur anthropologists, finally, they were to observe and describe the manners and morals of the Indian tribes they encountered, especially "the state of morality, religion and information among them," so that missionaries might "better civilize and instruct them." (The notes, mostly Lewis's, on trans-Mississippi Indian Tribes turned out to be among the most valuable "literary" results of the expedition.)

The variety and complexity of the information demanded of the Lewis and Clark expedition are representative of all the Government-sponsored expeditions into the West, including Frémont's and Powell's. And they demanded increasingly impressive "literary" credentials of the explorers. Frémont was a lieutenant in the Corps of Topographical Engineers, and he was assisted in his map-making by a trained topographer, Charles Preuss, who also sketched the landscapes they traversed. Powell, whose expedition to the last white space left on the maps of a continental United States "was not made for adventure, but purely for scientific purposes, geographic and geologic," was a scholarly geologist who had founded the U.S. Geological Survey.

The techniques for sketching sublime and picturesque scenery, finally, were at least as much in demand as the techniques of natural history in delineating Western landscapes. After Lewis's lament at the lack of a "camera obscura" to do justice to the "sublimely grand" and "pleasingly beautiful" scenery of the Great Falls of the Missouri, no major foray into the West went without its artist of the pen or pencil: Frémont had his Preuss, Maxmilian his Karl Bodmer. When photography came of age, photographers, too, went west.

In Western landscapes, it is evident that the science most helpful in educating the eye was geology. Geology was not only an absolute prerequisite for the explorer and, later, the miner, it was also indispensable for the linear and verbal sketches of Western scenery. The flat, treeless prairies and deserts and the Alpine Rockies could be pictured to best effect in the panoramic spatial and temporal perspectives natural to the geologist. In the East, the terrain was still largely covered by deciduous forest—the domain of the botanist. In the West, the chief visible facts of scenery were geological: riverbeds, sedimentary and volcanic deposits, mountains, canyons, the wonderfully weird sculptures of soft stone such as Maxmilian's White Castle, and the sulphurous effusions of the hot springs and geysers along the Yellowstone. When this river and rock scenery came to be sketched by artists of the picturesque, a knowledge of geology contributed to the freshness and force of the artist's play of mind. Powell, John Muir, and others, for example, could fancy Western landscapes as scenes in a theater more ancient, moving, and profound than Europe's rich theater of human events. Here in the West was a theater of natural events in which the violent turmoil in the earth and the endless changes brought about by wind, fire, and water artfully shaped the earth into natural monuments: grand estates, Parthenons, cathedrals. Here too was a theater of creation in full accord with the ideal design of the age of Darwin and the literary naturalists.

By the middle of the nineteenth century, another complex process was making the West an epochal scene in the great theater of human events. The flood of emigrants was spectacularly transforming the Western wilderness. "During the nineteenth century," writes Howard Mumford Jones, "no part of the republic moved with more rapidity from a state of nature to a state of industry. The population of Ohio in 1800 was estimated at about 45,000; just before the Civil War it was 2,339,511." Where gold, silver, and other valuable minerals were discovered, usually in arid wastelands of the Far West, boom towns sprang up without the usual transition through a pastoral middle ground that Crèvecœur, Jefferson, and others had envisioned. These towns were, indeed, chaotic mutations of the pastoral ideal or even, as in Davis's sketch of Oklahoma City, parodies of it. Meanwhile, the energies of the machine in the pastoral gardens were realizing themselves equally spectacularly in the West as in New England or the South. In the post-war Midwest and then in the Far West, the freeman's 160-acre garden was transformed into machine-run "bonanza farms" covering thousands of acres and functioning as a big business in an international market.

As with other sublime phenomena, the machine excited (and still excites) mixed emotions. Progressivists like C. C. Coffin, in "Dakota Wheat Fields," celebrated it as an ally in the cultivation of the garden. That seems to be the attitude, too, in the selection from Norris's *The Octopus,* where the landscape is less a garden than a primitive Earth Mother who must be forcefully seduced and impregnated by men with giant horse-drawn plows. But in the novel, Norris sets this heroic struggle in yet another perspective—that of a conflict between two corporate machines: the wheat growers' bonanza farms against the railroad, that "symbol of vast power, huge, terrible, flinging the echo of its thunder over all the reaches of the valley, . . . the leviathan, with tentacles of steel clutching into the soil." The farmers lose the conflict because of inferior mechanical force.

From the perspective many writers took after the Civil War and especially after the frontier closed—a conservationist perspective—the entry of the machine into the agricultural garden only made the ravaging of land more efficient. Reckless disregard of the need for fertilization and crop-rotation and the reckless use of crop sprays transformed rich soil into dust or poison; they ravaged the pastoral middle-ground in ways just as devastating as, if less immediate than, ways in which the wilderness and the city were being ravaged. The inevitable result was a landscape like that of Aldo Leopold's "Illinois Bus Ride" or Rachel Carson's "Realms of the Soil" (see Deformations) and a column of farmer-emigrants, like that of Steinbeck's in *Grapes of Wrath,* moving west to find another garden not yet become a wasteland.

Meriwether Lewis

From The Journals of Lewis and Clark

The Lewis and Clark expedition is treated at some length in the introduction to this section.

[The Great Falls of the Missouri]

June 13th, 1805

THIS MORNING we set out about sunrise after taking breakfast off our venison and fish. We again ascended the hills of the river and gained the level country. Fearing that the river bore to the south, and that I might pass the Falls if they existed between this and the snowy mountains, I altered my course nearly to the south and proceeded through the plain. I sent Fields on my right and Drouilliard and Gibson on my left, with orders to kill some meat and join me at the river, where I should halt for dinner.

I had proceeded on this course about two miles with Goodrich at some distance behind me, when my ears were saluted with the agreeable sound of a fall of water, and advancing a little further, I saw the spray rise above the plain like a column of smoke, which would frequently disappear again in an instant, caused, I presume, by the wind which blew pretty hard from the S.W. I did not, however, lose my direction to this point, which soon began to make a roaring too tremendous to be mistaken for any cause short of the Great Falls of the Missouri. Here I arrived about 12 o'clock, having traveled, by estimate, about 15 miles. I hurried down the hill, which was about 200 feet high and difficult of access, to gaze on this sublimely grand spectacle.

I took my position on the top of some rocks about 20 feet high opposite the center of the Falls. This chain of rocks appears once to have formed a part of those over which the waters tumbled, but in the course of time has been separated from it to the distance of 150 yards, lying parallel to it, and an abutment against which the water, after falling over the precipice, beats with great fury. This barrier extends on the right to the perpendicular cliff which forms that border of the river, but to the distance of 120 yards next to the cliff it is but a few feet above the level of the water, and here the water in very high tides appears to pass in a channel of 40 yards next to the higher part of the ledge of rocks. On the left, it extends within 80 or 90 yards of the larboard cliff, which is also perpendicular. Between this abrupt extremity of the ledge of rocks and the perpendicular bluff, the whole body of water passes with incredible swiftness.

Immediately at the cascade, the river is about 300 yards wide. About 90 or 100 yards of this, next the larboard bluff, is a smooth even sheet of water falling over a precipice of at least 80 feet; the remaining part, about 200 yards wide, on my right, forms the grandest sight I ever beheld. The height of the fall is the same as the other, but the irregular and somewhat projecting rocks below receive the water in its passage down, and break it into a perfect white foam which assumes a thousand forms in a moment, sometimes flying up in jets of sparkling foam to the height of fifteen or twenty feet, which are scarcely formed before large rolling bodies of the same beaten and foaming water are thrown over and conceal them. In short, the rocks seem to be most happily fixed to present a sheet of the whitest beaten froth for 200 yards in length and about 80 feet perpendicular.

The water, after descending, strikes against the abutment before mentioned, or that on which I stand, and seems to reverberate, and being met by the more impetuous current, they roll and swell into half-formed billows of great height which rise and again disappear in an instant. The abutment of rocks defends a handsome little bottom of about three acres which is diversified and agreeably shaded with some cottonwood trees.

In the lower extremity of the bottom there is a very thick grove of the same kind of trees which are small. In this wood, there are several Indian lodges formed of sticks. A few small cedar grow near the ledge of rocks where I rest. Below the point of these rocks, at a small distance, the river is divided by a large rock which rises several feet above the water, and extends downward with the stream for about 20 yards. About a mile before the water arrives at the pitch, it descends very rapidly, and is confined on the larboard side by a perpendicular cliff of about 100 feet. On the starboard side it is also perpendicular for about three hundred yards above the pitch, where it is then broken by the discharge of a small ravine, down which the buffalo have a large beaten road to the water, for it is but in very few places that these animals can obtain water near this place, owing to the steep and inaccessible banks. I see several skeletons of the buffalo lying in the edge of the water near the starboard bluff which I presume have been swept down by the current and precipitated over this tremendous fall.

About 300 yards below me, there is another abutment of solid rock with a perpendicular face and about 60 feet high, which projects from the starboard side at right angles to the distance of 134 yards, and terminates the lower part nearly of the bottom before mentioned, there being a passage around the end of this abutment, between it and the river, of about 20 yards. Here the river again assumes its usual width, soon spreading to near 300 yards but still continuing its rapidity. From the reflection of the sun on the spray or mist which arises from these Falls, there is a beautiful rainbow produced which adds not a little to the beauty of this majestically grand scenery.

After writing this imperfect description, I again viewed the Falls, and was so much disgusted with the imperfect idea which it conveyed of the scene, that

I determined to draw my pen across it and begin again; but then reflected that I could not perhaps succeed better than penning the first impressions of the mind. I wished for the pencil of Salvator Rosa, a Titian, or the pen of [*James*] Thomson, that I might be enabled to give to the enlightened world some just idea of this truly magnificent and sublimely grand object which has, from the commencement of time, been concealed from the view of civilized man. But this was fruitless and vain. I most sincerely regretted that I had not brought a camera obscura with me, by the assistance of which even I could have hoped to have done better, but alas, this was also out of my reach.

I therefore, with the assistance of my pen only, endeavored to trace some of the stronger features of this scene by the assistance of which, and my recollection aided by some able pencil, I hope still to give to the world some faint idea of an object which at this moment fills me with such pleasure and astonishment; and which of its kind, I will venture to assert, is second to but one in the known world. . . .

June 14th, 1805

. . . . About ten o'clock this morning, while the men were engaged with the meat, I took my gun and espontoon and thought I would walk a few miles and see where the rapids terminated above, and return to dinner. Accordingly, I set out and proceeded up the river about S.W. After passing one continued rapid and three small cascades of about four or five feet each at the distance of about five miles, I arrived at a fall of about 19 feet. The river is here about 400 yards wide. This pitch, which I called the Crooked Falls, occupies about three-fourths of the width of the river, commencing on the south side, extends obliquely upward about 150 yards, then, forming an acute angle, extends downward nearly to the commencement of four small islands lying near the N. shore. Among these islands and between them and the lower extremity of the perpendicular pitch, being a distance of 100 yards or upwards, the water glides down the side of a sloping rock with a velocity almost equal to that of its perpendicular descent. Just above this rapid the river makes a sudden bend to the right, or northwardly.

I should have returned from hence; but, hearing a tremendous roaring above me, I continued my route across the point of a hill a few hundred yards further, and was again presented by one of the most beautiful objects in nature—a cascade of about fifty feet perpendicular stretching at right angles across the river from side to side to the distance of at least a quarter of a mile. Here the river pitches over a shelving rock, with an edge as regular and as straight as if formed by art, without a niche or break in it. The water descends in one even and uninterrupted sheet to the bottom, where, dashing against the rocky bottom, it rises into foaming billows of great height and rapidly glides away, hissing, flashing, and sparkling as it departs. The spray rises, from one extremity to the other, to 50 feet. I now thought that if a skillful painter had been asked to make a beautiful cascade, he would most probably have presented the precise image of this one. Nor could I for some time determine on which of those two great cataracts to bestow the palm—on this, or that which I had discovered yesterday. At length I determined between these two great rivals for glory, that this was *pleasingly beautiful,* while the other was *sublimely grand*.

1809

Prince Maxmilian

From Travels in the Interior of North America

Like most natural historians of the nineteenth century, Maxmilian, Prussian Prince of Wied-Neuwied, had traveled through landscapes as a soldier (he fought in the Prussian army against Napoleon) before he traveled them as a field naturalist. He had made a two-year field trip to Brazil before he came to study the flora and fauna of the American West in 1833. Accompanied by Charles Bodmer, a young Swiss artist, he traveled up the Missouri on the boats of Astor's American Fur Company as far as Fort McKenzie (just north of the Great Falls of the Missouri), and it was on the last leg of this journey that he sighted the rock formations that he describes in the material reprinted here (Lewis and Clark had also been struck by them). They are in the area of what is now Fort Peck Reservoir in north central Montana.

[Rock Formations: The Missouri]

AT BREAK OF DAY the weather was extremely cool and disagreeable; the thermometer at half-past seven was only at 58°, and a bleak wind prevailed, which enabled us to use our sails. The part of the country called The Stone Walls, which now opened before us, has nothing like it on the whole course of the Missouri, and we did not leave the deck for a single moment the whole forenoon. Lewis and Clarke have given a short description of this remarkable tract, without, however, knowing the name of Stone Walls, which has since been given it. In this tract of twelve or fifteen miles, the valley of the Missouri has naked, moderately high mountains, rounded above, or extending like ridges, with tufts of low plants here and there, on which the thick strata of whitish coarse-grained friable sand-stone, which extends over all this country, are everywhere visible. As soon as we have passed Judith River this white sand-stone begins to stand out in some places, till we have passed Bighorn River, and entered the narrower valley of the Stone Walls, where the strata extend, without interruption, far through the country, and lie partly halfway up the mountain, and partly form the summits. They are the continuation of the white sand-stone which occurs in such singular forms at the Blackhills. At all the places which are bare of grass, they are visible, and there we see horizontal or perpendicular angles and ledges resembling walls, some of which contain caverns. This sandstone formation is the most striking when it forms the tops of more isolated mountains, separated by gentle valleys and ravines. Here, on both sides of the river, the most strange forms are seen, and you may fancy that you see colonnades, small round pillars with large globes or a flat slab at the top, little towers, pulpits, organs with their pipes, old ruins, fortresses, castles, churches, with pointed towers, etc., etc., almost every mountain bearing on its summit some similar structure.

Towards nine o'clock the valley began to be particularly interesting, for its fantastic forms were more and more numerous; every moment, as we proceeded along, new white fairy-like castles appeared, and a painter who had leisure might fill whole volumes with these original landscapes. As proofs of this we may refer to some of these figures, which Mr. Bodmer sketched very accurately. In many places the clay formed the summits of the hills; in these parts there were patches of *Juniperus repens,* and on the bank of the river, small and narrow strips covered with artemisia and the thorn with flesh-coloured leaves (*Sarcobatus nees.*). Long tracts of the sand-stone strata perfectly resembled a large blown-up fortress, because the stratification everywhere gave these walls a certain regularity, while, at the same time, they bore marks of having been destroyed by violence. In several places where the sandstone summit appeared plainly to represent an ancient knight's castle, another remarkable rock was seen to traverse the mountain in narrow perpendicular strata, like regularly built walls. These walls consist of a blackish-brown rock, in the mass of which large olive-green crystals are disseminated. They run in a perfectly straight line from the summits of the mountain to the foot, appearing to form the outworks of the old castles. The surface is divided by rents or furrows into pretty regular cubic figures like bricks, which renders their similarity to a work of art still more complete. The breadth of these perpendicular strata seldom exceeds one or two feet. One of these walls was particularly striking, which ran, without interruption, over the tops of three mountains, and through the clefts between them, and connected the three masses of white sand-stone on the summits in so regular a manner, that one could hardly fancy they were natural, but that they were a work of art. All these eminences are inhabited by numerous troops of the wild mountain sheep, of which we often saw thirty or fifty at a time climbing and springing over the sand-stone formation. These harmless animals often stood on a lofty peak, far beyond the reach of our rifles, while the outlines of their forms were clearly defined against the bright blue sky. As we passed a hollow lateral valley, we were shown the place at which the hunters of the keel-boat had, last year, hemmed in a whole herd of these animals in such a manner that not one escaped.

Early in the afternoon we came to a remarkable place where the Missouri seems to issue from a narrow opening, making a turn round a dark brown rugged painted towerlike rock on the south, to which the traders have given the name of the Citadel Rock. This singular isolated rock seems to consist of clay-slate, grauwacke, and a conglomerate of fragments of rock in yellowish clay, and is joined to the south bank by a ridge. On the bank opposite to it the white sand-stone runs over the ridge of the hills, which Mr. Bodmer has very accurately represented. After we had doubled the Citadel Rock we lay to on the south bank, and our people took their dinner. We did not stop long, and had to contend against a cold, very high wind, while the country was flatter and more open, with only a few of the oddly-fashioned rocks. Immediately above the Citadel there is a similar dark brown much smaller rock, and soon afterwards we saw, on the north bank, a jagged conical rock, which stands quite isolated on a hill covered with short grass. Two other less remarkable tops follow, of which the towers (according to the course of the river) resemble a small castle, while the other hills in this part have again the flat and rounded forms. A herd of wild sheep looked down upon us from these heights. We had, however, not yet taken leave of the extraordinary sand-stone valley, on the contrary, we now came to a most remarkable place. The stratum of sand-stone, regularly bedded in low hills, runs along both banks of the river, which is rather narrow, like a high, smooth, white wall, pretty equally horizontal above, with low pinnacles on the top. At some distance before us, the eye fell on an apparently narrow gate, the white walls in the two banks approaching so near to each other, that the river seemed to be very contracted in breadth as it passed between them, and this illusion was heightened by the turn which the Missouri makes in this place to the south-west. Looking backwards, the high, black, conical rock rose above the surrounding country; and on our right hand, there were, on the bank, dark perpendicular walls, seemingly divided into cubes, in the form of an ancient Gothic chapel with a chimney. Some pines grew singly about these walls, where there appear to be regular gateways formed by art. A little further on there was, on the north bank, a mass which much resembled a long barrack or some other considerable building, the corners of which were as regular as if they had been hewn and built up by a skilful workman. Beyond the rocky gate a herd of buffaloes were grazing on a small lateral valley; our hunters contrived to get near them and to kill four. As evening was come, and the people had to cut up the buffaloes, we lay to for the night on the north bank. I took this opportunity to ascend the remarkable eminences. I found the sand-stone so soft that it crumbled in my hand; whereas the yellowish-red sand-stone, which, in some places, formed the tops or roofs of the strange white masses, were of a rather harder grain. Extremely stunted and often strangely contorted cedars (*juniperus*) grew among these rocks; but the pines (*Pinus flexilis*) were well grown and flourishing, though not above forty feet high. When standing among the remarkable masses of the sand-stone, we fancied ourselves in a garden laid out in the old French style, where urns, obelisks, statues, as well as hedges and trees clipped into various shapes, surround the astonished spectator. The balls and slabs, often of a colossal size, which rested on the above-mentioned pedestals, were likewise soft and friable, but not so much as the white sand-stone, and there were in them many round holes. Stratification could be perceived in all these stones, for even round spherical blocks were easily divided into regular plates, nearly an inch thick. Among these fragments the tracks of the mountain sheep were everywhere discernible, and on the lower declivities, which were covered with grass, those of the buffaloes. In the prairie beyond the Stone Walls, *Cactus ferox* grew, and at their foot, the beautiful *Bartonia ornata,* with its large snow-white flowers.

We looked with impatience for the following day, the 7th, in order to reach what is called the Gate of the Stone Walls. We soon came to a dark brown rock, like a tower, rising in the middle of the white wall, the front of which had fallen down, and had a great number of boulders about it. From this tower it is between 600 and 800 paces to the place which appeared to us yesterday to form a narrow gate; before reaching it, there is, on the north bank, a stream called, by Lewis and Clark, Stonewall Creek, which is about fifty paces broad at the mouth, and its banks are bordered with high poplars. A cold wind blew from the gate, beyond which there was another tower-like dark brown rock, not so large as the other, while the white sand-stone walls decreased and became less regular. The hills became gradually lower, the sand-stone partly disappeared, and was only seen occasionally.

1839

Washington Irving

From Astoria

Though at the center of New York's first-generation literary circle, Irving had more than a passing dalliance with the West. In the early 1830's he traveled with a government commission to inspect Indian country put aside for dispossessed tribes, and out of that experience and his antiquarian's interest in American history came three Western narratives: *A Tour on the Prairies* (1835); *The Rocky Mountains; or Scenes, Incidents, and Adventures in the Far West* (1837), a digest of the journals of Captain

Benjamin Bonneville, an independent fur trader and mountain man; *Astoria; or Anecdotes of an Enterprise Beyond the Rocky Mountains* (1836), a narrative of John Jacob Astor's American Fur Company's explorations for overland trade routes from Astoria, Oregon, eastward. *Astoria* was commissioned by Astor himself. The two excerpts included in this section trace the movements of Wilson Hunt up the Missouri River in 1811 to the area of the Platte River where he turned west on a route that would become the Oregon Trail. The Bradbury mentioned in the text is John Bradbury, a botanist who accompanied Hunt. It is likely that Irving painted his "scenes"—as Francis Parkman would later in his histories—from personal memories and notes of his own Western tour.

[Prairie Country]

THE WEATHER continued rainy and ungenial for some days after Mr. Hunt's return to Nodowa; yet spring was rapidly advancing and vegetation was putting forth with all its early freshness and beauty. The snakes began to recover from their torpor and crawl forth into day; and the neighborhood of the wintering house seems to have been much infested with them. Mr. Bradbury, in the course of his botanical researches, found a surprising number in a half torpid state, under flat stones upon the banks which overhung the cantonment, and narrowly escaped being struck by a rattlesnake, which darted at him from a cleft in the rock, but fortunately gave him warning by his rattle.

The pigeons, too, were filling the woods in vast migratory flocks. It is almost incredible to describe the prodigious flights of these birds in the western wildernesses. They appear absolutely in clouds, and move with astonishing velocity, their wings making a whistling sound as they fly. The rapid evolutions of these flocks, wheeling and shifting suddenly as if with one mind and one impulse; the flashing changes of color they present, as their backs, their breasts, or the under part of their wings are turned to the spectator, are singularly pleasing. When they alight, if on the ground, they cover whole acres at a time; if upon trees, the branches often break beneath their weight. If suddenly startled while feeding in the midst of a forest, the noise they make in getting on the wing is like the roar of a cataract or the sound of distant thunder.

A flight of this kind, like an Egyptian flight of locusts, devours everything that serves for its food as it passes along. So great were the numbers in the vicinity of the camp that Mr. Bradbury, in the course of a morning's excursion, shot nearly three hundred with a fowling-piece. He gives a curious, though apparently a faithful, account of the kind of discipline observed in these immense flocks, so that each may have a chance of picking up food. As the front ranks must meet with the greatest abundance, and the rear ranks must have scanty pickings, the instant a rank finds itself the hindmost, it rises in the air, flies over the whole flock and takes its place in the advance. The next rank follows in its course, and thus the last is continually becoming first and all by turns have a front place at the banquet. . . .

The party continued their voyage [up the Missouri River] with delightful May weather. The prairies bordering on the river were gayly painted with innumerable flowers, exhibiting the motley confusion of colors of a Turkey carpet. The beautiful islands, also, on which they occasionally halted, presented the appearance of mingled grove and garden. The trees were often covered with clambering grapevines in blossom, which perfumed the air. Between the stately masses of the groves were grassy lawns and glades, studded with flowers, or interspersed with rose-bushes in full bloom. These islands were often the resort of the buffalo, the elk, and the antelope, who had made innumerable paths among the trees and thickets, which had the effect of the mazy walks and alleys of parks and shrubberies. Sometimes, where the river passed between high banks and bluffs, the roads, made by the tramp of buffaloes for many ages along the face of the heights, looked like so many well-travelled highways. At other places the banks were banded with great veins of iron ore, laid bare by the abrasion of the river. At one place the course of the river was nearly in a straight line for about fifteen miles. The banks sloped gently to its margin, without a single tree, but bordered with grass and herbage of a vivid green. Along each bank, for the whole fifteen miles, extended a stripe, one hundred yards in breadth, of a deep rusty brown, indicating an inexhaustible bed of iron, through the centre of which the Missouri had worn its way. Indications of the continuance of this bed were afterwards observed higher up the river. It is, in fact, one of the mineral magazines which nature has provided in the heart of this vast realm of fertility, and which, in connection with the immense beds of coal on the same river, seem garnered up as the elements of the future wealth and power of the mighty West.

The sight of these minerals treasures greatly excited the curiosity of Mr. Bradbury, and it was tantalizing to him to be checked in his scientific researches, and obliged to forego his usual rambles on shore; but they were now entering the fated country of the Sioux Tetons, in which it was dangerous to wander about unguarded.

This country extends for some days' journey along the river, and consists of vast prairies, here and there diversified by swelling hills, and cut up by ravines, the channels of turbid streams in the rainy seasons, but almost destitute of water during the heats of summer. Here and there on the sides of the hills, or along the alluvial borders and bottoms of the ravines, are groves and skirts of forest: but for the most part the country presented to the eye a boundless waste, covered with herbage, but without trees. . . .

The scenery and objects, as they proceeded, gave evidence that they were advancing deeper and deeper into the domains of savage nature. Boundless wastes kept extending to the eye, more and more animated by herds of buffalo. Sometimes these unwieldy animals were seen moving in long procession across the silent landscape; at other times they were scattered about, singly or in groups, on the broad, enameled prairies and green acclivities, some cropping the rich pasturage, others reclining amidst the flowery herbage; the whole scene realizing in a manner the old Scriptural descriptions of the vast pastoral countries of the Orient, with "cattle upon a thousand hills."

At one place the shores seemed absolutely lined with buffaloes; many were making their way across the stream, snorting, and blowing, and floundering. Numbers, in spite of every effort, were borne by the rapid current within shot of the boats, and several were killed. At another place a number were descried on the beach of a small island, under the shade of the trees, or standing in the water, like cattle, to avoid the flies and the heat of the day.

1836

[The Great American Desert]

WHILE MR. HUNT was diligently preparing for his arduous journey, some of his men began to lose heart at the perilous prospect before them; but before we accuse them of want of spirit, it is proper to consider the nature of the wilderness into which they were about to adventure. It was a region almost as vast and trackless as the ocean, and, at the time of which we treat, but little known, excepting through the vague accounts of Indian hunters. A part of their route would lay across an immense tract, stretching north and south for hundreds of miles along the foot of the Rocky Mountains, and drained by the tributary streams of the Missouri and the Mississippi. This region, which resembles one of the immeasurable steppes of Asia, has not inaptly been termed "the great American desert." It spreads forth into undulating and treeless plains, and desolate sandy wastes wearisome to the eye from their extent and monotony, and which are supposed by geologists to have formed the ancient floor of the ocean, countless ages since, when its primeval waves beat against the granite bases of the Rocky Mountains.

It is a land where no man permanently abides; for, in certain seasons of the year there is no food either for the hunter or his steed. The herbage is parched and withered; the brooks and streams are dried up; the buffalo, the elk and the deer have wandered to distant parts, keeping within the verge of expiring verdure, and leaving behind them a vast uninhabited solitude, seamed by ravines, the beds of former torrents, but now serving only to tantalize and increase the thirst of the traveller.

Occasionally the monotony of this vast wilderness is interrupted by mountainous belts of sand and limestone, broken into confused masses; with precipitous cliffs and yawning ravines, looking like the ruins of a world; or is traversed by lofty and barren ridges of rock, almost impassable, like those denominated the Black Hills. Beyond these rise the stern barriers of the Rocky

Mountains, the limits, as it were, of the Atlantic world. The rugged defiles and deep valleys of this vast chain form sheltering places for restless and ferocious bands of savages, many of them the remnants of tribes, once inhabitants of the prairies, but broken up by war and violence, and who carry into their mountain haunts the fierce passions and reckless habits of desperadoes.

Such is the nature of this immense wilderness of the far West; which apparently defies cultivation, and the habitation of civilized life. Some portions of it along the rivers may partially be subdued by agriculture, others may form vast pastoral tracts, like those of the East; but it is to be feared that a great part of it will form a lawless interval between the abodes of civilized man, like the wastes of the ocean or the deserts of Arabia; and, like them, be subject to the depredations of the marauder. Here may spring up new and mongrel races, like new formations in geology, the amalgamation of the "debris" and "abrasions" of former races, civilized and savage; the remains of broken and almost extinguished tribes; the descendants of wandering hunters and trappers; of fugitives from the Spanish and American frontiers; of adventurers and desperadoes of every class and country, yearly ejected from the bosom of society into the wilderness. We are contributing incessantly to swell this singular and heterogeneous cloud of wild population that is to hang about our frontier, by the transfer of whole tribes from the east of the Mississippi to the great wastes of the far West. Many of these bear with them the smart of real or fancied injuries; many consider themselves expatriated beings, wrongfully exiled from their hereditary homes, and the sepulchres of their fathers, and cherish a deep and abiding animosity against the race that has dispossessed them. Some may gradually become pastoral hordes, like those rude and migratory people, half shepherd, half warrior, who, with their flocks and herds, roam the plains of upper Asia; but others, it is to be apprehended, will become predatory bands, mounted on the fleet steeds of the prairies, with the open plains for their marauding grounds, and the mountains for their retreats and lurking-places. Here they may resemble those great hordes of the North, "Gog and Magog with their bands," that haunted the gloomy imaginations of the prophets. "A great company and a mighty host, all riding upon horses, and warring upon those nations which were at rest, and dwelt peaceably, and had gotten cattle and goods."

1836

John C. Frémont

From Report of the Exploring Expedition to the Rocky Mountains

Emigration to the gardens of Oregon began in the early 1830's with the Oregon Colonization Society of Nathaniel Wyeth, a Cambridge, Massachusetts, businessman. By the 1840's Frémont, a lieutenant in the Army Corps of Topographical Engineers, was ordered to conduct explorations and surveys of the overland route to Oregon. Of his two most important expeditions, one to the Rocky Mountains (1842), the other to Oregon and northern California (1843–1844), the first surveyed the Wind River Range in Wyoming, including the South Pass traversed by the California-Oregon Trail. His duties included the collecting of zoological, botanical, and geological specimens, the testing of soil and water, and the collecting of intelligence on potential sites of forts, towns, and roads. Two of the men accompanying him were Charles Preuss, who mapped and sketched the landscape, and Kit Carson.

[Frémont's Peak]

August 3.—AS WE PASSED over a slight rise near the river, we caught the first view of the Wind river mountains, appearing, at this distance of about seventy miles, to be a low and dark mountainous ridge. The view dissipated in a moment the pictures which had been created in our minds, by many descriptions of travellers, who have compared these mountains to the Alps in Switzerland, and speak of the glittering peaks which rise in icy majesty amidst the eternal glaciers nine or ten thousand feet into the region of eternal snows. The nakedness of the river was relieved by groves of willows, where we encamped at night, after a march of twenty-six miles; and numerous bright-colored flowers had made the river bottom look gay as a garden. . . .

August 10.—The air at sunrise is clear and pure, and the morning extremely cold, but beautiful. A lofty snow peak of the mountain is glittering in the first rays of the sun, which has not yet reached us. The long mountain wall to the east, rising two thousand feet abruptly from the plain, behind which we see the peaks, is still dark, and cuts clear against the glowing sky. A fog, just risen from the river, lies along the base of the mountain. A little before sunrise, the thermometer was at 35°, and at sunrise 33°. Water froze last night, and fires are very comfortable. The scenery becomes hourly more interesting and grand, and the view here is truly magnificent; but, indeed, it needs something to repay the long prairie journey of a thousand miles. The sun has just shot above the wall, and makes a magical change. The whole valley is glowing and bright, and all the mountain peaks are gleaming like silver. Though these snow mountains are not the Alps, they have their own character of grandeur and magnificence, and will doubtless find pens and pencils to do them justice. In the scene before us, we feel how much wood improves a view. The pines on the mountain seemed to give it much additional beauty. I was agreeably disappointed in the character of the streams on this side of the ridge. Instead of the creeks, which description had led me to expect, I find bold, broad streams, with three or four feet water, and a rapid current. The fork on which we are encamped is upwards of a hundred feet wide, timbered with groves or thickets of the low willow. We were now approaching the loftiest part of the Wind river chain; and I left the valley a few miles from our encampment, intending to penetrate the mountains as far as possible with the whole party. We were soon involved in very broken ground, among long ridges covered with fragments of granite. Winding our way up a long ravine, we came unexpectedly in view of a most beautiful lake, set like a gem in the mountains. The sheet of water lay transversely across the direction we had been pursuing; and, descending the steep, rocky ridge, where it was necessary to lead our horses, we followed its banks to the southern extremity. Here a view of the utmost magnificence and grandeur burst upon our eyes. With nothing between us and their feet to lessen the effect of the whole height, a grand bed of snow-capped mountains rose before us, pile upon pile, glowing in the bright light of an August day. Immediately below them lay the lake, between two ridges, covered with dark pines, which swept down from the main chain to the spot where we stood. Here, where the lake glittered in the open sunlight, its banks of yellow sand and the light foliage of aspen groves contrasted well with the gloomy pines. "Never before," said Mr. Preuss, "in this country or in Europe, have I seen such magnificent, grand rocks." I was so much pleased with the beauty of the place, that I determined to make the main camp here, where our animals would find good pasturage, and explore the mountains with a small party of men. Proceeding a little further, we came suddenly upon the outlet of the lake, where it found its way through a narrow passage between low hills. Dark pines, which overhung the stream, and masses of rock, where the water foamed along, gave it much romantic beauty. Where we crossed, which was immediately at the outlet, it is two hundred and fifty feet wide, and so deep, that with difficulty we were able to ford it. Its bed was an accumulation of rocks, boulders, and broad slabs, and large angular fragments, among which the animals fell repeatedly.

The current was very swift, and the water cold, and of a crystal purity. In crossing this stream, I met with a great misfortune in having my barometer broken. It was the only one. A great part of the interest of the journey for me was in the exploration of these mountains, of which so much had been said that was doubtful and contradictory; and now their snowy peaks rose majestically before me, and the only means of giving them authentically to science, the object of my anxious solicitude by night and day, was destroyed. We had brought this barometer in safety a thousand miles, and broke it almost among the snow of the mountains. The loss was felt by the whole camp—all had seen my anxiety, and aided me in preserving it. The height of these mountains, considered by the hunters and traders the highest in the whole range, had been a theme of constant discussion among them; and all had looked forward with pleasure to the moment when the instrument, which they believed to be true as the sun, should stand upon the summits, and decide their disputes. Their grief was only inferior to my own. . . .

August 12.— . . . We heard the roar, and had a glimpse of a waterfall as we rode along; and, crossing in our way two fine streams, tributary to the Colorado, in about two hours' ride we reached the top of the first row or range of the mountains. Here, again, a view of the most romantic beauty met our eyes. It seemed as if, from the vast expanse of uninteresting prairie we had passed over, Nature had collected all her beauties together in one chosen place. We were overlooking a deep valley, which was entirely occupied by three lakes, and from the brink the surrounding ridges rose precipitously five hundred and a thousand feet, covered with the dark green of the balsam pine, relieved on the border of the lake with the light foliage of the aspen. They all communicated with each other; and the green of the waters, common to mountain lakes of great depth, showed that it would be impossible to cross them. The surprise manifested by our guides when these impassable obstacles suddenly barred our progress proved that they were among the hidden treasures of the place, unknown even to the wandering trappers of the region. Descending the hill, we proceeded to make our way along the margin to the southern extremity. A narrow strip of angular fragments of rock sometimes afforded a rough pathway for our mules, but generally we rode along the shelving side, occasionally scrambling up, at a considerable risk of tumbling back into the lake.

The slope was frequently 60°; the pines grew densely together, and the ground was covered with the branches and trunks of trees. The air was fragrant with the odor of the pines; and I realized this delightful morning the pleasure of breathing that mountain air which makes a constant theme of the hunter's praise, and which now made us feel as if we had all been drinking some exhilarating gas. The depths of this unexplored forest were a place to delight the heart of a botanist. There was a rich undergrowth of plants, and numerous gay-colored flowers in brilliant bloom. We reached the outlet at length, where some freshly barked willows that lay in the water showed that beaver had been recently at work. There were some small brown squirrels jumping about in the pines, and a couple of large mallard ducks swimming about in the stream.

The hills on this southern end were low, and the lake looked like a mimic sea, as the waves broke on the sandy beach in the force of a strong breeze. There was a pretty open spot, with fine grass for our mules; and we made our noon halt on the beach, under the shade of some large hemlocks. We resumed our journey after a halt of about an hour, making our way up the ridge on the western side of the lake. In search of smoother ground, we rode a little inland; and, passing through groves of aspen, soon found ourselves again among the pines. Emerging from these, we struck the summit of the ridge above the upper end of the lake.

We had reached a very elevated point; and in the valley below, and among the hills, were a number of lakes at different levels; some two or three hundred feet above others, with which they communicated by foaming torrents. Even to our great height, the roar of the cataracts came up, and we could see them leaping down in lines of snowy foam. From this scene of busy waters, we turned abruptly into the stillness of a forest, where we rode among the open bolls of the pines, over a lawn of verdant grass, having strikingly the air of cultivated grounds. This led us, after a time, among masses of rock which had no vegetable earth but in hollows and crevices, though still the pine forest continued. Toward evening, we reached a defile, or rather a hole in the mountains, entirely shut in by dark pine-covered rocks. . . .

August 13.— . . . Having made an early dinner, we started again. We were soon involved in the most ragged precipices, nearing the central chain very slowly, and rising but little. The first ridge hid a succession of others; and when, with great fatigue and difficulty, we had climbed up five hundred feet, it was but to make an equal descent on the other side; all these intervening places were filled with small deep lakes, which met the eye in every direction, descending from one level to another, sometimes under bridges formed by huge fragments of granite, beneath which was heard the roar of the water. These constantly obstructed our path, forcing us to make long *detours;* frequently obliged to retrace our steps, and frequently falling among the rocks. Maxwell was precipitated toward the face of a precipice, and saved himself from going over by throwing himself flat on the ground. We clambered on, always expecting, with every ridge that we crossed, to reach the foot of the peaks, and always disappointed, until about 4 o'clock, when, pretty well worn out, we reached the shore of a little lake, in which there was a rocky island, and from which we obtained the view given in the frontispiece. We remained here a short time to rest, and continued on around the lake, which had in some places a beach of white sand, and in others was bound with rocks, over which the way was difficult and dangerous, as the water from innumerable springs made them very slippery.

By the time we had reached the further side of the lake, we found ourselves all exceedingly fatigued, and, much to the satisfaction of the whole party, we encamped. . . .

August 15.— . . . When we had secured strength for the day by a hearty breakfast, we covered what remained, which was enough for one meal, with rocks, in order that it might be safe from any marauding bird; and, saddling our mules, turned our faces once more towards the peaks. This time we determined to proceed quietly and cautiously, deliberately resolved to accomplish our object if it were within the compass of human means. We were of opinion that a long defile which lay to the left of yesterday's route would lead us to the foot of the main peak. We soon had the satisfaction to find ourselves riding along the huge wall which forms the central summits of the chain. There at last it rose by our sides, a nearly perpendicular wall of granite, terminating 2,000 to 3,000 feet above our heads in a serrated line of broken, jagged cones. We rode on until we came almost immediately below the main peak, which I denominated the Snow peak, as it exhibited more snow to the eye than any of the neighboring summits. . . .

. . . . Having divested ourselves of every unnecessary encumbrance, we commenced the ascent. This time, like experienced travellers, we did not press ourselves, but climbed leisurely, sitting down so soon as we found breath beginning to fail. At intervals we reached places where a number of springs gushed from the rocks, and about 1,800 feet above the lakes came to the snow line. From this point our progress was uninterrupted climbing. Hitherto I had worn a pair of thick moccasins, with soles of *parflêche;* but here I put on a light thin pair, which I had brought for the purpose, as now the use of our toes became necessary to a further advance. I availed myself of a sort of comb of the mountain, which stood against the wall like a buttress, and which the wind and the solar radiation, joined to the steepness of the smooth rock, had kept almost entirely free from snow. Up this I made my way rapidly. Our cautious method of advancing in the outset had spared my strength; and, with the exception of a slight disposition to headache, I felt no reamins of yesterday's illness. In a few minutes we reached a point where the buttress was overhanging, and there was no other way of surmounting the difficulty than by passing around one side of it, which was the face of a vertical precipice of several hundred feet.

Putting hands and feet in the crevices between the blocks, I succeeded in getting over it, and, when I reached the top, found my companions in a small valley below. Descending to them, we continued climbing, and in a short time reached the crest. I sprang upon the summit, and another step would have precipitated me into an immense snow field five hundred feet below. To the edge of this field was a sheer icy precipice; and then, with a gradual fall, the field sloped off for about a mile, until it struck the foot of another lower ridge. I stood on a narrow crest about three feet in width, with an inclination of about 20° N. 51° E. As soon as I had gratified the first feelings of curiosity, I descended, and each man ascended in his turn; for I would only allow one at a time to mount the unstable and precarious slab, which it seemed a breath would hurl into the abyss below. We mounted the barometer in the snow of the summit, and fixing a ramrod in a crevice, unfurled the national flag to wave in the breeze where never flag waved before. During our morning's ascent we had met no sign of animal life, except the small sparrow-like bird already mentioned. A stillness the most profound and a terrible solitude forced themselves constantly on the mind as the great features of the place. Here, on the summit, where the stillness was absolute, unbroken by any sound, and the solitude complete, we thought ourselves beyond the region of animated life; but while we were sitting on the rock, a solitary bee (*bromus, the humble bee*) came winging his flight from the eastern valley, and lit on the knee of one of the men.

It was a strange place, the icy rock and the highest peak of the Rocky mountains, for a lover of warm sunshine and flowers; and we pleased ourselves with the idea that he was the first of his species to cross the mountain barrier—a solitary pioneer to foretell the advance of civilization. I believe that a moment's thought would have made us let him continue his way unharmed; but we carried out the law of this country, where all animated nature seems at war; and, seizing him immediately, put him in at least a fit place—in the leaves of a large book, among the flowers we had collected on our way. The barometer stood at 18.293, the attached thermometer at 44°, giving for the elevation of this summit 13,570 feet above the Gulf of Mexico, which may be called the highest flight of the bee. It is certainly the highest known flight of that insect. From the description given by Mackenzie of the mountains where he crossed them, with that of a French officer still farther to the north, and Colonel Long's measurements to the south, joined to the opinion of the oldest traders of the country, it is presumed that this is the highest peak of the Rocky mountains. The day was sunny and bright, but a slight shining mist hung over the lower plains, which interfered with our view of the surrounding county. On one side we overlooked innumerable lakes and streams, the spring of the Colorado of the Gulf of California; and on the other was the Wind river valley, where were the heads of the Yellowstone branch of the Missouri; far to the north, we just could discover the snowy heads of the *Trois Tetons,* where were the sources of the Missouri and Columbia rivers; and at the southern extremity of the ridge, the peaks were plainly visible, among which were some of the springs of the Nebraska or Platte river. Around us, the whole scene had one main striking feature, which was that of terrible convulsion. Parallel to its length, the ridge was split into chasms and fissures; between which rose the thin lofty walls, terminated with slender minarets and columns, which is correctly represented in the view from the camp on Island lake. . . . Having now made what observations our means afforded, we proceeded to descend. We had accomplished an object of laudable ambition, and beyond the strict order of our instructions. We had climbed the loftiest peak of the Rocky mountains, and looked down upon the snow a thousand feet below, and, standing where never human foot had stood before, felt the exultation of first explorers. . . .

We reached our deposite of provisions at nightfall. Here was not the inn which awaits the tired traveller on his return from Mont Blanc, or the orange groves of South America, with their refreshing juices and soft fragrant air; but we found our little *cache* of dried meat and coffee undisturbed. Though the moon was bright, the road was full of precipices, and the fatigue of the day had been great. We therefore abandoned the idea of rejoining our friends, and lay down on the rock, and, in spite of the cold, slept soundly.

1845

George W. Kendall

From Across the Great Southwestern Prairies

The territory of America's Manifest Destiny came to include not only the Pacific Northwest but also the Southwest. The purpose of the expedition from Texas to Sante Fe as Kendall describes it was to open a trade route, but its secret political purpose was to urge New Mexicans to join the new Republic of Texas in a revolt against Mexico. The expedition was intercepted by the Mexican army, and the survivors were marched to Chihuahua. Kendall, an enterprising journalist who had founded the New Orleans *Picayune* and who joined the expedition in search of adventure and story material, wrote his book after he was freed. The book helped to raise popular sentiment for the Mexican War in 1848, as a result of which both Texas and New Mexico became U.S. possessions.

[Lost on the Prairie]

AN EARLY START was made the next morning, and near half the day was spent in climbing steep and abrupt hills, so rocky that the feet of the oxen suffered severely, and many of them had to be unyoked and turned loose. I thought I had previously seen a country in a state of nature, but this was the roughest part of "out doors" it had ever been my unfortunate lot to traverse. It appeared to have been just *got out* rough hewn, without a single finishing stroke in any quarter. Rough and mis-shapen hills, formed of rocks and sand, were piled up here and there without system or order, and not a bush or blade of grass could be found upon them to relieve their desolate appearance.

By noon we had partially extricated ourselves from the maze of hills on which our feet had been stumbling during that morning's march. Seeing what appeared to be a level and grassy prairie, a mile or a mile and a half to the left of our line of march, which seemed as though it might afford pasturage for a stray deer or antelope, myself and "Old Paint" rode off in that direction. As the old hunter expected, we quickly saw a drove of some fifteen deer; but they happened to see us first, and set off on a run. My companion was well enough versed in their "ways" not to think of following them; for after having once seen an enemy, the deer seldom allows him to come within gunshot.

My experience, in comparison with that of the veteran borderer, was limited, and I was simple enough not to resist the temptation of following the herd over a roll of the prairie, in the vain hope of obtaining a shot. They halted, as I supposed they would, but were on the lookout, and before I was within three hundred yards again bounded off across the prairie. Hope induced me to give one more trial, which terminated like the first. I now reluctantly gave up the chase and cast my eyes about for my fellow-hunter, but he was nowhere in sight. I tried hurriedly to ascertain the direction in which I had left him; but the result of my reflections convinced me that I was, to use a common expression, thoroughly "turned round"—lost. I put spurs to my horse and galloped to the highest roll of the prairie, with the hope of obtaining a sight of my companion or companions, but without success.

A sickening feeling of loneliness came over me on *finding* myself in that worst of all situations upon a prairie—*lost!* The sun was still high in the heavens, and I could not tell which was north or which south. I had my rifle and pistols with me, was well mounted, and had a sufficiency of ammunition, but I was not well enough acquainted with a prairie life to steer a course, even if I had known what course to start upon, neither was I hunter enough to feel confident that I could kill a sufficiency of meat in case I should be unsuccessful in finding my companions. Another thing, I had already found out what every hunter knows, that the more hungry a man grows upon the prairies the more unlikely he is to find game, and the more difficult it is to shoot it. There, then, I was, without a companion and without experience—starvation staring me in the face, or even if I was fortunate in obtaining meat, I still was almost certain to be killed and scalped by the Indians, or end my days in vain efforts to reach the settlements. I thought of home, and made up my mind firmly that if ever I was fortunate enough to reach it, I should be in no particular hurry to leave it again.

I dashed off to what appeared a still higher prairie swell than the one I now stood upon—nothing could I see except a solitary wolf, trotting stealthily along in the hollow below me: I even envied this most contemptible of the brute creation, for he knew where he was. I strained my eyes as though to penetrate beyond the limits of human vision; but all was a waste, a blank. I leaped from my horse and sat upon the ground for a moment; it was only for a moment, for in my uneasiness I could not remain motionless. I tried to reflect, to reason; but so fast did thoughts of starvation and of Indian perils crowd on my mind, that I could come to no definite conclusion as to my present position with reference to that of my companions. I tried to follow my own trail back to the point where I had so foolishly left "Old Paint," but the ground was so hard that my horse's hoofs had made little or no indentation, and I was too impatient to examine the face of the prairie with that searching scrutiny which might have resulted in success.

Yet I resolved to make one desperate effort, at least, to find the command. I knew enough of my situation to feel convinced that by circling about, from prairie roll to prairie roll, I might gallop my horse for hours, and at last find myself at the point I started from, "with confusion worse confounded"—travelling in a straight line alone might save me. Here was another difficulty; for the course I might adopt, even were I successful in keeping it, might leave me at a still greater distance from my friends. How I wished for the presence of Tom Hancock—the presence even of the greatest dullard in the command would have assisted in removing the mountain of torturing uncertainty that pressed upon my mind. Man never knows the full weight of *hopelessness* until he is made to bear it alone, with no human intelligence near from whose resources he can hope to draw something for his relief when he is too consciously aware that his own are exhausted. Even sympathy imparts something of hope. I felt that even my horse was some company to me: I patted him kindly on the neck and told him so, aloud.

"But," the reader will perchance inquire, "why did you not give your horse the reins and trust to his natural instinct for regaining his and your companions?" And again, "Why did you not wait until the sun was low in the western heavens, then reflect, for one moment, in what direction the command was travelling and the side on which you had left it? You knew that the sun would set in the west, and that as you faced it, north was to the right and south to the left—surely you could then steer a course, even if you could not while the sun was vertical."

Gentle reader, you have never been lost on a wide ocean of prairies, unskilled in border life, and little gifted with the power of first adopting a course to follow and then not deviating from it. You must recollect that there, as on the wide ocean, you find no trees, no friendly landmarks, to guide you—all is a wide waste of eternal sameness. *To be lost,* as I and others have experienced, has a complex and fearful meaning. It is not merely to stray from your friends, your path, but from yourself. With your way you lose your presence of mind. You attempt to reason, but the rudder and compass of your reflective faculties are gone. Self-confidence, too, is lost—in a word all is lost, except a maniacal impulse to despair, that is peculiar and indescribable.

In my case, fate, fortune, good luck, call it by what name you may—stepped into my assistance. While upon one of the highest rolls of the prairie I resolved to proceed in a certain direction, and, if possible to keep it without variation. Whether I did so or not I am unable to say—I only know that after travelling at a rapid pace, it may be some five miles, I suddenly found myself upon the brow of a high and steep declivity, overlooking a narrow but beautiful valley, through which a small creek was winding. I had examined the prairies in every direction, during my short ride, until my eyes ached from overstraining, yet had not for a moment allowed my horse to slacken his pace. I now paused to examine the valley before me. The reader may judge my feelings when, after an hasty glance I discovered the white tops of the waggons, far off in the distance to the right, slowly winding their way down a gentle slope into the valley. Never was the sight of friendly sail more welcome to the eye of a shipwrecked mariner than was the appearance of these waggons to me, and I fairly laughed aloud at my good fortune.

1845

Nathaniel Pitt Langford

From The Discovery of Yellowstone Park

Langford, a one-time bank clerk turned adventurer, was a collector of internal revenue for the Territory of Montana. In 1870, he became a promotion agent for Jay Cooke's Northern Pacific Railway. His job was to acquaint the public with the land the railroad was to traverse ("Jay Cooke's banana belt") and with the value of buying stock in the corporation. Under that impetus, he organized the expedition to the Yellowstone area and chose its leader, General Henry Dana Washburn, a Civil War veteran and the surveyor general of the territory of Montana. The Washburn expedition followed the Cook-Folsom-Peterson Expedition to the Yellowstone (1869) by a year, and Langford was its chief diarist. When the region became a National Park in 1872, Langford was its first superintendent.

Monday, August 29.—AT ABOUT ONE MILE below our camp the creek runs through a bed of volcanic ashes, which extends for a hundred yards on either side. Toiling on our course down this creek to the river we came suddenly upon a basin of boiling sulphur springs, exhibiting signs of activity and points of difference so wonderful as to fully absorb our curiosity. The largest of these, about twenty feet in diameter, is boiling like a cauldron, throwing water and fearful volumes of sulphurous vapor higher than our heads. Its color is a disagreeable greenish yellow. The central spring of the group, of dark leaden hue, is in the most violent agitation, its convulsive spasms frequently projecting large masses of water to the height of seven or eight feet. The spring lying to the east of this, more diabolical in appearance, filled with a hot brownish substance of the consistency of mucilage, is in constant noisy ebullition, emitting fumes of villainous odor. Its surface is covered with bubbles, which are constantly rising and bursting, and emitting sulphurous gases from various parts of its surface. Its appearance has suggested the name, which Hedges has given, of "Hell-Broth springs"; for, as we gazed upon the infernal mixture and inhaled the pungent sickening vapors, we were impressed with the idea that this was a most perfect realization of Shakespeare's image in Macbeth. It needed but the presence of Hecate and her weird band to realize that horrible creation of poetic fancy, and I fancied the "black and midnight hags" concocting a charm around this horrible cauldron. We ventured near enough to this spring to dip the end of a pine pole into it, which, upon removal, was covered an eighth of an inch thick with lead-colored sulphury slime. . . .

Friday, September 2.—To-day we have occupied ourselves in examining the springs and other wonders at this point. . . . Through a little coulee on the other side of the hill runs a small stream of greenish water, which issues from a small cavern, the mouth of which is about five feet high and the same dimension in width. From the mouth, the roof of the cavern descends at an angle of about fifteen degrees, till at the distance of twenty feet from the entrance it joins the surface of the water. The bottom of the cavern under the water seems to descend at about the same angle, but as the water is in constant ebullition, we cannot determine this fact accurately. The water is thrown out in regular spasmodic jets, the pulsations occurring once in ten or twelve seconds. The sides of the mouth of this cavern are covered with dark green deposits, some which we have taken with us for analysis. About two hundred yards farther on is another geyser, the flow of which occurs about every six hours, and when the crater is full the diameter of the surface is about fourteen feet, the sides of the crater being of an irregular funnel-shape, and the descending at an angle of about forty-five degrees. At the lowest point at which we saw the water it was about seven feet in diameter on the surface. One or another of our party watched the gradual rise of the water for four or five hours. The boiling commenced when the water had risen half way to the surface, occasionally breaking forth with great violence. When the water had reached its full height in the basin, the stream was thrown up with great force to a height of from twenty to thirty feet, the column being from seven to ten feet in diameter, at the midway height of the column, from bottom to top. The water was of a dark lead color, and those portions of the sides of the crater that were overflowed and then exposed by the rise and fall of the water were covered with stalagmites formed by the deposit from the geyser.

While surveying these wonders, our ears were constantly saluted by dull, thundering, booming sounds, resembling the reports of distant artillery. As we approached the spot whence they proceeded, the ground beneath us shook and trembled as from successive shocks of an earthquake. Ascending a small hillock, the cause of the uproar was found to be a mud volcano—the greatest marvel we have yet met with. It is about midway up a gentle pine-covered slope, above which on the lower side its crater, thirty feet in diameter, rises to a height of about thirty-five feet. Dense masses of steam issue with explosive force from this crater, into whose tapering mouth, as they are momentarily dispelled by the wind, we can see at a depth of about forty feet the regurgitating contents. The explosions are not uniform in force or time, varying from three to eight seconds, and occasionally with perfect regularity occurring every five seconds. They are very distinctly heard at the distance of half a mile, and the massive jets of vapor which accompany them burst forth like the smoke of burning gunpowder. . . .

Monday, September 19.—When we left Yellowstone lake two days ago, the desire for home had superceded all thought of further explorations. Five days of rapid travel would, we believed, bring us to the upper valley of the Madison, and within twenty-five miles of Virginia City . . . We had within a distance of fifty miles seen what we believed to be the greatest wonders on the continent. We were convinced that there was not on the globe another region where within the same limits Nature had crowded so much of grandeur and majesty with so much of novelty and wonder. Judge, then, of our astonishment on entering this basin, to see at no great distance before us an immense body of sparkling water, projected suddenly and with terrific force into the air to the height of over one hundred feet. We had found a real geyser. In the valley before us were a thousand hot springs of various sizes and character, and five hundred craters jetting forth vapor. In one place the eye followed through crevices in the crust a stream of hot water of considerable size, running at nearly right angles with the river, and in a direction, not towards, but away from the stream. We traced the course of this stream by the crevices in the surface for twenty or thirty yards. It is probable that it eventually flows into the Firehole, but there is nothing on the surface to indicate to the beholder the course of its underground passage to the river.

On the summit of a cone twenty-five feet high was a boiling spring seven feet in diameter, surrounded with beautiful incrustations, on the slope of which we gathered twigs encased in a crust a quarter of an inch in thickness. On an incrusted hill opposite our camp are four craters from three to five feet in diameter, sending forth steam jets and water to the height of four or five feet. But the marvelous features of this wonderful basin are its spouting geysers, of which during our brief stay of twenty-two hours we have seen twelve in action. Six of these threw water to the height of from fifteen to twenty feet, but in the presence of others of immense dimensions they soon ceased to attract attention.

Of the latter six, the one we saw in action on entering the basin ejected from a crevice of irregular form, and about four feet long by three wide, a column of water of corresponding magnitude in the height of one hundred feet. Around this crevice or mouth the sediment is piled in many capricious shapes, chiefly indented globules from six inches to two feet in diameter. Little hollows in the crust filled with water contained small white spheres of tufa, of the size of a nutmeg, formed as it seemed to me around some nuclei.

We gave such names to those of the geysers which we saw in action as we think will best illustrate their peculiarities. The one I have just described General Washburn has named "Old Faithful," because of the regularity of its eruptions, the intervals between which being from sixty to sixty-five minutes, the column of water being thrown at each eruption to the height of from eight to one hundred feet.

The "Fan" has a distorted pipe from which are projected two radiating sheets of water to the height of sixty feet, resembling a feather fan. Forty feet from this geyser is a vent connected with it, two feet in diameter, which, during the eruption, expels with loud reports dense volumes of vapor to the height of fifty feet.

The "Grotto," so named from the singularly winding apertures penetrating the sinter surrounding it, was at rest when we first discovered it. Externally it presented few indications of its character as a geyser. Private Williamson, one of our escort, crawled through an aperture and looked into the discharging orifice. When afterwards, he saw it belching forth a column of boiling water two feet in diameter to the height of sixty feet, and a scalding stream of two hundred square inches flowing from the cavern he had entered a short time before, he said that he felt like one who had narrowly escaped being summarily cooked.

The "Castle" is on the summit of an incrusted elevation. This name was given because of its resemblance to the ruins of some old tower with its broken down turrets. The silicious sinter composing the formation surrounding it takes the form of small globules, resembling a ripe cauliflower, and the massive nodules indicate that at some former period the flow of water must have been much larger than at present. The jet is sixty feet high by four feet in diameter, and the vent near it, which is in angry ebullition during the eruption, constantly flows with boiling water.

One of the most wonderful of the springs in this basin is that of ultramarine hue directly in front of the "Castle" geyser. It is nearly round, having diameters of about twenty and twenty-five feet, the sides being corrugated and funnel-shaped, and at the depth of thirty feet opening out into a cavern of unfathomable depth, the rim of the spring having beautifully escalloped edges. It does not boil over, but a very small stream of water flows from it, and it is not affected in its appearance by the spouting of the geyser in its immediate proximity. There is evidently no connection between this spring and the geyser.

The "Giant" is a rugged deposit presenting in form a miniature model of the Colosseum. It has an opening three feet in diameter. A remarkable characteristic of this geyser is the duration of its discharges, which yesterday afternoon continued for more than an hour in a steady stream about three feet in diameter and one hundred and forty feet high . . .

Near by is situated the "Giantess," the largest of all the geysers we saw in eruption. Ascending a gentle slope for a distance of sixty yards we came to a sink or well or an irregular oval shape, fifteen by twenty feet across, into which we could see to the depth of fifty feet or more, but we could discover no water, though we could distinctly hear it gurgling and boiling at a fearful rate afar down this vertical cavern. Suddenly it commenced spluttering and rising with incredible rapidity, causing a general stampede among our company, who all moved around to the windward side of the geyser. When the water had risen within about twenty-five feet of the surface, it became stationary, and we returned to look down upon the foaming water, which occasionally emitted hot jets nearly to the mouth of the orifice. As if tired of this sport the water began to ascend at the rate of five feet in a second, and when near the top it was expelled with terrific momentum in a column the full size of the immense aperture to a height of sixty feet. The column remained at this height for the space of about a minute, when from the apex of this vast aqueous mass five lesser jets or round columns of water varying in size from six to fifteen inches in diameter shot up into the atmosphere to the amazing height of two hundred and fifty feet.

This was without exception the most magnificent phenomenon I ever beheld. We were standing on the side of the geyser exposed to the sun, whose sparkling rays filled the ponderous column with what appeared to be the clippings of a thousand rainbows. These prismatic illusions disappeared, only to be succeeded by myriads of others which continually fluttered and sparkled through the spray during the twenty minutes the eruption lasted. These lesser jets, thrown so much higher than the main column and shooting through it, doubtless proceed from auxiliary pipes leading into the principal orifice near the bottom, where the explosive force is greater. The minute globules into which the spent column was diffused when falling sparkled like a shower of diamonds, and around every shadow produced by the column of steam hiding the sun was the halo so often represented in paintings as encircling the head of the Savior. We unhesitatingly agreed that this was the greatest wonder of our trip.

1905

John Wesley Powell

From The Exploration of the Colorado River and Its Canyons

Born in New York's Genesee Valley, Powell emigrated with his family, at an early age, to Wisconsin. Like Maxmilian and other Western explorers and naturalists, he was a soldier (he lost his right arm at Shiloh), hardened to life in the field, who became a field naturalist. Powell was more professional than many of his counterparts: he was a professor of geology at Illinois Wesleyan University and later director of the U.S. Geological Survey and founder of the Bureau of American Ethnology. It was as a professor that he began his explorations of the Colorado River, the Grand Canyon, and other areas of the Southwest (1869–1872). His *Exploration,* first published in 1895 as *Canyons of the Colorado,* is basically a journal of his river travels; "The Grand Canyon," its fifteenth and last chapter, is a kind of descriptive relation, which begins as a geological map, becomes a painting, and ends as song of praise.

From The Grand Canyon

THE GRAND CANYON is a gorge 217 miles in length, through which flows a great river with many storm-born tributaries. It has a winding way, as rivers are wont to have. Its banks are vast structures of adamant, piled up in forms rarely seen in the mountains.

Down by the river the walls are composed of black gneiss, slates, and schists, all greatly implicated and traversed by dikes of granite. Let this formation be called the black gneiss. It is usually about 800 feet in thickness.

Then over the black gneiss are found 800 feet of quartzites, usually in very thin beds of many colors, but exceedingly hard, and ringing under the hammer like phonolite. These beds are dipping and unconformable with the rocks above; while they make but 800 feet of the wall or less, they have a geological thickness of 12,000 feet. Set up a row of books aslant; it is 10 inches from the shelf to the top of the line of books, but there may be 3 feet of the books measured directly through the leaves. So these quartzites are aslant, and though of great geologic thickness, they make but 800 feet of the wall. Your books may have many-colored bindings and differ greatly in their contents; so these quartzites vary greatly from place to place along the wall, and in many places they entirely disappear. Let us call this formation the variegated quartzite.

Above the quartzites there are 500 feet of sandstones. They are of a greenish hue, but are mottled with spots of brown and black by iron stains. They usually stand in a bold cliff, weathered in alcoves. Let this formation be called the cliff sandstone.

Above the cliff sandstone there are 700 feet of bedded sandstones and limestones, which are massive sometimes and sometimes broken into thin strata. These rocks are often weathered in deep alcoves. Let this formation be called the alcove sandstone.

Over the alcove sandstone there are 1,600 feet of limestone, in many places a beautiful marble, as in Marble Canyon. As it appears along the Grand Canyon it is always stained a brilliant red, for immediately over it there are thin seams of iron, and the storms have painted these limestones with pigments from above. Altogether this is the red-wall group. It is chiefly limestone. Let it be called the red wall limestone.

Above the red wall there are 800 feet of gray and bright red sandstone, alternating in beds that look like vast ribbons of landscape. Let it be called the banded sandstone.

And over all, at the top of the wall, is the Aubrey limestone, 1,000 feet in thickness. This Aubrey has much gypsum in it, great beds of alabaster that are pure white in comparison with the great body of limestone below. In the same limestone there are enormous beds of chert, agates, and carnelians. This limestone is especially remarkable for its pinnacles and towers. Let it be called the tower limestone.

Now recapitulate: The black gneiss below, 800 feet in thickness; the variegated quartzite, 800 feet in thickness; the cliff sandstone, 500 feet in thickness; the alcove sandstone, 700 feet in thickness; the red wall limestone, 1,600 feet in thickness; the banded sandstone, 800 feet in thickness; the tower limestone, 1,000 feet in thickness.

These are the elements with which the walls are constructed, from black buttress below to alabaster tower above. All of these elements weather in different forms and are painted in different colors, so that the wall presents a highly complex façade. A wall of homogeneous granite, like that in the Yosemite, is but a naked wall, whether it be 1,000 or 5,000 feet high. Hundreds and thousands of feet mean nothing to the eye when they stand in a meaningless front. A mountain covered by pure snow 10,000 feet high has but little more effect on the imagination than a mountain of snow 1,000 feet high—it is but more of the same thing; but a façade of seven systems of rock has its sublimity multiplied sevenfold. . . .

Such are the vertical elements of which the Grand Canyon façade is composed. Its horizontal elements must next be considered. The river meanders in great curves, which are themselves broken into curves of smaller magnitude. The streams that head far back in the plateau on either side come down in gorges and break the wall into sections. Each lateral canyon has a secondary system of laterals, and the secondary canyons are broken by tertiary canyons; so the crags are forever branching, like the limbs of an oak. That which has been described as a wall is such only in its grand effect. In detail it is a series of structures separated by a ramification of canyons, each having its own walls. Thus, in passing down the canyon it seems to be inclosed by walls, but oftener by salients—towering structures that stand between canyons that run back into the plateau. Sometimes gorges of the second or third order have met before reaching the brink of the Grand Canyon, and then great salients are cut off from the wall and stand out as buttes—huge pavilions in the architecture of the canyon. The scenic elements thus described are fused and combined in very different ways. . . .

Stand at some point on the brink of the Grand Canyon where you can overlook the river, and the details of the structure, the vast labyrinth of gorges of which it is composed, are scarcely noticed; the elements are lost in the grand effect, and a broad, deep, flaring gorge of many colors is seen. But stand down among these gorges and the landscape seems to be composed of huge vertical elements of wonderful form. Above, it is an open, sunny gorge; below, it is deep and gloomy. Above, it is a chasm; below, it is a stairway from gloom to heaven.

The traveler in the region of mountains sees vast masses piled up in gentle declivities to the clouds. To see mountains in this way is to appreciate the masses of which they are composed. But the climber among the glaciers sees the elements of which this mass is composed,—that it is made of cliffs and towers and pinnacles, with intervening gorges, and the smooth billows of granite seen from afar are transformed into cliffs and caves and towers and minarets. These two aspects of mountain scenery have been seized by painters, and in their art two classes of mountains are represented: mountains with towering forms that seem ready to topple in the first storm, and mountains in masses that seem to frown defiance at the tempests. Both classes have told the truth. The two aspects are sometimes caught by our painters severally; sometimes they are combined. Church paints a mountain like a kingdom of glory. Bierstadt paints a mountain cliff where an eagle is lost from sight ere he reaches the summit. Thomas Moran marries these great characteristics, and in his infinite masses cliffs of immeasurable height are seen.

Thus the elements of the façade of the Grand Canyon change vertically and horizontally. The details of structure can be seen only at close view, but grand effects of structure can be witnessed in great panoramic scenes. Seen in detail, gorges and precipices appear; seen at a distance, in comprehensive views, vast massive structures are presented. The traveler on the brink looks from afar and is overwhelmed with the sublimity of massive forms; the traveler among the gorges stands in the presence of awful mysteries, profound, solemn, and gloomy. . . .

The Grand Canyon of the Colorado is a canyon composed of many canyons. It is a composite of thousands, of tens of thousands, of gorges. In like manner, each wall of the canyon is a composite structure, a wall composed of many walls, but never a repetition. Every one of these almost innumerable gorges is a world of beauty in itself. In the Grand Canyon there are thousands of gorges like that below Niagara Falls, and there are a thousand Yosemites. Yet all these canyons unite to form one grand canyon, the most sublime spectacle on the earth. Pluck up Mt. Washington by the roots to the level of the sea and drop it headfirst into the Grand Canyon, and the dam will not force its waters over the walls. Pluck up the Blue Ridge and hurl it into the Grand Canyon, and it will not fill it.

The carving of the Grand Canyon is the work of rains and rivers. The vast labyrinth of canyon by which the plateau region drained by the Colorado is dissected is also the work of waters. Every river has excavated its own gorge and every creek has excavated its gorge. When a shower comes in this land, the rills carve canyons—but a little at each storm; and though storms are far apart and the heavens above are cloudless for most of the days of the year, still, years are plenty in the ages, and an intermittent rill called to life by a shower can do much work in centuries of centuries.

The erosion represented in the canyons, although vast, is but a small part of the great erosion of the region, for between the cliffs blocks have been carried away far superior in magnitude to those necessary to fill the canyons. Probably there is no portion of the whole region from which there have not been more than a thousand feet degraded, and there are districts from which more than 30,000 feet of rock have been carried away. Altogether, there is a district of country more than 200,000 square miles in extent from which on the average more than 6,000 feet have been eroded. Consider a rock 200,000 square miles in extent and a mile in thickness, against which the clouds have hurled their storms and beat it into sands and the rills have carried the sands into the creeks and the creeks have carried them into the rivers and the Colorado has carried them into the sea. We think of the mountains as forming clouds about their brows, but the clouds have formed the mountains. Great continental blocks are upheaved from beneath the sea by internal geologic forces that fashion the earth. Then the wandering clouds, the tempest-bearing clouds, the rainbow-decked clouds, with mighty power and with wonderful skill, carve out valleys and canyons and fashion hills and cliffs and mountains. The clouds are the artists sublime.

In winter some of the characteristics of the Grand Canyon are emphasized. The black gneiss below, the variegated quartzite, and the green or alcove sandstone form the foundation for the mighty red wall. The banded sandstone entablature is crowned by the tower limestone. In winter this is covered with snow. Seen from below, these changing elements seem to graduate into the heavens, and no plane of demarcation between wall and blue firmament can be seen. The heavens constitute a portion of the façade and mount into a vast dome from wall to wall, spanning the Grand Canyon with empyrean blue. So the earth and the heavens are blended in one vast structure.

When the clouds play in the canyon, as they often do in the rainy season, another set of effects is produced. Clouds creep out of canyons and wind into other canyons. The heavens seem to be alive, not moving as move the heavens over a plain, in one direction with the wind, but following the multiplied courses of these gorges. In this manner the little clouds seem to be individualized, to have wills and souls of their own, and to be going on diverse errands—a vast assemblage of self-willed clouds, faring here and there, intent upon purposes hidden in their own breasts. In the imagination the clouds belong to the sky, and when they are in the canyon the skies come down into the gorges and cling to the cliffs and lift them up to immeasurable heights, for the sky must still be far away. Thus they lend infinity to the walls.

The wonders of the Grand Canyon cannot be adequately represented in symbols of speech, nor by speech itself. The resources of the graphic art are taxed beyond their powers in attempting to portray its features. Language and illustration combined must fail. The elements that unite to make the Grand Canyon the most sublime spectacle in nature are multifarious and exceedingly diverse. The Cyclopean forms which result from the sculpture of tempests through ages too long for man to compute, are wrought into endless details, to describe which would be a task equal in magnitude to that of describing the stars of the heavens or the multitudinous beauties of the forest with its traceries of foliage presented by oak and pine and poplar, by beech and linden and hawthorn, by tulip and lily and rose, by fern and moss and lichen. Besides the elements of form, there are elements of color, for here the colors of the heavens are rivaled by the colors of the rocks. The rainbow is not more replete with hues. But form and color do not exhaust all the divine qualities of the Grand

Canyon. It is the land of music. The river thunders in perpetual roar, swelling in floods of music when the storm gods play upon the rocks and fading away in soft and low murmurs when the infinite blue of heaven is unveiled. With the melody of the great tide rising and falling, swelling and vanishing forever, other melodies are heard in the gorges of the lateral canyons, while the waters plunge in the rapids among the rocks or leap in great cataracts. Thus the Grand Canyon is a land of song. Mountains of music swell in the rivers, hills of music billow in the creeks, and meadows of music murmur in the rills that ripple over the rocks. Altogether it is a symphony of multitudinous melodies. All this is the music of waters. The adamant foundations of the earth have been wrought into a sublime harp, upon which the clouds of the heavens play with mighty tempests or with gentle showers.

The glories and the beauties of form, color, and sound unite in the Grand Canyon—forms unrivaled even by the mountains, colors that vie with sunsets, and sounds that span the diapason from tempest to tinkling raindrop, from cataract to bubbling fountain. But more: it is a vast district of country. Were it a valley plain it would make a state. It can be seen only in parts from hour to hour and from day to day and from week to week and from month to month. A year scarcely suffices to see it all. It has infinite variety, and no part is ever duplicated. Its colors, though many and complex at any instant, change with the ascending and declining sun; lights and shadows appear and vanish with the passing clouds, and the changing seasons mark their passage in changing colors. You cannot see the Grand Canyon in one view, as if it were a changeless spectacle from which a curtain might be lifted, but to see it you have to toil from month to month through its labyrinths. It is a region more difficult to traverse than the Alps or the Himalayas, but if strength and courage are sufficient for the task, by a year's toil a concept of sublimity can be obtained never again to be equaled on the hither side of Paradise.

1895

Mark Twain

From Roughing It

After leaving his job as a Mississippi River steamboat pilot, Twain spent five years in the West: from 1861 to 1864 in Nevada, the boom years for mining (by the late 1860's the mines had largely exhausted themselves); from May 1864 to March 1866 in California. *Roughing It,* written in 1871 and published the next year, is a kind of factual counterpart to Bret Harte's fiction of local color (see Landscape as Environment).

In his sketch of Carson City, in Nevada Territory, Twain pictures a fairly typical mining boom town: it has risen so fast, built by energies as wild as those of the "Washoe wind," that it has no pastoral middle ground. It is a small civilization (stores, sidewalks, a Governor's house) "in the midst of solitude, silence and desolation." The camp Twain visits in the second excerpt is apparently Angel's Camp in Tuolumne, California, a boom town gone bust. Out of one of the tales he heard in this landscape of ruin, Twain composed "The Celebrated Jumping Frog of Calaveras County."

[Carson City, Nevada]

AT EIGHT IN THE MORNING we reached the remnant and ruin of what had been the important military station of "Camp Floyd," some forty-five or fifty miles from Salt Lake City. At four P.M. we had doubled our distance and were ninety or a hundred miles from Salt Lake. And now we entered upon one of that species of deserts whose concentrated hideousness shames the diffused and diluted horrors of Sahara—an *"alkali"* desert. For sixty-eight miles there was but one break in it. I do not remember that this was really a break; indeed it seems to me that it was nothing but a watering depot *in the midst* of the stretch of sixty-eight miles. If my memory serves me, there was no well or spring at this place, but the water was hauled there by mule and ox teams from the further side of the desert. There was a stage station there. It was forty-five miles from the beginning of the desert, and twenty-three from the end of it.

We plowed and dragged and groped along, the whole live-long night, and at the end of this uncomfortable twelve hours we finished the forty-five-mile part of the desert and got to the stage station where the imported water was. The sun was just rising. It was easy enough to cross a desert in the night while we were asleep; and it was pleasant to reflect, in the morning, that we in actual person *had* encountered an absolute desert and could always speak knowingly of deserts in presence of the ignorant thenceforward. And it was pleasant also to reflect that this was not an obscure, back country desert, but a very celebrated one, the metropolis itself, as you may say. All this was very well and very comfortable and satisfactory—but now we were to cross a desert in *daylight*. This was fine—novel—romantic—dramatically adventurous—*this*, indeed, was worth living for, worth traveling for! We would write home all about it.

This enthusiasm, this stern thirst for adventure, wilted under the sultry August sun and did not last above one hour. One poor little hour—and then we were ashamed that we had "gushed" so. The poetry was all in the anticipation—there is none in the reality. Imagine a vast, waveless ocean stricken dead and turned to ashes; imagine this solemn waste tufted with ash-dusted sage-bushes; imagine the lifeless silence and solitude that belong to such a place; imagine a coach, creeping like a bug through the midst of this shoreless level, and sending up tumbled volumes of dust as if it were a bug that went by steam; imagine this aching monotony of toiling and plowing kept up hour after hour, and the shore still as far away as ever, apparently; imagine team, driver, coach and passengers so deeply coated with ashes that they are all one colorless color; imagine ash-drifts roosting above moustaches and eyebrows like snow accumulations on boughs and bushes. This is the reality of it.

The sun beats down with dead, blistering, relentless malignity; the perspiration is welling from every pore in man and beast, but scarcely a sign of it finds its way to the surface—it is absorbed before it gets there; there is not the faintest breath of air stirring; there is not a merciful shred of cloud in all the brilliant firmament; there is not a living creature visible in any direction whither one searches the blank level that stretches its monotonous miles on every hand; there is not a sound—not a sigh—not a whisper—not a buzz, or a whir of wings, or distant pipe of bird—not even a sob from the lost souls that doubtless people that dead air. And so the occasional sneezing of the resting mules, and the champing of the bits, grate harshly on the grim stillness, not dissipating the spell but accenting it and making one feel more lonesome and forsaken than before.

The mules, under violent swearing, coaxing and whip-cracking, would make at stated intervals a "spurt," and drag the coach a hundred or may be two hundred yards, stirring up a billowy cloud of dust that rolled back, enveloping the vehicle to the wheel-tops or higher, and making it seem afloat in a fog. Then a rest followed, with the usual sneezing and bit-champing. Then another "spurt" of a hundred yards and another rest at the end of it. All day long we kept this up, without water for the mules and without ever changing the team. At least we kept it up ten hours, which, I take it, is a day, and a pretty honest one, in an alkali desert. It was from four in the morning till two in the afternoon. And it was so hot! and so close! and our water canteens went dry in the middle of the day and we got so thirsty! It was so stupid and tiresome and dull! and the tedious hours did lag and drag and limp along with such a cruel deliberation! It was so trying to give one's watch a good long undisturbed spell and then take it out and find that it had been fooling away the time and not trying to get ahead any! The alkali dust cut through our lips, it persecuted our eyes, it ate through the delicate membranes and made our noses bleed and *kept* them bleeding—and truly and seriously the romance all faded far away and disappeared, and left the desert trip nothing but a harsh reality—a thirsty, sweltering, longing, hateful reality!

Two miles and a quarter an hour for ten hours—that was what we accomplished. It was hard to bring the comprehension away down to such a snail-pace as that, when we had been used to making eight and ten miles an hour. When we reached the station on the farther verge of the desert, we were glad, for the first time, that the dictionary was along, because we never could have found language to tell how glad we were, in any sort of dictionary but an unabridged one with pictures in it. But there could not have been found in a whole library of dictionaries language sufficient to tell how tired those mules were after their twenty-three mile pull. To try to give the reader an idea of how *thirsty* they were, would be to "gild refined gold or paint the lily." . . .

On the seventeenth day we passed the highest mountain peaks we had yet seen, and although the day was very warm the night that followed upon its heels was wintry cold and blankets were next to useless.

On the eighteenth day we encountered the eastward-bound telegraph-constructors at Reese River station and sent a message to his Excellency Gov. Nye at Carson City (distance one hundred and fifty-six miles).

On the nineteenth day we crossed the Great American Desert—forty memorable miles of bottomless sand, into which the coach wheels sunk from six inches to a foot. We worked our passage most of the way across. That is to say, we got out and walked. It was a dreary pull and a long and thirsty one, for we had no water. From one extremity of this desert to the other, the road was white with the bones of oxen and horses. It would hardly be an exaggeration to say that we could have walked the forty miles and set our feet on a bone at every step! The desert was one prodigious graveyard. And the log-chains, wagon tyres, and rotting wrecks of vehicles were almost as thick as the bones. I think we saw log-chains enough rusting there in the desert, to reach across any State in the Union. Do not these relics suggest something of an idea of the fearful suffering and privation the early emigrants to California endured?

At the border of the Desert lies Carson Lake, or The "Sink" of the Carson, a shallow, melancholy sheet of water some eighty or a hundred miles in circumference. Carson River empties into it and is lost—sinks mysteriously into the earth and never appears in the light of the sun again—for the lake has no outlet whatever.

There are several rivers in Nevada, and they all have this mysterious fate. They end in various lakes or "sinks," and that is the last of them. Carson Lake, Humboldt Lake, Walker Lake, Mono Lake, are all great sheets of water without any visible outlet. Water is always flowing into them; none is ever seen to flow out of them, and yet they remain always level full, neither receding nor overflowing. What they do with their surplus is only known to the Creator.

On the western verge of the Desert we halted a moment at Ragtown. It consisted of one loghouse and is not set down on the map. . . .

We were approaching the end of our long journey. It was the morning of the twentieth day. At noon we would reach Carson City, the capital of Nevada Territory. We were not glad, but sorry. It had been a fine pleasure trip; we had fed fat on wonders every day; we were now well accustomed to stage life, and very fond of it; so the idea of coming to a stand-still and settling down to a humdrum existence in a village was not agreeable, but on the contrary depressing.

Visibly our new home was a desert, walled in by barren, snow-clad mountains. There was not a tree in sight. There was no vegetation but the endless sage-brush and greasewood. All nature was gray with it. We were plowing through great deeps of powdery alkali dust that rose in thick clouds and floated across the plain like smoke from a burning house. We were coated with it like millers; so were the coach, the mules, the mail-bags, the driver—we and the sage-bush and the other scenery were all one monotonous color. Long trains of freight wagons in the distance enveloped in ascending masses of dust suggested pictures of prairies on fire. These teams and their masters were the only life we saw. Otherwise we moved in the midst of solitude, silence and desolation. Every twenty steps we passed the skeleton of some dead beast of burthen, with its dust-coated skin stretched tightly over its empty ribs. Frequently a solemn raven sat upon the skull or the hips and contemplated the passing coach with meditative serenity.

By and by Carson City was pointed out to us. It nestled in the edge of a great plain and was a sufficient number of miles away to look like an assemblage of mere white spots in the shadow of a grim range of mountains overlooking it, whose summits seemed lifted clear out of companionship and consciousness of earthly things.

We arrived, disembarked, and the stage went on. It was a "wooden" town; its population two thousand souls. The main street consisted of four or five blocks of little white frame stores which were too high to sit down on, but not too high for various other purposes; in fact hardly high enough. They were packed close together, side by side, as if room were scarce in that mighty plain. The sidewalk was of boards that were more or less loose and inclined to rattle when walked upon. In the middle of the town, opposite the stores, was the "plaza" which is native to all towns beyond the Rocky Mountains—a large, unfenced, level vacancy, with a liberty pole in it, and very useful as a place for public auctions, horse trades, and mass meetings, and likewise for teamsters to camp in. Two other sides of the plaza were faced by stores, offices and stables. The rest of Carson City was pretty scattering.

We were introduced to several citizens, at the stage-office and on the way up to the Governor's from the hotel—among others, to a Mr. Harris, who was on horseback; he began to say something, but interrupted himself with the remark:

"I'll have to get you to excuse me a minute; yonder is the witness that swore I helped to rob the California coach—a piece of impertinent intermeddling, sir, for I am not even acquainted with the man."

Then he rode over and began to rebuke the stranger with a six-shooter, and the stranger began to explain with another. When the pistols were emptied, the stranger resumed his work (mending a whip-lash), and Mr. Harris rode by with a polite nod, homeward bound, with a bullet through one of his lungs, and several in his hips; and from them issued little rivulets of blood that coursed down the horse's sides and made the animal look quite picturesque. I never saw Harris shoot a man after that but it recalled to mind that first day in Carson.

This was all we saw that day, for it was two o'clock, now, and according to custom the daily "Washoe Zephyr" set in; a soaring dust-drift about the size of the United States set up edgewise came with it, and the capital of Nevada Territory disappeared from view. Still, there were sights to be seen which were not wholly uninteresting to new comers; for the vast dust cloud was thickly freckled with things strange to the upper air—things living and dead, that flitted hither and thither, going and coming, appearing and disappearing among the rolling billows of dust—hats, chickens and parasols sailing in the remote heavens; blankets, tin signs, sage-brush and shingles a shade lower; doormats and buffalo robes lower still; shovels and coal scuttles on the next grade; glass doors, cats and little children on the next; disrupted lumber yards, light buggies and wheelbarrows on the next; and down only thirty or forty feet above ground was a scurrying storm of emigrating roofs and vacant lots.

It was something to see that much. I could have seen more, if I could have kept the dust out of my eyes.

But seriously a Washoe wind is by no means a trifling matter. It blows flimsy houses down, lifts shingle roofs occasionally, rolls up tin ones like sheet music, now and then blows a stage coach over and spills the passengers; and tradition says the reason there are so many bald people there, is, that the wind blows the hair off their heads while they are looking skyward after their hats. Carson streets seldom look inactive on Summer afternoons, because there are so many citizens skipping around their escaping hats, like chambermaids trying to head off a spider.

The "Washoe Zephyr" (Washoe is a pet nickname for Nevada) is a peculiarly Scriptural wind, in that no man knoweth "whence it cometh." That is to say, where it *originates*. It comes right over the mountains from the West, but when one crosses the ridge he does not find any of it on the other side! It probably is manufactured on the mountain-top for the occasion, and starts from there. It is a pretty regular wind, in the summer time. Its office hours are from two in the afternoon till two the next morning; and anybody venturing abroad during those twelve hours needs to allow for the wind or he will bring up a mile or two to leeward of the point he is aiming at. And yet the first complaint a Washoe visitor to San Francisco makes, is that the sea winds blow so, there! There is a good deal of human nature in that.

[Pocket Mining: Tuolumne, California]

BY AND BY an old friend of mine, a miner, came down from one of the decayed mining camps of Tuolumne, California, and I went back with him. We lived in a small cabin on a verdant hillside, and there were not five other cabins in view over the wide expanse of hill and forest. Yet a flourishing city of two or three thousand population had occupied this grassy dead solitude during the flush times of twelve or fifteen years before, and where our cabin stood had once been the heart of the teeming hive, the centre of the city. When the mines gave out the town fell into decay, and in a few years wholly disappeared—streets, dwellings, shops, everything—and left no sign. The grassy slopes were as green and smooth and desolate of life as if they had never been disturbed. The mere handful of miners still remaining, had seen the town spring up, spread, grow and flourish in its pride; and they had seen it sicken and die, and pass away like a dream. With it their hopes had died, and their zest of life. They had long ago resigned themselves to their exile, and ceased to correspond with their distant friends or turn longing eyes toward their early homes. They had accepted banishment, forgotten the world and been forgotten of the world. They were far from telegraphs and railroads, and they stood, as it were, in a living grave, dead to the events that stirred the globe's great populations, dead to the common interests of men, isolated and outcast from brotherhood with their kind. It was the most singular, and almost the most touching and melancholy exile that fancy can imagine.—One of my associates in this locality, for two or three months, was a man who had had a university education; but now for eighteen years he had decayed there by inches, a bearded, rough-clad, clay-stained miner, and at times, among his sighings and soliloquizings, he unconsciously interjected vaguely remembered Latin and Greek sentences—dead and musty tongues, meet vehicles for the thoughts of one whose dreams were all of the past, whose life was a failure; a tired man, burdened with the present, and indifferent to the future; a man without ties, hopes, interests, waiting for rest and the end.

In that one little corner of California is found a species of mining which is seldom or never mentioned in print. It is called "pocket mining" and I am not aware that any of it is done outside of that little corner. The gold is not evenly distributed through the surface dirt, as in ordinary placer mines, but is collected in little spots, and they are very wide apart and exceedingly hard to find, but when you do find one you reap a rich and sudden harvest. There are not more than twenty pocket miners in that entire little region. I think I know every one of them personally. I have known one of them to hunt patiently about the hillsides every day for eight months without finding gold enough to make a snuff-box—his grocery bill running up relentlessly all the time—and then find a pocket and take out of it two thousand dollars in two dips of his shovel. I have known him to take out three thousand dollars in two hours, and go and pay up every cent of his indebtedness, then enter on a dazzling spree that finished the last of his treasure before the night was gone. And the next day he bought his groceries on credit as usual, and shouldered his pan and shovel and went off to the hills hunting pockets again happy and content. This is the most fascinating of all the different kinds of mining, and furnishes a very handsome percentage of victims to the lunatic asylum.

Pocket hunting is an ingenious process. You take a spadeful of earth from the hill-side and put it in a large tin pan and dissolve and wash it gradually away till nothing is left but a teaspoonful of fine sediment. Whatever gold was in that earth has remained, because, being the heaviest, it has sought the bottom. Among the sediment you will find half a dozen yellow particles no larger than pin-heads. You are delighted. You move off to one side and wash another pan. If you find gold again, you move to one side further, and wash a third pan. If you find *no* gold this time, you are delighted again, because you know you are on the right scent. You lay an imaginary plan, shaped like a fan, with its handle up the hill—for just where the end of the handle is, you argue that the rich deposit lies hidden, whose vagrant grains of gold have escaped and been washed down the hill, spreading farther and farther apart as they wandered. And so you proceed up the hill, washing the earth and narrowing your lines every time the absence of gold in the pan shows that you are outside the spread of the fan; and at last, twenty yards up the hill your lines have converged to a point—a single foot from that point you cannot find any gold. Your breath comes short and quick, you are feverish with excitement; the dinner-bell may ring its clapper off, you pay no attention; friends may die, weddings transpire, houses burn down, they are nothing to you; you sweat and dig and delve with a frantic interest—and all at once you strike it! Up comes a spadeful of earth and quartz that is all lovely with soiled lumps and leaves and sprays of gold. Sometimes that one spadeful is all—$500. Sometimes the next contains $10,000, and it takes you three or four days to get it all out. The pocket-miners tell of one nest that yielded $60,000 and two men exhausted it in two weeks, and then sold the ground for $10,000 to a party who never got $300 out of it afterward.

The hogs are good pocket hunters. All the summer they root around the bushes, and turn up a thousand little piles of dirt, and then the miners long for the rains; for the rains beat upon these little piles and wash them down and expose the gold, possibly right over a pocket. Two pockets were found in this way by the same man in one day. One had $5,000 in it and the other $8,000. That man could appreciate it, for he hadn't had a cent for about a year.

1872

Walt Whitman

From Specimen Days

This was Whitman's second Western tour (see the headnote to "Song of the Redwood-Tree" in Landscape as Idea: Romantic Prose and Poetry). Whitman is an ecstatic and uncritical witness to the Myth of the West: for him, both the land and its people were the fulfillment of America's Manifest Destiny.

[Western Tour]

BEGIN A LONG JAUNT WEST

The following three or four months (Sept. to Dec. '79) I made quite a western journey, fetching up at Denver, Colorado, and penetrating the Rocky Mountain region enough to get a good notion of it all. . . .

IN THE SLEEPER

What a fierce weird pleasure to lie in my berth at night in the luxurious palace-car, drawn by the mighty Baldwin—embodying, and filling me, too, full of the swiftest motion, and most resistless strength! It is late, perhaps midnight or after—distances join'd like magic—as we speed through Harrisburg, Columbus, Indianapolis. The element of danger adds zest to it all. On we go, rumbling and flashing, with our loud whinnies thrown out from time to time, or trumpet-blasts, into the darkness. Passing the homes of men, the farms, barns, cattle—the silent villages. And the car itself, the sleeper, with curtains drawn and lights turn'd down—in the berths the slumberers, many of them women and children—as on, on, on, we fly like lightning through the night—how strangely sound and sweet they sleep! (They say the French Voltaire in his time designated the grand opera and a ship of war the most signal illustrations of the growth of humanity's and art's advance beyond primitive barbarism. Perhaps if the witty philosopher were here these days, and went in the same car with perfect bedding and feed from New York to San Francisco, he would shift his type and sample to one of our American sleepers.)

MISSOURI STATE

. . . As I cross'd Missouri State the whole distance by the St. Louis and Kansas City Northern Railroad, a fine early autumn day, I thought my eyes had never looked on scenes of greater pastoral beauty. For over two hundred miles successive rolling prairies, agriculturally perfect view'd by Pennsylvania and New Jersey eyes, and dotted here and there with fine timber. Yet fine as the land is, it isn't the finest portion; (there is a bed of impervious clay and hard-pan beneath this section that holds water too firmly, "drowns the land in wet weather, and bakes it in dry," as a cynical farmer told me.) South are some richer tracts, though perhaps the beauty-spots of the State are the northwestern counties. Altogether, I am clear, (now, and from what I have seen and learn'd since,) that Missouri, in climate, soil, relative situation, wheat, grass, mines, railroads, and every important materialistic respect, stands in the front rank of the Union. Of Missouri averaged politically and socially I have heard all sorts of talk, some pretty severe—but I should have no fear myself of getting along safely and comfortably anywhere among the Missourians. They raise a good deal of tobacco. You see at this time quantities of the light greenish-gray leaves pulled and hanging out to dry on temporary frameworks or rows of sticks. Looks much like the mullein familiar to eastern eyes. . . .

THE PRAIRIES (*And an Undeliver'd Speech*)

At a large popular meeting at Topeka—the Kansas State Silver Wedding, fifteen or twenty thousand people—I had been erroneously bill'd to deliver a poem. As I seem'd to be made much of, and wanted to be good-natured, I hastily pencill'd out the following little speech. Unfortunately, (or fortunately,) I had such a good time and rest, and talk and dinner, with the U. boys, that I let the hours slip away and didn't drive over to the meeting and speak my piece. But here it is just the same:

> "My friends, your bills announce me as giving a poem; but I have no poem—have composed none for this occasion. And I can honestly say I am now glad of it. Under these skies resplendent in September beauty—amid the peculiar landscape you are used to, but which is new to me—these interminable and stately prairies—in the freedom and vigor and sane enthusiasm of this perfect western air and autumn sunshine—it seems to me a poem would be almost an impertinence. But if you care to have a word from me, I should speak it about these very prairies; they impress me most, of all the objective shows I see or have seen on this, my first real visit to the West. As I have roll'd rapidly hither for more than a thousand miles, through fair Ohio, through bread-raising Indiana and Illinois—through ample Missouri, that contains and raises everything; as I have partially explor'd your charming city during the last two days, and, standing on Oread hill, by the university, have launch'd my view across broad expanses of living green, in every direction—I have again been most impress'd, I say, and shall remain for the rest of my life most impress'd, with that feature of the topography of your western central world—that vast Something, stretching out on its own unbounded scale, unconfined, which there is in these prairies, combining the real and ideal, and beautiful as dreams.
>
> "I wonder indeed if the people of this continental inland West know how much of first-class *art* they have in these prairies—how original and all your own—how much of the influences of a character for your future humanity, broad, patriotic, heroic and new? how entirely they tally on

land the grandeur and superb monotony of the skies of heaven, and the ocean with its waters? how freeing, soothing, nourishing they are to the soul?

"Then is it not subtly they who have given us our leading modern Americans, Lincoln and Grant?—vast-spread, average men—their foregrounds of character altogether practical and real, yet (to those who have eyes to see) with finest backgrounds of the ideal, towering high as any. And do we not see, in them, foreshadowings of the future races that shall fill these prairies?

"Not but what the Yankee and Atlantic States, and every other part—Texas, and the States flanking the south-east and the Gulf of Mexico—the Pacific shore empire—the Territories and Lakes, and the Canada line (the day is not yet, but it will come, including Canada entire)—are equally and integrally and indissolubly this Nation, the *sine qua non* of the human, political and commercial New World. But this favor'd central area of (in round numbers) two thousand miles square seems fated to be the home both of what I would call America's distinctive ideas and distinctive realities." . . .

AN HOUR ON KENOSHA SUMMIT

Jottings from the Rocky Mountains, mostly pencill'd during a day's trip over the South Park RR., returning from Leadville, and especially the hour we were detain'd, (much to my satisfaction,) at Kenosha summit. As afternoon advances, novelties, far-reaching splendors, accumulate under the bright sun in this pure air. But I had better commence with the day.

The confronting of Platte cañon just at dawn, after a ten miles' ride in early darkness on the rail from Denver—the seasonable stoppage at the entrance of the cañon, and good breakfast of eggs, trout, and nice griddle-cakes—then as we travel on, and get well in the gorge, all the wonders, beauty, savage power of the scene—the wild stream of water, from sources of snows, brawling continually in sight one side—the dazzling sun, and the morning lights on the rocks—such turns and grades in the track, squirming around corners, or up and down hills—far glimpses of a hundred peaks, titanic necklaces, stretching north and south—the huge rightly-named Dome-rock—and as we dash along, others similar, simple, monolithic, elephantine.

AN EGOTISTICAL "FIND"

"I have found the law of my own poems," was the unspoken but more-and-more decided feeling that came to me as I pass'd, hour after hour, amid all this grim yet joyous elemental abandon—this plenitude of material, entire absence of art, untrammel'd play of primitive Nature—the chasm, the gorge, the crystal mountain stream, repeated scores, hundreds of miles—the broad handling and absolute uncrampedness—the fantastic forms, bathed in transparent browns, faint reds and grays, towering sometimes a thousand, sometimes two or three thousand feet high—at their tops now and then huge masses pois'd, and mixing with the clouds, with only their outlines, hazed in misty lilac, visible. ("In Nature's grandest shows," says an old Dutch writer, an ecclesiastic, "amid the ocean's depth, if so might be, or countless worlds rolling above at night, a man thinks of them, weighs all, not for themselves or the abstract, but with reference to his own personality, and how they may affect him or color his destinies.")

NEW SENSES: NEW JOYS

We follow the stream of amber and bronze brawling along its bed, with its frequent cascades and snow-white foam. Through the cañon we fly—mountains not only each side, but seemingly, till we get near, right in front of us—every rood a new view flashing, and each flash defying description—on the almost perpendicular sides, clinging pines, cedars, spruces, crimson sumach bushes, spots of wild grass—but dominating all, those towering rocks, rocks, rocks, bathed in delicate vari-colors, with the clear sky of autumn overhead. New senses, new joys, seem develop'd. Talk as you like, a typical Rocky Mountain cañon, or a limitless sea-like stretch of the great Kansas or Colorado plains, under favoring circumstances, tallies, perhaps expresses, certainly awakes, those grandest and subtlest element-emotions in the human soul, that all the marble temples and sculptures from Phidias to Thorwaldsen—all paintings, poems, reminiscences, or even music, probably never can.

STEAM-POWER, TELEGRAPHS, ETC.

I get out on a ten minutes' stoppage at Deer creek, to enjoy the unequal'd combination of hill, stone and wood. As we speed again, the yellow granite in the sunshine, with natural spires, minarets, castellated perches far aloft—then long stretches of straight-upright palisades, rhinoceros color—then gamboge and tinted chromos. Ever the best of my pleasures the cool-fresh Colorado atmosphere, yet sufficiently warm. Signs of man's restless advent and pioneerage, hard as Nature's face is—deserted dug-outs by dozens in the side-hills—the scantling-hut, the telegraph-pole, the smoke of some impromptu chimney or outdoor fire—at intervals little settlements of log-houses, or parties of surveyors or telegraph builders, with their comfortable tents. Once, a canvas office where you could send a message by electricity anywhere around the world! Yes, pronounc'd signs of the man of latest dates, dauntlessly grappling with these grisliest shows of the old kosmos. At several places steam saw-mills, with their piles of logs and boards, and the pipes puffing. Occasionally Platte cañon expanding into a grassy flat of a few acres. At one such place, toward the end, where we stop, and I get out to stretch my legs, as I look skyward, or rather mountain-topward, a huge hawk or eagle (a rare sight here) is idly soaring, balancing along the ether, now sinking low and coming quite near, and then up again in stately-lanquid circles—then higher, higher, slanting to the north, and gradually out of sight. . . .

ART FEATURES

Talk, I say again, of going to Europe, of visiting the ruins of feudal castles, or Coliseum remains, or kings' palaces—when you can come *here.* The alternations one gets, too; after the Illinois and Kansas prairies of a thousand miles—smooth and easy areas of the corn and wheat of ten million democratic farms in the future—here start up in every conceivable presentation of shape, these non-utilitarian piles, coping the skies, emanating a beauty, terror, power, more than Dante or Angelo ever knew. Yes, I think the chyle of not only poetry and painting, but oratory, and even the metaphysics and music fit for the New World, before being finally assimilated, need first and feeding visits here.

Mountain streams.—The spiritual contrast and etheriality of the whole region consist largely to me in its never-absent peculiar streams—the snows of inaccessible upper areas melting and running down through the gorges continually. Nothing like the water of pastoral plains, or creeks with wooded banks and turf, or anything of the kind elsewhere. The shapes that element takes in the shows of the globe cannot be fully understood by an artist until he has studied these unique rivulets.

Aerial effects.—But perhaps as I gaze around me the rarest sight of all is in atmospheric hues. The prairies—as I cross'd them in my journey hither—and these mountains and parks, seem to me to afford new lights and shades. Everywhere the aerial gradations and sky-effects inimitable; nowhere else such perspectives, such transparent lilacs and grays. I can conceive of some superior landscape painter, some fine colorist, after sketching awhile out here, discarding all his previous work, delightful to stock exhibition amateurs, as muddy, raw and artificial. Near one's eye ranges an infinite variety; high up, the bare whitey-brown, above timber line; in certain spots afar patches of snow any time of year; (no trees, no flowers, no birds, at those chilling altitudes.) As I write I see the Snowy Range through the blue mist, beautiful and far off. I plainly see the patches of snow.

1882

Richard Harding Davis

From The West from a Car Window

If Whitman was an enthusiastic booster of the myth of the frontier, Davis, in his descriptions of "what impressed an Eastern man in a hurried trip through the Western States," was an equally enthusiastic debunker of that myth. Instead of a "Wild West" he found a "mild West"—a West hungry for the money to be gained from mining, ranching, and real estate and anxiously eager to emulate the East in its fashions as well as in its values. Stephen Crane read Davis's book before he took his own Western tour, and Crane, too, tried to de-mythologize what he found there (see for example, "The Blue Hotel" in Landscape as Antagonist).

A Three-Year-Old City

THE ONLY INTEREST which the East can take in Oklahoma City for some time to come must be the same as that with which one regards a portrait finished by a lightning crayon artist, "with frame complete," in ten minutes. We may have seen better portraits and more perfect coloring, but we have never watched one completed, as it were, "while you wait." People long ago crowded to see Master Betty act, not because there were no better actors in those days, but because he was so very young to do it so very well. It was as a freak of nature, a Josef Hoffman of the drama, that they considered him, and Oklahoma City must content itself with being only of interest as yet as a freak of our civilization.

After it has decided which of the half-dozen claimants to each of its town sites is the only one, and the others have stopped appealing to higher and higher courts, and have left the law alone and have reduced their attention strictly to business, and the city has been burned down once or twice, and had its Treasurer default and its Mayor impeached, and has been admitted to the National Baseball League, it may hope to be regarded as a full-grown rival city; but at present, as far as it concerns the far East, it is interesting chiefly as a city that grew up overnight, and did in three years or less what other towns have accomplished only after half a century.

The history of its pioneers and their invasion of their undiscovered country not only shows how far the West is from the East, but how much we have changed our ways of doing things from the days of the Pilgrim Fathers to those of the modern pilgrims, the "boomers" and "sooners" of the end of the century. We have seen pictures in our school-books, and pictures which Mr. Boughton has made for us, of the *Mayflower's* people kneeling on the shore, the long, anxious voyage behind them, and the "rock-bound coast" of their new home before them, with the Indians looking on doubtfully from behind the pine-trees. It makes a very interesting picture—those stern-faced pilgrims in their knickerbockers and broad white collars; each man strong in the consciousness that he has resisted persecution and overcome the perils of the sea, and is ready to meet the perils of an unknown land. I should like you to place in contrast with this the opening of Oklahoma Territory to the new white settlers three years ago. These modern pilgrims stand in rows twenty deep, separated from the promised land not by an ocean, but by a line scratched in the earth with the point of a soldier's bayonet. The long row toeing this line are bending forward, panting with excitement, and looking with greedy eyes towards the new Canaan, the women with their dresses tucked up to their knees, the men stripped of coats and waistcoats for the coming race. And then, a trumpet call, answered by a thousand hungry yells from all along the line, and hundreds of men and women on foot and on horseback break away across the prairie, the stronger pushing down the weak, and those on horseback riding over and in some cases killing those on foot, in a mad, unseemly race for something which they are getting for nothing. These pilgrims do not drop on one knee to give thanks decorously, as did Columbus according to the twenty-dollar bills, but fall on both knees, and hammer stakes into the ground and pull them up again, and drive them down somewhere else, at a place which they hope will eventually become a corner lot facing the post-office, and drag up the next man's stake, and threaten him with a Winchester because he is on *their* land, which they have owned for the last three minutes. And there are no Indians in this scene. They have been paid one dollar and twenty-five cents an acre for the land, which is worth five dollars an acre as it lies, before a spade has been driven into it or a bit of timber cut, and they are safely out of the way.

Oklahoma Territory, which lies in the most fertile part of the Indian Territory, equally distant from Kansas and Texas, was thrown open to white settlers at noon on the 22d of April, 1889. To appreciate the Oklahoma City of this day, it is necessary to go back to the Oklahoma of three years ago. The city at that time consisted of a railroad station, a section house and water-tank, the home of the railroad agent, and four other small buildings. The rest was prairie-land, with low curving hills covered with high grass and bunches of thick timber; this as far as the eye could see, and nothing else. This land, which is rich and black and soft, and looks like chocolate where the plough has turned the sod, was thrown open by the proclamation of the President to white settlers, who could on such a day, at such an hour, "enter and occupy it" for homestead holdings. A homestead holding is one hundred and sixty acres of land. The proclamation said nothing about town sites, or of the division of town sites into "lots" for stores, or of streets and cross-streets. But several bodies of men in different parts of Kansas prepared plans long before the opening, for a town to be laid out around the station, the water-tank, and the other buildings where Oklahoma City now stands, and had their surveyors and their blue prints hidden away in readiness for the 22d of April. All of those who intended to enter this open-to-all-comers race for land knew that the prairie around the station would be laid out into lots. Hence that station and other stations which in time would become cities were the goals for which over forty thousand people raced from the borders of the new Territory. So many of these "beat the pistol" on the start and reached the goal first that, in consequence, the efforts ever since to run this race over again through the law courts has kept Oklahoma City from growing with even more marvellous rapidity than it already has done. . . .

It is much more pleasant to write of these early days of Oklahoma City than of the Oklahoma City of the present, although one of its citizens would not find it so, for he regards his adopted home with a fierce local pride and jealousy almost equal to a Chicagoan's love for Chicago, which is saying a very great deal. But to the transient visitor Oklahoma City of to-day, after he has recovered from the shock its extent and solidity give him, is dispiriting and unprofitable to a degree. This may partly be accounted for by the circumstance that his only means of entering it from the south by train is, or was at the time I visited it, at four o'clock in the morning. No one, after having been dragged out of his berth and dropped into a cold misty well of darkness, punctured only by the light from the brakeman's lantern and a smoking omnibus lamp, is in a mood to grow enthusiastic over the city about him. And the fact that the hotel is crowded, and that he must sleep with the barkeeper, does not tend to raise his spirits. I can heartily recommend this method of discouraging immigration to the authorities of any already overcrowded city.

But as the sun comes up, one sees the remarkable growth of this city—remarkable not only for its extent in so short a period, but for the come-to-stay air about many of its buildings. There are stone banks and stores, and an opera-house, and rows of brick buildings with dwelling-rooms above, and in the part of the city where the people go to sleep hundreds of wooden houses, fashioned after the architecture of the sea-shore cottages of the Jersey coast; for the climate is mild the best part of the year. There are also churches of stone and brick and stained glass, and a flour-mill, and three or four newspapers, and courts of law, and boards of trade. But with all of these things, which show a steadily improving growth after the mushroom nature of its birth, Oklahoma City cannot or has not yet shaken off the attributes with which it was born, and which in a community founded by law and purchase would not exist. For speculation in land, whether in lots on the main street or in homestead holdings on the prairie, and the excitement of real estate transfers, and the battle for rights in the courts, seem to be the prevailing and ruling passion of the place. Gambling in real estate is as much in the air as is the spirit of the Louisiana State Lottery in New Orleans. Every one in Oklahoma City seems to live, in part at least, by transferring real estate to some one else, and the lawyers and real-estate agents live by helping them to do it. It reminded me of that happy island in the Pacific seas where every one took in every one else's washing. This may sound unfair, but it is not in the least exaggerated. The town swarms with lawyers, and is overrun with real-estate offices. The men you meet and the men you pass in the street are not discussing the weather or the crops or the news of the outside world, but you hear them say: "I'll appeal it, by God!" "I'll spend every cent I've got, sir!" "They're a lot of 'sooners,' and I can prove it!" or, "Ted Hillman's lot on Prairie Avenue, that he sold for two hundred dollars, rose to three hundred in one week, and Abner Brown says he won't take six hundred for it now. . . ."

A man in Oklahoma City when the day's work is done has before him a prospect of broad red clayey streets, muddy after rain, bristling with dust after a drought, with the sun setting at one end of them into the prairie. He can go to his cottage, or to "The Turf," where he can lose some money at faro, or he can sit in one of the hotels, which are the clubs of the city, and talk cattle to strangers and real estate to citizens, or he can join a lodge and talk real estate there. Once or twice a week a "show" makes a one-night stand at the opera-house. The schools are not good for his children as yet, and the society that he is willing his wife should enjoy is limited. On Sunday he goes to church, and eats a large dinner in the middle of the day, and walks up to the top of the hill to look over the prairie where he and many others would like to build, but which must remain empty until the twelve different disputants for each holding have stopped appealing to higher courts. This is actually the case, and the reason the city has not spread as others around it have done. As the Romans shortened their swords to extend their boundaries, so the people of Oklahoma City might cut down some of their higher courts and increase theirs.

I have given this sketch of Oklahoma City as it impressed itself on me, because I think any man who can afford a hall bedroom and a gas-stove in New York City is better off than he would be as the owner of one hundred and sixty acres on the prairie, or in one of these small so-called cities.

At a New Mining Camp

MY ONLY IDEAS of a new mining camp before I visited Creede were derived from an early and eager study of Bret Harte. Not that I expected to see one of his mining camps or his own people when I visited Creede, but the few ideas of miners and their ways and manners that I had were those which he had given me. I should have liked, although I did not expect it, to see the outcasts of Poker Flat before John Oakhurst, in his well-fitting frock-coat, had left the outfit, and Yuba Bill pulling up his horses in front of the Lone Star saloon, where Colonel Starbuckle, with one elbow resting on the bar, and with his high white hat tipped to one side, waited to do him honor. I do not know that Bret Harte ever said that Colonel Starbuckle had a white hat, but I always pictured him in it, and with a black stock. I wanted to hear people say, "Waal, stranger," and to see auburn-haired giants in red shirts, with bags of gold-dust and nuggets of silver, and much should I have liked to meet Rose of Toulumne. But all that I found at Creede which reminded me of these miners and gamblers and the chivalric extravagant days of '49 were a steel pan, like a frying-pan without a handle, which I recognized with a thrill as the pan for washing gold, and a pick in the corner of a cabin; and once when a man hailed me as "Pardner" on the mountain-side, and asked "What luck?" The men and the scenes in this new silver camp showed what might have existed in the more glorious sunshine of California, but they were dim and commonplace, and lacked the sharp, clear-cut personality of Bret Harte's men and scenes. They were like the negative of a photograph which has been under-exposed, and which no amount of touching up will make clear. So I will not attempt to touch them up. . . .

Creede lies in a gully between two great mountains. In the summer the mountain streams wash down into this gully and turn it into a little river; but with the recklessness of true gamblers, the people who came to Creede built their stores, houses, and saloons as near the base of the great sides of the valley as they could, and if the stream comes next summer, as it has done for hundreds of years before, it will carry with it fresh pine houses and log huts instead of twigs and branches.

The train stopped at the opening of this gully, and its passengers jumped out into two feet of mud and snow. The ticket and telegraph office on one side of the track were situated in a freight car with windows and doors cut out of it, and with the familiar blue and white sign of the Western Union nailed to one end; that station was typical of the whole town in its rawness, and in the temporary and impromptu air of its inhabitants. If you looked back at the road over which you had just come, you saw the beautiful circle of the Wagon Wheel Gap, a chain of magnificent mountains white with snow, picked with hundreds of thousands of pine-trees so high above one that they looked like little black pins. The clouds, less white than the snow, lay packed in between the peaks of the range, or drifted from one to another to find a resting-place, and the sun, beating down on both a blinding glare, showed other mountains and other snow-capped ranges for fifty miles beyond. This is at the opening of Willow Gulch into which Creede has hurried and the sides of which it has tramped into mud and covered with hundreds of little pine boxes of houses and log-cabins, and the simple quadrangles of four planks which mark a building site. In front of you is a village of fresh pine. There is not a brick, a painted front, nor an awning in the whole town. It is like a city of fresh card-board, and the pine shanties seem to trust for support to the rocky sides of the gulch into which they have squeezed themselves. In the street are ox-teams, mules, men, and donkeys loaded with ore, crowding each other familiarly, and sinking knee-deep in the mud. Furniture and kegs of beer, bedding and canned provisions, clothing and half-open packing-cases, and piles of raw lumber are heaped up in front of the new stores—or those still to be built—stores of canvas only, stores with canvas tops and foundations of logs, and houses with the Leadville front, where the upper boards have been left square instead of following the sloping angle of the roof.

It is more like a circus-tent, which has sprung up overnight and which may be removed on the morrow, than a town, and you cannot but feel that the people about you are a part of the show. A great shaft of rock that rises hundreds of feet above the lower town gives the little village at its base an absurdly pushing, impudent air, and the silence of the mountains around from ten to fourteen thousand feet high, makes the confusion of hammers and the cries of the drivers swearing at their mules in the mud and even the random blasts from the mines futile and ridiculous. It is more strange and fantastic at night, when it appears to one looking down from half-way up the mountain like a camp of gypsies at the foot of a cañon. On the raw pine fronts shine electric lights in red and blue globes, mixing with the hot, smoky glare rising from the saloons and gambling-houses, and striking upward far enough to show the signs of The Holy Moses Saloon, The Theatre Comique, The Keno, and The Little Delmonico against the face of the great rock at their back doors, but only suggesting the greater mass of it which towers majestically above, hidden somewhere in the night. It is as incongruous as an excursion boat covered with colored lights, and banging out popular airs at the base of the Palisades.

The town of Creede is in what is known as the King Solomon district; it is three hundred and twenty miles from Denver, and lies directly in the pathway of the Great Divide. Why it was not discovered sooner, why, indeed, there is one square foot of land in Colorado containing silver not yet discovered, is something which the Eastern mind cannot grasp. Colorado is a State, not a country, and in that State the mines of Leadville, Aspen, Ouray, Clear Creek County, Telluride, Boulder, Silverton, and Cripple Creek, have yielded up in the last year forty million dollars. If the State has done that much, it can do more; and I could not understand why any one in Colorado should remain contentedly at home selling ribbons when there must be other mines to be had for the finding. A prospector is, after all, very much like a tramp, but with a knowledge of minerals, a pick, rations, a purpose, and—hope. We know how many tramps we have in the East; imagine, then, all of these, instead of wandering lazily and purposelessly from farm-house to farm-house, stopping instead to hammer at a bit of rock, or stooping to pick up every loose piece they find. One would think that with a regular army like this searching everywhere in Colorado no one acre of it would by this time have remained unclaimed. But this new town of Creede, once known only as Willow Gap, was discovered but twenty months ago, and it was not until December last that the railway reached it, and, as I have said, there is not a station there yet. . . .

The shaft of the Last Chance Mine is at the top of the Bachelor Mountain, and one has to climb and slip for an hour and a half to reach it. A very nice

Yale boy guided me there, and seemed as willing as myself to sit down in the snow every ten minutes and look at the scenery. But we saw much more of the scenery than of the mine, because there was more of it to see, and there was no general manager to prevent us from looking as long as we liked. The trail led over fallen logs and up slippery rocks caked with ice and through drifts of snow higher than one's head, and the pines accompanied us all the way with branches bent to the mountain-side with the weight of the snow, and a cold, cheery mountain stream appeared and disappeared from under long bridges of ice and mocked at us for our slow progress. But we gave it a very close race coming down. Sometimes we walked in the cold, dark shadows of the pines, where hardly a ray of sunlight came, and again the trail would cross a land-slide, and the wind brought strong odors of the pine and keen, icy blasts from the snow-capped ranges which stretched before us for fifty miles, and we could see Creede lying at our feet like a box of spilled jackstraws. Every now and then we met long lines of burros carrying five bags of ore each, with but twenty dollars' worth of silver scattered through each load, and we could hear the voice of the driver from far up above and the tinkle of the bell as they de-scended upon us. Sometimes they made way for us or halted timidly with curious, patient eyes, and sometimes they shouldered us promptly backward into three feet of snow. It was a lonely, impressive journey, and the wonderful beauty and silence of the mountain made words impertinent. And, again, we would come upon a solitary prospector tapping at the great rock in front of him, and only stopping to dip his hot face and blistered hands into the snow about him, before he began to drive the steel bar again with the help which hope gave him. His work but for this ingredient would seem futile, foolish, and impos-sible. Why, he would ask himself, should I work against this stone safe day after day only to bore a hole in its side as minute as a nail's point in the front of a house, and a thousand rods, probably, from where the hole should be? And then hope tells him that perhaps the very next stroke will make him a million-aire like Creede, and so he makes the next stroke, and the next, and the next.

If ever I own a silver mine, I am going to have it situated at the base of a mountain, and not at the top. I would not care to take that journey we made to the Chance every day. I would rather sit in the office below and read reports. After one gets there, the best has been seen. . . . which certainly ought to ac-count for several things. I expected to be led into a tunnel, and to be shown delicate veins of white silver running around the sides, which one could cut out with a penknife and make into scarf-pins and watch guards. If not, from whence, then, do the nuggets come that the young and disappointed lover sends as a wedding present to the woman who should have married him, when she marries some other man who has sensibly remained in the East—a present, in-deed, which has always struck me as extremely economical, and much cheaper than standing-lamps. But I saw no silver nuggets. One of the workmen showed us a hole in the side of the mountain which he assured us was the Last Chance Mine, and that out of this hole one hundred and eighty thousand dollars came every month. He then handed us a piece of red stone and a piece of black stone, and said that when these two stones were found together silver was not far off. To one thirsting for a sight of the precious metal this was about as satisfying as being told that after the invitations had been sent out and the awning stretched over the sidewalk there was a chance of a dance in the neighborhood. I was also told that the veins lie between walls of porphyry and trachyte, but that there is not a distinctly marked difference, as the walls resemble each other closely. This may or may not be true; it is certainly not interesting, and I regret that I cannot satisfy the mining expert as to the formation of the mine, or tell him whether or not the vein is a heavy galena running so much per cent of lead, or a dry silicious ore, or whether the ore bodies were north and south, and are or are not true fissures, and at what angle the contact or body veins cut these same fissures. All of this I should have ascertained had the general manager been more genial; but we cannot expect one man to combine the riches of Montezuma and the graces of Chesterfield. One is sure to destroy the other. . . .

Of the inner life of Creede I saw nothing; I mean the real business of the place—the speculation in real estate and in mines. Capitalists came every day, and were carried off up the mountains to look at a hole in the ground, and down again to see the assay tests of the ore taken from it. Prospectors scoured the sides of the mountains from sundawn to sunset, and at night their fires lit up the range, and their little heaps of stone and their single stick, with their name scrawled on it in pencil, made the mountains look like great burying-grounds. All of the land within two miles of Creede was claimed by these simple proofs of ownership—simple, yet as effectual as a parchment sealed and signed. When the snow has left the mountains, and these claims can be worked, it will be time enough to write the real history of the rise or fall of Creede.

1892

William Gilpin

From The Central Gold Region

The flamboyant Gilpin accompanied Frémont on his 1843 expedition to Oregon and Northern California, joined Thomas Hart Bention in promoting a central route for the transcontinental railroad and was first governor of the territory of Colorado. "Each of Gilpin's cosmic generalizations," writes Daniel Boorstin in *The Americans: The National Experience,* "resounded with booster overtones for the projects in which he happened to be interested." In the Mississippi Valley he proposed a new national capitol along that "supreme artery" the Missouri River at a site which he happened to own. When he moved to Denver, that city became his new "focal point of impregnable power in the topographical configuration of the continent." Gilpin thus demonstrates both the perennial allure of the pastoral ideal and its transformation, during the last half of the nineteenth century, into self-interested advertisement.

The Great Basin of the Mississippi

THE MOST REMARKABLE FEATURE of America is the Basin of the Mississippi. As yet the popular mind does not clearly comprehend its dimensions, and the understanding of its physical characteristics is indistinct and vague. It is bisected through its centre by a supreme artery, which above St. Louis has received the name of the Missouri, and below, the Mississippi river. This is 5000 miles in length, and its surface is a continuous inclined plane, descending seven inches in the mile. Into this central artery, as into a common *trough,* descend innumerable rivers, coming from the great mountain chains of the continent. All of the immense area thus drained, forms a single *basin,* of which the mountains form the rim. It may also be called an *amphitheatre,* embracing 1,123,100 miles of surface. This has been, during the antediluvian ages, the bed of a great ocean, such as is now the Gulf of Mexico or the Mediterranean, above the surface of which the mountains protruded themselves as islands. Gradually filled up by the filtration of the water during countless ages, it has reached its present altitude above the other basins, over which the oceans now still roll, and into which the waters have retired. The "Basin of the Mississippi" is then a pavement many thousand feet in depth, formed by the sediment of the superincumbent water, deposited stratum upon stratum, compressed by its weight and crystallized into rock by its chemical fermentation and pressure. It is in exact imitation of this sublime process of the natural world, that every housewife compresses the milk of her dairy into solid cheese and butter. It is, therefore, a homogeneous, undulating plain of the *secondary* or sedimentary formation, surmounted by a covering of soil from which springs the vegetation, as hair from the external skin of an animal. Through this coating of soil, and into the soft surface strata of rock, the descending fresh waters burrow their channels, converging everywhere from the circumferent rim to the lowest level and pass out to the sea. In this system, which is the same as the circulation of the blood in animal life, the Missouri river and the minutest rill that flows from a garden fountain has each its specific and conspicuous place. Hence the corresponding order in the undulations, the variety, and the complexity of contour in the surface and in its vegetation.

Such is this vast Basin, whose transverse diameter is 2500 miles, and so simple, homogeneous, and clear is the system of its geology and its waters. . . .

All that portion of the Mississippi Basin lying between the Mississippi river and the Atlantic, is densely timbered, excepting only a portion of Indiana, Illinois, and Wisconsin; so also are the States of Louisiana, Arkansas, and South Missouri. An irregular line from the head of Lake Erie, running towards the south and west into Texas, defines the cessation of the timber. Between this line and the sea exists a continuous forest region, perpetually moistened by showers from the ocean. Beyond this line, and deeper into the continent, the upland ceases to nourish timber, which is replaced by luxuriant annual grasses, though narrow lines of forest continue upon the saturated bottoms of the rivers and in the islands. This is the Prairie region of luxuriant, annual grasses, and soft, arable soil, over which the fires annually sweep after the decay of vegetation. The termination of this belt is marked by an irregular line parallel to the first, where the rains cease, and the timber entirely disappears. It is about 450 miles in width, and within it artificial irrigation is not practised, nor necessary, it being everywhere soft, arable, and fertile. To this succeeds the immense rainless region onward to the mountains, exclusively pastoral, of a compact soil, coated with the dwarf buffalo grass, without trees, and the abode of the aboriginal cattle. That no desert does or can exist within this Basin, is manifest from the abundance and magnitude of the rivers, the uniform calcareous formation, the absence of a tropical sun, its longitudinal position across the temperate zone, and the greatness and altitude of the mountains on its western rim. The river system of the Mississippi Basin resembles a fan of palm leaf. The stem in the State of Louisiana rests in the Gulf; above, the affluent rivers converge to it from all parts of the compass. From the east come in the Homochitta, the Yazoo, the Ohio, the Illinois, and the Upper Mississippi. From the west, the Red river, the Washita, the Arkansas, the White, St. Francis, and Osage rivers, the Kansas, the Triple Platte, the L'eau qui Cours, and the Yellowstone, all navigable rivers of great length and importance. These rivers present a continuous navigable channel of 22,500 miles, having 45,000 miles of shore, an amount of navigation and coast equal to the Atlantic Ocean.

The area of the Mississippi Basin classifies itself into one-and-a-half fifths of compactly-growing forest, the same of prairie, and two-fifths of great plains. Through all of these the river system is ramified as minutely complex as are the veins and arteries of the human system.

The population is at present 12,000,000. The capacity for population is indefinite. . . . The Basin of the Mississippi will . . . more easily contain and feed ten times the population, or 1,310,000,000 of inhabitants! If the calcareous plain extending to the Arctic Sea, the two maritime fronts, and the mountain formation, be added, and the whole compared to Europe and Asia, 2,000,000,000 will easily find room—a population double the existing human race! This Basin is all within the Temperate Zone; but upon the shores of the Gulf, at the level of the sea, tropical fruits, flowers, and vegetation are produced. On the high mountain slopes grows the vegetation of the Arctic Zone. Between these are found every kind of agricultural production, as we descend from the extremes to the central medium. In position it is exactly central to the continent. Not far remote from the west bank of the Missouri river, in the bosom of romantic scenery and fertile prairie, is a spot where the Smokyhill and Republican rivers, by their confluence, form the Kansas. This is the geographical centre at once of the North American Continent, and of the Basin of the Mississippi. The circle described from this centre with a radius to San Francisco will pass through Vancouver on the Columbia, the port of Severn river on Hudson's Bay, through Quebec, through Boston, through Havana, Vera Cruz, and the city of Mexico. With a radius to the 49th°, a circle will pass through Mobile, New Orleans, and Matagorda. This spot is, therefore, the geographical centre of the North American Continent and of the Basin of the Mississippi, both at once. It is also equally the centre of the American Union, as it is now blocked out into existing States and into prospective States, to occupy sites in the now-existing Territories! Moreover, it is equidistant from, and exactly in, the middle between the two halves of the human family, distinctly concentrated; the one half Christians, occupying Western Europe, to the number of 259,000,000 of population; the other half Pagans, occupying Oriental Asia and Polynesia, to the number of 650,000,000! Europe has all the outlets of its inland seas and rivers towards the west, debouching on to our Atlantic front, towards which its whole surface slopes. Asia similarly presents to our Pacific front, an Oriental slope, containing her great rivers, the densest masses of her population, and detached islands of great area, dense population, and infinite production. The distance from the European to the Asian shores (from Paris to Pekin), travelling straight by the continuous river line of the Potomac, Ohio, Missouri, Platte, and Snake rivers, and across the two oceans, is only 10,000 geographic miles. This straight line is the axis of that temperate zone of the Northern Hemisphere of the globe, thirty-three degrees in width, which contains four-fifths of the land, nine-tenths of the people, and all the white races, commercial activity, and industry of the civilized world. When, therefore, this interval of North America shall be filled up, the affiliation of mankind will be accomplished, proximity recognised, the distraction of intervening oceans and equatorial heats cease, the remotest nations be grouped together and fused into one universal and convenient system of immediate relationship.

Such are some of the extraordinary attractions presented to mankind, as a social mass, by the position and configuration of the Mississippi Basin. There is another and superlative prospective view. This presents itself in contrasting the physical configuration of North America with the other continents.

Europe, the smallest in area of the continents, culminates in its centre into the icy masses of the Alps. From the glaciers, where all the great rivers have their sources, they descend the declivities and radiate to the different seas. The Danube flows directly east to the Pontic Sea; the Po, to the Adriatic; the Rhone, to the Sea of Lyons; the Rhine, north to the German Sea. Walled off by the Pyrenean and Carpathian Mountains, divergent and isolated, are the Tagus, the

Elbe, and other single rivers, affluents of the Baltic, the Atlantic, the Mediterranean, and the Pontic Sea. Descending from common radiant points and diverging every way from one another, no intercommunication exists among the rivers of Europe towards their sources; navigation is petty and feeble; art and commerce have never, during thirty centuries, united so many small valleys, remotely isolated by impenetrable barriers. Hence upon each river dwells a distinct people, differing from all the rest in race, language, religion, interests, and habits. Though often politically amalgamated by conquest, they again relapse into fragments, from innate geographical incoherence. Religious creeds and diplomacy form no more enduring bond. The history of these nations is a story of perpetual war, of mutual extermination: an appalling dramatic catalogue of a few splendid tyrannies crushing multitudinous millions of submissive and unchronicled serfs.

Exactly similar to Europe, though grander in size and population, is Asia. From the stupendous central barrier of the Himalayas run the four great rivers of China, due east, to discharge themselves under the rising sun: towards the south run the rivers of Cochin China, the Ganges, and the Indus: towards the west, the rivers of the Caspian: and north, through Siberia to the Arctic Sea, many rivers of the first magnitude. During fifty centuries, as now, the Alps and Himalaya Mountains have proved insuperable barriers to the amalgamation of the nations around their bases and dwelling in the valleys that radiate from their slopes. The continents of Africa and South America, as far as we are familiar with the details of their surfaces, are even more than these perplexed into dislocated fragments.

In contrast, the interior of North America presents towards heaven an expanded bowl, to receive and fuse into harmony whatsoever enters within its rim. So, each of the other continents presenting a bowl reversed, scatter everything from a central apex into radiant distraction. Political societies and empires have in all ages conformed themselves to these emphatic geographical facts. This Democratic Republican empire of North America is then predestined to expand and fit itself to the continent; to control the oceans on either hand, and eventually the continents beyond them. Much is uncertain, yet through all the vicissitudes of the future, this much of eternal truth is discernible. In geography the antithesis of the old world, in society we are and will be the reverse. *Our* North America will rapidly accumulate a population equalling that of the rest of the world combined: a people one and indivisible, identical in manners, language, customs, and impulses: preserving the same civilization, the same religion; imbued with the same opinions, and having the same political liberties. Of this we have two illustrations now under our eye, the one passing away, the other advancing. The aboriginal Indian race, amongst whom, from Darien to the Esquimaux, and from Florida to Vancouver's Island, exists a perfect identity in hair, complexion, features, religion, stature, and language: and, second, in the instinctive fusion into one language and into one new race, immigrant Germans, English, Norwegians, Celts, and Italians, whose individualities are obliterated in a single generation.

Thus, the perpetuity and destiny of our sacred Union find their conclusive proof and illustration in the bosom of nature. The political storms that periodically rage are but the clouds and sunshine that give variety to the atmosphere and checker our history as we march. The possession of the Basin of the Mississippi, thus held in unity by the American people, is a supreme, a crowning mercy. Viewed alone in its wonderful position and capacity among the continents and the nations; viewed, also, as the dominating part of the great calcareous plain formed of the conterminous Basins of the Mississippi, St. Lawrence, Hudson's Bay, and Mackenzie, the amphitheatre of the world—here is supremely, indeed, the most magnificent dwelling-place marked out by God for man's abode.

Behold, then, rising now and in the future, the empire which industry and self-government create. The growth of half a century, hewed out of the wilderness—its weapons, the axe and plow; its tactics, labor and energy; its soldiers, free and equal citizens. Behold the oracular goal to which our eagles march, and whither the phalanx of our States and people moves harmoniously on, to plant a hundred States and consummate their civic greatness.

1860

C. C. Coffin

Dakota Wheat Fields

C. C. Coffin, a reporter for *Harper's New Monthly Magazine,* describes here the operation of one of the technologized "bonanza farms" of the Midwest, created after the Civil War by the application of large-scale production techniques to farming. Visiting a similar farm in Fargo, North Dakota, the poet Sidney Lanier wrote: "large farming is not farming at all. It is mining for wheat."

RIDE OVER these fertile acres of Dakota, and behold the working of this latest triumph of American genius. You are in a sea of wheat. On the farms managed by Oliver Dalrymple are 13,000 acres in one field. There are other farmers who cultivate from 160 to 6000 acres, The railroad train rolls through an ocean of grain. Pleasant the music of the rippling waves as the west wind sweeps over the expanse. We encounter a squadron of war chariots, not such as once swept over the Delta of the Nile in pursuit of an army of fugitive Israelites, not such as the warriors of Rome were wont to drive, with glittering knives projecting from the axles to mow a swath through the ranks of an enemy, to drench the ground with blood, to cut down the human race, as if men were noxious weeds, but chariots of peace, doing the work of human hands for the sustenance of men. There are twenty-five of them in this one brigade of the grand army of 115, under the marshalship of this Dakota farmer. A superintendent upon a superb horse, like a brigadier directing his forces, rides along the line, accompanied by his staff of two on horseback. They are fully armed and equipped, not with swords, but the implements of peace—wrenches, hammers, chisels. They are surgeons in waiting, with nuts and screws, or whatever may be needed.

This brigade of horse artillery sweeps by in echelon—in close order, reaper following reaper. There is a sound of wheels. The grain disappears an instant, then reappears; iron arms clasp it, hold it a moment in their embrace, wind it with wire, then toss it disdainfully at your feet. You hear in the rattling of the wheels the mechanism saying to itself, "See how easy I can do it!"

An army of "shockers" follow the reapers, setting up the bundles to ripen before threshing. The reaping must ordinarily all be done in fifteen days, else the grain becomes too ripe. The first fields harvested, therefore, are cut before the ripening is complete. Each reaper averages about fifteen acres per day, and is drawn by three horses or mules.

The reaping ended, threshing begins. Again memory goes back to early years, to the pounding out of the grain upon the threshing-floor with the flail—the slow, tedious work of the winter days. Poets no more will rehearse the music of the flail. The picture for February in the old *Farmer's Almanac* is obsolete. September is the month for threshing, the thresher doing its 600 or 700 bushels per day, driven by a steam-engine of sixteen horse-power. Remorseless that sharp-toothed devourer, swallowing its food as fast as two men can cut the wire bands, requiring six teams to supply its demands! And what a cataract of grain pours from its spout, faster than two men can bag it!

The latest triumph of invention in this direction is a straw-burning engine, utilizing the stalks of the grain for fuel.

The cost of raising wheat per bushel is from thirty-five to forty cents; the average yield, from twenty to twenty-five bushels per acre. The nearness of these lands to Lake Superior, and the rates established by the railroad—fifteen cents per bushel from any point between Bismarck and Duluth—give the Dakota farmers a wide margin of profit.

Since the first furrow was turned in the Red River Valley, in 1870, there has been no failure of crops from drought, excessive rains, blight, mildew, rust, or other influence of climatology. The chinch-bug has not made its appearance; the grasshoppers alone have troubled the farmers, but they have disappeared, and the fields are smiling with bounty. With good tilth, the farmer may count upon a net return of from eight to ten dollars per acre per annum. The employment of capital has accomplished a beneficent end, by demonstrating that the region, instead of being incapable of settlement, is one of the fairest sections of the continent. Nor is it a wonder that the land-offices are besieged by emigrants making entries, or that the surveyors find the lands ''squatted'' upon before they can survey them; that hotels are crowded; that on every hand there is activity. During the months of May, June, and July, 1879, the sales of government land were nearly 700,000 acres, and the entries for the year will probably aggregate 1,500,000, taken in homestead, pre-emption, and tree claims. There are other millions of acres, as fair and fertile, yet to be occupied.

1880

Mari Sandoz

From Old Jules

Mari Sandoz's book is a biography of her father, a Swiss emigrant to the upper Niobrara country in western Nebraska in 1884. It is also a chronicle of western frontier farmers, who are pitted in a struggle against desert, drought, floods, storms, land-stealing schemes, and cattlemen fighting to keep an open range. Jules Sandoz's life in the Nebraska panhandle is a series of frustrated attempts to make an orchard bloom and a community flourish. He died in 1928, at seventy-one, saying: "I got to start all over . . . build up—build—build—." In this excerpt Mary is his fourth wife; the storm occurs in June, near the beginning of the century.

From Hail on the Panhandle

DURING THE FALL and early spring Jules and Mary cleared a new orchard patch north of the house, sloping down over the Oglala camp site and the old Freese yard. With a few days' help from some of the more regular grub-line riders, free boarders, Mary wielded the axe, the spade, and the grub hoe against the bushes and trees. Her mother bound the brush into sheaves, piled the larger wood into ricks. Jules drilled holes under the stumps with a post-hole auger, planted charges of blasting powder, called the family together, and lighted the fuse. From behind a big tree they watched the stump fly into the air with an eruption of earth, a shaking of the ground underfoot, an echoing up and down the bluffs, and a smell of spent giant powder. When the weather was too cold for grubbing, Mary, using wedges, split the stumps, mostly ash, into heater chunks.

After the snow water was gone and the Niobrara growled surly within its banks, Jules planted his new orchard. Mary dug the holes, Jule and Marie carried little bundles of trees or ran to anthills for Indian beads. Jules consulted his plan, selected a tree, snipped the end of every rootlet with the pruning shears, and spread them as they had grown, pulverizing the soil about them, pressing it gently with his knuckles. Then he cut the stem back to encourage low growth as a protection against January sunburn, and limped on to the next hole.

Trees that winterkilled to the ground in the old orchard were grafted with hardy slips and staked with laths to prevent the fast-growing shoots from windbreakage. And when the meadow larks sang on the posts and the swallows living in the shed built against the lean-to skimmed over the blooming plum trees, Jules limped about the rows carrying sprigs of blossoms, tying them here and there, marking the branches and protecting them against other fertilizations.

And among the blossoming trees fluttered thousands of orange butterflies, so tame the children could catch them and let them walk on their palms, their feet tickling.

''Prospects look good for a fruit crop,'' Jules told Mary. . . .

Jules's orchard was becoming quite an important feature in the settlement of the country, denying the cattleman contention that nothing would grow. By crossing selected wild plums with choice tame varieties, but not quite hardy, he developed a new plum that stood the winter, was free of insect pests, of delicate flavor, and tender-skinned. In addition he experimented with cherries and apples, and grew all kinds of small fruit between the trees to hold the sand and the snow. Every spring he gave away wagonloads of shrubbery, sucker plums, asparagus, horseradish, and pie-plant roots to anyone who would promise to care for them. And in these activities he caught once more something of the early vision he had upon the top of the hill as he looked across Mirage Flats in 1884.

In recognition of his services, Jules's place was designated an experiment station and he was made director of the eighth district, from Cherry County to the Wyoming line. A bushel of Russian macaroni wheat was on the way for trial. Fruits, flowers, and grains for tryouts were available in reasonable quantities, from Washington.

''Well, Mary, you married an important man,'' he boasted.

''Yes, but I still have to wear men's shoes and carry home the wood.''

''Heah?—Oh, hell, can't you be pleasant one minute?''

It was true that the financial return was small. The orchard was young, experimental, and all comers were welcome to eat as much as they could hold. All summer gay dresses enlivened the long rows; boys ran in gangs searching for riper cherries, blacker berries. Jules limped through the crowd, his pipe at a happy angle.

But Mary was proud of the orchard too. This year she would take her friends through the cleanly hoed rows white with the snow of blossom time or redding with fruit. Then she might forget her leathery skin and her work-crippled hands. With her apron full of large, firm fruit for her guests she could forget the debts, Jules's quarrels with the government and the cattlemen, even the coming trial with Koller and Peters.

Surber spent his early summer vacation with his family. They visited many Sundays on the Niobrara. Walking through the trees, they talked of many things, of the fine fruit crop hanging thick along the young branches, of the Boer defeat and the disappearance of two republics from the world map, of the cattleman activities in local politics, working to fill the Republican convention with Kinkaid timber, of the fence fights, and of Jules's arrest for shooting at Koller.

"Why do you blacken your fine hands on such besotted sheep?" Surber wondered.

The last day of June the sun rose with a peculiar whiteness, casting a bluish shadow behind every post and bush. About six o'clock a gray cloud started directly overhead and spread. Two sharp, dry bolts of lightning sent the grandmother and the boys scurrying into the house.

"Ah, I don't like this *Donner* in the morning we have here in America. It brings only bad before the night," the old woman complained.

"We can use rain for the corn," Mary said as she strained the milk into pans.

Without answering the old woman went out again, to look at the clearing sky, shaking her head.

About eleven the five-year-old Marie ran into the house, jumping up and down in pale excitement. She and the boys had found a snake, a great big snake, right under the east window. Jules took the shotgun out and blew away the small head poised over the thick coils. Then picking the writhing thing up by the tail, he stretched his arm high—over six feet of the heavy, twisting mottled body, the largest bull snake he had ever seen.

"He could crush you like an egg," he told the children.

"Does he bite?" Jule asked.

"No, I don't think so."

The grandmother ran up to see. "I said it gives something bad to-day, and right under the window, with the children—Ach, don't do that!" she cried to Marie. "Ugly thing, you, stepping on the tail, still alive, and then laughing. Are you bewitched?"

The child drew away, still watching the twisting tail.

Because it was clouding up Mary didn't go to the field after dinner. By two o'clock the sky was covered and a great green sausage cloud rolled in over Mirage Flats.

"Still!" Jules commanded the children, who were noisily pushing dirt in upon the snake's grave. There was a faint rumble—such as the Indians had warned him against, like a thousand buffalo stampeding over far prairie, their sharp hoofs cutting the grass to powder.

"Oh, hell!—Mary! Hail coming—Oh, ruin me my corn and my trees."

Mary, coming through the garden gate, turned to follow Jules's pointing finger, her skirts still tucked high under her apron strings, the well-polished hoe over her shoulder.

"Ach!" She slammed the hoe on the fence. "So it goes! Work, work, and then the hail comes and takes it all. Marie, where is the baby?"

"Wo ist Grossmutter?" Jules fussed. "Why don't she come home when a storm's coming?" Just then she came through the trees, the short, plump old woman bent double under the weight of both Jule and the baby pickaback.

Sending them into the lean-to, Mary nailed old sheets and blankets over the windows to the west, while Jules carried a fifty-pound can of blasting powder out of the house and covered it with a wooden washtub. Then they huddled in the lean-to as far from the chimney as possible, Jules rolled in a feather tick, Mary and her mother on the floor with the children. By now the lightning was an almost continuous blinding violet; the thunder rocked the house.

Then suddenly the hail was upon them, a deafening pounding against the shingles and the side of the house, bouncing high from the ground in white sheets. One window after another crashed inward, the force of the wind blowing the blankets and sheets into the room, driving the hail in spurts across the floor, until white streaks reached clear across it. Water ran in streams through the wide cracks between the boards.

The wind turned, and the south windows, unprotected, crashed inward together, the house rocking with the blast. Mary ran to the bedroom, pushed the bed into a far corner, rolled the tick and covers into a pile. Outside the trees about the house were momentarily visible through the gusts of hail, only naked sticks, stripped of all fruit and foliage.

She walked the floor, the hail cracking under her heavy shoes, her knotted fingers twisting her apron, still tucked up.

"Ach, *Gott,* what must we do now Everything, everything gone."

The next two days the drifts of hail lay thick in the canyons under the summer sun hot on the naked fields and prairie. Even the mocking bird that lived in the brush pile east of the house was gone. The children found him washed against a post, the feathers stripped from his back, dead. Pete Staskiewicz helped them bury the bird, and stole a little of his mother's holy water for the cigar-box coffin.

Jules came in from the garden and sat hunched over on a box before the house. All the trees were stripped, barked on the west and south, gone. Where her garden had been Mary planted radishes and peas and turnips as though it were spring. The corn and wheat were pounded into the ground, the orchard gone, but still they must eat.

1935

Frank Norris

From The Octopus

Norris conceived of *The Octopus* as the first novel in an epic trilogy, *Epic of the Wheat,* on the production, the distribution (*The Pit*), and the consumption of wheat; but he died before finishing the project. Like Bret Harte he thought America's westward expansion to be the "last great epic in the history of civilization." A literary naturalist, he based his novel on a bloody battle called the Mussel Slough Affair—the culmination of a corporate power struggle between San Joaquin Valley "bonanza-farmers" and the Southern Pacific Railroad over land prices and freight rates, the determining factors in the control of wheat production. Norris saw this struggle as a reflection of the more primal struggle, delineated here in terms of a kind of mystical Darwinism, between man and "the mystical, unassailable, eternal power of the wheat-giving earth." Vanamee, around whom this scene takes place, is a self-exiled desert wanderer looking for purpose in life (it is he who finally finds it in the power of the earth); Quien Sabe (who knows?) is a four-thousand-acre wheat ranch.

[Planting: San Joaquin Valley]

THE DAY WAS FINE. Since the first rain of the season, there had been no other. Now the sky was without a cloud, pale blue, delicate, luminous, scintillating with morning. The great brown earth turned a huge flank to it, exhaling the moisture of the early dew. The atmosphere, washed clean of dust and mist, was translucent as crystal. Far off to the east, the hills on the other side of Broderson Creek stood out against the pallid saffron of the horizon as flat and as sharply outlined as if pasted on the sky. The campanile of the ancient Mission of San Juan seemed as fine as frost work. All about between the horizons, the carpet of the land unrolled itself to infinity. But now it was no longer parched with heat, cracked and warped by a merciless sun, powdered with dust. The rain had done its work; not a clod that was not swollen with fertility, not a fissure that did not exhale the sense of fecundity. One could not take a dozen steps upon the ranches without the brusque sensation that underfoot the land was alive; aroused at last from its sleep, palpitating with the desire of reproduction. Deep down there in the recesses of the soil, the great heart throbbed once more, thrilling with passion, vibrating with desire, offering itself to the caress of the plough, insistent, eager, imperious. Dimly one felt the deep-seated trouble of the earth, the uneasy agitation of its members, the hidden tumult of its womb, demanding to be made fruitful, to reproduce, to disengage the eternal renascent germ of Life that stirred and struggled in its loins.

The ploughs, thirty-five in number, each drawn by its team of ten, stretched in an interminable line, nearly a quarter of a mile in length, behind and ahead of Vanamee. They were arranged, as it were, *en echelon,* not in file—not one directly behind the other, but each succeeding plough its own width farther in the field than the one in front of it. Each of these ploughs held five shears, so that when the entire company was in motion, one hundred and seventy-five furrows were made at the same instant. At a distance, the ploughs resembled a great column of field artillery. Each driver was in his place, his glance alternating between his horses and the foreman nearest at hand. Other foremen, in their buggies or buckboards, were at intervals along the line, like battery lieutenants. Annixter himself, on horseback, in boots and campaign hat, a cigar in his teeth, overlooked the scene.

The division superintendent, on the opposite side of the line, galloped past to a position at the head. For a long moment there was a silence. A sense of preparedness ran from end to end of the column. All things were ready, each man in his place. The day's work was about to begin.

Suddenly, from a distance at the head of the line came the shrill trilling of a whistle. At once the foreman nearest Vanamee repeated it, at the same time turning down the line, and waving one arm. The signal was repeated, whistle answering whistle, till the sounds lost themselves in the distance. At once the line of ploughs lost its immobility, moving forward, getting slowly under way, the horses straining in the traces. A prolonged movement rippled from team to team, disengaging in its passage a multitude of sounds—the click of buckles, the creak of straining leather, the subdued clash of machinery, the cracking of whips, the deep breathing of nearly four hundred horses, the abrupt commands and cries of the drivers, and, last of all, the prolonged, soothing murmur of the thick brown earth turning steadily from the multitude of advancing shears.

The ploughing thus commenced, continued. The sun rose higher. Steadily the hundred iron hands kneaded and furrowed and stroked the brown, humid earth, the hundred iron teeth bit deep into the Titan's flesh. Perched on his seat, the moist living reins slipping and tugging in his hands, Vanamee, in the midst of this steady confusion of constantly varying sensation, sight interrupted by sound, sound mingling with sight, on this swaying, vibrating seat, quivering with the prolonged thrill of the earth, lapsed to a sort of pleasing numbness, in a sense, hypnotized by the weaving maze of things in which he found himself involved. To keep his team at an even, regular gait, maintaining the precise interval, to run his furrows as closely as possible to those already made by the plough in front—this for the moment was the entire sum of his duties. But while one part of his brain, alert and watchful, took cognizance of these matters, all the greater part was lulled and stupefied with the long monotony of the affair.

The ploughing, now in full swing, enveloped him in a vague, slow-moving whirl of things. Underneath him was the jarring, jolting, trembling machine; not a clod was turned, not an obstacle encountered, that he did not receive the swift impression of it through all his body, the very friction of the damp soil, sliding incessantly from the shiny surface of the shears, seemed to reproduce itself in his finger-tips and along the back of his head. He heard the horsehoofs by the myriads crushing down easily, deeply, into the loam, the prolonged clinking of trace-chains, the working of the smooth brown flanks in the harness, the clatter of wooden hames, the champing of bits, the click of iron shoes against pebbles, the brittle stubble of the surface ground crackling and snapping as the furrows turned, the sonorous, steady breaths wrenched from the deep, labouring chests, strap-bound, shining with sweat, and all along the line the voices of the men talking to the horses. Everywhere there were visions of glossy brown backs, straining, heaving, swollen with muscle; harness streaked with specks of froth, broad, cup-shaped hoofs, heavy with brown loam, men's faces red with tan, blue overalls spotted with axle-grease; muscled hands, the knuckles whitened in their grip on the reins, and through it all the ammoniacal smell of the horses, the bitter reek of perspiration of beasts and men, the aroma of warm leather, the scent of dead stubble—and stronger and more penetrating than everything else, the heavy, enervating odour of the upturned, living earth.

At intervals, from the tops of one of the rare, low swells of the land, Vanamee overlooked a wider horizon. On the other divisions of Quien Sabe the same work was in progress. Occasionally he could see another column of ploughs in the adjoining division—sometimes so close at hand that the subdued murmur of its movements reached his ear; sometimes so distant that it resolved itself into a long, brown streak upon the grey of the ground. Farther off to the west on the Osterman ranch other columns came and went, and, once, from the crest of the highest swell on his division, Vanamee caught a distant glimpse of the Broderson ranch. There, too, moving specks indicated that the ploughing was under way. And farther away still, far off there beyond the fine line of the horizons, over the curve of the globe, the shoulder of the earth, he knew were other ranches, and beyond these others, and beyond these still others, the immensities multiplying to infinity.

Everywhere throughout the great San Joaquin, unseen and unheard, a thousand ploughs up-stirred the land, tens of thousands of shears clutched deep into the warm, moist soil.

It was the long stroking caress, vigorous, male, powerful, for which the

Earth seemed panting. The heroic embrace of a multitude of iron hands, gripping deep into the brown, warm flesh of the land that quivered responsive and passionate under this rude advance, so robust as to be almost an assault, so violent as to be veritably brutal. There, under the sun and under the speckless sheen of the sky, the wooing of the Titan began, the vast primal passion, the two world-forces, the elemental Male and Female, locked in a colossal embrace, at grapples in the throes of an infinite desire, at once terrible and divine, knowing no law, untamed, savage, natural, sublime.

1901

John Steinbeck

From The Grapes of Wrath

Like Norris's, Steinbeck's novel deals with a historical event of great significance—here the dispossession of Oklahoma tenant farmers from their land in the 1930's and their great migration to California. For Steinbeck, the causes of the dispossession were related: topsoil drained by a one-crop economy (cotton); an economy dictated, in turn, by a depression and the need for a high-profit crop; a drought which stripped the drained topsoil and made Oklahoma a dust bowl; and foreclosure of mortgages on tenant farms by profit-minded banks and landlords who found in full scale mechanization cheaper and more efficient methods of farming. The passages included here from Steinbeck's novel function as a kind of loosely connected montage—a sequence of evocations, interspersed by scenes involving two tenant families, the Joads and the Wilsons, of the tenant farmers' western exodus. Those scenes humanize the situation; the passages included here elevate it to epic dimensions.

[Exodus]

THE TRACTORS came over the roads and into the fields, great crawlers moving like insects, having the incredible strength of insects. They crawled over the ground, laying the track and rolling on it and picking it up. Diesel tractors, puttering while they stood idle; they thundered when they moved, and then settled down to a droning roar. Snub-nosed monsters, raising the dust and sticking their snouts into it, straight down the country, across the country, through fences, through dooryards, in and out of gullies in straight lines. They did not run on the ground, but on their own roadbeds. They ignored hills and gulches, water courses, fences, houses.

The man sitting in the iron seat did not look like a man; gloved, goggled, rubber dust mask over nose and mouth, he was a part of the monster, a robot in the seat. The thunder of the cylinders sounded through the country, became one with the air and the earth, so that earth and air muttered in sympathetic vibration. The driver could not control it—straight across country it went, cutting through a dozen farms and straight back. A twitch at the controls could swerve the cat', but the driver's hands could not twitch because the monster that built the tractor, the monster that sent the tractor out, had somehow got into the driver's hands, into his brain and muscle, had goggled him and muzzled him—goggled his mind, muzzled his speech, goggled his perception, muzzled his protest. He could not see the land as it was, he could not smell the land as it smelled; his feet did not stamp the clods or feel the warmth and power of the earth. He sat in an iron seat and stepped on iron pedals. He could not cheer or beat or curse or encourage the extension of his power, and because of this he could not cheer or whip or curse or encourage himself. He did not know or own or trust or beseech the land. If a seed dropped did not germinate, it was nothing. If the young thrusting plant withered in drought or drowned in a flood of rain, it was no more to the driver than to the tractor.

He loved the land no more than the bank loved the land. He could admire the tractor—its machined surfaces, its surge of power, the roar of its detonating cylinders; but it was not his tractor. Behind the tractor rolled the shining disks, cutting the earth with blades—not plowing but surgery, pushing the cut earth to the right where the second row of disks cut it and pushed it to the left; slicing blades shining, polished by the cut earth. And pulled behind the disks, the harrows combing with iron teeth so that the little clods broke up and the earth lay smooth. Behind the harrows, the long seeders—twelve curved iron penes erected in the foundry, orgasms set by gears, raping methodically, raping without passion. The driver sat in his iron seat and he was proud of the straight lines he did not will, proud of the tractor he did not own or love, proud of the power he could not control. And when that crop grew, and was harvested, no man had crumbled a hot clod in his fingers and let the earth sift past his fingertips. No man had touched the seed, or lusted for the growth. Men ate what they had not raised, had no connection with the bread. The land bore under iron, and under iron gradually died; for it was not loved or hated, it had no prayers or curses. . . .

The houses were left vacant on the land, and the land was vacant because of this. Only the tractor sheds of corrugated iron, silver and gleaming, were alive; and they were alive with metal and gasoline and oil, the disks of the plows shining. The tractors had lights shining, for there is no day and night for a tractor and the disks turn the earth in the darkness and they glitter in the daylight. And when a horse stops work and goes into the barn there is a life and a vitality left, there is a breathing and a warmth, and the feet shift on the straw, and the jaws champ on the hay, and the ears and the eyes are alive. There is a warmth of life in the barn, and the heat and smell of life. But when the motor of a tractor stops, it is as dead as the ore it came from. The heat goes out of it like the living heat that leaves a corpse. Then the corrugated iron doors are closed and the tractor man drives home to town, perhaps twenty miles away, and he need not come back for weeks or months, for the tractor is dead. And this is easy and efficient. So easy that the wonder goes out of work, so efficient that the wonder goes out of land and the working of it, and with the wonder the deep understanding and the relation. And in the tractor man there grows the contempt that comes only to a stranger who has little understanding and no relation. For nitrates are not the land, nor phosphates; and the length of fiber in the cotton is not the land. Carbon is not a man, nor salt nor water nor calcium. He is all these, but he is much more, much more; and the land is so much more than its analysis. The man who is more than his chemistry, walking on the earth, turning his plow point for a stone, dropping his handles to slide over an outcropping, kneeling in the earth to eat his lunch; that man who is more than his elements knows the land that is more than its analysis. But the machine man, driving a dead tractor on land he does not know and love, understands only chemistry; and he is contemptuous of the land and of himself. When the corrugated iron doors are shut, he goes home, and his home is not the land.

The doors of the empty houses swung open, and drifted back and forth in the wind. Bands of little boys came out from the towns to break the windows and to pick over the debris, looking for treasures. And here's a knife with half the blade gone. That's a good thing. And—smells like a rat died here. And look what Whitey wrote on the wall. He wrote that in the toilet in school, too, an' teacher made 'im wash it off.

When the folks first left, and the evening of the first day came, the hunting cats slouched in from the fields and mewed on the porch. And when no one came out, the cats crept through the open doors and walked mewing through the empty rooms. And then they went back to the fields and were wild cats from then on, hunting gophers and field mice, and sleeping in ditches in the daytime. When the night came, the bats, which had stopped at the doors for fear of light, swooped into the houses and sailed about through the empty rooms, and in a little while they stayed in dark room corners during the day, folded their wings high, and hung headdown among the rafters, and the smell of their droppings was in the empty houses.

And the mice moved in and stored weed seeds in corners, in boxes, in the backs of drawers in the kitchens. And weasels came in to hunt the mice, and the brown owls flew shrieking in and out again.

Now there came a little shower. The weeds sprang up in front of the door-step, where they had not been allowed, and grass grew up through the porch boards. The houses were vacant, and a vacant house falls quickly apart. Splits started up the sheathing from the rusted nails. A dust settled on the floors, and only mouse and weasel and cat tracks disturbed it.

On a night the wind loosened a shingle and flipped it to the ground. The next wind pried into the hole where the shingle had been, lifted off three, and the next, a dozen. The midday sun burned through the hole and threw a glaring spot on the floor. The wild cats crept in from the fields at night, but they did not mew at the doorstep any more. They moved like shadows of a cloud across the moon, into the rooms to hunt the mice. And on windy nights the doors banged, and the ragged curtains fluttered in the broken windows.

Highway 66 is the main migrant road. 66—the long concrete path across the country, waving gently up and down on the map, from the Mississippi to Bakersfield—over the red lands and the gray lands, twisting up into the mountains, crossing the Divide and down into the bright and terrible desert, and across the desert to the mountains again, and into the rich California valleys.

66 is the path of a people in flight, refugees from dust and shrinking land, from the thunder of tractors and shrinking ownership, from the desert's slow northward invasion, from the twisting winds that howl up out of Texas, from the floods that bring no richness to the land and steal what little richness is there. From all of these the people are in flight, and they come into 66 from the tributary side roads, from the wagon tracks and the rutted country roads. 66 is the mother road, the road of flight.

Clarksville and Ozark and Van Buren and Fort Smith on 64, and there's an end of Arkansas. And all the roads into Oklahoma City, 66 down from Tulsa, 270 up from McAlester. 81 from Wichita Falls south, from Enid north. Edmond, McLoud, Purcell. 66 out of Oklahoma City; El Reno and Clinton, going west on 66. Hydro, Elk City, and Texola; and there's an end to Oklahoma. 66 across the Panhandle of Texas. Shamrock and McLean, Conway and Amarillo, the yellow. Wildorado and Vega and Boise, and there's an end of Texas. Tucumcari and Santa Rosa and into the New Mexican mountains to Albuquerque, where the road comes down from Santa Fe. Then down the gorged Rio Grande to Los Lunas and west again on 66 to Gallup, and there's the border of New Mexico.

And now the high mountains. Holbrook and Winslow and Flagstaff in the high mountains of Arizona. Then the great plateau rolling like a ground swell. Ashfork and Kingman and stone mountains again, where water must be hauled and sold. Then out of the broken sun-rotted mountains of Arizona to the Colrado, with green reeds on its banks, and that's the end of Arizona. There's California just over the river, and a pretty town to start it. Needles, on the river. But the river is a stranger in this place. Up from Needles and over a burned range, and there's the desert. And 66 goes on over the terrible desert, where the distance shimmers and the black center mountains hang unbearably in the distance. At last there's Barstow, and more desert until at last the mountains rise up again, the good mountains, and 66 winds through them. Then suddenly a pass, and below the beautiful valley, below orchards, and vine-yards and little houses, and in the distance a city. And, oh, my God, it's over.

The people in flight streamed out on 66, sometimes a single car, sometimes a little caravan. All day they rolled slowly along the road, and at night they stopped near water. In the day ancient leaky radiators sent up columns of steam, loose connecting rods hammered and pounded. And the men driving the trucks and the overloaded cars listened apprehensively. How far between towns? It is a terror between towns. If something breaks—well, if something breaks we camp right here while Jim walks to town and gets a part and walks back and—how much food we got? . . .

'F we can on'y get to California where the oranges grow before this here ol' jug blows up. 'F we on'y can.

And the tires—two layers of fabric worn through. On'y a four-ply tire. Might get a hunderd miles more outa her if we don't hit a rock an' blow her. Which'll we take—a hunderd, maybe, miles, or maybe spoil the tubes? Which? A hunderd miles. Well, that's somepin you got to think about. We got tube patches. Maybe when she goes she'll only spring a leak. How about makin' a boot? Might get five hundred more miles. Le's go on till she blows.

We got to get a tire, but, Jesus, they want a lot for a ol' tire. They look a fella over. They know he got to go on. They know he can't wait. And the price goes up.

Take it or leave it. I ain't in business for my health. I'm here a-sellin' tires. I ain't givin' 'em away. I can't help what happens to you. I got to think what happens to me.

How far's the nex' town?

I seen forty-two cars a you fellas go by yesterday. Where you all come from? Where all of you goin?

Well, California's a big State.

It ain't that big. The whole United States ain't that big. It ain't that big. It ain't big enough. There ain't room enough for you an' me, for your kind an' my kind, for rich and poor together all in one country, for thieves and honest men. For hunger and fat. Whyn't you go back where you come from?

This is a free country. Fella can go where he wants.

That's what you think! Ever hear of the border patrol on the California line? Police from Los Angeles—stopped you bastards, turned you back. Says, if you can't buy no real estate we don't want you. Says, got a driver's license? Le's see it. Tore it up. Says you can't come in without no driver's license.

It's a free country.

Well, try to get some freedom to do. Fella says you're jus' as free as you got jack to pay for it.

In California they got high wages. I got a han'bill here tells about it.

Baloney! I seen folks comin' back. Somebody's kiddin' you. You want that tire, or don't ya?

Got to take it, but, Jesus, mister, it cuts into our money! We ain't got much left.

Well, I ain't no charity. Take her along. . . .

Sound telegraphs through the frame.

There goes a gasket. Got to go on. Listen to her whistle. Find a nice place to camp an' I'll jerk the head off. But, God Almighty, the food's gettin' low. When we can't buy no more gas—what then?

Danny in the back seat wants a cup a water. Little fella's thirsty.

Listen to that gasket whistle.

Chee-rist! There she went. Blowed tube an' casing all to hell. Have to fix her. Save that casing to make boots; cut 'em out and stick 'em inside a weak place.

Cars pulled up beside the road, engine heads off, tires mended. Cars limping along 66 like wounded things, panting and struggling. Too hot, loose connections, loose bearings, rattling bodies. . . .

The people in flight from the terror behind—strange things happen to them, some bitterly cruel and some so beautiful that the faith is refired forever.

The ancient overloaded Hudson creaked and grunted to the highway at Sallisaw and turned west, and the sun was blinding. But on the concrete Al built up his speed because the flattened springs were not in danger any more. From Sallisaw to Gore is twenty-one miles and the Hudson was doing thirty-five miles an hour. From Gore to Warner thirteen miles; Warner to Checotah fourteen miles; Checotah a long jump to Henrietta—thirty-four miles, but a real town at the end of it. Henrietta to Castle nineteen miles, and the sun was overhead, and the red fields, heated by the high sun vibrated the air. . . .

Joads and Wilsons crawled westward as a unit: El Reno and Bridgeport, Clinton, Elk City, Sayre, and Texola. There's the border, and Oklahoma was behind. And this day the cars crawled on and on, through the Panhandle of Texas. Shamrock and Alanreed, Groom and Yarnell. They went through Amarillo in the evening, drove too long, and camped when it was dusk. They were tired and dusty and hot.

Joads and Wilsons were in flight across the Panhandle, the rolling gray country, lined and cut with old flood scars. They were in flight out of Oklahoma and across Texas. The land turtles crawled through the dust and the sun whipped the earth, and in the evening the heat went out of the sky and the earth sent up a wave of heat from itself.

Two days the families were in flight, but on the third the land was too huge for them and they settled into a new technique of living; the highway became their home and movement their medium of expression. Little by little they settled into the new life . . . The land rolled like great stationary ground swells. Wildorado and Vega and Boise and Glenrio. That's the end of Texas. New Mexico and the mountains. In the far distance, waved up against the sky, the mountains stood. And the wheels of the cars creaked around, the engines were hot, and the steam spurted around the radiator caps. They crawled to the Pecos River, and crossed at Santa Rosa. And they went on for twenty miles. . . .

The Joad family moved slowly westward, up into the mountains of New Mexico, past the pinnacles and pyramids of the upland. They climbed into the high country of Arizona, and through a gap they looked down on the Painted Desert. A border guard stopped them.

"Where are you going?"

"To California," said Tom.

"How long you plan to be in Arizona?"

"No longer'n we can get acrost her."

"Got any plants?"

"No plants."

"I ought to look your stuff over."

"I tell you we ain't got no plants."

The guard put a little sticker on the windshield.

"O.K. Go ahead, but you better keep movin'."

"Sure. We aim to."

They crawled up the slopes, and the low twisted trees covered the slopes. Holbrook, Joseph City, Winslow. And then the tall trees began, and the cars spouted steam and labored up the slopes. And there was Flagstaff over the great plateaus, and the road disappeared in the distance ahead. The water grew scarce, water was to be bought, five cents, ten cents, fifteen cents a gallon. The sun drained the dry rocky country, and ahead were jagged broken peaks, the western wall of Arizona. And now they were in flight from the sun and the drought. They drove all night, and came to the mountains in the night. And they crawled the jagged ramparts in the night, and their dim lights flickered on the pale stone walls of the road. They passed the summit in the dark and came slowly down in the late night, through the shattered stone debris of Oatman; and when the daylight came they saw the Colorado river below them. They drove to Topock, pulled up at the bridge while a guard washed off the windshield sticker. Then across the bridge and into the broken rock wilderness.

And although they were dead weary and the morning heat was growing, they stopped.

Pa called, "We're there—we're in California!" They looked dully at the broken rock glaring under the sun, and across the river the terrible ramparts of Arizona.

"We got the desert," said Tom. "We got to get to the water and rest."

The road runs parallel to the river, and it was well into the morning when the burning motors came to Needles, where the river runs swiftly among the reeds. . . .

The truck took the road and moved up the long hill, through the broken, rotten rock. The engine boiled very soon and Tom slowed down and took it easy. Up the long slope, winding and twisting through dead country, burned white and gray, and no hint of life in it. Once Tom stopped for a few moments to let the engine cool, and then he traveled on. They topped the pass while the sun was still up, and looked down on the desert—black cinder mountains in the distance, and the yellow sun reflected on the gray desert. The little starved bushes, sage and greasewood, threw bold shadows on the sand and bits of rock. The glaring sun was straight ahead. Tom held his hand before his eyes to see at all. They passed the crest and coasted down to cool the engine. They coasted down the long sweep to the floor of the desert, and the fan turned over to cool the water in the radiator. In the driver's seat, Tom and Al and Pa, and Winfield on Pa's knee, looked into the bright descending sun, and their eyes were stony, and their brown faces were damp with perspiration. The burnt land and the black, cindery hills broke the even distance and made it terrible in the reddening light of the setting sun.

Al said, "Jesus, what a place. How'd you like to walk acrost her?"

"People done it," said Tom. "Lots a people done it; an' if they could, we could." . . .

All night they bored through the hot darkness, and jackrabbits scuttled into the lights and dashed away in long jolting leaps. And the dawn came up behind them when the lights of Mojave were ahead. And the dawn showed high mountains to the west. They filled with water and oil at Mojave and crawled into the mountains, and the dawn was about them.

Tom said, "Jesus, the desert's past! Pa, Al, for Christ sakes! The desert's past!"

"I'm too goddamn tired to care," said Al.

"Want me to drive?"

"No, wait awhile."

They drove through Tehachapi in the morning glow, and the sun came up behind them, and then—suddenly they saw the great valley below them. Al jammed on the brake and stopped in the middle of the road, and, "Jesus Christ!

Look!'' he said. The vineyards, the orchards, the great flat valley, green and beautiful, the trees set in rows and the farm houses.

And Pa said, ''God Almighty!'' The distant cities, the little towns in the orchard land, and the morning sun, golden on the valley. A car honked behind them. Al pulled to the side of the road and parked.

''I want ta look at her.'' The grain fields golden in the morning, and the willow lines, the eucalyptus trees in rows.

Pa sighed, ''I never knowed they was anything like her.'' The peach trees and the walnut groves, and the dark green patches of oranges. And red roofs among the trees, and barns—rich barns. Al got out and stretched his legs.

He called, ''Ma—come look. We're there!''

Ruthie and Winfield scrambled down from the car, and then they stood, silent and awestruck, embarrassed before the great valley. The distance was thinned with haze, and the land grew softer and softer in the distance. A windmill flashed in the sun, and its turning blades were like a little heliograph, far away. Ruthie and Winfield looked at it, and Ruthie whispered, ''It's California.''

1939

Landscape as Environment

Local Color Landscapes

In 1899 Bret Harte published a retrospective account of "The Development of the American Short Story" in which he catalogued the deficiencies of pre-Civil War Romantic fiction. "It was not," he declared, "characteristic of American life. . . . It was not vital and instinct with the experience and observation of the average American." As for plot, "it had no sympathy with those dramatic contrasts and surprises which are the wonders of American civilization." And as for setting, "it took no account of the modifications of environment and of geographical limitations; indeed, it knew little of geography." The best Romantic writers, Harte judged, were "artistically contemplative of their own country, but seldom observant."

Harte's own fiction and that of other local colorists writing after the war served to define a new direction for American fiction—and not incidentally a new concept of setting. The local colorists wrote not of an America diffused into idea but of an America observed and present: a heterogeneous patchwork of regional environments each with its picturesquely distinctive manners and morals and its reflection, at the same time, of "characteristic American life."

Harte's "The Luck of Roaring Camp" and Kate Chopin's "Beyond the Bayou" will have to represent here a long catalogue of locales and of writers of local color: New England (Mary Wilkins Freeman, Sarah Orne Jewett); Louisiana (George Washington Cable, Kate Chopin, Lafcadio Hearn); the Far West of California and Nevada (Bret Harte, the early Mark Twain); the South (William Harben's delta country, Mary Noailles Murphree's Tennessee mountains, Charles Chesnutt's North Carolina); and finally, the latest of the major regions to emerge, the Midwest (E. W. Howe's Kansas, Hamlin Garland's Wisconsin and the Dakotas).

Local color writers did not ignore the visual aspects of landscapes, but they insisted on seeing landscape as part of an environmental continuum which included settlements as well as natural landscapes and the cultural as well as the natural atmosphere. "Local color in a novel," wrote Hamlin Garland, "means that it has such a quality of texture and back-ground that it could not have been written any other place or by anyone else than a native." By texture Garland seems to mean cultural qualities: matters of dress and speech, manners and morals and so on; by background, both landscape and regional history. And he implies that all of these demand a distinctive organic form in the literature which would re-create them.

The local color settings of both Harte and Chopin share with the best local color a faithful, minute, and sympathetic observation of their worlds ("no fastidious ignorings of its habitual expression . . . ; no moral determination except that which may affect the legitimate outcome of the story itself," Harte advised) and of even their lowliest inhabitants. They share, too, the sense of change in the air—a change both necessary and destructive. The "world beyond" Roaring Camp begins to soften the harshness of the place, but at the same time it lulls the men into forgetting that they are gamblers in life; the "world beyond" La Folle's bayou has both freed and terrorized her.

"The Luck of Roaring Camp" was published in 1868. By the end of the century, the fiction of local color—age-mate of Muir and Powell, of photography, sociology, transcontinental railroad travel—had reached its ascendency and was being incorporated into an aesthetics more profoundly and subtly regional in character. Thus the Nebraska of Crane's "The Blue Hotel," the Mississippi of Faulkner's story, and so on.

And yet even as regionalism deepened its hold on the fictional and poetic imagination, the regions themselves were being deformed by the new technological order in the "world beyond." *"The region,"* announced the Nebraskan novelist Wright Morris in the early 1960's,

> the region in the sense that once fed the imagination—is now for sale on the shelf with the maple-sugar Kewpies; the hand-loomed ties and hand-sewn moccasins are now available, along with food and fuel, at regular intervals on our turnpikes. The only regions left are those the artist must imagine. They lie beyond the usual forms of salvage. No matter where we go, in America today, we shall find what we just left . . . We have come to the end of what is raw in the material vein.

Bret Harte

The Luck of Roaring Camp

Harte, an émigré to California, contributed to what he called a "literature of the Pacific slope." Its historical moment was the epic adventure of gold-mining and the transformation of the West into a democratic society. Its characters were the immigrant-adventurers, the young and the outcast, who took the Cape Horn voyage or the California Trail (see The Ways West) and left behind them "the trammels of precedent or tradition in arranging their lives and making their rude homes." Add to this, Harte proclaimed, "the environment of magnificent scenery, a unique climate, and a vegetation that was marvelous in its proportions and spontaneity of growth; let it be further considered that the strongest relief was given to this picture by its setting among the crumbling ruins of early Spanish settlers— . . . whose legitimate Castilian descendents still lived and moved in picturesque and dignified contrast to their energetic invaders—and it must be admitted that a condition of romantic and dramatic possibilities was created unrivalled in history." "The Luck of Roaring Camp" was the first local color story.

THERE WAS COMMOTION in Roaring Camp. It could not have been a fight, for in 1850 that was not novel enough to have called together the entire settlement. The ditches and claims were not only deserted, but "Tuttle's grocery" had contributed its gamblers, who, it will be remembered, calmly continued their game the day that French Pete and Kanaka Joe shot each other to death over the bar in the front room. The whole camp was collected before a rude cabin on the outer edge of the clearing. Conversation was carried on in a low tone, but the name of a woman was frequently repeated. It was a name familiar enough in the camp,—"Cherokee Sal."

Perhaps the less said of her the better. She was a coarse, and it is to be feared, a very sinful woman. But at that time she was the only woman in Roaring Camp, and was just then lying in sore extremity, when she most needed the ministration of her own sex. Dissolute, abandoned, and irreclaimable, she was yet suffering a martyrdom hard enough to bear even when veiled by sympathizing womanhood, but now terrible in her loneliness. The primal curse had come to her in that original isolation which must have made the punishment of the first transgression so dreadful. It was, perhaps, part of the expiation of her sin, that, at a moment when she most lacked her sex's intuitive tenderness and care, she met only the half-contemptuous faces of her masculine associates. Yet a few of the spectators were, I think, touched by her sufferings. Sandy Tipton thought it was "rough on Sal," and, in the contemplation of her condition, for a moment rose superior to the fact that he had an ace and two bowers in his sleeve.

It will be seen, also, that the situation was novel. Deaths were by no means uncommon in Roaring Camp, but a birth was a new thing. People had been dismissed from the camp effectively, finally, and with no possibility of return; but this was the first time that anybody had been introduced *ab initio*. Hence the excitement.

''You go in there, Stumpy,'' said a prominent citizen known as ''Kentuck,'' addressing one of the loungers. ''Go in there, and see what you kin do. You've had experience in them things.''

Perhaps there was a fitness in the selection. Stumpy, in other climes, had been the putative head of two families; in fact, it was owing to some legal informality in these proceedings that Roaring Camp—a city of refuge—was indebted to his company. The crowd approved the choice, and Stumpy was wise enough to bow to the majority. The door closed upon the extempore surgeon and midwife, and Roaring Camp sat down outside, smoked its pipe, and awaited the issue.

The assemblage numbered about a hundred men. One or two of these were actual fugitives from justice, some were criminal, and all were reckless. Physically, they exhibited no indication of their past lives and character. The greatest scamp had a Raphael face, with a profusion of blond hair; Oakhurst, a gambler, had the melancholy air and intellectual abstraction of a Hamlet; the coolest and most courageous man was scarcely over five feet in height, with a soft voice and an embarrassed, timid manner. The term ''roughs'' applied to them was a distinction rather than a definition. Perhaps in the minor details of fingers, toes, ears, etc., the camp may have been deficient, but these slight omissions did not detract from their aggregate force. The strongest man had but three fingers on his right hand; the best shot had but one eye.

Such was the physical aspect of the men that were dispersed around the cabin. The camp lay in a triangular valley, between two hills and a river. The only outlet was a steep trail over the summit of a hill that faced the cabin, now illuminated by the rising moon. The suffering woman might have seen it from the rude bunk whereon she lay,—seen it winding like a silver thread until it was lost in the stars above.

A fire of withered pine boughs added sociability to the gathering. By degrees the natural levity of Roaring Camp returned. Bets were freely offered and taken regarding the result. Three to five that ''Sal would get through with it''; even, that the child would survive; side bets as to the sex and complexion of the coming stranger. In the midst of an excited discussion an exclamation came from those nearest the door, and the camp stopped to listen. Above the swaying and moaning of the pines, the swift rush of the river, and the crackling of the fire rose a sharp, querulous cry—a cry unlike anything heard before in the camp. The pines stopped moaning, the river ceased to rush, and the fire to crackle. It seemed as if Nature had stopped to listen too.

The camp rose to its feet as one man! It was proposed to explode a barrel of gun-powder, but, in consideration of the situation of the mother, better counsels prevailed, and only a few revolvers were discharged; for, whether owing to the rude surgery of the camp, or some other reason, Cherokee Sal was sinking fast. Within an hour she had climbed, as it were, that rugged road that led to the stars, and so passed out of Roaring Camp, its sin and shame forever. I do not think that the announcement disturbed them much, except in speculation as to the fate of the child. "Can he live now?" was asked of Stumpy. The answer was doubtful. The only other being of Cherokee Sal's sex and maternal condition in the settlement was an ass. There was some conjecture as to fitness, but the experiment was tried. It was less problematical than the ancient treatment of Romulus and Remus, and apparently as successful.

When these details were completed, which exhausted another hour, the door was opened, and the anxious crowd, who had already formed themselves into a queue, entered in single file. Beside the low bunk or shelf, on which the figure of the mother was starkly outlined below the blankets, stood a pine table. On this a candle-box was placed, and within it, swathed in staring red flannel, lay the last arrival at Roaring Camp. Beside the candle-box was placed a hat. Its use was soon indicated. "Gentlemen," said Stumpy, with a singular mixture of authority and *ex officio* complacency—"Gentlemen will please pass in at the front door, round the table, and out at the back door. Them as wishes to contribute anything toward the orphan will find a hat handy." The first man entered with his hat on; he uncovered, however, as he looked about him, and so, unconsciously, set an example to the next. In such communities good and bad actions are catching. As the procession filed in, comments were audible,—criticisms addressed, perhaps rather to Stumpy, in the character of showman,—"Is that him?" "Mighty small specimen"; "Hasn't more'n got the color"; "Ain't bigger nor a derringer." The contributions were as characteristic: A silver tobacco box; a doubloon; a navy revolver, silver mounted; a gold specimen; a very beautifully embroidered lady's handkerchief (from Oakhurst the gambler); a diamond breastpin, a diamond ring (suggested by the pin, with the remark from the giver that he "saw that pin and went two diamonds better"); a slung shot; a Bible (contributor not detected); a golden spur; a silver teaspoon (the initials, I regret to say, were not the giver's); a pair of surgeon's shears; a lancet; a Bank of England note for £5; and about $200 in loose gold and silver coin. During these proceedings Stumpy maintained a silence as impassive as the dead on his left—a gravity as inscrutable as that of the newly-born on his right. Only one incident occurred to break the monotony of the curious procession. As Kentuck bent over the candle-box half curiously, the child turned, and, in a spasm of pain, caught at his groping finger, and held it fast for a moment. Kentuck looked foolish and embarrassed. Something like a blush tried to assert itself in his weather-beaten cheek. "The d—d little cuss!" he said, as he extricated his finger, with, perhaps, more tenderness and care than he might have been deemed capable of showing. He held that finger a little apart from its fellows as he went out, and examined it curiously. The examination provoked the same original remark in regard to the child. In fact, he seemed to enjoy repeating it. "He rastled with my finger," he remarked to Tipton, holding up the member, "the d—d little cuss!"

It was four o'clock before the camp sought repose. A light burnt in the cabin where the watchers sat, for Stumpy did not go to bed that night. Nor did Kentuck. He drank quite freely and related with great gusto his experience, invariably ending with his characteristic condemnation of the newcomer. It seemed to relieve him of any unjust implication of sentiment, and Kentuck had the weaknesses of the nobler sex. When everybody else had gone to bed, he walked down to the river, and whistled reflectingly. Then he walked up the gulch, past the cabin, still whistling with demonstrative unconcern. At a large redwood tree he paused and retraced his steps, and again passed the cabin. Halfway down to the river's bank he again paused, and then returned and knocked at the door. It was opened by Stumpy. "How goes it?" said Kentuck, looking past Stumpy toward the candle-box. "All serene," replied Stumpy. "Anything up?" "Nothing." There was a pause—an embarrassing one—Stumpy still holding the door. Then Kentuck had recourse to his finger, which he held up to Stumpy. "Rastled with it,—the d—d little cuss," he said, and retired.

The next day Cherokee Sal had such rude sepulture as Roaring Camp afforded. After her body had been committed to the hillside, there was a formal meeting of the camp to discuss what should be done with her infant. A resolution to adopt it was unanimous and enthusiastic. But an animated discussion in regard to the manner and feasibility of providing for its wants at once sprung up. It was remarkable that the argument partook of none of those fierce personalities with which discussions were usually conducted at Roaring Camp. Tipton proposed that they should send the child to Red Dog—a distance of forty miles—where female attention could be procured. But the unlucky suggestion met with fierce and unanimous opposition. It was evident that no plan which entailed parting from their new acquisition would for a moment be entertained. "Besides," said Tom Ryder, "them fellows at Red Dog would swap it, and ring in somebody else on us." A disbelief in the honesty of other camps prevailed at Roaring Camp as in other places.

The introduction of a female nurse in the camp also met with objection. It was argued that no decent woman could be prevailed to accept Roaring Camp as her home, and the speaker urged that "they didn't want any more of the other kind." This unkind allusion to the defunct mother, harsh as it may seem, was the first spasm of propriety—the first symptom of the camp's regeneration. Stumpy advanced nothing. Perhaps he felt a certain delicacy in interfering with the selection of a possible successor in office. But when questioned, he averred stoutly that he and "Jinny"—the mammal before alluded to—could manage to rear the child. There was something original, independent, and heroic about the plan that pleased the camp. Stumpy was retained. Certain articles were sent for to Sacramento. ''Mind,'' said the treasurer, as he pressed a bag of gold-dust into the expressman's hand, ''the best that can be got—lace, you know, and filigree-work and frills,—d—n the cost!''

Strange to say, the child thrived. Perhaps the invigorating climate of the mountain camp was compensation for material deficiencies. Nature took the foundling to her broader breast. In that rare atmosphere of the Sierra foothills—that air pungent with balsamic odor, that ethereal cordial, at once bracing and exhilarating, he may have found food and nourishment, or a subtle chemistry that transmuted asses' milk to lime and phosphorus. Stumpy inclined to the belief that it was the latter and good nursing. ''Me and that ass,'' he would say, ''has been father and mother to him! Don't you,'' he would add, apostrophizing the helpless bundle before him, ''never go back on us.''

By the time he was a month old, the necessity of giving him a name became apparent. He had generally been known as ''the Kid,'' ''Stumpy's boy,'' ''the Cayote'' (an allusion to his vocal powers) and even by Kentuck's endearing diminutive of ''the d—d little cuss.'' But these were felt to be vague and unsatisfactory, and were at last dismissed under another influence. Gamblers and adventurers are generally superstitious, and Oakhurst one day declared that the baby had brought ''the luck'' to Roaring Camp. It was certain that of late they had been successful. ''Luck'' was the name agreed upon, with the prefix of Tommy for greater convenience. No allusion was made to the mother, and the father was unknown. ''It's better,'' said the philosophical Oakhurst, ''to take a fresh deal all round. Call him Luck, and start him fair.'' A day was accordingly set apart for the christening. What was meant by this ceremony the reader may imagine, who has already gathered some idea of the reckless irreverence of Roaring Camp. The master of ceremonies was one ''Boston,'' a noted wag, and the occasion seemed to promise the greatest facetiousness. This ingenious satirist had spent two days in preparing a burlesque of the church service, with pointed local allusions. The choir was properly trained, and Sandy Tipton was to stand godfather. But after the procession had marched to the grove with music and banners, and the child had been deposited before a mock altar, Stumpy stepped before the expectant crowd. ''It ain't my style to spoil fun, boys,'' said the little man, stoutly, eyeing the faces around him, ''but it strikes me that this thing ain't exactly on the squar. It's playing it pretty low down on this yer baby to ring in fun on him that he ain't goin' to understand. And ef there's going to be any god-fathers round, I'd like to see who's got any better rights than me.'' A silence followed Stumpy's speech. To the credit of all humorists be it said that the first man to acknowledge its justice was the satirist, thus stopped of his fun. ''But,'' said Stumpy, quickly, following up his advantage, ''we're here for a christening, and we'll have it. I proclaim you Thomas Luck, according to the laws of the United States and the State of California, so help me God.'' It was the first time that the name of the Deity had been uttered otherwise but profanely in the camp. The form of christening was perhaps even more ludicrous than the satirist had conceived; but strangely enough, nobody saw it and nobody laughed. ''Tommy'' was christened as seriously as he would have been under a Christian roof, and cried and was comforted in as orthodox fashion.

And so the work of regeneration began in Roaring Camp. Almost imperceptibly a change came over the settlement. The cabin assigned to ''Tommy Luck''—or ''The Luck,'' as he was more frequently called—first showed signs of improvement. It was kept scrupulously clean and whitewashed. Then it was boarded, clothed and papered. The rosewood cradle—packed eighty miles by mule—had, in Stumpy's way of putting it, ''sorter killed the rest of the furniture.'' So the rehabilitation of the cabin became a necessity. The men who were in the habit of lounging in at Stumpy's to see ''how The Luck got on'' seemed to appreciate the change, and, in self-defense, the rival establishment of ''Tuttle's grocery'' bestirred itself, and imported a carpet and mirrors. The reflections of the latter on the appearance of Roaring Camp tended to produce stricter habits of personal cleanliness. Again Stumpy imposed a kind of quarantine upon those who aspired to the honor and privilege of holding ''The Luck.'' It was a cruel mortification to Kentuck—who, in the carelessness of a large nature and the habits of frontier life, had begun to regard all garments as a second cuticle, which, like a snake's, only sloughed off through decay—to be debarred this privilege from certain prudential reasons. Yet such was the subtle influence of innovation that he thereafter appeared regularly every afternoon in a clean shirt, and face still shining from his ablutions. Nor were moral and social sanitary laws neglected. ''Tommy,'' who was supposed to spend his whole existence in a persistent attempt to repose, must not be disturbed by noise. The shouting and yelling which had gained the camp its infelicitous title were not permitted within hearing distance of Stumpy's. The men conversed in whispers, or smoked with Indian gravity. Profanity was tacitly given up in these sacred precincts, and throughout the camp a popular form of expletive, known as ''D—n the luck!'' and ''Curse the luck!'' was abandoned, as having a new personal bearing. Vocal music was not interdicted, being supposed to have a soothing, tranquilizing quality, and one song, sung by ''Man-o'-War Jack,'' an English sailor from Her Majesty's Australian colonies, was quite popular as a lullaby. It was a lugubrious recital of the exploits of ''the *Arethusa,* Seventy-four,'' in a muffled minor, ending with a prolonged dying fall at the burden of each verse, ''On b-o-o-o-ard of the *Arethusa.*'' It was a fine sight to see Jack holding The Luck, rocking from side to side as if with the motion of a ship, and crooning forth this naval ditty. Either through the peculiar rocking of Jack or the length of his song—it contained ninety stanzas, and was continued with conscientious deliberation to the bitter end—the lullaby generally had the desired effect. At such times the men would lie at full length under the trees, in the soft summer twilight, smoking their pipes and drinking in the melodious utterances. An indistinct idea that this was pastoral happiness pervaded the camp. "This 'ere kind o' think," said the Cockney Simmons, meditatively reclining on his elbow, "is 'evingly." It reminded him of Greenwich.

On the long summer days The Luck was usually carried to the gulch, from whence the golden store of Roaring Camp was taken. There, on a blanket spread over pine boughs, he would lie while the men were working in the ditches below. Latterly, there was a rude attempt to decorate this bower with flowers and sweet-smelling shrubs, and generally some one would bring him a cluster of wild honey-suckles, azaleas, or the painted blossoms of Las Mariposas. The men had suddenly awakened to the fact that there were beauty and significance in these trifles, which they had so long trodden carelessly beneath their feet. A flake of glittering mica, a fragment of variegated quartz, a bright pebble from the bed of the creek, became beautiful to eyes thus cleared and strengthened, and were invariably put aside for "The Luck." It was wonderful how many treasures the woods and hillsides yielded that "would do for Tommy." Surrounded by playthings such as never child out of fairyland had before, it is to be hoped that Tommy was content. He appeared to be serenely happy, albeit there was an infantine gravity about him, a contemplative light in his round gray eyes, that sometimes worried Stumpy. He was always tractable and quiet, and it is recorded that once, having crept beyond his "corral"—a hedge of tessellated pine boughs, which surrounded his bed—he dropped over the bank on his head in the soft earth, and remained with his mottled legs in the air in that position for at least five minutes with unflinching gravity. He was extricated without a murmur. I hesitate to record the many other instances of his sagacity, which rest, unfortunately, upon the statements of prejudiced friends. Some of them were not without a tinge of superstition. "I crep' up the bank just now," said Kentuck one day, in a breathless state of excitement, "and dern my skin if he wasn't a talking to a jaybird as was a-sittin on his lap. There they was, just as free and sociable as anything you please, a-jawin at each other just like two cherrybums." Howbeit, whether creeping over the pine boughs or lying lazily on his back, blinking at the leaves above him, to him the birds sang, the squirrels chattered, and the flowers bloomed. Nature was his nurse and playfellow. For him she would let slip between the leaves golden shafts of sunlight that fell just within his grasp; she would send wandering breezes to visit him with the balm of bay and resinous gums; to him the tall redwoods nodded familiarly and sleepily, the bumblebees buzzed, and the rooks cawed a slumbrous accompaniment.

Such was the golden summer of Roaring Camp. They were "flush times"—and the Luck was with them. The claims had yielded enormously. The camp was jealous of its privileges and looked suspiciously on strangers. No encouragement was given to immigration, and, to make their seclusion more perfect, the land on either side of the mountain wall that surrounded the camp they duly pre-empted. This, and a reputation for singular proficiency with the revolver, kept the reserve of Roaring Camp inviolate. The expressman—their only connecting link with the surrounding world—sometimes told wonderful stories of the camp. He would say, "They've a street up there in 'Roaring,' that would lay over any street up there in Red Dog. They've got vines and flowers round their houses, and they wash themselves twice a day. But they're mighty rough on strangers, and they worship an Ingin baby."

With the prosperity of the camp came a desire for further improvement. It was proposed to build a hotel in the following spring, and to invite one or two decent families to reside there for the sake of "The Luck," who might perhaps profit by female companionship. The sacrifice that this concession to the sex cost these men, who were fiercely skeptical in regard to its general virtue and usefulness, can only be accounted for by their affection for Tommy. A few still held out. But the resolve could not be carried into effect for three months, and the minority meekly yielded in the hope that something might turn up to prevent it. And it did.

The winter of '51 will long be remembered in the foothills. The snow lay deep on the Sierras, and every mountain creek became a river, and every river a lake. Each gorge and gulch was transformed into a tumultuous watercourse that descended the hillsides, tearing down giant trees and scattering its drift and debris along the plain. Red Dog had been twice under water, and Roaring Camp had been forewarned. "Water put the gold into them gulches," said Stumpy; "it's been here once and will be here again!" And that night the North Fork suddenly leaped over its banks, and swept up the triangular valley of Roaring Camp.

In the confusion of rushing water, crashing trees, and crackling timber, and the darkness which seemed to flow with the water and blot out the fair valley, but little could be done to collect the scattered camp. When the morning broke, the cabin of Stumpy nearest the river-bank was gone. Higher up the gulch they found the body of its unlucky owner; but the pride—the hope—the joy—the Luck—of Roaring Camp had disappeared. They were returning with sad hearts, when a shout from the bank recalled them.

It was a relief-boat from down the river. They had picked up, they said, a man and an infant, nearly exhausted, about two miles below. Did anybody know them, and did they belong here?

It needed but a glance to show them Kentuck lying there, cruelly crushed and bruised, but still holding The Luck of Roaring Camp in his arms. As they bent over the strangely assorted pair, they saw that the child was cold and pulseless. "He is dead," said one. Kentuck opened his eyes. "Dead?" he repeated feebly. "Yes, my man, and you are dying too." A smile lit the eyes of the expiring Kentuck. "Dying!" he repeated, "he's a-taking me with him—tell the boys I've got the Luck with me now"; and the strong man, clinging to the frail babe as a drowning man is said to cling to a straw, drifted away into the shadowy river that flows forever to the unknown sea.

1868

Kate Chopin
Beyond the Bayou

Kate Chopin (born O'Flaherty) grew up in St. Louis and after her marriage moved with her husband to Natchitoches Parish, Louisiana, the setting for most of her fiction. Her Louisiana seems to share nothing in common with Harte's California. Its landscape is a bayou. Its culture is an amalgam of French and Black American, and its historical moments—the age of plantation slavery and the Civil War—have passed. Like Irving's Sleepy Hollow, it seems an anachronistic backwater.

Her chief affinities as a writer are to Sarah Orne Jewett, George Washington Cable, and Walt Whitman, as well as to the French realists Maupassant and Flaubert.

THE BAYOU CURVED like a crescent around the point of land on which La Folle's cabin stood. Between the stream and the hut lay a big abandoned field, where cattle were pastured when the bayou supplied them with water enough. Through the woods that spread back into unknown regions the woman had drawn an imaginary line, and past this circle she never stepped. This was the form of her only mania.

She was now a large, gaunt black woman, past thirty-five. Her real name was Jacqueline, but every one on the plantation called her La Folle, because in childhood she had been frightened literally "out of her senses," and had never wholly regained them.

It was when there had been skirmishing and sharpshooting all day in the woods. Evening was near when P'tit Maître, black with powder and crimson with blood, had staggered into the cabin of Jacqueline's mother, his pursuers close at his heels. The sight had stunned her childish reason.

She dwelt alone in her solitary cabin, for the rest of the quarters had long since been removed beyond her sight and knowledge. She had more physical strength than most men, and made her patch of cotton and corn and tobacco like the best of them. But of the world beyond the bayou she had long known nothing, save what her morbid fancy conceived.

People at Bellissime had grown used to her and her way, and they thought nothing of it. Even when "Old Mis' " died, they did not wonder that La Folle had not crossed the bayou, but had stood upon her side of it, wailing and lamenting.

P'tit Maître was now the owner of Bellissime. He was a middle-aged man, with a family of beautiful daughters about him, and a little son whom La Folle loved as if he had been her own. She called him Chéri, and so did every one else because she did.

None of the girls had ever been to her what Chéri was. They had each and all loved to be with her, and to listen to her wondrous stories of things that always happened "yonda, beyon' de bayou."

But none of them had stroked her black hand quite as Chéri did, nor rested their heads against her knee so confidingly, nor fallen asleep in her arms as he used to do. For Chéri hardly did such things now, since he had become the proud possessor of a gun, and had had his black curls cut off.

That summer—the summer Chéri gave La Folle two black curls tied with a knot of red ribbon—the water ran so low in the bayou that even the little children at Bellissime were able to cross it on foot, and the cattle were sent to pasture down by the river. La Folle was sorry when they were gone, for she loved these dumb companions well, and liked to feel that they were there, and to hear them browsing by night up to her own inclosure.

It was Saturday afternoon, when the fields were deserted. The men had flocked to a neighboring village to do their week's trading, and the women were occupied with household affairs—La Folle as well as the others. It was then she mended and washed her handful of clothes, scoured her house, and did her baking.

In this last employment she never forgot Chéri. Today she had fashioned croquignoles [biscuits] of the most fantastic and alluring shapes for him. So when she saw the boy come trudging across the old field with his gleaming little new rifle on his shoulder, she called out gayly to him, "Chéri! Chéri!"

But Chéri did not need the summons, for he was coming straight to her. His pockets all bulged out with almonds and raisins and an orange that he had secured for her from the very fine dinner which had been given that day up at his father's house.

He was a sunny-faced youngster of ten. When he had emptied his pockets, La Folle patted his round red cheek, wiped his soiled hands on her apron, and smoothed his hair. Then she watched him as, with his cakes in his hand, he crossed her strip of cotton back of the cabin, and disappeared into the wood.

He had boasted of the things he was going to do with his gun out there.

"You think they got plenty deer in the wood, La Folle?" he had inquired, with the calculating air of an experienced hunter.

"Non, non!" the woman laughed. "Don't you look fo' no deer, Chéri.

Dat's too big. But you bring La Folle one good fat squirrel fo' her dinner to-morrow, an' she goin' be satisfi'."

One squirrel ain't a bite. I'll bring you mo' 'an one, LaFolle," he had boasted pompously as he went away.

When the woman, an hour later, heard the report of the boy's rifle close to the wood's edge, she would have thought nothing of it if a sharp cry of distress had not followed the sound.

She withdrew her arms from the tub of suds in which they had been plunged, dried them upon her apron, and as quickly as her trembling limbs would bear her, hurried to the spot whence the ominous report had come.

It was as she feared. There she found Chéri stretched upon the ground, with his rifle beside him. He moaned piteously:

"I'm dead, La Folle! I'm dead! I'm gone!"

"*Non, non!*" she exclaimed resolutely, as she knelt beside him. "Put you' arm 'roun' La Folle's nake, Chéri. Dat's nuttin'; dat goin' be nuttin'." She lifted him in her powerful arms.

Chéri had carried his gun muzzle-downward. He had stumbled—he did not know how. He only knew that he had a ball lodged somewhere in his leg, and he thought that his end was at hand. Now, with his head upon the woman's shoulder, he moaned and wept with pain and fright.

"Oh, La Folle! La Folle! it hurt so bad! I can' stan' it, La Folle!"

"Don't cry, *Mon bébé, mon bébé, mon Chéri!*" the woman spoke soothingly as she covered the ground with long strides. "La Folle goin' mine you; Doctor Bonfils goin' come make *mon Chéri* well agin."

She had reached the abandoned field. As she crossed it with her precious burden, she looked constantly and restlessly from side to side. A terrible fear was upon her,—the fear of the world beyond the bayou, the morbid and insane dread she had been under since childhood.

When she was at the bayou's edge she stood there, and shouted for help as if a life depended upon it:—

"Oh, P'tit Maître! P'tit Maître! Venez donc! Au secours! Au secours!" ["Come quick! Help! Help!"]

No voice responded. Chéri's hot tears were scalding her neck. She called for each and every one upon the place, and still no answer came.

She shouted, she wailed; but whether her voice remained unheard or unheeded, no reply came to her frenzied cries. And all the while Chéri moaned and wept and entreated to be taken home to his mother.

La Folle gave a last despairing look around her. Extreme terror was upon her. She clasped the child close against her breast, where he could feel her heart beat like a muffled hammer. Then shutting her eyes, she ran suddenly down the shallow bank of the bayou, and never stopped till she had climbed the opposite shore.

She stood there quivering an instant as she opened her eyes. Then she plunged into the footpath through the trees.

She spoke no more to Chéri, but muttered constantly, "Bon Dieu, ayez pitié La Folle! Bon Dieu, ayez pitié moi!" ["Good God, pity La Folle . . . pity me!"]

Instinct seemed to guide her. When the pathway spread clear and smooth enough before her, she again closed her eyes tightly against the sight of that unknown and terrifying world.

A child, playing in some weeds, caught sight of her as she neared the quarters. The little one uttered a cry of dismay.

"La Folle!" she screamed, in her piercing treble. "La Folle done cross de bayer!"

Quickly the cry passed down the line of cabins.

"Yonda, La Folle done cross de bayou!"

Children, old men, old women, young ones with infants in their arms, flocked to doors and windows to see this awe-inspiring spectacle. Most of them shuddered with superstitious dread of what it might portend. "She totin' Chéri!" some of them shouted.

Some of the more daring gathered about her, and followed at her heels, only to fall back with new terror when she turned her distorted face upon them. Her eyes were bloodshot and the saliva had gathered in a white foam on her black lips.

Some one had run ahead of her to where P'tit Maître sat with his family and guests upon the gallery.

"P'tit Maître! La Folle done cross de bayou! Look her! Look her yonda totin' Chéri!" This startling intimation was the first which they had of the woman's approach.

She was now near at hand. She walked with long strides. Her eyes were fixed desperately before her, and she breathed heavily, as a tired ox.

At the foot of the stairway, which she could not have mounted, she laid the boy in his father's arms. Then the world that had looked red to La Folle suddenly turned black—like that day she had seen powder and blood.

She reeled for an instant. Before a sustaining arm could reach her, she fell heavily to the ground.

When La Folle regained consciousness, she was at home again, in her own cabin and upon her own bed. The moon rays, streaming in through the open door and windows, gave what light was needed to the old black mammy who stood at the table concocting a tisane [tea] of fragrant herbs. It was very late.

Others who had come, and found that the stupor clung to her, had gone again. P'tit Maître had been there, and with him Doctor Bonfils, who said that La Folle might die.

But death had passed her by. The voice was very clear and steady with which she spoke to Tante Lizette, brewing her tisane there in a corner.

''Ef you will give me one good drink tisane, Tante Lizette, I b'lieve I'm goin' sleep, me.''

And she did sleep; so soundly, so healthfully, that old Lizette without compunction stole softly away, to creep back through the moonlit fields to her own cabin in the new quarters.

The first touch of the cool gray morning awoke La Folle. She arose, calmly, as if no tempest had shaken and threatened her existence but yesterday.

She donned her new blue cottonade and white apron, for she remembered that this was Sunday. When she had made for herself a cup of strong black coffee, and drunk it with relish, she quitted the cabin and walked across the old familiar field to the bayou's edge again.

She did not stop there as she had always done before, but crossed with a long, steady stride as if she had done this all her life.

When she had made her way through the brush and scrub cottonwood trees that lines the opposite bank, she found herself upon the border of a field where the white, bursting cotton, with the dew upon it, gleamed for acres and acres like frosted silver in the early dawn.

La Folle drew a long, deep breath as she gazed across the country. She walked slowly and uncertainly, like one who hardly knows how, looking about her as she went.

The cabins, that yesterday had sent a clamor of voices to pursue her, were quiet now. No one was yet astir at Bellissime. Only the birds that darted here and there from hedges were awake, and singing their matins.

When La Folle came to the broad stretch of velvety lawn that surrounded the house, she moved slowly and with delight over the springy turf, that was delicious beneath her tread.

She stopped to find whence came those perfumes that were assailing her senses with memories from a time far gone.

There they were, stealing up to her from the thousand blue violets that peeped out from green, luxuriant beds. There they were, showering down from the big waxen bells of the magnolias far above her head, and from the jessamine clumps around her.

There were roses, too, without number. To right and left palms spread in broad and graceful curves. It all looked like enchantment beneath the sparkling sheen of dew.

When La Folle had slowly and cautiously mounted the many steps that led up to the veranda, she turned to look back at the perilous ascent she had made. Then she caught sight of the river, bending like a silver bow at the foot of Bellissime. Exultation possessed her soul.

La Folle rapped softly upon a door near at hand. Chéri's mother soon cautiously opened it. Quickly and cleverly she dissembled the astonishment she felt at seeing La Folle.

"Ah, La Folle! Is it you, so early?"

"*Oui,* madame. I come ax how my po' li'le Chéri to, 's mo'nin'."

"He is feeling easier, thank you, La Folle. Dr. Bonfils says it will be nothing serious. He's sleeping now. Will you come back when he awakes?"

"*Non,* madame. I'm goin' wait yair tell Chéri wake up." La Folle seated herself upon the topmost step of the veranda.

A look of wonder and deep content crept into her face as she watched for the first time the sun rise upon the new, the beautiful world beyond the bayou.

1894

Landscape as Antagonist

The Literary Naturalists

The first generation of literary naturalists—Frank Norris, Theodore Dreiser, Jack London, and Stephen Crane—came to maturity around 1900; the second generation, including young Faulkner, during the 1910's and 1920's. Their imagination of the American environment during this time was caught and colored by two phenomena.

On the one hand, there was, as a contemporary critic, Warner Berthoff, observes, "the rapid and disruptive emergence of the modern cultural order": urban, technological, oppressive, and wholly taken up with the ideal of progress and with a capitalistic version of the survival of the fittest. For the literary naturalists, drawn as they were to its victims, the new order was "a condition of life as inexorable as the order of the seasons or the division of the sexes and as strictly determining." The literary naturalists were indeed determinists. With the care and apparent detachment of laboratory scientists they noted in their "documentary" fiction the determining effects both of biology (heredity, ego, hunger and sex drives, pathological "mind-sets," such as the Swede's in Crane's story) and of environment. They apprehended the urban environment in the same terms that the Puritans had apprehended the wilderness: it was wild (that is, beyond human control), inhuman, and dangerous. It was the abode of chaos and waste, and it was animated by alien energies now called "chemical" and "mechanical" rather than demonic.

On the other hand, there were those wilderness or waste landscapes still relatively untouched by the modern cultural order: the sea, the desert Southwest, the Pacific Northwest (Jack London's territory), the northern Great Plains ("The Blue Hotel"), and the rural South (Faulkner's Mississippi). Here the naturalists made the shocking discovery that the modern cultural order was not a departure from the laws of nature but a direct reflection of it. Here they discovered that though man must and could open his sensibilities to the natural world, nature—a nature "red in tooth and claw," a nature which, as Henry Adams wrote in his *Education,* had lost "the sugar-coating that she shows to youth"—was inhuman, arbitrary, and unforgivably impartial in its relationship to the human species.

Darwin and his scientific disciples had begun stripping the "sugar-coating" from nature in several areas. Christian orthodoxy, viewing the world-experience as a brief moment in eternity, tended to assert that the world was very young (perhaps 6000 years) and that if it had not been made literally in six days by God it had emerged just as suddenly and miraculously by cataclysm; Darwin, Charles Lyell, and others (including Muir) inaugurated, on the other hand, the new concept of a gradual and seemingly endless process of change in the natural world. In addition, Darwin's convincing theory of natural selection—which argued that within every species there was constant change that resulted from materialistic struggle—blurred the lines of distinction between species and suggested that no species, not even man, was immutable; man was connected by physical laws, laws which affected his very survival, to his environment and to the other living things in it. Finally, Darwin's very approach to nature as well as his findings suggested that life was not so much a matter of emotion or even of ethics, but of detachment, material force, and adaptability.

The emergence of Darwinian theory and of the new, remorseless urban environment were perhaps the chief factors in the new design of nature and of landscape which took shape after the Civil War, but they were not the only ones. At least two other factors were involved. One was the environment of the Far West—a wilderness somehow both more ominous and drearier than the deciduous forests of the east—over which spilled the post-war torrent of emigrants. The reports that came back from these emigrants (explorers, naturalists, tourists, and settlers) reinforced the sense of struggle and violence and the enormous and terrible indifference, the overwhelming elemental energies, the long epochs of mineral and pre-human existence that constituted the new design (see The Ways West). Even that ecstatic "John the Baptist" Muir, suited as he was by temperament to loneliness and to the physical energies of the Sierras, had his moments of disorientation and panic (see "A Near View of the High Sierras").

The other factor had to do precisely with the spectacularly rapid conversion of the Midwest and the trans-Mississippi West from what Howard Mumford Jones calls "a state of nature to a state of industry." That conversion could have been accomplished only by the new technological order with all of its energy and corruption: railroads, land-grabbing, and farm machines. The second half of The Ways West delineates some of the effects of the machine in the western gardens.

In their landscapes, the literary naturalists (and to a lesser extent the Southern and Midwestern regionalists) register the shock of these circumstances and the design of landscape which they gave shape to. For these writers the ancient spiritual cords connecting man and landscape seemed cut clean through. They experienced instead, with a sense of diminishment and victimization, the profound *physical* connection between man and a non-human universe. Wrote Henry Adams of his own shock of recognition when his sister died of convulsions after a cab bruised her foot:

> The first serious consciousness of Nature's gesture—her attitude towards life—took form . . . as a phantasm, a nightmare, an insanity of force. For

> the first time, the stage-scenery of the senses collapsed; the human mind felt itself stripped naked, vibrating in a void of shapeless energies, with resistless mass, colliding, crushing, wasting, and destroying what these same energies had created and labored from eternity to perfect. Society became fantastic, a vision of pantomime with a mechanical motion . . . The usual anodynes of social medicine became evident artifice. Stoicism was perhaps the best; religion was the most human; but the idea that any personal deity could find pleasure or profit in torturing a poor woman, by accident, with a fiendish cruelty known to man only in perverted and insane temperaments, could not be held for a moment . . . God might be, as the Church said, a Substance, but He could not be a Person.

The natural settings of the literary naturalists are an impressionistic embodiment of such a world-view. The landscapes are characteristically vast, and they are characteristically overwhelmed by spectacular and unrelenting discharges of energy (storms, blizzards, droughts, floods). The perspective does not achieve the physical and psychic distance characteristic of the Romantics. It is a perspective immersed and overwhelmed by sublimity and so threatened rather than elevated by it. In relation to the sublime, inhuman energies in which they are immersed, humans seem tiny and defenseless, and they are further reduced in significance by metaphoric equations with the lowest forms of animal life: ants, lice, and other vermin. In the meantime, the forces set loose in the landscape are magnified by equations with the mechanical forces being set loose by the new cultural order: note, for example, how Crane makes blizzard-driven snowflakes "bullets" and how Faulkner makes the Mississippi flood rumble like a "subway" or an "express train" toward the tiny thread of ant-men trying to contain it. Often the power of these forces is further magnified (in Crane's work, at least) by restricting the point of view to the people being buffeted by them—people who can feel and hear as well as see—to the point of losing everything but an immediate, fragmented, and disjointed perspective on the landscape.

Early nineteenth-century writers were able to transfigure the terror in sublimity (and in themselves) by seeing it as an instrument or a revelation of the power of God, a power ultimately benevolent. The literary naturalists, on the other hand, conceived of sublimity only as the arbitrary, implacable instrument of an infinitely indifferent mechanical universe. Like the new cultural order, the universe dominated, diminished, and victimized anything of merely human status. It was not simply the determinant of human life, but quite often its antagonist as well. In "The Blue Hotel," for example, Crane sets up the landscape as antagonist. Its cold penetrates every protection (clothes, buildings, even human charity), snuffing out physical and spiritual warmth, creating, as it shoots its snow like bullets, an apparently irresistible environment of frenzy and violence.

Yet, ironically, the naturalists' landscape-as-antagonist rarely kills. Subverting man's will to live, creating in him every expectation of death, it toys with him by anticlimactically denying him death: "One was a coxcomb not to die in it. However, the Swede found a saloon."

Even more significantly, the landscape in literary naturalism becomes passive enough at times to act as a reflection or prefiguration of the human psyche. At these moments it still wears, as Emerson would have said, "the colors of the spirit." In "The Blue Hotel" the spiritual colors of the Swede and his antagonists, for example, are symbolically projected onto the snow. Swede's manic mind-set deepens the blue of the evening and of the hotel, and when, after struggling through the blizzard, he opens the door of the saloon in which he will anticlimactically die, the light of the saloon stains the snow the color of blood.

Partly through the use of such symbolism, partly through explicit statement, Crane and other literary naturalists suggest that the inhuman actions of the universe are no excuse for the inhuman actions of men to each other or to themselves. Even if it is illusion, a person's conceit of his own value and significance must be "the very engine of life," for man's only hope for survival as man is in seeing clearly, without the coloration of sentiment, the way things really are and in refusing to take on the role of oppression even as he accepts the fact that oppression is part of the natural and social order of things.

The inheritance of the literary naturalists has been twofold. Quite clearly they bequeathed their vision and their techniques to modern landscapes of technological ruin, which deal with the devastating effects of mechanical force on landscape. But equally clearly, beneath the shock to the imagination, they register the consciousness of a symbiotic web which connects all physical being and which ecologists and other more contemporary writers would take as both an article of faith and a cause for celebration.

Stephen Crane

The Blue Hotel

Inspired by Frederic Remington's paintings and by the Mississippi of Mark Twain's work, Stephen Crane contracted with a newspaper syndicate to spend most of 1895 (his twenty-third year) on a tour of the West. In February he visited a desolate town in Nebraska and saw a hotel painted light blue: that, the landscape, some of the people he met, and a bar fight he was involved in became the raw material of "The Blue Hotel," which he finished three years later, in February 1898. The conflict between the Western myth which attracted him and the realities he witnessed is evident in many stories ("Moonlight in the Snow," "Twelve O'Clock," and "A Self-Made Man," for example, are parodies of Bret Harte's West). In this story, the conflict locates itself on the one hand in the Swede, who is obsessed with the "dime-novel" myth of violence, and on the other hand in Scully, who is a businessman bent on making colorful and profitable "seductions" of travelers and who boasts that "in two years Romper'll be a met-tro-pol-is." The violence which climaxes the story seems to be part of the human condition rather than of the Western frontier.

I

THE PALACE HOTEL at Fort Romper was painted a light blue, a shade that is on the legs of a kind of heron, causing the bird to declare its position against any background. The Palace Hotel, then, was always screaming and howling in a way that made the dazzling winter landscape of Nebraska seem only a grey swampish hush. It stood alone on the prairie, and when the snow was falling the town two hundred yards away was not visible. But when the traveller alighted at the railway station he was obliged to pass the Palace Hotel before he could come upon the company of low clapboard houses which composed Fort Romper, and it was not to be thought that any traveller could pass the Palace Hotel without looking at it. Pat Scully, the proprietor, had proved himself a master of strategy when he chose his paints. It is true that on clear days, when the great transcontinental expresses, long lines of swaying Pullmans, swept through Fort Romper, passengers were overcome at the sight, and the cult that knows the brown-reds and the subdivisions of the dark greens of the East expressed shame, pity, horror, in a laugh. But to the citizens of this prairie town and to the people who would naturally stop there, Pat Scully had performed a feat. With this opulence and splendour, these creeds, classes, egotisms, that streamed through Romper on the rails day after day, they had no colour in common.

As if the displayed delights of such a blue hotel were not sufficiently enticing, it was Scully's habit to go every morning and evening to meet the leisurely trains that stopped at Romper and work his seductions upon any man that he might see wavering, gripsack in hand.

One morning, when a snow-crusted engine dragged its long string of freight cars and its one passenger coach to the station, Scully performed the marvel of catching three men. One was a shaky and quick-eyed Swede, with a great shining cheap valise; one was a tall bronzed cowboy, who was on his way to a ranch near the Dakota line; one was a little silent man from the East, who didn't look it, and didn't announce it. Scully practically made them prisoners. He was so nimble and merry and kindly that each probably felt it would be the height of brutality to try to escape. They trudged off over the creaking board sidewalks in the wake of the eager little Irishman. He wore a heavy fur cap squeezed tightly down on his head. It caused his two red ears to stick out stiffly, as if they were made of tin.

At last, Scully, elaborately, with boisterous hospitality, conducted them through the portals of the blue hotel. The room which they entered was small. It seemed to be merely a proper temple for an enormous stove, which, in the centre, was humming with godlike violence. At various points on its surface the iron had become luminous and glowed yellow from the heat. Beside the stove Scully's son Johnnie was playing High-Five with an old farmer who had whiskers both grey and sandy. They were quarrelling. Frequently the old farmer turned his face toward a box of sawdust—coloured brown from tobacco juice—that was behind the stove, and spat with an air of great impatience and irritation. With a loud flourish of words Scully destroyed the game of cards, and bustled his son upstairs with part of the baggage of the new guests. He himself conducted them to three basins of the coldest water in the world. The cowboy and the Easterner burnished themselves fiery red with this water, until it seemed to be some kind of metal-polish. The Swede, however, merely dipped his fingers gingerly and with trepidation. It was notable that throughout this series of small ceremonies the three travellers were made to feel that Scully was very benevolent. He was conferring great favours upon them. He handed the towel from one to another with an air of philanthropic impulse.

Afterward they went to the first room, and, sitting about the stove, listened to Scully's officious clamour at his daughters, who were preparing the midday meal. They reflected in the silence of experienced men who tread carefully amid new people. Nevertheless, the old farmer, stationary, invincible in his chair near the warmest part of the stove, turned his face from the sawdust-box frequently and addressed a glowing commonplace to the strangers. Usually he was answered in short but adequate sentences by either the cowboy or the Easterner. The Swede said nothing. He seemed to be occupied in making furtive estimates of each man in the room. One might have thought that he had the sense of silly suspicion which comes to guilt. He resembled a badly frightened man.

Later, at dinner, he spoke a little, addressing his conversation entirely to Scully. He volunteered that he had come from New York, where for ten years he had worked as a tailor. These facts seemed to strike Scully as fascinating, and afterward he volunteered that he had lived at Romper for fourteen years. The Swede asked about the crops and the price of labour. He seemed barely to listen to Scully's extended replies. His eyes continued to rove from man to man.

Finally, with a laugh and a wink, he said that some of these Western communities were very dangerous; and after his statement he straightened his legs under the table, tilted his head, and laughed again, loudly. It was plain that the demonstration had no meaning to the others. They looked at him wondering and in silence.

II

As the men trooped heavily back into the front room, the two little windows presented views of a turmoiling sea of snow. The huge arms of the wind were making attempts—mighty, circular, futile—to embrace the flakes as they sped. A gate-post like a still man with a blanched face stood aghast amid this profligate fury. In a hearty voice Scully announced the presence of a blizzard. The guests of the blue hotel, lighting their pipes, assented with grunts of lazy masculine contentment. No island of the sea could be exempt in the degree of this little room with its humming stove. Johnnie, son of Scully, in a tone which defined his opinion of his ability as a card-player, challenged the old farmer of both grey and sandy whiskers to a game of High-Five. The farmer agreed with a contemptuous and bitter scoff. They sat close to the stove, and squared their knees under a wide board. The cowboy and the Easterner watched the game with interest. The Swede remained near the window, aloof, but with a countenance that showed signs of an inexplicable excitement.

The play of Johnnie and the grey-beard was suddenly ended by another quarrel. The old man arose while casting a look of heated scorn at his adversary. He slowly buttoned his coat, and then stalked with fabulous dignity from the room. In the discreet silence of all the other men the Swede laughed. His laughter rang somehow childish. Men by this time had begun to look at him askance, as if they wished to inquire what ailed him.

A new game was formed jocosely. The cowboy volunteered to become the partner of Johnnie, and they all then turned to ask the Swede to throw in his lot with the little Easterner. He asked some questions about the game, and, learning that it wore many names, and that he had played it when it was under an alias, he accepted the invitation. He strode toward the men nervously, as if he expected to be assaulted. Finally, seated, he gazed from face to face and laughed shrilly. This laugh was so strange that the Easterner looked up quickly, the cowboy sat intent and with his mouth open, and Johnnie paused, holding the cards with still fingers.

Afterward there was a short silence. Then Johnnie said, "Well, let's get at it. Come on now!" They pulled their chairs forward until their knees were bunched under the board. They began to play, and their interest in the game caused the others to forget the manner of the Swede.

The cowboy was a board-whacker. Each time that he held superior cards he whanged them, one by one, with exceeding force, down upon the improvised table, and took the tricks with a glowing air of prowess and pride that sent thrills of indignation into the hearts of his opponents. A game with a broad-whacker in it is sure to become intense. The countenances of the Easterner and the Swede were miserable whenever the cowboy thundered down his aces and kings, while Johnnie, his eyes gleaming with joy, chuckled and chuckled.

Because of the absorbing play none considered the strange ways of the Swede. They paid strict heed to the game. Finally, during a lull caused by a new deal, the Swede suddenly addressed Johnnie: "I suppose there have been a good many men killed in this room." The jaws of the others dropped and they looked at him.

"What in hell are you talking about?" said Johnnie.

The Swede laughed again his blatant laugh, full of a kind of false courage and defiance. "Oh, you know what I mean all right," he answered.

"I'm a liar if I do!" Johnnie protested. The card was halted, and the men stared at the Swede. Johnnie evidently felt that as the son of the proprietor he should make a direct inquiry. "Now, what might you be drivin' at, mister?" he asked. The Swede winked at him. It was a wink full of cunning. His fingers shook on the edge of the board. "Oh, maybe you think I have been to nowheres. Maybe you think I'm a tenderfoot?"

"I don't know nothin' about you," answered Johnnie, "and I don't give a damn where you've been. All I got to say is that I don't know what you're driving at. There hain't never been nobody killed in this room."

The cowboy, who had been steadily gazing at the Swede, then spoke: "What's wrong with you, mister?"

Apparently it seemed to the Swede that he was formidably menaced. He shivered and turned white near the corners of his mouth. He sent an appealing glance in the direction of the little Easterner. During these moments he did not forget to wear his air of advanced pot-valour. "They say they don't know what I mean," he remarked mockingly to the Easterner.

The latter answered after prolonged and cautious reflection. "I don't understand you," he said, impassively.

The Swede made a movement then which announced that he thought he had encountered treachery from the only quarter where he had expected sympathy, if not help. "Oh, I see you are all against me. I see—"

The cowboy was in a state of deep stupefaction. "Say," he cried, as he tumbled the deck violently down upon the board, "say, what are you gittin' at, hey?"

The Swede sprang up with the celerity of a man escaping from a snake on the floor. "I don't want to fight!" he shouted. "I don't want to fight!"

The cowboy stretched his long legs indolently and deliberately. His hands were in his pockets. He spat into the sawdust-box. "Well, who the hell thought you did?" he inquired.

The Swede backed rapidly toward a corner of the room. His hands were out protectingly in front of his chest, but he was making an obvious struggle to control his fright. "Gentlemen," he quavered, "I suppose I am going to be killed before I can leave this house! I suppose I am going to be killed before I can leave this house!" In his eyes was the dying-swan look. Through the windows could be seen the snow turning blue in the shadow of dusk. The wind tore at the house, and some loose thing beat regularly against the clapboards like a spirit tapping.

A door opened, and Scully himself entered. He paused in surprise as he noted the tragic attitude of the Swede. Then he said, "What's the matter here?"

The Swede answered him swiftly and eagerly: "These men are going to kill me."

"Kill you!" ejaculated Scully. "Kill you! What are you talkin'?"

The Swede made the gesture of a martyr.

Scully wheeled sternly upon his son. "What is this, Johnnie?"

The lad had grown sullen. "Damned if I know," he answered. "I can't make no sense to it." He began to shuffle the cards, fluttering them together with an angry snap. "He says a good many men have been killed in this room, or something like that. And he says he's goin' to be killed here too. I don't know what ails him. He's crazy, I shouldn't wonder."

Scully then looked for explanation to the cowboy, but the cowboy simply shrugged his shoulders.

"Kill you?" said Scully again to the Swede. "Kill you? Man, you're off your nut."

"Oh, I know," burst out the Swede. "I know what will happen. Yes, I'm crazy—yes. Yes, of course, I'm crazy—yes. But I know one thing—" There was a sort of sweat of misery and terror upon his face. "I know I won't get out of here alive."

The cowboy drew a deep breath, as if his mind was passing into the last stages of dissolution. "Well, I'm doggoned," he whispered to himself.

Scully wheeled suddenly and faced his son. "You've been troublin' this man!"

Johnnie's voice was loud with its burden of grievance. "Why, good Gawd, I ain't done nothin' to 'im."

The Swede broke in. "Gentlemen, do not disturb yourselves. I will leave this house. I will go away, because"—he accused them dramatically with his glance—"because I do not want to be killed."

Scully was furious with his son. "Will you tell me what is the matter, you young divil? What's the matter, anyhow? Speak out!"

"Blame it!" cried Johnnie in despair, "don't I tell you I don't know? He—he says we want to kill him, and that's all I know. I can't tell what ails him."

The Swede continued to repeat: "Never mind, Mr. Scully; never mind. I will leave this house. I will go away, because I do not wish to be killed. Yes, of course, I am crazy—yes. But I know one thing! I will go away. I will leave this house. Never mind, Mr. Scully; never mind. I will go away."

"You will not go 'way," said Scully. "You will not go 'way until I hear the reason of this business. If anybody has troubled you I will take care of him. This is my house. You are under my roof, and I will not allow any peaceable man to be troubled here." He cast a terrible eye upon Johnnie, the cowboy, and the Easterner.

"Never mind, Mr. Scully; never mind. I will go away. I do not wish to be killed." The Swede moved toward the door which opened upon the stairs. It was evidently his intention to go at once for his baggage.

"No, no," shouted Scully peremptorily; but the white-faced man slid by him and disappeared. "Now," said Scully severely, "what does this mane?"

Johnnie and the cowboy cried together: "Why, we didn't do nothin' to 'im!"

Scully's eyes were cold. "No," he said, "you didn't?"

Johnnie swore a deep oath. "Why, this is the wildest loon I ever see. We didn't do nothin' at all. We were jest sittin' here playin' cards, and he—"

The father suddenly spoke to the Easterner. "Mr. Blanc," he asked, "what has these boys been doin'?"

The Easterner reflected again. "I didn't see anything wrong at all," he said at last, slowly.

Scully began to howl. "But what does it mane?" He stared ferociously at his son. "I have a mind to lather you for this, me boy."

Johnnie was frantic. "Well, what have I done?" he bawled at his father.

III

"I think you are tongue-tied," said Scully finally to his son, the cowboy, and the Easterner; and at the end of this scornful sentence he left the room.

Upstairs the Swede was swiftly fastening the straps of his great valise. Once his back happened to be half turned toward the door, and, hearing a noise there, he wheeled and sprang up, uttering a loud cry. Scully's wrinkled visage showed grimly in the light of the small lamp he carried. This yellow effulgence, streaming upward, coloured only his prominent features, and left his eyes, for instance, in mysterious shadow. He resembled a murderer.

"Man! man!" he exclaimed, "have you gone daffy?"

"Oh, no! Oh, no!" rejoined the other. "There are people in this world who know pretty nearly as much as you do—understand?"

For a moment they stood gazing at each other. Upon the Swede's deathly pale cheeks were two spots brightly crimson and sharply edged, as if they had been carefully painted. Scully placed the light on the table and sat himself on the edge of the bed. He spoke ruminatively. "By cracky, I never heard of such a thing in my life. It's a complete muddle. I can't, for the soul of me, think how you ever got this idea into your head." Presently he lifted his eyes and asked: "And did you sure think they were going to kill you?"

The Swede scanned the old man as if he wished to see into his mind. "I did," he said at last. He obviously suspected that this answer might precipitate an outbreak. As he pulled on a strap his whole arm shook, the elbow wavering like a bit of paper.

Scully banged his hand impressively on the footboard of the bed. "Why, man, we're goin' to have a line of ilictric street-cars in this town next spring."

" 'A line of electric street-cars,' " repeated the Swede, stupidly.

"And," said Scully, "there's a new railroad goin' to be built down from Broken Arm to here. Not to mintion the four churches and the smashin' big brick school-house. Then there's the big factory, too. Why, in two years Romper'll be a met-tro-*pol*-is."

Having finished the preparation of his baggage, the Swede straightened himself. "Mr. Scully," he said, with sudden hardihood, "how much do I owe you?"

"You don't owe me anythin'," said the old man, angrily.

"Yes, I do," retorted the Swede. He took seventy-five cents from his pocket and tendered it to Scully; but the latter snapped his fingers in disdainful refusal. However, it happened that they both stood gazing in a strange fashion at three silver pieces on the Swede's open palm.

"I'll not take your money," said Scully at last. "Not after what's been goin' on here." Then a plan seemed to strike him. "Here," he cried, picking up his lamp and moving toward the door. "Here! Come with me a minute."

"No," said the Swede, in overwhelming alarm.

"Yes," urged the old man. "Come on! I want you to come and see a picter—just across the hall—in my room."

The Swede must have concluded that his hour was come. His jaw dropped and his teeth showed like a dead man's. He ultimately followed Scully across the corridor, but he had the step of one hung in chains.

Scully flashed the light high on the wall of his own chamber. There was revealed a ridiculous photograph of a little girl. She was leaning against a balustrade of gorgeous decoration, and the formidable bang to her hair was prominent. The figure was as graceful as an upright sled-stake, and, withal, it was of the hue of lead. "There," said Scully, tenderly, "that's the picter of my little girl that died. Her name was Carrie. She had the purtiest hair you ever saw! I was that fond of her, she—"

Turning then, he saw that the Swede was not contemplating the picture at all, but, instead, was keeping keen watch on the gloom in the rear.

''Look, man!'' cried Scully, heartily. ''That's the picter of my little gal that died. Her name was Carrie. And then here's the picter of my oldest boy, Michael. He's a lawyer in Lincoln, an' doin' well. I gave that boy a grand eddication, and I'm glad for it now. He's a fine boy. Look at 'im now. Ain't he bold as blazes, him there in Lincoln, an honoured an' respicted gintleman! An honoured and respicted gintleman,'' concluded Scully with a flourish. And, so saying, he smote the Swede jovially on the back.

The Swede faintly smiled.

''Now,'' said the old man, ''there's only one more thing.'' He dropped suddenly to the floor and thrust his head beneath the bed. The Swede could hear his muffled voice. ''I'd keep it under me piller if it wasn't for that boy Johnnie. Then there's the old woman—Where is it now? I never put it twice in the same place. Ah, now come out with you!''

Presently he backed clumsily from under the bed, dragging with him an old coat rolled into a bundle. ''I've fetched him,'' he muttered. Kneeling on the floor, he unrolled the coat and extracted from its heart a large yellow-brown whisky-bottle.

His first manœuvre was to hold the bottle up to the light. Reassured, apparently, that nobody had been tampering with it, he thrust it with a generous movement toward the Swede.

The weak-kneed Swede was about to eagerly clutch this element of strength, but he suddenly jerked his hand away and cast a look of horror upon Scully.

''Drink,'' said the old man affectionately. He had risen to his feet, and now stood facing the Swede.

There was a silence. Then again Scully said: ''Drink!''

The Swede laughed wildly. He grabbed the bottle, put it to his mouth; and as his lips curled absurdly around the opening and his throat worked, he kept his glance, burning with hatred, upon the old man's face.

IV

After the departure of Scully the three men, with the cardboard still upon their knees, preserved for a long time an astounded silence. Then Johnnie said: ''That's the doddangedest Swede I ever see.''

''He ain't no Swede,'' said the cowboy, scornfully.

''Well, what is he then?'' cried Johnnie. ''What is he then?''

''It's my opinion,'' replied the cowboy deliberately, ''he's some kind of a Dutchman.'' It was a venerable custom of the country to entitle as Swedes all light-haired men who spoke with a heavy tongue. In consequence the idea of the cowboy was not without its daring. ''Yes, sir,'' he repeated. ''It's my opinion this feller is some kind of a Dutchman.''

''Well, he says he's a Swede, anyhow,'' muttered Johnnie, sulkily. He turned to the Easterner: ''What do you think, Mr. Blanc?''

''Oh, I don't know,'' replied the Easterner.

''Well, what do you think makes him act that way?'' asked the cowboy.

''Why, he's frightened.'' The Easterner knocked his pipe against a rim of the stove. ''He's clear frightened out of his boots.''

''What at?'' cried Johnnie and the cowboy together.

The Easterner reflected over his answer.

''What at?'' cried the others again.

''Oh, I don't know, but it seems to me this man has been reading dime novels, and he thinks he's right out in the middle of it—the shootin' and stabbin' and all.''

''But,'' said the cowboy, deeply scandalized, ''this ain't Wyoming, ner none of them places. This is Nebrasker.''

''Yes,'' added Johnnie, ''an' why don't he wait till he gits *out West?''*

The travelled Easterner laughed. ''It isn't different there even—not in these days. But he thinks he's right in the middle of hell.''

Johnnie and the cowboy mused long.

''It's awful funny,'' remarked Johnnie at last.

''Yes,'' said the cowboy. ''This is a queer game. I hope we don't git snowed in, because then we'd have to stand this here man bein' around with us all the time. That wouldn't be no good.''

''I wish pop would throw him out,'' said Johnnie.

Presently they heard a loud stamping on the stairs, accompanied by ringing jokes in the voice of old Scully, and laughter, evidently from the Swede. The men around the stove stared vacantly at each other. ''Gosh!'' said the cowboy. The door flew open, and old Scully, flushed and anecdotal, came into the room. He was jabbering at the Swede, who followed him, laughing bravely. It was the entry of two roisterers from a banquet hall.

''Come now,'' said Scully sharply to the three seated men, ''move up and give us a chance at the stove.'' The cowboy and the Easterner obediently sidled their chairs to make room for the new-comers. Johnnie, however, simply arranged himself in a more indolent attitude, and then remained motionless.

''Come! Git over, there,'' said Scully.

''Plenty of room on the other side of the stove,'' said Johnnie.

''Do you think we want to sit in the draught?'' roared the father.

But the Swede here interposed with a grandeur of confidence. ''No, no. Let the boy sit where he likes,'' he cried in a bullying voice to the father.

''All right! All right!'' said Scully, deferentially. The cowboy and the Easterner exchanged glances of wonder.

The five chairs were formed in a crescent about one side of the stove. The Swede began to talk; he talked arrogantly, profanely, angrily. Johnnie, the cowboy, and the Easterner maintained a morose silence, while old Scully appeared to be receptive and eager, breaking in constantly with sympathetic ejaculations.

Finally the Swede announced that he was thirsty. He moved in his chair, and said that he would go for a drink of water.

"I'll git it for you," cried Scully at once.

"No," said the Swede, contemptuously. "I'll get it for myself." He arose and stalked with the air of an owner off into the executive parts of the hotel.

As soon as the Swede was out of hearing Scully sprang to his feet and whispered intensely to the others: "Upstairs he thought I was tryin' to poison 'im."

"Say," said Johnnie, "this makes me sick. Why don't you throw 'im out in the snow?"

"Why, he's all right now," declared Scully. "It was only that he was from the East, and he thought this was a tough place. That's all. He's all right now."

The cowboy looked with admiration upon the Easterner. "You were straight," he said. "You were on to that there Dutchman."

"Well," said Johnnie to his father, "he may be all right now, but I don't see it. Other time he was scared, but now he's too fresh."

Scully's speech was always a combination of Irish brogue and idiom, Western twang and idiom, and scraps of curiously formal diction taken from the story-books and newspapers. He now hurled a strange mass of language at the head of his son. "What do I keep? What do I keep? What do I keep?" he demanded, in a voice of thunder. He slapped his knee impressively, to indicate that he himself was going to make reply, and that all should heed. "I keep a hotel," he shouted. "A hotel, do you mind? A guest under my roof has sacred privileges. He is to be intimidated by none. Not one word shall he hear that would prijudice him in favour of goin' away. I'll not have it. There's no place in this here town where they can say they iver took in a guest of mine because he was afraid to stay here." He wheeled suddenly upon the cowboy and the Easterner. "Am I right?"

"Yes, Mr. Scully," said the cowboy, "I think you're right."

"Yes, Mr. Scully," said the Easterner, "I think you're right."

V

At six-o'clock supper, the Swede fizzed like a fire-wheel. He sometimes seemed on the point of bursting into riotous song, and in all his madness he was encouraged by old Scully. The Easterner was encased in reserve; the cowboy sat in wide-mouthed amazement, forgetting to eat, while Johnnie wrathily demolished great plates of food. The daughters of the house, when they were obliged to replenish the biscuits, approached as warily as Indians, and, having succeeded in their purpose, fled with ill-concealed trepidation. The Swede domineered the whole feast, and he gave it the appearance of a cruel bacchanal.

He seemed to have grown suddenly taller; he gazed, brutally disdainful, into every face. His voice rang through the room. Once when he jabbed out harpoon-fashion with his fork to pinion a biscuit, the weapon nearly impaled the hand of the Easterner, which had been stretched quietly out for the same biscuit.

After supper, as the men filed toward the other room, the Swede smote Scully ruthlessly on the shoulder. "Well, old boy, that was a good, square meal." Johnnie looked hopefully at his father; he knew that shoulder was tender from an old fall; and, indeed, it appeared for a moment as if Scully was going to flame out over the matter, but in the end he smiled a sickly smile and remained silent. The others understood from his manner that he was admitting his responsibility for the Swede's new view-point.

Johnnie, however, addressed his parent in an aside. "Why don't you license somebody to kick you downstairs?" Scully scowed darkly by way of reply.

When they were gathered about the stove, the Swede insisted on another game of High-Five. Scully gently deprecated the plan at first, but the Swede turned a wolfish glare upon him. The old man subsided, and the Swede canvassed the others. In his tone there was always a great threat. The cowboy and the Easterner both remarked indifferently that they would play. Scully said that he would presently have to go to meet the 6.58 train, and so the Swede turned menacingly upon Johnnie. For a moment their glances crossed like blades, and then Johnnie smiled and said, "Yes, I'll play."

They formed a square, with the little board on their knees. The Easterner and the Swede were again partners. As the play went on, it was noticeable that the cowboy was not board-whacking as usual. Meanwhile, Scully, near the lamp, had put on his spectacles and, with an appearance curiously like an old priest, was reading a newspaper. In time he went out to meet the 6.58 train, and, despite his precautions, a gust of polar wind whirled into the room as he opened the door. Besides scattering the cards, it chilled the players to the marrow. The Swede cursed frightfully. When Scully returned, his entrance disturbed a cosy and friendly scene. The Swede again cursed. But presently they were once more intent, their heads bent forward and their hands moving swiftly. The Swede had adopted the fashion of board-whacking.

Scully took up his paper and for a long time remained immersed in matters which were extraordinarily remote from him. The lamp burned badly, and once he stopped to adjust the wick. The newspaper, as he turned from page to page, rustled with a slow and comfortable sound. Then suddenly he heard three terrible words: "You are cheatin'!"

Such scenes often prove that there can be little of dramatic import in environment. Any room can present a tragic front; any room can be comic. This little den was now hideous as a torture-chamber. The new faces of the men themselves had changed it upon the instant. The Swede held a huge fist in front of Johnnie's face, while the latter looked steadily over it into the blazing orbs of his accuser. The Easterner had grown pallid; the cowboy's jaw had dropped in that expression of bovine amazement which was one of his important mannerisms. After the three words, the first sound in the room was made by Scully's paper as it floated forgotten to his feet. His spectacles had also fallen from his nose, but by a clutch he had saved them in air. His hand, grasping the spectacles, now remained poised awkwardly and near his shoulder. He stared at the card-players.

Probably the silence was while a second elapsed. Then, if the floor had been suddenly twitched out from under the men they could not have moved quicker. The five had projected themselves headlong toward a common point. It happened that Johnnie, in rising to hurl himself upon the Swede, had stumbled slightly because of his curiously instinctive care for the cards and the board. The loss of the moment allowed time for the arrival of Scully, and also allowed the cowboy time to give the Swede a great push which sent him staggering back. The men found tongue together, and hoarse shouts of rage, appeal, or fear burst from every throat. The cowboy pushed and jostled feverishly at the Swede, and the Easterner and Scully clung wildly to Johnnie; but through the smoky air, above the swaying bodies of the peace-compellers, the eyes of the two warriors ever sought each other in glances of challenge that were at once hot and steely.

Of course the board had been overturned, and now the whole company of cards was scattered over the floor, where the boots of the men trampled the fat and painted kings and queens as they gazed with their silly eyes at the war that was waging above them.

Scully's voice was dominating the yells. "Stop now! Stop, I say! Stop, now—"

Johnnie, as he struggled to burst through the rank formed by Scully and the Easterner, was crying, "Well, he says I cheated! He says I cheated! I won't allow no man to say I cheated! If he says I cheated, he's a —— ——!"

The cowboy was telling the Swede, "Quit, now! Quit, d'ye hear—"

The screams of the Swede never ceased: "He did cheat! I saw him! I saw him—"

As for the Easterner, he was importuning in a voice that was not heeded: "Wait a moment, can't you? Oh, wait a moment. What's the good of a fight over a game of cards? Wait a moment—"

In this tumult no complete sentences were clear. "Cheat"—"Quit"—"He says"—these fragments pierced the uproar and rang out sharply. It was remarkable that, whereas Scully undoubtedly made the most noise, he was the least heard of any of the riotous band.

Then suddenly there was a great cessation. It was as if each man had paused for breath; and although the room was still lighted with the anger of men, it could be seen that there was no danger of immediate conflict, and at once Johnnie, shouldering his way forward, almost succeeded in confronting the Swede. "What did you say I cheated for? What did you say I cheated for? I don't cheat, and I won't let no man say I do!"

The Swede said, "I saw you! I saw you!"

"Well," cried Johnnie, "I'll fight any man what says I cheat!"

"No, you won't," said the cowboy. "Not here."

"Ah, be still, can't you?" said Scully, coming between them.

The quiet was sufficient to allow the Easterner's voice to be heard. He was repeating, "Oh, wait a moment, can't you? What's the good of a fight over a game of cards? Wait a moment!"

Johnnie, his red face appearing above his father's shoulder, hailed the Swede again. "Did you say I cheated?"

The Swede showed his teeth. "Yes."

"Then," said Johnnie, "we must fight."

"Yes, fight," roared the Swede. He was like a demoniac. "Yes, fight! I'll show you what kind of a man I am! I'll show you who you want to fight! Maybe you think I can't fight! Maybe you think I can't! I'll show you, you skin, you card-sharp! Yes, you cheated! You cheated! You cheated!"

"Well, let's go at it, then, mister," said Johnnie, coolly.

The cowboy's brow was beaded with sweat from his efforts in intercepting all sorts of raids. He turned in despair to Scully. "What are you goin' to do now?"

A change had come over the Celtic visage of the old man. He now seemed all eagerness; his eyes glowed.

"We'll let them fight," he answered, stalwartly. "I can't put up with it any longer. I've stood this damned Swede till I'm sick. We'll let them fight."

VI

The men prepared to go out of doors. The Easterner was so nervous that he had great difficulty in getting his arms into the sleeves of his new leather coat. As the cowboy drew his fur cap down over his ears his hands trembled. In fact, Johnnie and old Scully were the only ones who displayed no agitation. These preliminaries were conducted without words.

Scully threw open the door. "Well, come on," he said. Instantly a terrific wind caused the flame of the lamp to struggle at its wick, while a puff of black smoke sprang from the chimney-top. The stove was in mid-current of the blast, and its voice swelled to equal the roar of the storm. Some of the scarred and bedabbled cards were caught up from the floor and dashed helplessly against the farther wall. The men lowered their heads and plunged into the tempest as into a sea.

No snow was falling, but great whirls and clouds of flakes, swept up from the ground by the frantic winds, were streaming southward with the speed of bullets. The covered land was blue with the sheen of an unearthly satin, and there was no other hue save where, at the low, black railway station—which seemed incredibly distant—one light gleamed like a tiny jewel. As the men floundered into a thigh-deep drift, it was known that the Swede was bawling out something. Scully went to him, put a hand on his shoulder, and projected an ear. ''What's that you say?'' he shouted.

''I say,'' bawled the Swede again, ''I won't stand much show against this gang. I know you'll all pitch on me.''

Scully smote him reproachfully on the arm. ''Tut, man!'' he yelled. The wind tore the words from Scully's lips and scattered them far alee.

''You are all a gang of—'' boomed the Swede, but the storm also seized the remainder of this sentence.

Immediately turning their backs upon the wind, the men had swung around a corner of the sheltered side of the hotel. It was the function of the little house to preserve here, amid this great devastation of snow, an irregular V-shape of heavily encrusted grass, which crackled beneath the feet. One could imagine the great drifts piled against the windward side. When the party reached the comparative peace of this spot it was found that the Swede was still bellowing.

''Oh, I know what kind of a thing this is! I know you'll all pitch on me. I can't lick you all!''

Scully turned upon him panther-fashion. ''You'll not have to whip all of us. You'll have to whip my son Johnnie. An' the man what troubles you durin' that time will have me to dale with.''

The arrangements were swiftly made. The two men faced each other, obedient to the harsh commands of Scully, whose face, in the subtly luminous gloom, could be seen set in the austere impersonal lines that are pictured on the countenances of the Roman veterans. The Easterner's teeth were chattering, and he was hopping up and down like a mechanical toy. The cowboy stood rock-like.

The contestants had not stripped off any clothing. Each was in his ordinary attire. Their fists were up, and they eyed each other in a calm that had the elements of leonine cruelty in it.

During this pause, the Easterner's mind, like a film, took lasting impressions of three men—the iron-nerved master of the ceremony; the Swede, pale, motionless, terrible; and Johnnie, serene yet ferocious, brutish yet heroic. The entire prelude had in it a tragedy greater than the tragedy of action, and this aspect was accentuated by the long, mellow cry of the blizzard, as it sped the tumbling and wailing flakes into the black abyss of the south.

''Now!'' said Scully.

The two combatants leaped forward and crashed together like bullocks.

There was heard the cushioned sound of blows, and of a curse squeezing out from between the tight teeth of one.

As for the spectators, the Easterner's pent-up breath exploded from him with a pop of relief, absolute relief from the tension of the preliminaries. The cowboy bounded into the air with a yowl. Scully was immovable as from supreme amazement and fear at the fury of the fight which he himself had permitted and arranged.

For a time the encounter in the darkness was such a perplexity of flying arms that it presented no more detail than would a swiftly revolving wheel. Occasionally a face, as if illumined by a flash of light, would shine out, ghastly and marked with pink spots. A moment later, the men might have been known as shadows, if it were not for the involuntary utterance of oaths that came from them in whispers.

Suddenly a holocaust of warlike desire caught the cowboy, and he bolted forward with the speed of a broncho. "Go it, Johnnie! go it! Kill him! Kill him!"

Scully confronted him. "Kape back," he said; and by his glance the cowboy could tell that this man was Johnnie's father.

To the Easterner there was a monotony of unchangeable fighting that was an abomination. This confused mingling was eternal to his sense, which was concentrated in a longing for the end, the priceless end. Once the fighters lurched near him, and as he scrambled hastily backward he heard them breathe like men on the rack.

"Kill him, Johnnie! Kill him! Kill him! Kill him!" The cowboy's face was contorted like one of those agony masks in museums.

"Keep still," said Scully, icily.

Then there was a sudden loud grunt, incomplete, cut short, and Johnnie's body swung away from the Swede and fell with sickening heaviness to the grass. The cowboy was barely in time to prevent the mad Swede from flinging himself upon his prone adversary. "No, you don't," said the cowboy, interposing an arm. "Wait a second."

Scully was at his son's side. "Johnnie! Johnnie, me boy!" His voice had a quality of melancholy tenderness. "Johnnie! Can you go on with it?" He looked anxiously down into the bloody, pulpy face of his son.

There was a moment of silence, and then Johnnie answered in his ordinary voice, "Yes, I—it—yes."

Assisted by his father he struggled to his feet. "Wait a bit now till you git your wind," said the old man.

A few paces away the cowboy was lecturing the Swede. "No, you don't! Wait a second!"

The Easterner was plucking at Scully's sleeve. "Oh, this is enough," he pleaded. "This is enough! Let it go as it stands. This is enough!"

"Bill," said Scully, "git out of the road." The cowboy stepped aside.

"Now." The combatants were actuated by a new caution as they advanced toward collision. They glared at each other, and then the Swede aimed a lightning blow that carried with it his entire weight. Johnnie was evidently half stupid from weakness, but he miraculously dodged, and his fist sent the overbalanced Swede sprawling.

The cowboy, Scully, and the Easterner burst into a cheer that was like a chorus of triumphant soldiery, but before its conclusion the Swede had scuffled agilely to his feet and come in berserk abandon at his foe. There was another perplexity of flying arms, and Johnnie's body again swung away and fell, even as a bundle might fall from a roof. The Swede instantly staggered to a little wind-waved tree and leaned upon it, breathing like an engine, while his savage and flame-lit eyes roamed from face to face as the men bent over Johnnie. There was a splendour of isolation in his situation at this time which the Easterner felt once when, lifting his eyes from the man on the ground, he beheld that mysterious and lonely figure, waiting.

"Are you any good yet, Johnnie?" asked Scully in a broken voice.

The son gasped and opened his eyes languidly. After a moment he answered, "No—I ain't—any good—any—more." Then, from shame and bodily ill, he began to weep, the tears furrowing down through the blood-stains on his face. "He was too—too—too heavy for me."

Scully straightened and addressed the waiting figure. "Stranger," he said, evenly, "it's all up with our side." Then his voice changed into that vibrant huskiness which is commonly the tone of the most simple and deadly announcements. "Johnnie is whipped."

Without replying, the victor moved off on the route to the front door of the hotel.

The cowboy was formulating new and unspellable blasphemies. The Easterner was startled to find that they were out in a wind that seemed to come direct from the shadowed arctic floes. He heard again the wail of the snow as it was flung to its grave in the south. He knew now that all this time the cold had been sinking into him deeper and deeper, and he wondered that he had not perished. He felt indifferent to the condition of the vanquished man.

"Johnnie, can you walk?" asked Scully.

"Did I hurt—hurt him any?" asked the son.

"Can you walk, boy? Can you walk?"

Johnnie's voice was suddenly strong. There was a robust impatience in it. "I asked you whether I hurt him any!"

"Yes, yes, Johnnie," answered the cowboy, consolingly; "he's hurt a good deal."

They raised him from the ground, and as soon as he was on his feet he went tottering off, rebuffing all attempts at assistance. When the party rounded the corner they were fairly blinded by the pelting of the snow. It burned their faces like fire. The cowboy carried Johnnie through the drift to the door. As they entered, some cards again rose from the floor and beat against the wall.

The Easterner rushed to the stove. He was so profoundly chilled that he almost dared to embrace the glowing iron. The Swede was not in the room. Johnnie sank into a chair and, folding his arms on his knees, buried his face in them. Scully, warming one foot and then the other at a rim of the stove, muttered to himself with Celtic mournfulness. The cowboy had removed his fur cap, and with a dazed and rueful air he was running one hand through his tousled locks. From overhead they could hear the creaking of boards, as the Swede tramped here and there in his room.

The sad quiet was broken by the sudden flinging open of a door that led toward the kitchen. It was instantly followed by an inrush of women. They precipitated themselves upon Johnnie amid a chorus of lamentation. Before they carried their prey off to the kitchen, there to be bathed and harangued with that mixture of sympathy and abuse which is a feat of their sex, the mother straightened herself and fixed old Scully with an eye of stern reproach. "Shame be upon you, Patrick Scully!" she cried. "Your own son, too. Shame be upon you!"

"There, now! Be quiet, now!" said the old man, weakly.

"Shame be upon you, Patrick Scully!" The girls, rallying to this slogan, sniffed disdainfully in the direction of those trembling accomplices, the cowboy and the Easterner. Presently they bore Johnnie away, and left the three men to dismal reflection.

VII

"I'd like to fight this here Dutchman myself," said the cowboy, breaking a long silence.

Scully wagged his head sadly. "No, that wouldn't do. It wouldn't be right. It wouldn't be right."

"Well, why wouldn't it?" argued the cowboy. "I don't see no harm in it."

"No," answered Scully, with mournful heroism. "It wouldn't be right. It was Johnnie's fight, and now we mustn't whip the man just because he whipped Johnnie."

"Yes, that's true enough," said the cowboy; "but—he better not get fresh with me, because I couldn't stand no more of it."

"You'll not say a word to him," commanded Scully, and even then they heard the tread of the Swede on the stairs. His entrance was made theatric. He swept the door back with a bang and swaggered to the middle of the room. No one looked at him. "Well," he cried, insolently, at Scully, "I s'pose you'll tell me now how much I owe you?"

The old man remained stolid. "You don't owe me nothin'."

"Huh!" said the Swede, "huh! Don't owe 'im nothin'."

The cowboy addressed the Swede. "Stranger, I don't see how you come to be so gay around here."

Old Scully was instantly alert. "Stop!" he shouted, holding his hand forth, fingers upward. "Bill, you shut up!"

The cowboy spat carelessly into the sawdust-box. "I didn't say a word, did I?" he asked.

"Mr. Scully," called the Swede, "how much do I owe you?" It was seen that he was attired for departure, and that he had his valise in his hand.

"You don't owe me nothin'," repeated Scully in the same imperturbable way.

"Huh!" said the Swede. "I guess you're right. I guess if it was any way at all, you'd owe me somethin'. That's what I guess." He turned to the cowboy. " 'Kill him! Kill him! Kill him!' " he mimicked, and then guffawed victoriously. " 'Kill him!' " He was convulsed with ironical humour.

But he might have been jeering the dead. The three men were immovable and silent, staring with glassy eyes at the stove.

The Swede opened the door and passed into the storm, giving one derisive glance backward at the still group.

As soon as the door was closed, Scully and the cowboy leaped to their feet and began to curse. They trampled to and fro, waving their arms and smashing into the air with their fists. "Oh, but that was a hard minute!" wailed Scully. "That was a hard minute! Him there leerin' and scoffin'! One bang at his nose was worth forty dollars to me that minute! How did you stand it, Bill?"

"How did I stand it?" cried the cowboy in a quivering voice. "How did I stand it? Oh!"

The old man burst into sudden brogue. "I'd loike to take that Swade," he wailed, "and hould 'im down on a shtone flure and bate 'im to a jelly wid a shtick!"

The cowboy groaned in sympathy. "I'd like to git him by the neck and ha-ammer him"—he brought his hand down on a chair with a noise like a pistolshot—"hammer that there Dutchman until he couldn't tell himself from a dead coyote!"

"I'd bate 'im until he—"

"I'd show *him* some things—"

And then together they raised a yearning, fanatic cry—"Oh-o-oh! if we only could—"

"Yes!"

"Yes!"

"And then I'd—"

"O-o-oh!"

VIII

The Swede, tightly gripping his valise, tacked across the face of the storm as if he carried sails. He was following a line of little naked, grasping trees which, he knew, must mark the way of the road. His face, fresh from the pounding of Johnnie's fists, felt more pleasure than pain in the wind and the driving snow. A number of square shapes loomed upon him finally, and he knew them as the houses of the main body of the town. He found a street and made travel along it, leaning heavily upon the wind whenever, at a corner, a terrific blast caught him.

He might have been in a deserted village. We picture the world as thick with conquering and elate humanity, but here, with the bugles of the tempest pealing, it was hard to imagine a peopled earth. One viewed the existence of man then as a marvel, and conceded a glamour of wonder to these lice which were caused to cling to a whirling, fire-smitten, ice-locked, disease-stricken, space-lost bulb. The conceit of man was explained by this storm to be the very engine of life. One was a coxcomb not to die in it. However, the Swede found a saloon.

In front of it an indomitable red light was burning, and the snowflakes were made blood-colour as they flew through the circumscribed territory of the lamp's shining. The Swede pushed open the door of the saloon and entered. A sanded expanse was before him, and at the end of it four men sat about a table drinking. Down one side of the room extended a radiant bar, and its guardian was leaning upon his elbows listening to the talk of the men at the table. The Swede dropped his valise upon the floor and, smiling fraternally upon the barkeeper, said, "Gimme some whisky, will you?" The man placed a bottle, a whisky-glass, and a glass of ice-thick water upon the bar. The Swede poured himself an abnormal portion of whisky and drank it in three gulps. "Pretty bad night," remarked the bartender, indifferently. He was making the pretension of blindness which is usually a distinction of his class; but it could have been seen that he was furtively studying the half-erased blood-stains on the face of the Swede. "Bad night," he said again.

"Oh, it's good enough for me," replied the Swede, hardily, as he poured himself some more whisky. The barkeeper took his coin and manœuvred it through its reception by the highly nickelled cash-machine. A bell rang; a card labelled "20 cts." had appeared.

"No," continued the Swede, "this isn't too bad weather. It's good enough for me."

"So?" murmured the barkeeper, languidly.

The copious drams made the Swede's eyes swim, and he breathed a trifle heavier. "Yes, I like this weather. I like it. It suits me." It was apparently his design to impart a deep significance to these words.

"So?" murmured the bartender again. He turned to gaze dreamily at the scroll-like birds and bird-like scrolls which had been drawn with soap upon the mirrors in back of the bar.

"Well, I guess I'll take another drink," said the Swede, presently. "Have something?"

"No, thanks; I'm not drinkin'," answered the bartender. Afterward he asked, "How did you hurt your face?"

The Swede immediately began to boast loudly. "Why, in a fight. I thumped the soul out of a man down here at Scully's hotel."

The interest of the four men at the table was at last aroused.

"Who was it?" said one.

"Johnnie Scully," blustered the Swede. "Son of the man what runs it. He will be pretty near dead for some weeks, I can tell you. I made a nice thing of him, I did. He couldn't get up. They carried him in the house. Have a drink?"

Instantly the men in some subtle way encased themselves in reserve. "No, thanks," said one. The group was of curious formation. Two were prominent local business men; one was the district attorney; and one was a professional gambler of the kind known as "square." But a scrutiny of the group would not have enabled an observer to pick the gambler from the men of more reputable pursuits. He was, in fact, a man so delicate in manner, when among people of fair class, and so judicious in his choice of victims, that in the strictly masculine part of the town's life he had come to be explicitly trusted and admired. People called him a thoroughbred. The fear and contempt with which his craft was regarded were undoubtedly the reason why his quiet dignity shone conspicuous above the quiet dignity of men who might be merely hatters, billiard-markers, or grocery clerks. Beyond an occasional unwary traveller who came by rail, this gambler was supposed to prey solely upon reckless and senile farmers, who, when flush with good crops, drove into town in all the pride and confidence of an absolutely invulnerable stupidity. Hearing at times in circuitous fashion of the despoilment of such a farmer, the important men of Romper invariably laughed in contempt of the victim, and if they thought of the wolf at all, it was with a kind of pride at the knowledge that he would never dare think of attacking their wisdom and courage. Besides, it was popular that this gambler had a real wife and two real children in a neat cottage in a suburb, where he led an exemplary home life; and when any one even suggested a discrepancy in his character, the crowd immediately vociferated descriptions of this virtuous family circle. Then men who led exemplary home lives, and men who did not lead exemplary home lives, all subsided in a bunch, remarking that there was nothing more to be said.

However, when a restriction was placed upon him—as, for instance, when a strong clique of members of the new Pollywog Club refused to permit him, even as a spectator, to appear in the rooms of the organization—the candour and gentleness with which he accepted the judgment disarmed many of his foes and made his friends more desperately partisan. He invariably distinguished between himself and a respectable Romper man so quickly and frankly that his manner actually appeared to be a continual broadcast compliment.

And one must not forget to declare the fundamental fact of his entire position in Romper. It is irrefutable that in all affairs outside his business, in all matters that occur eternally and commonly between man and man, this thieving card-player was so generous, so just, so moral, that, in a contest, he could have put to flight the consciences of nine tenths of the citizens of Romper.

And so it happened that he was seated in this saloon with the two prominent local merchants and the district attorney.

The Swede continued to drink raw whisky, meanwhile babbling at the barkeeper and trying to induce him to indulge in potations. "Come on. Have a drink. Come on. What—no? Well, have a little one, then. By gawd, I've whipped a man to-night, and I want to celebrate. I whipped him good, too. Gentlemen," the Swede cried to the men at the table, "have a drink?"

"Ssh!" said the barkeeper.

The group at the table, although furtively attentive, had been pretending to be deep in talk, but now a man lifted his eyes toward the Swede and said, shortly, "Thanks. We don't want any more."

At this reply the Swede ruffled out his chest like a rooster. "Well," he exploded, "it seems I can't get anybody to drink with me in this town. Seems so, don't it? Well!"

"Ssh!" said the barkeeper.

"Say," snarled the Swede, "don't you try to shut me up. I won't have it. I'm a gentleman, and I want people to drink with me. And I want 'em to drink with me now. *Now*—do you understand?" He rapped the bar with his knuckles.

Years of experience had calloused the bartender. He merely grew sulky. "I hear you," he answered.

"Well," cried the Swede, "listen hard then. See those men over there? Well, they're going to drink with me, and don't you forget it. Now you watch."

"Hi!" yelled the barkeeper, "this won't do!"

"Why won't it?" demanded the Swede. He stalked over to the table, and by chance laid his hand upon the shoulder of the gambler. "How about this?" he asked wrathfully. "I asked you to drink with me."

The gambler simply twisted his head and spoke over his shoulder. "My friend, I don't know you."

"Oh, hell!" answered the Swede, "come and have a drink."

"Now, my boy," advised the gambler, kindly, "take your hand off my shoulder and go 'way and mind your own business." He was a little, slim man, and it seemed strange to hear him use this tone of heroic patronage to the burly Swede. The other men at the table said nothing.

"What! You won't drink with me, you little dude? I'll make you, then! I'll make you!" The Swede had grasped the gambler frenziedly at the throat, and was dragging him from his chair. The other men sprang up. The barkeeper dashed around the corner of his bar. There was a great tumult, and then was seen a long blade in the hand of the gambler. It shot forward, and a human body, this citadel of virtue, wisdom, power, was pierced as easily as if it had been a melon. The Swede fell with a cry of supreme astonishment.

The prominent merchants and the district attorney must have at once tumbled out of the place backward. The bartender found himself hanging limply to the arm of a chair and gazing into the eyes of a murderer.

"Henry," said the latter, as he wiped his knife on one of the towels that hung beneath the bar rail, "you tell 'em where to find me. I'll be home, waiting for 'em." Then he vanished. A moment afterward the barkeeper was in the street dinning through the storm for help and, moreover, companionship.

The corpse of the Swede, alone in the saloon, had its eyes fixed upon a dreadful legend that dwelt atop of the cash-machine: "This registers the amount of your purchase."

IX

Months later, the cowboy was frying pork over the stove of a little ranch near the Dakota line, when there was a quick thud of hoofs outside, and presently the Easterner entered with the letters and the papers.

"Well," said the Easterner at once, "the chap that killed the Swede has got three years. Wasn't much, was it?"

"He has? Three years?" The cowboy poised his pan of pork, while he ruminated upon the news. "Three years. That ain't much."

"No. It was a light sentence," replied the Easterner as he unbuckled his spurs. "Seems there was a good deal of sympathy for him in Romper."

"If the bartender had been any good," observed the cowboy, thoughtfully, "he would have gone in and cracked that there Dutchman on the head with a bottle in the beginnin' of it and stopped all this here murderin'."

"Yes, a thousand things might have happened," said the Easterner, tartly.

The cowboy returned his pan of pork to the fire, but his philosophy continued. "It's funny, ain't it? If he hadn't said Johnnie was cheatin' he'd be alive this minute. He was an awful fool. Game played for fun, too. Not for money. I believe he was crazy."

"I feel sorry for that gambler," said the Easterner.

"Oh, so do I," said the cowboy. "He don't deserve none of it for killin' who he did."

"The Swede might not have been killed if everything had been square."

"Might not have been killed?" exclaimed the cowboy. "Everythin' square? Why, when he said that Johnnie was cheatin' and acted like such a jackass? And then in the saloon he fairly walked up to git hurt?" With these arguments the cowboy browbeat the Easterner and reduced him to rage.

"You're a fool!" cried the Easterner, viciously. "You're a bigger jackass than the Swede by a million majority. Now let me tell you one thing. Let me tell you something. Listen! Johnnie *was* cheating!"

" 'Johnnie,' " said the cowboy, blankly. There was a minute of silence, and then he said, robustly, "Why, no. The game was only for fun."

"Fun or not," said the Easterner, "Johnnie was cheating. I saw him. I know it. I saw him. And I refused to stand up and be a man. I let the Swede fight it out alone. And you—you were simply puffing around the place and wanting to fight. And then old Scully himself! We are all in it! This poor gambler isn't even a noun. He is kind of an adverb. Every sin is the result of a collaboration. We, five of us, have collaborated in the murder of this Swede. Usually there are from a dozen to forty women really involved in every murder, but in this case it seems to be only five men—you, I, Johnnie, old Scully; and that fool of an unfortunate gambler came merely as a culmination, the apex of a human movement, and gets all the punishment."

The cowboy, injured and rebellious, cried out blindly into this fog of mysterious theory: "Well, I didn't do anythin', did I?"

1898

William Faulkner

From The Wild Palms

In *The Wild Palms* (1927), Faulkner experimented with the device of juxtaposition (see introduction to Deformations) by alternating each of the five sections of one story, "Old Man," with a section from another story, "The Wild Palms"; both stories deal in separate ways with the loss of love and freedom. In this excerpt, part II of "Old Man" (the first two paragraphs come at the end of part I), the convict gains the temporary freedom he will in the end relinquish by finding his way back to prison when the flood recedes. The story is set not in Faulkner's mythical Yoknapatawpha County but in Parchman, Mississippi Delta country.

From Old Man

THEY WERE SLEEPING restlessly beneath the sound of the rain on the tin roof when at midnight the sudden glare of the electric bulbs and the guards' voices waked them and they heard the throbbing of the waiting trucks.

"Turn out of there!" the deputy shouted. He was fully dressed—rubber boots, slicker and shotgun. "The levee went out at Mound's Landing an hour ago. Get up out of it!"

II

When the belated and streaming dawn broke the two convicts, along with twenty others, were in a truck. A trusty drove, two armed guards sat in the cab with him. Inside the high, stall-like, topless body the convicts stood, packed like matches in an upright box or like the pencil-shaped ranks of cordite in a shell, shackled by the ankles to a single chain which wove among the motionless feet and swaying legs and a clutter of picks and shovels among which they stood, and was riveted by both ends to the steel body of the truck.

Then, and without warning, they saw the flood about which the plump convict had been reading and they listening for two weeks or more. The road ran south. It was built on a raised levee, known locally as a dump, about eight feet above the flat surrounding land, bordered on both sides by the barrow pits from which the earth of the levee had been excavated. These barrow pits had held water all winter from the fall rains, not to speak of the rain of yesterday, but now they saw that the pit on either side of the road had vanished and instead there lay a flat still sheet of brown water which extended into the fields beyond the pits, ravelled out into long motionless shreds in the bottom of the plow furrows and gleamed faintly in the gray light like the bars of a prone and enormous grating. And then (the truck was moving at good speed) as they watched quietly (they had not been talking much anyway but now they were all silent and quite grave, shifting and craning as one to look soberly off to the west side of the road) the crests of the furrows vanished too, and they now looked at a single perfectly flat and motionless steel-colored sheet in which the telephone poles and the straight hedgerows which marked section lines seemed to be fixed and rigid as though set in concrete.

It was perfectly motionless, perfectly flat. It looked, not innocent, but bland. It looked almost demure. It looked as if you could walk on it. It looked so still that they did not realize it possessed motion until they came to the first bridge. There was a ditch under the bridge, a small stream, but ditch and stream were both invisible now, indicated only by the rows of cypress and bramble which marked its course. Here they both saw and heard movement—the slow profound eastward and upstream ("It's running backward," one convict said quietly) set of the still rigid surface, from beneath which came a deep faint subaquean rumble which (though none in the truck could have made the comparison) sounded like a subway train passing far beneath the street, and which suggested a terrific and secret speed. It was as if the water itself were in three strata, separate and distinct, the bland and unhurried surface bearing a frothy scum and a miniature flotsam of twigs and screening, as though by vicious calculation, the rush and fury of the flood itself, and beneath this in turn the original stream trickle, murmuring along in the opposite direction, following undisturbed and unaware of its appointed course and serving its Lilliputian end, like a thread of ants between the rails on which an express train passes, they (the ants) as unaware of the power and fury as if it were a cyclone crossing Saturn.

Now there was water on both sides of the road and now, as if once they had become aware of movement in the water it had given over deception and concealment, they seemed to be able to watch it rising up the flanks of the dump; trees which a few miles back had stood on tall trunks above the water now seemed to burst from the surface at the level of the lower branches like decorative shrubs on barbered lawns. The truck passed a Negro cabin. The water was up to the window ledges. A woman clutching two children squatted on the ridgepole, a man and a halfgrown youth, standing waist-deep, were hoisting a squealing pig onto the slanting roof of a barn, on the ridgepole of which sat a row of chickens and a turkey. Near the barn was a haystack on which a cow stood tied by a rope to the center pole and bawling steadily; a yelling Negro boy on a saddleless mule which he flogged steadily, his legs clutching the mule's barrel and his body leaned to the drag of a rope attached to a second mule, approached the haystack, splashing and floundering. The woman on the housetop began to shriek at the passing truck, her voice carrying faint and melodious across the brown water, becoming fainter and fainter as the truck passed and went on, ceasing at last, whether because of distance or because she had stopped screaming those in the truck did not know.

Then the road vanished. There was no perceptible slant to it yet it had slipped abruptly beneath the brown surface with no ripple, no ridgy demarcation, like a flat thin blade slipped obliquely into flesh by a delicate hand, annealed into the water without disturbance, as if it had existed so for years, had been built that way. The truck stopped. The trusty descended from the cab and came back and dragged two shovels from among their feet, the blades clashing against the serpentining of the chain about their ankles. "What is it?" one said. "What are you fixing to do?" The trusty didn't answer. He returned to the cab, from which one of the guards had descended, without his shotgun. He and the trusty, both in hip boots and each carrying a shovel, advanced into the water, gingerly, probing and feeling ahead with the shovel handles. The same convict spoke again. He was a middle-aged man with a wild thatch of iron-gray hair and a slightly mad face. "What the hell are they doing?" he said. Again nobody answered him. The truck moved, on into the water, behind the guard and the trusty, beginning to push ahead of itself a thick slow viscid ridge of chocolate water. Then the gray-haired convict began to scream. "God damn it, unlock the chain!" He began to struggle, thrashing violently about him, striking at the men nearest him until he reached the cab, the roof of which he now hammered on with his fists, screaming. ''God damn it, unlock us! Unlock us! Son of a bitch!'' he screamed, addressing no one. ''They're going to drown us! Unlock the chain!'' But for all the answer he got the men within radius of his voice might have been dead. The truck crawled on, the guard and the trusty feeling out the road ahead with the reversed shovels, the second guard at the wheel, the twenty-two convicts packed like sardines into the truck bed and padlocked by the ankles to the body of the truck itself. They crossed another bridge—two delicate and paradoxical iron railings slanting out of the water, travelling parallel to it for a distance, then slanting down into it again with an outrageous quality almost significant yet apparently meaningless like something in a dream not quite nightmare. The truck crawled on.

Along toward noon they came to a town, their destination. The streets were paved; now the wheels of the truck made a sound like tearing silk. Moving faster now, the guard and the trusty in the cab again, the truck even had a slight bone in its teeth, its bow-wave spreading beyond the submerged sidewalks and across the adjacent lawns, lapping against the stoops and porches of houses where people stood among piles of furniture. They passed through the business district; a man in hip boots emerged knee-deep in water from a store, dragging a flat-bottomed skiff containing a steel safe.

At last they reached the railroad. It crossed the street at right angles, cutting the town in two. It was on a dump, a levee, also, eight or ten feet above the town itself; the street ran blankly into it and turned at right angles beside a cotton compress and a loading platform on stilts at the level of a freight-car door. On this platform was a khaki army tent and a uniformed National Guard sentry with a rifle and bandolier.

The truck turned and crawled out of the water and up the ramp which cotton wagons used and where trucks and private cars filled with household goods came and unloaded onto the platform. They were unlocked from the chain in the truck and, shackled ankle to ankle in pairs, they mounted the platform and into an apparently inextricable jumble of beds and trunks, gas and electric stoves, radios and tables and chairs and framed pictures, which a chain of Negroes under the eye of an unshaven white man in muddy corduroy and hip boots carried piece by piece into the compress, at the door of which another guardsman stood with his rifle, they (the convicts) not stopping here but herded on by the two guards with their shotguns into the dim and cavernous building where, among the piled heterogeneous furniture, the ends of cotton bales and the mirrors on dressers and sideboards gleamed with an identical mute and unreflecting concentration of pallid light.

They passed on through, onto the loading platform where the army tent and the first sentry were. They waited here. Nobody told them for what nor why. While the two guards talked with the sentry before the tent, the convicts sat in a line along the edge of the platform like buzzards on a fence, their shackled feet dangling above the brown motionless flood out of which the railroad embankment rose, pristine and intact, in a kind of paradoxical denial and repudiation of change and portent; not talking, just looking quietly across the track to where the other half of the amputated town seemed to float, house, shrub, and tree, ordered and pageant-like and without motion, upon the limitless liquid plain beneath the thick gray sky.

After a while the other four trucks from the Farm arrived. They came up, bunched closely, radiator to tail light, with their four separate sounds of tearing silk and vanished beyond the compress. Presently the ones on the platform heard the feet, the mute clashing of the shackles. The first truckload emerged from the compress, the second, the third; there were more than a hundred of them now in their bed-ticking overalls and jumpers and fifteen or twenty guards with rifles and shotguns. The first lot rose and they mingled, paired, twinned by their clanking and clashing umbilicals; then it began to rain, a slow steady gray drizzle like November instead of May. Yet not one of them made any move toward the open door of the compress. They did not even look toward it, with longing or hope or without it. If they thought at all, they doubtless knew that the available space in it would be needed for furniture, even if it were not already filled. Or perhaps they knew that, even if there were room in it, it would not be for them, not that the guards would wish them to get wet but that the guards would not think about getting them out of the rain. So they just stopped talking and, with their jumper collars turned up and shackled in braces like dogs at a field trial, they stood, immobile, patient, almost ruminant, their backs turned to the rain as sheep and cattle do.

After another while they became aware that the number of soldiers had increased to a dozen or more, warm and dry beneath rubberized ponchos, there was an officer with a pistol at his belt, then and without making any more toward it, they began to smell food and, turning to look, saw an army field kitchen set up just inside the compress door. But they made no move, they waited until they were herded into line, they inched forward, their heads lowered and patient in the rain, and received each a bowl of stew, a mug of coffee, two slices of bread. They ate this in the rain. They did not sit down because the platform was wet, they squatted on their heels as country men do, hunching forward, trying to shield the bowls and mugs into which nevertheless the rain splashed steadily as into miniature ponds and soaked, invisible and soundless, into the bread.

After they had stood on the platform for three hours, a train came for them. Those nearest the edge saw it, watched it—a passenger coach apparently running under its own power and trailing a cloud of smoke from no visible stack, a cloud which did not rise but instead shifted slowly and heavily aside and lay upon the surface of the aqueous earth with a quality at once weightless and completely spent. It came up and stopped, a single old-fashioned open-ended wooden car coupled to the nose of a pushing switch engine considerably smaller. They were herded into it, crowding forward to the other end where there was a small cast-iron stove. There was no fire in it, nevertheless they crowded about it—the cold and voiceless lump of iron stained with fading tobacco and hovered about by the ghosts of a thousand Sunday excursions to Memphis or Moorhead and return—the peanuts, the bananas, the soiled garments of infants—huddling, shoving for places near it. "Come on, come on," one of the guards shouted. "Sit down, now." At last three of the guards, laying aside their guns, came among them and broke up the huddle, driving them back and into seats.

There were not enough seats for all. The others stood in the aisle, they stood braced, they heard the air hiss out of the released brakes, the engine whistled four blasts, the car came into motion with a snapping jerk; the platform, the compress fled violently as the train seemed to transpose from immobility to full speed with that same quality of unreality with which it had appeared, running backward now though with the engine in front where before it had moved forward but with the engine behind.

When the railroad in its turn ran beneath the surface of the water, the convicts did not even know it. They felt the train stop, they heard the engine blow a long blast which wailed away unechoed across the waste, wild and forlorn, and they were not even curious; they sat or stood behind the rain-streaming windows as the train crawled on again, feeling its way as the truck had while the brown water swirled between the trucks and among the spokes of the driving wheels and lapped in cloudy steam against the dragging fire-filled belly of the engine; again it blew four short harsh blasts filled with the wild triumph and defiance yet also with repudiation and even farewell, as if the articulated steel itself knew it did not dare stop and would not be able to return. Two hours later in the twilight they saw through the streaming windows a burning plantation house. Juxtaposed to nowhere and neighbored by nothing it stood, a clear steady pyre-like flame rigidly fleeing its own reflection, burning in the dusk above the watery desolation with a quality paradoxical, outrageous and bizarre.

Sometime after dark the train stopped. The convicts did not know where they were. They did not ask. They would no more have thought of asking where they were than they would have asked why and what for. They couldn't even see, since the car was unlighted and the windows fogged on the outside by rain and on the inside by the engendered heat of the packed bodies. All they could see was a milky and sourceless flick and glare of flashlights. They could hear shouts and commands, then the guards inside the car began to shout; they were herded to their feet and toward the exit, the ankle chains clashing and clanking. They descended into a fierce hissing of steam, through ragged whisps of it blowing past the car. Laid-to alongside the train and resembling a train itself was a thick blunt motor launch to which was attached a string of skiffs and flat boats. There were more soldiers; the flashlights played on the rifle barrels and bandolier buckles and flicked and glinted on the ankle chains of the convicts as they stepped gingerly down into knee-deep water and entered the boats; now car and engine both vanished completely in steam as the crew began dumping the fire from the firebox.

After another hour they began to see lights ahead—a faint wavering row of red pin-pricks extending along the horizon and apparently hanging low in the sky. But it took almost another hour to reach them while the convicts squatted in the skiffs, huddled into the soaked garments (they no longer felt the rain any more at all as separate drops) and watched the lights draw nearer and nearer until at last the crest of the levee defined itself; now they could discern a row of army tents stretching along it and people squatting about the fires, the wavering reflections from which, stretching across the water, revealed an involved mass of other skiffs tied against the flank of the levee which now stood high and dark overhead. Flashlights glared and winked along the base, among the tethered skiffs; the launch, silent now, drifted in.

When they reached the top of the levee they could see the long line of khaki tents, interspersed with fires about which people—men, women and children, Negro and white—crouched or stood among shapeless bales of clothing, their heads turning, their eyeballs glinting in the firelight as they looked quietly at the striped garments and the chains; further down the levee, huddled together too though untethered, was a drove of mules and two or three cows. Then the taller convict became conscious of another sound. He did not begin to hear it all at once, he suddenly became aware that he had been hearing it all the time, a sound so much beyond all his experience and his powers of assimilation that up to this point he had been as oblivious of it as an ant or a flea might be of the sound of the avalanche on which it rides; he had been travelling upon water since early afternoon and for seven years now he had run his plow and harrow and planter within the very shadow of the levee on which he now stood, but this profound deep whisper which came from the further side of it he did not at once recognize. He stopped. The line of convicts behind jolted into him like a line of freight cars stopping, with an iron clashing like cars. "Get on!" a guard shouted.

"What's that?" the convict said. A Negro man squatting before the nearest fire answered him:

"Dat's him. Dat's de Ole Man."

"The old man?" the convict said.

"Get on! Get on up there!" the guard shouted. They went on; they passed another huddle of mules, the eyeballs rolling too, the long morose faces turning into and out of the firelight; they passed them and reached a section of empty tents, the light pup tents of a military campaign, made to hold two men. The guards herded the convicts into them, three brace of shackled men to each tent.

They crawled in on all fours, like dogs into cramped kennels, and settled down. Presently the tent became warm from their bodies. Then they became quiet and then all of them could hear it, they lay listening to the bass whisper deep, strong, and powerful. "The old man?" the train-robber convict said.

"Yah," another said. "He don't have to brag."

At dawn the guards waked them by kicking the soles of the projecting feet. Opposite the muddy landing and the huddle of skiffs an army field kitchen was set up, already they could smell the coffee. But the taller convict at least, even though he had had but one meal yesterday and that at noon in the rain, did not move at once toward the food. Instead and for the first time he looked at the River within whose shadow he had spent the last seven years of his life but had never seen before; he stood in quiet and amazed surmise and looked at the rigid steel-colored surface not broken into waves but merely slightly undulant. It stretched from the levee on which he stood, further than he could see—a slowly and heavily roiling chocolate-frothy expanse broken only by a thin line a mile away as fragile in appearance as a single hair, which after a moment he recognized. *It's another levee,* he thought quietly. *That's what we look like from there. That's what I am standing on looks like from there.* He was prodded from the rear; a guard's voice carried forward: "Go on! Go on! You'll have plenty of time to look at that!"

They received the same stew and coffee and bread as the day before; they squatted again with their bowls and mugs as yesterday, though it was not raining yet. During the night an intact wooden barn had floated up. It now lay jammed by the current against the levee while a crowd of Negroes swarmed over it, ripping off the shingles and planks and carrying them up the bank; eating steadily and without haste, the taller convict watched the barn dissolve rapidly down to the very water-line exactly as a dead fly vanished beneath the moiling industry of a swarm of ants.

They finished eating. Then it began to rain again, as upon a signal, while they stood or squatted in their harsh garments which had not dried out during the night but had merely become slightly warmer than the air. Presently they were haled to their feet and told off into two groups, one of which was armed from a stack of mud-clogged picks and shovels nearby, and marched away up the levee. A little later the motor launch with its train of skiffs came up across what was, fifteen feet beneath its keel, probably a cotton field, the skiffs loaded to the gunwales with Negroes and a scattering of white people nursing bundles on their laps. When the engine shut off the faint plinking of a guitar came across the water. The skiffs warped in and unloaded; the convicts watched the men and women and children struggle up the muddy slope, carrying heavy tow-sacks and bundles wrapped in quilts. The sound of the guitar had not ceased and now the convicts saw him—a young, black, lean-hipped man, the guitar slung by a piece of cotton plow line about his neck. He mounted the levee, still picking it. He carried nothing else, no food, no change of clothes, not even a coat.

The taller convict was so busy watching this that he did not hear the guard until the guard stood directly beside him shouting his name. "Wake up!" the guard shouted. "Can you fellows paddle a boat?"

"Paddle a boat where?" the taller convict said.

"In the water," the guard said. "Where in hell do you think?"

"I ain't going to paddle no boat nowhere out yonder," the tall convict said, jerking his head toward the invisible river beyond the levee behind him.

"No, it's on this side," the guard said. He stooped swiftly and unlocked the chain which joined the tall convict and the plump hairless one. "It's just down the road a piece." He rose. The two convicts followed him down to the boats. "Follow them telephone poles until you come to a filling station. You can tell it, the roof is still above water. It's on a bayou and you can tell the bayou because the tops of the trees are sticking up. Follow the bayou until you come to a cypress snag with a woman in it. Pick her up and then cut straight back west until you come to a cottonhouse with a fellow sitting on the ridgepole—" He turned, looking at the two convicts, who stood perfectly still, looking first at the skiff and then at the water with intense sobriety. "Well? What are you waiting for?"

"I can't row a boat," the plump convict said.

"Then it's high time you learned," the guard said. "Get in."

The tall convict shoved the other forward. "Get in," he said. "That water ain't going to hurt you. Ain't nobody going to make you take a bath."

As, the plump one in the bow and the other in the stern, they shoved away from the levee, they saw other pairs being unshackled and manning the other skiffs. "I wonder how many more of them fellows are seeing this much water for the first time in their lives too," the tall convict said. The other did not answer. He knelt in the bottom of the skiff, pecking gingerly at the water now and then with his paddle. The very shape of his thick soft back seemed to wear that expression of wary and tense concern.

Some time after midnight a rescue boat filled to the guard rail with homeless men and women and children docked at Vicksburg. It was a steamer, shallow of draft; all day long it had poked up and down cypress- and gum-choked bayous and across cotton fields (where at times instead of swimming it waded) gathering its sorry cargo from the tops of houses and barns and even out of trees, and now it warped into that mushroom city of the forlorn and despairing, where kerosene flares smoked in the drizzle and hurriedly strung electrics glared upon the bayonets of martial policemen and the Red-Cross brassards of doctors and nurses and canteen-workers. The bluff overhead was almost solid with tents, yet still there were more people than shelter for them; they sat or lay, single and by whole families, under what shelter they could find, or sometimes under the rain itself, in the little death of profound exhaustion while the doctors and the nurses and the soldiers stepped over and around and among them.

Among the first to disembark was one of the penitentiary deputy wardens, followed closely by the plump convict and another white man—a small man with a gaunt unshaven wan face still wearing an expression of incredulous outrage. The deputy warden seemed to know exactly where he wished to go. Followed closely by his two companions he threaded his way swiftly among the piled furniture and the sleeping bodies and stood presently in a fiercely lighted and hastily established temporary office, almost a military post of command in fact, where the Warden of the Penitentiary sat with two army officers wearing majors' leaves. The deputy warden spoke without preamble. "We lost a man," he said. He called the tall convict's name.

"Lost him?" the Warden said.

"Yah. Drowned." Without turning his head he spoke to the plump convict. "Tell him," he said.

"He was the one that said he could row a boat," the plump convict said. "I never. I told him myself—" he indicated the deputy warden with a jerk of his head "—I couldn't. So when we got to the bayou—"

"What's this?" the Warden said.

"The launch brought word in," the deputy warden said. "Woman in a cypress snag on the bayou, then this fellow—" he indicated the third man; the Warden and the two officers looked at the third man "—on a cottonhouse. Never had room in the launch to pick them up. Go on."

"So we come to where the bayou was," the plump convict continued in a voice perfectly flat, without any inflection whatever. "Then the boat got away from him. I don't know what happened. I was just sitting there because he was so positive he could row a boat. I never saw any current. Just all of a sudden the boat whirled clean around and begun to run fast backward like it was hitched to a train and it whirled around again and I happened to look up and there was a limb right over my head and I grabbed it just in time and that boat was snatched out from under me like you'd snatch off a sock and I saw it one time more upside down and that fellow that said he knew all about rowing holding to it with one hand and still holding the paddle in the other—" He ceased. There was no dying fall to his voice, it just ceased and the convict stood looking quietly at a half-full quart of whiskey sitting on the table.

"How do you know he's drowned?" the Warden said to the deputy. "How do you know he didn't just see his chance to escape, and took it?"

"Escape where?" the other said. "The whole Delta's flooded. There's fifteen foot of water for fifty miles, clean back to the hills. And that boat was upside down.''

''That fellow's drowned,'' the plump convict said. ''You don't need to worry about him. He's got his pardon; it won't cramp nobody's hand signing it, neither.''

''And nobody else saw him?'' the Warden said. ''What about the woman in the tree?''

''I don't know,'' the deputy said. ''I ain't found her yet. I reckon some other boat picked her up. But this is the fellow on the cotton house.''

Again the Warden and the two officers looked at the third man, at the gaunt, unshaven wild face in which an old terror, an old blending of fear and impotence and rage still lingered. ''He never came for you?'' the Warden said. ''You never saw him?''

''Never nobody came for me,'' the refugee said. He began to tremble though at first he spoke quietly enough. ''I set there on that sonabitching cotton house, expecting hit to go any minute. I saw that launch and them boats come up and they never had no room for me. Full of bastard niggers and one of them setting there playing a guitar but there wasn't no room for me. A guitar!'' he cried; now he began to scream, trembling, slavering, his face twitching and jerking. ''Room for a bastard nigger guitar but not for me—''

''Steady now,'' the Warden said. ''Steady now.''

''Give him a drink,'' one of the officers said. The Warden poured the drink. The deputy handed it to the refugee, who took the glass in both jerking hands and tried to raise it to his mouth. They watched him for perhaps twenty seconds, then the deputy took the glass from him and held it to his lips while he gulped, though even then a thin trickle ran from each corner of his mouth, into the stubble on his chin.

''So we picked him and—'' the deputy called the plump convict's name now ''—both up just before dark and come on in. But that other fellow is gone.''

''Yes,'' the Warden said. ''Well. Here I haven't lost a prisoner in ten years, and now, like this—I'm sending you back to the Farm tomorrow. Have his family notified, and his discharge papers filled out at once.''

''All right,'' the deputy said. ''And listen, chief. He wasn't a bad fellow and maybe he never had no business in that boat. Only he did say he could paddle one. Listen. Suppose I write on his discharge, Drowned while trying to save lives in the great flood of nineteen twenty-seven, and send it down for the Governor to sign it. It will be something nice for his folks to have, to hang on the wall when neighbors come in or something. Maybe they will even give his folks a cash bonus because after all they sent him to the Farm to raise cotton, not to fool around in a boat in a flood.''

''All right,'' the Warden said. ''I'll see about it. The main thing is to get his name off the books as dead before some politician tries to collect his food allowance."

"All right," the deputy said. He turned and herded his companions out. In the drizzling darkness again he said to the plump convict: "Well, your partner beat you. He's free. He's done served his time out but you've got a right far piece to go yet."

"Yah," the plump convict said. "Free. He can have it."

1927

Landscape into Myth and Ritual

The Shaman-poet is simply the man whose mind reaches easily out into all manner of shapes and other lives, and gives song to dreams.

—Gary Snyder, *Earth House Hold*

It is one of the many ironies of American culture that white Americans began to "discover" the rituals, myths, and folk traditions of the two minority groups they most feared only after the Civil War—at a time when they had almost succeeded in killing off one group, the American Indians, and were still treating the other, the Black Americans, as a lower caste group which might or might not be capable of assimilation into the mainstream but which, in any case, existed chiefly as a creature of debate. It is a further irony that the animistic and magical world-views of these two groups began to be discovered and recorded by proponents of the "new objectivity": scientists like John Wesley Powell, geologist and founder of the Bureau of Ethnology, factually minded journalists, and the sociological historians of local color. This new objectivity, endorsing as it did the theory of creation according to Darwin and Lyell, was at the same time devaluing, as merely myth, the Christian version of Genesis. Thus the mythical visions of creation in America, animistic and Christian alike, were both preserved and pushed underground by the new, scientific orthodoxy.

During this period of psychic and physical change, the cultural and natural history of landscape spanned several dimensions of time. In landscape one could see the past of one's childhood, the regional or national past, the past of Indian civilization (particularly, in the Midwest, that of the Moundbuilders and, in the Southwest, that of the Pueblos), and even the past of geological change and of evolution. These visible records of history gave landscape a dynamic quality: it was not inert or dreamlike but changeful and pulsing with dynamic and vitalistic energies.

Religious and mythical perception, on the other hand, focuses not on the physical but on the supernatural events and presences in landscape. Landscape is seen as redolent with animistic presences: the spirits of departed ancestors; local geniuses residing in the sun, the moon, tree groves, rivers, corn, canyons, bears, and so on; or gods who lead a disembodied existence but who can be summoned forth, if good, for help or, if evil or destructive, warded off. In such a perspective landscape becomes sacramentalized. "The sacramental perception is not one of order," writes Theodore Roszak in *The Making of a Counter Culture,* nor does it yield any sense of "accomplished and rounded off knowledge." It is, rather, an experience of power, which "may begin and end in an overwhelming sense of mystery. We are awed, not informed . . . We settle for celebrating the sheer, amazing fact that this wondrous thing is self-sufficiently there before us" though it might not be touched or photographed.

The recognition of animistic power in American landscape takes several verbal forms. There is, first, the ritual, incantatory poetry of shaman or priest devised to cast rhythmic spells. This is a poetry characterized by *apostrophe* (direct addresses to the spirits), by *litany* (repetition of words and phrases), and by other techniques of what we call free verse, chiefly structural repetition (that is, parallel construction), and sound repetition (alliteration). Then there are the mythological narrations on the origins and histories of spirits, the experiences of souls after death (often they transmigrate to objects in the landscape) or the origin of the world and the things in it. And finally there are the folk traditions which preserve fragments and vestiges of animistic magic and myth. Each of these forms is represented here by Indian or Afro-American examples.

Also represented here are examples of two of the forms in which animism came to be assimilated into the mainstream culture. One of the forms was the Christian liturgy, where Blacks fused (in gospel songs and especially in sermons) the traditions of West African religions and Christian enthusiasm and added, indirectly, the sorrowful testimony of their own experience in an American Egypt. Thus the Reverend C. C. Lovelace's sermon "The Wounds of Jesus," for example, was part of a traditional Black Christian repertoire, which assumes through rhapsodic inspiration the perspective of a person who has actually witnessed the creation of the world and of Christ's sacrifice.

The other form in which animism came to be assimilated into the mainstream culture was that of the *lie*—a kind of tall tale which amplifies an event, through comic overstatement, into mythical meaning and which thus makes that event a revelation of animistic power. It is no accident that the American form of the lie emerged from the "Old West" (Kentucky, Georgia, Arkansas, and so on), for there, according to scholars, vestigial African and Indian mythical traditions merged with the Celtic traditions of the Scotch-Irish settlers. Some of the Davy Crockett stories, for example, are apparently New World adaptations of Old World myths of the sun god; in them Davy Crockett is apotheosized into a New World Cuchulainn who must deal with such powers as magic bears and cosmic cold spells, all set in the Edenic or wilderness landscape of Christian myth.

Even when the humor of the lie seems to undercut its mythical truth, the lie itself has three very serious functions: to demonstrate the scope and flair, if not the magic, of the teller's imagination and verbal power (in the contest of liars he must "top" all competitors with the most outrageously possible explanation of an event or situation or narration of an exploit); to diminish the fear of a wild or hostile environment by exaggerating it, thus showing how the conditions could be worse; and finally to create heroes strong or guileful enough to cope with the conditions the teller and his audience face—to apotheosize heroes into beings capable of meeting force with force or even capable of restoring to creation its primal order and harmony. These last two functions were especially necessary to psychic survival in the harsh frontier landscapes of the Old and Far West: the miasmic swamps, the great rivers, the prairies with their rattlesnakes and bears, floods and tornadoes, blizzards and sudden arctic freezes. Like the frontier settlers, like the heroes of the literary naturalists, the hero of the lie must stand up to forces in a landscape which, in Henry Nash Smith's words, "throws the hero back in upon himself and accentuates his terrible and sublime isolation. He is an anarchic and self-contained atom—hardly even a monad—alone in a hostile, or at best neutral, universe." In such a situation a person has to summon his own powers through the self-fulfilling magic of the lie or the boast.

The reader attracted to the magical and mythical perception of landscape might be disposed to consider the entire anthology as an adumbration of America's mainstream culture-myth, an Adamic myth which perceives in landscape the divinely ordained genesis of America as a nation and its apocalyptic ascendence into a peaceful millennium. If the basis of the myth was tribal, its tellers nevertheless have had the liberty of adapting it inexhaustibly to particular historical and even individual circumstances, and they have had the duty not only of narrating, but also of advocating and advertising it. That is true even of the mainstream's first shaman, Walt Whitman, who, even while he invokes the magical powers of self and nationhood, must at the same time instruct and convince his listeners.

Frank Waters

From Masked Gods

This is an example of a contemporary impulse toward what might be called imaginative anthropology—a reinvigoration, as Clyde Kluckhohn writes in the Introduction to *Masked Gods*, of "the inner drama that lies beneath the surface of ethnological documentation."

The Rock

IN THE BEGINNING the people lived in several worlds below. Successively they emerged from them to a new world above. In the middle of this new world stood a great rock. Extending through all the previous underworlds and protruding above this one, it was the core of the universe, rooted in time and space. It was oriented to the four directions, and its sides glowed with their corresponding colors—white on the east, blue on the south, yellow-red on the west, black on the north.

Emerging from the world below, the people gathered at its foot. And when they planted seeds to make the earth spread out, and when they called to the Holy People to help them plant the Holy Mountains, it was around this great natal rock. Hence they called it simply the Mountain Around Which Moving Was Done, the Mountain Surrounded by Mountains, or the Encircled Mountain.

To the east of it they planted the Holy Mountain of the East, made of sand and white shell. To the south they planted the Mountain of the South, made of sand and blue-green turquoise. To the west, the Mountain of the West, of yellow-red sand and abalone. And to the north, the Mountain of the North, of black sand and jet. In each they placed a Holy Person, a Talking God to guard the mountain and to listen to the prayers and songs offered it. Extra mountains they transplanted, and seeds of the four sacred plants. They made a fire with four kinds of wood and a hogan with four logs. Everything—the stars, the winds, the seasons—they put in order and named, and they became. For "when you put a thing in order, give it a name, and you are all in accord: it becomes."

Thus the pattern of the Navaho world at the Emergence. The great central Encircled Mountain. The four directional Holy Mountains. The lesser transplanted mountains, the plants, the trees, with the winds, the seasons, and the sun and moon and stars above. A world spread out like a four-petalled flower as seen from above. This today in a Navaho sand-painting is the symbol of the great axial rock, the Encircled Mountain: a four-petalled flower, like a four-leafed clover, like a lotus.

The four sacred mountains still bounding the ancient Navaho homeland are physical mountains: the Mountain of the East variously identified as Mount

Blanca, in Colorado; Wheeler Peak, above Taos in the Sangre de Cristo range; or Pelado Peak, near the pueblo of Jemez; Mount Taylor, of the San Mateo range, as the Mountain of the South; the San Francisco peaks, in Arizona, as the Mountain of the West; and a peak in the La Plata or San Juan range as the Mountain of the North.

The Encircled Mountain is something else. It has been identified as Huerfano Peak, above Chaco Cañon, which bears its name. But by its very nature it cannot be so constricted. Being the core of the whole cosmos, it existed when the First People were still in the lower worlds; and spanning a time and space beyond our earth-dimensional comprehension, it is too great and too powerful to be visible. This is its metaphysical reality. El Huerfano is merely its material image, its physical counterpart.

The meaning of this is amplified by reference to the cosmography of Tibetan Buddhism, in which is found the most striking parallel to the Encircled Mountain.

The core of the cosmos is Mt. Meru. It is shaped like a truncated pyramid, three of its four sides glowing with the same directional colors of the Navaho world-axis: white on the east, blue on the south, red on the west, and yellow on the north. It is eighty thousand miles high and eighty thousand miles deep. Within it are several underworlds and several heavens. Around this mighty cosmic core are seven concentric circles of mountains separated by seven encircling oceans. Each of these fresh-water oceans and its corresponding wall of mountains is a separate universe with its own sun and moon and planets.

Outside these seven universes, and floating in the outer salt-water ocean of space, are four main continents or land masses spreading out in the four main directions. The eastern continent is crescent in shape, white in color, as are the faces of its inhabitants. It is nine thousand miles in diameter. The western continent is round in shape, red in color, as are the faces of its inhabitants; its diameter is eight thousand miles. The northern continent is the largest of all, being ten thousand miles in diameter. It is of square shape and yellow color, and its inhabitants have corresponding faces. The southern continent is our planet Earth. It is the smallest of the four, being seven thousand miles in diameter as now verified by our modern scientific measurements. It is pear-shaped—and we agree that rather than being round it is flattened at both ends and bulges in the middle. Blue is the color assigned to it; and the faces of its inhabitants are oval shaped and greyish blue.

Below this mighty Mt. Meru the cosmos thus spreads out like a great four-petalled flower, a lotus. Each of the world-petals is protected by a Pokapala, or World Guardian, as each of the four Holy Mountains of the Navahos is guarded by its Talking God. And just as the Navaho world and the Encircled Mountain is symbolized by a four-petalled flower, so is the Buddhistic cosmos represented as a lotus.

These are striking pictorial and mythological parallels. But their full significance would be lost without their metaphysical meaning. The whole cosmos is represented as a lotus; but this cosmos is also identical with the goddess-mother called "The Lotus"; and our earthly universe is located within her "at about the level of her waist." In its duality, then, it is both that which was created and that which created it. And each living being, himself created in the image of the Goddess Mother of creation, also duplicates within his own psyche the complete cosmos.

Only by this can we understand the cryptic opening sentence of the legend of the Navaho ceremonial *Where The Two Came to Their Father:* "When they put the extra mountains around, they took Mountain Around Which Moving Was Done out of First Woman's belt."

This too explains the Zuñi references to the Sacred Middle which their ancestors found at Zuñi after their emergence from the underworld, and the location of their corresponding Mountain of Generation as being just below the navel of the Earth Mother. Above all is their striking conception of the Earth Mother as the goddess-mother of creation, through whose successive womb-worlds they emerged to this one.

The conception of this four-cornered world structure is not confined to them alone in America. In the sacred *Popol Vuh,* recording the creation myth of the Quiché Maya, the world is described as "four-pointed, four-sided, four-bordered." In the *Chilan Balam of Mani* this cubical world-block is further alluded to as the altar of the gods. The truncated pyramid temples of the Toltecs, Zapotecs, and Aztecs themselves suggest such world axes.

Hence we understand now, at the outset, that in Pueblo and Navaho mythology we are dealing not with easily comprehended, childish legends, but with a cosmographic concept as abstract, imaginatively vast and old as that of any people on earth. It is strangely consistent that the area today still contains this mythological meaning in its name of the Four Corners. Its original prototype, its greatest physical image, may well have been, not El Huerfano, but the Colorado Pyramid, the high hinterland heart of America. Its central section, the Colorado plateau region, is still the sacred middle, their traditional homeland. The Pueblos and Navahos have always regarded life as dual: the physical and the psychical. And it is both of these realities of the Rock to which they have clung against the assault of erosion and materialism alike.

The Canyon

HERE IS THE VISIBLE WORLD, four-pointed, four cornered, bounded by the four directions. One terrace, one plane as it were, of the pyramidal universe extending below and above. One of its two great polarities is the Encircled Mountain, which extends invisibly upward towards the Sun Father.

The other is an equally tremendous hole, a naval, the *sipapu:* the place of emergence whence came man from the dark underworld, the place of beginning. It leads back down into the depths of the earth; into her who is known as the Goddess Mother of creation, Our Mother Earth.

It too is a mighty rock, as long as a mountain range, as high as its highest peak. But upside down. A deep cleft in the earth, a monstrous chasm. Like the Encircled Mountain, the Grand Canyon is impervious to time and change; and paradoxically, the more it has been assaulted the larger it has grown. Its spires and pinnacles have lengthened, its clefts and chasms have deepened, its buttes and mesas have broadened, until it seems as immeasurable and indestructible as the Rock itself.

This Upside Down Rock is visible. But unbelievable. In its abysmal depths whole mountains contract and expand. Clouds ebb in and out of the gorges like frothy tides. Everything changes shape constantly in the shifting light. And all these mutations of form, these permutations of substance, are suffused with infinite variations of color. Never static, never still, it is inconstant as the passing moment, and yet durable as time. It too is a realm of the fantastic unreal, Maya, "a world of illusion."

For us, as for the Hopi, Grand Canyon is the largest and deepest *sipapu* in the nebulous past.

Its walls are twisted, folded and compressed layers of rock three miles thick, one mile deep and 217 miles long. On the plateau out of which it has been cut there stand around it tall rock pillars like Vermilion Cliffs, Cedar Mountain, and Red Butte. On top of one of these lies a small pebble. And on this rests a speck of dust.

This speck of dust represents the age of the earth according to Archbishop Ussher, who, in the authorized version of the Bible of his time, sanctioned the statement that God created the world at 9 A.M., October 26, 4004 B.C.—scarcely six thousand years ago. . . . But there! It has blown away into the shifting, dissolving illusions of the canyon.

The small pebble represents the one million years since man first appeared on earth; the Age of Man, according to present scientists. In this little time-span man has walked through all history—lumbering out of a dark cave to discover fire, through the resplendent castles and kingdoms of vanished civilizations, to stand on the threshold of our Atomic Age. . . . But there. It has rolled off into the soundless depths of the canyon.

The pillar on which it rests is all that remains here of the sixty million years of the Cenozoic or Modern Era. In this short age of Mammals appeared all the forms of life now known on earth—the continents, mountains, seas, and rivers; the hardwood forests, cereals, fruits, and grasses; the birds; the mammals and man-apes. But the pillar is crumbling into the canyon. There! It is carried away by that river of time which in only twelve million years has carried away, sand by sand, all the great mountain peaks around it.

Another butte still totters on the edge. It is all that remains of the one hundred and forty million years of the Mesozoic or Medieval Era. This was the Age of Reptiles—of great, slimy monsters, huge, toothed birds, and mammoth dinosaurs; of insects; of tropical plants and flowers; of the almost immortal evergreens. Soon it too will crumble and wash away with all the footprints, skeletons, and fossils imbedded in its rock.

Here now are the upper rock layers of the canyon walls. Kaibab limestone, named for the plateau on the north rim, Kaibab being a Piute name meaning "Mountain Lying Down." Coconino sandstone, named for the plateau on the south rim. Then the Supai shale formations which form the walls of Cataract Canyon, in which the Supais still live. Redwall limestone. Finally the Tonto group. . . . Over 3,500 feet of rock remaining to attest the three hundred and forty million years of the Paleozoic or Ancient Era. The Age of Fishes and the Age of Amphibians, of shell-bearing mollusca and corals, and the first appearance of land plants.

Below all this lie the Grand Canyon series of formations, twelve thousand feet thick. The Unkar and Chuar groups containing Hotauta basal conglomerate, bright red Hakatai shale, and Shinumo quartzite, appropriately named for the old Hopi confederacy. These thick, complex formations leave a record of the Proterozoic or Primitive Era, fifteen hundred million years long. The Age of Marine Invertebrates, primitive marine forms of life, trilobites and brachiopods, little groveling crustaceans.

Thus in a three-mile thickness of rock, in a vertical drop of one mile, there lie the remnants of an earth at least two thousand million years old. A whole world rising and sinking beneath the sea and rising again with the almost imperceptible, rhythmic pulse of eternity. Really different worlds successively emerging, each with its own physical pattern, its own forms of life. All lost now and forgotten in the illusory depths of time. Mere kachina worlds, of which are left but fragments of their masks.

But here now at the bottom of the canyon protrudes the oldest rock system known, part of the original earth's crust. Great vertical layers of gneiss that formed before the planet had cooled. Huge blocks of granite forced into them in a molten state by heat and pressure. Pegmatite. Vishnu schist. In it are found traces of the earliest known larval life—bits of carbon remaining from microscopic plants and single-celled animals.

Now we know what it is. The Rock, a protruding fragment of the Mountain Around Which Moving Was Done, the cosmic core of the universe.

Vestiges of visible time go back no further than this Archeozoic Era. The lengthening pulse beat—one million years, sixty million, one hundred and forty million, three hundred and forty million, fifteen hundred million—grows into a steady hum. In a whirling nebula Archeozoic Time merges into Azoic Time and it into Cosmic Time; and in the fantastic unreality of this palpable fourth dimension, this beginning links with the Psychozoic Time yet to come.

All these names, these physical remnants of vanished worlds and vanished life forms are but discarded kachina masks. Through this *sipapu* we come to the deep underworld, the heart of the rock, the womb of Our Mother Earth. It is the revered Place of Beginning whence came man.

1950

Creation Myth (Zuñi)

This translation of the Creation Myth by Frank Cushing appeared in his *Outlines of Zuñi Creation Myths* in the Thirteenth Annual Report of the Bureau of American Ethnology (Washington, D. C., 1896). It appears (as do "The Buffalo Rock," "The Corn Spirit," and "Rain Song," following) in Margot Astrov's excellent anthology *American Indian Prose and Poetry* (New York, 1962). Astrov quotes the anthopologist Ruth Benedict to the effect that though Cushing's is a "poeticized version that draws heavily upon his interpretative powers," it still accurately reflects "Zuñi esoteric speculative attempts at synthesis of ceremonies, clans, societies, directions of the compass, colors and patron animals."

BEFORE THE BEGINNING of the new-making, Awonawilona solely had being. There was nothing else whatsoever throughout the great spaces of the ages save everywhere black darkness in it, and everywhere void desolation.

In the beginning of the new-made, Awonawilona conceived within himself and thought outward in space, whereby mists of increase, steams potent of growth, were evolved and uplifted. Thus, by means of his innate knowledge, the All-Container made himself in person and form of the Sun, whom we hold to be our father and who thus came to exist and appear. With his appearance came the brightening of the spaces with light, and with the brightening of the spaces the great mist-clouds were thickened and fell, whereby evolved water in water; yea, and the world-holding sea. With his substance of flesh outdrawn from the surface of his person, the Sun Father formed the seed-stuff of twin-worlds impregnating therewith the great waters, and lo! in the heat of his light these waters of the sea grew green and scums grew upon them waxing wide and weighty until, behold! they became Awitelin Tsita, the "Fourfold-Containing Mother Earth," and Apoyan Tachu, the "All-Covering Father Sky." From the lying together of these twain upon the great world-waters, so vitalizing, terrestrial life was conceived; whence began all beings of earth, men and the creatures, in the Fourfold Womb of the Earth. Thereupon the Earth Mother repulsed the Sky Father, growing big and sinking deep into the embrace of the waters below, thus separating from the Sky Father in the embrace of the waters above. . . .

Now, like all the surpassing beings, the Earth Mother and the Sky Father were changeable, even as smoke in the wind; transmutable at thought, manifesting themselves in any form at will, like as dancers may by mask making . . . Thus as a man and a woman spake they, one to another:

"Behold," said the Earth Mother, as a great terraced bowl appeared at her hand and within it water, "this is as upon me the homes of my tiny children shall be. On the rim of each world country they wander in, terraced mountains shall stand, . . . whereby country shall be known from country, and within each, place from place. Behold again!" said she as she spat on the water, and rapidly smote and stirred it with her fingers. Foam formed, gathering about the terraced rim, mounting higher and higher. "Yea," she said, "and from my bosom they shall draw nourishment, for in such as this shall they find the substance of life whence we were ourselves sustained. For see!"

Then with her warm breath she blew across the terraces; white flecks of the foam broke away, and floating over above the water, were shattered by the cold breath of the Sky Father attending, and forthwith shed downward abundantly fine mist and spray! "Even so shall white clouds float up from the great waters at the borders of the world, and clustering about the mountain terraces of the horizons be borne aloft and abroad by the breaths of the surpassing soul beings, and of the children, and shall be hardened and broken by the cold, shedding downward, in rain spray, the water of life, even in the hollow places of my lap. For therein shall chiefly nestle our children, mankind and creature-kind, for warmth in thy coldness! Even the trees on high mountains near the clouds . . . crouch low toward Mother Earth for warmth and protection.

"Even so!" said the Sky Father. "Yet not alone shalt thou be helpful unto our children, for behold!" and he spread his hand abroad with the palm downward and into all the wrinkles and crevices thereof he set the semblance of shining yellow corn grains; in the dark of the early world-dawn they gleamed like sparks of fire and moved as his hand was moved over the bowl, shining up from and also moving in the depth of the water therein.

Night Chant (Navaho)

First translated in 1907 by Washington Matthews in his *Navajo Myths, Prayers and Songs,* this chant reappears in George Cronyn's anthology *American Indian Poetry* (New York, 1972). It is excerpted here.

(*For the Ninth Song*)

In Tsegihi,
In the house made of dawn,

In the house made of evening twilight,
In the house made of dark cloud,
In the house made of rain and mist, of pollen, of grasshoppers,
Where the dark mist curtains the doorway,
The path to which is on the rainbow,
Where the zig-zag lightning stands high on top,
Where the he-rain stands high on top,
Oh, male divinity!
With your moccasins of dark cloud, come to us,
With your mind enveloped in dark cloud, come to us,
With the dark thunder above you, come to us soaring,
With the shapen cloud at your feet, come to us soaring.
With the far darkness made of the dark cloud over your head, come to us soaring,
With the far darkness made of the rain and the mist over your head, come to us soaring,
With the far darkness made of the rain and the mist over your head, come to us soaring.
With the zig-zag lightning flung out high over your head,
With the rainbow hanging high over your head, come to us soaring.
With the far darkness made of the dark cloud on the ends of your wings,
With the far darkness made of the rain and the mist on the ends of your wings, come to us soaring,
With the zig-zag lightning, with the rainbow hanging high on the ends of your wings, come to us soaring.
With the near darkness made of dark cloud of the rain and the mist, come to us,
With the darkness on the earth, come to us.

With these I wish the foam floating on the flowing water over the roots of the great corn,
I have made your sacrifice,
I have prepared a smoke for you,
My feet restore for me.
My limbs restore, my body restore, my mind restore, my voice restore for me.
Today, take out your spell for me,
Today, take away your spell for me.
Away from me you have taken it,
Far off from me it is taken,
Far off you have done it.

Happily I recover,
Happily I become cool,
My eyes regain their power, my head cools, my limbs regain their strength, I hear again.
Happily for me the spell is taken off,
Happily I walk; impervious to pain, I walk; light within, I walk; joyous, I walk.
Abundant dark clouds I desire,
An abundance of vegetation I desire,
An abundance of pollen, abundant dew, I desire.
Happily may fair white corn, to the ends of the earth, come with you,
Happily may fair yellow corn, fair blue corn, fair corn of all kinds, plants of all kinds, goods of all kinds, jewels of all kinds, to the ends of the earth, come with you.
With these before you, happily may they come with you,
With these behind, below, above, around you, happily may they come with you,
Thus you accomplish your tasks.

Happily the old men will regard you,
Happily the old women will regard you,
The young men and the young women will regard you,
The children will regard you,
The chiefs will regard you,
Happily, as they scatter in different directions, they will regard you,
Happily, as they approach their homes, they will regard you.

May their roads home be on the trail of peace,
Happily may they all return.
In beauty I walk,
With beauty before me, I walk,
With beauty behind me, I walk,
With beauty above and about me, I walk,
It is finished in beauty,
It is finished in beauty.

Rain Song (Pima)

"Rain Song" first appeared in Frank Russel's *The Pima Indians* in the Twenty-sixth Annual Report of the Bureau of American Ethnology (Washington, D.C., 1904). The drums both symbolize and conjure thunder; the feathers and down of the eagle, clouds.

Hi-iya naiho-o! The earth is rumbling
From the beating of our basket drums.
The earth is rumbling from the beating
Of our basket drums, everywhere humming.
Earth is rumbling, everywhere raining.

Hi-iya naiho-o! Pluck out the feathers
From the wing of the eagle and turn them
Toward the east where lie the large clouds.
Hi-iya naiho-o! Pluck out the soft down
From the breast of the eagle and turn it
Toward the west where sail the small clouds.
Hi-iya naiho-o! Beneath the abode
Of the rain gods it is thundering;
Large corn is there. *Hi-iya naiho-o!*
Beneath the abode of the rain gods
It is raining; small corn is there.

Three Black American Folk Tales

"Big Swamps of the Congaree" conjures a landscape familiar to Southern Blacks since slavery times, when the swamps offered the only refuge to fugitives because they would not be tracked there and because no one else inhabited them. The other two selections represent two kinds of lies.

Big Swamps of the Congaree

TAD: Gentlemens, how is you-all?

VOICE: Howdy! how you been?

SECOND VOICE: Tolerable.

TAD: I been down in de big swamps on de Congaree.

VOICE: Tell us, brother?

TAD: I been down to de Congaree in de big swamps, where de trees is tall an' de moss long an' gray, where de Bullace grow, an' where I hear de tune of de bird in de mornin'; down wey de wild turkey gobbles, way down on de Congaree; wey God's mornin' leads to de devil's night; down on de river, where night make her sign, where owls on a dead limb talks of de dead, talks wid de dead an laughs like de dead, way down in de big swamps of de Congaree; down where de blunt-tailed moccasin crawls in de grass, where de air is stink wid he smell; where de water is green, where de worms is spewed out of de groun', where de groun' is mud, where de trees sweat like a man; down in de home of de varmint an' bugs, down in de slick yallow mud, de black mud an' de brown, way down in de big swamps of de Congaree; down in de land of pizen, where de yallow-fly sting, in de home of de fever an' wey death is de king. Dat wey I been, down in de big swamps. Down in de land of mosquito, way down in de big swamps, down on de Congaree.

The Promised Land

YES, SIR, Boss Man, the niggers is easy fooled. They always is been that way, and we was fooled away from Alabama to Arkansas by them two Yankee mens, Mr. Van Fleet and Mr. Bill Bowman, what I told you about, that brung that hundred head of folks the time us come. They told us that in Arkansas the hogs just laying around already baked with the knives and the forks sticking in them ready for to be et, and that there was fritter ponds everywhere with the fritters a-frying in them ponds of grease, and that there was money trees where all you had to do was to pick the money offen 'em like picking cotton offen the stalk, and us was sure put out when us git here and find that the onliest meat to be had was that what was in the store, and them fritters had to be fried in the pans, and that there wa'n't no money trees a-tall.

Big Corn

THERE HAPPEN to be a young nigger there, back from the West for a visit, and he was a great bragger. He was telling 'bout corn in Texas. "There," he said, "corn grow twenty feet high, with stalks as big as the arm of John L. Sullivan, when he whupped Kilrain, and half a dozen big ears on each stalk." The crowd was thunderstruck.

My daddy cleared his throat and say: "That am nothing in the way of corn. One day I was walking past a forty-acre patch of corn, on the Governor Heyward plantation by the Combahee River, and the corn was so high and thick, I decide to ramble through it. 'Bout halfway over, I hears a commotion. I walks on and peeps. There stands a four-ox wagon backed up to the edge of the field, and two niggers was sawing down a stalk. Finally they drag it on the wagon and drive off. I seen one of them, in a day or two, and asks 'bout it. He say: "We shelled 356 bushels of corn from that one ear, and then we saw 800 feet of lumber from the cob."

That young man soon slip out from the crowd and has never been seen here since.

Zora Neale Hurston

From Mules and Men

An anthropology student of Franz Boas at Columbia and a novelist, Zora Hurston traveled the South in the late 1920's gathering the material which was to become *Mules and Men.* Both the story of the "two-head" or hoodoo doctor Marie Leveau and the sermon ("The Wounds of Jesus") which follows this excerpt conjure divinities or intermediaries capable of calling forth and of quieting the elements. In the case of Marie Leveau, the rituals are clearly a mixture of animism and of Catholicism.

[Hoodoo Doctor]

Now I was in New Orleans and I asked. They told me Algiers, the part of New Orleans that is across the river to the west. I went there and lived for four months and asked. I found women reading cards and doing mail order business in names and insinuations of well known factors in conjure. Nothing worth putting on paper. But they all claimed some knowledge and link with Marie Leveau. From so much of hearing the name I asked everywhere for this Leveau, and everybody told me differently. . . . I did a lot of stumbling and asking before I heard of Luke Turner, himself a hoodoo doctor, who says that he is her nephew.

When I found out about Turner, I had already studied under five two-headed doctors and had gone thru an initiation ceremony with each. So I asked Turner to take me as a pupil. He was very cold. In fact he showed no eagerness even to talk with me. He feels sure of his powers and seeks no one. . . .

I made three more trips before he would talk to me in any way that I could feel encouraged. He talked about Marie Leveau because I asked. I wanted to know if she was really as great as they told me. So he enlightened my ignorance and taught me. We sat before the soft coal fire in his grate.

"Time went around pointing out what God had already made. Moses had seen the Burning Bush. Solomon by magic knowed all wisdom. And Marie Leveau was a woman in New Orleans.

"She was born February 2, 1827. Anybody don't believe I tell the truth can go look at the book in St. Louis Cathedral. Her mamma and her papa, they wasn't married and his name was Christopher Glapion.

"She was very pretty, one of the Creole Quadroons and many people said she would never be a hoodoo doctor like her mamma and her grandma before her. She liked to go to balls very much where all the young men fell in love with her. But Alexander, the great two-headed doctor felt the power in her and so he tell her she must come to study with him. Marie, she rather dance and make love, but one day a rattlesnake come to her in her bedroom and spoke to her. So she went to Alexander and studied. But soon she could teach her teacher and the snake stayed with her always. . . .

"Out on Lake Pontchartrain at Bayou St. John she hold a great feast every year on the Eve of St. John's, June 24th. It is Midsummer Eve, and the Sun give special benefits then and need great honor. The special drum be played then. It is a cow-hide stretched over a half-barrel. Beat with a jaw-bone. Some say a man but I think they do not know. I think the jawbone of an ass or a cow. She hold the feast of St. John's partly because she is a Catholic and partly because of hoodoo.

"The ones around her altar fix everything for the feast. Nobody see Marie Leveau for nine days before the feast. But when the great crowd of people at the feast call upon her, she would rise out of the waters of the lake with a great communion candle burning upon her head and another in each one of her hands. She walked upon the waters to the shore. As a little boy I saw her myself. When the feast was over, she went back into the lake, and nobody saw her for nine days again.

"On the feast that I saw her open the waters, she looked hard at me and nodded her head so that her tignon shook. Then I knew I was called to take up her work. She was very old and I was a lad of seventeen. Soon I went to wait upon her Altar both on St. Anne Street and her house on Bayou St. John's.

"The rattlesnake that had come to her a little one when she was also young was very huge. He piled great upon his altar and took nothing from the food set before him. One night he sang and Marie Leveau called me from my sleep to look at him and see. 'Look well, Turner,' she told me. 'No one shall hear and see such as this for many centuries.'

"She went to the Great Altar and made great ceremony. The snake finished his song and seemed to sleep. She drove me back to my bed and went again to her Altar.

"The next morning the great snake was not at his altar. His hide was before the Great Altar stuffed with spices and things of power. Never did I know what become of his flesh. It is said that the snake went off to the woods alone after the death of Marie Leveau, but they don't know. This is his skin that I wear about my shoulders whenever I reach for power.

"Three days Marie, she set at the Altar with the great sun candle burning and shining in her face. She set the water upon the Altar and turned to the window, and looked upon the lake. The sky grew dark. The lightning raced to the seventeen quarters of the heavens and the lake heaved like a mighty herd of cattle rolling in a pasture. The house shook with the earth.

"She told me, 'You are afraid, That is right, you should fear. Go to your own house and build an altar. Power will come.' So I hurried to my mother's house and told them.

"Some who loved her hurried out to Bayou St. John and tried to enter the house but she try hard to send them off. They beat upon the door, but she will not open. The terrible strong wind at last tore the house away and set it in the lake. The thunder and lightning grow greater. Then the loving ones find a boat and went out to where her house floats on one side and break a window to bring her out, but she begs, 'No! Please, no,' she tell them. 'I want to die here in the lake,' but they would not permit her. She did not wish their destruction, so she let herself be drawn away from her altar in the lake. And the wind, the thunder and lightning, and the water all ceased the moment she set foot on dry land.

"That night she also sing a song and is dead, yes. So I have the snake skin and do works with the power she leave me."

"How did Marie Leveau do her work?" I asked feeling that I had gotten a little closer to him.

"She go to her great Altar and seek until she become the same as the spirit, then she come out into the room where she listens to them that come to ask. When they finish she answers them as a god. If a lady have a bad enemy and come to her she go into her altar room and when she come out and take her seat, the lady will say to her:

" 'Oh, Good Mother. I come to you with my heart bowed down and my shoulders drooping, and my spirits broken; for an enemy has sorely tried me; has caused my loved ones to leave me; has taken from me my worldly goods and my gold; has spoken meanly of me and caused my friends to lose faith in me. On my knees I pray to you, Good Mother, that you will cause confusion to reign in the house of my enemy and that you will take their power from them and cause them to be unsuccessful.'

"Marie Leveau is not a women when she answer the one who ask. No. She is a god, yes. Whatever she say, it will come so. . . .

By the time that Turner had finished his recitation he wasn't too conscious of me. In fact he gave me the feeling that he was just speaking, but not for my benefit. He was away off somewhere. He made a final dramatic gesture with open hands and hushed for a minute. Then he sank deeper into himself and went on:

"But when she put the last curse on a person, it would be better if that man was dead, yes."

With an impatient gesture he signalled me not to interrupt him.

"She set the altar for the curse with black candles that have been dressed in vinegar. She would write the name of the person to be cursed on the candle with a needle. Then she place fifteen cents in the lap of Death upon the altar to pay the spirit to obey her orders. Then she place her hands flat upon the table and say the curse-prayer.

" 'To The Man God: O great One, I have been sorely tried by my enemies and have been blasphemed and lied against. My good thoughts and my honest actions have been turned to bad actions and dishonest ideas. My home has been disrespected, my children have been cursed and ill-treated. My dear ones have been backbitten and their virtue questioned. O Man God, I beg that this that I ask for my enemies shall come to pass:

" 'That the South wind shall scorch their bodies and make them wither and shall not be tempered to them. That the North wind shall freeze their blood and numb their muscles and that it will not leave their hair to grow, and that their finger nails shall fall off and their bones shall crumble. That the East wind shall make their minds grow dark, their sight shall fail and their seed dry up so that they shall not multiply.

" 'I ask that their fathers and mothers from their furthest generation will not intercede for them before the great throne, and the wombs of their women shall not bear fruit except for strangers, and that they shall become extinct. I pray that the children who come shall be weak of mind and paralyzed of limb and that they themselves shall curse them in their turn for ever turning the breath of life into their bodies. I pray that disease and death shall be forever with them and that their worldly goods shall not prosper, and that their crops shall not multiply and that their cows, their sheep, and their hogs and all their living beasts shall die of thirst and starvation. I pray that their house shall be unroofed and that the rain, the thunder and lightning shall find the innermost recesses of their home and that the foundation shall crumble and the floods tear it asunder. I pray that the sun shall not shed its rays on them in benevolence, but instead it shall beat down on them and burn them and destroy them. I pray that the moon shall not give them peace, but instead shall deride them and decry them and cause their minds to shrivel. I pray that their friends shall betray them and cause them loss of power, of gold and of silver, and that their enemies shall smite them until they beg for mercy which shall not be given them. I pray that their tongues shall forget how to speak in sweet words, and that it shall be paralyzed and that all about them shall be desolation, pestilence, and death. O Man God, I ask you for all these things because they have dragged me in the dust and destroyed my good name; broken my heart and caused me to curse the day I was born. So be it.' "

Turner again made that gesture with his hands that meant the end. Then he sat in a dazed silence. My own spirits had been falling all during the terrible curse and he did not have to tell me to be quiet this time. After a long period of waiting I rose to go. "The Spirit say you come back tomorrow," he breathed as I passed his knees. I nodded that I had heard and went out. The next day he began to prepare me for my initiation ceremony, for rest assured that no one may approach the Altar without the crown, and none may wear the crown of power without preparation. *It must be earned.*

1935

The Reverend C. C. Lovelace

From The Wounds of Jesus

Zora Neale Hurston heard the Reverend C. C. Lovelace's sermon at Eau Gallie, Florida, in May 1929. She later incorporated it into her novel, *Jonah's Gourd Vine* (1934).

Jesus have always loved us from the foundation of the world.
When God
Stood out on the apex of His power
Before the hammers of creation
Fell upon the anvils of Time and hammered out the ribs of the earth
Before He made ropes
By the breath of fire
And set the boundaries of the ocean by gravity of His power
When God said, ha!
Let us make man
And the elders upon the altar cried, ha!
If you make man, ha!
He will sin.
God my master, ha!
Christ, yo' friend said
Father!! Ha-aa!
I am the teeth of Time
That comprehended de dust of de earth
And weighed de hills in scales
Painted de rainbow dat marks de end of de departing storm
Measured de seas in de holler of my hand
Held de elements in a unbroken chain of controllment.

Make man, ha!
If he sin, I will redeem him
I'll break de chasm of hell
Where de fire's never quenched
I'll go into de grave
Where de worm never dies, Ah—
So God A'mighty, ha!
Got his stuff together
He dipped some water out of de mighty deep
He got Him a handful of dirt, ha!
From de foundation sills of de earth
He seized a thimble full of breath, ha!
From de drums of de wind, ha!
God my master!
Now I'm ready to make man
Aa-aah!
Who shall I make him after? Ha!
Worlds within worlds begin to wheel and roll
De Sun, Ah!
Gathered up de fiery skirts of her garments
And wheeled around de throne, Ah!
Saying, Ah, make man after me, Ah!
God gazed upon the sun
And sent her back to her blood-red socket
And shook His head, ha!
De Moon, Ha!
Grabbed up de reins of de tides
And dragged a thousand seas behind her
As she walked around de throne—
Ah-h, please make man after me
But God said, No.
De stars bust from their diamond sockets
And circled de glitterin throne cryin
A-aah! Make man after me
God said, No!
I'll make man in my own image, ha!
I'll put him in de garden
And Jesus said, ha!
And if he sin,
I'll go his bond before yo mighty throne
Ah. He was yo friend
He made us all, ha!

Delegates to de judgment convention
Ah!
Faith hasn't got no eyes, but she's long-legged
But take de spy-glass of Faith
And look into dat upper room
When you are alone to yourself
When yo' heart is burnt with fire, ha!
When de blood is lopin thru yo veins
Like de iron monasters on de rail
Look into dat upper chamber, ha!
We notice at de supper table
As He gazed upon His friends, ha!
His eyes flowin wid tears, ha!
"My soul is exceedingly sorrowful unto death, ha!
For this night, ha!
One of you shall betray me, ha!
It were not a Roman officer, ha!
It were not a centurion soldier
But one of you
Who I have chosen my bosom friend
That sops in the dish with me shall betray me."
I want to draw a parable.
I see Jesus
Leaving heben with all of His Grandeur
Disrobin Hisself of His matchless honor
Yieldin up de sceptre of revolvin worlds
Clothing Hisself in de garment of humanity
Coming into de world to rescue His friends.
Two thousand years have went by on their rusty ankles
But with the eye of faith I can see Him,
Look down from His high towers of elevation
I can hear Him when He walks about the golden streets
I can hear 'em ring under His footsteps
Sol me-e-e, Sol do
Sol me-e-e, Sol do
I can see Him step out upon the rim bones of nothing
Crying I am de way
De truth and de light
Ah!
God A'mighty!
I see Him grab de throttle
Of de well ordered train of mercy

I see kingdoms crush and crumble
Whilst de arc angels held de winds in de corner chambers
I see Him arrive on dis earth
And walk de streets thirty and three years
Oh-h-hhh!
I see Him walking beside de sea of Galilee wid His disciples
This declaration gendered on His lips.
''Let us go on the other side''
God A'mighty!
Dey entered de boat
Wid their oarus stuck in de back
Sails unfurled to de evenin breeze
And de ship was now sailin
As she reached de center of de lake
Jesus was 'sleep on a pillow in de rear of de boat
And de dynamic powers of nature became disturbed
And de mad winds broke de heads of de western drums
And fell down on de Lake of Galilee
And buried themselves behind de gallopin waves
And de white-caps marbilized themselves like an army
And walked out like soldiers goin to battle
And de zig-zag lightning
Licked out her fiery tongue
And de flying clouds
Threw their wings in the channels of the deep
And bedded de waters like a road-plow
And faced de current of de chargin billows
And de terrific bolts of thunder—they bust in de clouds
And de ship begin to reel and rock
God A'mighty!
And one of de disciples called Jesus
''Master!! Carest thou not that we perish?''
And He arose
And de storm was in its pitch
And de lightnin played on His raiments as He stood on the prow of the boat
And placed His foot upon the neck of the storm
And spoke to the howlin winds
And de sea fell at His feet like a marble floor
And de thunders went back in their vault
Then He set down on de rim of de ship
And took de hooks of his power

And lifted de billows in His lap
And rocked de winds to sleep on His arm
And said, "Peace be still."
And de Bible says there was a calm.
I can see Him wid de eye of faith
When He went from Pilate's house
Wid the crown of 72 wounds upon His head
I can see Him as He mounted Calvary and hung upon de cross for our sins.
I can see-eee-ee
De mountains fall to their rocky knees when He cried
"My God, my God! Why hast thou forsaken me?"
The mountains fell to their rocky knees and trembled like a beast
From the stroke of the master's axe
One angel took the flinches of God's eternal power
And bled the veins of the earth
One angel that stood at the gate with a flaming sword
Was so well pleased with his power
Until he pierced the moon with his sword
And she ran down in blood
And de sun
Batted her fiery eyes and put on her judgement robe
And laid down in de cradle of eternity
And rocked herself into sleep and slumber.
He died until the great belt in the wheel of time
And de geological strata fell aloose
And a thousand angels rushed to de canopy of heben
With flamin swords in their hands
And placed their feet upon blue ether's bosom and looked back at de dazzlin throne
And de arc angels had veiled their faces
And de throne was draped in mournin
And de orchestra had struck silence for the space of half an hour
Angels had lifted their harps to de weepin willows
And God had looked off to-wards immensity
And blazin worlds fell off His teeth
And about that time Jesus groaned on de cross and said, "It is finished"
And then de chambers of hell explode
And de damnable spirits
Come up from de Sodomistic world and rushed into de smoky camps of eternal night
And cried "Woe! Woe! Woe!"

And then de Centurion cried out
"Surely this is the Son of God."
And about dat time
De angel of Justice unsheathed his flamin sword and ripped de veil of de temple
And de High Priest vacated his office
And then de sacrificial energy penetrated de mighty strata
And quickened de bones of de prophets
And they arose from their graves and walked about in de streets of Jerusalem.
I heard de whistle of de damnation train
Dat pulled out from Garden of Eden loaded wid cargo goin to hell
Ran at break-neck speed all de way thru de law
All de way thru de prophetic age
All de way thru de reign of kings and judges—
Plowed her way thru de Jurdan
And on her way to Calvary when she blew for de switch
Jesus stood out on her track like a rough-backed mountain
And she threw her cow-catcher in His side and His blood ditched de train,
He died for our sins.
Wounded in the house of His friends.
That's where I got off de damnation train
And dats where you must get off, ha!
For in dat mor-ornin', ha!
When we shall all be delegates, ha!
To dat judgement convention, ha!
When de two trains of Time shall meet on de trestle
And wreck de burnin axles of de unformed ether
And de mountains shall skip like lambs
When Jesus shall place one foot on de neck of de sea, ha!
One foot on dry land
When His chariot wheels shall be running hub-deep in fire
He shall take His friends thru the open bosom of a unclouded sky
And place in their hands de hosanna fan
And they shall stand round and round His beatific throne
And praise His name forever.

Amen.

1934

Constance Rourke

From Davy Crockett

This is an example of a tall tale, and it is given a general context in the introduction to this section.

From Sunrise in His Pocket

A FEW MEN had gathered about the fire in a tavern on the Forked Deer River in western Tennessee. The winter dusk had fallen. An old hunter was speaking, mournfully.

"Thar's a great rejoicing among the bears of the river country and the alligators of the Mississippi are rolling up their shining ribs to the sun. The rattlesnakes has been coming out of their holes this autumn to frolic in the clearings, and the foxes goes to sleep in the goose pens. It's because the rifle of Crockett is silent forever, and the print of his moccasins is found no more in our woods."

"The painters and bears will miss him," said another hunter.

"He never missed *them,*" said a man with red hair who was bending over the barrel of a flintlock, oiling it.

"I heard Davy never died at all," said a hunter.

"I heard he was roaming over the prairies of Texas with a bear," said a traveler.

"Named Death Hug," said the red-haired man.

"He was carrying messages for Sam Houston," said the traveler, "and he was stopped by a big party of Mexican scouts. Quick as lightning Crockett mounted Death Hug and leapt clean over their heads." There was a pause. "Another time when he was carrying those messages he met a squad of Mexicans just as he came up to a grove of oaks and Death Hug ran right up one of the oaks with Crockett on his back and then out on a limb as slick as a panther going to roost, and over to the limb of another oak, and another, and then they were down and away."

"And once he sighted a stallion on the prairie," said the old hunter, "wild as the whirlwind, and tall and strong. Crockett came within a hundred yards of him, and the stallion threw back his ears, spread his jaws, and came snorting at him. As the horse reared to plunge Crockett seized his mane and mounted him as easy as a cow bird sits on the back of a brindle bull. The stallion made off like lightning and a big thunderstorm came up. Lightning struck all around but it flashed to either side of the horse as he ran and never struck him. The horse was off to the west and Crockett thought he was going to be flung against the Rocky Mountains. He ran for three days and three nights until he came to the Mad River, that poured down the mountainside boiling and hissing. There the horse ran under a tree, trying to brush Crockett off his back, but Crockett pulled his mane and that stallion leapt over the tree and the boiling river besides. Then he stopped quiet and Crockett got off." . . .

In the Ozarks they tell of another time when Crockett was out hunting and traveled far from his cabin and spent the night in the woods. The next morning at daybreak he took a far jump and landed on the sun, thinking that he would be carried over the mountain to his cabin. But he had forgotten that he was west of his cabin instead of east. So, traveling with the sun for twenty-four hours, he saw the whole world, and dropped off the next morning and landed on his own doorstep.

During his own lifetime Crockett had been spoken of as consorting on easy terms with the moon, with shooting stars, a fiery comet, and the lightning. In all the stories his close companions were wind, water, fire, the earth, and the wild creatures of forest and prairie. In a last story he is portrayed as stronger than the sun, and he appears once more in the hunting country of Tennessee.

This story belongs to the Winter of the Big Snow, the winter of 1835, when Crockett set out for Texas, when snow fell early through the wide stretches of the North, crept farther and farther down through the hard wood forests of Michigan, then through the soft wood forests, through the long valleys of Wisconsin, down upon the prairie country of Illinois, into Kentucky and Tennessee. The story was told as if Crockett himself related it.

"On one of those winter mornings it was all screwen cold," said Crockett. "The forest trees were so stiff they couldn't shake and the very daybreak froze fast as it was trying to dawn. The tinder-box in my cabin would no more catch fire than a sunk raft at the bottom of the sea. All creation was in a fair way for freezing fast, so I thought I must strike a little fire from my fingers and travel out a few leagues and see what I could do about it. I brought my knuckles together like two thunderclouds, but the sparks froze up before I could collect 'em, so out I walked and tried to keep myself unfrozen by going along at a frolic gait, whistling the tune of 'Fire in the Mountains' and keeping going at three double quick time. Well, after I had walked about a hundred miles up Daybreak Hill I reached Peak o' Day, and there I discovered what was the matter. The earth had actually frozen fast on her axis and couldn't turn round, and the sun had got jammed between two cakes of ice under the wheels, and there he had been shining and working to get loose till he was frozen fast in his cold sweat.

" 'C-R-E-A-T-I-O-N,' thought I, 'this is the toughest sort of suspension, and it mustn't be endured—something must be done or human creation is done for!' It was so premature an antediluvian cold on top of Peak o' Day that my upper and lower teeth were all collapsed together as tight as a frozen oyster. So I took a big bear off my back that I'd picked up on my road and threw him down on the ice and soon there was hot sweet bear oil on all sides. I took and squeezed him over the earth's axis until I'd thawed it loose, and I poured about a ton of sweet bear oil over the sun's face. Then I gave the earth's cog wheel one kick backward till I got the sun free and whistled 'Push Along, Keep Moving.' In about fifteen seconds the earth gave a grunt and began to roll around easy, and the sun walked up most beautiful, saluting me with such a wind of gratitude it made me sneeze.

"I lit my pipe by the blaze of his topknot and walked home, introducing people to the fresh daylight with a piece of sunrise in my pocket."

So when Davy Crockett set out for Texas the earth was no longer screwed up stiff and frozen fast, but rolled around. The sun walked up in the morning and down at night, though the days were bitter cold and the snow lay deep.

1934

Affirming the Ancient Connections

Twentieth-Century Symbiotic Landscapes

". . . From an ecological viewpoint, we should not look
at the wilderness from the viewpoint of man,
which is by definition an external view,
but from the viewpoint of the wilderness community itself,
a view which is internal and self-evaluating."

—Stephen H. Spurr,
"The Value of Wilderness to Science"

For ecologists as well as for other modern and contemporary writers, the American landscape seems to be dominantly a landscape of ruin. "One of the penalties of an ecological education," writes Aldo Leopold, "is that one lives alone in a world of wounds." And where for ecologists the earth has not been visibly wounded, it has been made, less visibly to the layman, diseased—subtly robbed of its energy, sickened by blight and pollution. Ecologists do not share literary techniques with their contemporaries since they are concerned not with dream-logic but with biology and conservation economics, and they characteristically compose what might be called medical reports on the environment, more statistical and expository than pictorial. They do share, however, a range of tones, including nostalgia—a nostalgia for what Leopold calls the "perfect aboriginal health" of the wilderness. Ecologists are preoccupied with "sick" and mutilated landscapes; they are continually measuring, with more than a little nostalgia, what Emerson called "the contrast between us and our house" (the root meaning of "ecology" is "knowledge of the house," house holding).

Yet ecologists' ideal design of a symbiotic landscape—an affirmation of man's ancient connections to the earth—is both a demonstrable fact and a vision of harmony which does exist and which is eminently possible rather than wistfully, unobtainably nostalgic. Symbiosis is a dynamic state of being in which dissimilar organisms exist in union or in close association with each other, not as parasites but as beings mutually dependent on each other for existence. In a forest landscape viewed as an eco-system, for example, such organisms include bacteria, fungi, protozoa, arthropods, trees, shrubs, herbs, vertebrates (including man), dead organic matter, and such non-organic elements as oxygen, carbon dioxide, water, and minerals. All of these are, to a greater or less degree, in symbiotic relationship to each other.

Strictly speaking, the symbiotic landscape is the terrain of biology. Ecology, writes Stephen Spurr, is "the most complex and highest of the biological sciences." But the concepts of symbiosis and ecology have taken on enormous philosophical implications in the mid-twentieth century—in ethics, in aesthetics, even in metaphysics, as well as in political economics. We have come to recognize a cultural as well as a biological symbosis between man and land. The more humanistic ecologists, represented in this anthology by Aldo Leopold and Rachel Carson, are aware of this; it is an awareness they share with contemporary poets and with writers of the counter-culture (Jack Kerouac, for example). At the point where ecology discovers its philosophical implications, it joins an intellectual and spiritual nexus which includes geology and Darwinism; the nineteenth-century visionary naturalists, Emerson especially, who intuited and experienced a transcendent oneness in being; the metaphysics and the ethics of such Eastern religions as Taoism, Hinduism, and Buddhism (in their American incarnations); psychedelics; the shamanistic beliefs of American Indians and other primitive cultures discovered by anthropologists; and, in the Judaeo-Christian tradition, those minority traditions (Franciscanism, Hasidism) which sacramentalize natural objects as incarnations of God. Since all of these traditions are represented in various combinations here, a series of brief definitions and comments might be helpful.

Darwin, with his concepts of adaptation and evolution, made natural history a unified and coherent narrative of life-process rather than a series of disjointed descriptions. With ecology, the concept of evolution provides a new way of perceiving and valuing landscape. What Leopold calls "conservation esthetics" is a way of perceiving the landscape as an interplay of "the natural processes by which land and the living things upon it have achieved their characteristic forms (evolution) and by which they maintain their existence (ecology)." Darwin and the geologists, Leopold writes elsewhere, show us that

> men are only fellow-voyageurs with other creatures in the odyssey of evolution. This new knowledge should have given us, by this time, a sense of kinship with fellow-creatures; a wish to live and let live; a sense of wonder over the magnitude and duration of the biotic enterprise.

The concept of adaptation, in its miraculous manifestation in the "air-hoses" of the Syrphid flies—their larvae lying at the bottom of a microcosmic "lake" in a hollow tree—is the central focus of Edwin Way Teale's "Night in the Garden." The metaphor of evolution as an odyssey, or as a flowing from the "body" of the earth through time and change, is at the center of Loren Eiseley's "Flow of the River," as it is at the center of his book, *The Immense Journey,* from which the essay comes. In their prose, Teale and Eiseley re-enact what might be called scenes in a theater of adaptation.

Like evolutionists, *Eastern religions* (Taoism, Hinduism, Buddhism) perceive the world as flux and flow, though for these religions the flux is metaphysical. Things in nature, including man, are seen ideally as emerging from and merging back into the nirvanic no-thingness of "the Void." Nature becomes, as Gary Snyder Buddhistically defines it in *Earth House Hold,*

> . . . a vast set of conventions, totally arbitrary, patterns and stresses that come into being each instant; could disappear totally anytime; and continues only as a form of play: the cosmic/comic delight.

And because man and nature are both part of the flux, because all things are on "the long road nowhere" (that is, to the ineffable Void from which they have come), all things in nature should be tenderly respected for their shared selfhood, their miraculous just-so-ness.

Jack Kerouac's "Alone on a Mountaintop" embodies or implies most of the elements of this vision—a vision of a landscape of the Northwest imaged both in its just-so-ness and in its changeful flux: thus the recurrent images of mountains taking shape in the dawn and dissolving in fog or distance or night; of things looming in the night; of things swept by in the wind. Kerouac's essay is representative of a large literature in contemporary America which has drawn its vision of nature from Eastern religions, chiefly through the influence of Alan Watts, Gary Snyder, and Allen Ginsberg.

In religious rituals, fasting and herbs (peyote, for example) have been used since ancient times as means of experiencing *psychedelic visions,* as ways of breaking up habitual or rational perceptions of the world and of quickening the non-rational areas of consciousness. In this way, some people are able to attune themselves to a place—"the strains and stresses deep beneath one in the rock," as Snyder writes, "the flow and fabric of wildlife around, the human history of Indians on this continent."

The *shaman* is the primitive magician or holy man of a tribe. For him, every place, object, or phenomenon in the world is inhabited by powerful, invisible beings, each with his own mysterious purposes, his own mysterious ways. The shaman's magic involves a sympathetic understanding of these beings so that he can become a part of them and call on their power. They are not to be seen, they are not to be understood rationally, but they can be addressed as if they were sentient, as if they could be argued, coaxed, or hypnotized into sympathy with the shaman's will, imparting harmony, rain, endurance, power over enemies.

The shaman's verbal form is poetry—an address whose language and rhythms attune his own powers to those of the being he addresses (see Landscape into Myth and Ritual). Theologically the shaman differs from priest and rabbi: he believes in many animistic spirits, the Christian and the Jew in one transcendent God. And yet the shamans' and the Judaeo-Christians' prayerful litanies are not as far apart as they might seem. All share a sense of how things in the world may be made sacred, powerful, or uplifting by the divine presences which inhabit and thus sacramentalize them; all share a sense, too, of the power of language to address and call forth those presences and to merge with them.

To some extent all American poetry is part of the Judaeo-Christian tradition, and to that extent all of it partakes of litany, but the poets in this anthology who most closely approximate the poetry of the shaman or litanist are the poets in the free-verse tradition, poets who purposefully conjure and apostrophize: Whitman, Denise Levertov, Brother Antoninus, for example.

The vision of *St. Francis,* as it is now being rediscovered, is a vision of God's sacramentalizing presence in all of His creatures, not only in man, but also in animals and in "the lower and insensible creatures": flowers, wood, water, stones. For Francis all things can be seen as holy, living types in the scripture called Creation, and he treats them accordingly. "After fire," write the Franciscan authors of *The Mirror of Perfection,*

> he most singularly loved water, by which is figured holy penitence and tribulation, whereby the filth of the soul is washed away, and because the first ablution of the soul is by the water of baptism. Whence, when he washed his hands, he used to choose such a place that the water which fell should not be trodden by his feet. . . . He used also to say to the friar who made ready the wood for the fire, that he should never cut down the wood of a whole tree; but so that always some part of a tree should remain whole for the love of Him Who did work out our salvation on the wood of the cross.

Francis's desire to act in accordance with his sacramental vision of nature leads him away from the impulse to dominate and master non-human things toward an impulse of tender, reverent loving kindness. For him all things are creatures able in their own ways to give praise to their Creator, and thus all things, in his pan-psychic vision of man and nature, are brothers and sisters. Brother Sun, Wind, Fire; Sister Moon, Water, Earth—these are some of the "fellow creatures" he praisefully addresses in his "Song of Brother Sun."

Franciscans are rare among American poets, as they have been in the Christian tradition. Brother Antoninus, the most consciously Franciscan poet represented here, evokes both Francis's scriptural sense of typology (spring, for example, as a type of Advent) and his pan-psychism.

In its vision of nature at least, *Hasidism* (a mystical Judaism dating from about the eighteenth century) is a kind of Jewish counterpart of Franciscanism. In *Hasidism and Modern Man,* Martin Buber writes of the Hasidic sense of sacramentalism as it is embodied in the "myth of the holy sparks": "With the 'breaking of the world-vessels,' which in the era before creation could not withstand the creative overflow, sparks have fallen into all things and are now imprisoned in them until ever again a man uses a thing in holiness and this liberates the sparks that it conceals." Denise Levertov's long poem "A Tree Telling of Orpheus" evokes both the Orphic tradition of rapt song and the spirit of Hasidism. Raised in a Hasidic community, she writes: "The Hasidim were a little bit like the Franciscans . . . there was a recognition and joy in the physical world. And a sense of wonder at creation. . . ."

All of the contemporary landscapes represented in this section do not share the metaphysical beliefs of Buddhism, shamanism, or the Judaeo-Christian traditions. Neither are all of them informed by the concepts of evolution, ecology, or symbiosis. The landscapes of Stevens are a case in point. They could be called mindscapes rather than symbiotic landscapes, for their point of reference is not the "not-man" but the mind itself, and particularly the power of the imagination to create, shape, and order external reality. Like Emerson, Whitman, and Emily Dickinson, Stevens is a transcendentalist for whom there exists an ideal reality above the concrete. Where for Emerson that reality is Over-Soul, for Stevens that reality is imagination, the creative power of mind. Brother Antoninus, on the other hand (as one example), is not a transcendentalist but a sacramentalist, for whom there is no true division between the ideal and the real. For him the ideal is incarnate in the real, the spirit incarnate in the flesh.

Between the transcendentalist and the sacramentalist in American poetry, often in each American poet, there has always been a profound dialogue. Without doing more than mentioning the dialogue (it is about epistemology), it is possible to suggest some literary signals of transcendentalism and of sacramentalism. The transcendentalist tends to treat landscape allegorically, as a concrete projection of his or God's psyche; his images tend to be diffuse rather than concrete, and indeed he tends as much toward abstractions as he does toward images; he is philosophical more than pictorial. The sacramentalist, on the other hand, tends to treat landscape imagistically or symbolically, as the concrete embodiment of a meaning which is part of its embodiment; his images tend to be concrete; and the philosophical meaning of his poems tends to be implicit, symbolically communicated through the concrete surface.

Such differences aside, however, all of the writers represented in this section more or less share a common range of attitudes, both ethical and aesthetic, toward the natural landscape. The attitudes are connected with three essential metaphors of perception: organism, community, and flow.

The metaphor of *organism* suggests that a natural landscape (or eco-system) is itself a macro-organism composed of micro-organisms, including man, which exist in a close symbiotic or mental relationship. Man is thus only part of a larger organic whole operating according to its own laws. Often a landscape will be conceived as an intricate "web" of relationships. Often, too, the organic metaphors will give way to mechanical ones—as in "land mechanism," "eco-system," and so on—as if in reference to the divine machine of the universe of the eighteenth-century Deists. On the whole, this group of metaphors and that of community appears more often and more explicitly in terms of the symbiotic landscape.

The metaphor of *community* suggests that each part, each organism, of a community is a member-citizen. "That land is a community," writes Leopold, "is the basic concept of ecology, but that land is to be loved and respected is an extension of ethics." Leopold's "land ethic" "presupposes the existence of some mental image of land as a biotic mechanism. We can be ethical only in relation to something we can see, feel, understand, love, or otherwise have faith in." This "mental image" is often a personification, which, when it is most effective, sacramentally bestows sentience on inanimate objects or on animals without distorting scientific fact. In such a way the land ethic "changes the role of *Homo sapiens* from conqueror of the land-community to plain member and citizen of it."

The metaphor of *flow* suggests several kinds of motion. Ecologists speak of two kinds. One is the imperceptible flow of evolution. The other is the flow of energy: the food cycle (soil to tree to nut to squirrel to squirrel hunter to soil when the hunter dies), for example. Then there are the more perceptible flows: day into night, summer into winter. "The organisms constituting the forest eco-system," writes Stephen Spurr, "are continually in a state of flux . . . The forest eco-system exists only at a given instant in time and a given instant in space." This biological vision of flow is strikingly like that of Snyder's intuitive and mystical vision of nature, and it is not very different from the flow in Steven's mindscapes—the flow of psychic energy from reality to imagination and out again, into "imagined landscapes."

Ernest Hemingway

Big Two-Hearted River

Hemingway wrote in a letter to Gertrude Stein concerning "Big Two-Hearted River": "I'm trying to do the country like Cezanne." Like Cezanne, Hemingway represented this country (the environs of Seney, Michigan, to which Nick Adams is retreating from the devastations of World War I) with an eye to its healing solidity and to its geometrical relationships. For symbolic purposes, Hemingway altered the country around Seney in several ways: gave it a sunken road like the one in Italy where Nick Adams was wounded in "A Way You'll Never Be"; put in a hill outside the burnt town for Nick's spiritual ascent; changed Seney's Fox River to the Big Two-Hearted River, actually forty miles north of the town; and put a swamp in the river's path.

Part I

THE TRAIN went on up the track out of sight, around one of the hills of burnt timber. Nick sat down on the bundle of canvas and bedding the baggage man had pitched out of the door of the baggage car. There was no town, nothing but the rails and the burned-over country. The thirteen saloons that had lined the one street of Seney had not left a trace. The foundations of the Mansion House hotel stuck up above the ground. The stone was chipped and split by the fire. It was all that was left of the town of Seney. Even the surface had been burned off the ground.

Nick looked at the burned-over stretch of hillside, where he had expected to find the scattered houses of the town and then walked down the railroad track to the bridge over the river. The river was there. It swirled against the log spiles of the bridge. Nick looked down into the clear, brown water, colored from the pebbly bottom, and watched the trout keeping themselves steady in the current with wavering fins. As he watched them they changed their positions by quick angles, only to hold steady in the fast water again. Nick watched them a long time.

He watched them holding themselves with their noses into the current, many trout in deep, fast moving water, slightly distorted as he watched far down through the glassy convex surface of the pool, its surface pushing and swelling smooth against the resistance of the log-driven piles of the bridge. At the bottom of the pool were the big trout. Nick did not see them at first. Then he saw them at the bottom of the pool, big trout looking to hold themselves on the gravel bottom in a varying mist of gravel and sand, raised in spurts by the current.

Nick looked down into the pool from the bridge. It was a hot day. A kingfisher flew up the stream. It was a long time since Nick had looked into a stream and seen trout. They were very satisfactory. As the shadow of the kingfisher moved up the stream, a big trout shot upstream in a long angle, only his shadow marking the angle, then lost his shadow as he came through the surface of the water, caught the sun, and then, as he went back into the stream under the surface, his shadow seemed to float down the stream with the current, unresisting, to his post under the bridge where he tightened facing up into the current.

Nick's heart tightened as the trout moved. He felt all the old feeling.

He turned and looked down the stream. It stretched away, pebbly-bottomed with shallows and big boulders and a deep pool as it curved away around the foot of a bluff.

Nick walked back up the ties to where his pack lay in the cinders beside the railway track. He was happy. He adjusted the pack harness around the bundle, pulling straps tight, slung the pack on his back, got his arms through the shoulder straps and took some of the pull off his shoulders by leaning his forehead against the wide band of the tump-line. Still, it was too heavy. It was much too heavy. He had his leather rod-case in his hand and leaning forward to keep the weight of the pack high on his shoulders he walked along the road that paralleled the railway track, leaving the burned town behind in the heat, and then turned off around a hill with a high, fire-scarred hill on either side onto a road that went back into the country. He walked along the road feeling the ache from the pull of the heavy pack. The road climbed steadily. It was hard work walking up-hill. His muscles ached and the day was hot, but Nick felt happy. He felt he had left everything behind, the need for thinking, the need to write, other needs. It was all back of him.

From the time he had gotten down off the train and the baggage man had thrown his pack out of the open car door things had been different. Seney was burned, the country was burned over and changed, but it did not matter. It could not all be burned. He knew that. He hiked along the road, sweating in the sun, climbing to cross the range of hills that separated the railway from the pine plains.

The road ran on, dipping occasionally, but always climbing. Nick went on up. Finally the road after going parallel to the burnt hillside reached the top. Nick leaned back against a stump and slipped out of the pack harness. Ahead of him, as far as he could see, was the pine plain. The burned country stopped off at the left with the range of hills. On ahead islands of dark pine trees rose out of the plain. Far off to the left was the line of the river. Nick followed it with his eye and caught glints of the water in the sun.

There was nothing but the pine plain ahead of him, until the far blue hills that marked the Lake Superior height of land. He could hardly see them, faint and far away in the heat-light over the plain. If he looked too steadily they were gone. But if he only half-looked they were there, the far-off hills of the height of land.

Nick sat down against the charred stump and smoked a cigarette. His pack balanced on the top of the stump, harness holding ready, a hollow molded in it from his back. Nick sat smoking, looking out over the country. He did not need to get his map out. He knew where he was from the position of the river.

As he smoked, his legs stretched out in front of him, he noticed a grasshopper walk along the ground and up onto his woolen sock. The grasshopper was black. As he had walked along the road, climbing, he had started many grasshoppers from the dust. They were all black. They were not the big grasshoppers with yellow and black or red and black wings whirring out from their black wing sheathing as they fly up. These were just ordinary hoppers, but all a sooty black in color. Nick had wondered about them as he walked, without really thinking about them. Now, as he watched the black hopper that was nibbling at the wool of his sock with its fourway lip, he realized that they had all turned black from living in the burned-over land. He realized that the fire must have come the year before, but the grasshoppers were all black now. He wondered how long they would stay that way.

Carefully he reached his hand down and took hold of the hopper by the wings. He turned him up, all his legs walking in the air, and looked at his jointed belly. Yes, it was black too, iridescent where the back and head were dusty.

''Go on, hopper,'' Nick said, speaking out loud for the first time. ''Fly away somewhere.''

He tossed the grasshopper up into the air and watched him sail away to a charcoal stump across the road.

Nick stood up. He leaned his back against the weight of his pack where it rested upright on the stump and got his arms through the shoulder straps. He stood with the pack on his back on the brow of the hill looking out across the country, toward the distant river and then struck down the hillside away from the road. Underfoot the ground was good walking. Two hundred yards down the hillside the fire line stopped. Then it was sweet fern, growing ankle high, to walk through, and clumps of jack pines; a long undulating country with frequent rises and descents, sandy underfoot and the country alive again.

Nick kept his direction by the sun. He knew where he wanted to strike the river and he kept on through the pine plain, mounting small rises to see other rises ahead of him and sometimes from the top of a rise a great solid island of pines off to his right or his left. He broke off some sprigs of the heathery sweet fern, and put them under his pack straps. The chafing crushed it and he smelled it as he walked.

He was tired and very hot, walking across the uneven, shadeless pine plain. At any time he knew he could strike the river by turning off to his left. It could not be more than a mile away. But he kept on toward the north to hit the river as far upstream as he could go in one day's walking.

For some time as he walked Nick had been in sight of one of the big islands of pine standing out above the rolling high ground he was crossing. He dipped down and then as he came slowly up to the crest of the bridge he turned and made toward the pine trees.

There was no underbrush in the island of pine trees. The trunks of the trees went straight up or slanted toward each other. The trunks were straight and brown without branches. The branches were high above. Some interlocked to make a solid shadow on the brown forest floor. Around the grove of trees was a bare space. It was brown and soft underfoot as Nick walked on it. This was the over-lapping of the pine needle floor, extending out beyond the width of the high branches. The trees had grown tall and the branches moved high, leaving in the sun this bare space they had once covered with shadow. Sharp at the edge of this extension of the forest floor commenced the sweet fern.

Nick slipped off his pack and lay down in the shade. He lay on his back and looked up into the pine trees. His neck and back and the small of his back rested as he stretched. The earth felt good against his back. He looked up at the sky, through the branches, and then shut his eyes. He opened them and looked up again. There was a wind high up in the branches. He shut his eyes again and went to sleep.

Nick woke stiff and cramped. The sun was nearly down. His pack was heavy and the straps painful as he lifted it on. He leaned over with the pack on and picked up the leather rod-case and started out from the pine trees across the sweet fern swale, toward the river. He knew it could not be more than a mile.

He came down a hillside covered with stumps into a meadow. At the edge of the meadow flowed the river. Nick was glad to get to the river. He walked upstream through the meadow. His trousers were soaked with the dew as he walked. After the hot day, the dew had come quickly and heavily. The river made no sound. It was too fast and smooth. At the edge of the meadow, before he mounted to a piece of high ground to make camp, Nick looked down the river at the trout rising. They were rising to insects come from the swamp on the other side of the stream when the sun went down. The trout jumped out of water to take them. While Nick walked through the little stretch of meadow alongside the stream, trout had jumped high out of water. Now as he looked down the river, the insects must be settling on the surface, for the trout were feeding steadily all down the stream. As far down the long stretch as he could see, the trout were rising, making circles all down the surface of the water, as though it were starting to rain.

The ground rose, wooded and sandy, to overlook the meadow, the stretch of river and the swamp. Nick dropped his pack and rod-case and looked for a level piece of ground. He was very hungry and he wanted to make his camp before he cooked. Between two jack pines, the ground was quite level. He took the ax out of the pack and chopped out two projecting roots. That leveled a piece of ground large enough to sleep on. He smoothed out the sandy soil with his hand and pulled all the sweet fern bushes by their roots. His hands smelled good from the sweet fern. He smoothed the uprooted earth. He did not want anything making lumps under the blankets. When he had the ground smooth, he spread his three blankets. One he folded double, next to the ground. The other two he spread on top.

With the ax he slit off a bright slab of pine from one of the stumps and split it into pegs for the tent. He wanted them long and solid to hold in the ground. With the tent unpacked and spread on the ground, the pack, leaning against a jackpine, looked much smaller. Nick tied the rope that served the tent for a ridge-pole to the trunk of one of the pine trees and pulled the tent up off the ground with the other end of the rope and tied it to the other pine. The tent hung on the rope like a canvas blanket on a clothesline. Nick poked a pole he had cut up under the back peak of the canvas and then made it a tent by pegging out the sides. He pegged the sides out taut and drove the pegs deep, hitting them down into the ground with the flat of the ax until the rope loops were buried and the canvas was drum tight.

Across the open mouth of the tent Nick fixed cheesecloth to keep out mosquitoes. He crawled inside under the mosquito bar with various things from the pack to put at the head of the bed under the slant of the canvas. Inside the tent the light came through the brown canvas. It smelled pleasantly of canvas. Already there was something mysterious and homelike. Nick was happy as he crawled inside the tent. He had not been unhappy all day. This was different though. Now things were done. There had been this to do. Now it was done. It had been a hard trip. He was very tired. That was done. He had made his camp. He was settled. Nothing could touch him. It was a good place to camp. He was there, in the good place. He was in his home where he had made it. Now he was hungry.

He came out, crawling under the cheesecloth. It was quite dark outside. It was lighter in the tent.

Nick went over to the pack and found, with his fingers, a long nail in a paper sack of nails, in the bottom of the pack. He drove it into the pine tree, holding it close and hitting it gently with the flat of the ax. He hung the pack up on the nail. All his supplies were in the pack. They were off the ground and sheltered now.

Nick was hungry. He did not believe he had ever been hungrier. He opened and emptied a can of pork and beans and a can of spaghetti into the frying pan.

"I've got a right to eat this kind of stuff, if I'm willing to carry it," Nick said. His voice sounded strange in the darkening woods. He did not speak again.

He started a fire with some chunks of pine he got with the ax from a stump. Over the fire he stuck a wire grill, pushing the four legs down into the ground with his boot. Nick put the frying pan on the grill over the flames. He was hungrier. The beans and spaghetti warmed. Nick stirred them and mixed them together. They began to bubble, making little bubbles that rose with difficulty to the surface. There was a good smell. Nick got out a bottle of tomato catchup and cut four slices of bread. The little bubbles were coming faster now. Nick sat down beside the fire and lifted the frying pan off. He poured about half the contents out into the tin plate. It spread slowly on the plate. Nick knew it was too hot. He poured on some tomato catchup. He knew the beans and spaghetti were still too hot. He looked at the fire, then at the tent, he was not going to spoil it all by burning his tongue. For years he had never enjoyed fried bananas because he had never been able to wait for them to cool. His tongue was very sensitive. He was very hungry. Across the river in the swamp, in the almost dark, he saw a mist rising. He looked at the tent once more. All right. He took a full spoonful from the plate.

"Chrise," Nick said, "Geezus Chrise," he said happily.

He ate the whole plateful before he remembered the bread. Nick finished the second plateful with the bread, mopping the plate shiny. He had not eaten since a cup of coffee and a ham sandwich in the station restaurant at St. Ignace. It had been a very fine experience. He had been that hungry before, but had not been able to satisfy it. He could have made camp hours before if he had wanted to. There were plenty of good places to camp on the river. But this was good.

Nick tucked two big chips of pine under the grill. The fire flared up. He had forgotten to get water for the coffee. Out of the pack he got a folding canvas bucket and walked down the hill, across the edge of the meadow, to the stream. The other bank was in the white mist. The grass was wet and cold as he knelt on the bank and dipped the canvas bucket into the stream. It bellied and pulled hard in the current. The water was ice cold. Nick rinsed the bucket and carried it full up to the camp. Up away from the stream it was not so cold.

Nick drove another big nail and hung up the bucket full of water. He dipped the coffee pot half full, put some more chips under the grill onto the fire and put the pot on. He could not remember which way he made coffee. He could remember an argument about it with Hopkins, but not which side he had taken. He decided to bring it to a boil. He remembered now that was Hopkins's way. He had once argued about everything with Hopkins. While he waited for the coffee to boil, he opened a small can of apricots. He liked to open cans. He emptied the can of apricots out into a tin cup. While he watched the coffee on the fire, he drank the juice syrup of the apricots, carefully at first to keep from spilling, then meditatively, sucking the apricots down. They were better than fresh apricots.

The coffee boiled as he watched. The lid came up and coffee and grounds ran down the side of the pot. Nick took it off the grill. It was a triumph for Hopkins. He put sugar in the empty apricot cup and poured some of the coffee out to cool. It was too hot to pour and he used his hat to hold the handle of the coffee pot. He would not let it steep in the pot at all. Not the first cup. It should be straight Hopkins all the way. Hop deserved that. He was a very serious coffee drinker. He was the most serious man Nick had ever known. Not heavy, serious. That was a long time ago. Hopkins spoke without moving his lips. He had played polo. He made millions of dollars in Texas. He had borrowed carfare to go to Chicago, when the wire came that his first big well had come in. He could have wired for money. That would have been too slow. They called Hop's girl the Blonde Venus. Hop did not mind because she was not his real girl. Hopkins said very confidently that none of them would make fun of his real girl. He was right. Hopkins went away when the telegram came. That was on the Black River. It took eight days for the telegram to reach him. Hopkins gave away his .22 caliber Colt automatic pistol to Nick. He gave his camera to Bill. It was to remember him always by. They were all going fishing again next summer. The Hop Head was rich. He would get a yacht and they would all cruise along the north shore of Lake Superior. He was excited but serious. They said good-bye and all felt bad. It broke up the trip. They never saw Hopkins again. That was a long time ago on the Black River.

Nick drank the coffee, the coffee according to Hopkins. The coffee was bitter. Nick laughed. It made a good ending to the story. His mind was starting to work. He knew he could choke it because he was tired enough. He spilled the coffee out of the pot and shook the grounds loose into the fire. He lit a cigarette and went inside the tent. He took off his shoes and trousers, sitting on the blankets, rolled the shoes up inside the trousers for a pillow and got in between the blankets.

Out through the front of the tent he watched the glow of the fire, when the night wind blew on it. It was a quiet night. The swamp was perfectly quiet. Nick stretched under the blanket comfortably. A mosquito hummed close to his ear. Nick sat up and lit a match. The mosquito was on the canvas, over his head. Nick moved the match quickly up to it. The mosquito made a satisfactory hiss in the flame. The match went out. Nick lay down again under the blanket. He turned on his side and shut his eyes. He was sleepy. He felt sleep coming. He curled up under the blanket and went to sleep.

Part II

IN THE MORNING the sun was up and the tent was starting to get hot. Nick crawled out under the mosquito netting stretched across the mouth of the tent, to look at the morning. The grass was wet on his hands as he came out. He held his trousers and shoes in his hands. The sun was just up over the hill. There was the meadow, the river and the swamp. There were birch trees in the green of the swamp on the other side of the river.

The river was clear and smoothly fast in the early morning. Down about two hundred yards were three logs all the way across the stream. They made the water smooth and deep above them. As Nick watched, a mink crossed the river on the logs and went into the swamp. Nick was excited. He was excited by the early morning and the river. He was really too hurried to eat breakfast, but he knew he must. He built a little fire and put on the coffee pot.

While the water was heating in the pot he took an empty bottle and went down over the edge of the high ground to the meadow. The meadow was wet with dew and Nick wanted to catch grasshoppers for bait before the sun dried the grass. He found plenty of good grasshoppers. They were at the base of the grass stems. Sometimes they clung to a grass stem. They were cold and wet with the dew, and could not jump until the sun warmed them. Nick picked them up, taking only the medium-sized brown ones, and put them into the bottle. He turned over a log and just under the shelter of the edge were several hundred hoppers. It was a grasshopper lodging house. Nick put about fifty of the medium browns into the bottle. While he was picking up the hoppers the others warmed in the sun and commenced to hop away. They flew when they hopped. At first they made one flight and stayed stiff when they landed, as though they were dead.

Nick knew that by the time he was through with breakfast they would be as lively as ever. Without dew in the grass it would take him all day to catch a bottle full of good grasshoppers and he would have to crush many of them, slamming at them with his hat. He washed his hands at the stream. He was excited to be near it. Then he walked up to the tent. The hoppers were already jumping stiffly in the grass. In the bottle, warmed by the sun, they were jumping in a mass. Nick put in a pine stick as a cork. It plugged the mouth of the bottle enough, so the hoppers could not get out and left plenty of air passage.

He had rolled the log back and knew he could get grasshoppers there every morning.

Nick laid the bottle full of jumping grasshoppers against a pine trunk. Rapidly he mixed some buckwheat flour with water and stirred it smooth, one cup of flour, one cup of water. He put a handful of coffee in the pot and dipped a lump of grease out of a can and slid it sputtering across the hot skillet. On the smoking skillet he poured smoothly the buckwheat batter. It spread like lava, the grease spitting sharply. Around the edges the buckwheat cake began to firm, then brown, then crisp. The surface was bubbling slowly to porousness. Nick pushed under the browned under surface with a fresh pine chip. He shook the skillet sideways and the cake was loose on the surface. I won't try and flop it, he thought. He slid the chip of clean wood all the way under the cake, and flopped it over onto its face. It sputtered in the pan.

When it was cooked Nick regreased the skillet. He used all the batter. It made another big flapjack and one smaller one.

Nick ate a big flapjack and a smaller one, covered with apple butter. He put apple butter on the third cake, folded it over twice, wrapped it in oiled paper and put it in his shirt pocket. He put the apple butter jar back in the pack and cut bread for two sandwiches.

In the pack he found a big onion. He slicked it in two and peeled the silky outer skin. Then he cut one half into slices and made onion sandwiches. He wrapped them in oiled paper and buttoned them in the other pocket of his khaki shirt. He turned the skillet upside down on the grill, drank the coffee, sweetened and yellow brown with the condensed milk in it, and tidied up the camp. It was a good camp.

Nick took his fly rod out of the leather rod-case, jointed it, and shoved the rod-case back into the tent. He put on the reel and threaded the line through the guides. He had to hold it from hand to hand, as he threaded it, or it would slip back through its own weight. It was a heavy, double tapered fly line. Nick had paid eight dollars for it a long time ago. It was made heavy to lift back in the air and come forward flat and heavy and straight to make it possible to cast a fly which has no weight. Nick opened the aluminum leader box. The leaders were coiled between the damp flannel pads. Nick had wet the pads at the water cooler on the train up to St. Ignace. In the damp pads the gut leaders had softened and Nick unrolled one and tied it by a loop at the end to the heavy fly line. He fastened a hook on the end of the leader. It was a small hook; very thin and springy.

Nick took it from his hook book, sitting with the rod across his lap. He tested the knot and the spring of the rod by pulling the line taut. It was a good feeling. He was careful not to let the hook bite into his finger.

He started down to the stream, holding his rod, the bottle of grasshoppers hung from his neck by a thong tied in half hitches around the neck of the bottle. His landing net hung by a hook from his belt. Over his shoulder was a long flour sack tied at each corner into an ear. The cord went over his shoulder. The sack flapped against his legs.

Nick felt awkward and professionally happy with all his equipment hanging from him. The grasshopper bottle swung against his chest. In his shirt the breast pockets bulged against him with the lunch and his fly book.

He stepped into the stream. It was a shock. His trousers clung tight to his legs. His shoes felt the gravel. The water was a rising cold shock.

Rushing, the current sucked against his legs. Where he stepped in, the water was over his knees. He waded with the current. The gravel slid under his shoes. He looked down at the swirl of water below each leg and tipped up the bottle to get a grasshopper.

The first grasshopper gave a jump in the neck of the bottle and went out into the water. He was sucked under in the whirl by Nick's right leg and came to the surface a little way down stream. He floated rapidly, kicking. In a quick circle, breaking the smooth surface of the water, he disappeared. A trout had taken him.

Another hopper poked his face out of the bottle. His antennæ wavered. He was getting his front legs out of the bottle to jump. Nick took him by the head and held him while he threaded the slim hook under his chin, down through his thorax and into the last segments of his abdomen. The grasshopper took hold of the hook with his front feet, spitting tobacco juice on it. Nick dropped him into the water.

Holding the rod in his right hand he let out line against the pull of the grasshopper in the current. He stripped off line from the reel with his left hand and let it run free. He could see the hopper in the little waves of the current. It went out of sight.

There was a tug on the line. Nick pulled against the taut line. It was his first strike. Holding the now living rod across the current, he brought in the line with his left hand. The rod bent in jerks, the trout pumping against the current. Nick knew it was a small one. He lifted the rod straight up in the air. It bowed with the pull.

He saw the trout in the water jerking with his head and body against the shifting tangent of the line in the stream.

Nick took the line in his left hand and pulled the trout, thumping tiredly against the current, to the surface. His back was mottled the clear, water-over-gravel color, his side flashing in the sun. The rod under his right arm, Nick stooped, dipping his right hand into the current. He held the trout, never still, with his moist right hand, while he unhooked the barb from his mouth, then dropped him back into the stream.

He hung unsteadily in the current, then settled to the bottom beside a stone. Nick reached down his hand to touch him, his arm to the elbow under the water. The trout was steady in the moving stream, resting on the gravel, beside a stone. As Nick's fingers touched him, touched his smooth, cool, underwater feeling he was gone, gone in a shadow across the bottom of the stream.

He's all right, Nick thought. He was only tired.

He had wet his hand before he touched the trout, so he would not disturb the delicate mucus that covered him. If a trout was touched with a dry hand, a white fungus attacked the unprotected spot. Years before when he had fished crowded streams, with fly fishermen ahead of him and behind him, Nick had again and again come on dead trout, furry with white fungus, drifted against a rock, or floating belly up in some pool. Nick did not like to fish with other men on the river. Unless they were of your party, they spoiled it.

He wallowed down the stream, above his knees in the current, through the fifty yards of shallow water above the pile of logs that crossed the stream. He did not rebait his hook and held it in his hand as he waded. He was certain he could catch small trout in the shallows, but he did not want them. There would be no big trout in the shallows this time of day.

Now the water deepened up his thighs sharply and coldly. Ahead was the smooth dammed-back flood of water above the logs. The water was smooth and dark; on the left, the lower edge of the meadow; on the right the swamp.

Nick leaned back against the current and took a hopper from the bottle. He threaded the hopper on the hook and spat on him for good luck. Then he pulled several yards of line from the reel and tossed the hopper out ahead onto the fast, dark water. It floated down towards the logs, then the weight of the line pulled the bait under the surface. Nick held the rod in his right hand, letting the line run out through his fingers.

There was a long tug. Nick struck and the rod came alive and dangerous, bent double, the line tightening, coming out of water, tightening, all in a heavy, dangerous, steady pull. Nick felt the moment when the leader would break if the strain increased and let the line go.

The reel ratcheted into a mechanical shriek as the line went out in a rush. Too fast. Nick could not check it, the line rushing out, the reel note rising as the line ran out.

With the core of the reel showing, his heart feeling stopped with the excitement, leaning back against the current that mounted icily his thighs, Nick thumbed the reel hard with his left hand. It was awkward getting his thumb inside the fly reel frame.

As he put on pressure the line tightened into sudden hardness and beyond the logs a huge trout went high out of water. As he jumped, Nick lowered the tip of the rod. But he felt, as he dropped the tip to ease the strain, the moment when the strain was too great; the hardness too tight. Of course, the leader had broken. There was no mistaking the feeling when all spring left the line and it became dry and hard. Then it went slack.

His mouth dry, his heart down, Nick reeled in. He had never seen so big a trout. There was a heaviness, a power not to be held, and then the bulk of him, as he jumped. He looked as broad as a salmon.

Nick's hand was shaky. He reeled in slowly. The thrill had been too much. He felt, vaguely, a little sick, as though it would be better to sit down.

The leader had broken where the hook was tied to it. Nick took it in his hand. He thought of the trout somewhere on the bottom, holding himself steady over the gravel, far down below the light, under the logs, with the hook in his jaw. Nick knew the trout's teeth would cut through the snell of the hook. The hook would imbed itself in his jaw. He'd bet the trout was angry. Anything that size would be angry. That was a trout. He had been solidly hooked. Solid as a rock. He felt like a rock, too, before he started off. By God, he was a big one. By God, he was the biggest one I ever heard of.

Nick climbed out onto the meadow and stood, water running down his trousers and out of his shoes, his shoes squlchy. He went over and sat on the logs. He did not want to rush his sensations any.

He wriggled his toes in the water, in his shoes, and got out a cigarette from his breast pocket. He lit it and tossed the match into the fast water below the logs. A tiny trout rose at the match, as it swung around in the fast current. Nick laughed. He would finish the cigarette.

He sat on the logs, smoking, drying in the sun, the sun warm on his back, the river shallow ahead entering the woods, curving into the woods, shallows, light glittering, big water-smooth rocks, cedars along the bank and white birches, the logs warm in the sun, smooth to sit on, without bark, gray to the touch; slowly the feeling of disappointment left him. It went away slowly, the feeling of disappointment that came sharply after the thrill that made his shoulders ache. It was all right now. His rod lying out on the logs, Nick tied a new hook on the leader, pulling the gut tight until it grimped into itself in a hard knot.

He baited up, then picked up the rod and walked to the far end of the logs to get into the water, where it was not too deep. Under and beyond the logs was a deep pool. Nick walked around the shallow shelf near the swamp shore until he came out on the shallow bed of the stream.

On the left, where the meadow ended and the woods began, a great elm tree was uprooted. Gone over in a storm, it lay back into the woods, its roots clotted with dirt, grass growing in them, rising a solid bank beside the stream. The river cut to the edge of the uprooted tree. From where Nick stood he could see deep channels, like ruts, cut in the shallow bed of the stream by the flow of the current. Pebbly where he stood and pebbly and full of boulders beyond; where it curved near the tree roots, the bed of the stream was marly and between the ruts of deep water green weed fronds swung in the current.

Nick swung the rod back over his shoulder and forward, and the line, curving forward, laid the grasshopper down on one of the deep channels in the weeds. A trout struck and Nick hooked him.

Holding the rod far out toward the uprooted tree and sloshing backward in the current, Nick worked the trout, plunging the rod bending alive, out of the danger of the weeds into the open river. Holding the rod, pumping alive against the current, Nick brought the trout in. He rushed, but always came, the spring of the rod yielding to the rushes, sometimes jerking under water, but always bringing him in. Nick eased downstream with the rushes. The rod above his head he led the trout over the net, then lifted.

The trout hung heavy in the net, mottled trout back and silver sides in the meshes. Nick unhooked him; heavy sides, good to hold, big undershot jaw, and slipped him, heaving and big sliding, into the long sack that hung from his shoulders in the water.

Nick spread the mouth of the sack against the current and it filled, heavy with water. He held it up, the bottom in the stream, and the water poured out through the sides. Inside at the bottom was the big trout, alive in the water.

Nick moved downstream. The sack out ahead of him sunk heavy in the water, pulling from his shoulders.

It was getting hot, the sun hot on the back of his neck.

Nick had one good trout. He did not care about getting many trout. Now the stream was shallow and wide. There were trees along both banks. The trees of the left bank made short shadows on the current in the forenoon sun. Nick knew there were trout in each shadow. In the afternoon, after the sun had crossed toward the hills, the trout would be in the cool shadows on the other side of the stream.

The very biggest ones would lie up close to the bank. You could always pick them up there on the Black. When the sun was down they all moved out into the current. Just when the sun made the water blinding in the glare before it went down, you were liable to strike a big trout anywhere in the current. It was almost impossible to fish then, the surface of the water was blinding as a mirror in the sun. Of course, you could fish upstream, but in a stream like the Black, or this, you had to wallow against the current and in a deep place, the water piled up on you. It was no fun to fish upstream with this much current.

Nick moved along through the shallow stretch watching the banks for deep holes. A beech tree grew close beside the river, so that the branches hung down into the water. The stream went back in under the leaves. There were always trout in a place like that.

Nick did not care about fishing that hole. He was sure he would get hooked in the branches.

It looked deep though. He dropped the grasshopper so the current took it under water, back in under the overhanging branch. The line pulled hard and Nick struck. The trout threshed heavily, half out of water in the leaves and branches. The line was caught. Nick pulled hard and the trout was off. He reeled in and holding the hook in his hand, walked down the stream.

Ahead, close to the left bank, was a big log. Nick saw it was hollow; pointing up river the current entered it smoothly, only a little ripple spread each side of the log. The water was deepening. The top of the hollow log was gray and dry. It was partly in the shadow.

Nick took the cork out of the grasshopper bottle and a hopper clung to it. He picked him off, hooked him and tossed him out. He held the rod far out so that the hopper on the water moved into the current flowing into the hollow log. Nick lowered the rod and the hopper floated in. There was a heavy strike. Nick swung the rod against the pull. It felt as though he were hooked into the log itself, except for the live feeling.

He tried to force the fish out into the current. It came, heavily.

The line went slack and Nick thought the trout was gone. Then he saw him, very near, in the current, shaking his head, trying to get the hook out. His mouth was clamped shut. He was fighting the hook in the clear flowing current.

Looping in the line with his left hand, Nick swung the rod to make the line taut and tried to lead the trout toward the net, but he was gone, out of sight, the line pumping. Nick fought him against the current, letting him thump in the water against the spring of the rod. He shifted the rod to his left hand, worked the trout upstream, holding his weight, fighting on the rod, and then let him down into the net. He lifted him clear of the water, a heavy half circle in the net, the net dripping, unhooked him and slid him into the sack.

He spread the mouth of the sack and looked down in at the two big trout alive in the water.

Through the deepening water, Nick waded over to the hollow log. He took the sack off, over his head, the trout flopping as it came out of water, and hung it so the trout were deep in the water. Then he pulled himself up on the log and sat, the water from his trouser and boots running down into the stream. He laid his rod down, moved along to the shady end of the log and took the sandwiches out of his pocket. He dipped the sandwiches in the cold water. The current carried away the crumbs. He ate the sandwiches and dipped his hat full of water to drink, the water running out through his hat just ahead of his drinking.

It was cool in the shade, sitting on the log. He took a cigarette out and struck a match to light it. The match sunk into the gray wood, making a tiny furrow. Nick leaned over the side of the log, found a hard place and lit the match. He sat smoking and watching the river.

Ahead the river narrowed and went into a swamp. The river became smooth and deep and the swamp looked solid with cedar trees, their trunks close together, their branches solid. It would not be possible to walk through a swamp like that. The branches grew so low. You would have to keep almost level with the ground to move at all. You could not crash through the branches. That must be why the animals that lived in swamps were built the way they were, Nick thought.

He wished he had brought something to read. He felt like reading. He did not feel like going on into the swamp. He looked down the river. A big cedar slanted all the way across the stream. Beyond that the river went into the swamp.

Nick did not want to go in there now. He felt a reaction against deep wading with the water deepening up under his armpits, to hook big trout in places impossible to land them. In the swamp the banks were bare, the big cedars came together overhead, the sun did not come through, except in patches; in the fast deep water, in the half light, the fishing would be tragic. In the swamp fishing was a tragic adventure. Nick did not want it. He did not want to go down the stream any further today.

He took out his knife, opened it and stuck it in the log. Then he pulled up the sack, reached into it and brought out one of the trout. Holding him near the tail, hard to hold, alive, in his hand, he whacked him against the log. The trout quivered, rigid. Nick laid him on the log in the shade and broke the neck of the other fish the same way. He laid them side by side on the log. They were fine trout.

Nick cleaned them, slitting them from the vent to the tip of the jaw. All the insides and the gills and tongue came out in one piece. They were both males; long gray-white strips of milt, smooth and clean. All the insides clean and compact, coming out all together. Nick tossed the offal ashore for the minks to find.

He washed the trout in the stream. When he held them back up in the water they looked like live fish. Their color was not gone yet. He washed his hands and dried them on the log. Then he laid the trout on the sack spread out on the log, rolled them up in it, tied the bundle and put it in the landing net. His knife was still standing, blade stuck in the log. He cleaned it on the wood and put it in his pocket.

Nick stood up on the log, holding his rod, the landing net hanging heavy, then stepped into the water and splashed ashore. He climbed the bank and cut up into the woods, toward the high ground. He was going back to camp. He looked back. The river just showed through the trees. There were plenty of days coming when he could fish the swamp.

1925

Edwin Way Teale

Night in the Garden

A visible majority of contemporary naturalists seem to have roots in the Midwest. Teale spent his summers as a boy on his grandfather's farm in the dune country of Indiana, and he early kept a notebook of observations on wildlife and particularly on insects, his chief love. In 1936, Teale writes in *Near Horizons: The Story of an Insect Garden,* he planted on Long Island (where the Milburn School of Baldwin was later built) "the shrubs and vines, the annuals and perennials, the wildflowers and the cultivated plants which are most attractive to the insects"—an insect garden where he could observe and photograph insect life. That is the larger setting of the microcosmic landscape of "Night in the Garden."

THE YELLOW PENCIL which writes these words is moving at the bottom of a truncated cone of illumination spreading downward from the glass bull's-eye of a flashlight. It is ten o'clock at night and the month is September.

All around, bushes and twisted trees—so familiar in my garden by daylight—stand mysterious and still. The wild-cherry tangle, the Lincoln Tree, the reared hulk of the old barn, are massed in silhouette against a faintly luminous sky. The night has engulfed the hillside in blackness. It has concentrated all visible life into the little area illuminated by my torch.

I move the beam, like an elongated, magic finger, among the jungles of grass, across the bushes, into the trees, and as the light swings from place to place, successive little realms of life are spotlighted in its illumination. Like some mythical astrologer of old, working amid the shadows of a high-ceilinged room, I produce my night-magic, making this succession of worlds materialize and vanish at a pressure of my thumb.

Occasionally, when I have been traveling by train on stormy nights, I have caught fleeting glimpses of unfamiliar landscapes illuminated for a moment by flashes from the sky. They appeared and disappeared in an instant and left me wishing I could see more clearly these isolated spots picked out at random by the chance glare of a thunderbolt. Something of the same feeling comes on nights like tonight when my beam shifts from point to point and I go exploring among the nocturnal dwellers of my garden. But here I can hold the lightning, so to speak, and keep the beam of my torch illuminating some scene of special interest.

There is always the spice of the unexpected in one of these after-dark safaris. Tonight, beneath one of the oldest of my apple trees, I pause and listen to the vast, swelling orchestration of the snowy tree-crickets, that mellow, rhythmical ''waa-waa-waa'' which fills the air with the coming of late summer dusks. Part of the mellow sound comes from overhead. I swing the flashlight in that direction. The beam glides up the trunk of the tree, zigzags along the limbs, leaps from branch to branch. Then, only a few feet above my head, it comes to rest on the gray-brown bark of a limb jutting out almost at right angles from the trunk. In the center of the white disk of illumination, two pale-green, fairylike creatures, hardly an inch in length, stand out against the somber background of the bark. One has its gauzy wings raised straight above its back. Like cards sliding past each other in an arc, they rub together to produce the enchanting sound I hear. For this nocturnal musician is the male snowy tree cricket.

Its companion, a silent female, remains close as though charmed by the rhythm of the performance. Then, as I watch, the listening female does a curious thing. She mounts the back of her companion and thrusts her head almost against the vibrating wings. She appears to be crowding closer the better to hear the melody. In reality, she is feeding on a fatty secretion which has collected in two tiny, saucerlike depressions on the back of the male cricket. This secretion has a powerful attraction for the female. Her companion continues to fiddle on, providing music as well as food for this strange nocturnal banquet.

Other insects, far less melodious, are adding an ear-piercing volume of sound. The night is noisy. It is filled with continuous metallic chirps and trills and buzzes. One sound suggests a stick running with increasing speed along a tiny picket fence. Another is a metallic simmer. A third is a high-pitched bur-r-r so piercing it hurts the ears.

My beam swings downward to the grass at my feet. In the circle of light other musicians, black field crickets, stream through the grass like dark fish darting among the underwater vegetation of a pond. The hillside is alive with these autumn insects. The high tide of their fecundity comes late in the season, comes at a time when only short weeks remain before autumn frost eliminates them all.

In the grass tangle above the noisy crickets, a red-legged locust slumbers on, clinging to an upright stalk, oblivious to the activity around it. On nimble legs, an ashy hued daddy longlegs hurries past as though intent on keeping an appointment. Near by a spider, equally gray, pauses in the light, the green arc of its blade of grass swinging up and down with its weight. A moment later, in the doorway of a knothole, I come upon another nocturnal spider, peering ogre-like from the darkness within. Its eyes glint like red coals and its lair is partially curtained with the silk of a fragmentary web.

Other silk-makers have plied their craft among the dead twigs of the lower branches. Their tiny jewel-like webs, only two or three inches across, gleam in the light as though formed of threads of burnished silver. I count thirty-seven orb webs among the twigs of a single branch. As I run my beam through the twigs, the light seems to leap from web to web, glinting each time as though momentarily ensnared among the glistening threads, then plunging on into the comparative darkness of the black-brown twigs beyond.

Where the tallest maple soars high above the path to the swamp stream, a dead branch hangs low with its terminal twigs curving upward like the crooked fingers of a hand. I run my light along a dozen of these thin dry fingers of wood. At the tip of each, a robber fly is anchored for the night. When I move the flashlight close, concentrating the beam upon the great compound eyes of one of the sleepers, it immediately awakens and rapidly rubs its eyes with its forelegs.

I poke the fly gently with the tip of my yellow pencil. It drops to the underside of the twig and clings there, upsidedown. My pencil follows. The great-eyed insect appears on top again, completing the circle like a Cossack horseman at the circus. Again and again the robber fly repeats this maneuver. Finally its patience gives out. Quitting the perch, it darts to another twig outside the beam of my light but visible against the sky.

Of all the insects I have encountered asleep during after-dark explorations, the one most dead to the world was a small bumblebee. I found it one windy night, clamped fast with feet and jaws to the underside of an apple leaf. The leaf was at the very tip of a branch lashing wildly about in a boisterous wind. I thrust my light within half an inch of the insect's eyes. It slumbered on. I poked it with the point of my pencil. It gave no response. I shook the branch, I shouted, I tapped its antennae with a twig. Still it was lost in the heavy sleep of the laborer. I left it more than half convinced that it had died in its clinging position. But early the next morning the bee was gone. Soon after daylight, I suppose, it had awakened and gone about its business with—if bumblebees ever have bumblebee dreams—a faint recollection of a nightmare that had vaguely troubled its slumbers.

In addition to the insects sleeping through the hours of darkness and the nocturnal musicians filling the air with sound, a host of varied creatures are working in silence amid the bushes, the trees and the tangles of grass. In the spotlight, they stand out, the beam arresting them in the midst of action. Black carpenter ants are toiling up and down the trunk of a pear tree. A lacewing fly is fluttering on gauzy wings from hollyhock to hollyhock. Brown beetles are feeding at the centers of sunflowers. Two walking sticks, almost side by side, are nibbling leaves near the wild-cherry tangle while, over the green plateau of a bushtop, a praying mantis is stalking catwise across the leaves. In the flashlight's beam, its eyes appear brown like dry cocoa.

I hold my watch in the beam of the flashlight and find it is past midnight. The sky has become overcast. The smell of rain is in the night air. Moths flutter about from plant to plant. I find three crowding close and drinking sap from the broken stem of a sunflower leaf. A slow rain begins. Then the falling drops increase their tempo. I take shelter under the green arc of the biggest apple tree. And here, while the sound of the rain becomes a steady drumming, I meet the culminating adventure of the night.

For a moment I listen in the darkness before I switch on my light. The beam glides upward along the gray tree trunk. Five feet from the ground, it encounters the black, unblinking eye of a knothole. A dozen times a day, in full sunlight, I have passed this opening without a second glance. But now, surrounded by the vast blackness of the night the three-inch opening assumes a new interest.

Rain from previous showers has collected in the hollow within. In the beam of my flashlight the scene resembles some unexplored cave or subterranean lake in miniature. The weathered wood, sloping downward along the roof of this teacup-sized cavern, has the appearance of shelving rock. Half a dozen sow bugs, like trilobites from a remote geological past, glide away on the flowing action of a succession of slender legs, to crowd into the darker corners of the cave. Two black ants are bending down at the edge of the water as though drinking at the shore of a lake.

On the surface of this knothole pool floats the body of a dead crane-fly. While looking at it, I catch a glimpse of one of the sow bugs hurrying from one dark corner to another with a baby sow bug clinging firmly to its back.

From the debris at the bottom of the flooded cavern rise a score or more slender white stalks, apparently sprouts from seeds scattered singly and in little clusters. As the beam of my flashlight shoots low over the water, I observe a curious thing. The surface is not smooth but has a dozen dimples that suggest the "knots" in an imperfect pane of glass. Under each dimple there are from one to seven of the sprouts. Where there are more than one, the thin stalks come together like the poles of a tepee. Some attraction seems to pull them to a common center. Using a straw, I push one of these clusters apart. With a slow, stately motion, the component stalks swing back and assume their former position.

The dimples above such clusters are larger than where a single sprout reaches the surface. And here is another surprising thing: Not one sprout is pushed above the water. All reach exactly to the surface and no farther. I am puzzling over this when an amazing thing takes place before my eyes.

One of the sprouts, as I watch it, telescopes slowly downward like a moving picture running in reverse. It steadily becomes shorter until it reaches the debris below. The other stalks remain as before. But something has happened at the spot where the descending sprout has reached the debris. Half an inch of white is moving among the black decayed wood of the pond-bottom. In a flash, I know. These are no sprouts. These slender stalklike columns are the air-hoses of the world's first diving suits. At the bottom of my knothole cavern are not seeds but some of the strangest, most incredible creatures of the insect world.

These larvae of a Syrphid fly, *Eristalis tenax,* feed upon decaying matter underwater. Their tubelike, telescoping tails reach to the surface and carry air to the creatures below. Aeons before man first appeared on earth, Nature thus invented the prototype of the diving gear. Réaumur, the great natural scientist of Eighteenth Century France, studied and named this larva. He called it "the rat-tailed maggot" and the name has struck.

The larvae themselves are at most only two-thirds of an inch long. But their remarkable tails, formed of two tubes, one sliding within the other and both capable of tremendous elongation and contraction, can be extended as much as eight times the length of the larva's body. In his pioneer researches, Réaumur added water, little by little, to a vessel in which several of these creatures were feeding. He saw the breathing tubes extend to each new level until the water reached a height of almost six inches. The tails, now no thicker than horsehairs, had stretched to their limit. When more water was added, the larvae either crept up the side of the vessel or floated up to a height from which their breathing tubes could reach the air supply.

At the bottom of my knothole cavern, I discovered, these larvae root among decaying matter like clusters of white pigs, feeding upon organic particles by the means of tiny hooklets which are attached to a head that is soft and capable of changing its shape. Other hooklets form a double circle on the bottom of each of twelve of its fourteen feet. On the front pair of stubby legs, the hooklets point forward like fingernails.

Later when I took some of these strange little larvae home and established them in a glass dish near my desk, I found they could use these hooklet-studded feet in a remarkable way. By means of them, they are able to walk on the underside of the surface film like a fly crawling across the ceiling.

At the end of its larval period, the rat-tailed maggot leaves the water. Its color changes from white to yellow. Its body becomes shorter and thicker. Its larval skin grows hard and opaque, forming the chrysalis within which the transformation into the adult fly occurs. Two pairs of horns appear at the head of this pupa case. They provide respiratory organs for the period of transformation.

This period lasts for from eight to ten days. At the end of that time, what appears to be a honeybee—in shape, size, color and furry thorax—crawls from the pupa case. Like the bee, this fly haunts flowers and lives on nectar and pollen. The adults appear in spring and autumn. Before they die, the females deposit their eggs in some cranny filled with decaying matter and stagnant water.

As amazing as anything in the life story of these strange creatures of my knothole, is the chronicle of a myth with which they are connected. These insects are believed to be responsible for one of the most tenacious errors of science, the world-wide, centuries-old belief in the ox-born bee. Because such flies are often seen about the carcasses of animals, in the fluids of which they deposit their eggs, the ancients—mistaking them for honeybees—concluded that the nectar gatherers were engendered in the decaying carcasses of larger animals. The myth of the ox-born bee is one of those contagious misconceptions which spread to all parts of the globe. It stands as a monument to the intellectual sloth of mankind. For the simplest kind of experiment—an attempt to obtain honey from such insects—would at any time, have proved its falsity.

Like the legend which it produced, the fly, *Eristalis tenax,* has spread from country to country. As a stowaway on shipboard, it has traveled widely. About the time of the Civil War, the bee-like Syrphid flies and their rat-tailed larvae were first recorded in America. For me, the story of these insects took on added interest because I had picked up the thread of their history under unusual circumstances; because within the space of a knothole cavern on a night of rain, my flashlight had illuminated the silent drama of their early lives.

1942

Loren Eiseley

The Flow of the River

Eiseley, the son of homesteaders in the Nebraska territory, is Benjamin Franklin Professor of Anthropology and the History of Science at the University of Pennsylvania. In college he was editor of the *Prairie Schooner*—an indication of his literary engagements. As an anthropologist, he has worked extensively in the high plains, mountains, and deserts bordering the Rocky Mountains. A lyrical Darwinist, he takes as his recurrent theme in *The Immense Journey,* from which "The Flow of the River" comes, the enormous capacity of life to extend itself in space, adapting itself to new environments, and in time (a capacity peculiar to the human brain). "The most enormous extension of vision of which life is capable," he writes, "is the projection of itself into other lives. This is the lonely, magnificent power of humanity."

IF THERE IS MAGIC on this planet, it is contained in water. Its least stir even, as now in a rain pond on a flat roof opposite my office, is enough to bring me searching to the window. A wind ripple may be translating itself into life. I have a constant feeling that some time I may witness that momentous miracle on a city roof, see life veritably and suddenly boiling out of a heap of rusted pipes and old television aerials. I marvel at how suddenly a water beetle has come and is submarining there in a spatter of green algae. Thin vapors, rust, wet tar and sun are an alembic remarkably like the mind; they throw off odorous shadows that threaten to take real shape when no one is looking.

Once in a lifetime, perhaps, one escapes the actual confines of the flesh. Once in a lifetime, if one is lucky, one so merges with sunlight and air and running water that whole eons, the eons that mountains and deserts know, might pass in a single afternoon without discomfort. The mind has sunk away into its beginnings among old roots and the obscure tricklings and movings that stir inanimate things. Like the charmed fairy circle into which a man once stepped, and upon emergence learned that a whole century had passed in a single night, one can never quite define this secret; but it has something to do, I am sure, with common water. Its substance reaches everywhere; it touches the past and prepares the future; it moves under the poles and wanders thinly in the heights of air. It can assume forms of exquisite perfection in a snowflake, or strip the living to a single shining bone cast up by the sea.

Many years ago, in the course of some scientific investigations in a remote western county, I experienced, by chance, precisely the sort of curious absorption by water—the extension of shape by osmosis—at which I have been hinting. You have probably never experienced in yourself the meandering roots of a whole watershed or felt your outstretched fingers touching, by some kind of clairvoyant extension, the brooks of snow-line glaciers at the same time that you were flowing toward the Gulf over the eroded debris of worn-down mountains. A poet, MacKnight Black, has spoken of being "limbed . . . with waters gripping pole and pole." He had the idea, all right, and it is obvious that these sensations are not unique, but they are hard to come by; and the sort of extension of the senses that people will accept when they put their ear against a sea shell, they will smile at in the confessions of a bookish professor. What makes it worse is the fact that because of a traumatic experience in childhood, I am not a swimmer, and am inclined to be timid before any large body of water. Perhaps it was just this, in a way, that contributed to my experience.

As it leaves the Rockies and moves downward over the high plains towards the Missouri, the Platte River is a curious stream. In the spring floods, on occasion, it can be a mile-wide roaring torrent of destruction, gulping farms and bridges. Normally, however, it is a rambling, dispersed series of streamlets flowing erratically over great sand and gravel fans that are, in part, the remnants of a mightier Ice Age stream bed. Quicksands and shifting islands haunt its waters. Over it the prairie suns beat mercilessly throughout the summer. The Platte, "a mile wide and an inch deep," is a refuge for any heat-weary pilgrim along its shores. This is particularly true on the high plains before its long march by the cities begins.

The reason that I came upon it when I did, breaking through a willow thicket and stumbling out through ankle-deep water to a dune in the shade, is of no concern to this narrative. On various purposes of science I have ranged over a good bit of that country on foot, and I know the kinds of bones that come gurgling up through the gravel pumps, and the arrowheads of shining chalcedony that occasionally spill out of water-loosened sand. On that day, however, the sight of sky and willows and the weaving net of water murmuring a little in the shallows on its way to the Gulf stirred me, parched as I was with miles of walking, with a new idea: I was going to float. I was going to undergo a tremendous adventure.

The notion came to me, I suppose, by degrees. I had shed my clothes and was floundering pleasantly in a hole among some reeds when a great desire to stretch out and go with this gently insistent water began to pluck at me. Now to this bronzed, bold, modern generation, the struggle I waged with timidity while standing there in knee-deep water can only seem farcical; yet actually for me it was not so. A near-drowning accident in childhood had scarred my reactions; in addition to the fact that I was a nonswimmer, this "inch-deep river" was treacherous with holes and quicksands. Death was not precisely infrequent along its wandering and illusory channels. Like all broad wastes of this kind, where neither water nor land quite prevails, its thickets were lonely and untraversed. A man in trouble would cry out in vain.

I thought of all this, standing quietly in the water, feeling the sand shifting away under my toes. Then I lay back in the floating position that left my face to the sky, and shoved off. The sky wheeled over me. For an instant, as I bobbed into the main channel, I had the sensation of sliding down the vast tilted face of the continent. It was then that I felt the cold needles of the alpine springs at my fingertips, and the warmth of the Gulf pulling me southward. Moving with me, leaving its taste upon my mouth and spouting under me in dancing springs of sand, was the immense body of the continent itself, flowing like the river was flowing, grain by grain, mountain by mountain, down to the sea. I was streaming over ancient sea beds thrust aloft where giant reptiles had once sported; I was wearing down the face of time and trundling cloud-wreathed ranges into oblivion. I touched my margins with the delicacy of a crayfish's antennae, and felt great fishes glide about their work.

I drifted by stranded timber cut by beaver in mountain fastnesses; I slid over shallows that had buried the broken axles of prairie schooners and the mired bones of mammoth. I was streaming alive through the hot and working ferment of the sun, or oozing secretively through shady thickets. I *was* water and the unspeakable alchemies that gestate and take shape in water, the slimy jellies that under the enormous magnification of the sun writhe and whip upward as great barbeled fish mouths, or sink indistinctly back into the murk out of which they arose. Turtle and fish and the pinpoint chirpings of individual frogs are all watery projections, concentrations—as man himself is a concentration—of that indescribable and liquid brew which is compounded in varying proportions of salt and sun and time. It has appearances, but at its heart lies water, and as I was finally edged gently against a sand bar and dropped like any log, I tottered as I rose. I knew once more the body's revolt against emergence into the harsh and unsupporting air, its reluctance to break contact with that mother element which still, at this late point in time, shelters and brings into being nine tenths of everything alive.

As for men, those myriad little detached ponds with their own swarming corpuscular life, what were they but a way that water has of going about beyond the reach of rivers? I, too, was a microcosm of pouring rivulets and floating driftwood gnawed by the mysterious animalcules of my own creation. I was three fourths water, rising and subsiding according to the hollow knocking in my veins: a minute pulse like the eternal pulse that lifts Himalayas and which, in the following systole, will carry them away.

Thoreau, peering at the emerald pickerel in Walden Pond, called them "animalized water" in one of his moments of strange insight. If he had been possessed of the geological knowledge so laboriously accumulated since his time, he might have gone further and amusedly detected in the planetary rumblings and eructations which so delighted him in the gross habits of certain frogs, signs of that dark interior stress which has reared sea bottoms up to mountainous heights. He might have developed an acute inner ear for the sound of the surf on Cretaceous beaches where now the wheat of Kansas rolls. In any case, he would have seen, as the long trail of life was unfolded by the fossil hunters, that his animalized water had changed its shapes eon by eon to the beating of the earth's dark millennial heart. In the swamps of the low continents, the amphibians had flourished and had their day; and as the long skyward swing—the isostatic response of the crust—had come about, the era of the cooling grasslands and mammalian life had come into being.

A few winters ago, clothed heavily against the weather, I wandered several miles along one of the tributaries of that same Platte I had floated down years before. The land was stark and ice-locked. The rivulets were frozen, and over the marshlands the willow thickets made such an array of vertical lines against the snow that tramping through them produced strange optical illusions and dizziness. On the edge of a frozen backwater, I stopped and rubbed my eyes. At my feet a raw prairie wind had swept the ice clean of snow. A peculiar green object caught my eye; there was no mistaking it.

Staring up at me with all his barbels spread pathetically, frozen solidly in the wind-ruffled ice, was a huge familiar face. It was one of those catfish of the twisting channels, those dwellers in the yellow murk, who had been about me and beneath me on the day of my great voyage. Whatever sunny dream had kept him paddling there while the mercury plummeted downward and that Cheshire smile froze slowly, it would be hard to say. Or perhaps he was trapped in a blocked channel and had simply kept swimming until the ice contracted around him. At any rate, there he would lie till the spring thaw.

At that moment I started to turn away, but something in the bleak, whiskered face reproached me, or perhaps it was the river calling to her children. I termed it science, however—a convenient rational phrase I reserve for such occasions—and decided that I would cut the fish out of the ice and take him home. I had no intention of eating him. I was merely struck by a sudden impulse to test the survival qualities of high-plains fishes, particularly fishes of this type who get themselves immured in oxygenless ponds or in cut-off oxbows buried in winter drifts. I blocked him out as gently as possible and dropped him, ice and all, into a collecting can in the car. Then we set out for home.

Unfortunately, the first stages of what was to prove a remarkable resurrection escaped me. Cold and tired after a long drive, I deposited the can with its melting water and ice in the basement. The accompanying corpse I anticipated I would either dispose of or dissect on the following day. A hurried glance had revealed no signs of life.

To my astonishment, however, upon descending into the basement several hours later, I heard stirrings in the receptacle and peered in. The ice had melted. A vast pouting mouth ringed with sensitive feelers confronted me, and the creature's gills labored slowly. A thin stream of silver bubbles rose to the surface and popped. A fishy eye gazed up at me protestingly.

''A tank,'' it said. This was no Walden pickerel. This was a yellow-green, mud-grubbing, evil-tempered inhabitant of floods and droughts and cyclones. It was the selective product of the high continent and the waters that pour across it. It had outlasted prairie blizzards that left cattle standing frozen upright in the drifts.

"I'll get the tank," I said respectfully.

He lived with me all that winter, and his departure was totally in keeping with his sturdy, independent character. In the spring a migratory impulse or perhaps sheer boredom struck him. Maybe, in some little lost corner of his brain, he felt, far off, the pouring of the mountain waters through the sandy coverts of the Platte. Anyhow, something called to him, and he went. One night when no one was about, he simply jumped out of his tank. I found him dead on the floor next morning. He had made his gamble like a man—or, I should say, a fish. In the proper place it would not have been a fool's gamble. Fishes in the drying shallows of intermittent prairie streams who feel their confinement and have the impulse to leap while there is yet time may regain the main channel and survive. A million ancestral years had gone into that jump, I thought as I looked at him, a million years of climbing through prairie sunflowers and twining in and out through the pillared legs of drinking mammoth.

"Some of your close relatives have been experimenting with air breathing," I remarked, apropos of nothing, as I gathered him up. "Suppose we meet again up there in the cottonwoods in a million years or so."

I missed him a little as I said it. He had for me the kind of lost archaic glory that comes from the water brotherhood. We were both projections out of that timeless ferment and locked as well in some greater unity that lay incalculably beyond us. In many a fin and reptile foot I have seen myself passing by—some part of myself, that is, some part that lies unrealized in the momentary shape I inhabit. People have occasionally written me harsh letters and castigated me for a lack of faith in man when I have ventured to speak of this matter in print. They distrust, it would seem, all shapes and thoughts but their own. They would bring God into the compass of a shopkeeper's understanding and confine Him to those limits, lest He proceed to some unimaginable and shocking act—create perhaps, as a casual afterthought, a being more beautiful than man. As for me, I believe nature capable of this, and having been part of the flow of the river, I feel no envy—any more than the frog envies the reptile or an ancestral ape should envy man.

Every spring in the wet meadows and ditches I hear a little shrilling chorus which sounds for all the world like an endlessly reiterated "We're here, we're here, we're here." And so they are, as frogs, of course. Confident little fellows. I suspect that to some greater ear than ours, man's optimistic pronouncements about his role and destiny may make a similar little ringing sound that travels a small way out into the night. It is only its nearness that is offensive. From the heights of a mountain, or a marsh at evening, it blends, not too badly, with all the other sleepy voices that, in croaks or chirrups, are saying the same thing.

After a while the skilled listener can distinguish man's noise from the katydid's rhythmic assertion, allow for the offbeat of a rabbit's thumping, pick up the autumnal monotone of crickets, and find in all of them a grave pleasure without admitting any to a place of preëminence in his thoughts. It is when all these voices cease and the waters are still, when along the frozen river nothing cries, screams or howls, that the enormous mindlessness of space settles down upon the soul. Somewhere out in that waste of crushed ice and reflected stars, the black waters may be running, but they appear to be running without life toward a destiny in which the whole of space may be locked in some silvery winter of dispersed radiation.

It is then, when the wind comes straitly across the barren marshes and the snow rises and beats in endless waves against the traveler, that I remember best, by some trick of the imagination, my summer voyage on the river. I remember my green extensions, my catfish nuzzlings and minnow wrigglings, my gelatinous materializations out of the mother ooze. And as I walk on through the white smother, it is the magic of water that leaves me a final sign.

Men talk much of matter and energy, of the struggle for existence that molds the shape of life. These things exist, it is true; but more delicate, elusive, quicker than the fins in water, is that mysterious principle known as "organization," which leaves all other mysteries concerned with life stale and insignificant by comparison. For that without organization life does not persist is obvious. Yet this organization itself is not strictly the product of life, nor of selection. Like some dark and passing shadow within matter, it cups out the eyes' small windows or spaces the notes of a meadow lark's song in the interior of a mottled egg. That principle—I am beginning to suspect—was there before the living in the deeps of water.

The temperature has risen. The little stinging needles have given way to huge flakes floating in like white leaves blown from some great tree in open space. In the car, switching on the lights, I examine one intricate crystal on my sleeve before it melts. No utilitarian philosophy explains a snow crystal, no doctrine of use or disuse. Water has merely leapt out of vapor and thin nothingness in the night sky to array itself in form. There is no logical reason for the existence of a snowflake any more than there is for evolution. It is an apparition from that mysterious shadow world beyond nature, that final world which contains—if anything contains—the explanation of men and catfish and green leaves.

1957

Jack Kerouac

Alone on a Mountaintop

Kerouac, one of the lights of the beat generation, "read the life of Jack London at 18 and decided to also be an adventurer, a lonesome traveler." During the fifties, the heyday of the beats, he spent six years "writing whatever came into my head, hopping freights, hitchhiking, and working as a railroad brakeman, deckhand and scullion on merchant ships, government fire lookout, and hundreds of assorted jobs." Out of these experiences came not only *Lonesome Traveler,* from which "Alone on a Mountaintop" comes, but also *On the Road* (1957) and other novels. "In scope and purpose," Kerouac describes *Lonesome Traveler* as "simply poetry, or, natural description." "Alone on a Mountaintop" came from his experiences as a forest service fire lookout in 1956—a job many of his friends and fellow readers of the Oriental mystics have had, including Gary Snyder and Philip Whalen.

AFTER ALL THIS KIND OF FANFARE, and even more, I came to a point where I needed solitude and just stop the machine of "thinking" and "enjoying" what they call "living," I just wanted to lie in the grass and look at the clouds——

They say, too, in ancient scripture:——"Wisdom can only be obtained from the viewpoint of solitude."

And anyway I was sick and tired of all the ships and railroads and Times Squares of all time——

I applied with the U.S. Agriculture Department for a job as a fire lookout in the Mount Baker National Forest in the High Cascades of the Great Northwest.

Just to look at these words made me shiver to think of cool pine trees by a morning lake.

I beat my way out to Seattle three thousand miles from the heat and dust of eastern cities in June.

Anybody who's been to Seattle and missed Alaskan Way, the old water front, has missed the point——here the totem-pole stores, the waters of Puget Sound washing under old piers, the dark gloomy look of ancient warehouses and pier sheds, and the most antique locomotives in America switching boxcars up and down the water front, give a hint, under the pure cloud-mopped sparkling skies of the Northwest, of great country to come. Driving north from Seattle on Highway 99 is an exciting experience because suddenly you see the Cascade Mountains rising on the northeast horizon, truly *Komo Kulshan* under their uncountable snows.——The great peaks covered with trackless white, worlds of huge rock twisted and heaped and sometimes almost spiraled into fantastic unbelievable shapes.

All this is seen far above the dreaming fields of the Stilaquamish and Skagit valleys, agricultural flats of peaceful green, the soil so rich and dark it is proudly referred to by inhabitants as second only to the Nile in fertility. At Milltown Washington your car rolls over the bridge across the Skagit River.——To the left——seaward, westward——the Skagit flows into Skagit Bay and the Pacific Ocean.——At Burlington you turn right and head for the heart of the mountains along a rural valley road through sleepy little towns and one bustling agricultural market center known as Sedro-Woolley with hundreds of cars parked aslant on a typical country-town Main Street of hardware stores, grain-and-feed stores and five-and-tens.——On deeper into the deepening valley, cliffs rich with timber appearing by the side of the road, the narrowing river rushing more swiftly now, a pure translucent green like the green of the ocean on a cloudy day but a saltless rush of melted snow from the High Cascades——almost good enough to drink north of Marblemount.——The road curves more and more till you reach Concrete, the last town in Skagit Valley with a bank and a five-and-ten——after that the mountains rising secretly behind foothills are so close that now you don't see them but begin to feel them more and more.

At Marblemount the river is a swift torrent, the work of the quiet mountains.——Fallen logs beside the water provide good seats to enjoy a river wonderland, leaves jiggling in the good clean northwest wind seem to rejoice, the topmost trees on nearby timbered peaks swept and dimmed by low-flying clouds seem contented.——The clouds assume the faces of hermits or of nuns, or sometimes look like sad dog acts hurrying off into the wings over the horizon.——Snags struggle and gurgle in the heaving bulk of the river.——Logs rush by at twenty miles an hour. The air smells of pine and sawdust and bark and mud and twigs——birds flash over the water looking for secret fish.

As you drive north across the bridge at Marblemount and on to Newhalem the road narrows and twists until finally the Skagit is seen pouring over rocks, frothing, and small creeks come tumbling from steep hillsides and pile right in.——The mountains rise on all sides, only their shoulders and ribs visible, their heads out of sight and now snowcapped.

At Newhalem extensive road construction raises a cloud of dust over shacks and cats and rigs, the dam there is the first in a series that create the Skagit watershed which provides all the power for Seattle.

The road ends at Diablo, a peaceful company settlement of neat cottages and green lawns surrounded by close packed peaks named Pyramid and Colonial and Davis.——Here a huge lift takes you one thousand feet up to the level of Diablo Lake and Diablo Dam.——Over the dam pours a jet roar of water through which a stray log could go shooting out like a toothpick in a one-thousand-foot arc.——Here for the first time you're high enough really to begin to see the Cascades. Dazzles of light to the north show where Ross Lake sweeps back all the way to Canada, opening a view of the Mt. Baker National Forest as spectacular as any vista in the Colorado Rockies.

The Seattle City Light and Power boat leaves on regular schedule from a little pier near Diablo Dam and heads north between steep timbered rocky cliffs toward Ross Dam, about half an hour's ride. The passengers are power employees, hunters and fishermen and forestry workers. Below Ross Dam the footwork begins——you must climb a rocky trail one thousand feet to the level of the dam. Here the vast lake opens out, disclosing small resort floats offering rooms and boats for vacationists, and just beyond, the floats of the U.S. Forestry Service. From this point on, if you're lucky enough to be a rich man or a forest-fire lookout, you can get packed into the North Cascade Primitive Area by horse and mule and spend a summer of complete solitude.

I was a fire lookout and after two nights of trying to sleep in the boom and slap of the Forest Service floats, they came for me one rainy morning——a powerful tugboat lashed to a large corral float bearing four mules and three horses, my own groceries, feed, batteries and equipment.——The muleskinner's name was Andy and he wore the same old floppy cowboy hat he'd worn in Wyoming twenty years ago. "Well, boy, now we're gonna put you away where we cant reach ya——you better get ready."

"It's just what I want, Andy, be alone for three solid months nobody to bother me."

"It's what you're saying' now but you'll change your tune after a week."

I didn't believe him.——I was looking forward to an experience men seldom earn in this modern world: complete and comfortable solitude in the wilderness, day and night, sixty-three days and nights to be exact. We had no idea how much snow had fallen on my mountain during the winter and Andy said: "If there didnt it means you gotta hike two miles down that hard trail every day or every other day with two buckets, boy. I aint envyin' you——I been back there. And one day it's gonna be hot and you're about ready to broil, and bugs you cant even count 'em, and next day a li'l' ole summer blizzard come hit you around the corner of Hozomeen which sits right there near Canada in your back yard and you wont be able to stick logs fast enough in that potbelly stove of yours."——But I had a full rucksack loaded with turtleneck sweaters and warm shirts and pants and long wool socks bought on the Seattle water front, and gloves and an earmuff cap, and lots of instant soup and coffee in my grub list.

"Shoulda brought yourself a quart of brandy, boy," says Andy shaking his head as the tug pushed our corral float up Ross Lake through the log gate and around to the left dead north underneath the immense rain shroud of Sourdough Mountain and Ruby Mountain.

"Where's Desolation Peak?" I asked, meaning my own mountain (*A mountain to be kept forever,* I'd dreamed all that spring) (O lonesome traveler!)

"You aint gonna see it today till we're practically on top it and by that time you'll be so soakin' wet you wont care."

Assistant Ranger Marty Gohlke of Marblemount Ranger Station was with us too, also giving me tips and instructions. Nobody seemed to envy Desolation Peak except me. After two hours pushing through the storming waves of the long rainy lake with dreary misty timber rising steeply on both sides and the mules and horses chomping on their feedbags patient in the downpour, we arrived at the foot of Desolation Trail and the tugman (who'd been providing us with good hot coffee in the pilot cabin) eased her over and settled the float against a steep muddy slope full of bushes and fallen trees.—The muleskinner whacked the first mule and she lurched ahead with her double-sided pack of batteries and canned goods, hit the mud with forehoofs, scrambled, slipped, almost fell back in the lake and finally gave one mighty heave and went skittering out of sight in the fog to wait on the trail for the other mules and her master.——We all got off, cut the barge loose, waved to the tug man, mounted our horses and started up a sad and dripping party in heavy rain.

At first the trail, always steeply rising, was so dense with shrubbery we kept getting shower after shower from overhead and against our out-saddled knees.——The trail was deep with round rocks that kept causing the animals to slip.——At one point a great fallen tree made it impossible to go on until Old Andy and Marty went ahead with axes and cleared a short cut around the tree, sweating and cursing and hacking as I watched the animals.——By-and-by they were ready but the mules were afraid of the rough steepness of the short cut and had to be prodded through with sticks.——Soon the trail reached alpine meadows powdered with blue lupine everywhere in the drenching mists, and with little red poppies, tiny-budded flowers as delicate as designs on a small Japanese teacup.——Now the trail zigzagged widely back and forth up the high meadow.——Soon we saw the vast foggy heap of a rock-cliff face above and Andy yelled "Soon's we get up high as that we're almost there but that's another two thousand feet though you think you could reach up and touch it!"

I unfolded my nylon poncho and draped it over my head, and, drying a little, or, rather, ceasing to drip, I walked alongside the horse to warm my blood and began to feel better. But the other boys just rode along with their heads bowed in the rain. As for altitude all I could tell was from some occasional frightening spots on the trail where we could look down on distant treetops.

The alpine meadow reached to timber line and suddenly a great wind blew shafts of sleet on us.——"Gettin' near the top now!" yelled Andy——and suddenly there was snow on the trail, the horses were chumping through a foot of slush and mud, and to the left and right everything was blinding white in the gray fog.——"About five and a half thousand feet right now" said Andy rolling a cigarette as he rode in the rain.——

We went down, then up another spell, down again, a slow gradual climb, and then Andy yelled "There she is!" and up ahead in the mountaintop gloom I saw a little shadowy peaked shack standing alone on the top of the world and gulped with fear:

"This my home all summer? And *this* is summer?"

The inside of the shack was even more miserable, damp and dirty, leftover groceries and magazines torn to shreds by rats and mice, the floor muddy, the windows impenetrable.——But hardy Old Andy who'd been through this kind of thing all his life got a roaring fire crackling in the potbelly stove and had me lay out a pot of water with almost half a can of coffee in it saying "Coffee aint no good 'less it's *strong!*" and pretty soon the coffee was boiling a nice brown aromatic foam and we got our cups out and drank deep.——

Meanwhile I'd gone out on the roof with Marty and removed the bucket from the chimney and put up the weather pole with the anemometer and done a few other chores——when we came back in Andy was frying Spam and eggs in a huge pan and it was almost like a party.——Outside, the patient animals chomped on their supper bags and were glad to rest by the old corral fence built of logs by some Desolation lookout of the Thirties.

Darkness came, incomprehensible.

In the gray morning after they'd slept in sleeping bags on the floor and I on the only bunk in my mummy bag, Andy and Marty left, laughing, saying, "Well, whatayou think now hey? We been here twelve hours and you still aint been able to see more than twelve feet!"

"By gosh that's right, what am I going to do for watching fires?"

"Dont worry boy, these clouds'll roll away and you'll be able to see a hunnerd miles in every direction."

I didn't believe it and I felt miserable and spent the day trying to clean up the shack or pacing twenty careful feet each way in my "yard" (the ends of which appeared to be sheer drops into silent gorges), and I went to bed early.——About bedtime I saw my first star, briefly, then giant phantom clouds billowed all around me and the star was gone.——But in that instant I thought I'd seen a mile-down maw of grayblack lake where Andy and Marty were back in the Forest Service boat which had met them at noon.

In the middle of the night I woke up suddenly and my hair was standing on end——I saw a huge black shadow in my window.——Then I saw that it had a star above it, and realized that this was Mt. Hozomeen (8080 feet) looking in my window from miles away near Canada.——I got up from the forlorn bunk with the mice scattering underneath and went outside and gasped to see black mountain shapes gianting all around, and not only that but the billowing curtains of the northern lights shifting behind the clouds.——It was a little too much for a city boy——the fear that the Abominable Snowman might be breathing behind me in the dark sent me back to bed where I buried my head inside my sleeping bag.——

But in the morning——Sunday, July sixth——I was amazed and overjoyed to see a clear blue sunny sky and down below, like a radiant pure snow sea, the clouds making a marshmallow cover for all the world and all the lake while I abided in warm sunshine among hundreds of miles of snow-white peaks.——I brewed coffee and sang and drank a cup on my drowsy warm doorstep.

At noon the clouds vanished and the lake appeared below, beautiful beyond belief, a perfect blue pool twenty five miles long and more, and the creeks like toy creeks and the timber green and fresh everywhere below and even the joyous little unfolding liquid tracks of vacationists' fishingboats on the lake and in the lagoons.——A perfect afternoon of sun, and behind the shack I discovered a snowfield big enough to provide me with buckets of cold water till late September.

My job was to watch for fires. One night a terrific lightning storm made a dry run across the Mt. Baker National Forest without any rainfall.——When I saw that ominous black cloud flashing wrathfully toward me I shut off the radio and laid the aerial on the ground and waited for the worst.——Hiss! hiss! said the wind, bringing dust and lightning nearer.——Tick! said the lightning rod, receiving a strand of electricity from a strike on nearby Skagit Peak.——Hiss! tick! and in my bed I felt the earth move.——Fifteen miles to the south, just east of Ruby Peak and somewhere near Panther Creek, a large fire raged, a huge orange spot.——At ten o'clock lightning hit it again and it flared up dangerously.——

I was supposed to note the general area of lightning strikes.——By midnight I'd been staring so intently out the dark window I got hallucinations of fires everywhere, three of them right in Lightning Creek, phosphorescent orange verticals of ghost fire that seemed to come and go.

In the morning, there at 177° 16′ where I'd seen the big fire was a strange brown patch in the snowy rock showing where the fire had raged and sputtered out in the all-night rain that followed the lightning. But the result of this storm was disastrous fifteen miles away at McAllister Creek where a great blaze had outlasted the rain and exploded the following afternoon in a cloud that could be seen from Seattle. I felt sorry for the fellows who had to fight these fires, the smoke-jumpers who parachuted down on them out of planes and the trail crews who hiked to them, climbing and scrambling over slippery rocks and scree slopes, arriving sweaty and exhausted only to face the wall of heat when they got there. As a lookout I had it pretty easy and only had to concentrate on reporting the exact location (by instrument findings) of every blaze I detected.

Most days, though, it was the routine that occupied me.——Up at seven or so every day, a pot of coffee brought to a boil over a handful of burning twigs, I'd go out in the alpine yard with a cup of coffee hooked in my thumb and leisurely make my wind speed and wind direction and temperature and moisture readings——then, after chopping wood, I'd use the two-way radio and report to the relay station at Sourdough.——At 10 AM I usually got hungry for breakfast, and I'd make delicious pancakes, eating them at my little table that was decorated with bouquets of moutain lupine and sprigs of fir.

Early in the afternoon was the usual time for my kick of the day, instant chocolate pudding with hot coffee.——Around two or three I'd lie on my back on the meadowside and watched the clouds float by, or pick blueberries and eat them right there. The radio was on loud enough to hear any calls for Desolation.

Then at sunset I'd roust up my supper out of cans of yams and Spam and peas, or sometimes just pea soup with corn muffins baked on top of the wood stove in aluminum foil.——Then I'd go out to that precipitous snow slope and shovel my two pails of snow for the water tub and gather an armful of fallen firewood from the hillside like the proverbial Old Woman of Japan.——For the chipmunks and conies I put pans of leftovers under the shack, in the middle of the night I could hear them clanking around. The rat would scramble down from the attic and eat some too.

Sometimes I'd yell questions at the rocks and trees, and across gorges, or yodel——"What is the meaning of the void?" The answer was perfect silence, so I knew.——

Before bedtime I'd read by kerosene lamp whatever books were in the shack.——It's amazing how people in solitary hunger after books.——After poring over every word of a medical tome, and the synopsized versions of Shakespeare's plays by Charles and Mary Lamb, I climbed up in the little attic and put together torn cowboy pocket books and magazines the mice had ravaged——I also played stud poker with three imaginary players.

Around bedtime I'd bring a cup of milk almost to a boil with a tablespoon of honey in it, and drink that for my lamby nightcap, then I'd curl up in my sleeping bag.

No man should go through life without once experiencing healthy, even bored solitude in the wilderness, finding himself depending solely on himself and thereby learning his true and hidden strength.——Learning, for instance, to eat when he's hungry and sleep when he's sleepy.

Also around bedtime was my singing time. I'd pace up and down the well-worn path in the dust of my rock singing all the show tunes I could remember, at the top of my voice too, with nobody to hear except the deer and the bear.

In the red dusk, the mountains were symphonies in pink snow——Jack Mountain, Three Fools Peak, Freezeout Peak, Golden Horn, Mt. Terror, Mt. Fury, Mt. Despair, Crooked Thumb Peak, Mt. Challenger and the incomparable Mt. Baker bigger than the world in the distance——and my own little Jackass Ridge that completed the Ridge of Desolation.——Pink snow and the clouds all distant and frilly like ancient remote cities of Buddhaland splendor, and the wind working incessantly——whish, whish——booming, at times rattling my shack.

For supper I made chop suey and baked some biscuits and put the leftovers in a pan for deer that came in the moonlit night and nibbled like big strange cows of peace—long-antlered buck and does and babies too——as I meditated in the alpine grass facing the magic moon-laned lake.——And I could see firs reflected in the moonlit lake five thousand feet below, upside down, pointing to infinity.——

And all the insects ceased in honor of the moon.

Sixty-three sunsets I saw revolve on that perpendicular hill—— mad raging sunsets pouring in sea foams of cloud through unimaginable crags like the crags you grayly drew in pencil as a child, with every rose-tint of hope beyond, making you feel just like them, brilliant and bleak beyond words.——

Cold mornings with clouds billowing out of Lightning Gorge like smoke from a giant fire but the lake cerulean as ever.

August comes in with a blast that shakes your house and augurs little Augusticity——then that snowy-air and woodsmoke feeling——then the snow comes sweeping your way from Canada, and the wind rises and dark low clouds rush up as out of a forge. Suddenly a green-rose rainbow appears right on your ridge with steamy clouds all around and an orange sun turmoiling . . .

What is a rainbow
Lord?—a hoop
For the lowly

. . . and you go out and suddenly your shadow is ringed by the rainbow as you walk on the hilltop, a lovely-haloed mystery making you want to pray.——

A blade of grass jiggling in the winds of infinity, anchored to a rock, and for your own poor gentle flesh no answer.

Your oil lamp burning in infinity.

One morning I found bear stool and signs of where the monster had taken a can of frozen milk and squeezed it in his paws and bit into it with one sharp tooth trying to suck out the paste.——In the foggy dawn I looked down the mysterious Ridge of Starvation with its fog-lost firs and its hills humping into invisibility, and the wind blowing the fog by like a faint blizzard and I realized that somewhere in the fog stalked the bear.

And it seemed as I sat there that this was the Primordial Bear, and that he owned all the Northwest and all the snow and commanded all the mountains.——He was King Bear, who could crush my head in his paws and crack my spine like a stick and this was his house, his yard, his domain.——Though I looked all day, he would not show himself in the mystery of those silent foggy slopes——he prowled at night among unknown lakes, and in the early morning the pearl-pure light that shadowed mountainsides of fir made him blink with respect.——He had millenniums of prowling here behind him, he had seen the Indians and Redcoats come and go, and would see much more.——He continuously heard the reassuring rapturous rush of silence, except when near creeks, he was aware of the light material the world is made of, yet he never discoursed, nor communicated by signs, nor wasted a breath complaining——he just nibbled and pawed and lumbered along snags paying no attention to things inanimate or animate.——His big mouth chew-chewed in the night, I could hear it across the mountain in the starlight.——Soon he would come out of the fog, huge, and come and stare in my window with big burning eyes.——He was Avalokitesvara the Bear, and his sign was the gray wind of autumn.——

I was waiting for him. He never came.

Finally the autumn rains, all-night gales of soaking rain as I lie warm as toast in my sleeping bag and the mornings open cold wild fall days with high wind, racing fogs, racing clouds, sudden bright sun, pristine light on hill patches and my fire crackling as I exult and sing at the top of my voice.——Outside my window a wind-swept chipmunk sits up straight on a rock, hands clasped he nibbles an oat between his paws——the little nutty lord of all he surveys.

Thinking of the stars night after night I begin to realize "The stars are words" and all the innumerable worlds in the Milky Way are words, and so is this world too. And I realize that no matter where I am, whether in a little room full of thought, or in this endless universe of stars and mountains, it's all in my mind. There's no need for solitude. So love life for what it is, and form no preconceptions whatever in your mind.

What strange sweet thoughts come to you in the mountain solitudes!——One night I realized that when you give people understanding and encouragement a funny little meek childish look abashes their eyes, no matter what they've been doing they weren't sure it was right——lambies all over the world.

For when you realize that God is Everything you know that you've got to love everything no matter how bad it is, in the ultimate sense it was neither good nor bad (consider the dust), it was just *what was,* that is, what was made to appear.——Some kind of drama to teach something to something, some "despiséd substance of divinest show."

And I realized I didnt have to hide myself in desolation but could accept society for better or for worse, like a wife——I saw that if it wasnt for the six senses, of seeing, hearing, smelling, touching, tasting and thinking, the self of that, which is non-existent, there would be no phenomena to perceive at all, in fact no six senses or self.——The fear of extinction is much worse than extinction (death) itself.——To chase after extinction in the old Nirvanic sense of Buddhism is ultimately silly, as the dead indicate in the silence of their blissful sleep in Mother Earth which is an Angel hanging in orbit in Heaven anyway.——

I just lay on the mountain meadowside in the moonlight, head to grass, and heard the silent recognition of my temporary woes.——Yes, so to try to *attain* to Nirvana when you're already there, to attain to the top of a mountain when you're already there and only have to stay——thus, to *stay* in the Nirvana Bliss, is all I have to do, you have to do, no effort, no path really, no discipline but just to know that all is empty and awake, a Vision and a Movie in God's Universal Mind (*Alaya-Vijnana*) and to stay more or less wisely in that.——Because silence itself is the sound of diamonds which can cut through anything, the sound of Holy Emptiness, the sound of extinction and bliss, that graveyard silence which is like the silence of an infant's smile, the sound of eternity, of the blessedness surely to be believed, the sound of nothing-ever-happened-except-God (which I'd soon hear in a noisy Atlantic tempest).——What exists is God in His Emanation, what does not exist is God in His peaceful Neutrality, what neither exists nor does not exist is God's immortal primordial dawn of Father Sky (this world this very minute).——So I said:——"Stay in that, no dimensions here to any of the mountains or mosquitos and whole milky ways of worlds——" Because sensation is emptiness, old age is emptiness.——'T's only the Golden Eternity of God's Mind so practise kindness and sympathy, remember that men are *not responsible in themselves as men* for their ignorance and unkindness, they should be pitied, God does pity it, because who says anything about anything since everything is just what it is, free of interpretations.——God is not the "attainer," he is the "farer" in that which everything is, the "abider"——one caterpillar, a thousand hairs of God.——So know constantly that this is only you, God, empty and awake and eternally free as the unnumerable atoms of emptiness everywhere.——

I decided that when I would go back to the world down there I'd try to keep my mind clear in the midst of murky human ideas smoking like factories on the horizon through which I would walk, forward . . .

When I came down in September a cool old golden look had come into the forest, auguring cold snaps and frost and the eventual howling blizzard that would cover my shack completely, unless those winds at the top of the world would keep her bald. As I reached the bend in the trail where the shack would disappear and I would plunge down to the lake to meet the boat that would take me out and home, I turned and blessed Desolation Peak and the little pagoda on top and thanked them for the shelter and the lesson I'd been taught.

1960

N. Scott Momaday

The Priest of the Sun

A chapter from Momaday's *House Made of Dawn,* "The Priest of the Sun" recalls two journeys: one made by the Kiowa Indians during the sixteenth century when they migrated from the headwaters of the Yellowstone River (in western Montana) to the Oklahoma plains; the other made by the speaker, Tosamah. The story reappears as the Introduction to Momaday's *The Way to Rainy Mountains* (1970), a collection of the legends, myths, and history of the Kiowas. It is clear from this context that the speaker is Momaday himself, who, on pilgrimage to the grave of his grandmother, followed the route of his ancestors in their journey to a new home.

January 27

TOSAMAH, orator, physician, Priest of the Sun, son of Hummingbird, spoke:

"A single knoll rises out of the plain in Oklahoma, north and west of the Wichita range. For my people it is an old landmark, and they gave it the name Rainy Mountain. There, in the south of the continental trough, is the hardest weather in the world. In winter there are blizzards which come down the Williston corridor, bearing hail and sleet. Hot tornadic winds arise in the spring, and in summer the prairie is an anvil's edge. The grass turns brittle and brown, and it cracks beneath your feet. There are green belts along the rivers and creeks, linear groves of hickory and pecan, willow and witch hazel. At a distance in July or August the steaming foliage seems almost to writhe in fire. Great green and yellow grasshoppers are everywhere in the tall grass, popping up like corn to sting the flesh, and tortoises crawl about on the red earth, going nowhere in the plenty of time. Loneliness is there as an aspect of the land. All things in the plain are isolate; there is no confusion of objects in the eye, but *one* hill or *one* tree or *one* man. At the slightest elevation you can see to the end of the world. To look upon that landscape in the early morning, with the sun at your back, is to lose the sense of proportion. Your imagination comes to life, and this, you think, is where Creation was begun.

"I returned to Rainy Mountain in July. My grandmother had died in the spring, and I wanted to be at her grave. She had lived to be very old and at last infirm. Her only living daughter was with her when she died, and I was told that in death her face was that of a child.

"I like to think of her as a child. When she was born, the Kiowas were living the last great moment of their history. For more than a hundred years they had controlled the open range from the Smoky Hill River to the Red, from the headwaters of the Canadian to the fork of the Arkansas and Cimarron. In alliance with the Comanches, they had ruled the whole of the Southern Plains. War was their sacred business, and they were the finest horsemen the world has ever known. But warfare for the Kiowas was pre-eminently a matter of disposition rather than survival, and they never understood the grim, unrelenting advance of the U.S. Cavalry. When at last, divided and ill-provisioned, they were driven onto the Staked Plain in the cold autumn, they fell into panic. In Palo Duro Canyon they abandoned their crucial stores to pillage and had nothing then but their lives. In order to save themselves, they surrendered to the soldiers at Fort Sill and were imprisoned in the old stone corral that now stands as a military museum. My grandmother was spared the humiliation of those high gray walls by eight or ten years, but she must have known from birth the affliction of defeat, the dark brooding of old warriors.

"Her name was Aho, and she belonged to the last culture to evolve in North America. Her forebears came down from the high north country nearly three centuries ago. The earliest evidence of their existence places them close to the source of the Yellowstone River in western Montana. They were a mountain people, a mysterious tribe of hunters whose language has never been classified in any major group. In the late seventeenth century they began a long migration to the south and east. It was a journey toward the dawn, and it led to a golden age. Along the way the Kiowas were befriended by the Crows, who gave them the culture and religion of the plains. They acquired horses, and their ancient nomadic spirit was suddenly free of the ground. They acquired Tai-me, the sacred sun dance doll, from that moment the chief object and symbol of their worship, and so shared in the divinity of the sun. Not least, they acquired the sense of destiny, therefore courage and pride. When they entered upon the Southern Plains, they had been transformed. No longer were they slaves to the simple necessity of survival; they were a lordly and dangerous society of fighters and thieves, hunters and priests of the sun. According to their origin myth, they entered the world through a hollow log. From one point of view, their migration was the fruit of an old prophecy, for indeed they emerged from a sunless world.

"I could see that. I followed their ancient way to my grandmother's grave. Though she lived out her long life in the shadow of Rainy Mountain, the immense landscape of the continental interior—all of its seasons and its sounds—lay like memory in her blood. She could tell of the Crows, whom she had never seen, and of Black Hills, where she had never been. I wanted to see in reality what she had seen more perfectly in the mind's eye.

"I began my pilgrimage on the course of the Yellowstone. There, it seemed to me, was the top of the world, a region of deep lakes and dark timber, canyons and waterfalls. But, beautiful as it is, one might have the sense of confinement there. The skyline in all directions is close at hand, the high wall of the woods and deep cleavages of shade. There is a perfect freedom in the mountains, but it belongs to the eagle and the elk, the badger and the bear. The Kiowas reckoned their stature by the distance they could see, and they were bent and blind in the wilderness.

"Descending eastward, the highland meadows are a stairway to the plain. In July the inland slope of the Rockies is luxuriant with flax and buckwheat, stonecrop and larkspur. The earth unfolds and the limit of the land recedes. Clusters of trees, and animals grazing far in the distance, cause the vision to reach away and wonder to build upon the mind. The sun follows a longer course in the day, and the sky is immense beyond all comparison. The great billowing clouds that sail upon it are shadows that move upon the grass and grain like water, dividing light. Farther down, in the land of the Crows and the Blackfeet, the plain is yellow. Sweet clover takes hold of the hills and bends upon itself to cover and seal the soil. There the Kiowas paused on their way; they had come to the place where they must change their lives. The sun is at home on the plains. Precisely there does it have the certain character of a god. When the Kiowas came to the land of the Crows, they could see the dark lees of the hills at dawn across the Bighorn River, the profusion of light on the grain shelves, the oldest deity ranging after the solstices. Not yet would they veer south to the caldron of the land that lay below; they must wean their blood from the northern winter and hold the mountains a while longer in their view. They bore Tai-me in procession to the east.

''A dark mist lay over the Black Hills, and the land was like iron. At the top of a ridge I caught sight of Devils Tower—the uppermost extremity of it, like a file's end on the gray sky—and then it fell away behind the land. I was a long time then in coming upon it, and I did not see it again until I saw it whole, suddenly there across the valley, as if in the birth of time the core of the earth had broken through its crust and the motion of the world was begun. It stands in motion, like certain timeless trees that aspire too much into the sky, and imposes an illusion on the land. There are things in nature which engender an awful quiet in the heart of man; Devils Tower is one of them. Man must account for it. He must never fail to explain such a thing to himself, or else he is estranged forever from the universe. Two centuries ago, because they could not do otherwise, the Kiowas made a legend at the base of the rock. My grandmother said:

> Eight children were there at play, seven sisters and their brother. Suddenly the boy was struck dumb; he trembled and began to run upon his hands and feet. His fingers became claws, and his body was covered with fur. There was a bear where the boy had been. The sisters were terrified; they ran, and the bear after them. They came to the stump of a great tree, and the tree spoke to them. It bade them climb upon it, and as they did so it began to rise into the air. The bear came to kill them, but they were just beyond its reach. It reared against the tree and scored the bark all around with its claws. The seven sisters were borne into the sky, and they became the stars of the Big Dipper.

''From that moment, and so long as the legend lives, the Kiowas have kinsmen in the night sky. Whatever they were in the mountains, they could be no more. However tenuous their well-being, however much they had suffered and would suffer again, they had found a way out of the wilderness.

"The first man among them to stand on the edge of the Great Plains saw farther over land than he had ever seen before. There is something about the heart of the continent that resides always in the end of vision, some essence of the sun and wind. That man knew the possible quest. There was nothing to prevent his going out; he could enter upon the land and be alive, could bear at once the great hot weight of its silence. In a sense the question of survival had never been more imminent, for no land is more the measure of human strength. But neither had wonder been more accessible to the mind nor destiny to the will.

"My grandmother had a reverence for the sun, a certain holy regard which now is all but gone out of mankind. There was a wariness in her, and an ancient awe. She was a Christian in her later years, but she had come a long way about, and she never forgot her birthright. As a child, she had been to the sun dances; she had taken part in that annual rite, and by it she had learned the restoration of her people in the presence of Tai-me. She was about seven years old when the last Kiowa sun dance was held in 1887 on the Washita River above Rainy Mountain Creek. The buffalo were gone. In order to consummate the ancient sacrifice—to impale the head of a buffalo bull upon the Tai-me tree—a delegation of old men journeyed into Texas, there to beg and barter for an animal from the Goodnight herd. She was ten when the Kiowas came together for the last time as a living sun dance culture. They could find no buffalo; they had to hang an old hide from the sacred tree. That summer was known to my grandmother as Ä'poto Etódă-de K'ádó, Sun Dance When the Forked Poles Were Left Standing, and it is entered in the Kiowa calendars as the figure of a tree standing outside the unfinished framework of a medicine lodge. Before the dance could begin, a company of armed soldiers rode out from Fort Sill under orders to disperse the tribe. Forbidden without cause the essential act of their faith, having seen the wild herds slaughtered and left to rot upon the ground, the Kiowas back away forever from the tree. That was July 20, 1890, at the great bend of the Washita. My grandmother was there. Without bitterness, and for as long as she lived, she bore a vision of deicide.

"Now that I can have her only in memory, I see my grandmother in the several postures that were peculiar to her: standing at the wood stove on a winter morning and turning meat in a great iron skillet; sitting at the south window, bent above her beadwork, and afterward, when her vision failed, looking down for a long time into the fold of her hands; going out upon a cane, very slowly as she did when the weight of age came upon her; praying. I remember her most often at prayer. She made long, rambling prayers out of suffering and hope, having seen many things. I was never sure that I had the right to hear, so exclusive were they of all mere custom and company. The last time I saw her, she prayed standing by the side of her bed at night, naked to the waist, the light of a kerosene lamp moving upon her dark skin. Her long black hair, always drawn and braided in the day, lay upon her shoulders and against her breasts like a shawl. I did not always understand her prayers; I believe they were made of an older language than that of ordinary speech. There was something inherently sad in the sound, some slight hesitation upon the syllables of sorrow. She began in a high and descending pitch, exhausting her breath to silence; then again and again—and always the same intensity of effort, of something that is, and is not, like urgency in the human voice. Transported so in the dim and dancing light among the shadows of her room, she seemed beyond the reach of time, as if age could not lay hold of her. But that was illusion; I think I knew then that I should not see her again.

"Houses are like sentinels in the plain, old keepers of the weather watch. There, in a very little while, wood takes on the appearance of great age. All colors soon wear away in the wind and rain, and then the wood is burned gray and the grain appears and the nails turn red with rust. The windowpanes are black and opaque; you imagine there is nothing within, and indeed there are many ghosts, bones given up to the land. They stand here and there against the sky, and you approach them for a longer time than you expect. They belong in the distance; it is their domain.

"My grandmother lived in a house near the place where Rainy Mountain Creek runs into the Washita River. Once there was a lot of sound in the house, a lot of coming and going, feasting and talk. The summers there were full of excitement and reunion. The Kiowas are a summer people; they abide the cold and keep to themselves, but when the season turns and the land becomes warm and vital they cannot hold still; an old love of going returns upon them. The old people have a fine sense of pageantry and a wonderful notion of decorum. The aged visitors who came to my grandmother's house when I was a child were men of immense character, full of wisdom and disdain. They dealt in a kind of infallible quiet and gave but one face away; it was enough. They were made of lean and leather, and they bore themselves upright. They wore great black hats and bright ample shirts that shook in the wind. They rubbed fat upon their hair and wound their braids with strips of colored cloth. Some of them painted their faces and carried the scars of old and cherished enmities. They were an old council of war lords, come to remind and be reminded of who they were. Their wives and daughters served them well. The women might indulge themselves; gossip was at once the mark and compensation of their servitude. They made loud and elaborate talk among themselves, full of jest and gesture, fright and false alarm. They went abroad in fringed and flowered shawls, bright beadwork and German silver. They were at home in the kitchen, and they prepared meals that were banquets.

"There were frequent prayer meetings, and great nocturnal feasts. When I was a child, I played with my cousins outside, where the lamplight fell upon the ground and the singing of the old people rose up around us and carried away into the darkness. There were a lot of good things to eat, a lot of laughter and surprise. And afterward, when the quiet returned, I lay down with my grandmother and could hear the frogs away by the river and feel the motion of the air.

"Now there is a funeral silence in the rooms, the endless wake of some final word. The walls have closed in upon my grandmother's house. When I returned to it in mourning, I saw for the first time in my life how small it was. It was late at night, and there was a white moon, nearly full. I sat for a long time on the stone steps by the kitchen door. From there I could see out across the land; I could see the long row of trees by the creek, the low light upon the rolling plains, and the stars of the Big Dipper. Once I looked at the moon and caught sight of a strange thing. A cricket had perched upon the handrail, only a few inches away from me. My line of vision was such that the creature filled the moon like a fossil. It had gone there, I thought, to live and die, for there of all places was its small definition made whole and eternal. A warm wind rose up and purled like the longing within me.

"The next morning I awoke at dawn and went out of my grandmother's house to the scaffold of the well that stands near the arbor. There was a stillness all around, and night lay still upon the pecan groves away by the river. The sun rose out of the ground, powerless for a long time to burn the air away, dim and nearly cold like the moon. The orange arc grew upon the land, curving out and downward to an impossible diameter. It must not go on, I thought, and I began to be afraid; then the air dissolved and the sun backed away. But for a moment I had seen to the center of the world's being. Every day in the plains proceeds from that strange eclipse.

"I went out on the dirt road to Rainy Mountain. It was already hot, and the grasshoppers began to fill the air. Still, it was early in the morning, and birds sang out of the shadows. The long yellow grass on the mountain shone in the bright light, and a scissortail hied above the land. There, where it ought to be, at the end of a long and legendary way, was my grandmother's grave. She had at last succeeded to that holy ground. Here and there on the dark stones were the dear ancestral names. Looking back once, I saw the mountain and came away."

1968

William Carlos Williams

The introduction to this section suggests the existence of a dialogue between the transcendentalist and the sacramentalist in American poetry. One of the historical manifestations of this dialogue was the appearance, during the 1910's and 1920's, of Imagist and Symbolist poems. In the three poems following, Williams shows his affinity to the Imagist, a sacramental, poetry. William Pratt, in his excellent anthology *The Imagist Poem,* defines Imagism this way:

> What is the image of the Imagist poem? Essentially, it is a moment of revealed truth, rather than a structure of consecutive events or thoughts. The plot or argument of older poetry is replaced by a single dominant image, or a quick succession of related images: its effect is meant to be instantaneous rather than cumulative. And most often, the image is drawn from common life—either natural, . . . or man-made. . . . Whatever its source, the test of the image was that it be rendered exactly, in as few words as possible and with maximum of visual content. Imagist poetry aimed at complete objectivity, leaving out all rational and moral content; but in the Imagist poem, the human content is implied rather than stated.

Flowers by the Sea

When over the flowery, sharp pasture's
edge, unseen, the salt ocean

lifts its form—chicory and daisies
tied, released, seem hardly flowers alone

but color and the movement—or the shape
perhaps—of restlessness, whereas

the sea is circled and sways
peacefully upon its plantlike stem

1935

Dawn

Ecstatic bird songs pound
the hollow vastness of the sky
with metallic clinkings—
beating color up into it
at a far edge,—beating it, beating it
with rising, triumphant ardor,—

stirring it into warmth,
quickening in it a spreading change,—
bursting wildly against it as
dividing the horizon, a heavy sun
lifts himself—is lifted—
bit by bit above the edge
of things,—runs free at last
out into the open—! lumbering
glorified in full release upward—
songs cease.

1917

The Trees

The trees—being trees
thrash and scream
guffaw and curse—
wholly abandoned
damning the race of men—

Christ, the bastards
haven't even sense enough
to stay out in the rain—

Wha ha ha ha

Wheeeeee
clacka tacka tacka
tacka tacka
wha ha ha ha ha
ha ha ha

knocking knees, buds
bursting from each pore
even the trunk's self
putting out leafheads—
Loose desire!
we naked cry to you—
"Do what you please."

You cannot!

—ghosts
sapped of strength

wailing at the gate
heartbreak at the bridgehead—
desire
dead in the heart

haw haw haw haw
—and memory broken

wheeeeee

There were never satyrs
never maenads
never eagle-headed gods—
These were men
from whose hands sprung
love
bursting the wood—

Trees their companions
—a cold wind winterlong
in the hollows of our flesh
icy with pleasure—

no part of us untouched

1934

Wallace Stevens

If William Carlos Williams shows his affinity to the Imagist, a sacramental, poetry, Wallace Stevens shows (with Robert Frost) an affinity to the Symbolist, a transcendentalist, poetry. In his excellent anthology *The Symbolist Poem,* Edward Engelberg defines a Symbolist poem as

> a fairly short lyric in which the poet assumes no prior agreement with the reader as to the manner in which he will use his language or as to how he will fashion his context to yield "meaning." . . . A Symbolist poem differs

from other poetry, such as narrative, satire, or epic, by using language to evoke and to suggest, rather than to describe or to declare.

"The Snow Man," for example, suggests how it might feel to experience "nothingness" and so suggests what nothingness might be. In characteristic Symbolist fashion it uses images, but only as a part of the poem, and it diffuses their concreteness in order to evoke an ideal reality.

Looking Across the Fields and Watching the Birds Fly

Among the more irritating minor ideas
Of Mr. Homburg during his visits home
To Concord, at the edge of things, was this:

To think away the grass, the trees, the clouds,
Not to transform them into other things,
Is only what the sun does every day,

Until we say to ourselves that there may be
A pensive nature, a mechanical
And slightly detestable *operandum,* free

From man's ghost, larger and yet a little like,
Without his literature and without his gods . . .
No doubt we live beyond ourselves in air,

In an element that does not do for us,
So well, that which we do for ourselves, too big,
A thing not planned for imagery or belief,

Not one of the masculine myths we used to make,
A transparency through which the swallow weaves,
Without any form or any sense of form,

What we know in what we see, what we feel in what
We hear, what we are, beyond mystic disputation,
In the tumult of integrations out of the sky,

And what we think, a breathing like the wind,
A moving part of a motion, a discovery
Part of a discovery, a change part of a change,

A sharing of color and being part of it.
The afternoon is visibly a source,
Too wide, too irised, to be more than calm,

Too much like thinking to be less than thought,
Obscurest parent, obscurest patriarch,
A daily majesty of meditation,

That comes and goes in silences of its own.
We think, then, as the sun shines or does not.
We think as wind skitters on a pond in a field

Or we put mantles on our words because
The same wind, rising and rising, makes a sound
Like the last muting of winter as it ends.

A new scholar replacing an older one reflects
A moment on this fantasia. He seeks
For a human that can be accounted for.

The spirit comes from the body of the world,
Or so Mr. Homburg thought: the body of a world
Whose blunt laws make an affectation of mind,

The mannerism of nature caught in a glass
And there become a spirit's mannerism,
A glass aswarm with things going as far as they can.

1954

The Snow Man

One must have a mind of winter
To regard the frost and the boughs
Of the pine-trees crusted with snow;

And have been cold a long time
To behold the junipers shagged with ice,
The spruces rough in the distant glitter

Of the January sun; and not to think
Of any misery in the sound of the wind,
In the sound of a few leaves,

Which is the sound of the land
Full of the same wind
That is blowing in the same bare place

For the listener, who listens in the snow,
And, nothing himself, beholds
Nothing that is not there and the nothing that is.

1923

Robert Frost

Desert Places

Snow falling and night falling fast, oh, fast
In a field I looked into going past,
And the ground almost covered smooth in snow,
But a few weeds and stubble showing last.

The woods around it have it—it is theirs.
All animals are smothered in their lairs.
I am too absent-spirited to count;
The loneliness includes me unawares.

And lonely as it is, that loneliness
Will be more lonely ere it will be less—
A blanker whiteness of benighted snow
With no expression, nothing to express.

They cannot scare me with their empty spaces
Between stars—on stars where no human race is.
I have it in me so much nearer home
To scare myself with my own desert places.

1939

Directive

Back out of all this now too much for us,
Back in a time made simple by the loss
Of detail, burned, dissolved, and broken off
Like graveyard marble sculpture in the weather,
There is a house that is no more a house
Upon a farm that is no more a farm
And in a town that is no more a town.
The road there, if you'll let a guide direct you
Who only has at heart your getting lost,
May seem as if it should have been a quarry—
Great monolithic knees the former town
Long since gave up pretense of keeping covered.
And there's a story in a book about it:
Besides the wear of iron wagon wheels
The ledges show lines ruled southeast-northwest,
The chisel work of an enormous Glacier
That braced his feet against the Arctic Pole.
You must not mind a certain coolness from him
Still said to haunt this side of Panther Mountain.
Nor need you mind the serial ordeal
Of being watched from forty cellar holes
As if by eye pairs out of forty firkins.
As for the woods' excitement over you
That sends light rustle rushes to their leaves,
Charge that to upstart inexperience.
Where were they all not twenty years ago?
They think too much of having shaded out
A few old pecker-fretted apple trees.
Make yourself up a cheering song of how
Someone's road home from work this once was,
Who may be just ahead of you on foot
Or creaking with a buggy load of grain.
The height of the adventure is the height
Of country where two village cultures faded
Into each other. Both of them are lost.
And if you're lost enough to find yourself
By now, pull in your ladder road behind you
And put a sign up CLOSED to all but me.
Then make yourself at home. The only field
Now left's no bigger than a harness gall.

First there's the children's house of make-believe,
Some shattered dishes underneath a pine,
The playthings in the playhouse of the children.
Weep for what little things could make them glad.
Then for the house that is no more a house,
But only a belilaced cellar hole,
Now slowly closing like a dent in dough.
This was no playhouse but a house in earnest.
Your destination and your destiny's
A brook that was the water of the house,
Cold as a spring as yet so near its source,
Too lofty and original to rage.
(We know the valley streams that when aroused
Will leave their tatters hung on barb and thorn.)
I have kept hidden in the instep arch
Of an old cedar at the waterside
A broken drinking goblet like the Grail
Under a spell so the wrong ones can't find it,
So can't get saved, as Saint Mark says they mustn't.
(I stole the goblet from the children's playhouse.)
Here are your waters and your watering place.
Drink and be whole again beyond confusion.

1949

West-Running Brook

"Fred, where is north?"
"North? North is there, my love.
The brook runs west."
"West-Running Brook then call it."
(West-Running Brook men call it to this day.)
"What does it think it's doing running west
When all the other country brooks flow east
To reach the ocean? It must be the brook
Can trust itself to go by contraries
The way I can with you—and you with me—
Because we're—we're—I don't know what we are.
What are we?"
"Young or new?"
"We must be something.

We've said we two. Let's change that to we three.
As you and I are married to each other,
We'll both be married to the brook. We'll build
Our bridge across it, and the bridge shall be
Our arm thrown over it asleep beside it.
Look, look, it's waving to us with a wave
To let us know it hears me."

"Why, my dear,
That wave's been standing off this jut of shore—"
(The black stream, catching on a sunken rock,
Flung backward on itself in one white wave,
And the white water rode the black forever,
Not gaining but not losing, like a bird
White feathers from the struggle of whose breast
Flecked the dark stream and flecked the darker pool
Below the point, and were at last driven wrinkled
In a white scarf against the far-shore alders.)
"That wave's been standing off this jut of shore
Ever since rivers, I was going to say,
Were made in heaven. It wasn't waved to us."

"It wasn't, yet it was. If not to you,
It was to me—in an annunciation."

"Oh, if you take it off to lady-land,
As't were the country of the Amazons
We men must see you to the confines of
And leave you there, ourselves forbid to enter—
It is your brook! I have no more to say."

"Yes, you have, too. Go on. You thought of something."

"Speaking of contraries, see how the brook
In that white wave runs counter to itself.
It is from that in water we were from
Long, long before we were from any creature.
Here we, in our impatience of the steps,
Get back to the beginning of beginnings,
The stream of everything that runs away.
Some say existence like a Pirouot
And Pirouette, forever in one place,
Stands still and dances, but it runs away;

It seriously, sadly, runs away
To fill the abyss's void with emptiness.
It flows beside us in this water brook,
But it flows over us. It flows between us
To separate us for a panic moment.
It flows between us, over us, and *with* us.
And it is time, strength, tone, light, life, and love—
And even substance lapsing unsubstantial;
The universal cataract of death
That spends to nothingness—and unresisted,
Save by some strange resistance in itself,
Not just a swerving, but a throwing back,
As if regret were in it and were sacred.
It has this throwing backward on itself
So that the fall of most of it is always
Raising a little, sending up a little.
Our life runs down in sending up the clock.
The brook runs down in sending up our life.
The sun runs down in sending up the brook.
And there is something sending up the sun.
It is this backward motion toward the source,
Against the stream, that most we see ourselves in,
The tribute of the current to the source.
It is from this in nature we are from.
It is most us."

"Today will be the day
You said so."

"No, today will be the day
You said the brook was called West-Running Brook."

"Today will be the day of what we both said."

1930

Robinson Jeffers

Apology for Bad Dreams

I

In the purple light, heavy with redwood, the slopes drop seaward,
Headlong convexities of forest, drawn in together to the steep ravine.
    Below, on the sea-cliff,
A lonely clearing; a little field of corn by the streamside; a roof under
    spared trees. Then the ocean
Like a great stone someone has cut to a sharp edge and polished to shin-
    ing. Beyond it, the fountain
And furnace of incredible light flowing up from the sunk sun. In the little
    clearing a woman
Is punishing a horse; she had tied the halter to a sapling at the edge of the
    wood, but when the great whip
Clung to the flanks the creature kicked so hard she feared he would snap
    the halter; she called from the house
The young man her son; who fetched a chain tie-rope, they working
    together
Noosed the small rusty links round the horse's tongue
And tied him by the swollen tongue to the tree.
Seen from this height they are shrunk to insect size,
Out of all human relation. You cannot distinguish
The blood dripping from where the chain is fastened,
The beast shuddering; but the thrust neck and the legs
Far apart. You can see the whip fall on the flanks . . .
The gesture of the arm. You cannot see the face of the woman.
The enormous light beats up out of the west across the cloud-bars of the
    trade-wind. The ocean
Darkens, the high clouds brighten, the hills darken together. Unbridled
    and unbelievable beauty
Covers the evening world . . . not covers, grows apparent out of it, as
    Venus down there grows out
From the lit sky. What said the prophet? "I create good: and I create evil:
    I am the Lord."

II

This coast crying out for tragedy like all beautiful places,
(The quiet ones ask for quieter suffering: but here the granite cliff the
    gaunt cypresses crown
Demands what victim? The dykes of red lava and black what Titan? The
    hills like pointed flames

Beyond Soberanes, the terrible peaks of the bare hills under the sun, what immolation?)
This coast crying out for tragedy like all beautiful places: and like the passionate spirit of humanity
Pain for its bread: God's, many victims', the painful deaths, the horrible transfigurements: I said in my heart,
"Better invent than suffer: imagine victims
Lest your own flesh be chosen the agonist, or you
Martyr some creature to the beauty of the place." And I said,
"Burn sacrifices once a year to magic
Horror away from the house, this little house here
You have built over the ocean with your own hands
Beside the standing boulders: for what are we,
The beast that walks upright, with speaking lips
And little hair, to think we should always be fed,
Sheltered, intact, and self-controlled? We sooner more liable
Than the other animals. Pain and terror, the insanities of desire; not accidents but essential,
And crowd up from the core." I imagined victims for those wolves, I made the phantoms to follow,
They have hunted the phantoms and missed the house. It is not good to forget over what gulfs the spirit
Of the beauty of humanity, the petal of a lost flower blown seaward by the night-wind, floats to its quietness.

III

Boulders blunted like an old bear's teeth break up from the headland; below them
All the soil is thick with shells, the tide-rock feasts of a dead people.
Here the granite flanks are scarred with ancient fire, the ghosts of the tribe
Crouch in the nights beside the ghost of a fire, they try to remember the sunlight,
Light has died out of their skies. These have paid something for the future
Luck of the country, while we living keep old griefs in memory: though God's
Envy is not a likely fountain of ruin, to forget evil calls down
Sudden reminders from the cloud; remembered deaths be our redeemers;
Imagined victims our salvation: white as the half moon at midnight
Someone flamelike passed me, saying, "I am Tamar Cauldwell, I have my desire,"
Then the voice of the sea returned, when she had gone by, the stars to their towers.

. . . Beautiful country burn again, Point Pinos down to the Sur Rivers
Burn as before with bitter wonders, land and ocean and the Carmel water.

IV

He brays humanity in a mortar to bring the savor
From the bruised root: a man having bad dreams, who invents victims, is only the ape of that God.
He washes it out with tears and many waters, calcines it with fire in the red crucible,
Deforms it, makes it horrible to itself: the spirit flies out and stands naked, he sees the spirit,
He takes it in the naked ecstasy; it breaks in his hand, the atom is broken, the power that massed it
Cries to the power that moves the stars, "I have come home to myself, behold me.
I bruised myself in the flint mortar and burnt me
In the red shell, I tortured myself, I flew forth,
Stood naked of myself and broke me in fragments,
And here am I moving the stars that are me."
I have seen these ways of God: I know of no reason
For fire and change and torture and the old returnings.
He being sufficient might be still. I think they admit no reason; they are the ways of my love.
Unmeasured power, incredible passion, enormous craft: no thought apparent but burns darkly
Smothered with its own smoke in the human brain-vault: no thought outside: a certain measure in phenomena:
The fountains of the boiling stars, the flowers on the foreland, the ever-returning roses of dawn.

1930

Theodore Roethke

Meditation at Oyster River

I

Over the low, barnacled, elephant-colored rocks,
Come the first tide-ripples, moving, almost without sound, toward me,
Running along the narrow furrows of the shore, the rows of dead clam
shells;
Then a runnel behind me, creeping closer,
Alive with tiny striped fish, and young crabs climbing in and out of the
water.

No sound from the bay. No violence.
Even the gulls quiet on the far rocks,
Silent, in the deepening light,
Their cat-mewing over,
Their child whimpering.

At last one long undulant ripple,
Blue-black from where I am sitting,
Makes almost a wave over a barrier of small stones,
Slapping lightly against a sunken log.
I dabble my toes in the brackish foam sliding forward,
Then retire to a rock higher up on the cliff-side.
The wind slackens, light as a moth fanning a stone:
A twilight wind, light as a child's breath
Turning not a leaf, not a ripple.
The dew revives on the beach-grass;
The salt-soaked wood of a fire crackles;
A fish raven turns on its perch (a dead tree in the rivermouth),
Its wings catching a last glint of the reflected sunlight.

II

The self persists like a dying star,
In sleep, afraid. Death's face rises afresh,
Among the shy beasts, the deer at the salt-lick,
The doe with its sloped shoulders loping across the highway,
The young snake, poised in green leaves, waiting for its fly,
The hummingbird, whirring from quince-blossom to morning-glory—
With these I would be.

And with water: the waves coming forward, without cessation,
The waves, altered by sand-bars, beds of kelp, miscellaneous driftwood,

Topped by cross-winds, tugged at by sinuous undercurrents
The tide rustling in, sliding between the ridges of stone,
The tongues of water, creeping in, quietly.

III

In this hour,
In this first heaven of knowing,
The flesh takes on the pure poise of the spirit,
Acquires, for a time, the sandpiper's insouciance,
The hummingbird's surety, the kingfisher's cunning—
I shift on my rock, and I think:
Of the first trembling of a Michigan brook in April,
Over a lip of stone, the tiny rivulet;
And what wrist-thick cascade tumbling from a cleft rock,
Its spray holding a double rain-bow in early morning,
Small enough to be taken in, embraced, by two arms,—
Or the Tittebawasee, in the time between winter and spring,
When the ice melts along the edges in early afternoon.
And the midchannel begins cracking and heaving from the pressure beneath,
The ice piling high against the iron-bound spiles,
Gleaming, freezing hard again, creaking at midnight—
And I long for the blast of dynamite,
The sudden sucking roar as the culvert loosens its debris of branches and sticks,
Welter of tin cans, pails, old bird nests, a child's shoe riding a log,
As the piled ice breaks away from the battered spiles,
And the whole river begins to move forward, its bridges shaking.

IV

Now, in this waning of light,
I rock with the motion of morning;
In the cradle of all that is,
I'm lulled into half-sleep
By the lapping of water,
Cries of the sandpiper.
Water's my will, and my way,
And the spirit runs, intermittently,
In and out of the small waves,
Runs with the intrepid shorebirds—
How graceful the small before danger!

In the first of the moon,
All's a scattering,
A shining.

1960

Robert Hayden

A Road in Kentucky

And when that ballad lady went
    to ease the lover whose life she broke,
oh surely this is the road she took,
    road all hackled through barberry fire,
through cedar and alder and sumac and thorn.

Red clay stained her flounces
    and stones cut her shoes
and the road twisted on to his loveless house
    and his cornfield dying
in the scarecrow's arms.

And when she had left her lover lying
    so stark and so stark, with the Star-of-Hope
drawn over his eyes, oh this is the road
    that lady walked in the cawing light,
so dark and so dark in the briary light.

1966

The Ballad of Nat Turner

Then fled, O brethren, the wicked juba
    and wandered wandered far
from curfew joys in the Dismal's night.
    Fool of St. Elmo's fire

In scary night I wandered, praying,
    Lord God my harshener,

speak to me now or let me die;
    speak, Lord, to this mourner.

And came at length to livid trees
    where Ibo warriors
hung shadowless, turning in wind
    that moaned like Africa,

Their belltongue bodies dead, their eyes
    alive with the anger deep
in my own heart. Is this the sign,
    the sign forepromised me?

The spirits vanished. Afraid and lonely
    I wandered on in blackness.
Speak to me now or let me die.
    Die, whispered the blackness.

And wild things gasped and scuffled in
    the night; seething shapes
of evil frolicked upon the air.
    I reeled with fear, I prayed.

Sudden brightness clove the preying
    darkness, brightness that was
itself a golden darkness, brightness
    so bright that it was darkness.

And there were angels, their faces hidden
    from me, angels at war
with one another, angels in dazzling
    combat. And oh the splendor,

The fearful splendor of that warring.
    Hide me, I cried to rock and bramble.
Hide me, the rock, the bramble cried. . . .
    How tell you of that holy battle?

The shock of wing on wing and sword
    on sword was the tumult of
a taken city burning. I cannot
    say how long they strove,

For the wheel in a turning wheel which is time
in eternity had ceased
its whirling, and owl and moccasin,
panther and nameless beast

And I were held like creatures fixed
in flaming, in fiery amber.
But I saw I saw oh many of
those mighty beings waver,

Waver and fall, go streaking down
into swamp water, and the water
hissed and steamed and bubbled and locked
shuddering shuddering over

The fallen and soon was motionless.
Then that massive light
began a-folding slowly in
upon itself, and I

Beheld the conqueror faces and, lo,
they were like mine, I saw
they were like mine and in joy and terror
wept, praising praising Jehovah.

Oh praised my honer, harshener
till a sleep came over me,
a sleep heavy as death. And when
I awoke at last free

And purified, I rose and prayed
and returned after a time
to the blazing fields, to the humbleness.
And bided my time.

1966

Michael S. Harper

Oak

She lifts the two boys on
the overturned rowboat, a galley
plank as a slide;
gummy paint on the underside
sticks to their shoes;
as they walk the eggshell
white blackens the swaying birch boat.

She lifts cracked plaster,
glass, rock from the foundation,
hunting for nails, her pigtailed
sway the break of oars
beating the lake overturned;
she works for new grass
that springs up, the three oaks
burned to death in winter,
mistook victims of our rubbish pile.
A hundred-gallon garbage can
freezes in its burned tracks;
a wire cylinder holds our burned
paper; near the chain fence
we chew the burned oak
with a two-man saw.

In the attic is an old bed;
I hear its thumping as I watch her
leafing seeds to the hoed land
in foot-deep holes in our thawing ground,
trees that must grow in gravel.

We begin to live in the old way:
fertile eggs in a poaching tin,
cooked meal, kneaded bread rising
on the open-air rack,
stumps at our garden table.

As the spring thaws she plants,
uncovers, hoes, digs for the rich
earth; in gravel we take up the saw;
in the old way we cut dead oak.

1972

Dead Oaks

I eat on all fours
over the dank hole
where my 200-year-
old oak once was
now in a pile at
the cord-wound corral.
I think of the smell
of this earth,
earth that poisons
this brimmed cemetery,
burial ground
long since forgotten.

On a farm in the eastern
half of this state,
an old woman sat
on her porch whistling
an Indian tune
though whittling
in Norwegian.

I listen to her son
sing of the death of his
brother in war,
his brothers dying
in the old ancestral
earth of the Far East
or in African mines
plaqued in its gold
to our commercial hearth.

I chop at the tree
to make kindling
as the fire arches
out of sight, food
in this old place, this hole
in the cosmic earth.

Pale in his death heat,
the son of the mother

on the porch, having
heard of her death,
reading of his brother's
death, reading of the death
of his brothers:
Indian, Norwegian,
sits on this old stump
and whittles, whistling:
congress of the last
poetic word, this damp
ceremonial hill, this oak.

1972

A. R. Ammons

Conserving the Magnitude of Uselessness

Spits of glitter in lowgrade ore,
precious stones too poorly surrounded for harvest,
to all things not worth the work
of having,

brush oak on a sharp slope, for example,
the balk tonnage of woods-lodged boulders,
the irreparable desert,
drowned river mouths, lost shores where

the winged and light-footed go,
take creosote bush that possesses
ground nothing else will have,
to all things and for all things

crusty or billowy with indifference,
for example, incalculable, irremovable water
or fluvio-glacial deposits
larch or dwarf aspen in the least breeze sometimes shiver in—

suddenly the salvation of waste betides,
the peerlessly unsettled seas that shape the continents,
take the gales wasting and in waste over
Antarctica and the sundry high shoals of ice,

for the inexcusable (the worthless abundant) the
merely tiresome, the obviously unimprovable,
to these and for these and for their undiminishment
the poets will yelp and hoot forever

probably,
rank as weeds themselves and just as abandoned:
nothing useful is of lasting value:
dry wind only is still talking among the oldest stones.

1970

Possibility Along a Line of Difference

At the crustal
discontinuity
I went down and
walked
on the gravel bottom,
head below gully rims

tufted with
clumpgrass and
through-free roots:
prairie flatness crazed
by that difference,
I grew

excited with
the stream's image left
in dust
and farther down
in confined rambling
I

found a puddle
green, iridescent

with a visitation of daub-singing wasps,
sat down and watched
tilted shadow untilting
fill the trough,

imagined cloudbursts
and
scattered pillars of rain,
buffalo at night routed
by lightning,
leaping,

falling back,
wobble-kneed calves
tumbling, gully-caught;
coyote, crisp-footed
on the gravel,
loping up the difference.

1970

Robert Pack

The Hummingbird

hums with her wings, I am
in flight again. Surely
I can master the air suspended
at a rose to stay
while the sun pivots around me
another hour, another day.
I have entered her heart within
a fraction of an inch,
within her nest no larger
than a walnut shell, laced
with lichen and with spider webs,
while wind bulges,
leaves blare and the petaled sun
pivots around me. My wings,

you cannot see them move, I am here to stay
as the rose lifts up
forever in the sun. I pivot
to my nest, warming
two unbelievably tiny eggs,
for that is the way,
it must be repeated at another hour
on another day.
Having entered her heart, the heart of the rose,
I whirl with the sun,
I enter humming two tiny eggs
repeating the way
as the rose lifts mastering the air,
suspended in the sun
in flight unbelievably with wings—
a hummingbird
who hums the ruby color at his throat
sipping the rose
as I hum sipping at the sun.
I enter his heart, her heart,
their nest, their eggs, I am in flight
until the petals
unbelievably burn away
in the humming air
at another hour on another day.

1972

Make Way

The first phoebe startles the dawn.
Dawn startles my house
dreaming the way I am awake.
The apple trees shake themselves.
Foxes tune their ears.
I make way for the yellow push of light
and the streak of the thrush.
A slow wind enters.
Loosened pines attend.
I am new here—
what can I say to please them?

An insect admires its gauzy wings.
My pride measures the stone wall
at the slope edge of the field.
The mountains have not changed,
have not changed.
The night resides there still,
and the night before.
The grass does not hurry:
everything has taken place.
What am I needed for?
My hands remember the slick green
of the apple skin,
and the fuzz on the ears of my dog.
My feet remember their way,
both up and down.
It is still dawn, a chill tells me
I am awakening, make way.

My house hushes over my children,
trying to breathe,
as it used to, long ago.

1973

Denise Levertov

A Tree Telling of Orpheus

White dawn. Stillness.   When the rippling began
    I took it for sea-wind, coming to our valley with rumors
    of salt, of treeless horizons. But the white fog
didn't stir; the leaves of my brothers remained outstretched,
unmoving.
            Yet the rippling drew nearer—and then
my own outermost branches began to tingle, almost as if
fire had been lit below them, too close, and their twig-tips
were drying and curling.
                        Yet I was not afraid, only
                        deeply alert.

I was the first to see him, for I grew
        out on the pasture slope, beyond the forest.
He was a man, it seemed: the two
moving stems, the short trunk, the two
arm-branches, flexible, each with five leafless
                                        twigs at their ends,
and the head that's crowned by brown or gold grass,
bearing a face not like the beaked face of a bird,
        more like a flower's.
                                He carried a burden made of
some cut branch bent while it was green,
strands of a vine tight-stretched across it. From this,
when he touched it, and from his voice
which unlike the wind's voice had no need of our
leaves and branches to complete its sound,
                                        came the ripple.
But it was now no longer a ripple (he had come near and
stopped in my first shadow) it was a wave that bathed me
            as if rain
                    rose from below and around me
            instead of falling.
And what I felt was no longer a dry tingling:
        I seemed to be singing as he sang, I seemed to know
        what the lark knows; all my sap
            was mounting towards the sun that by now
                had risen, the midst was rising, the grass
was drying, yet my roots felt music moisten them
deep under earth.

            He came still closer, leaned on my trunk:
            the bark thrilled like a leaf still-folded.
Music! There was no twig of me not
                                trembling with joy and fear.

Then as he sang
it was no longer sounds only that made the music:
he spoke, and as no tree listens I listened, and language
                came into my roots
                                out of the earth,
                    into my bark
                                out of the air,
                    into the pores of my greenest shoots,
                                gently as dew

and there was no word he sang but I knew its meaning.
He told of journeys,
of where sun and moon go while we stand in dark,
of an earth-journey he dreamed he would take some day
deeper than roots . . .
He told of the dreams of man, wars, passions, griefs,
and I, a tree, understood words—ah, it seemed
my thick bark would split like a sapling's that
grew too fast in the spring
when a late frost wounds it.

Fire he sang,
that trees fear, and I, a tree, rejoiced in its flames.
New buds broke forth from me though it was full summer.
As though his lyre (now I knew its name)
were both frost and fire, its chords flamed
up to the crown of me.
I was seed again.
I was fern in the swamp.
I was coal.

And at the heart of my wood
(so close I was to becoming man or a god)
there was a kind of silence, a kind of sickness,
something akin to what men call boredom,
something
(the poem descended a scale, a stream over stones)
that gives to a candle a coldness
in the midst of its burning, he said.

It was then,
when in the blaze of his power that
reached me and changed me
I thought I should fall my length,
that the singer began
to leave me. Slowly
moved from my noon shadow
to open light,
words leaping and dancing over his shoulders
back to me
rivery sweep of lyre-tones becoming
slowly again
ripple.

And I
in terror
but not in doubt of
what I must do
in anguish, in haste,
wrenched from the earth root after root,
the soil heaving and cracking, the moss tearing asunder—
and behind me the others: my brothers
forgotten since dawn. In the forest
they too had heard,
and were pulling their roots in pain
out of a thousand years' layers of dead leaves,
rolling the rocks away,
breaking themselves
out of
their depths.
You would have thought we would lose the sound of the lyre,
of the singing
so dreadful the storm-sounds were, where there was no storm,
no wind but the rush of our
branches moving, our trunks breasting the air.
But the music!
The music reached us.

Clumsily,
stumbling over our own roots,
rustling our leaves
in answer,
we moved, we followed.

All day we followed, up hill and down.
We learned to dance,
for he would stop, where the ground was flat,
and words he said
taught us to leap and to wind in and out
around one another in figures the lyre's measure designed.
The singer
laughed till he wept to see us, he was so glad.
At sunset
we came to this place I stand in, this knoll
with its ancient grove that was bare grass then.
In the last light of that day his song became
farewell.

He stilled our longing.
He sang our sun-dried roots back into earth,
watered them: all-night rain of music so quiet
we could almost
not hear it in the
moonless dark.
By dawn he was gone.
We have stood here since,
in our new life.
We have waited.
He does not return.
It is said he made his earth-journey, and lost
what he sought.
It is said they felled him
and cut up his limbs for firewood.
And it is said
his head still sang and was swept out to sea singing.
Perhaps he will not return.
But what we have lived
comes back to us.
We see more.
We feel, as our rings increase,
something that lifts our branches, that stretches our furthest
leaf-tips
further.
The wind, the birds,
do not sound poorer but clearer,
recalling our agony, and the way we danced.
The music!

1966

Brother Antoninus

Advent

Fertile and rank and rich the coastal rains
Walked on the stiffened weeds and made them bend;
And stunned November chokes the cottonwood creeks
For Autumn's end.

And the hour of Advent draws on the small eyed seeds
That spilled in the pentacostal drought from the fallen cup:
Swept in the riddled summer-shrunken earth;
Now the eyes look up.

Faintly they glint, they glimmer; they try to see;
They pick at the crust; they touch at the wasted rind.
Winter will pinch them back but now they know,
And will not stay blind.

And all Creation will gather its glory up
Out of the clouded winter-frigid womb;
And the sudden Eye will swell with the gift of sight,
And split the tomb.

?1949

The South Coast

Salt creek mouths unflushed by the sea
And the long day shuts down.
Whose hand stacks rock, cairn-posted,
Churched to the folded sole of this hill,
And Whose mind conceives? Three herons
Gig their necks in the tule brake
And the prying mudhen plies.
Long down, far south to Sur, the wind lags,
Slosh-washes his slow heel,
Lays off our coast, rump of the domed
Mountain, woman-backed, bedded
Under his lea. Salt grasses here,
Fringes, twigging the crevice slips,
And the gagging cypress

Wracked away from the sea.
God *makes*. On earth, in us, most instantly,
On the very now,
His own means conceives.
How many strengths break out unchoked
Where He, Whom all declares,
Delights to make be!

1959

Appendix

William Bartram

Introduction to *Travels*

THE ATTENTION of a traveller, should be particularly turned, in the first place, to the various works of Nature, to mark the distinctions of the climates he may explore, and to offer such useful observations on the different productions as may occur. Men and manners undoubtedly hold the first rank—whatever may contribute to our existence is also of equal importance, whether it be found in the animal or vegetable kingdoms; neither are the various articles, which tend to promote the happiness and convenience of mankind, to be disregarded. How far the writer of the following sheets has succeeded in furnishing information on these subjects, the reader will be capable of determining. From the advantages the journalist enjoyed under his father JOHN BARTRAM, botanist to the king of Great-Britain, and fellow of the Royal Society, it is hoped that his labours will present new as well as useful information to the botanist and zoologist.

This world, as a glorious apartment of the boundless palace of the sovereign Creator, is furnished with an infinite variety of animated scenes, inexpressibly beautiful and pleasing, equally free to the inspection and enjoyment of all his creatures.

Perhaps there is not any part of creation, within the reach of our observations, which exhibits a more glorious display of the Almighty hand, than the vegetable world. Such a variety of pleasing scenes, ever changing, throughout the seasons, arising from various causes and assigned each to the purpose and use determined.

It is difficult to pronounce which division of the earth, within the polar circles, produces the greatest variety. The tropical division certainly affords those which principally contribute to the more luxurious scenes of splendor. . . .

But the temperate zone (including by far the greater portion of the earth, and a climate the most favourable to the increase and support of animal life, as well as for the exercise and activity of the human faculties) exhibits scenes of infinitely greater variety, magnificence and consequence, with respect to human economy, in regard to the various uses of vegetables.

For instance, Triticum Cereale, which affords us bread, and is termed, by way of eminence, the staff of life, the most pleasant and nourishing food—to all terrestrial animals. Vitis vinifera, whose exhilarating juice is said to cheer the hearts of gods and men. Oryza, Zea, Pyrus, Pyrus malus, Prunus, Pr. cerasus, Ficus, Nectarin, Apricot, Cydonia. Next follow the illustrious families of forest-trees, as the Magnolia grandiflora and Quercus sempervirens, which form the venerated groves and solemn shades, on the Mississipi, Alatamaha and Florida, the magnificent Cupressus disticha of Carolina and Florida, the beautiful Water Oak, whose vast hemispheric head, presents the likeness of a distant grove in the fields and savannas of Carolina. The gigantic Black Oak, Platanus occidentalis, Liquid-amber styraciflua, Liriodendron tulipifera, Fagus castania, Fagus sylvatica, Juglans nigra, Juglans cinerea, Jug. pecan, Ulmus, Acher sacharinum, of Virginia and Pennsylvania; Pinus phoenix, Pinus toeda, Magnolia acuminata, Nyssa aquatica, Populus heterophylla and the floriferous Gordonia lasianthus, of Carolina and Florida; the exalted Pinus strobus, Pin. balsamica, Pin. abies, Pin. Canadensis, Pin. larix, Fraxinus excelsior, Robinia pseudacacia, Guilandina dioica, Æsculus Virginica, Magnolia acuminata, of Virginia, Maryland, Pennsylvania, New-Jersey, New-York, New-England, Ohio and the regions of Erie and the Illinois; and the aromatic and floriferous shrubs, as Azalea coccinia, Azalea rosea, Rosa, Rhododendron, Kalmia, Syringa, Gardinia, Calycanthus, Daphne, Franklinia, Styrax and others equally celebrated.

In every order of nature, we perceive a variety of qualities distributed amongst individuals, designed for different purposes and uses, yet it appears evident, that the great Author has impartially distributed his favours to his creatures, so that the attributes of each one seem to be of sufficient importance to manifest the divine and inimitable workmanship. The pompous Palms of Florida, and glorious Magnolia, strike us with the sense of dignity and magnificence; the expansive umbrageous Live-Oak with awful veneration, the Carica papaya, supercilious with all the harmony of beauty and gracefulness; the Lillium superbum represents pride and vanity; Kalmia latifolia and Azalea coccinea, exhibit a perfect show of mirth and gaiety; the Illisium Floridanum, Crinum Floridanum, Convalaria majalis of the Cherokees, and Calycanthus floridus, charm with their beauty and fragrance. Yet they are not to be compared for usefulness with the nutritious Triticum, Zea, Oryza, Solanum tuberosa, Musa, Convolvulous, Batata, Rapa, Orchis, Vitis vinifera, Pyrus, Olea; for clothing, Linum, Canabis, Gossypium, Morus; for medical virtues, Hyssopus, Thymus, Anthemis nobilis, Papaver somniferum, Quinqina, Rheum rhabarbarum, Pisum, &c. though none of these most useful tribes are conspicuous for stateliness, figure or splendor, yet their valuable qualities and virtues, excite love, gratitude and adoration to the great Creator, who was pleased to endow them with such eminent qualities, and reveal them to us for our sustenance, amusement and delight.

But there remain of the vegetable world, several tribes that are distinguished by very remarkable properties, which excite our admiration, some for the elegance, singularity and splendor of their vestment, as the Tulipa, Fritillaria, Colchicum, Primula, Lillium superbum, Kalmia, &c. Others astonish us by their figure and disposal of their vestiture, as if designed only to embellish and please the observer, as in the Nepenthes distillatoria, Ophrys insectoria, Cypripedium calceolus, Hydrangia quercifolia, Bartramia bracteata, Viburnum Canadense, Bartsea, &c.

Observe these green meadows how they are decorated; they seem enamelled with the beds of flowers. The blushing Chironia and Rhexia, the spiral Ophrys with immaculate white flowers, the Limodorum, Arethusa pulcherima, Sarracenia purpurea, Sarracenia galeata, Sarracenia lacunosa, Sarracenia flava. Shall we analyze these beautiful plants, since they seem cheerfully to invite us? How greatly the flowers of the yellow Sarracenia represent a silken canopy, the yellow pendant petals are the curtains, and the hollow leaves are not unlike the cornucopia or Amaltheas horn, what a quantity of water a leaf is capable of containing, about a pint! taste of it—how cool and animating—limpid as the morning dew: nature seems to have furnished them with this cordated appendage or lid, which turns over, to prevent a too sudden, and copious supply of water from heavy showers of rain, which would bend down the leaves, never to rise again; because their straight parallel nerves, which extend and support them, are so rigid and fragile, the leaf would inevitably break when bent down to a right angle; therefore I suppose these waters which contribute to their supplies, are the rebounding drops or horizontal streams wafted by the winds, which adventitiously find their way into them, when a blast of wind shifts the lid; see these short stiff hairs, they all point downwards, which direct the condensed vapours down into the funiculum; these stiff hairs also prevent the varieties of insects, which are caught, from returning, being invited down to sip the mellifluous exuvia, from the interior surface of the tube, where they inevitably perish; what quantities there are of them! These latent waters undoubtedly contribute to the support and refreshment of the plant; perhaps designed as a reservoir in case of long continued droughts, or other casualties, since these plants naturally dwell in low savannas liable to overflows, from rain water: for although I am not of the opinion that vegetables receive their nourishment, only through the ascending part of the plant, as the stem, branches, leaves, &c. and that their descending part, as the root and fibres, only serve to hold and retain them in their places, yet I believe they imbibe rain and dews through their leaves, stems and branches, by extremely minute pores, which open on both surfaces of the leaves and on the branches, which may communicate to little auxiliary ducts or vessels; or, perhaps the cool dews and showers, by constricting these pores, and thereby preventing a too free perspiration, may recover and again invigorate the languid nerves, of those which seem to suffer for want of water, in great heats and droughts; but whether the insects caught in their leaves, and which dissolve and mix with the fluid, serve for aliment or support to these kind of plants, is doubtful. All the Sarracenia are insect catchers, and so is the Drossea rotundiflolia.

But admirable are the properties of the extraordinary Dionea muscipula! A great extent on each side of that serpentine rivulet, is occupied by those sportive vegetables—let us advance to the spot in which nature has seated them. Astonishing production! see the incarnate lobes expanding, how gay and ludicrous they appear! ready on the spring to intrap incautious deluded insects, what artifice! there behold one of the leaves just closed upon a struggling fly, another has got a worm, its hold is sure, its prey can never escape—carnivorous vegetable! Can we after viewing this object, hesitate a moment to confess, that vegetable beings are endued with some sensible faculties or attributes, similar to those that dignify animal nature; they are organical, living and self-moving bodies, for we see here, in this plant, motion and volition.

What power or faculty is it, that directs the cirri of the Cucurbita, Momordica, Vitis and other climbers, towards the twigs of shrubs, trees and other friendly support? we see them invariably leaning, extending and like the fingers of the human hand, reaching to catch hold of what is nearest, just as if they had eyes to see with, and when their hold is fixed, to coil the tendril in a spiral form, by which artifice it becomes more elastic and effectual, than if it had remained in a direct line, for every revolution of the coil adds a portion of strength, and thus collected, they are enabled to dilate and contract as occasion or necessity require, and thus by yielding to, and humouring the motion of the limbs and twigs, or other support on which they depend, are not so liable to be torn off by sudden blasts of wind or other assaults; is it sense or instinct that influences their actions? it must be some impulse; or does the hand of the Almighty act and perform this work in our sight?

The vital principle or efficient cause of motion and action, in the animal and vegetable system, perhaps, may be more familiar than we generally apprehend. Where is the essential difference between the seed of peas, peaches and other tribes of plants and trees, and that of oviparous animals? as the eggs of birds, snakes or butterflies, spawn of fish, &c. Let us begin at the source of terrestrial existence. Are not the seed of vegetables, and the eggs of oviparous animals fecundated, or influenced with the vivific principle of life, through the approximation and intimacy of the sexes, and immediately after the eggs and seeds are hatched, the young larva and infant plant, by heat and moisture, rise into existence, increase, and in due time arrive to a state of perfect maturity. The physiologists agree in opinion, that the work of generation in viviparous animals, is exactly similar, only more secret and enveloped. The mode of operation that nature pursues in the production of vegetables, and oviparous animals is infinitely more uniform and manifest, than that which is or can be discovered to take place in viviparous animals.

The most apparent difference between animals and vegetables is, that animals have the powers of sound, and are locomotive, whereas vegetables are not able to shift themselves from the places where nature has planted them: yet vegetables have the power of moving and exercising their members, and have the means of transplanting or colonising their tribes almost over the surface of the whole earth, some seeds, for instance, grapes, nuts, smilax, peas, and others, whose pulp or kernel is food for animals, such seed will remain several days without injuring in stomachs of pigeons and other birds of passage; by this means such sorts are distributed from place to place, even across seas; indeed some seeds require this preparation, by the digestive heat of the stomach of animals, to dissolve and detach the oily, viscid pulp, and to soften the hard shells of others. Small seeds are sometimes furnished with rays of hair or down, and others with thin light membranes attached to them, which serve the purpose of wings, on which they mount upward, leaving the earth, float in the air, and are carried away by the swift winds to very remote regions before they settle on the earth; some are furnished with hooks, which catch hold of the wool and hair of animals passing by them, are by that means spread abroad; other seeds ripen in pericarps, which open with elastic force, and shoot their seed to a very great distance round about; some other seeds, as of the Mosses and Fungi, are so very minute as to be invisible, light as atoms, and these mixing with the air, are wafted all over the world.

The animal creation also, excites our admiration, and equally manifests the almighty power, wisdom and beneficence of the Supreme Creator and Sovereign Lord of the universe; some in their vast size and strength, as the mammoth, the elephant, the whale, the lion and alligator; others in agility; others in their beauty and elegance of colour, plumage and rapidity of flight, have the faculty of moving and living in the air; others for their immediate and indispensable use and convenience to man, in furnishing means for our clothing and sustenance, and administering to our help in the toils and labours through life; how wonderful is the mechanism of these finely formed, self-moving beings, how complicated their system, yet what unerring uniformity prevails through every tribe and particular species! the effect we see and contemplate, the cause is invisible, incomprehensible, how can it be otherwise? when we cannot see the end or origin of a nerve or vein, while the divisibility of matter or fluid, is infinite. We admire the mechanism of a watch, and the fabric of a piece of brocade, as being the production of art; these merit our admiration, and must excite our esteem for the ingenious artist or modifier, but nature is the work of God omnipotent: and an elephant, even this world is comparatively but a very minute part of his works. If then the visible, the mechanical part of the animal creation, the mere material part is so admirably beautiful, harmonious and incomprehensible, what must be the intellectual system? that inexpressibly more essential principle, which secretly operates within? that which animates the inimitable machines, which gives them motion, impowers them to act, speak and perform, this must be divine and immortal?

I am sensible that the general opinion of philosophers, has distinguished the moral system of the brute creature from that of mankind, by an epithet which implies a mere mechanical impulse, which leads and impels them to necessary actions, without any premeditated design or contrivance, this we term instinct, which faculty we suppose to be inferior to reason in man.

The parental, and filial affections seem to be as ardent, their sensibility and attachment, as active and faithful, as those observed to be in human nature.

When travelling on the East coast of the isthmus of Florida, ascending the South Musquitoe river, in a canoe, we observed numbers of deer and bears, near the banks, and on the islands of the river, the bear were feeding on the fruit of the dwarf creeping Chamerops, (this fruit is of the form and size of dates, and is delicious and nourishing food:) we saw eleven bears in the course of the day, they seemed no way surprized or affrighted at the sight of us; in the evening my hunter, who was an excellent marksman, said that he would shoot one of them, for the sake of the skin and oil, for we had plenty and variety of provisions in our bark. We accordingly, on sight of two of them, planned our approaches, as artfully as possible, by crossing over to the opposite shore, in order to get under cover of a small island, this we cautiously coasted round, to a point, which we apprehended would take us within shot of the bear, but here finding ourselves at too great a distance from them, and discovering that we must openly show ourselves, we had no other alternative to effect our purpose, but making oblique approaches; we gained gradually on our prey by this artifice, without their noticing us, finding ourselves near enough, the hunter fired, and laid the largest dead on the spot, where she stood, when presently the other, not seeming the least moved, at the report of our piece, approached the dead body, smelled, and pawed it, and appearing in agony, fell to weeping and looking upwards, then towards us, and cried out like a child. Whilst our boat approached very near, the hunter was loading his rifle in order to shoot the survivor, which was a young cub, and the slain supposed to be the dam; the continual cries of this afflicted child, bereft of its parent, affected me very sensibly, I was moved with compassion, and charging myself as if accessary to what now appeared to be a cruel murder, and endeavoured to prevail on the hunter to save its life, but to no effect! for by habit he had become insensible to compassion towards the brute creation, being now within a few yards of the harmless devoted victim, he fired, and laid it dead, upon the body of the dam.

If we bestow but a very little attention to the economy of the animal creation, we shall find manifest examples of premeditation, perseverance, resolution, and consummate artifice, in order to effect their purpose. The next morning, after the slaughter of the bears whilst my companions were striking our tent and preparing to re-embark, I resolved to make a little botanical excursion alone; crossing over a narrow isthmus of sand hills which separated the river from the ocean, I passed over a pretty high hill, its summit crested with a few Palm trees, surrounded with an Orange grove; this hill, whose base was washed on one side, by the floods of the Musquitoe river, and the other side by the billows of the ocean, was about one hundred yards diameter, and seemed to be an entire heap of sea hills. I continued along the beach, a quarter of a mile, and came up to a forest of the Agave vivipara (though composed of herbaceous plants, I term it a forest, because their scapes or flower-stems arose erect near

30 feet high) their tops regularly branching in the form of a pyramidal tree, and these plants growing near to each other, occupied a space of ground of several acres: when their seed is ripe they vegetate, and grow on the branches, until the scape dries when the young plants fall to the ground, take root, and fix themselves in the sand: the plant grows to a prodigious size before the scape shoots up from its centre. Having contemplated this admirable grove, I proceeded towards the shrubberies on the banks of the river, and though it was now late in December, the aromatic groves appeared in full bloom. The broad leaved sweet Myrtus, Erythrina corrallodendrum, Cactus cochenellifer, Cacalia suffruticosa, and particularly, Rhizophora conjugata, which stood close to, and in the salt water of the river, were in full bloom, with beautiful white sweet scented flowers, which attracted to them, two or three species of very beautiful butterflies, one of which was black, the upper pair of its wings very long and narrow, marked with transverse stripes of pale yellow, with some spots of a crimson colour near the body. Another species remarkable for splendor, was of a larger size, the wings were undulated and obtusely crenated round their ends, the nether pair terminating near the body, with a long narrow forked tail; the ground light yellow, striped oblique-transversely, with stripes of pale celestial blue, the ends of them adorned with little eyes encircled with the finest blue and crimson, which represented a very brilliant rosary. But those which were the most numerous were as white as snow, their wings large, their ends lightly crenated and ciliated, forming a fringed border, faintly marked with little black crescents, their points downward, with a cluster of little brilliant orbs of blue and crimson, on the nether wings near the body; the numbers were incredible, and there seemed to be scarcely a flower for each fly, multitudinous as they were, besides clouds of them hovering over the mellifluous groves. Besides these papilios[?], a variety of other insects come in for share, particularly several species of bees.

As I was gathering specimens of flowers from the shrubs, I was greatly surprised at the sudden appearance of a remarkable large spider on a leaf, of the genus Araneus saliens, at sight of me he boldly faced about, and raised himself up as if ready to spring upon me; his body was about the size of a pigeons egg, of a buff colour, which with his legs were covered with short silky hair, on the top of the abdomen was a round red spot or ocellus encircled with black; after I had recovered from the surprise, and observing the wary hunter had retired under cover, I drew near again, and presently discovered that I had surprised him on predatory attempts against the insect tribes, I was therefore determined to watch his proceedings, I soon noticed that the object of his wishes was a large fat bomble bee (apis bombylicus) that was visiting the flowers, and piercing their nectariferous tubes; this cunning intrepid hunter (conducted his subtil approaches, with the circumspection and perseverance of a Siminole, when hunting a deer) advancing with slow steps obliquely, or under cover of dense foliage, and behind the limbs, and when the bee was engaged in probing a flower he would leap nearer, and then instantly retire out of sight, under a leaf or behind a branch, at the same time keeping a sharp eye upon me; when he had now got within two feet of his prey, and the bee was intent on sipping the delicious nectar from a flower, with his back next the spider, he instantly sprang upon him, and grasped him over the back and shoulder, when for some moments they both disappeared, I expected the bee had carried of his enemy, but to my surprise they both together rebounded back again, suspended at the extremity of a strong elastic thread or web, which the spider had artfully let fall, or fixed on the twig, the instant he leaped from it; the rapidity of the bee's wings, endeavouring to extricate himself, made them both together appear as a moving vapor, until the bee became fatigued by whirling round, first one way and then back again; at length, in about a quarter of an hour, the bee quite exhausted by his struggles, and the repeated wounds of the butcher, became motionless, and quickly expired in the arms of the devouring spider, who, ascending the rope with his game, retired to feast on it under cover of leaves; and perhaps before night became himself, the delicious evening repast of a bird or lizard.

Birds are in general social and benevolent creatures; intelligent, ingenious, volatile, active beings; and this order of animal creation consists of various nations, bands or tribes, as may be observed from their different structure, manners and languages or voice, as each nation, though subdivided into many different tribes, retain their general form or structure, a similarity of customs, and a sort of dialect or language, particular to that nation or genus from which they seem to have descended or separated: what I mean by a language in birds, is the common notes or speech, that they use when employed in feeding themselves and their young, calling on one another, as well as their menaces against their enemy; for their songs seem to be musical compositions, performed only by the males, about the time of incubation, in part to divert and amuse the female, entertaining her with melody, &c. this harmony, with the tender solicitude of the male, alleviates the toils, cares and distresses of the female, consoles her in solitary retirement whilst setting, and animates her with affection and attachment to himself in preference to any other. The volatility of their species, and operation of their passions and affections, are particularly conspicuous in the different tribes of the thrush, famous for song; on a sweet May morning we see the red thrushes (turdus rufus) perched on an elevated sprig of the snowy Hawthorn, sweet flowering Crab, or other hedge shrubs, exerting their accomplishments in song, striving by varying and elevating their voices to excel each other, we observe a very agreeable variation, not only in tone but in modulation; the voice of one is shrill, another lively and elevated, others sonorous and quivering. The mock-bird (turdus polyglottos) who excels, distinguishes himself in variety of action as well as air; from a turret he bounds aloft with the celerity of an arrow, as it were to recover or recall his very soul, expired in the last elevated strain. The high forests are filled with the symphony of the song or wood-thrush (turdus minor.)

Both sexes of some tribes of birds sing equally fine, and it is remarkable, that these reciprocally assist in their domestic cares, as building their nests and setting on their eggs, feeding and defending their young brood, &c. The oriolus (icterus, Cat.) is an instance in this case, and the female of the icterus minor is a bird of more splendid and gay dress than the male bird. Some tribes of birds will relieve and rear up the young and helpless, of their own and other tribes, when abandoned. Animal substance seems to be the first food of all birds, even the granivorous tribes.

Having passed through some remarks, which appeared of sufficient consequence to be offered to the public, and which were most suitable to have a place in the introduction, I shall now offer such observations as must necessarily occur, from a careful attention to, and investigation of the manners of the Indian nations; being induced, while travelling among them, to associate with them, that I might judge for myself whether they were deserving of the severe censure, which prevailed against them among the white people, that they were incapable of civilization.

In the consideration of this important subject it will be necessary to enquire, whether they were inclined to adopt the European modes of civil society? whether such a reformation could be obtained, without using coercive or violent means? and lastly, whether such a revolution would be productive of real benefit to them, and consequently beneficial to the public? I was satisfied in discovering that they were desirous of becoming united with us, in civil and religious society. It may, therefore, not be foreign to the subject, to point out the propriety of sending men of ability and virtue, under the authority of government, as friendly visitors, into their towns; let these men be instructed to learn perfectly their languages, and by a liberal and friendly intimacy, become acquainted with their customs and usages, religious and civil; their system of legislation and police, as well as their most ancient and present traditions and history. These men thus enlightened and instructed, would be qualified to judge equitably, and when returned to us, to make true and just reports, which might assist the legislature of the United States to form, and offer to them a judicious plan, for their civilization and union with us.

But I presume not to dictate in these high concerns of government, and I am fully convinced that such important matters are far above my ability; the duty and respect we owe to religion and rectitude, the most acceptable incense we can offer to the Almighty, as an atonement for our negligence, in the care of the present and future well being of our Indian brethren, induces me to mention this matter, though perhaps of greater concernment than we generally are aware of.

1791

Thomas Cole

Essay on American Scenery

THE ESSAY, which is here offered, is a mere sketch of an almost illimitable subject—American Scenery; and in selecting the theme the writer placed more confidence in its overflowing richness, than in his own capacity for treating it in a manner worthy of its vastness and importance.

It is a subject that to every American ought to be of surpassing interest; for, whether he beholds the Hudson mingling waters with the Atlantic—explores the central wilds of this vast continent, or stands on the margin of the distant Oregon, he is still in the midst of American scenery—it is his own land; its beauty, its magnificence, its sublimity—all are his; and how undeserving of such a birthright, if he can turn towards it an unobserving eye, an unaffected heart!

Before entering into the proposed subject, in which I shall treat more particularly of the scenery of the Northern and Eastern States, I shall be excused for saying a few words on the advantages of cultivating a taste for scenery, and for exclaiming against the apathy with which the beauties of external nature are regarded by the great mass, even of our refined community.

It is generally admitted that the liberal arts tend to soften our manners; but they do more—they carry with them the power to mend our hearts.

Poetry and Painting sublime and purify thought, by grasping the past, the present, and the future—they give the mind a foretaste of its immortality, and thus prepare it for performing an exalted part amid the realities of life. And *rural nature* is full of the same quickening spirit—it is, in fact, the exhaustless mine from which the poet and the painter have brought such wondrous treasures—an unfailing fountain of intellectual enjoyment, where all may drink, and be awakened to a deeper feeling of the works of genius, and a keener perception of the beauty of our existence. For those whose days are all consumed in the low pursuits of avarice, or the gaudy frivolities of fashion, unobservant of nature's loveliness, are unconscious of the harmony of creation—

> Heaven's roof to them
> Is but a painted ceiling hung with lamps;
> No more—that lights them to their purposes—
> They wander 'loose about;' they nothing see,
> Themselves except, and creatures like themselves,
> Short lived, short sighted.

What to them is the page of the poet where he describes or personifies the skies, the mountains, or the streams, if those objects themselves have never awakened observation or excited pleasure? What to them is the wild Salvator Rosa, or the aerial Claude Lorrain?

This essay appeared in *The American Monthly Magazine,* I (January 1836).

There is in the human mind an almost inseparable connection between the beautiful and the good, so that if we contemplate the one the other seems present; and an excellent author has said, "it is difficult to look at any objects with pleasure—unless where it arises from brutal and tumultuous emotions—without feeling that disposition of mind which tends towards kindness and benevolence; and surely, whatever creates such a disposition, by increasing our pleasures and enjoyments, cannot be too much cultivated."

It would seem unnecessary to those who can see and feel, for me to expatiate on the loveliness of verdant fields, the sublimity of lofty mountains, or the varied magnificence of the sky; but that the number of those who *seek* enjoyment in such sources is comparatively small. From the indifference with which the multitude regard the beauties of nature, it might be inferred that she had been unnecessarily lavish in adorning this world for beings who take no pleasure in its adornment. Who in grovelling pursuits forget their glorious heritage. Why was the earth made so beautiful, or the sun so clad in glory at his rising and setting, when *all* might be unrobed of beauty without affecting the insensate multitude, so they can be "lighted to their purposes?"

It *has not* been in vain—the good, the enlightened of all ages and nations, have found pleasure and consolation in the beauty of the rural earth. Prophets of old retired into the solitudes of nature to wait the inspiration of heaven. It was on Mount Horeb that Elijah witnessed the mighty wind, the earthquake, and the fire; and heard the "still small voice"—that voice is YET heard among the mountains! St. John preached in the desert;—the wilderness is YET a fitting place to speak of God. The solitary Anchorites of Syria and Egypt, though ignorant that the busy world is man's noblest sphere of usefulness, well knew how congenial to religious musings are the pathless solitudes.

He who looks on nature with a "loving eye," cannot move from his dwelling without the salutation of beauty; even in the city the deep blue sky and the drifting clouds appeal to him. And if to escape its turmoil—if only to obtain a free horizon, land and water in the play of light and shadow yields delight—let him be transported to those favored regions, where the features of the earth are more varied, or yet add the sunset, that wreath of glory daily bound around the world, and he, indeed, drinks from pleasure's purest cup. The delight such a man experiences is not merely sensual, or selfish, that passes with the occasion leaving no trace behind; but in gazing on the pure creations of the Almighty, he feels a calm religious tone steal through his mind, and when he has turned to mingle with his fellow men, the chords which have been struck in that sweet communion cease not to vibrate.

In what has been said I have alluded to wild and uncultivated scenery; but the cultivated must not be forgotten, for it is still more important to man in his social capacity—necessarily bringing him in contact with the cultured; it encompasses our homes, and, though devoid of the stern sublimity of the wild, its quieter spirit steals tenderly into our bosoms mingled with a thousand domestic affections and heart-touching associations—human hands have wrought, and human deeds hallowed all around.

And it is here that taste, which is the perception of the beautiful, and the knowledge of the principles on which nature works, can be applied, and our dwelling-places made fitting for refined and intellectual beings.

If, then, it is indeed true that the contemplation of scenery can be so abundant a source of delight and improvement, a taste for it is certainly worthy of particular cultivation; for the capacity for enjoyment increases with the knowledge of the true means of obtaining it.

In this age, when a meager utilitarianism seems ready to absorb every feeling and sentiment, and what is sometimes called improvement in its march makes us fear that the bright and tender flowers of the imagination shall all be crushed beneath its iron tramp, it would be well to cultivate the oasis that yet remains to us, and thus preserve the germs of a future and a purer system. And now, when the sway of fashion is extending widely over society—poisoning the healthful streams of true refinement, and turning men from the love of simplicity and beauty, to a senseless idolatry of their own follies—to lead them gently into the pleasant paths of Taste would be an object worthy of the highest efforts of genius and benevolence. The spirit of our society is to contrive but not to enjoy—toiling to produce more toil—accumulating in order to aggrandize. The pleasures of the imagination, among which the love of scenery holds a conspicuous place, will alone temper the harshness of such a state; and, like the atmosphere that softens the most rugged forms of the landscape, cast a veil of tender beauty over the asperities of life.

Did our limits permit I would endeavor more fully to show how necessary to the complete appreciation of the Fine Arts is the study of scenery, and how conducive to our happiness and well-being is that study and those arts; but I must now proceed to the proposed subject of this essay—American Scenery!

There are those who through ignorance or prejudice strive to maintain that American scenery possesses little that is interesting or truly beautiful—that it is rude without picturesqueness, and monotonous without sublimity—that being destitute of those vestiges of antiquity, whose associations so strongly affect the mind, it may not be compared with European scenery. But from whom do these opinions come? From those who have read of European scenery, of Grecian mountains, and Italian skies, and never troubled themselves to look at their own; and from those travelled ones whose eyes were never opened to the beauties of nature until they beheld foreign lands, and when those lands faded from the sight were again closed and forever; disdaining to destroy their trans-atlantic impressions by the observation of the less fashionable and unfamed American scenery. Let such persons shut themselves up in their narrow shell of prejudice—I hope they are few,—and the community increasing in intelligence, will know better how to appreciate the treasures of their own country.

I am by no means desirous of lessening in your estimation the glorious scenes of the old world—that ground which has been the great theater of human events—those mountains, woods, and streams, made sacred in our minds by heroic deeds and immortal song—over which time and genius have suspended an imperishable halo. No! But I would have it remembered that nature has shed over *this* land beauty and magnificence, and although the character of its scenery may differ from the old world's, yet inferiority must not therefore be inferred; for though American scenery is destitute of many of those circumstances that give value to the European, still it has features, and glorious ones, unknown to Europe.

A very few generations have passed away since this vast tract of the American continent, now the United States, rested in the shadow of primæval forests, whose gloom was peopled by savage beasts, and scarcely less savage men; or lay in those wide grassy plains called prairies—

> The Gardens of the Desert, these
> The unshorn fields, boundless and beautiful.

And, although an enlightened and increasing people have broken in upon the solitude, and with activity and power wrought changes that seem magical, yet the most distinctive, and perhaps the most impressive, characteristic of American scenery is its wildness.

It is the most distinctive, because in civilized Europe the primitive features of scenery have long since been destroyed or modified—the extensive forests that once overshadowed a great part of it have been felled—rugged mountains have been smoothed, and impetuous rivers turned from their courses to accommodate the tastes and necessities of a dense population—the once tangled wood is now a grassy lawn; the turbulent brook a navigable stream—crags that could not be removed have been crowned with towers, and the rudest valleys tamed by the plough.

And to this cultivated state our western world is fast approaching; but nature is still predominant, and there are those who regret that with the improvements of cultivation the sublimity of the wilderness should pass away: for those scenes of solitude from which the hand of nature has never been lifted, affect the mind with a more deep toned emotion than aught which the hand of man has touched. Amid them the consequent associations are of God the creator—they are his undefiled works, and the mind is cast into the contemplation of eternal things.

As mountains are the most conspicuous objects in landscape, they will take the precedence in what I may say on the elements of American scenery.

It is true that in the eastern part of this continent there are no mountains that vie in altitude with the snow-crowned Alps—that the Alleghanies and the Catskills are in no point higher than five thousand feet; but this is no inconsiderable height; Snowdon in Wales, and Ben-Nevis in Scotland, are not more lofty; and in New Hampshire, which has been called the Switzerland of the United States, the White Mountains almost pierce the region of perpetual snow. The Alleghanies are in general heavy in form; but the Catskills, although not broken into abrupt angles like the most picturesque mountains of Italy, have varied, undulating, and exceedingly beautiful outlines—they heave from the valley of the Hudson like the subsiding billows of the ocean after a storm.

American mountains are generally clothed to the summit by dense forests, while those of Europe are mostly bare, or merely tinted by grass or heath. It may be that the mountains of Europe are on this account more picturesque in form, and there is a grandeur in their nakedness; but in the gorgeous garb of the American mountains there is more than an equivalent; and when the woods "have put their glory on," as an American poet has beautifully said, the purple heath and yellow furze of Europe's mountains are in comparison but as the faint secondary rainbow to the primal one.

But in the mountains of New Hampshire there is a union of the picturesque, the sublime, and the magnificent; there the bare peaks of granite, broken and desolate, cradle the clouds; while the vallies and broad bases of the mountains rest under the shadow of noble and varied forests; and the traveller who passes the Sandwich range on his way to the White Mountains, of which it is a spur, cannot but acknowledge, that although in some regions of the globe nature has wrought on a more stupendous scale, yet she has nowhere so completely married together grandeur and loveliness—there he sees the sublime melting into the beautiful, the savage tempered by the magnificent.

I will now speak of another component of scenery, without which every landscape is defective—it is water. Like the eye in the human countenance, it is a most expressive feature: in the unrippled lake, which mirrors all surrounding objects, we have the expression of tranquillity and peace—in the rapid stream, the headlong cataract, that of turbulence and impetuosity.

In this great element of scenery, what land is so rich? I would not speak of the Great Lakes, which are in fact inland seas—possessing some of the attributes of the ocean, though destitute of its sublimity; but of those smaller lakes, such as Lake George, Champlain, Winnipisiogee, Otsego, Seneca, and a hundred others, that stud like gems the bosom of this country. There is one delightful quality in nearly all these lakes—the purity and transparency of the water. In speaking of scenery it might seem unnecessary to mention this; but independent of the pleasure that we all have in beholding pure water, it is a circumstance which contributes greatly to the beauty of landscape; for the reflections of surrounding objects, trees, mountains, sky, are most perfect in the clearest water; and the most perfect is the most beautiful.

I would rather persuade you to visit the "Holy Lake," the beautiful "Horican," than attempt to describe its scenery—to behold you rambling on its storied shores, where its southern expanse is spread, begemmed with isles of emerald, and curtained by green receding hills—or to see you gliding over its bosom, where the steep and rugged mountains approach from either side, shadowing with black precipices the innumerable islets—some of which bearing a solitary tree, others a group of two or three, or a "goodly company," seem to have been sprinkled over the smiling deep in Nature's frolic hour. These scenes are classic—History and Genius have hallowed them. War's shrill clarion once waked the echoes from these now silent hills—the pen of a living master has portrayed them in the pages of romance—and they are worthy of the admiration of the enlightened and the graphic hand of Genius.

Though differing from Lake George, Winnipisiogee resembles it in multitudinous and uncounted islands. Its mountains do not stoop to the water's edge, but through varied screens of forest may be seen ascending the sky softened by the blue haze of distance—on the one hand rise the Gunstock Mountains; on the other the dark Ossipees, while above and far beyond, rear the "cloud capt" peaks of the Sandwich and White Mountains.

I will not fatigue with a vain attempt to describe the lakes that I have named; but would turn your attention to those exquisitely beautiful lakes that are so numerous in the Northern States, and particularly in New Hampshire. In character they are truly and peculiarly American. I know nothing in Europe which they resemble; the famous lakes of Albano and Nemi, and the small and exceedingly picturesque lakes of Great Britain may be compared in size, but are dissimilar in almost every other respect. Embosomed in the primitive forest, and sometimes overshadowed by huge mountains, they are the chosen places of tranquillity; and when the deer issues from the surrounding woods to drink the cool waters, he beholds his own image as in a polished mirror,—the flight of the eagle can be seen in the lower sky; and if a leaf falls, the circling undulations chase each other to the shores unvexed by contending tides.

There are two lakes of this description, situated in a wild mountain gorge called the Franconia Notch, in New Hampshire. They lie within a few hundred feet of each other, but are remarkable as having no communication—one being the source of the wild Amonoosuck, the other of the Pemigiwasset. Shut in by stupendous mountains which rest on crags that tower more than a thousand feet above the water, whose rugged brows and shadowy breaks are clothed by dark and tangled woods, they have such an aspect of deep seclusion, of utter and unbroken solitude, that, when standing on their brink a lonely traveller, I was overwhelmed with an emotion of the sublime, such as I have rarely felt. It was not that the jagged precipices were lofty, that the encircling woods were of the dimmest shade, or that the waters were profoundly deep; but that over all, rocks, wood, and water, brooded the spirit of repose, and the silent energy of nature stirred the soul to its inmost depths.

I would not be understood that these lakes are always tranquil; but that tranquillity is their great characteristic. There are times when they take a far different expression; but in scenes like these the richest chords are those struck by the gentler hand of nature.

And now I must turn to another of the beautifiers of the earth—the Waterfall; which in the same object at once presents to the mind the beautiful, but apparently incongruous idea, of fixedness and motion—a single existence in which we perceive unceasing change and everlasting duration. The waterfall may be called the voice of the landscape, for, unlike the rocks and woods which utter sounds as the passive instruments played on by the elements, the waterfall strikes its own chords, and rocks and mountains re-echo in rich unison. And this is a land abounding in cataracts; in these Northern States where shall we turn and not find them? Have we not Kaaterskill, Trenton, the Flume, the Genesee, stupendous Niagara, and a hundred others named and nameless ones, whose exceeding beauty must be acknowledged when the hand of taste shall point them out?

In the Kaaterskill we have a stream, diminutive indeed, but throwing itself headlong over a fearful precipice into a deep gorge of the densely wooded mountains—and possessing a singular feature in the vast arched cave that extends beneath and behind the cataract. At Trenton there is a chain of waterfalls of remarkable beauty, where the foaming waters, shadowed by steep cliffs, break over rocks of architectural formation, and tangled and picturesque trees mantle abrupt precipices, which it would be easy to imagine crumbling and "time disparting towers."

And Niagara! that wonder of the world!—where the sublime and beautiful are bound together in an indissoluble chain. In gazing on it we feel as though a great void had been filled in our minds—our conceptions expand—we become a part of what we behold! At our feet the floods of a thousand rivers are poured out—the contents of vast inland seas. In its volume we conceive immensity; in its course, everlasting duration; in its impetuosity, uncontrollable power. These are the elements of its sublimity. Its beauty is garlanded around in the varied hues of the water, in the spray that ascends the sky, and in that unrivalled bow which forms a complete cincture round the unresting floods.

The river scenery of the United States is a rich and boundless theme. The Hudson for natural magnificence is unsurpassed. What can be more beautiful than the lake-like expanses of Tapaan and Haverstraw, as seen from the rich orchards of the surrounding hills? hills that have a legend, which has been so sweetly and admirably told that it shall not perish but with the language of the land. What can be more imposing than the precipitous Highlands; whose dark foundations have been rent to make a passage for the deep-flowing river? And, ascending still, where can be found scenes more enchanting? The lofty Catskills stand afar off—the green hills gently rising from the flood, recede like steps by which we may ascend to a great temple, whose pillars are those everlasting hills, and whose dome is the blue boundless vault of heaven.

The Rhine has its castled crags, its vine-clad hills, and ancient villages; the Hudson has its wooded mountains, its rugged precipices, its green undulating shores—a natural majesty, and an unbounded capacity for improvement by art. Its shores are not besprinkled with venerated ruins, or the palaces of princes; but there are flourishing towns, and neat villas, and the hand of taste has already been at work. Without any great stretch of the imagination we may anticipate the time when the ample waters shall reflect temple, and tower, and dome, in every variety of picturesqueness and magnificence.

In the Connecticut we behold a river that differs widely from the Hudson. Its sources are amid the wild mountains of New Hampshire; but it soon breaks into a luxuriant valley, and flows for more than a hundred miles, sometimes beneath the shadow of wooded hills, and sometimes glancing through the green expanse of elm-besprinkled meadows. Whether we see it at Haverhill, Northampton, or Hartford, it still possesses that gentle aspect; and the imagination can scarcely conceive Arcadian vales more lovely or more peaceful than the valley of the Connecticut—its villages are rural places where trees overspread every dwelling, and the fields upon its margin have the richest verdure.

Nor ought the Ohio, the Susquehannah, the Potomac, with their tributaries, and a thousand others, be omitted in the rich list of the American rivers—they are a glorious brotherhood; but volumes would be insufficient for their description.

In the Forest scenery of the United States we have that which occupies the greatest space, and is not the least remarkable; being primitive, it differs widely from the European. In the American forest we find trees in every stage of vegetable life and decay—the slender sapling rises in the shadow of the lofty tree, and the giant in his prime stands by the hoary patriarch of the wood—on the ground lie prostrate decaying ranks that once waved their verdant heads in the sun and wind. These are circumstances productive of great variety and picturesqueness—green umbrageous masses—lofty and scathed trunks—contorted branches thrust athwart the sky—the mouldering dead below, shrouded in moss of every hue and texture, from richer combinations than can be found in the trimmed and planted grove. It is true that the thinned and cultivated wood offers less obstruction to the feet, and the trees throw out their branches more horizontally, and are consequently more umbrageous when taken singly; but the true lover of the picturesque is seldom fatigued—and trees that grow widely apart are often heavy in form, and resemble each other too much for picturesqueness. Trees are like men, differing widely in character; in sheltered spots, or under the influence of culture, they show few contrasting points; peculiarities are pruned and trained away, until there is a general resemblance. But in exposed situations, wild and uncultivated, battling with the elements and with one another for the possession of a morsel of soil, or a favoring rock to which they may cling—they exhibit striking peculiarities, and sometimes grand originality.

For variety, the American forest is unrivalled: in some districts are found oaks, elms, birches, beeches, planes, pines, hemlocks, and many other kinds of trees, commingled—clothing the hills with every tint of green, and every variety of light and shade.

There is a peculiarity observable in some mountainous regions, where trees of a genus band together—there often may be seen a mountain whose foot is clothed with deciduous trees, while on its brow is a sable crown of pines; and sometimes belts of dark green encircle a mountain horizontally, or are stretched in well-defined lines from the summit to the base. The nature of the soil, or the courses of rivulets, are the causes of this variety;—and it is a beautiful instance of the exhaustlessness of nature; often where we should expect unvarying monotony, we behold a charming diversity. Time will not permit me to speak of the American forest trees individually; but I must notice the elm, that paragon of beauty and shade; the maple, with its rainbow hues; and the hemlock, the sublime of trees, which rises from the gloom of the forest like a dark and ivy-mantled tower.

There is one season when the American forest surpasses all the world in gorgeousness—that is the autumnal;—then every hill and dale is riant in the luxury of color—every hue is there, from the liveliest green to deepest purple—from the most golden yellow to the intensest crimson. The artist looks despairingly upon the glowing landscape, and in the old world his truest imitations of the American forest, at this season, are called falsely bright, and scenes in Fairy Land.

The sky will next demand our attention. The soul of all scenery, in it are the fountains of light, and shade, and color. Whatever expression the sky takes, the features of the landscape are affected in unison, whether it be the serenity of the summer's blue, or the dark tumult of the storm. It is the sky that makes the earth so lovely at sunrise, and so splendid at sunset. In the one it breathes over the earth the crystal-like ether, in the other liquid gold. The climate of a great part of the United States is subject to great vicissitudes, and we complain; but nature offers a compensation. These very vicissitudes are the abundant sources of beauty—as we have the temperature of every clime, so have we the skies—we have the blue unsearchable depths of the northern sky—we have the upheaped thunder-clouds of the Torrid Zone, fraught with gorgeousness and sublimity—we have the silver haze of England, and the golden atmosphere of Italy. And if he who has travelled and observed the skies of other climes will spend a few months on the banks of the Hudson, he must be constrained to acknowledge that for variety and magnificence American skies are unsurpassed. Italian skies have been lauded by every tongue, and sung by every poet, and who will deny their wonderful beauty? At sunset the serene arch is filled with alchemy that transmutes mountains, and streams, and temples, into living gold.

But the American summer never passes without many sunsets that might vie with the Italian, and many still more gorgeous—that seem peculiar to this clime.

Look at the heavens when the thunder shower has passed, and the sun stoops behind the western mountains—there the low purple clouds hang in festoons around the steeps—in the higher heaven are crimson bands interwoven with feathers of gold, fit for the wings of angels—and still above is spread that interminable field of ether, whose color is too beautiful to have a name.

It is not in the summer only that American skies are beautiful; for the winter evening often comes robed in purple and gold, and in the westering sun the iced groves glitter as beneath a shower of diamonds—and through the twilight heaven innumerable stars shine with a purer light than summer ever knows.

I will now venture a few remarks on what has been considered a grand defect in American scenery—the want of associations, such as arise amid the scenes of the old world.

We have many a spot as umbrageous as Vallombrosa, and as picturesque as the solitudes of Vaucluse; but Milton and Petrarch have not hallowed them by their footsteps and immortal verse. He who stands on Mont Albano and looks down on ancient Rome, has his mind peopled with the gigantic associations of the storied past; but he who stands on the mounds of the West, the most venerable remains of American antiquity, *may* experience the emotion of the sublime, but it is the sublimity of a shoreless ocean un-islanded by the recorded deeds of man.

Yet American scenes are not destitute of historical and legendary associations—the great struggle for freedom has sanctified many a spot, and many a mountain, stream, and rock has its legend, worthy of poet's pen or the painter's pencil. But American associations are not so much of the past as of the present and the future. Seated on a pleasant knoll, look down into the bosom of that secluded valley, begirt with wooded hills—through those enamelled meadows and wide waving fields of grain, a silver stream winds lingeringly along—here, seeking the green shade of trees—there, glancing in the sunshine: on its banks are rural dwellings shaded by elms and garlanded by flowers—from yonder dark mass of foliage the village spire beams like a star. You see no ruined tower to tell of outrage—no gorgeous temple to speak of ostentation; but freedom's offspring—peace, security, and happiness, dwell there, the spirits of the scene. On the margin of that gentle river the village girls may ramble unmolested—and the glad school-boy, with hook and line, pass his bright holiday—those neat dwellings, unpretending to magnificence, are the abodes of plenty, virtue, and refinement. And in looking over the yet uncultivated scene, the mind's eye may see far into futurity. Where the wolf roams, the plough shall glisten; on the gray crag shall rise temple and tower—mighty deeds shall be done in the now pathless wilderness; and poets yet unborn shall sanctify the soil.

It was my intention to attempt a description of several districts remarkable for their picturesqueness and truly American character; but I fear to trespass longer on your time and patience. Yet I cannot but express my sorrow that the beauty of such landscapes are quickly passing away—the ravages of the axe are daily increasing—the most noble scenes are made desolate, and oftentimes with a wantonness and barbarism scarcely credible in a civilized nation. The way-side is becoming shadeless, and another generation will behold spots, now rife with beauty, desecrated by what is called improvement; which, as yet, generally destroys Nature's beauty without substituting that of Art. This is a regret rather than a complaint; such is the road society has to travel; it may lead to refinement in the end, but the traveller who sees the place of rest close at hand, dislikes the road that has so many unnecessary windings.

I will now conclude, in the hope that, though feebly urged, the importance of cultivating a taste for scenery will not be forgotten. Nature has spread for us a rich and delightful banquet. Shall we turn from it? We are still in Eden; the wall that shuts us out of the garden is our own ignorance and folly. We should not allow the poet's words to be applicable to us—

> Deep in rich pasture do thy flocks complain?
> Not so; but to their master is denied
> To share the sweet serene.

May we at times turn from the ordinary pursuits of life to the pure enjoyment of rural nature; which is in the soul like a fountain of cool waters to the way-worn traveller; and let us

> Learn
> The laws by which the Eternal doth sublime
> And sanctify his works, that we may see
> The hidden glory veiled from vulgar eyes.

1835

Ralph Waldo Emerson

Nature

Introduction

OUR AGE is retrospective. It builds the sepulchres of the fathers. It writes biographies, histories, and criticism. The foregoing generations beheld God and nature face to face; we, through their eyes. Why should not we also enjoy an original relation to the universe? Why should not we have a poetry and philosophy of insight and not of tradition, and a religion by revelation to us, and not the history of theirs? Embosomed for a season in nature, whose floods of life stream around and through us, and invite us by the powers they supply, to action proportioned to nature, why should we grope among the dry bones of the past, or put the living generation into masquerade out of its faded wardrobe? The sun shines to-day also. There is more wool and flax in the fields. There are new lands, new men, new thoughts. Let us demand our own works and laws and worship.

Undoubtedly we have no questions to ask which are unanswerable. We must trust the perfection of the creation so far, as to believe that whatever curiosity the order of things has awakened in our minds, the order of things can satisfy. Every man's condition is a solution in hieroglyphic to those inquiries he would put. He acts it as life, before he apprehends it as truth. In like manner, nature is already, in its forms and tendencies, describing its own design. Let us interrogate the great apparition, that shines so peacefully around us. Let us inquire, to what end is nature?

All science has one aim, namely, to find a theory of nature. We have theories of races and of functions, but scarcely yet a remote approximation to an idea of creation. We are now so far from the road to truth, that religious teachers dispute and hate each other, and speculative men are esteemed unsound and frivolous. But to a sound judgment, the most abstract truth is the most practical. Whenever a true theory appears, it will be its own evidence. Its test is, that it will explain all phenomena. Now many are thought not only unexplained but inexplicable; as language, sleep, dreams, beasts, sex.

Philosophically considered, the universe is composed of Nature and the Soul. Strictly speaking, therefore, all that is separate from us, all which Philosophy distinguishes as the NOT ME, that is, both nature and art, all other men and my own body, must be ranked under this name, NATURE. In enumerating the values of nature and casting up their sum, I shall use the word in both senses;—in its common and in its philosophical import. In inquiries so general as our present one, the inaccuracy is not material; no confusion of thought will occur. *Nature,* in the common sense, refers to essences unchanged by man; space, the air, the river, the leaf. *Art* is applied to the mixture of his will with the same things, as in a house, a canal, a statue, a picture. But his operations taken together are so insignificant, a little chipping, baking, patching, and washing, that in an impression so grand as that of the world on the human mind, they do not vary the result.

Chapter I

TO GO INTO SOLITUDE, a man needs to retire as much from his chamber as from society. I am not solitary whilst I read and write, though nobody is with me. But if a man would be alone, let him look at the stars. The rays that come from those heavenly worlds, will separate between him and vulgar things. One might think the atmosphere was made transparent with this design, to give man, in the heavenly bodies, the perpetual presence of the sublime. Seen in the streets of cities, how great they are! If the stars should appear one night in a thousand years, how would men believe and adore; and preserve for many generations the remembrance of the city of God which had been shown! But every night come out these preachers of beauty, and light the universe with their admonishing smile.

The stars awaken a certain reverence, because though always present, they are always inaccessible; but all natural objects make a kindred impression, when the mind is open to their influence. Nature never wears a mean appearance. Neither does the wisest man extort all her secret, and lose his curiosity by finding out all her perfection. Nature never became a toy to a wise spirit. The flowers, the animals, the mountains, reflected all the wisdom of his best hour, as much as they had delighted the simplicity of his childhood.

When we speak of nature in this manner, we have a distinct but most poetical sense in the mind. We mean the integrity of impression made by manifold natural objects. It is this which distinguishes the stick of timber of the woodcutter, from the tree of the poet. The charming landscape which I saw this morning, is indubitably made up of some twenty or thirty farms. Miller owns this field, Locke that, and Manning the woodland beyond. But none of them owns the landscape. There is a property in the horizon which no man has but he whose eye can integrate all the parts, that is, the poet. This is the best part of these men's farms, yet to this their land-deeds give them no title.

To speak truly, few adult persons can see nature. Most persons do not see the sun. At least they have a very superficial seeing. The sun illuminates only the eye of the man, but shines into the eye and the heart of the child. The lover of nature is he whose inward and outward senses are still truly adjusted to each other; who has retained the spirit of infancy even into the era of manhood. His intercourse with heaven and earth, becomes part of his daily food. In the presence of nature, a wild delight runs through the man, in spite of real sorrows. Nature says,—he is my creature, and maugre all his impertinent griefs, he shall be glad with me. Not the sun or the summer alone, but every hour and season yields its tribute of delight; for every hour and change corresponds to and authorizes a different state of the mind, from breathless noon to grimmest midnight. Nature is a setting that fits equally well a comic or a mourning piece. In good health, the air is a cordial of incredible virtue. Crossing a bare common, in snow puddles, at twilight, under a clouded sky, without having in my thoughts any occurrence of special good fortune, I have enjoyed a perfect exhilaration. Almost I fear to think how glad I am. In the woods too, a man casts off his years, as the snake his slough, and at what period soever of life, is always a child. In the woods, is perpetual youth. Within these plantations of God, a decorum and sanctity reign, a perennial festival is dressed, and the guest sees not how he should tire of them in a thousand years. In the woods, we return to reason and faith. There I feel that nothing can befall me in life,—no disgrace, no calamity, (leaving me my eyes), which nature cannot repair. Standing on the bare ground,—my head bathed by the blithe air, and uplifted into infinite space,—all mean egotism vanishes. I become a transparent eye-ball. I am nothing. I see all. The currents of the Universal Being circulate through me; I am part or particle of God. The name of the nearest friend sounds then foreign and accidental. To be brothers, to be acquaintances,—master or servant, is then a trifle and a disturbance. I am the lover of uncontained and immortal beauty. In the wilderness, I find something more dear and connate than in streets or villages. In the tranquil landscape, and especially in the distant line of the horizon, man beholds somewhat as beautiful as his own nature.

The greatest delight which the fields and woods minister, is the suggestion of an occult relation between man and the vegetable. I am not alone and unacknowledged. They nod to me and I to them. The waving of the boughs in the storm, is new to me and old. It takes me by surprise, and yet is not unknown. Its effect is like that of a higher thought or a better emotion coming over me, when I deemed I was thinking justly or doing right.

Yet it is certain that the power to produce this delight, does not reside in nature, but in man, or in a harmony of both. It is necessary to use these pleasures with great temperance. For, nature is not always tricked in holiday attire, but the same scene which yesterday breathed perfume and glittered as for the frolic of the nymphs, is overspread with melancholy today. Nature always wears the colors of the spirit. To a man laboring under calamity, the heat of his own fire hath sadness in it. Then, there is a kind of contempt of the landscape felt by him who has just lost by death a dear friend. The sky is less grand as it shuts down over less worth in the population.

Chapter II

COMMODITY

Whoever considers the final cause of the world, will discern a multitude of uses that enter as parts into that result. They all admit of being thrown into one of the following classes: Commodity; Beauty; Language; and Discipline.

Under the general name of Commodity, I rank all those advantages which our senses owe to nature. This, of course, is a benefit which is temporary and mediate, not ultimate, like its service to the soul. Yet although low, it is perfect in its kind, and is the only use of nature which all men apprehend. The misery of man appears like childish petulance, when we explore the steady and prodigal provision that has been made for his support and delight on this green ball which floats him through the heavens. What angels invented these splendid ornaments, these rich conveniences, this ocean of air above, this ocean of water beneath, this firmament of earth between? this zodiac of lights, this tent of dropping clouds, this striped coat of climates, this fourfold year? Beasts, fire, water, stones, and corn serve him. The field is at once his floor, his work-yard, his play-ground, his garden, and his bed.

> "More servants wait on man
> Than he'll take notice of."———

Nature, in its ministry to man, is not only the material, but is also the process and the result. All the parts incessantly work into each other's hands for the profit of man. The wind sows the seed; the sun evaporates the sea; the wind blows the vapor to the field; the ice, on the other side of the planet, condenses rain on this; the rain feeds the plant; the plant feeds the animal; and thus the endless circulations of the divine charity nourish man.

The useful arts are but reproductions or new combinations by the wit of man, of the same natural benefactors. He no longer waits for favoring gales, but by means of steam, he realizes the fable of Æolus's bag, and carries the two and thirty winds in the boiler of his boat. To diminish friction, he paves the road with iron bars, and, mounting a coach with a ship-load of men, animals, and merchandise behind him, he darts through the country, from town to town, like an eagle or a swallow through the air. By the aggregate of these aids, how is the face of the world changed, from the era of Noah to that of Napoleon! The private poor man hath cities, ships, canals, bridges, built for him. He goes to the post-office, and the human race run on his errands; to the book-shop, and the human race read and write of all that happens, for him; to the court-house, and nations repair his wrongs. He sets his house upon the road, and the human race go forth every morning, and shovel out the snow, and cut a path for him.

But there is no need of specifying particulars in this class of uses. The catalogue is endless, and the examples so obvious, that I shall leave them to the reader's reflection, with the general remark, that this mercenary benefit is one which has respect to a farther good. A man is fed, not that he may be fed, but that he may work.

Chapter III

BEAUTY

A nobler want of man is served by nature, namely, the love of Beauty.

The ancient Greeks called the world κοσμος, beauty. Such is the constitution of all things, or such the plastic power of the human eye, that the primary forms, as the sky, the mountain, the tree, the animal, give us a delight *in and for themselves;* a pleasure arising from outline, color, motion, and grouping. This seems partly owing to the eye itself. The eye is the best of artists. By the mutual action of its structure and of the laws of light, perspective is produced, which integrates every mass of objects, of what character soever, into a well colored and shaded globe, so that where the particular objects are mean and unaffecting, the landscape which they compose, is round and symmetrical. And as the eye is the best composer, so light is the first of painters. There is no object so foul that intense light will not make beautiful. And the stimulus it affords to the sense, and a sort of infinitude which it hath, like space and time, make all matter gay. Even the corpse hath its own beauty. But beside this general grace diffused over nature, almost all the individual forms are agreeable to the eye, as is proved by our endless imitations of some of them, as the acorn, the grape, the pine-cone, the wheat-ear, the egg, the wings and forms of most birds, the lion's claw, the serpent, the butterfly, sea-shells, flames, clouds, buds, leaves, and the forms of many trees, as the palm.

For better consideration, we may distribute the aspects of Beauty in a threefold manner.

1. First, the simple perception of natural forms is a delight. The influence of the forms and actions in nature, is so needful to man, that, in its lowest functions, it seems to lie on the confines of commodity and beauty. To the body and mind which have been cramped by noxious work or company, nature is medicinal and restores their tone. The tradesman, the attorney comes out of the din and craft of the street, and sees the sky and the woods, and is a man again. In their eternal calm, he finds himself. The health of the eye seems to demand a horizon. We are never tired, so long as we can see far enough.

But in other hours, Nature satisfies the soul purely by its loveliness, and without any mixture of corporeal benefit. I have seen the spectacle of morning from the hilltop over against my house, from day-break to sun-rise, with emotions which an angel might share. The long slender bars of cloud float like fishes in the sea of crimson light. From the earth, as a shore, I look out into that silent sea. I seem to partake its rapid transformations: the active enchantment reaches my dust, and I dilate and conspire with the morning wind. How does Nature deify us with a few and cheap elements! Give me health and a day, and I will make the pomp of emperors ridiculous. The dawn is my Assyria; the sun-set and moon-rise my Paphos, and unimaginable realms of faerie; broad noon shall be my England of the senses and the understanding; the night shall be my Germany of mystic philosophy and dreams.

Not less excellent, except for our less susceptibility in the afternoon, was the charm, last evening, of a January sunset. The western clouds divided and subdivided themselves into pink flakes modulated with tints of unspeakable softness; and the air had so much life and sweetness, that it was a pain to come within doors. What was it that nature would say? Was there no meaning in the live repose of the valley behind the mill, and which Homer or Shakspeare could not re-form for me in words? The leafless trees become spires of flame in the sunset, with the blue east for their background, and the stars of the dead calices of flowers, and every withered stem and stubble rimed with frost, contribute something to the mute music.

The inhabitants of cities suppose that the country landscape is pleasant only half the year. I please myself with observing the graces of the winter scenery, and believe that we are as much touched by it as by the genial influences of summer. To the attentive eye, each moment of the year has its own beauty, and in the same field, it beholds, every hour, a picture which was never seen before, and which shall never be seen again. The heavens change every moment, and reflect their glory or gloom on the plains beneath. The state of the crop in the surrounding farms alters the expression of the earth from week to week. The succession of native plants in the pastures and roadsides, which make the silent clock by which time tells the summer hours, will make even the divisions of the day sensible to a keen observer. The tribes of birds and insects, like the plants punctual to their time, follow each other, and the year has room for all. By water-courses, the variety is greater. In July, the blue pontederia or pickerel-weed blooms in large beds in the shallow parts of our pleasant river, and swarms with yellow butterflies in continual motion. Art cannot rival this pomp of purple and gold. Indeed the river is a perpetual gala, and boasts each month a new ornament.

But this beauty of Nature which is seen and felt as beauty, is the least part. The shows of day, the dewy morning, the rainbow, mountains, orchards in blossom, stars, moonlight, shadows in still water, and the like, if too eagerly hunted, become shows merely, and mock us with their unreality. Go out of the house to see the moon, and 't is mere tinsel; it will not please as when its light shines upon your necessary journey. The beauty that shimmers in the yellow afternoons of October, who ever could clutch it? Go forth to find it, and it is gone: 't is only a mirage as you look from windows of diligence.

2. The presence of a higher, namely, of the spiritual element is essential to its perfection. The high and divine beauty which can be loved without effeminacy, is that which is found in combination with the human will, and never separate. Beauty is the mark God sets upon virtue. Every natural action is graceful. Every heroic act is also decent, and causes the place and the by-

standers to shine. We are taught by great actions that the universe is the property of every individual in it. Every rational creature has all nature for his dowry and estate. It is his, if he will. He may divest himself of it; he may creep into a corner, and abdicate his kingdom, as most men do, but he is entitled to the world by his constitution. In proportion to the energy of his thought and will, he takes up the world into himself. ''All those things for which men plough, build, or sail, obey virtue''; said an ancient historian. ''The winds and waves,'' said Gibbon, ''are always on the side of the ablest navigators.'' So are the sun and moon and all the stars of heaven. When a noble act is done,—perchance in a scene of great natural beauty; when Leonidas and his three hundred martyrs consume one day in dying, and the sun and moon come each and look at them once in the steep defile of Thermopylæ; when Arnold Winkelried, in the high Alps, under the shadow of the avalanche, gathers in his side a sheaf of Austrian spears to break the line for his comrades; are not these heroes entitled to add the beauty of the scene to the beauty of the deed? When the bark of Columbus nears the shore of America;—before it, the beach lined with savages, fleeing out of all their huts of cane; the sea behind; and the purple mountains of the Indian Archipelago around, can we separate the man from the living picture? Does not the New World clothe his form with her palm-groves and savannahs as fit drapery? Ever does natural beauty steal in like air, and envelope great actions. When Sir Harry Vane was dragged up the Tower-hill, sitting on a sled, to suffer death, as the champion of the English laws, one of the multitude cried out to him, ''You never sate on so glorious a seat.'' Charles II, to intimidate the citizens of London, caused the patriot Lord Russel to be drawn in an open coach, through the principal streets of the city, on his way to the scaffold. ''But,'' to use the simple narrative of his biographer, ''the multitude imagined they saw liberty and virtue sitting by his side.'' In private places, among sordid objects, an act of truth or heroism seems at once to draw to itself the sky as its temple, the sun as its candle. Nature stretcheth out her arms to embrace man, only let his thoughts be of equal greatness. Willingly does she follow his steps with the rose and the violet, and bend her lines of grandeur and grace to the decoration of her darling child. Only let his thoughts be of equal scope, and the frame will suit the picture. A virtuous man is in unison with her works, and makes the central figure of the visible sphere. Homer, Pindar, Socrates, Phocion, associate themselves fitly in our memory with the whole geography and climate of Greece. The visible heavens and earth sympathize with Jesus. And in common life, whosoever has seen a person of powerful character and happy genius, will have remarked how easily he took all things along with him,—the persons, the opinions, and the day, and nature became ancillary to a man.

3. There is still another aspect under which the beauty of the world may be viewed, namely, as it becomes an object of the intellect. Beside the relation of things to virtue, they have a relation to thought. The intellect searches out

the absolute order of things as they stand in the mind of God, and without the colors of affection. The intellectual and the active powers seem to succeed each other in man, and the exclusive activity of the one, generates the exclusive activity of the other. There is something unfriendly in each to the other, but they are like the alternate periods of feeding and working in animals; each prepares and certainly will be followed by the other. Therefore does beauty, which, in relation to actions, as we have seen, comes unsought, and comes because it is unsought, remain for the apprehension and pursuit of the intellect; and then again, in its turn, of the active power. Nothing divine dies. All good is eternally reproductive. The beauty of nature reforms itself in the mind, and not for barren contemplation, but for new creation.

All men are in some degree impressed by the face of the world. Some men even to delight. This love of beauty is Taste. Others have the same love in such excess, that, not content with admiring, they seek to embody it in new forms. The creation of beauty is Art.

The production of a work of art throws a light upon the mystery of humanity. A work of art is an abstract or epitome of the world. It is the result or expression of nature, in miniature. For although the works of nature are innumerable and all different, the result or the expression of them all is similar and single. Nature is a sea of forms radically alike and even unique. A leaf, a sunbeam, a landscape, the ocean, make an analogous impression on the mind. What is common to them all,—that perfectness and harmony, is beauty. Therefore the standard of beauty is the entire circuit of natural forms,—the totality of nature; which the Italians expressed by defining beauty "il piu nell' uno." Nothing is quite beautiful alone: nothing but is beautiful in the whole. A single object is only so far beautiful as it suggests this universal grace. The poet, the painter, the sculptor, the musician, the architect, seek each to concentrate this radiance of the world on one point, and each in his several work to satisfy the love of beauty which stimulates him to produce. Thus is Art, a nature passed through the alembic of man. Thus in art, does nature work through the will of a man filled with the beauty of her first works.

The world thus exists to the soul to satisfy the desire of beauty. Extend this element to the uttermost, and I call it an ultimate end. No reason can be asked or given why the soul seeks beauty. Beauty, in its largest and profoundest sense, is one expression for the universe. God is the all-fair. Truth, and goodness, and beauty, are but different faces of the same All. But beauty in nature is not ultimate. It is the herald of inward and eternal beauty, and is not alone a solid and satisfactory good. It must therefore stand as a part and not as yet the last or highest expression of the final cause of Nature.

Chapter IV

LANGUAGE

A third use which Nature subserves to man is that of Language. Nature is the vehicle of thought, and in a simple, double, and threefold degree.

1. Words are signs of natural facts.
2. Particular natural facts are symbols of particular spiritual facts.
3. Nature is the symbol of spirit.

1. Words are signs of natural facts. The use of natural history is to give us aid in supernatural history. The use of the outer creation is to give us language for the beings and changes of the inward creation. Every word which is used to express a moral or intellectual fact, if traced to its root, is found to be borrowed from some material appearance. *Right* originally means *straight; wrong* means *twisted. Spirit* primarily means *wind; transgression,* the crossing of a *line; supercilious,* the *raising of the eye-brow.* We say the *heart* to express emotion, the *head* to denote thought; and *thought* and *emotion* are, in their turn, words borrowed from sensible things, and now appropriated to spiritual nature. Most of the process by which this transformation is made, is hidden from us in the remote time when language was framed; but the same tendency may be daily observed in children. Children and savages use only nouns or names of things, which they continually convert into verbs, and apply to analogous mental acts.

2. But this origin of all words that convey a spiritual import,—so conspicuous a fact in the history of language,—is our least debt to nature. It is not words only that are emblematic; it is things which are emblematic. Every natural fact is a symbol of some spiritual fact. Every appearance in nature corresponds to some state of the mind, and that state of the mind can only be described by presenting that natural appearance as its picture. An enraged man is a lion, a cunning man is a fox, a firm man is a rock, a learned man is a torch. A lamb is innocence; a snake is subtle spite; flowers express to us the delicate affections. Light and darkness are our familiar expression for knowledge and ignorance; and heat for love. Visible distance behind and before us, is respectively our image of memory and hope.

Who looks upon a river in a meditative hour, and is not reminded of the flux of all things? Throw a stone into the stream, and the circles that propagate themselves are the beautiful type of all influence. Man is conscious of a universal soul within or behind his individual life, wherein, as in a firmament, the natures of Justice, Truth, Love, Freedom, arise and shine. This universal soul, he calls Reason: it is not mine or thine or his, but we are its; we are its property and men. And the blue sky in which the private earth is buried, the sky with its eternal calm, and full of everlasting orbs, is the type of Reason. That which, intellectually considered, we call Reason, considered in relation to nature, we call Spirit. Spirit is the Creator. Spirit hath life in itself. And man in all ages and countries, embodies it in his language, as the FATHER.

It is easily seen that there is nothing lucky or capricious in these analogies, but that they are constant, and pervade nature. These are not the dreams of a few poets, here and there, but man is an analogist, and studies relations in all objects. He is placed in the centre of beings, and a ray of relation passes from every other being to him. And neither can man be understood without these objects, nor these objects without man. All the facts in natural history taken by themselves, have no value, but are barren like a single sex. But marry it to human history, and it is full of life. Whole Floras, all Linnæus' and Buffon's volumes, are but dry catalogues of facts; but the most trivial of these facts, the habit of a plant, the organs, or work, or noise of an insect, applied to the illustration of a fact in intellectual philosophy, or, in any way associated to human nature, affects us in the most lively and agreeable manner. The seed of a plant,—to what affecting analogies in the nature of man, is that little fruit made use of, in all discourse, up to the voice of Paul, who calls the human corpse a seed,—"It is sown a natural body; it is raised a spiritual body." The motion of the earth round its axis, and round the sun, makes the day, and the year. These are certain amounts of brute light and heat. But is there no intent of an analogy between man's life and the seasons? And do the seasons gain no grandeur or pathos from that analogy? The instincts of the ant are very unimportant considered as the ant's; but the moment a ray of relation is seen to extend from it to man, and the little drudge is seen to be a monitor, a little body with a mighty heart, then all its habits, even that said to be recently observed, that it never sleeps, become sublime.

Because of this radical correspondence between visible things and human thoughts, savages, who have only what is necessary, converse in figures. As we go back in history, language becomes more picturesque, until its infancy, when it is all poetry; or, all spiritual facts are represented by natural symbols. The same symbols are found to make the original elements of all languages. It has moreover been observed, that the idioms of all languages approach each other in passages of the greatest eloquence and power. And as this is the first language, so is it the last. This immediate dependence of language upon nature, this conversion of an outward phenomenon into a type of somewhat in human life, never loses its power to affect us. It is this which gives that piquancy to the conversation of a strong-natured farmer or back-woodsman, which all men relish.

Thus is nature an interpreter, by whose means man converses with his fellow men. A man's power to connect his thought with its proper symbol, and so utter it, depends on the simplicity of his character, that is, upon his love of truth and his desire to communicate it without loss. The corruption of man is followed by the corruption of language. When simplicity of character and the sovereignty of ideas is broken up by the prevalence of secondary desires, the desire of riches, the desire of pleasure, the desire of power, the desire of praise,—and duplicity and falsehood take place of simplicity and truth, the power over nature as an interpreter of the will, is in a degree lost; new imagery ceases to be created, and old words are perverted to stand for things which are not; a paper currency is employed when there is no bullion in the vaults. In due time, the fraud is manifest, and words lose all power to stimulate the understanding or the affections. Hundreds of writers may be found in every long-civilized nation, who for a short time believe, and make others believe, that they see and utter truths, who do not of themselves clothe one thought in its natural garment, but who feed unconsciously upon the language created by the primary writers of the country, those, namely, who hold primarily on nature.

But wise men pierce this rotten diction and fasten words again to visible things; so that picturesque language is at once a commanding certificate that he who employs it, is a man in alliance with truth and God. The moment our discourse rises above the ground line of familiar facts, and is inflamed with passion or exalted by thought, it clothes itself in images. A man conversing in earnest, if he watch his intellectual processes, will find that always a material image, more or less luminous, arises in his mind, cotemporaneous with every thought, which furnishes the vestment of the thought. Hence, good writing and brilliant discourse are perpetual allegories. This imagery is spontaneous. It is the blending of experience with the present action of the mind. It is proper creation. It is the working of the Original Cause through the instruments he has already made.

These facts may suggest the advantage which the country-life possesses for a powerful mind, over the artificial and curtailed life of cities. We know more from nature than we can at will communicate. Its light flows into the mind evermore, and we forget its presence. The poet, the orator, bred in the woods, whose senses have been nourished by their fair and appeasing changes, year after year, without design and without heed,—shall not lose their lesson altogether, in the roar of cities or the broil of politics. Long hereafter, amidst agitation and terror in national councils,—in the hour of revolution,—these solemn images shall reappear in their morning lustre, as fit symbols and words of the thoughts which the passing events shall awaken. At the call of a noble sentiment, again the woods wave, the pines murmur, the river rolls and shines, and the cattle low upon the mountains, as he saw and heard them in his infancy. And with these forms, the spells of persuasion, the keys of power are put into his hands.

3. We are thus assisted by natural objects in the expression of particular meanings. But how great a language to convey such pepper-corn informations! Did it need such noble races of creatures, this profusion of forms, this host of orbs in heaven, to furnish man with the dictionary and grammar of his munici-

pal speech? Whilst we use this grand cipher to expedite the affairs of our pot and kettle, we feel that we have not yet put it to its use, neither are able. We are like travellers using the cinders of a volcano to roast their eggs. Whilst we see that it always stands ready to clothe what we would say, we cannot avoid the question, whether the characters are not significant of themselves. Have mountains, and waves, and skies, no significance but what we consciously give them, when we employ them as emblems of our thoughts? The world is emblematic. Parts of speech are metaphors because the whole of nature is a metaphor of the human mind. The laws of moral nature answer to those of matter as face to face in a glass. "The visible world and the relation of its parts, is the dial plate of the invisible." The axioms of physics translate the laws of ethics. Thus, "the whole is greater than its part"; "reaction is equal to action"; "the smallest weight may be made to lift the greatest, the difference of weight being compensated by time"; and many the like propositions, which have an ethical as well as physical sense. These propositions have a much more extensive and universal sense when applied to human life, than when confined to technical use.

In like manner, the memorable words of history, and the proverbs of nations, consist usually of a natural fact, selected as a picture or parable of a moral truth. Thus: A rolling stone gathers no moss; A bird in the hand is worth two in the bush; A cripple in the right way, will beat a racer in the wrong; Make hay whilst the sun shines; 'T is hard to carry a full cup even; Vinegar is the son of wine; The last ounce broke the camel's back; Long-lived trees make roots first;—and the like. In their primary sense these are trivial facts, but we repeat them for the value of their analogical import. What is true of proverbs, is true of all fables, parables, and allegories.

This relation between the mind and matter is not fancied by some poet, but stands in the will of God, and so is free to be known by all men. It appears to men, or it does not appear. When in fortunate hours we ponder this miracle, the wise man doubts, if, at all other times, he is not blind and deaf;

> ——— "Can these things be,
> And overcome us like a summer's cloud,
> Without our special wonder?"

for the universe becomes transparent, and the light of higher laws than its own, shines through it. It is the standing problem which has exercised the wonder and the study of every fine genius since the world began; from the era of the Egyptians and the Brahmins, to that of Pythagoras, of Plato, of Bacon, of Leibnitz, of Swedenborg. There sits the Sphinx at the road-side, and from age to age, as each prophet comes by, he tries his fortune at reading her riddle. There seems to be a necessity in spirit to manifest itself in material forms; and day and night, river and storm, beast and bird, acid and alkali, preëxist in necessary

Ideas in the mind of God, and are what they are by virtue of preceding affections, in the world of spirit. A Fact is the end or last issue of spirit. The visible creation is the terminus or the circumference of the invisible world. ''Material objects,'' said a French philosopher, ''are necessarily kinds of *scoriæ* of the substantial thoughts of the Creator, which must always preserve an exact relation to their first origin; in other words, visible nature must have a spiritual and moral side.''

This doctrine is abstruse, and though the images of ''garment,'' ''scoriæ,'' ''mirror,'' &c., may stimulate the fancy, we must summon the aid of subtler and more vital expositors to make it plain. ''Every scripture is to be interpreted by the same spirit which gave it forth,''—is the fundamental law of criticism. A life in harmony with nature, the love of truth and of virtue, will purge the eyes to understand her text. By degrees we may come to know the primitive sense of the permanent objects of nature, so that the world shall be to us an open book, and every form significant of its hidden life and final cause.

A new interest surpises us, whilst, under the view now suggested, we contemplate the fearful extent and multitude of objects; since ''every object rightly seen, unlocks a new faculty of the soul.'' That which was unconscious truth, becomes, when interpreted and defined in an object, a part of the domain of knowledge,—a new amount to the magazine of power.

Chapter V

DISCIPLINE

In view of this significance of nature, we arrive at once at a new fact, that nature is a discipline. This use of the world includes the preceding uses, as parts of itself.

Space, time, society, labor, climate, food, locomotion, the animals, the mechanical forces, give us sincerest lessons, day by day, whose meaning is unlimited. They educate both the Understanding and the Reason. Every property of matter is a school for the understanding,—its solidity or resistance, its inertia, its extension, its figure, its divisibility. The understanding adds, divides, combines, measures, and finds everlasting nutriment and room for its activity in this worthy scene. Meantime, Reason transfers all these lessons into its own world of thought, by perceiving the analogy that marries Matter and Mind.

1. Nature is a discipline of the understanding in intellectual truths. Our dealing with sensible objects is a constant exercise in the necessary lessons of difference, of likeness, of order, of being and seeming, of progressive arrangement; of ascent from particular to general; of combination to one end of manifold forces. Proportioned to the importance of the organ to be formed, is the extreme care with which its tuition is provided,—a care pretermitted in no single case. What tedious training, day after day, year after year, never ending, to

form the common sense; what continual reproduction of annoyances, inconveniences, dilemmas; what rejoicing over us of little men; what disputing of prices, what reckonings of interest,—and all to form the Hand of the mind;—to instruct us that "good thoughts are no better than good dreams, unless they be executed!"

The same good office is performed by Property and its filial systems of debt and credit. Debt, grinding debt, whose iron face the widow, the orphan, and the sons of genius fear and hate;—debt, which consumes so much time, which so cripples and disheartens a great spirit with cares that seem so base, is a preceptor whose lessons cannot be foregone, and is needed most by those who suffer from it most. Moreover, property, which has been well compared to snow,—"if it fall level to-day, it will be blown into drifts to-morrow,"—is merely the surface action of internal machinery, like the index on the face of a clock. Whilst now it is the gymnastics of the understanding, it is hiving in the foresight of the spirit, experience in profounder laws.

The whole character and fortune of the individual are affected by the least inequalities in the culture of the understanding; for example, in the perception of differences. Therefore is Space, and therefore Time, that man may know that things are not huddled and lumped, but sundered and individual. A bell and a plough have each their use, and neither can do the office of the other. Water is good to drink, coal to burn, wool to wear; but wool cannot be drunk, nor water spun, nor coal eaten. The wise man shows his wisdom in separation, in gradation, and his scale of creatures and of merits, is as wide as nature. The foolish have no range in their scale, but suppose every man is as every other man. What is not good they call the worst, and what is not hateful, they call the best.

In like manner, what good heed, nature forms in us! She pardons no mistakes. Her yea is yea, and her nay, nay.

The first steps in Agriculture, Astronomy, Zoölogy, (those first steps which the farmer, the hunter, and the sailor take,) teach that nature's dice are always loaded; that in her heaps and rubbish are concealed sure and useful results.

How calmly and genially the mind apprehends one after another the laws of physics! What noble emotions dilate the mortal as he enters into the counsels of the creation, and feels by knowledge the privilege to BE! His insight refines him. The beauty of nature shines in his own breast. Man is greater that he can see this, and the universe less, because Time and Space relations vanish as laws are known.

Here again we are impressed and even daunted by the immense Universe to be explored. "What we know, is a point to what we do not know." Open any recent journal of science, and weigh the problems suggested concerning Light, Heat, Electricity, Magnetism, Physiology, Geology, and judge whether the interest of natural science is likely to be soon exhausted.

Passing by many particulars of the discipline of nature we must not omit to specify two.

The exercise of the Will or the lesson of power is taught in every event. From the child's successive possession of his several senses up to the hour when he saith, "thy will be done!" he is learning the secret, that he can reduce under his will, not only particular events, but great classes, nay the whole series of events, and so conform all facts to his character. Nature is thoroughly mediate. It is made to serve. It receives the dominion of man as meekly as the ass on which the Saviour rode. It offers all its kingdoms to man as the raw material which he may mould into what is useful. Man is never weary of working it up. He forges the subtile and delicate air into wise and melodious words, and gives them wing as angels of persuasion and command. More and more, with every thought, does his kingdom stretch over things, until the world becomes, at last, only a realized will,—the double of the man.

2. Sensible objects conform to the premonitions of Reason and reflect the conscience. All things are moral; and in their boundless changes have an unceasing reference to spiritual nature. Therefore is nature glorious with form, color, and motion, that every globe in the remotest heaven; every chemical change from the rudest crystal up to the laws of life; every change of vegetation from the first principle of growth in the eye of a leaf, to the tropical forest and antediluvian coal-mine; every animal function from the sponge up to Hercules, shall hint or thunder to man the laws of right and wrong, and echo the Ten Commandments. Therefore is nature always the ally of Religion: lends all her pomp and riches to the religious sentiment. Prophet and priest, David, Isaiah, Jesus, have drawn deeply from this source.

This ethical character so penetrates the bone and marrow of nature, as to seem the end for which it was made. Whatever private purpose is answered by any member or part, this is its public and universal function, and is never omitted. Nothing in nature is exhausted in its first use. When a thing has served an end to the uttermost, it is wholly new for an ulterior service. In God, every end is converted into a new means. Thus the use of Commodity, regarded by itself, is mean and squalid. But it is to the mind an education in the great doctrine of Use, namely, that a thing is good only so far as it serves; that a conspiring of parts and efforts to the production of an end, is essential to any being. The first and gross manifestation of this truth, is our inevitable and hated training in values and wants, in corn and meat.

It has already been illustrated, in treating of the significance of material things, that every natural process is but a version of a moral sentence. The moral law lies at the centre of nature and radiates to the circumference. It is the pith and marrow of every substance, every relation, and every process. All things with which we deal, preach to us. What is a farm but a mute gospel! The chaff and the wheat, weeds and plants, blight, rain, insects, sun,—it is a sacred emblem from the first furrow of spring to the last stack which the snow of winter overtakes in the fields. But the sailor, the shepherd, the miner, the merchant, in their several resorts, have each an experience precisely parallel and leading to the same conclusions. Because all organizations are radically alike. Nor can it be doubted that this moral sentiment which thus scents the air, and grows in the grain, and impregnates the waters of the world, is caught by man and sinks into his soul. The moral influence of nature upon every individual is that amount of truth which it illustrates to him. Who can estimate this? Who can guess how much firmness the sea-beaten rock has taught the fisherman? how much tranquillity has been reflected to man from the azure sky, over whose unspotted deeps the winds forevermore drive flocks of stormy clouds, and leave no wrinkle or stain? how much industry and providence and affection we have caught from the pantomime of brutes? What a searching preacher of self-command is the varying phenomenon of Health!

Herein is especially apprehended the Unity of Nature,—the Unity in Variety,—which meets us everywhere. All the endless variety of things make a unique, an identical impression. Xenophanes complained in his old age, that, look where he would, all things hastened back to Unity. He was weary of seeing the same entity in the tedious variety of forms. The fable of Proteus has a cordial truth. Every particular in nature, a leaf, a drop, a crystal, a moment of time is related to the whole, and partakes of the perfection of the whole. Each particle is a microcosm, and faithfully renders the likeness of the world.

Not only resemblances exist in things whose analogy is obvious, as when we detect the type of the human hand in the flipper of the fossil saurus, but also in objects wherein there is great superficial unlikeness. Thus architecture is called "frozen music," by De Stael and Goethe. "A Gothic church," said Coleridge, "is a petrified religion." Michael Angelo maintained, that, to an architect, a knowledge of anatomy is essential. In Haydn's oratorios, the notes present to the imagination not only motions, as, of the snake, the stag, and the elephant, but colors also; as the green grass. The granite is differenced in its laws only by the more or less of heat, from the river that wears it away. The river, as it flows, resembles the air that flows over it; the air resembles the light which traverses it with more subtile currents; the light resembles the heat which rides with it through Space. Each creature is only a modification of the other; the likeness in them is more than the difference, and their radical law is one and the same. Hence it is, that a rule of one art, or a law of one organization, holds true throughout nature. So intimate is this Unity, that, it is easily seen, it lies under the undermost garment of nature, and betrays its source in universal Spirit. For, it pervades Thought also. Every universal truth which we express in words, implies or supposes every other truth. *Omne verum vero consonat.* It is like a great circle on a sphere, comprising all possible circles; which, however, may be drawn, and comprise it, in like manner. Every such truth is the absolute Ens seen from one side. But it has innumerable sides.

The same central Unity is still more conspicuous in actions. Words are finite organs of the infinite mind. They cannot cover the dimensions of what is in truth. They break, chop, and impoverish it. An action is the perfection and publication of thought. A right action seems to fill the eye, and to be related to all nature. "The wise man, in doing one thing, does all; or, in the one thing he does rightly, he sees the likeness of all which is done rightly."

Words and actions are not the attributes of mute and brute nature. They introduce us to that singular form which predominates over all other forms. This is the human. All other organizations appear to be degradations of the human form. When this organization appears among so many that surround it, the spirit prefers it to all others. It says, "From such as this, have I drawn joy and knowledge. In such as this, have I found and beheld myself. I will speak to it. It can speak again. It can yield me thought already formed and alive." In fact, the eye,—the mind,—is always accompanied by these forms, male and female; and these are incomparably the richest informations of the power and order that lie at the heart of things. Unfortunately, every one of them bears the marks as of some injury; is marred and superficially defective. Nevertheless, far different from the deaf and dumb nature around them, these all rest like fountain-pipes on the unfathomed sea of thought and virtue whereto they alone, of all organizations, are the entrances.

It were a pleasant inquiry to follow into detail their ministry to our education, but where would it stop? We are associated in adolescent and adult life with some friends, who, like skies and waters, are coextensive with our idea; who, answering each to a certain affection of the soul, satisfy our desire on that side; whom we lack power to put at such focal distance from us, that we can mend or even analyze them. We cannot chuse but love them. When much intercourse with a friend has supplied us with a standard of excellence, and has increased our respect for the resources of God who thus sends a real person to outgo our ideal; when he has, moreover, become an object of thought, and, whilst his character retains all its unconscious effect, is converted in the mind into solid and sweet wisdom,—it is a sign to us that his office is closing, and he is commonly withdrawn from our sight in a short time.

Chapter VI

IDEALISM

Thus is the unspeakable but intelligible and practicable meaning of the world conveyed to man, the immortal pupil, in every object of sense. To this one end of Discipline, all parts of nature conspire.

A noble doubt perpetually suggests itself, whether this end be not the Final Cause of the Universe; and whether nature outwardly exists. It is a sufficient account of that Appearance we call the World, that God will teach a human mind, and so makes it the receiver of a certain number of congruent sensations, which we call sun and moon, man and woman, house and trade. In my utter impotence to test the authenticity of the report of my senses, to know whether the impressions they make on me correspond with outlying objects, what difference does it make, whether Orion is up there in heaven, or some god paints the image in the firmament of the soul? The relations of parts and the end of the whole remaining the same, what is the difference, whether land and sea interact, and worlds revolve and intermingle without number or end,—deep yawning under deep, and galaxy balancing galaxy, throughout absolute space, or, whether, without relations of time and space, the same appearances are inscribed in the constant faith of man. Whether nature enjoy a substantial existence without, or is only in the apocalypse of the mind, it is alike useful and alike venerable to me. Be it what it may, it is ideal to me, so long as I cannot try the accuracy of my senses.

The frivolous make themselves merry with the Ideal theory, as if its consequences were burlesque; as if it affected the stability of nature. It surely does not. God never jests with us, and will not compromise the end of nature, by permitting any inconsequence in its procession. Any distrust of the permanence of laws, would paralyze the faculties of man. Their permanence is sacredly respected, and his faith therein is perfect. The wheels and springs of man are all set to the hypothesis of the permanence of nature. We are not built like a ship to be tossed, but like a house to stand. It is a natural consequence of this structure, that, so long as the active powers predominate over the reflective, we resist with indignation any hint that nature is more short-lived or mutable than spirit. The broker, the wheelwright, the carpenter, the tollman, are much displeased at the intimation.

But whilst we acquiesce entirely in the permanence of natural laws, the question of the absolute existence of nature, still remains open. It is the uniform effect of culture on the human mind, not to shake our faith in the stability of particular phenomena, as of heat, water, azote; but to lead us to regard nature as a phenomenon, not a substance; to attribute necessary existence to spirit; to esteem nature as an accident and an effect.

To the senses and the unrenewed understanding, belongs a sort of instinctive belief in the absolute existence of nature. In their view, man and nature are indissolubly joined. Things are ultimates, and they never look beyond their sphere. The presence of Reason mars this faith. The first effort of thought tends to relax this despotism of the senses, which binds us to nature as if we were a part of it, and shows us nature aloof, and, as it were, afloat. Until this higher agency intervened, the animal eye sees, with wonderful accuracy, sharp outlines and colored surfaces. When the eye of Reason opens, to outline and surface are at once added, grace and expression. These proceed from imagination and affection, and abate somewhat of the angular distinctness of objects. If the

Reason be stimulated to more earnest vision, outlines and surfaces become transparent, and are no longer seen; causes and spirits are seen through them. The best, the happiest moments of life, are these delicious awakenings of the higher powers, and the reverential withdrawing of nature before its God.

Let us proceed to indicate the effects of culture.

1. Our first institution in the Ideal philosophy is a hint from nature herself.

Nature is made to conspire with spirit to emancipate us. Certain mechanical changes, a small alteration in our local position apprizes us of a dualism. We are strangely affected by seeing the shore from a moving ship, from a balloon, or through the tints of an unusual sky. The least change in our point of view, gives the whole world a pictorial air. A man who seldom rides, needs only to get into a coach and traverse his own town, to turn the street into a puppet-show. The men, the women,—talking, running, bartering, fighting,—the earnest mechanic, the lounger, the beggar, the boys, the dogs, are unrealized at once, or, at least, wholly detached from all relation to the observer, and seen as apparent, not substantial beings. What new thoughts are suggested by seeing a face of country quite familiar, in the rapid movement of the rail-road car! Nay, the most wonted objects, (make a very slight change in the point of vision,) please us most. In a camera obscura, the butcher's cart, and the figure of one of our own family amuse us. So a portrait of a well-known face gratifies us. Turn the eyes upside down, by looking at the landscape through your legs, and how agreeable is the picture, though you have seen it any time these twenty years!

In these cases, by mechanical means, is suggested the difference between the observer and the spectacle,—between man and nature. Hence arises a pleasure mixed with awe; I may say, a low degree of the sublime is felt from the fact, probably, that man is hereby apprized, that, whilst the world is a spectacle, something in himself is stable.

2. In a higher manner, the poet communicates the same pleasure. By a few strokes he delineates, as on air, the sun, the mountain, the camp, the city, the hero, the maiden, not different from what we know them, but only lifted from the ground and afloat before the eye. He unfixes the land and the sea, makes them revolve around the axis of his primary thought, and disposes them anew. Possessed himself by a heroic passion, he uses matter as symbols of it. The sensual man conforms thoughts to things; the poet conforms things to his thoughts. The one esteems nature as rooted and fast; the other, as fluid, and impresses his being thereon. To him, the refractory world is ductile and flexible; he invests dust and stones with humanity, and makes them the words of the Reason. The imagination may be defined to be, the use which the Reason makes of the material world. Shakespeare possesses the power of subordinating nature for the purposes of expression, beyond all poets. His imperial muse tosses the creation like a bauble from hand to hand, to embody any capricious

shade of thought that is uppermost in his mind. The remotest spaces of nature are visited, and the farthest sundered things are brought together, by a subtile spiritual connexion. We are made aware that magnitude of material things is merely relative, and all objects shrink and expand to serve the passion of the poet. Thus, in his sonnets, the lays of birds, the scents and dyes of flowers, he finds to be the *shadow* of his beloved; time, which keeps her from him, is his *chest;* the suspicion she has awakened, is her *ornament;*

> The ornament of beauty is Suspect,
> A crow which flies in heaven's sweetest air.

His passion is not the fruit of chance; it swells, as he speaks, to a city, or a state.

> No, it was builded far from accident;
> It suffers not in smiling pomp, nor falls
> Under the brow of thralling discontent;
> It fears not policy, that heretic,
> That works on leases of short numbered hours,
> But all alone stands hugely politic.

In the strength of his constancy, the Pyramids seem to him recent and transitory. And the freshness of youth and love dazzles him with its resemblance to morning.

> Take those lips away
> Which so sweetly were forsworn;
> And those eyes,—the break of day,
> Lights that do mislead the morn.

The wild beauty of this hyperbole, I may say, in passing, it would not be easy to match in literature.

This transfiguration which all material objects undergo through the passion of the poet,—this power which he exerts, at any moment, to magnify the small, to micrify the great,—might be illustrated by a thousand examples from his Plays. I have before me the Tempest, and will cite only these few lines.

> ARIEL. The strong based promontory
> Have I made shake, and by the spurs plucked up
> The pine and cedar.

Prospero calls for music to soothe the frantic Alonzo, and his companions;

> A solemn air, and the best comforter
> To an unsettled fancy, cure thy brains
> Now useless, boiled within thy skull.

Again;

> The charm dissolves apace
> And, as the morning steals upon the night,
> Melting the darkness, so their rising senses
> Begin to chase the ignorant fumes that mantle
> Their clearer reason.
> Their understanding
> Begins to swell: and the approaching tide
> Will shortly fill the reasonable shores
> That now lie foul and muddy.

The perception of real affinities between events, (that is to say, of *ideal* affinities, for those only are real,) enables the poet thus to make free with the most imposing forms and phenomena of the world, and to assert the predominance of the soul.

3. Whilst thus the poet delights us by animating nature like a creator, with his own thoughts, he differs from the philosopher only herein, that the one proposes Beauty as his main end; the other Truth. But, the philosopher, not less than the poet, postpones the apparent order and relations of things to the empire of thought. "The problem of philosophy," according to Plato, "is, for all that exists conditionally, to find a ground unconditioned and absolute." It proceeds on the faith that a law determines all phenomena, which being known, the phenomena can be predicted. That law, when in the mind, is an idea. Its beauty is infinite. The true philosopher and the true poet are one, and a beauty, which is truth, and a truth, which is beauty, is the aim of both. Is not the charm of one of Plato's or Aristotle's definitions, strictly like that of the Antigone of Sophocles? It is, in both cases, that a spiritual life has been imparted to nature; that the solid seeming block of matter has been pervaded and dissolved by a thought; that this feeble human being has penetrated the vast masses of nature with an informing soul, and recognised itself in their harmony, that is, seized their law. In physics, when this is attained, the memory disburthens itself of its cumbrous catalogues of particulars, and carries centuries of observation in a single formula.

Thus even in physics, the material is ever degraded before the spiritual. The astronomer, the geometer, rely on their irrefragable analysis, and disdain the results of observation. The sublime remark of Euler on his law of arches, "This will be found contrary to all experience, yet is true"; had already transferred nature into the mind, and left matter like an outcast corpse.

4. Intellectual science has been observed to beget invariably a doubt of the existence of matter. Turgot said, "He that has never doubted the existence of matter, may be assured he has no aptitude for metaphysical inquiries." It fastens the attention upon immortal necessary uncreated natures, that is, upon

Ideas; and in their beautiful and majestic presence, we feel that our outward being is a dream and a shade. Whilst we wait in this Olympus of gods, we think of nature as an appendix to the soul. We ascend into their region, and know that these are the thoughts of the Supreme Being. "These are they who were set up from everlasting, from the beginning, or ever the earth was. When he prepared the heavens, they were there; when he established the clouds above, when he strengthened the fountains of the deep. Then they were by him, as one brought up with him. Of them took he counsel."

Their influence is proportionate. As objects of science, they are accessible to few men. Yet all men are capable of being raised by piety or by passion, into their region. And no man touches these divine natures, without becoming, in some degree, himself divine. Like a new soul, they renew the body. We become physically nimble and lightsome; we tread on air; life is no longer irksome, and we think it will never be so. No man fears age or misfortune or death, in their serene company, for he is transported out of the district of change. Whilst we behold unveiled the nature of Justice and Truth, we learn the difference between the absolute and the condition or relative. We apprehend the absolute. As it were, for the first time, *we exist*. We become immortal, for we learn that time and space are relations of matter; that, with a perception of truth, or a virtuous will, they have no affinity.

5. Finally, religion and ethics, which may be fitly called,—the practice of ideas, or the introduction of ideas into life,—have an analogous effect with all lower culture, in degrading nature and suggesting its dependence on spirit. Ethics and religion differ herein, that the one is the system of human duties commencing from man; the other, from God. Religion includes the personality of God; Ethics does not. They are one to our present design. They both put nature under foot. The first and last lesson of religion is, "The things that are seen, are temporal; the things that are unseen are eternal." It puts an affront upon nature. It does that for the unschooled, which philosophy does for Berkeley and Viasa. The uniform language that may be heard in the churches of the most ignorant sects, is,—"Contemn the unsubstantial shows of the world; they are vanities, dreams, shadows, unrealities; seek the realities of religion." The devotee flouts nature. Some theosophists have arrived at a certain hostility and indignation towards matter, as the Manichean and Plotinus. They distrusted in themselves any looking back to these flesh-pots of Egypt. Plotinus was ashamed of his body. In short, they might all better say of matter, what Michael Angelo said of external beauty, "it is the frail and weary weed, in which God dresses the soul, which he has called into time."

It appears that motion, poetry, physical and intellectual science, and religion, all tend to affect our convictions of the reality of the external world. But I own there is something ungrateful in expanding too curiously the particulars of the general proposition, that all culture tends to imbue us with idealism. I have no hostility to nature, but a child's love to it. I expand and live in the warm day like corn and melons. Let us speak her fair. I do not wish to fling stones at my beautiful mother, nor soil my gentle nest. I only wish to indicate the true position of nature in regard to man, wherein to establish man, all right education tends; as the ground which to attain is the object of human life, that is, of man's connexion with nature. Culture inverts the vulgar views of nature, and brings the mind to call that apparent, which it uses to call real, and that real, which it uses to call visionary. Children, it is true, believe in the external world. The belief that it appears only, is an afterthought, but with culture, this faith will as surely arise on the mind as did the first.

The advantage of the ideal theory over the popular faith, is this, that it presents the world in precisely that view which is most desirable to the mind. It is, in fact, the view which Reason, both speculative and practical, that is, philosophy and virtue, take. For, seen in the light of thought, the world always is phenomenal; and virtue subordinates it to the mind. Idealism sees the world in God. It beholds the whole circle of persons and things, of actions and events, of country and religion, not as painfully accumulated, atom after atom, act after act, in an aged creeping Past, but as one vast picture, which God paints on the instant eternity, for the contemplation of the soul. Therefore the soul holds itself off from a too trivial and microscopic study of the universal tablet. It respects the end too much, to immerse itself in the means. It sees something more important in Christianity, than the scandals of ecclesiastical history or the niceties of criticism; and, very incurious concerning persons or miracles, and not at all disturbed by chasms of historical evidence, it accepts from God the phenomenon, as it finds it, as the pure and awful form of religion in the world. It is not hot and passionate at the appearance of what it calls its own good or bad fortune, at the union or opposition of other persons. No man is its enemy. It accepts whatsoever befalls, as part of its lesson. It is a watcher more than a doer, and it is a doer, only that it may the better watch.

Chapter VII

SPIRIT

It is essential to a true theory of nature and of man, that it should contain somewhat progressive. Uses that are exhausted or that may be, and facts that end in the statement, cannot be all that is true of this brave lodging wherein man is harbored, and wherein all his faculties find appropriate and endless exercise. And all the uses of nature admit of being summed in one, which yields the activity of man an infinite scope. Through all its kingdoms, to the suburbs and outskirts of things, it is faithful to the cause whence it had its origin. It always speaks of Spirit. It suggests the absolute. It is a perpetual effect. It is a great shadow pointing always to the sun behind us.

The aspect of nature is devout. Like the figure of Jesus, she stands with bended head, and hands folded upon the breast. The happiest man is he who learns from nature the lesson of worship.

Of that ineffable essence which we call Spirit, he that thinks most, will say least. We can foresee God in the coarse and, as it were, distant phenomena of matter; but when we try to define and describe himself, both language and thought desert us, and we are as helpless as fools and savages. That essence refuses to be recorded in propositions, but when man has worshipped him intellectually, the noblest ministry of nature is to stand as the apparition of God. It is the great organ through which the universal spirit speaks to the individual, and strives to lead back the individual to it.

When we consider Spirit, we see that the views already presented do not include the whole circumference of man. We must add some related thoughts.

Three problems are put by nature to the mind; What is matter? Whence is it? and Whereto? The first of these questions only, the ideal theory answers. Idealism saith: matter is a phenomenon, not a substance. Idealism acquaints us with the total disparity between the evidence of our own being, and the evidence of the world's being. The one is perfect; the other, incapable of any assurance; the mind is a part of the nature of things; the world is a divine dream, from which we may presently awake to the glories and certainties of day. Idealism is a hypothesis to account for nature by other principles than those of carpentry and chemistry. Yet, if it only deny the existence of matter, it does not satisfy the demands of the spirit. It leaves God out of me. It leaves me in the splendid labyrinth of my perceptions, to wander without end. Then the heart resists it, because it baulks the affections in denying substantive being to men and women. Nature is so pervaded with human life, that there is something of humanity in all, and in every particular. But this theory makes nature foreign to me, and does not account for that consanguinity which we acknowledge to it.

Let it stand then, in the present state of our knowledge, merely as a useful introductory hypothesis, serving to apprize us of the eternal distinction between the soul and the world.

But when, following the invisible steps of thought, we come to inquire, Whence is matter? and Whereto? many truths arise to us out of the recesses of consciousness. We learn that the highest is present to the soul of man, that the dread universal essence, which is not wisdom, or love, or beauty, or power, but all in one, and each entirely, is that for which all things exist, and that by which they are; that spirit creates; that behind nature, throughout nature, spirit is present; that spirit is one and not compound; that spirit does not act upon us from without, that is, in space and time, but spiritually, or through ourselves. Therefore, that spirit, that is, the Supreme Being, does not build up nature around us, but puts it forth through us, as the life of the tree puts forth new branches and leaves through the pores of the old. As a plant upon the earth, so a man rests upon the bosom of God; he is nourished by unfailing fountains, and draws, at his need, inexhaustible power. Who can set bounds to the possibilities of man? Once inspire the infinite, by being admitted to behold the absolute natures of justice and truth, and we learn that man has access to the entire mind of the Creator, is himself the creator in the finite. This view, which admonishes me where the sources of wisdom and power lie, and points to virtue as to

> "The golden key
> Which opes the palace of eternity,"

carries upon its face the highest certificate of truth, because it animates me to create my own world through the purification of my soul.

The world proceeds from the same spirit as the body of man. It is a remoter and inferior incarnation of God, a projection of God in the unconscious. But it differs from the body in one important respect. It is not, like that, now subjected to the human will. Its serene order is inviolable by us. It is therefore, to us, the present expositor of the divine mind. It is a fixed point whereby we may measure our departure. As we degenerate, the contrast between us and our house is more evident. We are as much strangers in nature, as we are aliens from God. We do not understand the notes of birds. The fox and the deer run away from us; the bear and tiger rend us. We do not know the uses of more than a few plants, as corn and the apple, the potato and the vine. Is not the landscape, every glimpse of which hath a grandeur, a face of him? Yet this may show us what discord is between man and nature, for you cannot freely admire a noble landscape, if laborers are digging in the field hard by. The poet finds something ridiculous in his delight, until he is out of the sight of men.

Chapter VIII

PROSPECTS

In inquiries respecting the laws of the world and the frame of things, the highest reason is always the truest. That which seems faintly possible—it is so refined, is often faint and dim because it is deepest seated in the mind among the eternal verities. Empirical science is apt to cloud the sight, and, by the very knowledge of functions and processes, to bereave the student of the manly contemplation of the whole. The savant becomes unpoetic. But the best read naturalist who lends an entire and devout attention to truth, will see that there remains much to learn of his relation to the world, and that it is not to be learned by any addition or subtraction or other comparison of known quantities, but is arrived at by untaught sallies of the spirit, by a continual self-recovery, and by entire humility. He will perceive that there are far more excellent qualities in the student than preciseness and infallibility; that a guess is often more fruitful than an indisputable affirmation, and that a dream may let us deeper into the secret of nature than a hundred concerted experiments.

For, the problems to be solved are precisely those which the physiologist and the naturalist omit to state. It is not so pertinent to man to know all the individuals of the animal kingdom, as it is to know whence and whereto is this tyrannizing unity in his constitution, which evermore separates and classifies things, endeavouring to reduce the most diverse to one form. When I behold a rich landscape, it is less to my purpose to recite correctly the order and superposition of the strata, than to know why all thought of multitude is lost in a tranquil sense of unity. I cannot greatly honor minuteness in details, so long as there is no hint to explain the relation between things and thoughts; no ray upon the *metaphysics* of conchology, of botany, of the arts, to show the relation of the forms of flowers, shells, animals, architecture, to the mind, and build science upon ideas. In a cabinet of natural history, we become sensible of a certain occult recognition and sympathy in regard to the most bizarre forms of beast, fish, and insect. The American who has been confined, in his own country, to the sight of buildings designed after foreign models, is surprised on entering York Minster or St. Peter's at Rome, by the feeling that these structures are imitations also,—faint copies of an invisible archetype. Nor has science sufficient humanity, so long as the naturalist overlooks that wonderful congruity which subsists between man and the world; of which he is lord, not because he is the most subtile inhabitant, but because he is its head and heart, and finds something of himself in every great and small thing, in every mountain stratum, in every new law of color, fact of astronomy, or atmospheric influence which observation or analysis lays open. A perception of this mystery inspires the muse of George Herbert, the beautiful psalmist of the seventeenth century. The following lines are part of his little poem on Man.

"Man is all symmetry,
Full of proportions, one limb to another,
And to all the world besides.
Each part may call the farthest, brother;
For head with foot hath private amity,
And both with moons and tides.

"Nothing hath got so far
But man hath caught and kept it as his prey;
His eyes dismount the highest star;
He is in little all the sphere.
Herbs gladly cure our flesh, because that they
Find their acquaintance there.

"For us, the winds do blow,
The earth doth rest, heaven move, and fountains flow;
Nothing we see, but means our good,
As our delight, or as our treasure;
The whole is either our cupboard of food,
Or cabinet of pleasure.

"The stars have us to bed:
Night draws the curtain; which the sun withdraws.
Music and light attend our head.
All things unto our flesh are kind,
In their descent and being; to our mind,
In their ascent and cause.

"More servants wait on man
Than he'll take notice of. In every path,
He treads down that which doth befriend him
When sickness makes him pale and wan.
Oh mighty love! Man is one world, and hath
Another to attend him."

The perception of this class of truths makes the eternal attraction which draws men to science, but the end is lost sight of in attention to the means. In view of this half-sight of science, we accept the sentence of Plato, that, "poetry comes nearer to vital truth than history." Every surmise and vaticination of the mind is entitled to a certain respect, and we learn to prefer imperfect theories, and sentences, which contain glimpses of truth, to digested systems which have no one valuable suggestion. A wise writer will feel that the ends of study and composition are best answered by announcing undiscovered regions of thought, and so communicating, through hope, new activity to the torpid spirit.

I shall therefore conclude this essay with some traditions of man and nature, which a certain poet sang to me; and which, as they have always been in the world, and perhaps reappear to every bard, may be both history and prophecy.

"The foundations of man are not in matter, but in spirit. But the element of spirit is eternity. To it, therefore, the longest series of events, the oldest chronologies are young and recent. In the cycle of the universal man, from whom the known individuals proceed, centuries are points, and all history is but the epoch of one degradation.

"We distrust and deny inwardly our sympathy with nature. We own and disown our relation to it, by turns. We are, like Nebuchadnezzar, dethroned, bereft of reason, and eating grass like an ox. But who can set limits to the remedial force of spirit?

"A man is a god in ruins. When men are innocent, life shall be longer, and shall pass into the immortal, as gently as we awake from dreams. Now, the world would be insane and rabid, if these disorganizations should last for hundreds of years. It is kept in check by death and infancy. Infancy is the perpetual Messiah, which comes into the arms of fallen men, and pleads with them to return to paradise.

"Man is the dwarf of himself. Once he was permeated and dissolved by spirit. He filled nature with his overflowing currents. Out from him sprang the sun and moon; from man, the sun; from woman, the moon. The laws of his mind, the periods of his actions externized themselves into day and night, into the year and the seasons. But, having made for himself this huge shell, his waters retired; he no longer fills the veins and veinlets; he is shrunk to a drop. He sees, that the structure still fits him, but fits him colossally. Say, rather, once it fitted him, now it corresponds to him from far and on high. He adores timidly his own work. Now is man the follower of the sun, and woman the follower of the moon. Yet sometimes he starts in his slumber, and wonders at himself and his house, and muses strangely at the resemblance betwixt him and it. He perceives that if his law is still paramount, if still he have elemental power, 'if his word is sterling yet in nature,' it is not conscious power, it is not inferior but superior to his will. It is Instinct." Thus my Orphic poet sang.

At present, man applies to nature but half his force. He works on the world with his understanding alone. He lives in it, and masters it by a penny-wisdom; and he that works most in it, is but a half-man, and whilst his arms are strong and his digestion good, his mind is imbruted and he is a selfish savage. His relation to nature, his power over it, is through the understanding; as by manure; the economic use of fire, wind, water, and the mariner's needle; steam, coal, chemical agriculture; the repairs of the human body by the dentist and the surgeon. This is such a resumption of power, as if a banished king should buy his territories inch by inch, instead of vaulting at once into his throne. Meantime, in the thick darkness, there are not wanting gleams of a better light,—occasional examples of the action of man upon nature with his entire force,—with reason as well as understanding. Such examples are: the traditions of miracles in the earliest antiquity of all nations; the history of Jesus Christ; the achievement of a principle, as in religious and political revolutions, and in the abolition of the Slave-trade; the miracles of enthusiasm, as those reported of Swedenborg, Hohenlohe, and the Shakers; many obscure and yet contested facts, now arranged under the name of Animal Magnetism; prayer; eloquence; self-healing; and the wisdom of children. These are examples of Reason's momentary grasp of the sceptre; the exertions of a power which exists not in time or space, but an instantaneous in-streaming causing power. The difference between the actual and the ideal force of man is happily figured by the schoolmen, in saying, that the knowledge of man is an evening knowledge, *vespertina cognitio,* but that of God is a morning knowledge, *matutina cognitio.*

The problem of restoring to the world original and eternal beauty, is solved by the redemption of the soul. The ruin or the blank, that we see when we look at nature, is in our own eye. The axis of vision is not coincident with the axis of things, and so they appear not transparent but opaque. The reason why the world lacks unity, and lies broken and in heaps, is, because man is disunited with himself. He cannot be a naturalist, until he satisfies all the demands of the spirit. Love is as much its demand, as perception. Indeed, neither can be perfect without the other. In the uttermost meaning of the words, thought is devout, and devotion is thought. Deep calls unto deep. But in actual life, the marriage is not celebrated. There are innocent men who worship God after the tradition of their fathers, but their sense of duty has not yet extended to the use of all their faculties. And there are patient naturalists, but they freeze their subject under the wintry light of understanding. Is not prayer also a study of truth,—a sally of the soul into the unfound infinite? No man ever prayed heartily, without learning something. But when a faithful thinker, resolute to detach every object from personal relations, and see it in the light of thought, shall, at the same time, kindle science with the fire of the holiest affections, then will God go forth anew into the creation.

It will not need, when the mind is prepared for study, to search for objects. The invariable mark of wisdom is to see the miraculous in the common. What is a day? What is a year? What is summer? What is woman? What is a child? What is sleep? To our blindness, these things seem unaffecting. We make fables to hide the baldness of the fact and conform it, as we say, to the higher law of the mind. But when the fact is seen under the light of an idea, the gaudy fable fades and shrivels. We behold the real higher law. To the wise, therefore, a fact is true poetry, and the most beautiful of fables. These wonders are brought to our own door. You also are a man. Man and woman, and their social life, poverty, labor, sleep, fear, fortune, are known to you. Learn that none of these things is superficial, but that each phenomenon hath its roots in the faculties and affections of the mind. Whilst the abstract question occupies your intellect, nature brings it in the concrete to be solved by your hands. It were a wise inquiry for the closet, to compare, point by point, especially at remarkable crises in life, our daily history, with the rise and progress of ideas in the mind.

So shall we come to look at the world with new eyes. It shall answer the endless inquiry of the intellect,—What is truth? and of the affections,—What is good? by yielding itself passive to the educated Will. Then shall come to pass what my poet said: ''Nature is not fixed but fluid. Spirit alters, moulds, makes it. The immobility or bruteness of nature, is the absence of spirit; to pure spirit, it is fluid, it is volatile, it is obedient. Every spirit builds itself a house; and beyond its house, a world; and beyond its world, a heaven. Know then, that the world exists for you. For you is the phenomenon perfect. What we are, that only can we see. All that Adam had, all that Cæsar could, you have and can do. Adam called his house, heaven and earth; Cæsar called his house, Rome; you perhaps call yours, a cobbler's trade; a hundred acres of ploughed land; or a scholar's garret. Yet line for line and point for point, your dominion is as great as theirs, though without fine names. Build, therefore, your own world. As fast as you conform your life to the pure idea in your mind, that will unfold its great proportions. A correspondent revolution in things will attend the influx of the spirit. So fast will disagreeable appearances, swine, spiders, snakes, pests, mad-houses, prisons, enemies, vanish; they are temporary and shall be no more seen. The sordor and filths of nature, the sun shall dry up, and the wind exhale. As when the summer comes from the south, the snow-banks melt, and the face of the earth becomes green before it, so shall the advancing spirit create its ornaments along its path, and carry with it the beauty it visits, and the song which enchants it; it shall draw beautiful faces, and warm hearts, and wise discourse, and heroic acts, around its way, until evil is no more seen. The kingdom of man over nature, which cometh not with observation,—a dominion such as now is beyond his dream of God,—he shall enter without more wonder than the blind man feels who is gradually restored to perfect sight."

1836

Aldo Leopold
From Round River

Conservation

CONSERVATION is a bird that flies faster than the shot we aim at it.

I can remember the day when I was sure that reforming the Game Commission would give us conservation. A group of us worked like Trojans cleaning house at the Capitol. When we got through we found we had just started. We learned that you can't conserve game by itself; to rebuild the game resource you must first rebuild the game range, and this means rebuilding the people who use it, and all of the things they use it for. The job we aspired to perform with a dozen volunteers is now baffling a hundred professionals. The job we thought would take five years will barely be started in fifty.

Our target, then, is a receding one. The task grows greater year by year, but so does its importance. We begin by seeking a few trees or birds; to get them we must build a new relationship between men and land.

Conservation is a state of harmony between men and land. By land is meant all of the things on, over, or in the earth. Harmony with land is like harmony with a friend; you cannot cherish his right hand and chop off his left. That is to say, you cannot love game and hate predators; you cannot conserve the waters and waste the ranges; you cannot build the forest and mine the farm. The land is one organism. Its parts, like our own parts, compete with each other and co-operate with each other. The competitions are as much a part of the inner workings as the co-operations. You can regulate them—cautiously—but not abolish them.

The outstanding scientific discovery of the twentieth century is not television, or radio, but rather the complexity of the land organism. Only those who know the most about it can appreciate how little we know about it. The last word in ignorance is the man who says of an animal or plant: 'What good is it?' If the land mechanism as a whole is good, then every part is good, whether we understand it or not. If the biota, in the course of aeons, has built something we like but do not understand, then who but a fool would discard seemingly useless parts? To keep every cog and wheel is the first precaution of intelligent tinkering.

Have we learned this first principle of conservation: to preserve all the parts of the land mechanism? No, because even the scientist does not yet recognize all of them.

In Germany there is a mountain called the Spessart. Its south slope bears the most magnificent oaks in the world. American cabinetmakers, when they want the last word in quality, use Spessart oak. The north slope, which should be the better, bears an indifferent stand of Scotch pine. Why? Both slopes are part of the same state forest; both have been managed with equally scrupulous care for two centuries. Why the difference?

Kick up the litter under the oaks and you will see that the leaves rot almost as fast as they fall. Under the pines, though, the needles pile up as a thick duff; decay is much slower. Why? Because in the Middle Ages the south slope was preserved as a deer forest by a hunting bishop; the north slope was pastured, plowed, and cut by settlers, just as we do with our woodlots in Wisconsin and Iowa today. Only after this period of abuse was the north slope replanted to pines. During this period of abuse something happened to the microscopic flora and fauna of the soil. The number of species was greatly reduced, i.e. the digestive apparatus of the soil lost some of its parts. Two centuries of conservation have not sufficed to restore these losses. It required the modern microscope, and a century of research in soil science, to discover the existence of these 'small cogs and wheels' which determine harmony or disharmony between men and land in the Spessart.

American conservation is, I fear, still concerned for the most part with show pieces. We have not yet learned to think in terms of small cogs and wheels. Look at our own back yard: at the prairies of Iowa and southern Wisconsin. What is the most valuable part of the prairie? The fat black soil, the chernozem. Who built the chernozem? The black prairie was built by the prairie plants, a hundred distinctive species of grasses, herbs, and shrubs; by the prairie fungi, insects, and bacteria; by the prairie mammals and birds, all interlocked in one humming community of co-operations and competitions, one biota. This biota, through ten thousand years of living and dying, burning and growing, preying and fleeing, freezing and thawing, built that dark and bloody ground we call prairie.

Our grandfathers did not, could not, know the origin of their prairie empire. They killed off the prairie fauna and they drove the flora to a last refuge on railroad embankments and roadsides. To our engineers this flora is merely weeds and brush; they ply it with grader and mower. Through processes of plant succession predictable by any botanist, the prairie garden becomes a refuge for quack grass. After the garden is gone, the highway department employs landscapers to dot the quack with elms, and with artistic clumps of Scotch pine, Japanese barberry, and Spiraea. Conservation Committees, en route to some important convention, whiz by and applaud this zeal for roadside beauty.

Some day we may need this prairie flora not only to look at but to rebuild the wasting soil of prairie farms. Many species may then be missing. We have our hearts in the right place, but we do not yet recognize the small cogs and wheels.

In our attempts to save the bigger cogs and wheels, we are still pretty naïve. A little repentance just before a species goes over the brink is enough to make us feel virtuous. When the species is gone we have a good cry and repeat the performance.

The recent extermination of the grizzly from most of the western stock-raising states is a case in point. Yes, we still have grizzlies in the Yellowstone. But the species is ridden by imported parasites; the rifles wait on every refuge boundary; new dude ranches and new roads constantly shrink the remaining range; every year sees fewer grizzlies on fewer ranges in fewer states. We console ourselves with the comfortable fallacy that a single museum-piece will do, ignoring the clear dictum of history that a species must be saved *in many places* if it is to be saved at all.

The ivory-billed woodpecker, the California condor, and the desert sheep are the next candidates for rescue. The rescues will not be effective until we discard the idea that one sample will do; until we insist on living with our flora and fauna in as many places as possible.

We need knowledge—public awareness—of the small cogs and wheels, but sometimes I think there is something we need even more. It is the thing that *Forest and Stream,* on its editorial masthead, once called 'a refined taste in natural objects.' Have we made any headway in developing 'a refined taste in natural objects'?

In the northern parts of the lake states we have a few wolves left. Each state offers a bounty on wolves. In addition, it may invoke the expert services of the U. S. Fish and Wildlife Service in wolf-control. Yet both this agency and the several conservation commissions complain of an increasing number of localities where there are too many deer for the available feed. Foresters complain of periodic damage from too many rabbits. Why, then, continue the public policy of wolf-extermination? We debate such questions in terms of economics and biology. The mammalogists assert the wolf is the natural check on too many deer. The sportsmen reply they will take care of excess deer. Another decade of argument and there will be no wolves to argue about. One conservation inkpot cancels another until the resource is gone. Why? Because the basic question has not been debated at all. The basic question hinges on 'a refined taste in natural objects.' Is a wolfless north woods any north woods at all?

The hawk and owl question seems to me a parallel one. When you band a hundred hawks in fall, twenty are shot and the bands returned during the subsequent year. No four-egged bird on earth can withstand such a kill. Our raptors are on the toboggan.

Science has been trying for a generation to classify hawks and owls into 'good' and 'bad' species, the 'good' being those that do more economic good than harm. It seems to me a mistake to call the issue on economic grounds, even sound ones. The basic issue transcends economics. The basic question is whether a hawkless, owl-less countryside is a livable countryside for Americans with eyes to see and ears to hear. Hawks and owls are a part of the land mechanism. Shall we discard them because they compete with game and poultry? Can we assume that these competitions which we perceive are more important than the co-operations which we do not perceive?

The fish-predator question is likewise parallel. I worked one summer for a club that owns (and cherishes) a delectable trout stream, set in a matrix of virgin forest. There are 30,000 acres of the stuff that dreams are made on. But look more closely and you fail to see what 'a refined taste in natural objects' demands of such a setting. Only once in a great while does a kingfisher rattle his praise of rushing water. Only here and there does an otter-slide on the bank tell the story of pups rollicking in the night. At sunset you may or may not see a heron; the rookery has been shot out. This club is in the throes of a genuine educational process. One faction wants simply more trout; another wants trout plus all the trimmings, and has employed a fish ecologist to find ways and means. Superficially the issue again is 'good' and 'bad' predators, but basically the issue is deeper. Any club privileged to own such a piece of land is morally obligated to keep all its parts, even though it means a few less trout in the creel.

In the lake states we are proud of our forest nurseries, and of the progress we are making in replanting what was once the north woods. But look in these nurseries and you will find no white cedar, no tamarack. Why no cedar? It grows too slowly, the deer eat it, the alders choke it. The prospect of a cedarless north woods does not depress our foresters; cedar has, in effect, been purged on grounds of economic inefficiency. For the same reason beech has been purged from the future forests of the Southeast. To these voluntary expungements of species from our future flora, we must add the involuntary ones arising from the importation of diseases: chestnut, persimmon, white pine. Is it sound economics to regard any plant as a separate entity, to proscribe or encourage it on the grounds of its individual performance? What will be the effect on animal life, on the soil, and on the health of the forest as an organism? Is there not an aesthetic as well as an economic issue? Is there, at bottom, any real distinction between aesthetics and economics? I do not know the answers, but I can see in each of these questions another receding target for conservation.

I had a bird dog named Gus. When Gus couldn't find pheasants he worked up an enthusiasm for Sora rails and meadowlarks. This whipped-up zeal for unsatisfactory substitutes masked his failure to find the real thing. It assuaged his inner frustration.

We conservationists are like that. We set out a generation ago to convince the American landowner to control fire, to grow forests, to manage wildlife. He did not respond very well. We have virtually no forestry, and mighty little range management, game management, wildflower management, pollution control, or erosion control being practiced voluntarily by private landowners. In many instances the abuse of private land is worse than it was before we started. If you don't believe that, watch the strawstacks burn on the Canadian prairies; watch the fertile mud flowing down the Rio Grande; watch the gullies climb the hillsides in the Palouse, in the Ozarks, in the riverbreaks of southern Iowa and western Wisconsin.

To assuage our inner frustration over this failure, we have found us a meadowlark. I don't know which dog first caught the scent; I do know that every dog on the field whipped into an enthusiastic backing-point. I did myself. The meadowlark was the idea that if the private landowner won't practice conservation, let's build a bureau to do it for him.

Like the meadowlark, this substitute has its good points. It smells like success. It is satisfactory on poor land which bureaus can buy. The trouble is that it contains no device for preventing good private land from becoming poor public land. There is danger in the assuagement of honest frustration; it helps us forget we have not yet found a pheasant.

I'm afraid the meadowlark is not going to remind us. He is flattered by his sudden importance.

Why is it that conservation is so rarely practiced by those who must extract a living from the land? It is said to boil down, in the last analysis, to economic obstacles. Take forestry as an example: the lumberman says he will crop his timber when stumpage values rise high enough, and when wood substitutes quit underselling him. He said this decades ago. In the interim, stumpage values have gone down, not up; substitutes have increased, not decreased. Forest devastation goes on as before. I admit the reality of this predicament. I suspect that the forces inherent in unguided economic evolution are not all beneficent. Like the forces inside our own bodies, they may become malignant, pathogenic. I believe that many of the economic forces inside the modern body-politic are pathogenic in respect to harmony with land.

What to do? Right now there is a revival of the old idea of legislative compulsion. I fear it's another meadowlark. I think we should seek some organic remedy—something that works from the inside of the economic structure.

We have learned to use our votes and our dollars for conservation. Must we perhaps use our purchasing power also? If exploitation-lumber and forestry-lumber were each labeled as such, would we prefer to buy the conservation product? If the wheat threshed from burning strawstacks could be labeled as such, would we have the courage to ask for conservation-wheat, and pay for it? If pollution-paper could be distinguished from clean paper, would we pay the extra penny? Over-grazing beef vs. range-management beef? Corn from chernozem, not subsoil? Butter from pasture slopes under 20 per cent? Celery from ditchless marshes? Broiled whitefish from five-inch nets? Oranges from unpoisoned groves? A trip to Europe on liners that do not dump their bilgewater? Gasoline from capped wells?

The trouble is that we have developed, along with our skill in the exploitation of land, a prodigious skill in false advertising. I do not want to be told by advertisers what is a conservation product. The only alternative is a consumer-discrimination unthinkably perfect, or else a new batch of bureaus to certify 'this product is clean.' The one we can't hope for, the other we don't want. Thus does conservation in a democracy grow ever bigger, ever farther.

Not all the straws that denote the wind are cause for sadness. There are several that hearten me. In a single decade conservation has become a profession and a career for hundreds of young 'technicians.' Ill-trained, many of them; intellectually tethered by bureaucratic superiors, most of them; but in dead earnest, nearly all of them. I look at these youngsters and believe they are hungry to learn new cogs and wheels, eager to build a better taste in natural objects. They are the first generation of leaders in conservation who ever learned to say, 'I don't know.' After all, one can't be too discouraged about an idea which hundreds of young men believe in and live for.

Another hopeful sign: Conservation research, in a single decade, has blown its seeds across three continents. Nearly every university from Oxford to Oregon State has established new research or new teaching in some field of conservation. Barriers of language do not prevent the confluence of ideas.

Once poor as a church mouse, American conservation research now dispenses 'federal aid' of several kinds in many ciphers.

These new foci of cerebration are developing not only new facts, which I hope is important, but also a new land philosophy, which I know is important. Our first crop of conservation prophets followed the evangelical pattern; their teachings generated much heat but little light. An entirely new group of thinkers is now emerging. It consists of men who first made a reputation in science, and now seek to interpret the land mechanism in terms any scientist can approve and any layman understand, men like Robert Cushman Murphy, Charles Elton, Fraser Darling. Is it possible that science, once seeking only easier ways to live off the land, is now to seek better ways to live with it?

We shall never achieve harmony with land, any more than we shall achieve justice or liberty for people. In these higher aspirations the important thing is not to achieve, but to strive. It is only in mechanical enterprises that we can expect that early or complete fruition of effort which we call 'success.'

The problem, then, is how to bring about a striving for harmony with land among a people many of whom have forgotten there is any such thing as land, among whom education and culture have become almost synonymous with landlessness. This is the problem of 'conservation education.'

When we say 'striving,' we admit at the outset that the thing we need must grow from within. No striving for an idea was ever injected wholly from without.

When we say 'striving,' I think we imply an effort of the mind as well as a disturbance of the emotions. It is inconceivable to me that we can adjust ourselves to the complexities of the land mechanism without an intense curiosity to understand its workings and an habitual personal study of those workings. The urge to comprehend must precede the urge to reform.

When we say 'striving,' we likewise disqualify at least in part the two vehicles which conservation propagandists have most often used: fear and indignation. He who by a lifetime of observation and reflection has learned much about our maladjustments with land is entitled to fear, and would be something less than honest if he were not indignant. But for teaching the fresh mind, these are outmoded tools. They belong to history.

My own gropings come to a dead end when I try to appraise the profit motive. For a full generation the American conservation movement has been substituting the profit motive for the fear motive, yet it has failed to motivate. We can all see profit in conservation practice, but the profit accrues to society rather than to the individual. This, of course, explains the trend, at this moment, to wish the whole job on the government.

When one considers the prodigious achievements of the profit motive in wrecking land, one hesitates to reject it as a vehicle for restoring land. I incline to believe we have overestimated the scope of the profit motive. Is it profitable for the individual to build a beautiful home? To give his children a higher education? No, it is seldom profitable, yet we do both. These are, in fact, ethical and aesthetic premises which underlie the economic system. Once accepted, economic forces tend to align the smaller details of social organization into harmony with them.

No such ethical and aesthetic premise yet exists for the condition of the land these children must live in. Our children are our signature to the roster of history; our land is merely the place our money was made. There is as yet no social stigma in the possession of a gullied farm, a wrecked forest, or a polluted stream, provided the dividends suffice to send the youngsters to college. Whatever ails the land, the government will fix it.

I think we have here the root of the problem. What conservation education must build is an ethical underpinning for land economics and a universal curiosity to understand the land mechanism. Conservation may then follow.

1953

Further Reading

Deformations

Of the two chief causes of technological ruin, war and industry, the latter has had the greater impact on the American landscape. There is some attention to ruin in the literature of the Civil War: see especially Ambrose Bierce's story "Affair at Coulter's Notch" and passages in Stephen Crane's *The Red Badge of Courage*. The ruin of World War I, as I have suggested, registered as more devastating, though its effects on American literature were indirect. Edmund Blunden's *Undertones of War* (New York, 1965), a British book with a French landscape, traces in overwhelming detail every stage of battle ruin from deformation to primordial desolation and so provides an extraordinary gauge with which to measure the violence and desolation of American technological ruin. T. S. Eliot's *The Waste Land,* though its landscape is that of London, revolutionized the techniques of imaging landscapes of ruin, especially the technique of juxtaposition.

In the literature of "eco-catastrophe," the following books are particularly effective in rendering the effects of technological ruin: Harry Caudill's *Night Comes to the Cumberlands* (Boston, 1962); Barry Commoner's *The Closing Circle* (New York, 1972); and Raymond Dasmann's *The Destruction of California* (New York, 1965). This list is not exclusive; for a particularly fine bibliography of the literature of ecology (including eco-catastrophe), see Dave Hupp's "Annotated Bibliography" (distributed by Boston Area Ecology Action, 925 Massachusetts Avenue, Cambridge, Mass.).

The fiction of eco-catastrophe and technological apocalypse is growing:

Kurt Vonnegut's novels (particularly *Cat's Cradle*) and Walker Percy's *Love in the Ruins* (New York, 1972) are especially fine apocalyptic novels.

The aesthetics of contemporary literature as they affect landscape (the notions of discontinuity, spatial form, expressionism, surrealism, the grotesque, and so on) is a complex subject which gets much illumination from such critical books as these: Waldo Frank's "Spatial Form in Modern Literature" in his *The Widening Gyre* (Bloomington, 1968); Wolfgang Kayser's *The Grotesque in Art and Literature* (New York, 1966) and Wylie Sypher's *Rococo to Cubism in Art and Literature* (New York, 1960); Marshall McLuhan's *The Interior Landscape* (Eugene McNamara, ed.; New York, 1971), which in the course of several essays traces the idea of discontinuity from the aesthetics of the picturesque; and Frederick Hoffman's *The Mortal No* (Princeton, 1964), especially Chapter 6, "The Imagery of Catastrophe," which deals with the landscape and the psychology of violence with relation to World War I. The reader is warned that he must do his own job of focusing the concerns of these books on the subject of American landscape, for none of them are primarily concerned with the American landscape per se.

Early Explorations

The most accessible sources of material by both Renaissance maritime explorers and later settlers and continental explorers (through the nineteenth century) are J. Franklin Jameson's *Original Narratives of Early American History*, 18 vols. (New York, 1906–1917), and the March of America Facsimile Series, 101 vols. (Ann Arbor, 1966), volume 101 being a very fine descriptive bibliography of the series. The French exploration of the New World is fully documented in *The Jesuit Relations*, 73 vols. (Cleveland, 1896–1901), and the English exploration in Richard Hakluyt's *The Principal Navigations, Voyages, Traffiques and Discoveries of the English Nation*, 12 vols. (Glasgow, 1903–1905).

Two learned and luminous critical sources are, for the "history" of the New World from 400–1587 (from St. Brendan's voyage to the founding of the Virginia colonies), Samuel Eliot Morison's *The European Discovery of America: The Northern Voyages* (New York, 1971), and, for the "image" of the New World, Howard Mumford Jones's *O Strange New World* (New York, 1964), especially Chapters 1 and 2 ("The Image of the New World" and "The Anti-Image").

The Cultivation of the Promised Land, 1620–1800

For the cultivation and settlement of the Eastern seaboard through the eighteenth century, J. Franklin Jameson's *Original Narratives of Early American History,* 18 vols. (New York, 1906–1917), and the March of America Facsimile Series (MAFS), 101 vols. (Ann Arbor, 1966), remain the most accessible and comprehensive series. Albert Bushnell Hart's anthology, *American History Told by Contemporaries,* especially Vol. I, *Era of Colonization* (New York, 1897), presents a composite portrait of colonial landscapes from Massachusetts and Rhode Island to Virginia and Georgia, though the reader is warned again that the logic of all pre-Revolution prose is only intermittently pictorial and that the pictures tend to be more diffuse than concrete.

For the settlement westward, seven books in the MAFS focus especially closely on cultivation (for other perspectives, see The Ways West): John Filson's *The Discovery, Settlement and Present State of Kentucke,* (# 50), John Stillman Wright's *Letters from the West; or a Caution to Emigrants . . . ,* 1819 (# 64), Catherine Stewart's *New Homes in the West,* 1843 (# 68), Charles Fenno Hoffman's *A Winter in the West,* 1835 (# 75), William Oliver's *Eight Months in Illinois,* 1843 (# 81), Alonzo Delano's *Life on the Plains and Among the Diggings . . . ,* 1854 (# 89), Miriam Colt's *Went to Kansas; . . . An Ill-Fated Expedition,* 1862 (#91).

The fiction of New England, Southern, and Midwestern regionalists is a very fine register of the impact of the machine, of soil exhaustion, and of urban migration on the American garden (see Landscape as Environment). James Agee's *Let Us Now Praise Famous Men* (New York, 1960) is a magnificent portrait of Southern tenant farmers and farms in the 1930's, and Donald Hall's *String Too Short To Be Saved* (New York, 1964) is an equally grand portrait of decaying New England farmers and farms at about the same period.

The critical literature on the garden and the wilderness is vast, but these works stand out: Perry Miller's *Errand into the Wilderness* (Cambridge, Mass., 1970); Arthur K. Moore's *The Frontier Mind* (New York, 1963); Daniel J. Boorstin's *The Americans: The National Experience* (New York, 1965); Dorothy Anne Dondore's *The Prairie and the Making of Middle America: Four Centuries of Description* (Cedar Rapids, Iowa, 1926); Walter Prescott Webb's *The Great Plains* (New York, 1971); Leo Marx's *The Machine in the Garden* (New York, 1969); R. W. B. Lewis's *The American Adam* (Chicago, 1964); Charles Sanford's *The Quest for Paradise* (Urbana, 1961); and Chapter II of Howard Mumford Jones's *The Age of Energy: Varieties of American Experience, 1865–1915* (New York, 1971). A very fine anthology is Martin Ridge's and Ray Allen Billington's *America's Frontier Story: A Documentary History of Westward Expansion* (New York, 1969).

Eighteenth-Century Perspectives

For eighteenth- and early-nineteenth-century travels and natural histories, these are of major interest: William Byrd's *History of the Dividing Line Betwixt Virginia and North Carolina,* in *The London Diary, 1717–1721, and Other Writings* (Louis B. Wright and Marion Tinting, eds.; New York, 1958); Peter Kalm, *Travels in North America,* 2 vols. (New York, 1966); Francis Hobert Herrick's *Delineations of American Scenery and Character by John James Audubon* (New York, 1926); and, in the March of America Facsimile Series (MAFS, 101 vols., Ann Arbor, 1966), the works by John Lederer (# 25), John Lawson (# 35) and John Bartram (# 41).

In the critical literature on natural history in America, three books are especially helpful: Daniel Boorstin's *The Americans: The Colonial Experience* (New York, 1958), especially Parts 5–9; Henry Savage's *Lost Heritage* (New York, 1970); and Philip Marshall Hicks's *The Development of the Natural History Essay in American Literature* (Philadelphia: University of Pennsylvania dissertation, 1924).

For more on the sublime, see Samuel Monk's *The Sublime* (Ann Arbor, 1960), the classic history of English aesthetic theory on the subject; and Chapter 8 (''National Self-consciousness and the Concept of the Sublime'') of Charles Sanford's *The Quest for Paradise, op. cit.* For the Puritan reading of the ''book'' of creation, see Chapter VIII (''Nature'') on Perry Miller's *The New England Mind: The Seventeenth Century* (Boston, 1961) and Ursula Brumm's *American Thought and Religious Typology* (New Brunswick, N.J., 1970); and for more insight into the method of reading scripture, see Charles Donahue's ''Patristic Exigesis: Summation,'' in *Critical Approaches to Medieval Literature,* Dorothy Bethurum, ed. (New York, 1960).

The Poetry of Scene

There is a large literature of travel in the East during the period 1800–1900 (most of it deservedly forgotten), and by the 1830's it begins to expand westward (see The Ways West). The most durable work is by painters and writers. Some notable books: Jeremy Belknap, *Journal of a Tour to the White Mountains in 1784,* Charles Deane, ed. (Boston, 1876); William Cullen Bryant, *Picturesque America,* 2 vols. (New York, 1872–1874); Joel T. Headley, *The Adirondack; or Life in the Woods* (New York, 1849); Washington Irving, Bryant, Cooper, and others, *The Home Book of the Picturesque; or American Scenery, Art and Literature* (Gainesville, Fla., 1967); and Frederick W. Kilbourne, *Chronicles of the White Mountains* (Boston, 1916). There are several contemporary gift-book anthologies on the Hudson River, the Catskills, and other regions traversed by the American Grand Tour.

Hans Huth's *Nature and the American Mind* (University of Nebraska Press, 1972), especially Chapter 5 ("The Poetry of Travelling"), is the best single source on Romantic tourism in America. For more on picturesque scenery, see Ashur B. Durand's "Letters on Landscape Painting," anthologized in *American Art, 1700–1960,* John W. McCoubrey, ed. (Englewood Cliffs, N.J., 1965); William Gilpin's *Three Essays on Picturesque Beauty; on Picturesque Travel; and on Sketching Landscape* (London, 1808); Christopher Hussey's *The Picturesque: Studies in a Point of View* (London, 1967); and Martin Price's "The Picturesque Moment," in *From Sensibility to Romanticism,* Frederick W. Hilles and Harold Bloom, eds. (New York, 1970).

Landscape as Idea: The Transcendentalists

It is difficult to overemphasize the importance of journals and notebooks in the process of perceiving and rendering landscapes. The Transcendentalists were voluminous journal-writers, and they make a fine case in point. The journals of Emerson (Ralph L. Rusk, ed.; 10 vols., Boston, 1909–1914) and Thoreau (Bradford Torrey and F. H. Allen, eds.; 14 vols., Boston, 1906) are available, and there are excellent paperback excerpts from them; Muir's journals are available in Linnie Marsh Wolfe's *John of the Mountains* (New York, 1938). All of Thoreau's major work is represented here, with the exception of *A Week on the Concord and Merrimack Rivers,* but each work, of course, has much more on landscape than could be excerpted here. The reader caught up by John Muir should know of his *Writings* (William F. Bade, ed.; 10 vols., Boston, c. 1915–1924); especially interesting are his *My First Summer in the Sierra, Thousand Mile Walk to the Gulf,* and *The Yosemite,* the latter available in paperback (Garden City, N.Y., 1962).

Another man who should be represented in the company of the Transcendentalists (he, too, was a student of Emerson, and of Whitman as well) is John Burroughs, a master of the nature essay. See his *Works* (23 vols., Boston, 1904–1922) and *The Heart of Burroughs' Journals* (Clara Barrus, ed.).

The critical literature on the American Renaissance and the Transcendentalists, Emerson and Thoreau in particular, is enormous, but no better books could be consulted than Norman Foerster's *Nature in American Literature* (New York, 1923), F. O. Matthiessen's *American Renaissance* (New York, 1941; now in paper), and Sherman Paul's book on Thoreau, *The Shores of America* (New York, 1958). Howard Mumford Jones sets Burroughs and Muir beautifully into the context of *The Age of Energy, 1865–1915* (New York, 1971), a context which clearly limits the extent of their affinities to Emerson.

Landscape as Idea: Romantic Fiction and Poetry

For sketches of fancy, see Poe's "Silence—A Fable," "The Colloquy of Monos and Una," and "The Conversation of Eiros and Charmion," and Hawthorne's "The New Adam and Eve" and "Earth's Holocaust." For the beautiful in landscape, see Poe's "Morning on the Wissahiccon," "The Landscape Garden," "The Domain of Arnheim," and "Landor's Cottage"; for the sublime, Poe's "Descent into the Maelstrom" and Hawthorne's "Ethan Brand." The fiction of Melville is filled with sublime or picturesque scenes and with meditative sketches (Ishmael's reveries and meditations in *Moby Dick,* for example), and his "Encantadas" is a series of meditative sketches of fancy.

Hawthorne's preoccupation with New England landscapes (not always geographically locatable) as theater of historical or moral events can be seen in such stories as "The Gentle Boy," "The Maypole of Merry Mount," "Roger Malvin's Burial," "The Great Carbuncle," and "The Great Stone Face." The problem in some of these stories is to decide to what extent the theater is historical and to what extent moral (a matter of allegory or parable).

Each of the poets represented here is well worth pursuing on matters of landscape. For more on the notion of organic form, see F. O. Matthiessen's *American Renaissance* (under the Index heading "Organic Principle").

The Ways West

For explorers, surveyors, and natural scientists, see Zebulon Pike's *An account of expeditions to the sources of the Mississippi* (Philadelphia, 1810; March of America Facsimile Series MAFS, 101 vols., Ann Arbor, 1966, # 57); John Bradbury's *Travels in the Interior of America* (Liverpool, 1817; MAFS # 59); Thomas Nuttall's *A Journal of Travels into the Arkansas Territory* (Philadelphia, 1821); the "Annual Report of F. V. Hayden," one of the great Western surveyors, in each of twelve *Annual Reports of the United States Geological and Geographical Survey of the Territories* (Washington, D.C., 1868–1883); Charles Cook's, David Folsom's and William Peterson's *An Exploration of the Headwaters of the Yellowstone River in the Year 1869;* and Clarence King's *Mountaineering in the Sierra Nevada,* 1872 (New York, 1935), a little-known classic.

For emigrants' and settlers' perspectives, see bibliography in *The Cultivation of the Promised Land.* For those of mountain men, see Osbourne Russell's *Journal of a Trapper, 1834–1843,* Aubrey L. Haines, ed. (Lincoln, Neb., 1969) and Zenas Leonard's *Narrative of the adventures of Zenas Leonard . . .* (Clearfield, Pa., 1839; MAFS # 69). For the perspectives of tourists, see

Estwick Evans's *A Pedestrious Tour of 4,000 Miles through the Western States . . .* (Concord, N.H., 1819); James Hall's *Letters from the West* (London, 1828); Timothy Flint's *Recollections of the Last Ten Years . . . in the Valley of the Mississippi* (Boston, 1826); Samuel Bowles, *Across the Continent* (New York, 1866); and Montgomery Schuyler's *Westward the Course of Empire: "Out West" and "Back East" on the First Trip of the "Los Angeles County Limited"* (New York, 1905).

With MAFS, two other series of original narratives are extremely fruitful: Reuben Gold Thwaites's *Early Western Travels, 1748–1846,* 25 vols. (Cleveland, 1906), and the University of Oklahoma's Exploration and Travel Series, 47 vols. (Norman, 1939–1965).

The following secondary sources are particularly helpful: Bernard De Voto's *The Course of Empire* (Boston, 1960) and *Across the Wide Missouri* (Boston, 1947), the first a history of westward expansion from Columbus to Lewis and Clark, the second a history of the Western fur trade; Irene D. Paden's *The Wake of the Prairie Schooner* (Carbondale, Ill., 1970; with an extensive bibliography of emigrant journals and memoirs) and George R. Stewart's *The California Trail,* The American Trail Series (New York, 1971), both of which retrace the routes and the vicissitudes of the California-Oregon Trail; Richard A. Bartlett, *Great Surveys of the American West* (Norman, 1966); Wallace Stegner's *Beyond the Hundredth Meridian: John Wesley Powell and the Second Opening of the West* (Boston, 1954); Frederick Jackson Turner's *The Frontier in American History* (New York, 1920), which proclaims the end of the frontier. Books more concerned with mythical and literary perspectives on the "Old West" include Henry Nash Smith's epochal *Virgin Land* (New York, 1961); Edwin Fussell's *Frontier: American Literature and the American West* (Princeton, 1965), which focuses on the writers of the American Renaissance; and Harold P. Simonson's *The Closed Frontier,* which examines the effect of the closed frontier on the work of Mark Twain, Ole Rölvaag, and Nathaniel West.

Landscape as Environment

Since the difference between local color and regional fiction seems to me mostly a matter of sophistication—a difference between boosterism and nostalgia on the one hand, and an atmosphere or "spirit of place" on the other; a difference in the degree of subtlety and complexity with which setting-as-environment is handled—I shall focus here on three regions, leaving the reader to gauge for himself the impact on them of naturalism and other modern literary currents.

New England. Rose Terry Cooke's *Somebody's Neighbors* (1881); Sarah Orne Jewett's *The Country of the Pointed Firs and Other Stories* (New York,

1956) and *The World of Dunnet Landing* (Lincoln, Neb., 1962); the Tillbury Town poetry of E. A. Robinson; and the poetry of Robert Frost and Robert Lowell.

The Midwest. Edgar Watson Howe's *The Story of a Country Town* (New Haven, 1962); Charles Neider, ed., *The Complete Short Stories of Mark Twain* (New York, 1964); Hamlin Garland's *Main-Travelled Roads* (New York, 1956); Willa Cather's *O Pioneers!* (Boston, 1913) and other of her novels and short fiction; Edgar Lee Masters's *Spoon River Anthology;* Sherwood Anderson's *Winesburg, Ohio;* Glenway Wescott's *Good-Bye Wisconsin* (New York, 1964); Sinclair Lewis's *Main Street;* Hemingway's Nick Adams stories; and, most recently, Truman Capote's *In Cold Blood.*

The South. Thomas Nelson Page's *In Ole Virginia* (1887), representative of the post-Civil War ''plantation tradition''; George Washington Cable's *Creoles and Cajuns* (New York, 1959) and *Old Creole Days* (1879); Ellen Glasgow's fiction; Faulkner's *Go Down, Moses* and his Yoknapatawpha County novels; and such Southern Gothic fiction as Carson McCullers's *Collected Short Stories* and *The Ballad of the Sad Cafe,* Eudora Welty's short fiction, Flannery O'Connor's novels and her *Collected Short Stories,* and currently the novels of Harry Crews and Barry Hannah. Also, the poetry of Sidney Lanier, Henry Timrod, the Southern Fugitives (Allen Tate and Robert Penn Warren particularly), and James Dickey.

For some Black perspectives on the Southern landscape, from slavery to tenant farming and rural industry: Charles Chesnutt's *The Conjure Woman* (Ann Arbor, 1969); Jean Toomer's *Cane* (New York, 1969); Richard Wright's *Uncle Tom's Children;* William Attaway's *Blood on the Forge* (New York, 1970), a novel of the Great Migration; William Melvin Kelley's *A Different Drummer* (Garden City, 1969); Sarah Wright's *This Child's Gonna Live* (New York, 1969); and the fiction of Ernest Gaines, most recently *Miss Jane Pittman.*

Any list of the literature of the Far West would have to include the weird and grotesque California landscapes of Nathaniel West (*Day of the Locust* especially), Norman Mailer's *Deer Park,* and Joan Didion.

For the rise of local color and other manifestations of literary realism, see Warner Berthoff's *The Ferment of Realism* (New York, 1965), which has a chapter on naturalism as well; and Jay Martin's *Harvest of Change* (Englewood Cliffs, N.J., 1967).

Landscape as Antagonist

There is a good collection of Jack London's *Short Stories* in paperback (Maxwell Geismar, ed.; New York, 1968); see also *The Complete Short Stories and Sketches of Stephen Crane* (Thomas A. Gullason, ed.; Garden City, N.Y.,

1963), or for a good, inexpensive anthology Crane's *Stories and Tales* (Robert Wooster Stallman, ed.; New York, 1955). Much of the regional literature at the turn of the century is naturalistic in outlook: the early poetry of E. A. Robinson and Edgar Lee Masters, for example, and even a book as recent as Richard Wright's *Uncle Tom's Children,* first published in 1939.

Malcolm Cowley's "A Natural History of American Naturalism," included in *Documents of Modern Literary Realism* (George J. Becker, ed.; Princeton, 1967), is a particularly fine essay on the subject. Richard Hofstadter's *Social Darwinism in American Thought* (Boston, 1964), especially Chapter 1, "The Coming of Darwinism," provides a clear intellectual context in which to set the literary naturalists.

Landscape into Myth and Ritual

For one who is, as I am, unversed in folklore or anthropology, the anthologies of Indian prose and poetry by Margot Astrov and by George Cronyn, the anthologies of Black American folklore by Langston Hughes and Arna Bontemps and by B. A. Botkin, and Zora Neale Hurston's *Mules and Men* are really excellent sources. They are cited in the headnotes of Landscape into Myth and Ritual. Astrov's anthology contains an extensive bibliography of Indian material; for Black American material see Elizabeth W. Miller's *The Negro in America: A Bibliography* (Cambridge, Mass., 1965). An excellent source book on folklore is Maria Leach's *Standard Dictionary of Folklore, Mythology and Legend* (New York, 1972).

Affirming the Ancient Connections

The humanistically scientific affirmation of our ancient connections to landscape is well represented by these books: Marston Bates's *The Nature of Natural History* (New York, 1950); G. E. Hutchinson's *The Ecological Theatre and the Evolutionary Play* (New Haven, 1965); John McHale's *The Ecological Context* (New York, 1970); *Voices for the Wilderness,* William Schwartz, ed. (New York, 1969); Paul Shepard's *Man in the Landscape* (New York, 1967). Close in spirit to these are the contemporary nature essayists, whose works are readily available in paperback. Their attention seems focused on two areas. The Northeast: Henry Beston's *The Outermost House* (New York, 1971); John Hay's *In Defense of Nature* (New York, 1970), *Nature's Year* (New York, 1971), and *The Great Beach* (New York, 1972); Edward Hoagland's *Walking the Dead Diamond River* (New York, 1973); Edwin Way Teale's *North With Spring* (New York, 1951); Walter Teller's *Cape Cod and the Offshore Islands*

(Englewood Cliffs, N.J., 1970); William Chapman White's *Adirondack Country* (New York, 1954). And the Southwest: Mary Austin, *The Land of Little Rain* (Garden City, N.Y., 1962); Joseph Wood Krutch's *Grand Canyon* (Garden City, N.Y., 1962) and *The Best Nature Writing of Joseph Wood Krutch* (New York, 1971); Edward Abbey's *Desert Solitaire* (New York, 1968).

The ancient traditions of the West and the East in relation to nature which are now being reclaimed by the ''counter culture'' are well represented by such books as these: Carlos Castaneda's trilogy on ''the teachings of Don Juan''; Stephen Diamond's *What the Trees Said* (New York, 1971) and Raymond Mungo's *Total Loss Farm* (New York, 1971), two books on communes; Gary Snyder's *Earth Household* (New York, 1969), which ranges between Buddhism and American Indian shamanism; Frank Waters's *Masked Gods: Navaho and Pueblo Ceremonialism* (cited in Landscape into Myth and Ritual); Lynn White's ''The Historical Roots of Our Ecologic Crisis'' (*Science,* March 10, 1967), which reopens the matter of Franciscanism.

Further reading in modern fiction might include William Faulkner's ''The Bear'' and D. H. Lawrence's ''The Woman Who Rode Away''; but in modern and contemporary literature it is poetry rather than fiction which seems to have taken on itself the voice of affirmation (fiction seems more drawn to deformations). Any of the poets represented here is well worth further study.